GANDHI & CHURCHILL

ALSO BY ARTHUR HERMAN

How the Scots Invented the Modern World

To Rule the Waves: How the British Navy Shaped the Modern World

GANDHI & CHURCHILL

THE EPIC RIVALRY THAT DESTROYED AN EMPIRE AND FORGED OUR AGE

Arthur Herman

HUTCHINSON
LONDON

Published by Hutchinson 2008

2 4 6 8 10 9 7 5 3 1

Book design by Glen M. Edelstein
Maps by David Lindroth

Published by arrangement with Bantam Dell, a division of
Random House, Inc., New York, New York, USA

First published in Great Britain in 2008 by
Hutchinson
Random House, 20 Vauxhall Bridge Road,
London SW1V 2SA

www.rbooks.co.uk

Addresses for companies within The Random House Group Limited can be found at:
www.randomhouse.co.uk/offices.htm

The Random House Group Limited Reg. No. 954009

A CIP catalogue record for this book is available from the British Library

ISBN 9780091797164 (hardback)
ISBN 9780091921323 (trade paperback)

The Random House Group Limited supports The Forest Stewardship
Council (FSC), the leading international forest certification organisation. All our
titles that are printed on Greenpeace approved FSC certified paper carry the FSC logo.
Our paper procurement policy can be found at www.rbooks.co.uk/environment

Mixed Sources
Product group from well-managed
forests and other controlled sources
www.fsc.org Cert no. TT-COC-2139
© 1996 Forest Stewardship Council
FSC

Printed and bound in Great Britain by
CPI Mackays, Chatham, Kent ME5 8TD

To Beth, with all my love,
for her unfailing help and support.

CONTENTS

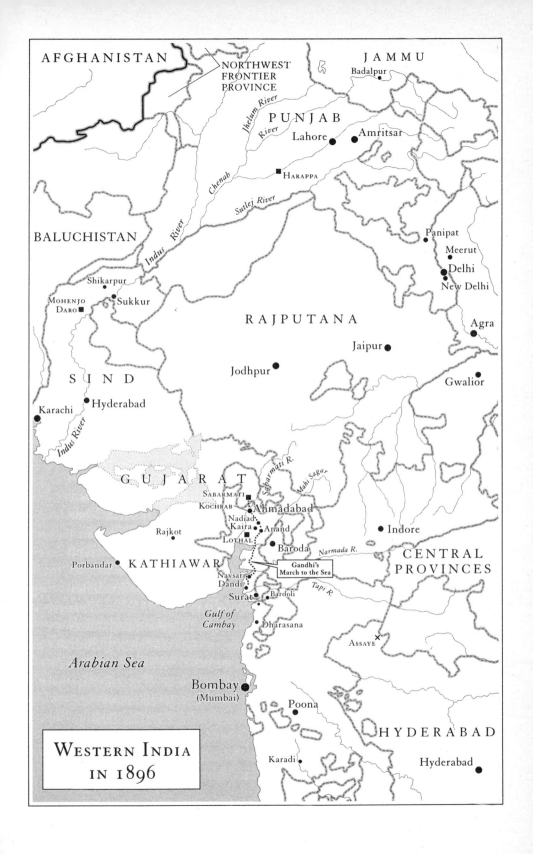

AFGHANISTAN

NORTHWEST
FRONTIER
PROVINCE

JAMMU

Badalpur

PUNJAB

Jhelum River

River

Lahore

Amritsar

Chenab

HARAPPA

Sutlej River

BALUCHISTAN

Indus River

Panipat

Meerut

Delhi

New Delhi

Shikarpur

MOHENJO
DARO

Sukkur

RAJPUTANA

Agra

SIND

Jodhpur

Jaipur

Gwalior

Karachi

Hyderabad

Indus River

GUJARAT

Sabarmati R.

Mahi Sagar

SABARMATI

KOCHRAB

Ahmadabad

Nadiad

Kaira

Anand

LOTHAL

Baroda

Indore

CENTRAL
PROVINCES

Rajkot

Narmada R.

Porbandar

KATHIAWAR

Navsari

Dandi

Tapi R.

Gandhi's
March to the Sea

Surat

Bardoli

*Gulf of
Cambay*

Dharasana

Arabian Sea

ASSAYE ×

Bombay
(Mumbai)

Poona

HYDERABAD

Karadi

Hyderabad

WESTERN INDIA
IN 1896

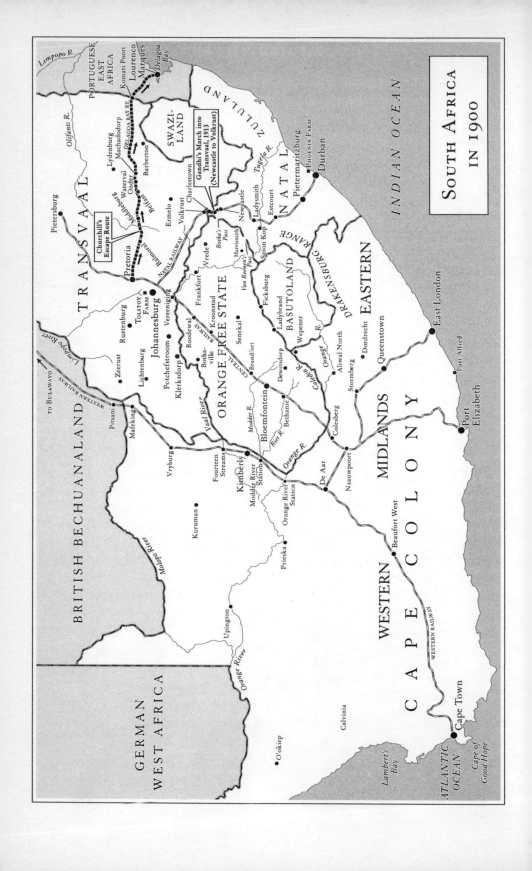

SOUTH AFRICA IN 1900

Limpopo R.

PORTUGUESE EAST AFRICA

Komati Poort
Lourenço Marques
Delagoa Bay

Olifants R.

TRANSVAAL

Pietersburg

Lydenburg
Machadodorp
Waterval
Onder
Barberton

DELAGOA BAY RY.

SWAZILAND

Gandhi's March into Transvaal, 1913 (Newcastle to Volkrust)

Charlestown
Volkrust
Ermelo
Newcastle

Churchill's Escape Route

Pretoria

Middelburg
Belfast

NATAL RAILWAY

Ladysmith
Estcourt

Pietermaritzburg

PHOENIX FARM
Durban

Z U L U L A N D

Tugela R.

INDIAN OCEAN

Botha's Pass
Harrismith
Van Reenen's Pass
Spion Kop

Vrede

Frankfort

TOLSTOY FARM

Johannesburg

Rustenburg

Zeerust

Lichtenburg

Potchefstroom

Klerksdorp

Roodewal

Kroonstad

CENTRAL

Senekal

Ficksburg

Ladybrand
Wepener

BASUTOLAND

Dordrecht

DRAKENSBURG RANGE

EASTERN

East London

to Bulawayo

WESTERN RAILWAY

Limpopo River

BRITISH BECHUANALAND

Pitsani
Mafeking

Vryburg

Kuruman

Molopo River

Botha-ville

Vaal River

Vereeniging

RAILWAY

ORANGE FREE STATE

Modder R.

Brand fort

Bloemfontein
Bethanie

Dewetsdorp

Caledon R.

Orange R.

Aliwal North

Stormberg

Queenstown

Port Alfred

Port Elizabeth

Fourteen Streams

Kimberley
Modder River Station

Orange River Station

Orange R.

Colesberg

De Aar

Naauwpoort

MIDLANDS

Beaufort West

GERMAN WEST AFRICA

Upington

Prieska

Orange River

Calvinia

O'okiep

Lambert's Bay

WESTERN

CAPE COLONY

WESTERN RAILWAY

Cape Town

ATLANTIC OCEAN

Cape of Good Hope

GANDHI & CHURCHILL

PROLOGUE

I see no being which lives in the world without violence.

MAHABHARATA

MUTINY. THE NEWS HAD SPREAD THROUGH the hot dusty streets of Cawnpore and its European quarters like a monsoon wind. The native *sepoys* or soldiers at the garrison at Meerut just outside Delhi had shot their British officers and were marching on the ancient Mughal capital. Other sepoys, it was said, were scrambling to join them. Cawnpore's English families, ensconced in their comfortable bungalows and surrounded by native servants, felt uneasy. Between Calcutta to the southeast and Peshawar to the north, a distance of thirteen hundred miles, there was exactly one battalion of British troops of seven hundred men. Very suddenly, in a few short days in May 1857, British rule in India, which had seemed so stable and secure for the past half-century, found itself on the edge of the abyss.

One question burned in everyone's mind. Would the sepoy regiments in Cawnpore remain loyal or join the rebels? One of those wondering was William Shepherd. He served in the garrison's Commissariat Office and had just moved his widowed sister's family to Cawnpore. Like many who worked for the British in India, Shepherd was of mixed race, half-Indian and half-English. "Everyone in the station seemed to think something dreadful was about to happen."[1] He knew that the small garrison town on the bank of the Ganges was weak and isolated, and that the native troops in Cawnpore outnumbered the whites by ten to one. If they mutinied, the nearest help would be more than fifty miles away in Lucknow, assuming the soldiers *there* remained loyal. Shepherd also sensed that he and other so-called half-castes, or anyone who worked with the British, would be in mortal danger if the Cawnpore sepoys joined the rebellion.

But would they? Shepherd certainly thought so. In an unguarded moment, some of them had revealed the depth of their resentment toward the British, and their paranoia. "See what deep plots are being laid against us," the Cawnpore sepoys told him. They had already refused the new cartridges issued from the arsenal at Dum Dum for their Enfield rifles, which rumor said were smeared with pig grease so that any Muslim soldier would be polluted and any Hindu soldier would break his caste. It was fear of those same cartridges that had set off the mutiny in Meerut. Now the rumor was that their British officers were secretly mixing the commissariat flour with pig and cow bones, for the same purpose: to make them all *badhurrum,* or outcastes.

Shepherd knew this was a lie but did not dare to contradict them. But he did ask why they would wish to attack civilians and others like himself who had done them no harm. They gathered menacingly around him, shouting over and over: *Suffun suffa! Suffun suffa!* "Enough is enough!" It was time to wipe the slate clean. Time to drive the British out of India.

One veteran sepoy, with bristling mustache and piercing eyes, almost rushed at Shepherd.

"Oh you are all one, all of the same breed," he cried. "You are serpents, and not one of you shall be spared!" That night Shepherd moved his family out of the city and into Cawnpore's only entrenched position, the old dragoon hospital, to the west of town.[2]

There he found the mood had degenerated to hysteria. Europeans and Eurasians were scrambling to get their families inside the compound, unnerved by rumors of impending trouble and angry stares from the locals. Trunks, suitcases, valises, bundles, and boxes were piled in profusion. Children ran under foot while weary officers tried to maintain order and their wives and sisters sat exhausted in the heat. Native servants and *ayahs* crouched fearfully in the corner. The hospital overflowed with "people...of every color, sect, or profession," an officer remembered later, "all in terror of the imaginary foe."[3]

But Major-General Hugh Wheeler, commander of the garrison, was still confident. Wheeler was sixty-seven. He had been born and raised in India; even his wife was Indian. He thought he knew his sepoys as well as anyone did, and like most old-school British officers, he spoke fluent Hindustani. On May 18, even as panicky whites were pouring into the hospital and laborers were put to work building a four-foot mud wall around it, Wheeler was writing to officials in Calcutta, "All is well in Cawnpore."[4]

Besides, if any real trouble did break out, Wheeler knew he could count on the support of the local raja of Bithur. The raja, generally known as Nana Sahib, was one of the literally hundreds of local Indian princes who kept their independence from the British East India Company and still governed more than half of India. Nana Sahib was not one of the great princes like the nizam of Hyderabad or the maharaja of Mysore, who between them ruled more territory than France and Germany put together. But he was wealthy, well spoken, and at thirty-five years old in the prime of life. He and Wheeler had dined together; played billiards and hunted tigers together. Nana Sahib belonged to the same Hindu caste as Wheeler's wife. There was no Indian Wheeler trusted more. So when the raja appeared at the end of May with five hundred troops and cavalry dressed in glittering breastplates and helmets and flowing robes, to pledge his support to the British, Wheeler was so grateful he turned the garrison's treasury over to the prince for safekeeping.

It was a fatal mistake. After Nana Sahib's father died in 1851, the government in Calcutta had decided in its infinite wisdom to cut off the raja's pension. Nana Sahib appealed to the East India Company's directors in Leadenhall Street in London; they refused to interfere. In 1857 Nana Sahib faced total ruin.[5] Behind his sleek demeanor Nana Sahib hated the British, and he was already scheming to become the sepoys' leader.

On the warm night of June 4 Shepherd and his family were sleeping out on the hospital's veranda when a commotion woke him up. An anxious crowd of whites had gathered. Shepherd asked what was wrong.

Someone hissed, "Listen!" and pointed in the direction of the tents of the native Second Light Cavalry. In the predawn blackness Shepherd could hear the sounds of men saddling horses. There were cries and shouts. Then a sudden blaze of light split the darkness.

The native troopers had set the regimental riding master's house on fire and cut down their senior native officer, or *rissaldar-major,* who refused to join them. The next morning he was brought back still alive to the hospital enclave, his body covered with saber wounds. He died in agony a few days later. By then another body had been discovered, that of Mr. Murphy of the East India Railway, with three bullets in his head.

On June 6 the mutineers, with Nana Sahib at their head, set up cannon around the enclave, while others ran riot through the city and shot any remaining Europeans or native Christians they found. The siege of Cawnpore had begun.[6]

It would last for eighteen terrible days. More than nine hundred people, men, women, and children, Europeans and Indians, were jammed into the hospital enclosure and its two brick buildings, one of which had only a thatched roof. They had no way to reach the garrison at Lucknow, who were about to be besieged themselves. Everyone who volunteered to try to sneak out to find help (including eventually William Shepherd) was either killed or captured. The Cawnpore "garrison"—in fact, not even a third were soldiers—was critically short of food, water, and ammunition, and protected by only a shallow trench and the four-foot mud wall around the main building. Cannonballs swept down on the helpless crowd night and day.

Wheeler's own son, Lieutenant Godfrey Wheeler, was one of the first to die, beheaded by a round shot even as his sister was treating his wound from an earlier firefight. Another shot killed a soldier as he was trying to comfort his wife and her twin babies, then passed through his wife's arm to maim one of their infants. Still another claimed Shepherd's infant daughter on June 18. He and his wife had to watch her linger in agony for nearly thirty-six hours, "dying away gradually until she resembled the faded bud of a delicate flower." Shepherd then wrapped her tiny body in some old clothes and buried it in a hole he scratched out with a knife. It was his and his wife's seventh wedding anniversary.[7]*

With temperatures rising past one hundred degrees during the day, and with the dust and tension, people became desperate for water. There was only one well in the compound, which was exposed to sniper fire from every side. One by one those who volunteered to draw water from it were killed. When a cannonball shattered the well house and winch, the garrison had to crawl under fire to lower the bucket by hand sixty feet down.

Meanwhile the two hundred or so British soldiers and handful of loyal sepoys, as well as every man who could fire a musket, managed to beat off attack after attack. Surrounded by unburied dead bodies fester-

---

* Shortly afterward Shepherd volunteered to carry a message to the garrison at Lucknow. He was captured and held by Nana Sahib's men until European troops freed him. However, his wife, his sister, and the rest of the family perished in the siege.

ing in the heat, living on a handful of flour a day, they watched their loved ones die with no hope of relief or salvation. One stark fear drove them all: what would happen if they or their families were captured by the mutineers. They had heard that in Delhi women and children had been hacked to death or shot, as well as soldiers and civilian males. In Jhansi on June 8 rebels had rounded up every European man, woman, and child and murdered them all.

So it was Nana Sahib, not the Cawnpore garrison, who finally offered terms. He and his men were impatient to end the fruitless siege and move on. On June 24 he sent a message that those in the compound who were not part of the administration in Calcutta, and were willing to lay down their arms, would have guaranteed passage to Allahabad, where the British still had a garrison.

Wheeler opposed any deal with a man whose word was manifestly worthless. However, his brother officers persuaded him that once the rainy season began (and it was already overdue) their last remaining trenches and ramparts would be washed away in the monsoon. And what else could they do, they said, "with such a mixed multitude, in which there was a woman and a child for every man"?[8] They would have to trust Nana Sahib and hope for the best.

Wheeler, surrounded by the sick and dying, was sick himself. He finally gave way. He agreed to a deal by which the garrison would be allowed to march under arms down to the Ganges and embark on boats to carry them downstream to Allahabad and safety.

"A truly strange spectacle" greeted the dawn in the entrenchment on June 27, remembered Lieutenant Mowbray Thomson, as a crowd of gaunt and exhausted men, women, and children emerged from the battered hospital buildings. Some were barefoot, and most were in rags. Soldiers had given up their shirts and women their dresses in order to make bandages for the wounded. Many were shivering with fever. According to Thomson, "never, surely, was there such an emaciated, ghostly party of human beings as we"—emaciated and ghostly, certainly, for a party of Europeans in India.[9] They loaded up willy-nilly into bullock carts, palanquins, and on some sixteen elephants Nana Sahib provided and began a slow, sad procession through the city. A great crowd followed them down to the river, and many of the sepoys gathered to jeer, although some were weeping with shame and offered to help their former officers and their families carry their few last belongings.

At last the procession reached the riverbank. The men and women gingerly descended the steep ravine, thick with prickly pear and elephant grass, to the beach where a dozen dilapidated barges with thatched roofs were drawn up in the mud. The crowd pressed forward, as Thomson and the other soldiers set down their muskets and waded out to the boats. They were standing waist deep in the water to help to load the women and children, when a sudden bugle call made everyone turn and glance back.

The bank above them was suddenly thick with armed sepoys, all of them pointing their muskets into the helpless crowd. There was a tremendous crash as they poured out a volley, while from nearby houses hidden cannon opened up with grapeshot. With a shout, troopers from the Second Light Cavalry charged down the bank with drawn swords.

A soldier's wife saw one cut down General Wheeler with a saber cut across the neck. "My son was killed near him," she recalled later. "Some were stabbed with bayonets; others cut down. Children were stabbed and thrown into the river." She heard the youngest daughter of Colonel Williams (who had been killed in the siege) say to a soldier who was about to bayonet her, " 'My father was always kind to sepoys.' He turned away, [but] just then a villager struck her on the head with his club, and she fell into the water."[10]

Men hurled torches into the boats, which soon became blazing pyres. "The air resounded with the shrieks of the women and children," remembered another eyewitness, "and agonized prayers to God for mercy. The water was red with blood. My poor little sister…crying all the while: 'Oh Amy don't leave me!' A few yards away I saw the boat containing my poor mother slowly burning, and I cowered on the deck overwhelmed with grief."[11]

Lieutenant Thomson and a few of the men managed to climb into one of the barges. The boat's oars were gone, and the rudder was shot away. It slowly drifted into the current while bullets whizzed and chipped at the gunwales. "The wounded and the dead were entangled in the bottom of the boat," Thomson remembered. As they floated out of range, the men looked back with helpless rage at what was happening on the shore.

Smoke from the musketry and cannon, and from boats that had been set on fire, hung thick over the riverbank. When the shooting stopped, all the surviving men were dragged away and killed. The remaining women and children, about 125 in all, were herded up the bank. Seven girls—four British and three Eurasians, including Wheeler's youngest daughter—were taken away by sepoys from the Second Cavalry.* The rest were herded back through town to await whatever fate Nana Sahib and the mutineers had in store for them.

Meanwhile, in Allahabad, General Henry Havelock was struggling to pull together his tiny army for the relief of Cawnpore. There were few troops to be found. When the mutiny started, twelve of twenty-nine army battalions were far to the west in the Punjab, and another three were to the east in Burma—one reason the uprising was able to spread so quickly. Havelock's scratch force numbered one thousand men from four different British regiments; 150 loyal Sikh infantry; a tiny detachment of native irregulars; and twenty-odd volunteer cavalrymen. Most of the latter were stranded officers from sepoy regiments that had mutinied and civilian clerks and employees from the East India Company. Many had volunteered to avenge the deaths of friends or loved ones— loved ones killed by the same natives whom they had thought they trusted, and had dominated, for more than a century.[12]

If personal revenge drove some of Havelock's men, anger and a thirst for retribution drove the rest. One was Colonel James Neill of the First Madras Fusiliers. A bulky, hard-headed Scot with fierce whiskers and bushy eyebrows—"the finest-looking man I ever saw," as one contemporary put it—Neill commanded one of the East India Company's few European regiments. He had ruthlessly restored order in Allahabad when native regiments there killed their officers and threatened to join the rebellion. Neill's battle-hardened Fusiliers, together with the Sikhs, had shot and hacked their way through Allahabad's streets, then summarily hanged every man they found in a sepoy uniform, rebel or not.

An English officer wrote to his mother, "Every day ten or a dozen niggers are hanged." For the next three months bullock carts would roam at night, collecting the bodies dangling by twos or threes from the Allahabad gallows, from tree branches, and from signposts in the market place, and take them to be dumped into the Ganges.[13]

"God grant that I may have acted with justice," Neill wrote on June 17.

---

* The four British women were eventually returned and perished with the rest. However, two of the Eurasian girls married their sepoy captors to escape further abuse. The first, Amelia Horne, eventually escaped. Miss Wheeler, however, became a Muslim and died a very old lady in Cawnpore after telling her extraordinary story to a Catholic priest on her deathbed.

"I know I have acted with severity." A devout Christian, he firmly believed that "the Word of God gives no authority to the modern tenderness for human life."[14] But he had restored British control, first in Benares and then in Allahabad.

For the past three weeks Neill had been desperately anxious to push on to save the garrison at Cawnpore. Finally on July 7 Havelock was marching to the rescue. On the twelfth Havelock's troops beat a sepoy force near the Mughal princely residence of Fatehpur and pillaged and burned its ancient mosques. Marching under a blazing sun that left men dying of heatstroke, then under a drenching downpour as the monsoon rolled across the plain, Havelock and his men grimly made their way to the outskirts of Cawnpore, hanging "rebels" as they went.

By now they all knew the story of Nana Sahib's treachery and of the women who had been taken hostage. "By God's help, " Havelock told his tired and hungry men (all their meat had spoiled in the heat and they were living on hard biscuits), "we shall save them, or every man of us die in the attempt."[15]

The rebels made a final stand outside the city: they broke before a last-minute charge led by Havelock's son. Nana Sahib galloped away in panic, while his demoralized army fled. By afternoon British soldiers took possession of Cawnpore and began looking for the house where they had been told the women and children were being held.

The streets and bazaar were deserted. The residents of Cawnpore had almost all gone into hiding, terrified of what the British would do once they learned the truth. In the eerie silence the ragged men finally came upon the house, called the Bibighar, off a side street—ironically, a house a British officer had built for his Indian mistress.[16] Once inside, the soldiers dashed frantically from room to room but found no one, only a tremendous litter of women and children's clothes, petticoats, straw hats, slippers, toys, pages from ripped Bibles, and the occasional daguerreotype in a cracked case. All of it was soaked in blood.

At last they were able to follow the grisly trail out the back and down into the courtyard, then to the well at the corner of the garden. With the help of reluctant eyewitnesses, they were able to reconstruct what had happened. As Havelock's troops closed on the city, Nana Sahib decided that the English and Eurasian women and children—tightly jammed into the tiny house and dying daily from heat, dysentery, and cholera— would make inconvenient witnesses. On July 16 he or one of his henchmen had ordered all of them, every last woman and child, put to death.

Even sepoys who had participated in the earlier attack at the river re-fused to carry out this cold-blooded act of slaughter. Finally five men—two local Muslim butchers, two indigent Hindu peasants, and a member of Nana Sahib's bodyguard—were found who were willing to enter the Bibighar with *tulwar*s (a type of scimitar) and complete the job. All day the screams and shrieks from inside the house reverberated through Cawnpore's streets. Even after the killers left at nightfall, the terrible sounds continued.[17]

The next morning a huge crowd had gathered, many standing on the garden wall as low-caste sweepers were sent in to take the bodies out. "The bodies were dragged out, most of them by the hair of the head," testified an eyewitness later. "Those who had clothes worth taking were stripped. Some of the women were alive. I cannot say how many." So were three little boys. They were running in circles, screaming hys-terically, as the mutilated bodies were dragged down to the well and thrown in.[18]

Finally the little boys were killed and thrown in as well: one of them had his brains dashed out against a tree. The British soldiers could still see "an eye glazed and withered...smashed into the coarse bark."

Giddy with exhaustion, thirst, and horror, some soldiers were in tears. Some vomited at the sight. Their commanding officer, Major Bingham, gazed down into the well, where naked bodies, limbs, and heads could be clearly seen in the bloodred water. "The *poor poor* crea-tures!" he exclaimed in sobbing tones.[19]

It seemed an unbelievable act. The deliberate butchery of innocent women and children touched a raw nerve in the Victorian sensibility.[20] What had been a desire for retribution became a general bloodlust.

Captain Neill set the tone. He had arrived on July 20 and immedi-ately ordered that every sepoy prisoner be taken to the Bibighar before execution. There each would be made to kneel and lick up the blood on the floor: he specifically ordered that "the task will be as revolting...to each miscreant's feeling as possible," knowing full well that touching blood was deeply abhorrent to high-caste Hindus.[21] Some prisoners had to be whipped for ten minutes before they would do the disgusting act. Neill was unmoved: "No one who has witnessed the scenes of murder, mutilation, and massacre can ever listen to the word 'mercy' applied to these fiends."

Other English took their own informal revenge. Bingham's men had caught one of Nana Sahib's officials when they entered the city. "We broke his caste," Bingham wrote later. "We stuffed pork, beef, and everything which would possibly break his caste down his throat." After the men had finished with their prisoner, Bingham was amazed the man was still alive when he was finally dragged to a tree and hanged, "which I had the pleasure of witnessing." One tree alone was soon festooned with more than 150 battered native corpses. "No doubt this is strange law," Neill said at the time, "but it suits the occasion well."[22]

Almost every white in India agreed. As the story of the Bibighar massacre spread, the facts took on more and more grotesque dimensions. Stories circulated that the women had been systematically raped and forced to commit what Victorians would only call "unspeakable acts" before they died. Given the sexually repressed society of the British Raj and the hysterical fear that the mutiny had triggered, almost any lurid atrocity story found believers.

There were stories of English matrons being sold in the bazaars to the highest bidder; of children being roasted alive; of an officer's wife at Meerut being stripped and her breasts cut off. And it was not just British men who were turned into bloodthirsty killers by the rumors. In far-off peaceful Bombay Mrs. Fanny Duberly, wife of a hussar officer, wrote in her diary: "I can only look forward with awe to the day of vengeance, when our hands shall be dipped in the blood of our enemies, and the tongues of our dogs shall be red with the same."[23]

As British soldiers left Cawnpore, they swore oaths that for every white woman and child killed they would kill one hundred of the enemy. That "enemy" was now anyone with a colored skin. An appalling trail of bodies followed Havelock's advance on Lucknow. The slaughter intensified when the main British Army returned from the Punjab and began its march on Delhi; and it reached its height in September as they retook the Mughal capital.

On September 11, 1857, cannon and howitzers fired their opening barrage on the city. Three days later British, Sikh, Pathan, and Gurkha troops stormed through the Kashmir Gate. Savage hand-to-hand fighting carried the attackers over the walls, into Delhi's maze of narrow, twisting streets and into nearly every house. British soldiers broke into the cellars of merchants who sold European beer and liquor and were soon drunk on port and brandy.

"The demon of destruction seemed to have enjoyed a perfect revel," commented the officer leading the assault on Delhi. Smashed walls and buildings, bayoneted bodies, and abandoned wagons and artillery pieces clogged every avenue, as the killing continued.[24] Men, young and old, sepoy or not, were mowed down without compunction. Indian women and children were generally spared. However, one officer met an old school chum in the street, a civilian volunteer from the Bengal Civil Service whose sister had been murdered by the mutineers. He told the officer that "he had put to death all he had come across, not excepting women and children." Judging by the man's crazed face and blood-soaked clothes, the officer added, "I quite believe he told me the truth."[25]

After the seventh day of fighting, on September 21, the Union Jack flew over the royal citadel, the famed Red Fort. Six out of every ten men in the British force had been killed or wounded. Dead rebels and civilians were beyond count. Refugees streamed out of the city, including the man in whose name the mutiny had been raised, seventy-year-old Bahadur Shah II, the king of Delhi and the last surviving Mughal ruler. Captain William Hodson of Hodson's Horse rode after him with fifty of his crack Sikh troopers. They were lean whipcord men, men with hawklike faces who never shaved or cut their hair. But the Sikhs were renowned across India for their bravery in battle, their skill with sword and musket, and their light dun-colored or *karki* clothes, which more and more British soldiers were substituting for their traditional scarlet coats.* Hodson and his men caught up with the would-be emperor and his entourage six miles south of the city at the great tomb of Emperor Humayun.

Hodson guaranteed the old man's safety if he surrendered; the safety of his three sons was another matter. The rumor was that they had ordered every English woman in Delhi to be put to death, forcing them to drink the blood of their own children before being murdered.

Bahadur Shah sent a messenger to ask if the princes' lives would be spared if they surrendered. "Unconditional surrender" was Hodson's only reply. At last the princes gave up and were loaded into a bullock cart for transport back to Delhi. When they were a mile from the Red Fort, Hodson pushed them out of the cart and ordered them to strip. He then shot each of the princes in the head with a carbine he borrowed from one of his men.

His grim-eyed Sikh troopers "shouted with delight." Their greatest

---

* British soldiers during the siege of Delhi discovered that the khaki cloth was not only lighter and cooler but also made them less conspicuous targets. It was a discovery that the rest of the British Army made during the Boer War, after losing too many men to enemy snipers, and led to its general adoption.

leader, Guru Teg Bahadur, had been murdered by Delhi's emperor in 1675, and prophecy had told them that a white man would lead them to the ancient capital and avenge the killing.[26] Hodson even dumped the princes' bodies in the exact spot where the Sikh leader's head had been displayed in 1675—and where the blood of the dead English women murdered in the uprising in May still stained the ground.

Hodson went to bed that night "very tired but very much satisfied with the day's work." On all sides, he wrote, he received congratulations "for my success in destroying the enemies of our race."[27] The heirs to the last Mughal emperor, direct descendants of the great Tamurlaine, were dead. British rule in India was secure. Bit by bit order was restored. The last rebel holdout, at Gwalior, fell on June 19, 1858. In March Bahadur Shah was tried by a military court and found guilty on all charges. He was sentenced to exile for life to Rangoon, in far-off Burma, where he died and was buried four years later in November 1862.

However, one rebel leader escaped capture. Nana Sahib had faked suicide after the fall of Cawnpore in hopes of eluding his British pursuers. His aide and general, Tania Tope, was caught and executed in April 1859. But Nana Sahib was never found. Hodson had said hanging him would have been "a positive pleasure." There were persistent rumors that Nana eventually died of fever in Nepal, but they were never confirmed. For decades officers in remote hill stations in northern and western India would report sightings of the ever-elusive raja of Bithur. The last would be in 1895.

Like some Victorian Osama bin Laden, the memory of the man Havelock called a "devil incarnate" would haunt the British Raj down to its final hours. The retribution for what he had done would scar India forever. Today Cawnpore has been renamed Kanpur, and the marble angel that once stood on the site of the Bibighar well is gone. But the red-brick neo-Gothic church built to the memory of the European victims still remains.

It serves as a reminder that for a few terrible months in 1857, violence had been met with violence, and the seeds of future violence had been sown. The British Empire in India, which seemed stronger than ever in the years after the Great Mutiny, would one day reap the whirlwind.

Meanwhile, on the west coast of India in Porbandar, an ancient port overlooking the Arabian Sea, the events of the Mutiny seemed as far away as events on the moon. British soldiers and officials were almost unknown in the city. Porbandar was one of many parts of India untouched by the uprising. Instead, its prosperous Hindu and Muslim merchants were still ruled, as they always had been, by their local prince, the rana of Porbandar. That same year, when the streets of Cawnpore and Delhi were flowing with blood, the rana's *diwan* or chief counselor, Karamchand Gandhi, was taking his new wife and bride through Porbandar's happily bustling avenues to his family home.

Karamchand was forty, tall, and distinguished looking. His bride was barely twelve. This was Karamchand Gandhi's fourth marriage. His first two wives had died before being able to produce him a male heir; the third had been terminally ill when he made his marriage contract in the traditional Hindu way with the family of his new bride, Putlibai. For her family, it was a good match. The Gandhis belonged to a higher *jati,* or subcaste, and Karamchand was an important man of affairs, as well as a man of property and piety. His house stood near the center of town, next to a temple dedicated to Lord Krishna and surrounded by elegant buildings made of a bright luminescent limestone that gave Porbandar the name of the White City. At sunset Karamchand and Porbandar's other residents would set small lamps on their doorsteps as part of some religious festivals, bathing the white limestone in a gentle amber glow.[28]

Karamchand Gandhi's house was a fine one, with three stories, that his grandfather had bought from a Brahmin woman eighty years earlier. (The original deed, written in the local language of Gujarati, and witnessed with the seal and swastika* of the rana himself, still survives.) The top floor, sunlit and fanned by the sea breezes, was where Karamchand's father conducted his daily prayers every morning for two hours. All the Gandhis were members of the Bania caste, devout Hindus, and Vaishnavas, or devotees to the cult of Vishnu and Lord Krishna, whose temple next door they visited twice a day.

In the bottom floor of the house was a room less than twenty feet long and thirteen wide, where Karamchand's bride would spend her entire life. It was dark, so dark that even at midday one needed to light the oil lamp to see, and stifling hot in summer. Yet it was the center of life for the household and the women in the Gandhi family. There she arose

---

* An ancient Indian solar disk and traditional sign of good luck that the Nazis later made into a symbol of Aryan racial purity.

every morning before anyone else and retired after everyone else had gone to bed.[29] On one side was a tiny kitchen, where she prepared the family meals: on the other, an even tinier room where her mother and sister lived. It was into that room that Putlibai, on October 2, 1869, retired to give birth to her fifth and last child.

In a Vaishnava household like the Gandhis, everything related to childbirth was considered a gross form of pollution. No one else entered the room except a midwife of the lowest caste: after the child's birth the room would be subject to days of ritual purification and cleansing. Karamchand's mother, however, was allowed to speak to Putlibai through the doorway. It was she who would inform the wives of her other sons and her granddaughters that Putlibai had given birth to a son. They would be jealous; surely Putlibai must be favored by the gods, since only one of her four children was a girl.[30]

For the next ten days, Putlibai and her new infant lay together in the sweltering chamber, lit by only a single oil lamp. But the baby was safe and well. Another daughter would have been problematic: the *Aitareya Brahmana* had proclaimed to Hindus for three thousand years that "to have a daughter is misery," and female infanticide, officially forbidden by the British, was not unknown in the region.[31] But this was a son, with a large head and hands, and a priest astrologer was immediately brought in to cast his horoscope. It was favorable, and out of the letters he recommended as most auspicious his parents formed a name: Mohandas.

He would be Putlibai's favorite, the spoiled youngest child in a large, pious, active household. His mother prayed daily that Lord Krishna should make her Mohandas a hero among heroes. But as life in the house of Gandhi returned to normal, and the tiny glowing lamps were set out on the doorstep for evening worship, even she could never have guessed what a hero he would become, or how.

Chapter One

THE CHURCHILLS AND THE RAJ

And Blenheim's Tower shall triumph
O'er Whitehall.
ANONYMOUS PAMPHLETEER, 1705

ON NOVEMBER 30, 1874, ANOTHER BABY boy was born on the other side of the world. This one also first saw light in his grandfather's house, but on a far grander scale—indeed, in the biggest private home in Britain.

Surrounded by three thousand acres of "green lawns and shining water, banks of laurel and fern, groves of oak and cedar, fountains and islands," Blenheim Palace boasted 187 rooms.[1] It was in a drafty bedroom on the first floor that Jennie Jerome Churchill gave birth to her first child. "Dark eyes and hair" was how her twenty-five-year-old husband, Randolph Churchill, described the boy to Jennie's mother, and "wonderfully very pretty everybody says."[2]

The child's baptized name would be Winston Leonard Spencer Churchill. If the Gandhis were unknown outside their tiny Indian state, the Churchill name was steeped in history. John Churchill, the first Duke of Marlborough, had been Europe's most acclaimed general and the most powerful man in Britain. His series of victories over France in the first decade of the eighteenth century had made Britain a world-class power. A grateful Queen Anne gave him the royal estate at Woodstock on which to build a palace, which he named after his most famous victory. For Winston Churchill, Blenheim Palace would always symbolize a heritage of glory and a family born to greatness.

Yet the first Duke of Marlborough had been followed by a succession of nonentities. If the power and wealth of England expanded to unimagined heights over the next century, that of the Churchills steadily declined.

The vast fortune that the first duke accumulated in the age of Queen Anne was squandered by his successors. When Randolph's father inherited the title in 1857, the same year the Great Mutiny raged in India, he had been faced, like his father and grandfather before him, by debts of Himalayan proportions and slender means with which to meet them. Randolph's grandfather had already turned Blenheim into a public museum, charging visitors one shilling admission. Randolph's father would have to sell off priceless paintings (including a Raphael and Van Dyck's splendid equestrian portrait of King Charles I, still the largest painting in the National Gallery), the fabulous Marlborough collection of gems, and the eighteen-thousand-volume Sunderland library, in order to make ends meet.[3]

In the financial squeeze which was beginning to affect nearly all the Victorian aristocracy, the Spencer-Churchills felt the pinch more than most. For Randolph Churchill, the Marlborough legacy was a bankrupt inheritance. In a crucial sense, it was no inheritance at all. His older brother, Lord Blandford, would take over the ducal title, Blenheim Palace, and the remaining estates. What was left for him, and for his heirs, was relatively paltry (although much more than the patrimony of the great majority of Britons), with £4,200 a year and the lease on a house in Mayfair.[4]

So the new father, twenty-five-year-old Randolph, was going to have to cut his own way into the world, just as his son would later. And both would choose the same way: politics.

Randolph was the family rebel, a natural contrarian and malcontent. Beneath his pale bulging eyes, large exquisite mustache, and cool aristocratic hauteur was the soul of a headstrong alpha male. As he told his friend Lord Rosebery, "I like to be the boss."[5] Young Lord Randolph was determined to make a name for himself as a member of Parliament. All he needed was an issue.

In 1874 an issue was not easy to find. At the time when Winston Churchill was born, British politics reflected a consensus that the country had not known in nearly a hundred years—and soon would never know again.[6] The last big domestic battle had been fought over the Second Reform Bill, when crowds in London clashed in the streets with police and tore up railings around Hyde Park. Passage of the act of 1867 opened the door to Britain's first working-class voters. But almost a decade later neither Conservatives nor Liberals were inclined to let it swing open any wider.

Both parties agreed that free trade was the cornerstone of the British economy, still the most productive in the world. Both agreed on the importance of keeping the gold standard. They even agreed that social reform was best left in private and local hands, although Parliament would occasionally give its approval to a round of slum clearances or a comprehensive health act. A twelve-hour day for the average workman, and ten and a half hours for women and young persons older than thirteen, made eminent good sense economically and morally. Giving them a government retirement pension or an unemployment check did not.[7]

Tories and Liberals also agreed on maintaining an empire that was without rival and on defending it with a navy that was second to none. In 1874 that empire was not only the most extensive but the most cohesive on the planet.[8] It emcompassed Britain itself, with England, Wales, Scotland, and Ireland all welded together under a single government and crown. Across the Atlantic there were the islands of the West Indies and also Canada, the empire's first self-governing "dominion"—a word that would loom large in the later battles between Churchill and Gandhi.

Then there were the prosperous and stable colonies of white settlers in New Zealand and Australia which, although more than ten thousand miles away, felt a strong bond of loyalty to Britain and the Crown. Britain also directed the fate of two colonies in southern Africa, the Cape Colony and Natal, in addition to Lagos in Nigeria. Hong Kong, Singapore, and some scattered possessions in Asia and the Mediterranean completed the collection.

But the centerpiece of the empire was India, where Britain was the undisputed master of more than a quarter billion people. In 1874 two out of every three British subjects was an Indian. Since the Mutiny both political parties had closed ranks about dealing with India. The power of the British system of governance, or the Raj as it was called after the Mutiny, had become more palpable but also more streamlined. The opening of the Suez Canal in 1869 had also made it much easier to reach the ancient subcontinent than in the days before the Mutiny.

Most Britons still knew almost nothing about the subcontinent or its peoples. Nonetheless, the fact that they possessed India, and governed it virtually as a separate empire, gave Britons a halo of superpower status that no other people or nation could match. The attitude was summed up nine years later in Rudyard Kipling's poem "Ave Imperatrix":

> *And all are bred to do your will*
> *By land and sea—wherever flies*

The Flag, to fight and follow still,
And work your Empire's destinies.

In the midst of this triumphant march to the future, the only hint of trouble was Ireland. The question of whether the Catholic Irish would ever enjoy any degree of "home rule" had become a live issue in Irish politics. In 1875 it sent Charles Stewart Parnell to Parliament, but otherwise Irish nationalism hardly registered in Westminster; nor did any other issue.*

There seemed to be no burning questions to divide public opinion, no bitter clash of interests, no looming threats on the horizon for an unknown but ambitious politician to seize upon. By 1880 Randolph realized he had only one way to get attention in Parliament: by becoming a nuisance and stirring things up.

The issue Winston's father seized upon was the Bradlaugh case. Charles Bradlaugh was a Liberal and a radical atheist who, when elected to Parliament that year, refused to take the oath of allegiance needed to take his seat in the Commons, because it contained the words "so help me God." The question of whether Bradlaugh should be allowed to take his seat anyway stirred the hearts of many Conservative members, and Randolph's friend Sir Henry Drummond Wolff asked his help against Bradlaugh.

Randolph soon discovered that Bradlaugh made an easy target.[9] He was not only a free thinker but a socialist, an advocate of birth control, and even a critic of Empire. Bradlaugh was also a radical republican who denounced the monarchy and aristocrats like Randolph in heated terms.† So when Randolph made his speech on May 24, 1880, condemning Bradlaugh for his atheism, he also read aloud from one of Bradlaugh's pamphlets calling the royal family "small German breast-beating wanderers, whose only merit is their loving hatred of one another." He then hurled the pamphlet on the floor and stamped on it.

The House was ecstatic. "Everyone was full of it," Jennie wrote, who

---

* It would be registering sooner than most realized. Ironically, Kipling's triumphant poem was composed in 1882, after the exposure of an Irish plot to assassinate Queen Victoria, to reassure the British public. Winston Churchill's earliest childhood memory was of wandering through Dublin's Phoenix Park and seeing the spot where the British viceroy had been murdered only a couple of years earlier.

† He would also be one of the first champions of Indian nationalism. When he died in 1891 and was buried in London's Brookwood Cemetery, among the three thousand mourners who attended the funeral would be a young Mohandas Gandhi.

had watched the speech from the gallery, "and rushed up and congratu-lated me to such an extent that I felt as though I had made it."[10] Lord Randolph Churchill's career was launched as a sensational, even outra-geous, headline-grabber. Together with Wolff and another friend, Sir Henry Gorst, he formed what came to be known as the Fourth Party,* a junta of Tory mavericks who ripped into their own party leaders any time they sided with the government—to the delight of journalists and newspaper readers.

Suddenly, thanks to Randolph Churchill, politics was fun again. When Bradlaugh was reelected in spite of being denied his seat, Randolph attacked him again, carefully playing it for laughs and for the gallery and the news media; when the voters of Northampton insisted on returning Bradlaugh again, Randolph did the same thing. And then a fourth and a fifth time: at one point Bradlaugh had to be escorted out of the House chamber by police and locked up in the Big Ben tower. Some people began to joke that Randolph must be bribing Northampton voters to keep voting for Bradlaugh, since they were also keeping Randolph in the headlines.[11]

Lord Randolph had the good sense to realize that while the Bradlaugh case had launched his political rise, he needed more substan-tial issues to sustain it. He tried Ireland for a while, taking up the cause of Ulster Protestants in the North and lambasting the Irish nationalists of the south. He tested a new catchphrase, "Tory Democracy," urging Conservatives to win votes and allies among Britain's newly enfran-chised working class—but the phrase had more media appeal than sub-stance or thought behind it. He even tried Egypt, furiously denouncing the Liberal government's support of its corrupt ruler. Finally in the sum-mer of 1884, the man an American journalist was calling "the political sensation of England" turned to India.

Crucial though India was to Britain, few politicians had any expertise in the empire's greatest possession. In November 1884 Churchill planned a major tour of India. His friend Wilfred Blunt, who had al-ready traveled widely there, set up the key introductions. He predicted "a great future for any statesman who will preach Tory Democracy in India."[12] Lord Randolph left in December and did not return to London until April 1885, after logging more than 22,800 miles. He then deliv-ered a round of fiery speeches denouncing the Gladstone government's

---

* After the Liberals, Tories, and Irish Nationalists.

policies there, from neglecting the threat from Russia to failing to gain more native participation in the Raj. The speeches established him as the Conservatives' "front line spokesman on India."[13] So when the Tories returned to power in June that year, he was the obvious candidate for secretary of state for India.

In terms of direct influence over people's lives, it was the single most powerful position in the cabinet, even more powerful than prime minister. At age thirty-six, Randolph Churchill would be overseeing an imperial domain that was, as he discovered in his travels and readings, unique in British history—perhaps unique in human history.

How the British built an empire in India, conquering one of the most ancient and powerful civilizations in the world, is an epic of heroism, sacrifice, ruthlessness, and greed. But it is also the story of a growing sense of mission, even destiny: the growing conviction that the British were meant to rule India not only for their own interests but for the sake of the Indians as well. That belief would decisively shape the character not only of the British Empire in India but also of Randolph's son Winston Churchill—the man into whose hands the destiny of the Raj would ultimately fall.

Ironically, that empire's founding fathers, the group of God-fearing merchants living in Shakespeare's London who created the Honorable East India Company, never intended to go to India at all—any more than Queen Elizabeth I expected them to when she gave them a royal charter on the last day of 1600. Their aim was to get to the Spice Islands (the Molucca Islands in today's Indonesia), where Spanish, Portuguese, and Dutch merchants and adventurers were battling over fortunes in nutmeg, cloves, and mace. The East India Company's initial stop at Surat, on India's west coast, was supposed to be only a layover for ventures farther east.

But when the Dutch tortured and murdered ten of their merchants in the island of Amboyne in 1623 and foisted the English out of the Spice Islands, the London-based company had nowhere else to go.[14] By 1650, the year John Churchill was born in Devon, the East India Company found itself precariously perched in a tiny settlement near Surat called Fort St. George, doing business at the pleasure of the rulers of India, the Mughal emperors—at the time probably the richest human beings in the world. In 1674 the company acquired a similar outpost at Bombay, which King Charles II had received as a wedding present from the king of Portugal. Then in 1690 it built another, in Bengal at Kalikat, which the English pronounced Calcutta.

The English were only one of several European communities doing business in the region. The Portuguese had a thriving settlement in Goa, where Portuguese and Indian Christians worshipped in a cathedral that contained the bones of Saint Francis Xavier. The Dutch dominated Ceylon; the Danes were set up at Tranquebar. The French East Indies Company, founded in 1668, had large "factories" or warehouses at Pondicherry and Chandernagar for its cargos of indigo, sugar, and pepper. In the blazing heat and stifling humidity, surrounded by disease and flies, everyone's energies were concentrated on making money and staying on the Mughal emperor's good side.

Then in 1712 Emperor Bahadur Shah I died at his palace at Lahore, surrounded by his courtiers, generals, and concubines—even as the Duke of Marlborough's workmen were erecting the stately towers of Blenheim Palace four thousand miles away. Although no one realized it, Bahadur was India's last great ruler. After his death the magnificent Mughal Empire came apart with alarming speed.

Bahadur's death left that empire split in two, with competing Mughal capitals at Delhi in the north and Hyderabad in the south. External enemies like the Afghans and Persians, and internal ones like the Sikhs and Hindu warrior clans of Marathas and Rajputs, made their move. When the old nizam of Hyderabad died in 1748, the French and British merchant communities in India were forced, almost against their will,[15] to choose sides in the struggle for control of the southern half of the empire before it crumbled into chaos.

The Frenchman Joseph François Dupleix was the first to grasp that by throwing the power of his Compagnie de l'Indie Ouest behind a candidate for the nizam's throne, he could shape events decisively to his side. But it was his rival Robert Clive who put that insight to work as a formula for empire-building.

In 1751 Clive was just another underpaid East India Company clerk in Madras, tormented by fever and prickly heat and bouts of manic depression. Twice he had tried to commit suicide, and twice the pistol he used had failed to fire. He had no military experience at all when his superiors suddenly decided to put him in charge of taking the nizam's fortress at Arcot.

But Clive grasped better than anyone else that power in India came literally out of the barrel of a gun. India was descending into anarchy. In order to protect its interests against both local marauders and the French, the East India Company had created its own army, with regiments of native soldiers (or *sepoys*) and cavalrymen (or *sowars*) serving under British officers and using modern muskets and European-style discipline and training.[16] Recruited largely from north India and the Hindu and Muslim villages between Bihar and Agra, these British-trained sepoys were far superior to troops any native ruler could field. So with a few hundred of them and some supporting European troops, Clive was able to take Arcot, hold it against all comers, and then form an alliance with a local Maratha chieftain to begin driving the French out of southern India—and to make himself a fortune.

From Hyderabad Clive went to Bengal, the Mughal Empire's richest province, where he and his barefoot sepoys did the same thing. By the time Clive routed France's Bengali allies at the Battle of Plassey in 1758, he had turned the East India Company's mercenary army into an unstoppable engine of conquest. The emperor in Delhi was forced to appoint Clive governor of Bengal, with British control over Bihar and Orissa as part of the deal.

The pattern for the future was set. With a rising tide of conflict and chaos on the subcontinent, no Indian prince could afford to be without British help. Yet the more a prince relied on British help, the more it weakened his own ability to control events or maintain order, leading to more conflict and chaos. Under these uncertain conditions, the one sure bet was the East India Company and its invincible army. And the company's soldiers, horses, and cannon were all paid for by revenues of the territories it conquered, which were then collected and administered by the local princes it left in place. Only eight years after Clive appeared on the scene, the East India Company had become a power, and a law, unto itself.

It was a setting that inevitably led to corruption. Clive himself set the standard with his looting of Bengal. As another future East India Company servant put it, Clive "walked between heaps of gold and silver, crowned with rubies and diamonds, and was at liberty to help himself." It took two hundred boats to carry the first load of booty down to Calcutta. It was estimated that in 1757 alone Clive and his cronies extorted more than 1.2 million pounds sterling from the ruler of Bengal, enough to build a duplicate Blenheim Palace. By 1781 the figure rose to nearly five million pounds.[17] Yet the remaining wealth of Bengal made even that amount seem paltry. "My God," Clive exclaimed when questioned in the House of Commons, "at this moment I stand astonished by my own moderation."

Clive bought a fabulous estate in Shropshire (where eventually he succeeded in taking his own life). Another company general, Eyre Coote, came away with enough to buy country homes in Ireland, estates in Hampshire and Wiltshire, and a comfortable house in London. The golden age of the nabob had arrived, as other company men used their trade monopoly with Bengal to make their fortunes.[18] Meanwhile the Bengalis starved and the company itself teetered on bankruptcy.

The situation got so bad that London finally dispatched Warren Hastings as governor-general to straighten things out, giving him executive powers over the East India Company's enclaves in Bombay and Madras as well. Hastings's reforms, along with the Regulating Act of 1773 and India Act of 1783, finally regularized British rule in India. They set up a governing council in Calcutta headed by a governor-general, as well as a board of control in London; and they made the East India Company and all its military and civil staff functionaries of the British government.

It was a pivotal moment. The bulk of the country, of course, was still in Indian hands, with a Mughal emperor still in Delhi. Neither Whitehall nor Leadenhall Street nor the council in Calcutta wanted to change that. But their refusal to assume responsibility for the fate of the rest of the Mughal Empire did not allow the British to escape dealing with its problems. Predatory outside powers, aggressive and well-armed local princes, independent-minded Indian *nawabs* or viceroys with their own power base, and self-assertive warrior communities like the Maharathas and the Sikhs were all poised to make their own bid for hegemony on the subcontinent.

Maintaining law and order was a problem going back millennia in India. "Whoever is superior in power shall wage war," wrote the author of the fifteen-hundred-year-old *Arthashastra* or *Treatise on State-Craft,* "whoever is rising in power shall break the agreement of peace." In thirty centuries of history, no Indian ruler had ever managed to defeat every challenger or fend off every marauder. Yet the English, in their arrogance and ignorance, were willing to give it a try.

So one by one the independent princelings and their armies of followers fell to British armies of sepoys and sowars, increasingly backed by white European troops. Hyderabad's ruler, the nizam, surrendered his last shreds of independence in 1798. Then the rulers of Mysore and the armies of the Maratha Confederacy were defeated in a series of campaigns that established Sir Arthur Wellesley's reputation as Britain's most brilliant soldier since the Duke of Marlborough.*

Then it was the turn of the marauding Pindaris; the peshwa of Poona, the last great Maratha prince, was defeated in 1818. Then the Rajputs; then the amir of Sind, followed by the Sikhs. With the annexation of Lower Burma in 1826, the Punjab in 1849, and the kingdom of Oudh in 1854, the map of British India that Winston Churchill would study as a schoolboy at Harrow was almost complete.

To the process of conquest and governance, the East India Company itself had become more and more irrelevant. Its trade monopoly was abolished in 1833. What was left was a military, judicial, and administrative network dominating the lives of tens of millions of Indians and affecting millions more. The government of India had gone through reforms since Warren Hastings, but it remained relatively simple. Beyond keeping order and collecting taxes, it largely left locals to their own devices, for better or—when famine or epidemic hit—for worse. Governor-General William Bentinck had set a precedent of cracking down on Hindu practices that were the most egregious in Western eyes, such as *suttee*, or burning widows to death on their husbands' funeral pyres, and *thugee*, the ritual murders committed by fanatical worshippers of the goddess Kali.

But on the whole, although they never doubted their superiority over Indians, British administrators were careful to avoid any head-on conflict with the indigenous culture. When Henry Lawrence took over administration of the Punjab in 1850, his only instructions to his young subordinates, some of whom were taking over districts the size of England, were: "Settle the country; make the people happy; and take care there are no rows."[19]

It was when Governor-General Lord Dalhousie tried to exceed these minimalist bounds that Indian resentment of British rule exploded into the Great Mutiny of 1857. By any standard, Dalhousie's progressive program was well meant. It brought India its first railways and telegraphs; it created a national postal service; it included laws banning child marriage and female infanticide, and it set up the first school for girls in India.[20] In his eight years in office, from January 1848 to February 1856,

---

* In 1815, as the Duke of Wellington, he would defeat Napoleon at Waterloo.

Dalhousie brought more changes to India than it had seen for centuries—more, in fact, than Indians could stomach. The sepoys' revolt against rumors of animal-greased cartridges was only the pretext. (It was also Dalhousie who cut off Nana Sahib's pension.) Offended Hindus and outraged Muslims all across north central India rose up in a ferocious attempt to turn back the clock and drive the British out.

They failed. The British used their victory in 1858 to clear away any alternative to their authority, whether military or political—or, just as important, moral. The last vestiges of the East India Company disappeared; native Indian regiments lost their artillery, and the number of British soldiers in India increased from just under 35,000 to 65,000.[21] The last Mughal emperor lost his throne, and every other prince forfeited his independent authority, including his private armies. The British emerged from the Mutiny stronger than ever, unquestioned masters of more than 250 million people. The Raj had begun.

But the British were careful to wear that mastership lightly. On November 1, 1858, Queen Victoria proclaimed the new order in India. Henceforth everyone, brown or white, rich or poor, Hindu or Muslim, Sikh or Christian, would "enjoy the equal and impartial protection of the law," she assured her Indian subjects. Any interference or intrusion on their religious beliefs would incur "our deepest displeasure." All would be "freely or impartially admitted to offices of our service." The proclamation ended with a promise and a prayer, penned by Victoria herself:

> In their prosperity will be our strength, in their contentment our security, and in their gratitude our best reward.... And may the God of all power grant to us, and those in authority under us, strength to carry out these our wishes for the good of our people.[22]

The Queen's proclamation would be the founding document of the British Raj. Behind the displays of fireworks and celebrations, from cites like Calcutta to remote hill stations like Massoorie, lay hope for a better future after the violence and bitterness of the Mutiny. Years later Mohandas Gandhi would remember the Queen's Proclamation as a model of benevolent motherly power.

Queen Victoria herself took up learning Hindi. She took on two Indian servants, one of whom became her confidential secretary. Meanwhile the British loosed their creative energies to remake India in their own image and, they believed, make India better. They built bridges, roads, railroads (by the 1860s there were more than five thousand miles of track), and factories generating iron and textiles.[23] They organized ambitious irrigation schemes to help feed India's masses and public health measures to reduce disease.

They set up schools and even universities for educating Indian youth, creating an elite of Western-educated Hindus and Muslims who edited and read English-language newspapers, wrote novels, studied law and engineering, and quoted Shakespeare and Keats. In 1861 the British introduced a legal code that was more impartial and more progressive than the one in Britain. (It protected, for instance, the right of married women to their own property.)[24] They maintained an efficient police force and a corps of judges and administrators in every province and district who would make the Indian Civil Service the model of paternal government for the rest of the world.

The British also kept order along the volatile Northwest Frontier, where mountain tribes fought each other as they had for centuries; it had been the gateway for foreign invaders since Alexander the Great. In the eighteenth century the chief threat to India had been from Persia. Under the British, and even before the Mutiny, the challenge seemed to be imperial Russia, which was busy building its own eastern empire through Tashkent and Khokand right up to the Pamir Mountains, the Bam-y-Dunya or Roof of the World, which lay only a few miles from the Indian frontier.[25]

The need for anti-Russian countermeasures gave birth to the so-called Great Game, which became both an imperial strategy and a geopolitical outlook. For some members of the Indian Civil Service, who are immortalized in the works of Rudyard Kipling, it became almost a calling. The Great Game required generations of political officers to work to maintain a cat's cradle of alliances with the various mountain tribes, as well as armed garrisons to patrol the rugged lunar landscape of the tribal areas. It meant keeping Afghanistan as a neutral buffer, while being on alert for any sudden Russian moves in Persia or Central Asia.

The Great Game also justified maintaining a large and active secret service in India (immortalized in Rudyard Kipling's *Kim*), in order to spy on the local population for any signs of Russian-inspired subversion or agitation against British rule (or later, any nationalist sentiment). It justified keeping a large native Indian army, 153,000 men in 1887 and all at the expense of Indian taxpayers,[26] ostensibly to protect them from the Russian Menace but also to help secure the Raj's authority as well as garrison tropical outposts of the empire from Egypt and Somalia to Hong Kong and Singapore.

In the two and a half decades after the Mutiny, the Raj fulfilled the queen's promise, or so it seemed. India's population was on the increase; average life expectancy rose from twenty-one years to thirty-two; even the per capita income of Indians was showing improvement (albeit an invisible one by British home standards).[27] The Indian Civil Service was a byword for incorruptibility, diligence, and dedication, symbolized by Kipling *Binks of Hezabad:*

> *"Why is my district death-rate low?"*
> *Said Binks of Hezabad.*
> *"Wells, drains and sewage-outfalls are*
> *My own peculiar fad."*

But if Britain had changed India, India had also changed Britain.

Britain enjoyed, for example, a host of Indian products from the imperial relationship. There was tea, which the East India Company had been exporting from China since the seventeenth century until a Scottish scientist discovered how to grow it in India. By the time Winston Churchill was born in 1874, production from Darjeeling had reached four million pounds weight a year, and Indian tea was becoming a mainstay of the British diet.

There was also jute, woven into ropes, cordage, and sturdy sacks for agricultural and industrial products. The jute industry became one of the fastest-growing and most profitable enterprises in both India and Britain. It virtually put the industrial city of Dundee on the map. Then there was cotton: when the American Civil War interrupted Britain's vital imports of cotton from the southern states, the Indian version kept the mills of Lancashire turning and the profits growing. By the same token, India got the bulk of its finished cotton cloth from England and was thus a crucial market for the output of Britain's Industrial Revolution.[28]

Finally there was opium, which the East India Company had smuggled from the poppy fields of India into China for decades until the Convention of Peking of 1861 legalized its sale, fatally weakening the Chinese empire and leading to the establishment of the British colony at Hong Kong. Similarly, it was an East India Company employee, Thomas

Raffles, who founded Singapore in 1819, and another, James Brooke, who established a British presence in Sarawak. In short, the British Empire in India fostered important imperial offshoots, indeed demanded them, from Asia to Suez and the Horn of Africa (the last two being vital for the sea link to India).

New words expanded and enriched the English vocabulary: palanquin, coolie, bungalow, jungle (from the Hindi *jangal*), cash (from the Tamil *kasu*), loot, tycoon, pundit, dinghy, dungaree, nabob, memsahib, thug (named after the Thugees, the murderous worshippers of Kali), and juggernaut (from the town of Jugarnath, where religious festivals included a great chariot under whose wheels worshippers would sometimes throw themselves). At the same time khaki (from the Hindi *khoko,* meaning "dusty"), puggarees (the cloth band covering a pith helmet), gymkhanas, cots, bangalores, and dum dum bullets (made at the Indian munitions factory in Dum Dum) became fixtures of British military life, not only in India but throughout the empire.

India deeply affected Britain's relations with other countries. In the eighteenth and nineteenth centuries the need to protect British interests there had fueled the rivalry with France (Napoleon's own conquest of Egypt of 1798 had been conceived as only a stepping-stone for restoring France's dominance in India) as well as Russia. It spurred close ties with the rulers of Egypt (home of the Suez Canal) and Turkey, whose sultan was the spiritual leader for millions of Indian Muslims. By 1884 protecting India was essential to British foreign policy. Virtually any diplomatic deal Britain struck with non-Western powers from Egypt and Abyssinia to China and Japan had to pass the scrutiny of the viceroy from his headquarters at Calcutta or lodgings nearby in Barrackpore, or was even handled directly by his personal envoys.

Finally, India taught Britons the habits of empire. It served as the training ground for generations of soldiers from Wellington to Lord Wavell; administrators from Elihu Yale (a former governor of Madras who also founded Yale College in America) to Thomas Raffles and Viscount Halifax (the man who almost replaced Winston Churchill as prime minister during World War II). Experiences there inspired writers from Thomas Macaulay and Kipling to E. M. Forster and George Orwell,* and philosophers James Fitzjames Stephen and James Mill.

---

* Orwell served in Burma from 1922 to 1927, at which date Burmese administration was still the responsibility of the Indian government.

The Indian Civil Service even helped to keep Britain's exclusive public schools in business, as Eton, Harrow, and the rest churned out young men by the hundreds, trained in Latin and Greek, who were useless for any jobs in a modern society but were willing to go to some remote Northwest Frontier hill station or to serve in the jungles of East Bengal as district commissioner for £300 a year. John Bright's famous remark (falsely attributed to John Stuart Mill) that the British Empire was a "vast system of outdoor relief for the upper classes" applied more to India than anywhere else.[29]

But India also taught Britons the habits of racial prejudice. The Raj thrived on an ugly pattern of racial and cultural attitudes that belied British protestations about their concerns for Indians' welfare and that undercut the moral basis of British rule.

This prejudice was largely the result of the Mutiny. In Clive's day or even Dalhousie's, race per se had counted for little in British India; social class or religion, much more.[30] Anglo-Indians of mixed race like Cawnpore's William Shepherd, although completely shunned by the Hindu community, were crucial to the building of the Raj. Eyre Coote, victor of Wandiwash, had been one; so was James Skinner, who created arguably the best regiment of the Indian Army, Skinner's Horse, just as the British Army's most distinguished soldier, Field Marshal Sir Frederick Roberts, was the grandson of a Rajput princess. An Anglo-Indian even became prime minister of England. Lord Liverpool, who oversaw the final defeat of Napoleon at Waterloo, was the grandson of a Calcutta woman who had married one of Clive's cronies.[31]

Liverpool had been a deeply controversial, even hated figure, but at the time none of his Whig opponents saw fit to mention his ancestry. Fifty years later any politician with Liverpool's racial background would have been instantly denounced as a "half-caste" or even "black." One reason for this change was the new theories about race and culture coming from the Continent, reinforced by Charles Darwin.[32] But at its core was the experience of the Mutiny. The events of 1857–58 left a permanent stamp of race fear in England, just as the uprising's defeat reinforced the lesson that the British were born to rule and the Indians to obey.

After 1858 Britons in India sensed they were a garrisoned community. "We are among the natives," as one of them put it, "as a ship on the wide and fathomless ocean constantly at the mercy of the wind, waves, and hidden rocks."[33] Uncertainty and anxiety turned India into an increasingly segregated society. Unlike the laws of South Africa or the

American South, Indian laws were ostensibly, even ostentatiously, color blind. But the new railways carefully reserved first-class compartments for whites only. Public restrooms were marked "European" and "Native." In some Anglican churches Indian Christians were not allowed to sit in the cooler parts of the church or under the fans.[34]

So paradoxically, even as the British were coming to India in record numbers and were becoming more involved in organizing Indian life than ever, they also were becoming more distant. The only natives with whom most Indian Britons had contact were servants or other passive objects of British rules and regulations. After work whites retreated to their bungalows or their private clubs, which excluded natives or even persons of mixed race. The basic attitude was summed up in one of Kipling's epigrams: "Let the White go to the White, and the Black to the Black." This policy not only seemed the best way to prevent racial discord, or even another Mutiny; it also ensured that whites and only whites remained in charge.

By 1884 British society in India had become a collection of self-enclosed boxes, each more exclusive and narrower than the one before. Class, education, and even ethnic distinctions (for example, Irish versus Scot and English versus Jew) sharply compartmentalized white society, from the Viceregal Lodge in Calcutta to the most remote hill stations. But these barriers bowed down to the most important distinction of all, the one that separated European from the native—even from the richest or highest-born native. The social and physical distance reinforced cultural and racial stereotypes that would carry right through into Winston Churchill's day.

Hindus, for example, were supposed to be weak and superstitious but also "intriguing, cunning... Falsehood and dissimulation, the most contemptible and degrading vices of which human beings can be guilty, are the national vices of Hindus."[35] Muslims, on the other hand, were considered physically strong but intellectually dim, while Sikhs were loyal but unstable, "the most militant and turbulent race in India."[36]

This system of racial stereotyping was born in the Indian Army. For decades its British commanders preferred to recruit their soldiers from the sturdy (mostly Muslim) peasant stock of northwestern India or from mountain tribes like Gurkhas and Garhwalis of the Himalaya foothills, rather than from the upper-caste Hindus who had dominated the pre-1857 army and were suspected of fomenting the Great Mutiny. What had begun as a strategy for avoiding a second national uprising became a rough-and-ready classification of Indians into those who were intelligent and educated but also weak and cowardly and the "martial races," those who were strong and brave but slow and backward. "Only British gentlemen combined both the intelligence and courage" needed to command troops in battle or to govern a subcontinent like India.[37]

On the whole, the average white in India believed that a typical native might make a good servant or a loyal soldier. In a few cases, a Bengali or high-caste Rajput might be ready to absorb a full Western education, studying Shakespeare sonnets and Latin grammar at Elphinstone College in Bombay or the Muslim Anglo-Oriental College in Aligarh. In truly extraordinary cases, he might even test into the Indian Civil Service. (Satyendranath Tagore was the first to do so, in 1863.)

But to the British they were still all "niggers," incapable of accomplishing anything without British help. Race allowed a half-educated Irish shipping clerk in Bombay to dismiss Tagore or his Nobel Prize–winning poet brother Rabindranath as pencil-pushing "babus." As late as 1922 one British colonel would directly attribute Gandhi's success to his support among the so-called nonfighting classes, "educated, discontented, cowardly agitators" who would quickly back down if the Raj stood firm—a view echoed by Winston Churchill a decade later.[38]

But as in all apartheid societies, beneath the contempt lay fear—especially fear for white women. The horrors in the garden at Bibighar cast an enormous and lurid shadow over British attitudes for nearly a century, especially as the numbers of British women in India grew after 1858. In a world in which whites were outnumbered ten thousand to one, and white women even more so, informal rules of sexual as well as racial segregation were rigorously applied.

White women were never to travel, or meet alone, with an Indian man; Indian males were never to speak to a European woman unless spoken to, let alone stare at or touch one. Those who dared to transgress those rules, male or female, became objects of scandal, even physical violence. Such incidents became the subject of sensational fiction from Kipling to E. M. Forster's *A Passage to India*. Bizarre as they were, the rules lasted almost as long as the Raj. As late as 1925 an Indian newspaperman could remember not being allowed to wander near a beach reserved for white women, in case an Indian male caught sight of an English lady in her bathing costume.[39]

The Raj taught that Indians were incapable of self-restraint, self-discipline, or self-help, let alone self-rule. J. F. Stephen, law member of the viceroy's council in the early 1870s, stated the case plainly and suc-cinctly. Centuries, even thousands of years, of conflict and native misrule had left India "worn to the bone." It was white rule, and the Raj's ab-solute authority, that had brought "peace, order, the supremacy of law, the prevention of crime [and] the construction of public works" to the subcontinent. Native rule would mean a return to chaos. The English mission in India was to impose "European principles" of law and progress and peace on a people who had known none. It was a just peace, Stephen stated, but ultimately a "peace compelled by force."[40]

So when Victoria was declared empress of India in 1877 (taking on, as it were, the formal mantle of the Mughals), she was, for all her maternal interest in her Indian subjects, also shutting the door on any change in their servile status. The only hope for Indians in the future, according to Sir John Strachey, a prominent post-Mutiny official in the Indian Civil Service, was "the long continuance of the benevolent but strong govern-ment of Englishmen"—whether Indians liked it or not.[41] Yet even in the midst of India's official celebrations of Victoria's new title in 1877, to which the viceroy, Lord Lytton, invited nearly seventy thousand guests and seventy-seven rajas and princes in their jeweled robes and finery, famine was breaking out across India. The monsoons had failed that year. Starvation soon spread to Bombay and Madras and Hyderabad, touching nearly thirty million people and lasting until mid-1878.[42]

Lytton, the son of novelist Edward Bulwer-Lytton and a friend of Prime Minister Benjamin Disraeli, was like most viceroys conscientious and hardworking. He set in motion a famine-control program that would, with only a single exception, prevent another major outbreak for nearly seventy years.* Yet his attitude about India and Indians was typi-cal. He believed that the majority of Indians were "an inert mass," inca-pable of generating effort or taking care of themselves, while the Western-trained elite were feckless "Baboos whom we have educated to write semi-seditious articles in the Press." The best the British could hope for, Lytton insisted, was good relations with the princes and the large landowners, who in turn kept the rest of the population in line. "We certainly cannot afford to give them any increased political power independent of our own."[43]

His successor in 1881, George Frederick Robinson, Lord Ripon, son of a Liberal prime minister (he had even been born at Number 10

---

* The record ended in 1943, when Winston Churchill was prime minister.

Downing Street), stood at the opposite pole to the conservative Lytton. In fact, Lytton and Ripon set off a debate about what to do about India that would last right down to the end of the Raj—and shape the lives and attitudes of both Gandhi and Winston Churchill.

Like Lytton, Ripon firmly believed in Britons' imperial mission in India. But he also believed that the Indians themselves had a role to play. His ideal was to create a nation of people who would be, as Thomas Macaulay stated in his famous *Minute on Indian Education* of 1835, "Indian in blood and colour, but English in taste, in opinions, in morals and in intellect." Ripon believed building a bond of trust and cooperation with educated Indians was crucial to creating the kind of color-blind India embodied in the Queen's Proclamation and to ensuring the future of the Raj. "We must make [the natives] feel that England wishes to govern India not only *for* India but *through* India."[44]

It was a noble dream, but Ripon's efforts to implement it would set off a firestorm, later called the White Mutiny, that seared away the moral facade of British rule and its self-justifications.

At issue were native judges in the civil service. When Ripon found out they were not allowed to try white defendants, only native ones, he and his equally liberal and high-principled law member of the Council, Courtenay Ilbert, introduced a bill in 1883 to correct this anomaly. The Ilbert Bill affected only a handful of senior judges, barely twenty in all of India. But the reaction from the British community was furious, even hysterical.

In February 1883 mass meetings were held in Bombay, Calcutta, and Madras attacking the bill, Ripon, and the native Indians, the "Bengalee Baboos," who seemed intent on promoting equality with whites. "It has always been an understood thing," said a distinguished member of the Madras Chamber of Commerce, "that a European—a white man—wherever he went, represented the governing race," and that any examination of his conduct would be only by a person "of the same class," namely another European. Indians lacked the character to act as judges in cases involving whites. Even the best-educated Indians, declared Judge C. D. Field of the Calcutta High Court, "do not make a habit of speaking the truth."[45]

Thousands turned out for the meeting in Calcutta's town hall, where speakers conjured up images of scheming dark-skinned Indians deciding the fates of helpless white Britons—even of their wives and daughters. "We cannot govern the natives, putting them side by side with ourselves," said one speaker. "We must either rule or we pander." The meeting ended with a rousing chorus of "God Save the Queen," while the *Bombay Gazette* reported that "the abuse of the natives set the audience beside itself with delight."[46]

The race rage shocked Ripon. "I had no idea that any large number of Englishmen in India were animated by such sentiments," he wrote. "The knowledge gives me a feeling akin to despair as to the future of this country." The backlash extended to London, where a committee to represent the feelings of Indian Britons was formed and petitions sent to Parliament. The London *Times* itself took up their cause.

Meanwhile, in India, Britons wrote indignant letters to leading British newspapers accusing Ripon and Ilbert of betraying the interests of their race and even British womanhood. "Have we not enough to endure in India, isolated as we often are?" wrote one lady to the *Englishman*. "Has Lord Ripon no feeling of regard for his country women that he should seek to expose hundreds of them to an anxiety so real?"[47] Ilbert was burned in effigy. Some proposed rebellion rather than allow their wives "to be torn from our homes...by half clad natives": there was even a plot to kidnap the viceroy himself.

Shaken by the opposition both at home and in India, Ripon had to back down. He and Ilbert presented a watered-down version of the bill, which passed but satisfied no one. The Indian Briton community was now on guard, determined that they would never, *ever* relinquish their power and privilege—even as Indians themselves watched, listened, and learned.

It had been India's worst crisis since 1857, and Conservatives were quick to blame the White Mutiny on Ripon and his liberal "meddling." When the Tories came back into power in June 1885, it would be left to their new secretary of state for India, Lord Randolph Churchill, to pick up the pieces.

Chapter Two

LORD RANDOLPH TAKES CHARGE

Without India, England would cease to be a nation.
RANDOLPH CHURCHILL, MAY 1885

RANDOLPH CHURCHILL LEFT LONDON IN DECEMBER 1884, reached Bombay on New Year's Eve, and did not return home until April 1885. It was no casual sightseeing expedition. His tour of India was part of his campaign to become the Conservatives' leading expert on Indian politics, which he believed would ultimately propel him to Number 10 Downing Street and the premiership itself. His letters describing the tour were carefully preserved and later published by his son Winston.[1] They provide a revealing look at the Raj in its heyday. They also form the background not only for Randolph's tenure as secretary of state for India but for the issues that would pit Randolph's son against Mohandas Gandhi.

On December 12 Randolph's ship SS *Rohilla* passed through the Suez Canal. The canal was the vital gateway to India and shaved more than two months off the old voyage around the Cape of Good Hope. Although still relatively new, the canal had already made Egypt almost as crucial to the fate of the British Empire as India itself. Randolph found "very much what I expected," he wrote to Jennie, "a dirty ditch with nothing remarkable except the multitudes of flamingos, pelicans, and wild fowl in the lakes we passed."[2] But it also enabled the *Rohilla* to reach Bombay by New Year's Eve.

Once ruled by the Portuguese, Bombay was India's Venice, a cosmopolitan commercial center where merchants from three continents and all races walked the streets and bazaars. Randolph found it enchantingly exotic. He told Jennie, "The complete novelty and originality of everything is remarkable, and one is never tired of staring and wondering."[3]

The city was also residence of the governor-general of the Bombay Presidency and a thriving center for India's Western-educated elite, who were still smarting from the racial backlash of the White Mutiny. They now hoped the progenitor of Tory Democracy might bring some of it their way. Many were prepared to greet Randolph Churchill as Lord Ripon reborn, and he did nothing to discourage them. B. M. Malabari, the editor of the *Indian Spectator,* India's biggest native newspaper, arranged for him to meet with Indian intellectuals who "set forth with great ability their various grievances." Churchill urged them to "instruct the British public... with their wants and wishes" regarding their desire to participate in some way in governing their country. Later he wrote enthusiastically to his friend T. H. S. Escott, "I feel little doubt that their moderation and caution is equal to their intelligence and their knowledge." He added, "I never cease to rejoice that I was able to come out here."[4]

Malabari was a Parsi. In Bombay Lord Randolph met with other leading members of the city's most important religious minority and visited their famous Towers of Silence. Emigrants from Persia since the eighth century, the Parsis were Zoroastrians and still set out their dead to be consumed by vultures in the old manner. Randolph walked through the towers' elaborate gardens, while clouds of great blackbirds swooped overhead. On the large flat towers lay the exposed bodies of men, women, and children, where the bones would be picked clean and then bleached by the sun and wind, and finally swept into the pit at the center of each tower.

The Parsis were more than just another exotic Indian religious group. The most literate of all Indians (with 40 percent able to read and write in 1872, compared to 15 percent of Hindus and even fewer Muslims), Parsi businessmen were transforming India. They had been shipbuilders in the eighteenth century and were becoming India's cotton mill engineers and owners, iron and steel manufacturers, and mine owners. Whereas the Bombay Presidency had had only thirteen cotton mills in 1865, it had fifty-one in 1877, including three in Cawnpore. The largest of all was J. N. Tata's Empress Mills in Nagpur, which had machinery equal to any factory in Liverpool or Manchester.[5] Thanks to Parsis like Tata, a new India was being born in the midst of the old, one

that Britons and Indians alike, including Mohandas Gandhi, would have to reckon with.

From Bombay Randolph traveled northeast to Gwalior, where fierce Maratha chieftains had once ruled from their white sandstone fortress which had been the last stronghold of the Mutiny, and then continued on to another former Maratha state, Indore. Both belonged to two of India's nearly six hundred independent princes, whose states still covered more than a third of India. Englishmen liked to believe the Indian princes were spoiled despots, even slightly mad, and incapable of rule without British supervision. It was true that none could make treaties on their own or defend themselves without British help; many were eccentric, a few were spendthrifts, and some were drunkards. The raja of Kapurthala once told Viceroy Curzon he was only really happy drinking champagne in Paris.[6]

But Randolph found Indore's maharaja, Holkar Tukoji Rao, and his son to be "most gracious and intelligent." After dinner there were "fireworks, Hindoo drama, Nautch,* conjurors etc." In the morning the holkar arranged for a hunting party to chase black buck with a cheetah, but the cheetah "was sulky" and refused to hunt. So Randolph and his friend Colonel Thomas set out into the bush with rifles and bagged five deer between them.[7]

All this was of intense interest to Randolph's ten-year-old son Winston. Winston Churchill had grown up the forgotten child, shuttled from one boarding school to another and scarcely noticed by his parents. His mother's obsessions were flirting with fashionable young men and fox hunting: Winston's most vivid early image of her would be her riding breeches, "fitting like a skin and beautifully spotted with mud."[8] Winston was now at school in Brighton, neglected and lonely, and his letters had a sad, plaintive air. "Do you think Papa will stay long in India?" he wrote to his mother on January 28. "Have you heard from him lately?"

On February 13 Winston wrote a letter to Randolph. "I hope you are enjoying yourself in India," it read. "I hear you have been out shooting…and shot some animals. When are you coming home again? I hope it will not be long!" He then asked if Randolph was planning to go

---

* A traditional dance performed by young women or Nautch girls, whom Ensign Winston Churchill would find as charming as his father had.

on a tiger hunt, adding: "Are the Indians funny?" And finally: "I am longing to see you so much."[9]

In fact, Randolph had gone on a tiger hunt two weeks earlier in Dudna, in the foothills of the Himalayas, which he described in a letter not to his son but to his mother. It described how they had spent "all day careering around on elephants after game" and how he found elephants to be "the best means of conveyance I know…Nothing stops them; if tree [is] in the way they pull it down; never crash or fall and don't run away." He also described shooting his tiger, a nine-and-a-half-foot specimen: "Heavens! How he growled and what a rage he was in!" The tiger skin "will, I think, look very well in Grosvenor Square," his mother's London house where he and Jennie were now living. Tiger hunting, Randolph pronounced, was "the very acme of sport."[10]

By now Randolph had a guide and companion in Sir Lepel Griffin, government agent for Central India and the embodiment of the hard line since the White Mutiny. Indian Britons were seething about Randolph's friendly visit with native politicians in Bombay. Griffin saw his chance to bring him around. Together they went to Agra, to see the Taj Mahal by moonlight, "an unequaled sight," and to Lucknow on the twenty-first. Both cities had been besieged during the Mutiny. Both flanked Cawnpore, and the well at Bibighar with its memorial and marble angel, and the red brick Cawnpore Memorial Church. Everything here was a reminder of what hard-liners said would happen if the British grip on India slipped.

Then on February 7 Randolph and Griffin reached Calcutta, the residence of Viceroy Lord Dufferin and the capital of the Raj. There a single white man and his executive council directed the lives of a quarter billion people, with powers far surpassing those of any European head of state. The viceroy built and ran India's railways; he controlled the sale of opium and salt; he supervised the manufacture of all the Indian Army's supplies and ammunition and, together with its commander in chief, decided where and when it would fight. The Raj's vast numbers of public works projects made him the largest employer in India. Compared to the prime minister in laissez-faire Britain, he supervised a "mixed economy" on a massive scale.

The viceroy surrounded himself with the pomp and splendor befitting his imperial powers, with echoes of Mughal ceremonial. When he traveled about the capital in his horse-drawn barouche, he was accompanied by eighteen postillions and guards. Each Indian servant was dressed in scarlet livery with the viceroy's monogram set out in gold. When he arrived at any dinner with more than twenty-four guests, the band was required to play "God Save the Queen," and all ladies were required to curtsy as he entered the room. At some ceremonies ladies found themselves having to curtsy eighteen separate times.

Randolph met Lord Dufferin at his country house in Barrackpore, north of the city. He found the viceroy "very kind and easy-going." Dufferin's children had just enjoyed a birthday party, complete with band, magician, and elephant rides.[11] Elephants notwithstanding, life in Barrackpore, and in the viceroy's summer residence in Simla (where Dufferin was building a magnificent Viceregal Lodge complete with ballroom for eight hundred people), looked to visitors far more like the Home Counties than India. Croquet on the lawn, tea in the afternoon, Gothic churches standing beside houses built in the Tudor timbered style: it must have seemed to Randolph like England in a dream.

But in Calcutta itself Randolph could not escape the darker side of British rule. Local police were rounding up the city's water carriers to send them to the Sudan, where the British Army was organizing an expedition to relieve Gordon at Khartoum. For these poor low-caste Hindus, it meant separation from their families and almost certain death in the desert. Randolph told his mother that one poor wretch saw him standing nearby and threw himself at the English lord's feet, begging not to be sent, until the police dragged him screaming away.

The whole incident shocked Lord Randolph and made him "very angry." He confessed that it "goes far to explain why we make no progress in popularity among the people. The arrogance or rather self-complacency of Indian officials is beyond all belief." He was "shattered" by the "great gulf between the government and the natives," he said: "the government know less than nothing of the native mind," and "refuse to allow for a moment that anyone outside their circle can know anything." At the same time he praised the Bengali intellectuals he met as "equal to any European in information, extent of reading, and public spirit." Surely these were men with whom the British could form some sort of partnership for India's future.[12]

On February 22 Randolph reached Benares, India's holiest city. He took a boat down the Ganges and could observe the other gulf between the Raj and India's masses: the religious one. Along the riverbanks thousands were bathing as "part of their religion," he wrote, as they had done since time immemorial. "The water is very dirty, but they lap it up in

quantities, as it is very 'holy.' " Then he saw the *ghats* with burning funeral pyres set along the bank, where the Hindu dead were cremated,
the darkly burning fires sending thick clouds of smoke heavenward as
relatives wept and prayed. "There were five bodies burning, each on its
little pile of faggots," he told his mother; "the whole sight was most curious, and I am going again this morning to have another look."[13]

On the whole, he found his experience in India sobering. On his way
back to Bombay, he wrote a melancholy letter to General Frederick
Roberts, whom he had met in Hyderabad. "After a century or so of rule
you have so little convinced (not the bulk of people) but the leaders of the
people of its excellence and merits," he warned, "that any great reverse
from the Russians would leave you powerless."[14] Less than a week later,
on March 20, 1885, he was on a steamship headed back to London.

By now he knew there was a growing political crisis at home. Irish
Fenians had set off a bomb in the House of Commons on January 24;
Khartoum had fallen to the armies of the Madhi, and Gordon had
been killed on February 21. On board ship Randolph had time to
reflect on all he had heard and seen. He thought about "how incredibly
strong and at the same time incredibly slender, our position in India
is." An all-powerful government cut off from the people it ruled; a
Western-educated native elite that felt slighted and betrayed; a British
community bristling with prejudice and fear; above all, a country that
after a century of British rule was still a world apart, with its ancient
religious rituals and darkly burning funeral pyres fading into the night.
At the end, he might have agreed with the reflection H. G. Wells published a few years later on the British in India.

"We are there like a man who has fallen off a ladder onto the back of
an elephant," Wells wrote. "[He] doesn't know what to do or how to get
down. Until something happens, there he remains."[15] Randolph would
slowly realize that his job was to see that nothing did happen and that
the embarrassment and danger of dismounting were put off as long as
possible. By the time he finally took office as secretary of state for India
on June 11, 1885, Randolph was set on a course that would take him
from would-be reformer to hard-line reactionary.

The India Office was in King Charles Street, in the heart of
Whitehall. Built in 1867, with an exterior by Gilbert Scott and a magnificent three-story inner courtyard of neoclassical marble columns and
tiled friezes, it oversaw the London end of what Winston Churchill
would call "the magnificent organization of the government of India,"

from the Indian Army to taxes and famine relief, all in close coordination with the viceroy.[16] It was also maintained at the expense of the Indian taxpayer, since every salary, every expense account, every official trip, and every retirement pension came from revenues paid by the subjects of the Raj.

Upstairs was the Council Chamber, paneled with mahogany and lined with gold leaf; its magnificent gilt marble fireplace depicted Britannia receiving the riches of the East. In this room sat by royal appointment the Council of India, made up of retired soldiers and civil servants who had served in the Raj and who approved whatever decisions the secretary of state wanted to make. Most were elderly. The first time the thirty-six-year-old Randolph sat down with them, he compared it to being "an Eton boy presiding at a meeting of the Masters."[17] Randolph learned to treat the council with respect, but he intended to run the India Office as he and no one else saw fit.

This was relatively easy. India was different from other parts of the empire. As secretary he was responsible only to his prime minister, not to Parliament. Not a single parliamentary committee oversaw his work or his dealings with the viceroy in Calcutta.[18] This suited Randolph. From the start he reacted badly to any perceived interference, even from the queen.* In general, he was free to do as he liked, and under the influence of men like Lepel Griffin, "the hammer of the babus," and General Frederick Roberts, his earlier doubts about the Raj were swept away, or at least swept under the rug. Under Randolph Churchill, the India Office position on India hardened and crystallized. The British would rule and the Indians would obey, and things were to stay that way—not just because the British were so good at ruling, but because Indians were so bad at everything else.

Roberts set the tone. He had actually been born in Cawnpore in 1832 and as a young ensign helped to put down the Mutiny. His memoirs, *Forty-one Years in India, from Subaltern to Commander-in-Chief,* conjured up the image of a primitive country where the vast bulk of the population

---

* The queen asked Prime Minister Salisbury to learn Viceroy Dufferin's opinion about appointing her son the Duke of Connaught as commander in chief for the Bombay Presidency. When Randolph found out, he exploded. By going over his head, she had directly challenged his authority to oversee all appointments, he raged; his authority had been "completely demolished." He even hinted he might resign. Eventually, a compromise was reached and ruffled feathers smoothed. But privately Salisbury and others wondered at Randolph's increasingly erratic behavior and mood swings—though none except his wife knew the real reason for them.

is illiterate, ninety-nine out of one hundred persons have no sense of civic association, and "the various races and religious sects possess no bond of national union." Under these conditions, Roberts said, forcing British-style constitutional reforms "on a community which is not prepared for them, does not want them, and cannot understand them" could only lead to chaos or even a replay of the Great Mutiny.

"The best government for India will be the intelligent and benevolent despotism which at present rules the country," Roberts concluded. The best thing politicians in London could do was ignore "the utterances of self-appointed agitators who pose as the mouth-pieces of an oppressed population" and listen to the officials on the spot, who "have a deeper insight into, and a greater sympathy with, the feelings and prejudices of Asiatics."

This is what Randolph proceeded to do. He learned to dismiss educated Indians as "a deadly legacy" from woolly-headed reformers of the past, who "cannot be anything else than opposition in quiet times, rebels in times of troubles."[19] On taking office, he had promised to launch a parliamentary inquiry into the Indian government, but there was never any chance that Indians themselves would be part of it— or that it would challenge the prevailing view from Calcutta. Faced by financial difficulties, Randolph did not hesitate to raise the Indians' taxes; he raided the Famine Insurance Fund to help pay for general expenses. He shut down any plans to make it easier for natives to enter the Indian Civil Service. In short, the "benevolent despotism" of Churchill's regime marked the end of any hope of major reform in India for nearly two decades.

Randolph may have rejected reform, but he was drawn to the other, more glamorous aspect of the Raj: the Great Game. It raised his energies to a fever pitch. He gave speeches about the impending advance of "the countless hosts of Russia upon the North-West Frontier of India," and began an expansion of the Indian Army by thirty thousand men—yet another excuse to raise Indians' taxes. He badgered the viceroy to contemplate a march on Kandahar, and Lord Salisbury to work with the Germans on an anti-Russian strategy in Persia, since German engineers were hoping to build a railway connecting Baghdad to Constantinople. He even proposed that the India Office take over all diplomatic dealings with Persia and China, and he envisaged Calcutta becoming under his guidance "the center of Asiatic politics," a great cynosure of British influence spreading from one end of the Eastern

Hemisphere to the other.[20] Salisbury soon wearied of Randolph's mega-lomaniacal schemes, and all came to nothing. All, that is, except Burma.

That kingdom to the east was already closely linked to India. Lower Burma, a lush triangle of jungle and rice fields surrounding the mouth of the Irawaddy River along with a strip of coastline on the eastern shore of the Bay of Bengal, had been annexed in 1826 and was administered from Calcutta. But Upper Burma had remained independent. Local British teak and cotton merchants worried that its king might work out an exclusive deal with the French, who were pressing in westward from Indo-China. In fact, in January 1883 King Theebaw signed a commercial agreement with France. British merchants assumed that the withdrawal of their own privileges would follow.

So the Rangoon Chamber of Commerce and its lobbyists in Parliament went into high gear, pushing for annexation of Upper Burma. Gladstone and Viceroy Lord Ripon had ignored them, but when the Tories came in, their new secretary of state for India paid more attention. Churchill soon worked himself into a state of alarm about French ambitions in the East, about dark (and largely untrue) accounts of Theebaw the "ignorant, arrogant, drunken boy king," surrounded by a band of greedy and savage sycophants, and the dangers to India from the ever-menacing Russians if the British "lost" Burma.[21]

Lord Randolph also understood the political benefits of launching a preemptive war there, and how "a government never fails to derive a certain amount of benefit from a successful military operation," as he told Viceroy Dufferin. He too would benefit, by becoming the Man Who Added Burma to the British Empire.

And so although neither the prime minister nor the viceroy had any plans or even desire to invade Burma, Randolph took matters in his own hands. His ultimatum to Theebaw, demanding that he withdraw his treaty with the French, reached the Burmese capital, Mandalay, on October 30, 1885. However, Randolph had effectively declared war a week earlier in a speech in Birmingham, and British and Indian troops were already headed for Rangoon. On December 1 the British entered Mandalay. That year Lord Randolph celebrated the New Year, as he always did, at his friends the Fitzpatricks' house in Dublin. As the clock struck twelve, Randolph raised his glass and announced to the assembled guests that Burma was now officially annexed to the British Crown: "a New Year's gift to the Empress and all her subjects."[22]

But it was too late to save him or his government. The voters had gone to the polls more than a month earlier, on November 24 and 25, 1885, and handed Salisbury and the Tories a resounding defeat. The Liberals were back, and Randolph Churchill's brief but hectic tenure as secretary of state for India was over. The next time he was back in office, it would be as chancellor of the exchequer. He would never grace the halls of the India Office, or worry about Indian policy, again.

But in his five short months Randolph had left a mark on Indian affairs that would last more than a lifetime. His blocking of any serious reform of the governance of India had offended a large portion of India's educated elite. And instead of producing the short sharp victory that he had envisaged, the war in Burma turned into a protracted ulcer. The Burmese were among the hardiest warriors in the world; they launched an effective insurgency against the British that would drag on for three years, tie up 35,000 British and Indian troops, and cost ten times as much as the war's original estimate, to the fury of India's taxpayers. Educated Indians already felt betrayed by the man they had championed during his visit as "a liberal in all but name." His war with Burma was the final straw.

Thus in late December 1885, just as the guerrilla war was breaking out in the jungles of Burma, a group of well-to do Bombay businessmen and landlords from Bengal met to form a new organization, the Indian National Congress. Almost all were Western-educated, with Parsis and high-caste Hindu Brahmins predominating. Although a few sported turbans, almost all wore Western suits and ties. Some were even white, including the Congress's moving spirit, Allan Octavian Hume, a distinguished former civil servant and veteran of the Great Mutiny. The Congress's goals, at least initially, were loyalist and respectful; in the words of one historian, "they were cautious moderate men who were confident in the ultimate fairness of the British people."[23] Viceroy Dufferin even welcomed the Congress as a useful safety valve for grievances and resentment.

But the founding of the Congress opened a new era for India, and a new kind of political movement in the subcontinent. For the next three decades it remained a tiny detached elite, what Randolph Churchill would dismiss as a gathering of "Bengalee baboos"—until a thin bespectacled man dressed in peasant clothes revealed its unexpected strength.

* * *

Defeated and out of office, Randolph Churchill was asked what he would do next. He said, "I shall lead the Opposition for five years. Then I shall be Prime Minister for five years. Then I shall die."[24]

Only the last prediction would come true. For already Lord Randolph could feel the hand of the dread disease that he had kept hidden from his family but that was slowly sapping his physical and mental powers—even his sanity. Doctors diagnosed it then and later as syphilis (although modern medical authorities diagnose it as a brain tumor). As he left the India Office, his illness was entering its final horrible stage.

Randolph's first severe attack, in 1881, had left him partially paralyzed and almost unable to speak; but he had then recovered, remission had set in, and he had seemed fine. Jennie, on the other hand, feared the worst. They had already ceased to sleep together. Her second son, Jack, was born in February 1880. Rumors flew that it was almost certainly not Randolph's child.[25]

At the India Office, the bouts of mental instability grew worse. They may even have affected his decision to wage his wars on Burma and on Indian reform. When the Tories returned to power in June 1886, Lord Randolph was well enough to step up as chancellor of the exchequer and his party's virtual leader in the House of Commons. But his quarrels with Lord Salisbury grew so bitter that on December 20, while staying at Windsor Castle, he impulsively sent in a letter of resignation.

To Randolph's shock, Salisbury accepted it. He too sensed something was wrong with his wayward younger colleague and was relieved to see him go. Although Randolph talked to others about one day returning to office, even becoming prime minister, his political career was over. Now it was left to his family to deal with the growing physical and mental wreck that was Lord Randolph Churchill, and with his bouts of delirium and rage, especially against his eldest son.

Winston became a major focus of his father's diseased wrath. Years later, in a very rare moment of candor about his father, he told friends: "He treated me as if I had been a fool; barked at me whenever I questioned him...He wouldn't listen to me or consider anything I said...He was so self-centered no one else existed for him."[26]

When Winston was eleven and at school in Brighton in October 1885, he learned his father had been in town but hadn't bothered to visit. "Dearest Papa," he wrote, "I cannot think why you did not come to see me, while you were in Brighton, I was very disappointed but I suppose

you were too busy to come." When Winston came down with pneumonia the following March and nearly died, Randolph barely interrupted
his London routine to come to Brighton. When the boy recovered, he
left again almost at once.[27]

All this took its toll on Winston's personality. At twelve he already
had the reputation of being a fiery troublemaker (ironically, just like his
father). "The naughtiest little boy in the world," one of his teachers at
Brighton remembered. A fellow student, Maurice Baring, said, "His
naughtiness appeared to have surpassed anything. He had been flogged
for taking sugar from the pantry, and so far from being penitent, had
taken the Headmaster's sacred straw hat from where it hung over the
door and kicked it to pieces. His sojourn at the school had been one long
feud with authority."[28]

And one long feud with his father. Exasperated with the boy,
Randolph had him transferred to the Harrow school. There he went
from being the naughtiest boy to the loneliest, shunned by his classmates
and ignored by his parents. Jennie had just taken up with her latest
lover, the Hungarian Count Kinsky—the list of paramours would grow
steadily as her husband's illness grew worse. With an unavailable
mother and a father descending into madness, young Winston was a
volatile bundle of verbal aggression and repressed anger. One classmate
who tangled with him remembered him as small but "hard as nails."
Years later, while boar hunting in India, the man remembered seeing a
cornered boar with "the same little beady eyes of warning" as it poised to
charge, and had a "mental flash" of Winston Churchill at Harrow.[29]

Another classmate was Leopold Amery. More than half a century
later, Amery would be Churchill's secretary of state for India, but in
1889 he was captain of the school while Winston sat in the school's bottom class. One day Winston, acting as class bully, shoved Amery into the
swimming pool when his back was turned. Winston later apologized,
saying he mistook Amery for a younger boy, because "you are so small."
Then he added, with pathetic pride, "My father too is small and he is
also a great man."

In fact, Randolph was now virtually out of control. When he made a
rare visit to the House of Commons, embarrassed spectators described
the speeches by this once-gifted orator as "foaming and incoherent." He
began traveling abroad widely and wildly as if to escape his terrible illness, sometimes taking Jennie with him, sometimes not.

An old friend who saw him in his last days was horrified at his changed appearance, with the haggard face, "his hair greyish and very thin on top...the heavy gummy bags under his miserable eyes, the shaking hand," but also the "gleams of hate, anger, and fear in his eyes, the dreadful fear of those who have learned how close madness is."[30]

In this state, Randolph's reaction when he received reports about Winston at Harrow can be imagined. "You have demonstrated beyond refutation your slovenly, harum scarum style of work throughout your schooldays," he raged, "always behind hand, never advancing in your class, incessant complaints and total want of application." If Winston carried on like this any further, his father concluded, "my responsibility for you is over."

But Randolph had, in a moment of lucidity, made the decision that would change his miserable son's life forever, and for the better. He allowed him to take the exam to enter Sandhurst as an army cadet.

It was a decision born in Winston's room at Portman Square when he was fourteen. Randolph had entered to find Winston's toy soldiers drawn up in magnificent battle order on the floor, all fifteen hundred of them. His father examined the formations for almost twenty minutes and then asked Winston if he thought he might want to join the army. Winston, delighted at the rare and unexpected attention, immediately said yes—thinking, as he recounted years later, that his father had discerned in his toy battle the makings of a military genius. "But I was told later that he had only come to the conclusion that I was not clever enough to go to the Bar" and that the only place left for his wayward and willful son was the Royal Military College at Sandhurst.

Winston tried twice to pass the exam for Sandhurst and failed. His father's rages were almost beyond bearing. Then finally on the third try, after tremendous cramming and concentration, he officially passed the prelim exam in January 1893 and entered Sandhurst in September, ranked ninety-second out of 102 cadets.

He wrote to his father, "I will try to modify your opinion of me by my work and conduct at Sandhurst...My...low place in passing in will have no effect whatever on my chance there." In fact, for the first time he found a life at school that suited him. Classes on drill and map-reading, riding and gymnastics, topography, tactics, and fortification suited him better than Brighton and Harrow's dreary years of Latin, French, and mathematics.[31]

His only quarrel with his father now was over which branch of service he would enter. Randolph insisted on the infantry, but Winston's heart was set on the cavalry, even though that meant paying an extra two hundred pounds a year for care and feeding of his mount. In the end, Winston won out. Finally, as a young cavalry cadet, Winston Churchill had found a secure place and an identity that made him useful and happy.

But even then he was thinking ahead. In January 1891, when he was sixteen and had just passed the first prelim exam for Sandhurst, he asked a London doctor, a distinguished specialist, what to do about his annoying lisp. The doctor told him it was minor and certainly wouldn't hinder his career in the army. Whereupon Winston explained that his goal in the military was not a career but an experience that he could use to enter his father's field: politics.

Of course he would finish at the Royal Military College, he told the doctor, and join a hussar regiment and serve for a year or two in India (all of which in fact he did). But after that, young Winston announced, he was going to become a great statesman like his father; he certainly didn't intend to be held back by being unable to pronounce his s's properly. After his patient left, the amazed doctor told his wife: "I have just seen the most extraordinary young man I have ever met."[32]

His father's approval meant everything to Winston, and he allowed literally nothing to stand in his way of winning it. As a present for entering the R.M.C., his father gave him a gold watch and warned him not to lose it. Deep in his second term Winston was walking along Sandhurst's Wish Stream when the watch bounced out of his pocket and into six feet of water, "the only deep place for miles." Winston instantly plunged in after it but after repeated dives couldn't find it.

The next day he had the pool dredged; still nothing. Then he got permission from Sandhurst to requisition twenty-three soldiers, who under his orders dug a new course for the stream and rerouted it. Then with a large pump from the local fire station, they drained the pool—and found the watch.[33]

Unfortunately, Randolph had no approval left for his son to win, or anything else. Randolph's illness was in its last horrible stages. Gaunt, incoherent, and shuffling, he planned one final round the world trip with his wife. One of the places he chose he had visited a decade earlier, and it still represented the only permanent achievements of his career: India. It is unclear what drew him back. Perhaps he wanted to see once more the vultures swooping over the Towers of Silence, or the Taj Mahal by moonlight, or the smoky glare of the funeral pyres along the banks of the Ganges, with the thousands bathing in its sacred waters—to see human beings at peace with themselves and their gods.

In any case, the couple arrived from Singapore in November 1893. But when they reached Madras, a doctor took one look at him and advised them to return at once to London. Randolph managed to reach his mother's house in Grosvenor Square in the last days of December 1894. He would not leave it alive.

Grief-stricken, Winston waited out Randolph's last days in the house of friends: his father could no longer even recognize him. Lord Randolph Spencer Churchill lingered on through the first three weeks of January 1895, rarely leaving his room; the morphine he took for the pain was increasingly ineffective, so that his screams reverberated through the house.

Finally, on January 22, after two terrible bouts of mania, he went into a coma and two days later slipped away. Winston was devastated. "All my dreams of companionship with him, of entering Parliament at his side and in his support were ended," he wrote later. "There remained for me only to pursue his aims and vindicate his memory."[34]

And to a large extent, his political career would be an attempt to resurrect a father he never knew, and to win the parental approval he had never found. A decade later Randolph's old friend Wilfred Blunt would notice how much young Winston resembled his father, as "a strange replica" of the dead Randolph, "with all his father's suddenness and assurance and I should say more than his father's ability." Even Winston Churchill's distinctive manner of speaking, later so famous, was directly modeled on his father's.

Above all, Blunt found "something touching" in the fact that Winston had embraced all his father's old causes and even his enmities.[35] Opposition to Home Rule and hatred of Russia; support for free trade and a conservative populism embedded in the catchphrase Tory Democracy: Winston Churchill the politician would embrace them all.

But on one issue he would remain adamant and true to his father's principles to the end. This was India and its place in the British Empire. Winston would be leaving for India in little more than a year, an experience that would change his life. And from his father he had absorbed two lessons about the place to which he was headed.

The first was that the British were essential to the survival and happiness of the subcontinent. He liked to quote one of Randolph's speeches in which his father had told listeners, "Your rule in India is, as it were, a sheet of oil spread out over the surface of, and keeping calm and quiet and unruffled by storms, an immense and profound ocean of humanity." Britain's mission was to use "your knowledge, your law, and higher civilization" to bind India's 230 million people "into a great, united people," Randolph had said. "That is your task for India. That is your raison d'etre in India. That is your title to India"—and Winston Churchill never forgot it.[36]

But he also remembered his father's other vital lesson. While Britain was essential to India, India was also essential to Britain. Randolph had remarked often on how India's vast import market kept British manufacturers in business, and how it mattered more than Europe or America. "India," he would say, "is the only free foreign market we have." Randolph had calculated that more than two and a half million Britons were dependent on that connection, including 50,000 to 60,000 British seamen and the 100,000 salaried employees in India and their families.[37] To lose India would not only be a strategic blunder and a devastating blow to British prestige. It would also tip Britain into economic chaos. As Winston Churchill himself put it years later, the loss of India would be "final and fatal to us."

In 1885 the father had warned, "Without India, England would cease to be a nation."[38] In 1931 the son warned that without India, the British Empire "would pass at a stroke out of life into history." Winston Churchill would dedicate his life to preventing that from happening, even as another man would dedicate his life to making it come true.

Chapter Three

ILLUSIONS OF POWER

The Gandhis, India, and British Rule

From the unreal lead me to the real!
BRIHADARANYAKA UPANISHAD, EIGHTH CENTURY B.C.E.

WINSTON CHURCHILL GREW UP AT THE very center of empire. By contrast, Mohandas Gandhi grew up in a small but prosperous town of less than fifteen thousand people set in a small princely state in the western Indian province of Gujarat.[1] He saw the world from a tiny corner of a vast subcontinent, distant from the momentous crosscurrents set off by the Raj. Gandhi never even saw an Englishman until the family moved to Rajkot when he was seven.

While Churchill was isolated and neglected as a child, Gandhi had constant attention from a large and loving family.[2] "Mohan" was his mother's darling, a mischievous boy with a large head and ears, and thin, ungainly legs. He would disappear from the house without warning, and his nursemaid would find him climbing trees or hiding from her in the temple. A servant would take him for a ride in a bullock cart through the villages around Porbandar. "As I was the son of a *diwan*," Gandhi remembered decades later, "people fed me on the way with *juwar roti* [millet cakes] and gave me eight anna pieces."[3]

This carefree life was overshadowed by his dignified and strict father, a figure of distinction in his child's mind and also in the community's. Karamchand was the *diwan* or chief adviser to the local *rana,* a post he had held since 1847 and that his father held before that.[4] "My father was a lover of his clan," Gandhi tells us in his autobiography, "truthful, brave, and generous, but short-tempered."[5] Karamchand Gandhi was an important player in local politics, the classic big frog in a small pond.* Every morning groups of suitors would squat on his veranda, hoping to ask some favor or tell some grievance. Every evening twenty or thirty men would appear for dinner to discuss the latest events, while "Kaba" (Karamchand's family nickname) presided and solemnly peeled vegetables for the meal.[6]

Gandhi's father was a man of piety, a member of the Hindu Modh Bania caste. The Banias were a commercial caste; at one time the Gandhis had been moneylenders. (The name itself means "seller of per-fumes.") But more central to the Gandhi household were the colorful rites and rituals of the Vaishnava sect, whose *bhakti* or devotion to Lord Krishna were part of daily routine. The Vaishnava temple next to the Gandhi house overflowed with songs and music, with men and women setting out ceremonial meals and masses of red, pink, blue, and yellow flowers. One of Gandhi's earliest memories would be of the sharp, musty smell of rotting flowers as he visited the temple every day with his mother.[7]

Putlibai joined the Gandhis in their Vaishnava rites and prayers. But she belonged to another local Hindu sect, the Pranamis, and went to daily worship at their temple just two hundred yards away. Pranamis abstained from alcohol and practiced vegetarianism and moderation in all things. Their festivals included a striking blend of Hindu and Muslim practices. (Muslims numbered about a fifth of the population of Gujarat.) On the altar in the Pranami temple there was even a copy of the Koran. At least one biographer has seen Pranami's influence on Gandhi's later religious outlook, including his respect for Islam.[8]

Gandhi himself tells us that his earliest and most valuable religious lesson came from his nursemaid. When he was not much more than four or five, she taught him to recite the *Ramanama,* saying the name of the god Rama over and over again, as a way to assuage his fear of ghosts and evil spirits in the dark. Rama was the divine hero of the Hindu na-tional epic; a shrine to Rama stood in Karamchand's office. And so recit-ing the *Ramanama* became the bedrock of Gandhi's Hindu faith, his "infallible remedy" in times of crisis and even disease.

"*Ramanama* purifies while it cures," he liked to say, "and therefore it

---

* Small did not necessarily mean dull. When Mohandas's grandfather Uttamchand sheltered a clerk from the wrath of his rana's widow, she ordered cannon wheeled down the Porbandar streets and had her troops fire on the Gandhi house. The cracks in the wall from the cannonballs are still visible today. Meanwhile Uttamchand fled to a neighboring Muslim principality until things were smoothed over. This defiance of princely authority on principle later became part of the Gandhi legacy for Mohandas.

elevates." Gandhi would credit the simple little prayer with curing one of his father's friends of leprosy. Later, he would tell women whose husbands had been massacred by Muslims to recite the *Ramanama* as consolation. It would be on Gandhi's lips when he died.[9]

Highbrow Hindus would dismiss all this as part of Gandhi's small-town outlook. Indeed, high-caste Brahmins considered the exuberant Vaishnava rites vulgar and unseemly.[10] Later, when Gandhi would explore the deeper reaches of Hindu philosophy, he too would find popular Hinduism's endless round of boisterous, even bawdy, festivals and garishly decorated temples distasteful. The smell of the decaying temple flowers he remembered had also made him sick; and when he witnessed the sacrifices to the goddess Kali in her temple in Calcutta in 1901, with rivulets of blood flowing down the stones, he was horrified.

All the same, his childhood in provincial Porbandar, instead of a Westernized city like Calcutta or a cosmopolitan one like Bombay, gave Gandhi a simple and straightforward religious base that he could share with millions of poor people from every region of India, people whose lives were still untouched by the Clives, Ripons, and Randolph Churchills. It would be one of the principal bonds between them. It helps to explain why throughout Gandhi's life people would walk miles to remote rail stations where he was supposed to stop, and wait hours, sometimes days, hoping to catch a glimpse of him, touch his feet, and recite the *Ramanama* with him.

This humble link is crucial, not just for understanding Gandhi but for putting the whole British Raj in perspective. For the British, their experience in India was full of drama, change, and progress. "To have found a great people sunk in the lowest depths of slavery and superstition," as one of them, Thomas Macaulay, enthused, and then to have brought India "the imperishable empire of our arts, and morals, our literature and our laws," was "the proudest day in English history."[11]

But the vast majority of Indians spread out over a subcontinent the size of Europe without Russia experienced no change. What change occurred, they had been taught to see as largely an illusion. Indians had seen plenty of history over four thousand years, but what mattered to them in this vast, slow-moving society was precisely the forces that resisted history: their land, their religion, and the very nature of Indian society itself.

That society's roots ran incredibly deep, as deep as the world's oldest civilizations. They still do. The *Rig Veda* is certainly the oldest religious hymn in daily use. Four-thousand-year-old rites associated with the worship of Shiva are still performed today, making it the oldest continuous religious cult in the world. Villagers still worship at shrines dedicated to gods and goddesses with roots in the Stone Age.[12] Compared to this unequaled staying power, the British Raj seemed very transitory—like every other ruler or conqueror in Indian history. Gandhi made his own view plain in 1909, in his *Hind Swaraj*. "History is really a record of every interruption of the even working of love or of the soul," he wrote, "a record of the interruption of the course of nature." In short, from Gandhi's perspective, history was meaningless: perhaps no other view separated him so much from a man like Winston Churchill. But here Gandhi reflected the larger Indian cultural experience, in which everything that happens is only another brief turn "of the supreme wheel of the empire of Truth." From the Indian perspective, even the British appeared as only a dot on the vast canvas of Indian civilization.[13]

That civilization had its beginnings not very far from Gujarat, in the Indus River Valley at Mohenjo-Daro and Harappa, cities which are today in Pakistan. Lothal, the active port of Harappan civilization, was less than two hundred miles from Rajkot. There, more than thirty centuries before Gandhi's birth, great merchants and priest-kings conducted trade across the Indian Ocean with their counterparts in the ancient Fertile Crescent, in Akkad and Sumer. By 2200 B.C.E., five hundred years before Hammurabi issued his law code in Babylon, the civilization of the Indus Valley was a flourishing urban world of small brick houses and straight narrow streets, clean, efficient, and uniform, ruled by all-powerful theocrats whose temples were the very cities themselves.[14]

Eventually every trace of the great cities vanished, as did their counterparts in the Fertile Crescent. When Gandhi was born, few Indians even knew of the Harappans' existence. But their successors left their mark on India, such as the Hindi words for money *(pana)* and trader *(vanik)*. Even Gandhi's own caste (Bania) is a derivation of the name that the Indus Valley's successors gave to these wealthy and businesslike people, the Panis. The earliest representations of the god Shiva in the typical yoga pose appear on ceramic seals from Mohenjo-Daro, as does the humped bull. The Harappans also cultivated a taste for body ornaments, bracelets, and bangles that would survive down to Gandhi's day and beyond. Once, when Gandhi visited a museum at the ancient

Gandharan city of Takshashila or Taxila displaying some of these ancient bracelets, he exclaimed with surprise, "Just like my mother used to wear."[15]

For all their sophistication, however, the Indus Valley peoples had no iron, and as the centuries passed, their basic technologies remained unchanged. Their society's very uniformity and efficiency became a trap. In the third millennium before the Christian era, when invaders from Central Asia swept down, the peoples of the Indus Valley were either unable or unwilling to resist. Their world was finished. The Aryans, horsemen warriors who were part of a great incursion that swept across Iran and Europe at the same time, had arrived.

The Aryans were as arrogant as they were tough: their very name, *Arya,* meant "master" or "noble." Scholars now agree there was probably no invasion at all, merely a slow, steady migration of Aryan tribes and clans into the perimeter of a civilization that was in a state of advanced decay, until one day they realized they were in charge.

Like their distant cousins the primitive Greeks, who took over the Mycenaean world at almost the same time, the Aryans found themselves possessors of the remnants of a society more sophisticated than their own. Like the Greeks, they brought to the cultural table their own set of gods: Varuna the sky god (like the Greeks' Uranus), Agni the fire god and god of ritual sacrifice, and Indra the god of war. Out of this aggressively masculine religious framework the Aryan priests (or *brahmins*) and warriors (or *rajyas*) built a stratified society of conqueror and conquered. The Brahmins accompanied their elaborate rituals with recitations in a distinct priestly language (later written down as Sanskrit), which would generate the *Vedas,* the oldest extant body of religious literature in the world. The Aryans also composed two of the world's greatest (and longest) epic poems, the *Ramayana* and the *Mahabharata,* which is eight times longer than the *Iliad* and *Odyssey* put together and three times longer than the Bible—all without the benefit of writing. These Vedic recitations, both sacred and secular, form the bedrock of Indian and Hindu culture.

The Aryans carried their culture with them as they gradually spread eastward from the Indus Valley. By now they had divided themselves into four distinct classes or *varnas*: a priest elite of *brahmanas* or Brahmins; the warrior ruling class of *rajyas* or *kshatriyas*; farmers and artisans or *vaishyas*; and at the very bottom, almost ignored by the Vedic religious conventions, the *shudras,* or serfs and laborers. Everyone else, from the survivors of the Indus Valley people to the aboriginal tribes they encountered on their wanderings, were *niravasita,* "excluded" or *candala.* They were forbidden to live in sight of an Aryan village and were relegated to the most menial tasks, such as cremating the dead. These *candala* would be the original "untouchables"—people so despised that they could not even enter a town without first striking a wooden clapper to warn the inhabitants of the approaching pollution.[16]

Eventually the original *classes* of Vedic society became the social *castes* of Hindu society. Hundreds of *jatis* or subdivisions and *gotras* or subcastes were scattered in every region of India, but all found their place within the hierarchic whole. Originally caste membership determined how you worshipped the gods and participated in the Vedic ceremonies. But eventually its rules dictated whom you married, where you lived, what you ate and how you ate it, and how you dressed and marked your body—even how you moved your bowels and when you had sex.[17]

Membership in a caste brings formal rules and rituals to follow, an unwritten guidebook for life on how to avoid pollution and loss of caste in this life and, since Hinduism embraces the notion of reincarnation, the next. It even (except for Brahmins) offers a council to perfect the rules or decide difficult cases for caste members. For the believer, caste and *gotra* formed, as it were, a giant support group that reconciled them to their lot in life and showed them how to achieve holiness, even as part of the lowest caste. To be an outcaste in traditional Hindu society was more than just a social or religious stigma. It meant to be thrown out of the most basic relationships that make life meaningful, to be relegated to cultural squalor, to *tamas* or a terrible darkness—a fate that, since it carried over into the next life, was literally worse than death.[18]

In short, caste gave every Hindu a social identity that was confirmed and sanctified by religious ritual, while at the same time it gave every religious rite in Hinduism a solid and concrete place in the social bedrock. It was so concrete, in fact, that the basic framework would remain unchallenged for more than two thousand years. Far from being rigid or outmoded, the caste system would adapt to new conditions, occupations, and even religious trends. As any visitor to India knows, it is still going strong today. There are more than five thousand castes in India, and new ones spring up every day.[19]

But the coming of the caste system also generated a creative tension. This was a tension between what one had to do as part of the Vedic hierarchy—one's duty or *dharma*—and the impulse to break free from that rigid system, to escape to a higher level of individual spiritual wholeness and freedom.

That impulse was embodied first in the ancient set of commentaries on the *Vedas* called the *Upanishads,* which offered a path to becoming one with a higher reality, the World Spirit or Brahman.[20] It would continue with the Jains and their spiritual leader Mahavira, who respected the sanctity of all life, compared to the blood-soaked Vedic sacrifices, and were nonviolent. (Gandhi would be a great admirer of the Jains.) In the sixth century c.e. that same impulse would reach its crescendo in the teachings of India's greatest and most influential spiritual figure, Gautama Buddha.

For fifty years this former north Indian prince taught others his unique path to liberation or *nirvana,* creating small retreats or *ashramas* of disciples and converts—the first monastic communities in the world. After the Buddha's death, his disciples continued to spread his message of the Middle Way, of how to be "free from anger, fear from malice, pure in mind, and master of oneself," with a missionary zeal. Four hundred years before the birth of Jesus Christ, Buddhism would become the first truly universal religion, spreading from India to Ceylon, Tibet, China, Japan, and Indonesia. By 700 c.e. Buddhism was the largest single spiritual faith in the world.

But the Buddha's presence on his own country and culture was marginal. Over the centuries his followers would steadily shrink away, except in certain parts of the south. Even in his home region he became forgotten. It was British scholars, not Indians, who would eventually discover that the Buddha was Indian and would even pinpoint his birthplace—all less than thirty years before Gandhi was born.[21]

For in the end, the traditional Hindu foundation was too strong and too flexible to be overturned or replaced. It ended up absorbing its Buddhist challenger, just as it had absorbed pre-Vedic gods like Shiva and the festivals, myths, and legends of the myriad peoples and cultures who lived on the subcontinent. Hinduism had become India itself. Nothing else held it together. Over the centuries it would face down all challengers, either by words or by swords.

Among the first challengers were the Greeks. One hundred and fifty years after the Buddha's death, Alexander the Great arrived on the banks of the Indus with his Macedonian army, after a twenty-two-thousand-mile thirteen-year march and fresh from his conquest of Persia. For two years he fought against a civilization that already included one-quarter of the world's population.[22] He defeated a great king on the banks of the Jhelum River and had coins struck in Babylon bearing an image of an elephant to commemorate his victory. He nearly lost his life in combat against a wild warrior tribe in the hill country of western Punjab; he had the West's first encounter with Indian yogis;* and he eventually declared victory and headed back to Persia. Yet he barely cracked the outer shell of a civilization that was now centered on cities rising along the mighty river Ganges, from Delhi and Benares to Patna and Calcutta. Like the Ganges itself, it was a vast and slow-moving world that stood aloof from its neighbors to the west and to the east, thanks to its unique religion and its distinct social and cultural patterns. The basic lesson of Indian history was already established. Material power like kingdoms, and kings, including Alexander the Great, comes and goes. But spiritual power, embodied in religion and caste and spiritual unity with Brahman, the changeless essence of the universe, lasts forever.

Prime exhibits of the transitory nature of political power were India's own dynasties. In 305 B.C.E. a prince from the central Ganges Valley named Chandragupta Maurya rose up against the princes Alexander had left behind and seized lands beyond the Indus, turning Kandahar and Kabul into the western outposts of a mighty Indian Empire. His son Bindusara and grandson Ashoka would push that empire to the south and southeast, with the conquest of the kingdom of Kalinga. The Mauryas were the equivalent of China's Chin dynasty, political unifiers of a great civilization for the first time in its history.

Wall paintings at Ajanta reveal the magnificence of Mauryan rule. They show the king surrounded by noblemen, Brahmin priests, acrobats, snake charmers, standard-bearers, musicians blowing conch shells, and horses and elephants arrayed in pearls, plumes, and gold pendants. Moving just one pillar for Ashoka's palace at Palipurta required a cart of forty-two wheels, drawn by 8,400 men. The imperial storehouses held gold and silver by the ton, diamonds and rubies by the pound.[23]

Amassing all this wealth and power required incessant war of the

---

* These Gymnosophs, as the Greeks called them (literally "naked philosophers"), were unclothed and expounded their teachings sitting on the floor, like prototype Mahatmas. What they said made little sense to their Greek listeners. But at least one intellectual in Alexander's entourage, Pyrrho, went home to Greece greatly disturbed. Seeing and listening to the Gymnosophs (probably Jains), he had realized that "men disagree on the nature of the good"—and a new Western philosophy, Pyrrhonism or skepticism, was born.

most brutal and merciless kind. According to the Greek ambassador at their court, the Mauryans maintained the largest standing army on earth, with more than 700,000 men, 9,000 elephants, and 10,000 chariots. The court's treatise on strategy and diplomacy, the *Arthashastra,* India's equivalent of Machiavelli's *The Prince,* prescribes an eighteen-day cycle of torture for captured rebels or traitors, suggesting a different method of torture for each day. Ashoka's own inscriptions tell us that in order to complete the conquest of Kalinga, he killed 100,000 people and ethnically cleansed another 150,000, while tens of thousands more died of starvation and exposure.[24]

But Ashoka grew sick of the endless cycle of slaughter and conquest and turned to the teachings of the Buddha for his own peace of mind, and to reform his kingdom. All humanity were his children, he declared, and he would henceforth rule through the Law of Righteousness and *ahimsa,* or nonviolence: "For the Beloved of the Gods [i.e., Ashoka] desires safety, self-control, justice and happiness for all beings." He established a new class of officials to look after the well-being of his subjects, and he banned animal sacrifice. He had fruit trees planted along the empire's roads in order to provide travelers with food and shade, collected more than seven thousand relics of the Buddha, and invited Buddhist monks into his court while sending others to foreign capitals.[25]

His high-mindedness and renunciation of violence would earn him the admiration of future generations of Indians, including Gandhi. His four-lion crowned pillars became the official seal of India. But perhaps not surprisingly, his legacy did not last. The kingdom fell apart shortly after his death in 232 B.C.E., and within fifty years the Mauryan Empire had vanished. The old ruthless laws of the jungle replaced the Law of Righteousness, and it would take five hundred years of chaos before another dynasty of worthy successors arose, the Guptas.

The Gupta Empire marks the "classical" period of Indian history, with a flourishing of architecture and art, including Buddhist and Hindu carvings of exquisite splendor and complexity; of language, with the poetry of Kalidasa, the "Shakespeare of India" and author of the Sanskrit drama *Shakuntala;* and of religious thought, along with wars of breathtaking savagery. Under the Guptas a Hindu society of clearly defined castes first emerged, built around an agricultural economy of landlords and peasants; it would survive right down to Gandhi's time and beyond. By the time the dynasty collapsed under assault by the Huns in the sixth century C.E., Indian civilization was ready to survive, and even defy, the next waves of catastrophic change.

The first was the coming of Islam and the rise of the Mughals. Despite their name, the Mughals were not Mongols at all but Turks. However, the dynasty's founder, Babur, claimed descent both from Tamurlaine and from the mighty Genghis Khan, and so the Mongol or Mughal appellation stuck. In 1526 Babur's army crushed his Muslim rival's forces at Panipat, only fifty miles from Delhi, scattering his enemy's elephants with artillery. A year later he defeated the proud Hindu Rajput princes. The empire of Babur and his successors, Akbar, Shah Jahan (builder of the Taj Mahal), and Aurangzeb, would possess more territory, wealth, and splendor than any kingdom India had ever seen—except with Muslims instead of Hindus in charge.

The two religions could not have been more different. Islam preached the existence of one God, Allah, instead of the pantheon of gods and goddesses of the Hindus. It preached the brotherhood of all believers, instead of the hierarchic inequalities and inequities of caste. And it condemned all religious imagery, like Hindu temple carvings and the statues surrounding Buddhist shrines, as blasphemous idolatry. Islamic zealots destroyed thousands of Hindu sites or converted them into mosques. Buddhist sites were virtually obliterated.[26] The complexity of Hindu caste law and dietary ritual also made little sense to Muslims, who butchered and ate the Brahmin cows that Hindus treated as sacrosanct.

But under the Mughals, both Hindus and Muslims in India found a *modus vivendi,* if not exactly common ground. Babur and Akbar patronized Hindu artists and builders. High-caste Hindus served as administrators and tax collectors for their empire, and Hindu generals and soldiers became the core of their army. In turn, Muslims became a permanent part of the social landscape of India, making up almost one-quarter of the population in the Punjab, Sind, and Baluchistan to the west and in Bengal to the east—although only 14 percent in Gandhi's home province of Gujarat and less than a tenth in the center and south of India were Muslims.[27]

Some Hindu princelings, especially among the Marathas and the Rajputs, never submitted to Muslim rule. Fierce insurgencies raged back and forth across the Hindu heartland of central India for more than a century. Babur's great-grandson Aurangzeb was engaged in crushing one in 1690, when the East India Company made its first appearance in Calcutta.

To the Mughals, the English, like other Europeans in India, seemed only a minor distraction. They were too few in number and too paltry in wealth and power to worry about, especially since Babur's successors had their hands full keeping their empire together and dealing with outside intruders from Afghanistan and Persia. When Bahadur Shah I died in 1712, no Indian could have imagined that these uncouth and (from a religious point of view) unclean Europeans or *feringhi* would soon hold the balance of power in the subcontinent.

They gained it precisely because they offered the two things everyone needed in the dog-eat-dog world of late Mughal politics: guns and soldiers. Mughal official and Hindu insurgent alike saw the French, the British, and their sepoy regiments as allies of convenience for their own power grabs. It was the Maratha chieftain Morari Rao who chose to back Clive at Arcot against a hated Muslim rival, and it was the emperor's renegade viceroy in Bengal, Siraj-ad-Daula, who mobilized his army in support of the French until Clive's victory at Plassey stripped him of power.

Some fought hard against the seemingly inexorable British conquest, just as they had against the Mughals. Haidar Ali was a Muslim adventurer, unable to read or write, who carved out a territory for himself around Mysore in southern India. He and his son Tipu Sahib fought bravely against the British for nearly three decades until Tipu finally succumbed to Lord Wellesley's sepoys and British infantry at the siege of Seringapatam in 1799.

Similarly, the proud Marathas were a warrior caste who had converted to Hinduism after settling in India from central Asia many centuries before. They seized the opportunity of collapsing Mughal rule to make their own bid for control of the entire empire, British or no British. Maratha power was finally checkmated at the Battle of Panipat in 1761, this time not by a European power but by a combined Afghan-Mughal army.

Panipat was the Gettysburg of Indian history. Never again would Maratha fortunes rise so high or their armies march so far north. Never again would any native Indian ruler have a chance of dominating the subcontinent. After Panipat the only power left that could hold India together was the East India Company, and the British.

In general, most Indians, whether Hindu or Muslim, preferred British rule to chaos. They also preferred trade with the English to being plundered by Persians or Afghans or their own homegrown bandits. It was true the British were foreigners, but the Mughals had been foreigners, too—although the new language of governance was English instead of Persian, and the new rulers' religion was Christianity instead of Islam. Privately, high-caste Hindus were horrified by the English, who wore leather gloves and hats made from dead animals next to their skins, who ate food that any Brahmin would call disgusting offal, who allowed their women to talk and argue loudly at the dinner table, and who made low-caste and untouchable Indians their intimate servants— in some cases, even their mistresses.[28]

But for those at the top of Indian society, British rule brought an administration that was fair, uncorrupt, and comfortably distant. Indian elites in the three presidencies of Bengal, Madras, and Bombay were content to submit to the East India Company's rules, serve in its armies, and help it collect money to pay for them as long as they were left alone to get on with their normal affairs. It was for those at the bottom, especially in eastern India, that the British brought disaster.

This was the result of the land tenure "reform" wrought by Governor-General Lord Charles Cornwallis in the 1790s. Cornwallis, fresh from his defeat at the hands of the Americans in Yorktown, had been determined to make this imperial venture succeed. He turned the old sliding scale of rents paid by peasants to their landlords, or *zemindars,* into a permanent fixed amount, to be collected by the zemindar; any disagreements were to be adjudicated in the local district court instead of by often-corrupt officials on the ground.

The reforms were well meant, according to Western standards of fairness and efficiency, but they broke the back of the old village communities. Local landlords who could not collect the fixed amount in times of shortage or famine simply sold their land to the highest bidder, including new merchants from cities like Bombay and Calcutta now getting rich from British trade.[29] As the practice spread from Bengal and Bihar to the other presidencies, the result was a rural landscape of destitute peasants and absentee landlords, and a growing wall of separation between the values of urban and rural India. It was this impoverished world that Gandhi would find when he toured the villages of Bihar more than a hundred years later, in 1917.

Cornwallis's land reform scheme was also part of a growing shift in British attitudes. The collapse and breakdown of civil order in eighteenth-century India (to which the British had contributed more than any other single power) had revised their opinion of Indians downward. Clive had fought beside and against Hindus and Muslims, made friends with them, and cheated and lied to them more or less as equals. Even Warren Hastings, the first governor-general, had said, "The people of this country do not require our aid to furnish them with a rule of conduct or a standard for their property."[30]

But their successors took a very different approach. "Every native of India, I verily believe," Cornwallis said, "is corrupt," and he dismissed every native official who worked for the East India Company. As one historian has put it, "He thought of the English as ruling Indians for their own good, but on European rather than Indian lines."[31] As their power grew, the English came to see India as a social science experiment, to be studied, to be worked over and tinkered with, regardless of how Indians themselves felt—especially since, from the European standpoint, Indian values and culture were at the root of the problem.

James Mill, writing his *History of British India* for the East India Company, pronounced Hindu caste society a cesspool of injustice and superstition.[32] Fifteen years later in 1835, while sitting in Calcutta on the governor-general's executive council, historian Thomas B. Macaulay concluded that "a single shelf of books from a good European library was worth more than the whole native literature of India and Arabia."[33]

The debate had become not whether the British were going to change India but how. Macaulay and others pushed for funding a Western-style education system that would supplant and eventually replace traditional Hindu learning, with its "medical doctrines which would disgrace an English farrier, [and] astronomy which would move laughter in girls at an English boarding school." To have found "a great people sunk in the lowest depths of slavery and superstition, to have so ruled them as to have made them desirous and capable of all the privileges of citizens, would indeed be a title to glory all our own," Macaulay affirmed.[34]

But without realizing it, the British were playing with cultural dynamite. Indian soldiers were proud to serve the British according to a military tradition reaching back to the Aryans. The Bengali writer Ram Mohan Roy could see that English rule, "though a foreign yoke, would lead most speedily and surely to the amelioration of the native inhabitants," including an end to suttee, which Roy calculated cost the lives of more than three hundred widows a year in Calcutta alone. At the same time British Orientalist scholars like William Jones and Henry Colebrooke were rediscovering and editing some of Sanskrit's most precious texts, including the *Bhagavad Gita,* and passing that knowledge to successive generations of Indian students.[35]

However, if British rule meant a daily assault on millennia-old traditions and beliefs; or a daily challenge to Hindus and Muslims by aggressive Christian missionaries sanctioned by the government; or legal changes that undermined the status of India's elites and its last autonomous rulers—then Indian cooperation, which the British took for granted, was going to turn into fierce resistance.

All these things happened and reached their culmination under Governor-General Lord Dalhousie. He took office in 1848, the year revolutions were convulsing the capitals of Europe. From Government House in Calcutta, Dalhousie would set off one of his own. He pushed radical reform on every front, economic, cultural, and political, including annexing Indian states like the kingdom of Oudh, whose rulers failed to produce a male heir. Dalhousie's annexations were a direct challenge to India's remaining power-holders, even as their rural tenants were finding their world turned upside down by legal and economic forces they could not understand.[36] Dalhousie left India "in peace within and without," as he put it, in 1856. But it was already too late to prevent the explosion of the Great Mutiny.

The Mutiny of 1857 was a watershed event not just in the history of British rule in India but for India. In May the native regiments in Meerut rose up, murdered their British officers, and marched on Delhi, where they proclaimed the last Mughal emperor, the powerless and pitiful seventy-year-old Bahadur Shah II, their ruler. Some who joined were encouraged by prophecies that the one hundredth anniversary of the Battle of Plassey would see the end of British rule. Others believed rumors that a Russian army would march down to help them restore Mughal rule and Muslim supremacy.[37] Still others, like the Maratha Nana Sahib, joined in hopes of restoring lost pride and glory; others in hopes of plunder; and some because they were afraid not to, if the British really were driven out.

But all agreed that the cumulative effect of a half-century of British rule had been to make them feel like strangers in their own country, and that the only way to turn back the tide was to drive the British out. For almost a year the mutineers controlled an area the size of Britain. Some local Hindu rulers and communities in northern and central India joined the revolt, but most of the subcontinent, like the Gandhis' hometown of Porbandar, remained quiet. The fact that the Sikhs, the Hindu military-religious brotherhood in the Punjab who had fought every power-holder in India since the fifteenth century, remained loyal to the British cause probably did more to smash the Mutiny than any other single factor. Certainly none of the mutineers or their princely allies had the skills or experience necessary to beat the British Army once it was fully aroused and mobilized.

By June 1858 British troops had crushed the sepoys and the last rebel prince, the Maharaja of Gwalior. British rule, having survived its gravest crisis, was stronger than ever. It was now "the Raj," successor to the Mughals and fount of all order and authority. But if the crisis of the Mutiny drove the British together, it ultimately drove Indians apart. Sikh loyalty, and apathy in southern India, doomed the revolt, but so did the limited and often self-interested motives of its organizers. In order to defeat the British, the mutineers had summoned up the spirits of the past: the Meerut mutineers looked to a restored Mughal empire, Nana Sahib and his followers to a revived Maratha confederacy of faith and resistance. They had failed. The result, paradoxically, was that now Indians were more dependent on the British than ever. For millions of Indians after 1858, the Raj was the one remaining fixed point in a world permanently in flux. Wherever it led, they had no choice but to follow.

For the British, too, there was no going back. The changes that the new India Office and the Queen's Proclamation brought were all based on a single principle: that the British would never again let down their guard. They would be patient with the Indians, and they would be more circumspect in introducing change. They would even consult with Indians, when necessary (as in 1886, when Viceroy Dufferin included Indians in a commission to study admitting more natives to the civil service). But the prospect vanished that the British would ever trust the Indians or give them any significant role in running their own affairs.

Meanwhile economic and communication growth, with the coming of factories, mines, and railroads, was creating a new industrial India side by side with the old. This too was a legacy of the Mutiny's defeat. The end of the last independent states removed the final barriers to India's integration into the British imperial economy. Only a few years after the massacre in the Bibighar, Cawnpore became a major textile center, "the Manchester of the East." Likewise Ahmedabad, some three hundred miles east of Rajkot, was where cotton grown in Gujarati fields was woven into cloth for India's toiling millions. Ahmedabad's Indian millionaires would become Gandhi's first important political contributors.

Yet by the 1890s India's mills were still producing only about eight percent of its cloth consumption.[38] While India's economy was *de jure* free from interference from the government in London (which was why

Randolph Churchill and his son could talk about India's "free markets"), *de facto* British rule kept it a captive market for British industrial goods, including cotton—even as the Indian national currency, the rupee, became subject to the fluctuations of the British pound and British exports. Some Indians benefited from the imperial economy, like the Parsis and other enterprising businessmen in the cities. But the vast majority of Indians remained trapped in a system of rural poverty, interspersed with cycles of floods, drought, and famine. They paid the taxes, including a tax on salt, that subsidized British rule. But they saw little or no return for shouldering most of the imperial burden. For most, the British present was no worse than the Mughal or even Gupta past. But apart from famine relief and other humanitarian efforts, it was hardly much better.

In the meantime traditional India, as embedded as ever, could offer no alternative to British rule. The defeat of the Mutiny had fractured the old order and destroyed the credibility of the traditional political class of rajas and *zemindar* landlords. Instead, what the future held for India would depend even more on a new elite, a Western-educated one, that saw the imperial relationship with Britain in a wholly new light.

This new elite was the product of the sweeping educational reforms set in motion by Thomas Macaulay and his successors. In 1838 there were forty English schools operating under the supervision of the General Committee of Public Instruction. By the 1870s some 6,000 Indian students were enrolled in English-speaking colleges and universities and another 200,000 in secondary schools. When Randolph Churchill did his tour of India in 1885, there were more than twenty-one colleges in Bengal alone and twenty-four in Madras.

The students were almost entirely Hindu and almost all upper caste, drawn from distinguished families like the Boses, Ghoses, and Tagores of Bengal—and all males. Only a few went into a business or technical field; most became lawyers, teachers, and journalists. Fully a fifth entered the government, even though by 1880 only four Indians had managed to enter the exalted ranks of the Indian Civil Service. These Western-educated Indians were inspired by an earlier figure, Ram Mohan Roy, the Brahmin-born intellectual and civil servant who could read Latin and Greek as well as Persian and Arabic.

"Perhaps no other Bengali," writes one distinguished scholar, "with the exception of Rabindranath Tagore, has been so thoroughly identified with the cultural self-image of the Indian people," or at least its educated elite.[39] Roy published India's first home newspaper. He lived in England as the Mughals' ambassador until his death in 1833. Roy also claimed to find in the *Upanishads* and other Hindu works a theory of reason and human rights equal to that of the West. He was also the first to advocate a new cultural pluralism for India, one that incorporated Christian ideals alongside Hindu and Muslim texts, just as Gandhi would do a century later.

This Ram Mohan Roy–inspired, Western-educated elite was never monolithic its views, including its views on British rule. It included fierce loyalists like Bholanath Chunder, whose *Travels of a Hindu,* published the year Gandhi was born, argued that the British constitution was the greatest in the world and that India had had no real political culture until the British arrived. It included fierce critics like Sayyid Ahmad Khan, whose *Causes of the Indian Revolt* put the rebellion's blame squarely on the British and warned that "security never [will be] acquired unless the people are allowed a share in the consultations of government."[40] The elite included many who proudly imbibed the Hindu classics alongside the Western ones (ignoring the irony that it was in British schools that they received the most rigorous education in their own culture). Still others discovered in writers like Milton, Locke, Edmund Burke, and John Stuart Mill an ideal of national self-government and asked why it should apply to whites but not to nonwhites.

These were the kind of men whom Randolph Churchill met during his tour of India and who had impressed him with their keen intelligence and understanding. Indian traditionalists considered them traitors for abandoning traditional ways and taking up Western dress and manners. The British in India mocked them as "babus." It was against them that the White Mutiny of 1883 was directed, and it was they who organized a massive rally in support of Lord Ripon when he left India, which Randolph Churchill described as "the first real assertion of the people of India of their...right and intention to exercise a more or less controlling influence over Indian Government."[41] And it was this same Western-educated elite who set up the Indian National Congress three years later.

Justifiably, these men saw themselves as India's future leaders, but they remained a tiny minority. During Randolph Churchill's tenure less than one percent of Indians could read or write English. Those who could, and who had the chance to travel or even study in England or Europe, were fired with Western liberal ideas. But the institutions of the

Raj would not allow them near the levers of powers. In addition, most found themselves educated beyond their means or India's needs, leaving them "in an economic strait jacket, caught between rising prices and badly paid employment or unemployment."[42]

But their anger and discontent also had another, deeper source. After 1857 the British classification of "martial races" and "non-fighting races" had covered India's best and brightest with a cloak of shame.[43] Put bluntly, in British eyes a Hindu, especially one from Bengal or southern India, was not a true man. An educated Hindu was even worse. As a result, young men of Gandhi's generation found themselves caught in a British cultural vise that stigmatized them as unmanly poltroons on one side, but as untrustworthy and "too clever by half" on the other. Gandhi and many others would spend their lives struggling to break free from that vise and the psychological scars it left. In a profound sense Gandhi's entire theory of satyagraha or civil disobedience as manly "soul force," requiring soldierly virtues like courage and self-sacrifice, sprang from the urgent need to fill the hole that Western education had left in his countrymen's souls.

Nonetheless, most Indians saw no alternative to Western education as the path to the future. This was true even in provincial Gujarat. In January 1879 Gandhi's father would send his son to the English school in Rajkot, in order to prepare him to enter that elite rank. It was Karamchand's way of recognizing that a new era had dawned, and that the traditional ways, around which he had built his life, were no longer enough.

And so, even as Queen Victoria settled into her new role as Empress of India, young Mohandas Gandhi was about to embark on a decade-and-a-half odyssey, across cultures but also across lands. It would take him thousands of miles from home—and then unexpectedly and paradoxically, it would also bring him back to his roots.

Chapter Four

AWAKENING:
Gandhi in London and South Africa, 1888–1895

You would have me sit at your feet; I will not do so.
MOHANDAS K. GANDHI, 1893

THE GANDHIS MOVED TO RAJKOT WHEN Mohandas was six. In 1874 Karamchand had become diwan for another Gujarati prince, the rani of Rajkot. He regularly made the two-hundred-mile, five-day journey from Porbandar by oxcart until his family was ready to join him. Small and dust-bitten, set on a flat featureless plain, Rajkot had no decent roads, no telegraph, and no post office. But here the Gandhis had their first encounter with the India the British had made.

Rajkot was the headquarters of the British resident in Kathiawar. A court of appeal sat in judgment of natives and Europeans alike. Under the Raj Rajkot had become in effect two towns. There was a British quarter, with neat white houses and streets running in straight right angles, and an Indian one, with dark winding alleyways and fifteen thousand people crammed into 137 acres of living space.[1] As diwan, Karamchand had to attend official durbars when the governor of Bombay came to call. Gandhi would remember the upheaval it caused in his household when his father put on European-style garb for the visit. "If I was a painter," he recalled, "I would paint my father's disgust and torture on his face as he was putting his legs into his stockings and feet into ill-fitting and uncomfortable boots." At home or at work Karamchand never wore anything but soft leather slippers. The ordeal of wearing boots was the price he had to pay for becoming a cog in the wheels of British power.[2]

Gandhi himself was getting his first dose of Western-style education in the local Rajkot school. A shy, timid student, he dutifully made his way through English grammar, arithmetic, penmanship, Sanskrit, and geography (his weakest subject). In 1881 he tested into the Kathiawar High School, where mostly Parsi teachers led their pupils through twenty-nine hours of lessons a week, including ten hours of training in English.

"I had not any high regard for my ability," Gandhi remembered of his school days, and he was amazed whenever he won a prize or award. "Everything had to be learned through English," he recalled fifty years later. "The tyranny of English was so great that even Sanskrit or Persian had to be learned through English, not through the mother tongue," that is, Gujarati. Since neither his father nor his mother spoke the language of the Raj, "I was fast becoming a stranger in my home," Gandhi remembered.[3]

Then one day he returned from school to learn he was going to be married. He was thirteen—certainly not too young for the prearranged marital match that was considered essential to a Hindu household. His bride Kasturbai Makanji, also thirteen, was the daughter of a merchant who lived only a few doors down from the Gandhis' old house in Porbandar. The ceremony took place in Porbandar. To save expense, it was celebrated together with the marriages of his older brother Karsandas and of a cousin.

Amid the music, incense, and banks of food and fragrant flowers, Mohandas exchanged vows and the traditional sweet wheat cake with his child bride. Kasturbai was small, shy, and plain. She had not learned how to read or write and never would. Yet Gandhi would write in his autobiography, "I was passionately fond of her." Although child brides customarily spent more than half their time in their father's, rather than their husband's, home, "separation was unbearable" to Mohandas. "I used to keep her awake til late at night with my idle talk." She was also the delightful, if passive, outlet for his adolescent sexual energies.[4]

Marriage marked the first crucial life change for Gandhi. The death of his father was the second. While traveling from Rajkot to Porbandar, Karamchand suffered from a road accident and never recovered. He spent the last three years of his life as an invalid. Almost every night Mohandas would go to his father's room and massage his withering limbs, "but while my hands were busy massaging my father's legs, my mind was hovering above the bed-room," with lustful thoughts about his bride Kasturbai. As soon as the massage was done, Mohandas would go straight into her bed, even though she was now pregnant with their first child.

One night he finished his father's massage late, around ten-thirty or eleven o'clock. He had to wake up Kasturbai in order to have sex; after a few minutes a frantic knock came at the door. "Get up!" one of the servants was shouting. "Father is very ill!" By the time Mohandas had opened the door and raced down the hall, he learned the stunning truth. Karamchand Gandhi, the family patriarch, was dead. He had been only fifty-six.

As he watched his mother and uncle and brothers dissolve into tears and heard the servants wailing, Mohandas was swept by a wave of intense shame. The thought that he had been having sex at the very moment his father died—that his "animal passion," as he called it, might even have somehow contributed to his father's death—would haunt Gandhi for the rest of his life. "It is a blot I have never been able to efface or forget," Gandhi confessed years later. To cap it all, the child that Kasturbai had been carrying that night died shortly after it was born.[5]

Sexual relations with his wife would never be the same. Although Mohandas and Kasturbai would have four more children (all sons), Gandhi's decision at age thirty-seven to take a vow of chastity or *brahmacharya* was more than just an act of self-denial.[6] It was also a way of trying to close a horrifying chapter in his life, one that marked and marred his relations with women until his death.

Karamchand's dying thoughts had been about his son. "Manu here will keep up my reputation," he said. "He will increase the fame of our lineage." Since 1879 there had been talk about sending Gandhi to England to study law. A friend of the family, a Brahmin, had told Karamchand that it was relatively easy to become a barrister. The course of study at one of London's Inns of Court was short and informal, and a law degree would not only earn Mohandas a good living but open the doors for him to become a diwan like his father. Even the proud Karamchand realized that an English education and a knowledge of British law were the new path to success in his profession.[7]

Somehow the family scraped together the money needed to send him to London. Mohandas even sold some of Kasturbai's gold necklaces to pay for the steamship ticket.[8] In that dry hot summer of 1888, as his brother announced that he would accompany him as far as Bombay (which Mohandas had never visited) and his fellow high school students stared at him with admiration, a trip to the moon must have seemed less of an undertaking. By any measure, going to England meant making a momentous break with his culture, his past life, his family, and even his marriage, because Kasturbai would remain in India while he was studying in London.

Then, even as Mohandas was poised on the brink of his new life, the values of old India asserted themselves. When he and his brother arrived in Bombay, they learned that other members of their Modh Bania caste were in an uproar. No Modh Bania had ever traveled to England; none should now. In fact, devout Hindus commonly feared "crossing the black water," as the ocean was called, meant pollution and breaking one's caste. The danger that one might have to eat and drink with Europeans or other nonbelievers, and perhaps eat what they did, was considered too great a risk. So Mohandas was summoned to a meeting of the caste council, where the *seth* or headman told him point-blank that he could not go to England.

Gandhi was nervous but angry. He explained that a learned Brahmin had approved the trip; so had his brother and mother.

"But will you disregard the orders of the caste?" the seth demanded.

Gandhi shrugged. "I am really helpless," he said. "I think the caste should not interfere in the matter." The seth and the council were furious. They declared him an outcaste and forbade anyone to give him money or to see him off at the dock, on pain of a fine of one rupee four annas. It was a humiliating sentence, but "I sat unmoved," Gandhi later remembered.[9] It was also a turning point. Going to England meant breaking with the ancient bonds that had held together India for centuries and that now, in the wake of the modern age, seemed to hold it back. But Gandhi had resolved that those bonds did not apply to him unless *he* decided they should. It was more than just an act of courage and will; it was a declaration of personal independence.

Besides, he could tell himself, he had broken with his caste but not his family. Before he left Rajkot, his mother had made him take a vow that he would not touch three things during his stay in England: wine, women, or animal flesh. It was that vow that he told himself he would uphold as his religious obligation, instead of the arbitrary and impersonal rules of his caste. And so on September 4, 1888, after frantic days of final packing and restless nights of anxious nightmares, he set sail from Bombay, leaving behind everything he knew to "see England, the land of philosophers and poets, the very centre of civilization."[10]

*   *   *

Certainly London was the largest city on the planet, with more than five and a half million inhabitants in 1888.[11] It was the nerve center of the world's financial system, the capital of the world's most admired government, and the summit of the world's mightiest empire. Someone once asked Gandhi what had led him to London. He answered with one word: "Ambition."[12] If true, then he had certainly come to the right place.

Ambitious foreigners had been flocking to London for years, making it Europe's premier cosmopolitan capital. The American novelist Henry James had settled there in 1876 and soon became a favorite of London's West End social elite and a close friend of Churchill's mother. Another American, the painter James McNeill Whistler, had left London for Paris, but John Singer Sargent had exhibited at the Royal Academy the previous year and was poised to become the high-paid portraitist of Britain's rich and powerful. Latin Americans, Jews from Eastern Europe, and Italians, as well as Indians, Arabs, and subjects from other parts of the British Empire were becoming a common sight in the streets of central London and the East End. At the same time new shops and department stores attracted hordes of shoppers to Oxford Street and Piccadilly in the West End.

But London also had another, darker side when Gandhi arrived there. Even as he was settling into the Victoria Hotel on October 1, 1888, all England was talking about the series of grisly murders in the slums of Whitechapel. The victims were all women and all prostitutes. The first had occurred on August 31; the second on September 8; and the third and fourth on September 30, just the day after Gandhi arrived.[13] That same afternoon the police received a note from the killer, signed "Jack the Ripper."

The Ripper murders would terrorize the city until mid-November. They also exposed to the British public the violence and squalor of an underclass London that was located only a few short minutes from wealthy homes like that of the Churchills in Grosvenor Square. In 1883 George Sims had published the first study of London slum housing, entitled *How the Poor Live*. Two years later W. T. Stead wrote his sensational exposé of child prostitution in London, "The Maiden Tribute of Babylon." A new era of social consciousness was under way. The Ripper murders (in November they ceased as mysteriously as they had begun and were never solved) would highlight the ugly reality lurking behind the confident facade of Western-style progress, "a dark continent that is within easy walking distance of the General Post Office."[14]

Gandhi's diary never mentions the murders, nor any of the famous sights of London that impressed every other visitor, like Big Ben and the British Museum. In fact, from the day of his arrival he seems to have virtually barricaded himself first in his hotel room, then in a boardinghouse in Baron's Court Road in West Kensington owned by an Anglo-Indian lady. He read the newspapers every day, including the *Daily Telegraph* and the *Pall Mall Gazette*. He met with several people from his home province living in London, including other Indians studying with him at the Inns of Court. (By 1907 Indians at the Inns of Court numbered more than three hundred.)[15]

But Gandhi found himself a fish out of water in London, isolated and homesick. "I would think continually of my home and country," he recalled forty years later. "At night the tears would stream down my cheeks." Speaking English was a constant battle: he bought a copy of *The Standard Elocutionist* by renowned speech therapist Alexander Melville Bell to help him practice but without much success.* He also had his struggles with Western dress. The ties, stiff collars, hard shoes, top hats, and thick wool suits (in a moment of extravagance Gandhi even bought an evening suit from a shop in Bond Street) that he needed to appear respectable, and to protect himself against the unfamiliar cold and damp of a London autumn, all grated on his nerves, not to mention on his pocketbook.[16]

Above all, he struggled with the issue of food. Life as an Inner Temple student required attending six dinners "in Hall" every term. Somewhat surprisingly for a boy who never enjoyed books, Gandhi threw himself into his legal studies with gusto. He made his diligent way through a shelf of textbooks on common and Roman law, civil and criminal procedure, and even read William Douglas Edwards's daunting 508-page *The Law of Property in Land* "with interest."

But the term dinners were a torment to him. Remembering his vow to his mother, Gandhi stuck to a meatless diet, but the only vegetables English cooks prepared were, then as now, "tasteless and insipid."[17] The special vegetarian meals he asked for tasted like cardboard, while the beef or mutton on other people's plates, and the decanters of claret and

---

* Bell was father of the inventor of the telephone, Alexander Graham Bell.

port on the table, reminded him that others were enjoying themselves even as he tried to keep his vow.

This was the temptation that the other members of his caste, and his mother, had feared. For what was at stake was not just a personal vow or even religious law. At stake was a fundamental part of Gandhi's identity as a Hindu.

"Meat is indeed the best kind of food," the *Vedas* had said.[18] In early India meat had been the food of the gods, literally so in the Vedic ritual sacrifices; meat was naturally also the food of kings and the ruling class. The Vedic social pecking order was resolutely and proudly carnivorous. "The mongoose eats mice," runs a passage in the *Mahabharata,* "just as the cat eats the mongoose; the dog devours the cat, O king, and wild beasts eat the dog. Man eats them all," the passage adds, "see *dharma* for what it is! Everything that moves and is still is food for life."[19]

The Brahminic cultural order of later Hinduism reversed every Vedic value. Glory, worldly wealth, power attained at the pain of others, all became "bad" or at least spiritually empty, and self-renunciation became "good." Likewise, meat became "bad," fit only for the lower castes and untouchables, while a purely vegetarian diet symbolized spiritual purity, just like other acts of renunciation and self-denial. For an Indian like Gandhi, vegetarianism was more than just a matter of diet. It upheld spiritual values that had ingrained themselves in Hindu culture and its social order. The rituals of vegetarianism had permeated his father's household and Gandhi's own sense of self-worth.

To yield on this issue, Gandhi had come to feel, would be to yield on everything. There would be nothing left, either of his culture or himself. "Daily I would pray for God's protection," he remembered later, "and get it."[20] He steered clear of the Englishman's diet. Once again Gandhi's willpower had prevailed.

Still, the problem remained: how to stay on a meatless regimen without dying of boredom. It was his kindly landlady who solved his difficulty. Three weeks after he moved in, she told him about a vegetarian restaurant she knew on High Holborn Street. On the way there Gandhi passed another vegetarian café, called the Central, off Farrington Street and not far from the Inner Temple. "The sight filled me with joy," Gandhi would write in his autobiography, and it would change his life.

In the front window was a stack of pamphlets, entitled *A Plea for Vegetarianism,* by Dr. Henry Salt. Gandhi bought a copy for a shilling and read it with his meal. For the first time he realized there was a "modern" Western philosophical case for not eating flesh of any kind, as well as the traditional Hindu one. Later, Gandhi saw Dr. Salt at high tea at the Central. "My name is Gandhi," he said, extending his hand to the tall, bearded middle-aged author. "You have of course never heard of it." The two remained friends until Salt's death in 1939.

Henry Salt was unlike any Englishman Gandhi had ever met. He had been born in India, the son of an army colonel who returned to England five years before the Great Mutiny when Henry was an infant. Educated at Eton and Cambridge, Salt fit the conventional mold of Victorian middle-class life in everything except his growing disgust with meat. By 1884 he moved to Surrey to cultivate an enormous vegetable garden and author a growing pile of pamphlets and books and poems, many of them centering on an issue that would come to be called animal rights.

"All practices which inflict unnecessary pain on sentient beings," Salt wrote, "are...incompatible with the higher instincts of humanity," including killing animals for food or sport or scientific research. (Salt was also a founder of the anti–fox-hunting Humanitarian League and very active in the Anti-Vivisection Society.)[21] In short, the basis of Salt's vegetarianism was not religious but secular and liberal. It was part of the new social consciousness in Britain and carried over from animal rights to opposition to the death penalty, corporal punishment, and industrialization's despoiling of the countryside—Salt's favorite book was Henry David Thoreau's *Walden*.*[22] Salt's wide circle of friends also included such unconventional figures as George Bernard Shaw and Sidney and Beatrice Webb, the sexologist Havelock Ellis, and the Catholic journalist G. K. Chesterton—the latter a figure whose work would have a decisive impact on Gandhi later on.

"From the date of reading" *A Plea for Vegetarianism,* Gandhi tells us, "I may claim to have become a vegetarian by choice." It also marked his first acquaintance with Late Victorian London's emerging counterculture. These counterculture gurus wore frock coats and top hats, not beads and sandals, while the ladies wore crinoline dresses. They read Shelley and John Ruskin, not Kerouac and Marcuse. But they were no less challenging to the official culture around them.

The official London of aristocrats like the Churchills and their friends,

---

* Salt even wrote a biography of Thoreau, and some scholars suspect it was Salt who first introduced Gandhi to Thoreau's writings, especially his *Civil Disobedience*.

Henry James and John Singer Sargent, was resolutely cosmopolitan, materialistic, and self-consciously modern. It endorsed all forms of progress as long as they had firm foundations in historical tradition. That sentiment was made visible by the new Houses of Parliament, which had been designed in a neo-Gothic style in order to underline modern self-government's continuity with its medieval past.

Therefore the official culture's opponents decided they would be esoteric, spiritual, and resolutely antimodern. Although their politics tilted sharply to the left, in their minds the transformation of politics was less important than the transformation of the inner self. They saw themselves as standard-bearers of a new dawn of spiritual and moral values for Western man and a new beginning for society. Their utopian vision of the future was summed up by the title of one of their magazines: *The New Age.*

Gandhi became friends with many of these New Age figures through Salt's Vegetarian Society. They included Josiah Oldfield, leader of the Esoteric Christian Union, who taught Gandhi the unity of all religions from Jesus and Buddha to Muhammad, and explained that the true realm of religion is the mind and heart of the individual.[23]

He met T. R. Allinson, a keen advocate of birth control as well as vegetarianism, whose writings on health and hygiene had a profound impact on Gandhi. He met Edward Carpenter, author of *Civilization: Its Cause and Cure,* a devastating moral critique of the modern industrial West. He met J. B. Paton, whose views on modern society were summed up in his *Back to the Land.* And finally he met Annie Besant, the estranged wife of an Anglican clergyman and a key figure in the Anti-Vivisection Society as well as the Social Democratic Federation.

Besant's life and Gandhi's would become strongly intertwined over the years, both in England and in India. She was in many ways a powerful role model (although later a bitter rival) for Gandhi. In fact, a year earlier in 1887 she had organized what could be called the first great display of the power of mass civil disobedience: a huge demonstration in Trafalgar Square against British rule in Ireland. It took fifteen hundred policemen and two hundred Life Guards to disperse a crowd numbering in the tens of thousands. Three people were killed and hundreds more thrown into prison, including Besant herself. Some protesters even chained themselves to iron railings before being dragged away to jail. Both Henry Salt and Edward Carpenter had been there that day, later remembered as "Bloody Sunday." Another supporter had been

Randolph Churchill's old nemesis, Charles Bradlaugh, who was a political mentor to many of Gandhi's New Age friends.

A young man from Kathiawar who found official London so strange and cold was exhilarated to be part of this marginal but active and intellectually alert elite. Gandhi enthusiastically joined the Vegetarian Society of London, and he read and eventually wrote articles for its house organ, *The Vegetarian*. He went to several meetings of the Esoteric Christian Union; later in South Africa he would list himself as a member of the Union and sell its pamphlets door to door. He attended Bradlaugh's funeral at Woking cemetery, "as I believe every Indian in London did."[24]

Gandhi's introduction to London's New Age counterculture was only just starting. At the end of 1889 two young Englishmen stopped at his table at the Central Café. They were reading the *Bhagavad Gita,* they explained, and had some questions about it. Since Gandhi was Indian, they were hoping he would discuss it with them.

"I felt ashamed," Gandhi remembered in his autobiography, "as I had read the divine poem neither in Sanskrit or in Gujarati," even though it had been his father's favorite book before he died. So he agreed to join their little reading group and learned that they were members of another New Age group called the Theosophical Society. (Annie Besant had recently also become a member.) They brought him to one of their meetings, where Gandhi met the woman who, more than any other single person, changed his view of India and its place in the world's future.

Helena Petrovna Blavatsky had been born in the Ukraine, the daughter of an army officer of German descent and wife of a Russian civil servant. Her passion, however, was for all forms of religious experience and the occult. That passion led her to travel extensively through Europe, Latin America, the Middle East, and India. In 1856 she had even tried to enter the forbidden Buddhist kingdom of Tibet to meet the Dalai Lama. Madame Blavatsky, as she was known, became a believer in reincarnation and the supernatural: she even claimed it was a guardian spirit who warned her to leave India just before the Mutiny.[25]

In 1875 she founded the Theosophical Society in New York City to proclaim the essential unity of all the world's religions, then moved to Madras in 1882 and to London five years later. Short and squat, a chain smoker with bulging penetrating eyes and dramatic gestures, Madame Blavatsky drew large crowds to her lectures and occult séances. Official London found her absurd, even a charlatan. One London wit called her "the low clown of the world to come." But London's New Age counter-culture was drawn to her idea that humanity was on the brink of a great spiritual breakthrough.

Gandhi listened intently as Blavatsky told her white European audience that their path to enlightenment lay in finding the hidden truths of Hinduism and Buddhism, the world's oldest spiritual systems. Indeed, "Pre-Vedic Brahmanism and Buddhism are the double source from which all religions sprung," including Christianity, she had written at the conclusion of her massive two-volume manifesto, *Isis Unveiled*. Blavatsky insisted that Brahmanism and Buddhism also set the spiritual standard for all other faiths, adding that, "Nirvana is the ocean to which all [religions] tend."[26] Gandhi was not alone in being impressed. Blavatsky's thesis that religion represented a higher form of knowledge than science, indeed that science was only an offshoot of religion, attracted some of the most intelligent minds of the age. Annie Besant became a Theosophist convert, as did the poet William Butler Yeats. Both James Joyce and D. H. Lawrence read her works with admiration. Throughout his life Albert Einstein kept a copy of *Isis Unveiled* on his desk.[27]

To the young Gandhi, however, Blavatsky's message was a double revelation. He was never comfortable with the more esoteric side of her Theosophist system, and her experiments with contacting the dead left him cold. But the chain-smoking Russian spiritualist "disabused me of the notion fostered by the missionaries that Hinduism was rife with superstition" and lifted a burden of shame that had weighed on him since he first started school. His native culture was suddenly revealed to him as offering a set of radiant truths relevant to all humanity. Finally he was ready to sit down to read the *Bhagavad Gita* for the first time, in the translation by the famed British Orientalist Edwin Arnold.

This experience, too, would change him forever, and once again it was a Westerner, Edwin Arnold, who sparked his spiritual awakening to one of the great texts of Indian culture.* It is no exaggeration to call the *Gita* the most important book in Gandhi's life. Reading Arnold's verse translation cannot have been easy for Gandhi. In fact, he mentions having to use an English dictionary to struggle through its

---

* Edwin Arnold had been a schoolteacher in India and wrote two best sellers that proved hugely popular with New Agers on both sides of the Atlantic. One was a biography of Gautama Buddha, called *The Light of Asia*; the other was his verse translation of the *Gita,* under the title *The Song Celestial*.

pseudo-archaic and allusive poetic stanzas heavily modeled on Lord Tennyson's *Idylls of the King*. Yet the *Bhagavad Gita* itself is short and its story simple, almost deceptively so.

It describes the eve of the climactic battle in the sprawling Vedic epic poem the *Mahabharata*. As the hero Arjuna prepares for battle, he suddenly realizes he no longer has the stomach for the fight. Martial glory and the endless cycle of kill or be killed, which is celebrated in mainstream Vedic culture, have lost their savor for him. Furthermore, fighting this battle will mean having to kill warriors on the other side who are friends and even relatives. Why should he even bother to show up? he asks his chariot driver, the blue-skinned Krishna. What Arjuna does not realize is that his driver is actually the god Vishnu.

Krishna proceeds to give him not one but three reasons to fight the battle. Do it for your own sake, he tells Arjuna, and your honor as a soldier and warrior. Fight the battle also for its own sake, Krishna says, as a task that, like every task in life, deserves to be done well, regardless of what it is or what the consequences might be. And then, Krishna adds, do it for *my* sake, as he reveals himself to be the incarnation of Vishnu in all his power and glory—in short, do it as an act of obedience and homage to God.

Arjuna discovers the truth that every reader learns by reading the *Bhagavad Gita*. By acting fearlessly and doing what we know is right, and without worrying about any reward, we can achieve holiness and oneness with God:

> *Do thine allotted task!*
> *Work is more excellent than idleness...*
> *There is a task of holiness to do,*
> *Unlike world-binding toil, which bindeth not*
> *the faithful soul; such earthly duty do*
> *Free from desire and thou shalt perform*
> *Thy heavenly purpose.*

The *Gita* marked a turning point in Indian thought and also for Gandhi. It became his "infallible guide of conduct," as he tells us in his autobiography, and a "daily reference" for the rest of his life. He spent time every day committing its verses to memory. Later he even published his own translation and commentary in Gujarati, although the

Arnold translation, for all its Late Victorian fussiness, always remained his favorite version.

Gandhi came to believe that the *Gita*'s "cardinal teaching" was that human beings must resolve to do the right thing without thinking about or considering its fruits or rewards. "He who broods over results," Gandhi would later write, "is ever distracted, he says goodbye to all scruples, everything is right in his estimation and he therefore resorts to means fair and foul to attain his end." In Gandhi's mind, detaching ourselves from results was an act of renunciation as spiritually powerful as any form of self-denial, the moral equivalent of renouncing worldly possessions or sexual desire. It brought holiness to man and peace to his soul. "Man is not at peace with himself til he has become like unto God" in renouncing worldly reward for his actions.

Bhagavad Gita literally means "The Song of God." It celebrates the active life as a form of worship of a particular god, Vishnu. Madame Blavatsky had shown Gandhi that the Hindu concept of God had first revealed the face of divinity to mankind. But was that face now too limited to serve the needs of the modern age and the New Age to come? The Esoteric Christian Union's Edward Maitland argued that Christianity did that job best. He had given Gandhi his first look at the Sermon on the Mount, and Gandhi was deeply impressed by what he read. We also know Gandhi attended Christian services in various London churches, including the City Temple Congregationalist Church (where another attendee at almost the same time was David Lloyd George). He attended marches by the Salvation Army. He had even met the Roman Catholic Cardinal Manning.[28]

Gandhi admitted he was strongly drawn to Christianity, especially to the figure of Jesus Christ. The principles of turning the other cheek and doing unto others as you would have them do unto you, Gandhi confessed later, "went straight to my heart."[29] But this attraction was tempered by his encounters with organized Christianity. His run-ins with missionaries and their zealous push to convert him to their message left him unmoved, no less than Madame Blavatsky's séances. Still, the sense that believing Christians had unlocked a door that was still closed to him, and that they found a peace and inner strength he still lacked, haunted him.

"But beyond this," Gandhi recalled later, "I could not go, as reading for the examination left me scarcely any time for outside subjects." After months of intense study he took his final law exam in June 1890. It was not until the following January that he learned he had passed, placing thirty-fourth out of 109 candidates. He was now a barrister, authorized to plead cases in British courts, including the High Court in Bombay.[30] His great task was over. He could now go home—regretfully so, since he was just becoming comfortable with his New Age circle.

The Vegetarian Society hosted a farewell dinner for Gandhi on June 11, 1891. Guests expressed regret that he was leaving but also confidence that his return to India would mean "even greater work for vegetarianism." In a "very graceful though somewhat nervous speech" Gandhi thanked the members and said how happy he was to see "the abstinence from animal flesh progressing in England." It was a bittersweet occasion, everyone agreed, but all felt that congratulating Gandhi on his professional success "should take the place of personal wailings."[31]

The voyage home was a sad one, and his homecoming even more dismal. The Bombay docks were bathed in a misting monsoon rain as he landed on July 5, 1891.[32] Not even the reunion with Kasturbai and his family could lift the gloom—or a growing "sense of helplessness and fear." Within a few months of trying to start his own law practice in Rajkot, he confesses in his autobiography, "I had serious doubts as to whether I should be able even to earn a living."

Things had changed at home. His mother had died, although his brothers did not tell him until he landed in Bombay. The family now drank coffee and cocoa and used Western-style plates for dinner. Kasturbai had even begun wearing some Western clothes.[33] The Gandhi family had high hopes for his success as a barrister. He went through a ritual cleansing ceremony in the holy Godavari River in order to restore good relations with his Modh Bania caste. Some, however, including his own sister, continued to shun him as an outcaste.

Gandhi took it all in with indifference. Even his beloved mother's death left him dry-eyed. He carried on, as he tells us, "as if nothing had happened."[34] For Gandhi, it was like seeing life through the wrong end of a telescope. It was not just that he knew little about Indian law (although he read whatever books he could get his hands on) or about how to plead or present a case in court. He had just spent three years in the capital of the British Empire, meeting people who were dealing with momentous spiritual and cultural issues. The old routines of home seemed unbearably restricting and dull. Everything, including his first law cases, seeming small and petty compared to the life he had left behind in London.

For almost two years he endured this routine with a sour peevishness. At one point he quarreled with Kasturbai and sent her packing home to her father, "not letting her come home until I made her thoroughly miserable," he confessed years later. But then in March 1893 an offer crossed his desk that woke him out of his depression.

A Kathiawar merchant named Dada Abdullah owned a large and successful shipping business in South Africa. A distant cousin in Johannesburg owed Abdullah £40,000; he needed a lawyer to plead his case there. So Abdullah's partner came to see Gandhi. The two partners were Muslims. Still, they preferred having a fellow Kathiawari handle the case, albeit a Hindu. For Gandhi it meant going to South Africa for at least a year.

"It won't be a difficult job," Abdullah's partner reassured him. "We have big Europeans as our friends, whose acquaintance you will make."

Gandhi asked him about pay. The partner told him they would pay for his expenses and a first-class ticket, plus a fee of £105.

"This was not going as a barrister," Gandhi remembered thinking to himself, "it was going as a servant of the firm."[35] But he knew he had to leave India and escape the boredom of his normal life. South Africa would be just the respite he needed.

So Gandhi accepted the offer virtually on the spot. He did feel a pang of regret on leaving Kasturbai and their two tiny children, but he told her they would certainly meet again in a year. (In fact, it would be more than three years.) And so in April 1893 he set sail from Bombay again. It never occurred to him that he was setting off on a personal and political journey that would consume nearly a quarter-century of his life and make him famous. Or that it would also lead to his first and only meeting with Winston Churchill.

In 1893 South Africa lay divided in four parts. North of the Vaal River were the independent Transvaal Republic and Orange Free State, both ruled by the Dutch-descended Boers. To the south were the Cape Colony and Natal, ruled by the British. Durban was Natal's capital and principal port. As the ship arrived there, Gandhi and the other passengers could see red sand hills streaked by vivid green foliage, dotted by the gray thatched huts of native villages and the occasional white house.[36]

Durban numbered twenty-seven thousand inhabitants. Its streets

were lined with large resort bungalows belonging to European whites
and with rows of shanties where black Africans lived, as well as the trim
brick and clapboard houses of Durban's Indian merchant community.
Many of Natal's Indian merchants came from Gujarat. They were
renowned businessmen, considered shrewd and frugal, and like
Gandhi's employers, many were Muslims. Gujaratis enjoyed wealth as
well as political connections to the colonial governor's mansion, and
most had acquired a Western-style education from schools in India.
They were as respectable and bourgeois a Victorian business class as
their white counterparts in Manchester or Sydney or Ottawa, and they
were standing on the Durban wharf in their suits and turbans, with
white whiskers and grave miens, in order to greet their new barrister as
he disembarked.

Gandhi would be staying in Durban. For most of his fellow
European passengers, however, this was just a brief overnight stop en
route to the Vaal River, where seven years earlier there had been a huge
gold strike. Now thousands of immigrants were heading for the
Transvaal, looking for instant wealth and in the process rapidly changing the character of South Africa and British rule there.

For decades South Africa's Cape Colony had been important to the
British largely as a stopover on the passage to India. But the discovery of
diamonds in 1872, and then gold in 1886, forced huge changes in
Britain's dealings both with the native black Africans and with the
white settlers of Dutch descent, the Boers. British business interests, led
by Cecil Rhodes and his Rothschild investors in London, were keen to
expand their reach into the Boer-controlled gold fields, especially in the
Republic of the Transvaal. British political interests, also led from
London, were eager to halt Boer depredations against the native tribes
and saw the gold rush in the Transvaal as an excuse for intervention.

Boers and Britons had already fought one war over control of the
Transvaal and would soon be fighting another. Meanwhile the influx of
would-be prospectors and adventurers—not only Englishmen but
Americans, Germans, and East Europeans—swelled the population of
every city in South Africa, from Capetown and Durban to Johannesburg,
the Transvaal's largest city and the hub of the gold rush.

The whole region, including Natal, was in the grip of gold fever.
"People here think of little except gold," Gandhi noted as he arrived.[37]
But even in a world where every immigrant dreamed of striking it rich,
someone still had to do the work of keeping the British colonies (Cape

Colony and Natal) and the Boer republics (Transvaal and Orange Free State) fed and clothed and producing the goods and services essential to any urban economy. That job fell to many German and English Jews, businessmen like Hermann Kallenbach and Henry Polak, who would become close friends of Gandhi; it also fell to South Africa's Indians.

Indians had been arriving in large numbers since 1860. Some were wealthy merchants like Dada Abdullah and his partners, but many more were poor indentured laborers. They arrived in conditions of virtual slavery and lived in shantytowns adjoining the sugarcane plantations and coal mines where they worked to earn their freedom and a meager income. By 1891 there were more than 41,000 of these laborers in Natal. A decade later it was close to 100,000.[38]

Although few cared to admit it, this was the other essential contribution India had made to the British Empire: providing literally hundreds of thousands of manual laborers to replace the black slaves who had been set free in 1837, when slavery was abolished. Poor illiterate Indians did the jobs, and kept down the wages, that enabled the British imperial economy to remain profitable and productive, from the West Indies to Mauritius in the Indian Ocean and Fiji in the Pacific. Thousands flocked from India's rural areas to East Africa, and many more to Natal and the Cape Colony.*

Their lives were miserable, although probably not as miserable as they would have been if they had remained in their diseased and hunger-ridden homes in India. Every other group in South Africa took ruthless advantage of them, including their own countrymen. Gujarati merchants lent them money at exorbitant interest rates, as historian Maureen Swan has shown. Indeed, many of the ships that brought them from India in unsafe and unsanitary conditions were actually owned by Gandhi's client Dada Abdullah.[39]

These indentured "coolies" (another English word borrowed from Hindi-Urdu roots) and their offspring were the backbone of South Africa's domestic economy. So were the well-to-do Indian merchants. Yet both groups, rich and poor, found themselves under growing social pressure. South Africa's whites, especially but not exclusively the Boers, deeply resented their dark-skinned presence. Natal's colonial legislature

---

* In the 1920s Gandhi would also take up the plight of Indians of East Africa, especially Kenya. He would thereby create another source of conflict and friction with Churchill, who firmly believed in the right of British colonies to run their affairs as their white residents saw fit.

threatened several times to cut off immigration, and legislators generally looked for ways to shrink their influence and visibility. No one was ready to expel the Indian immigrants, as the Orange Free State had in 1891; not with the Colonial Office watching, or the British government in India, which steadfastly stood up for the rights of its subjects living abroad. But every Indian living in Durban felt the heat, including Gandhi.

Issues of race and racism permeated every part of the British Empire at that time, but they were far more blatant and intense in South Africa than anything Gandhi had experienced in England or India. In London, Gandhi had found that his skin color and accent had rarity value and made him the object of respectful curiosity more than hostility. A fellow student from Madras even told *Indian Magazine* in April 1888 that his one regret about living in London was that his skin wasn't blacker.[40] When Gandhi had returned to Rajkot, he had the unpleasant experience of being treated rudely by a British civil servant with whom he had been friends in England, but put it down to the typical behavior of the white *sahib* under the Raj.

In Durban the lash of white supremacy was more naked and obvious. On Gandhi's very first day in court, the European judge refused to speak to him until he took off his turban—which, to a respectable Indian, was a deliberate insult.[41] Abdullah's partner explained that whites treated every Indian like an ignorant coolie because of his or her skin color, regardless of their actual status or income or education. Hence he and the other Muslim Gujarati merchants preferred to describe themselves as "Arabs," and the Parsis in town called themselves "Persians." It was the first important discovery Gandhi made about the color bar in South Africa: it made everyone deny who they really were, in order to fit into a scheme dreamed up and imposed by whites.

Just a few days after he arrived in Durban, Dada Abdullah asked Gandhi to go to the Transvaal's capital, Pretoria, where the case against his cousin was being tried. Gandhi took his seat in the first-class section of the train. A European entered the carriage at Maritzburg, took one look at Gandhi, and left. He came back with a railroad official who told Gandhi, "Come along, you must go to the van compartment." That was where blacks and Indian laborers were supposed to travel, as Gandhi well knew.

"But I have a first-class ticket," Gandhi protested.

"That doesn't matter," the official said, "You must leave this compartment, or else I shall have to call a police constable to push you out."[42]

Gandhi still refused to leave, and so a constable threw him and his luggage out onto the train platform. It was close to midnight and very cold. Gandhi's coat was in his luggage. He ended up spending the night there, becoming angrier by the minute at the unfair treatment.

Worse was to come. The next train dropped him in Charlestown, where the next stage of the journey was by stagecoach. The stage driver denied him a seat inside and ordered him to sit outside, at the coach driver's feet. Gandhi became furious. He said, "You would have me sit at your feet. I will not do so, but I am prepared to sit inside."

The conductor started punching Gandhi until the passengers inside protested: "Man, leave him alone. Don't beat him. He is not to blame. He is right." The conductor gave up, and finally Gandhi ended up taking the outside seat reserved for the black African servant. The coach got under way, but "my heart was beating fast within my breast," Gandhi remembered, "and I was wondering whether I should ever reach my destination alive."[43]

He did, but in Pretoria more humiliations lay ahead. He was denied a room at the main hotel, and a table in the dining room at another. With each incident whites expressed sympathy, even embarrassment. "I have no color prejudice," protested one, but if Gandhi were given the same table as a European, she said, "the other guests might be offended and go away." This was Gandhi's second discovery: whites, or at least some of them, seemed to be as embarrassed by the color bar as he and his fellow Indians were. Yet they refused to do anything about it. When he complained to Abdullah's trade representative, the man only laughed. "This country is not for men like you... Only *we* can live in a land like this, because, for making money, we do not mind pocketing insults." He advised Gandhi to do the same.[44]

But Gandhi could not. Later biographers would suggest that the train ride to Pretoria in 1893 formed a watershed in his life. His remarks in an interview with Dr. J. R. Mott and passages in his autobiography, written thirty years after the event, imply as much.[45] But nothing at the time indicated that it radically changed his worldview or turned him into a fearless opponent of racism or colonialism. Gandhi was certainly furious. His dignity had been deeply offended, as had his sense of what the British called "fair play." He fired off a long letter to the directors of the railway company, spoke to a gathering of Indian businessmen urging them to protest the treatment they were receiving from South African whites, and wrote an editorial for the *Natal Advertiser* that concluded: "Is this Christian-like, is this fair play, is this justice, is this civilization?"[46]

What really outraged Gandhi was he had been treated as if his education and professional status counted for nothing. He had risked physical injury rather than be forced to sit where, as he put it, the "Hottentot" sat. For Gandhi still believed in Queen Victoria's Proclamation, the Indian Magna Carta. Loyal Indians of "superior abilities" like himself deserved to be treated like any similar white person, not like ignorant coolies, let alone like African blacks. Whatever his views later, in 1893 Gandhi thought of himself as a Briton first and an Indian second. On the dividing line between European civilization and "barbarism," which is to say non-Western cultural standards, Gandhi still came down firmly on the side of civilization. Nothing about his spiritual awakening in London with Salt and Blavatsky had changed that.

Besides, he had no time for lengthy recriminations. His legal case was wrapping up; it was time to return to India. At the end of May 1894 his clients threw a farewell party in Durban. Someone thrust into his hands a newspaper announcing that the Legislative Assembly would soon vote on a bill to strip Indians of the vote in Natal. Gandhi confronted Dada Abdullah, who shrugged his shoulders and said, "What can we understand about these matters? We can only understand things that affect our trade."

"It is the first nail in our coffin," Gandhi warned Abdullah. "It strikes at the root of our self-respect."[47] At that moment, Gandhi tells us, he decided to stay in South Africa to help to organize Indians to fight the disenfranchisement bill and save them from oppression by whites. This is the account in Gandhi's autobiography, and most of his biographers have accepted it as true. The full story is somewhat different. Neither Abdullah nor the other Indian merchants were as naïve as Gandhi's account suggests. In fact, well before Gandhi appeared on the scene, Natal's Indian merchants and storeowners had been organizing and lobbying to protect not only their own rights but the rights of fellow Indian businessmen in the Boer Republics of Transvaal and Orange Free State. In 1891 and 1892 they had sent protests to Bombay and Calcutta as well as London. They even enlisted in their cause the former viceroy Lord Ripon, who was now secretary of state for India in the new Liberal government.[48]

Abdullah and the others did not need Gandhi to alert them to what the so-called Franchise Adjustment Bill might mean for them and their business interests. What they did need was someone who could give them legal help, since so much of the battle was couched in terms of interpreting existing laws both in Natal and in Great Britain, and someone willing to handle the busywork and administrative details in English. On both counts Gandhi was their man.

So in June 1894 Gandhi agreed to stay on in Durban and help with the political lobbying. He drew up a so-called "monster petition" to the Natal Assembly protesting the effort to deprive Indians of the vote. Based on his London studies, he cited various British scholarly authorities on the civilized character of Indians and their capacity for self-government. He did not hesitate to stoop to race history. He reminded the Natal premier that legal scholars like Sir Henry Maine and Orientalist linguists had established beyond doubt that Anglo-Saxons and Indians are "sprung from the same Aryan stock, or rather the Indo-European" peoples. They shared the superior propensity toward freedom and civilization; unlike black Africans, Indians were racially fit to exercise the franchise.*

"For it is justice we want and that only," Gandhi concluded the petition. The "flower of the British and Indian nations" did not deserve to be treated like "Asian dirt." Gandhi and his well-to-do merchant friends were entitled to be treated better than the poor Indian laborers in their midst, let alone the native blacks.[49]

This elitist view should come as no surprise. Pictures of Gandhi in those years show a smartly dressed and self-assured man, dressed in expensive business suits, with a gold watch chain and an elegant straw boater. His legal business would soon earn him more than £5,000 a year, and his house at Beach Grove Villa was filled with graceful furniture and an extensive library.[50] To be sure, Gandhi never set aside his New Age interests. He found time to finish a how-to "Guide to London" for Indians traveling abroad, advising them where to get vegetarian meals (he included the entire menu from the Central) and how to keep their expenses to a minimum. He experimented with a new vegetable and fruit "vital diet" and kept a meticulous diary on its health benefits. He took up an intense correspondence with one of his father's old Brahmin

---

* Ironically, this was precisely the same argument Hitler and others would mobilize for their "Aryan" nation; and allowed them to appropriate the Indian swastika as the emblem of the Third Reich.

friends on the meaning of Hinduism and on the *Gita,* while at the same time he peddled pamphlets from the Esoteric Christian Union.

But in every other respect Gandhi's dress, lifestyle, and attitudes were resolutely British imperial. When he sailed back to Bombay in the spring of 1896 to drum up support against the disenfranchisement bill and to gather his family, he still thought of himself as a child of the empire: "Hardly ever have I known anyone to cherish such loyalty as I did to the British constitution."[51]

Except perhaps for the well-born young man, five years his junior, who was to arrive in India only a few months later.

Chapter Five

AWAKENING II:
Churchill in India, 1896–1899

East of Suez Democratic reins are impossible.
India must be governed on old principles.
WINSTON CHURCHILL, 1897

GANDHI RETURNED TO INDIA ON JULY 4, 1896, to collect his family from Rajkot. He had not seen his wife Kasturbai in almost three years, nor his sons Manilal and Harilal. But his real focus was on drumming up support against the Natal Franchise Adjustment Bill among India's leading native politicians.

At this point Gandhi was not a major player in the South Africa protest movement, let alone its leader. But his fellow members of the Natal Indian Congress, which he had helped to found in 1894, had decided that the twenty-seven-year-old barrister was the right person to reach out to Indian public opinion, especially to the nine-year-old Indian National Congress, and mobilize it behind their cause. Their strategy was not radical but imperial: they intended to stir up one part of the British Empire in order to induce London to bring pressure on another part. Gandhi made that point clear when he composed his so-called Green Pamphlet that summer (so called because of the color of its cover). Give us our rights as Indians and as Britons, ran its theme. Do not let South African whites treat us like ignorant coolies, let alone like blacks.[1]

On September 26 Gandhi was in Bombay speaking to a public meeting organized by Congress stalwart and fellow barrister Pherozeshah Mehta. Six days later, not far from where Gandhi was planning his trip to Poona to meet other Congress heavyweights, a ship pulled into the harbor. It was the troopship *Britannia* carrying the Fourth Hussars cavalry regiment to their camp in Bangalore, including a twenty-one-year-old subaltern who had joined them the previous year after graduating from Sandhurst: Lieutenant Winston Churchill.

He was arriving in India just as he had predicted to his doctor five years before. He would stay for three years, longer than Gandhi had stayed in London. India would change his life almost as decisively as London had changed Gandhi's. Some historians claim that Churchill disliked India. Of this there is no evidence in either his writings or his letters. Biographer John Charmley is closer to the mark when he says India represented Churchill's lost youth.[2] However, Churchill's connection to India ran deeper. His years there were an intellectual, even spiritual, awakening for Churchill, as much as Gandhi's years in New Age London had been. It was in India that Winston Churchill first discovered who he was, what he could do, and who he wanted to be.

Here too he absorbed an ideal of the British Empire that he would carry with him the rest of his life: the idea of empire as a moral force, an institution of order and civilization, as well as national and racial supremacy. Churchill's experiences gave him "the keenest realization of the great work which England was doing in India," he wrote later, "and of her high mission to rule these primitive but agreeable races for their welfare and our own."[3] Astonishingly, it was a sentiment with which the Gandhi of 1896 would largely have agreed.

In a few short years, however, Gandhi's perspective on empire and on India would drastically change. Churchill's never would. His memories of India as a young officer remained with him until his death. They became his window on the non-Western world, and the scale by which he weighed Gandhi and all he represented. Ultimately, they even formed the scale in which Churchill would weigh his own life.

His very first view of India was from the deck of the *Britannia*. It "pulled up a curtain," he would write, on a world that "might well have been a different planet." Twenty-one days earlier the Fourth Hussars had left Southampton. Their commanding officer, Colonel Brabazon, had told them in his peculiar upper-class lisp that they were bound for "India, that famous apanage of the Bwitish Cwown." Brabazon, a distinguished soldier and friend to the Prince of Wales, had taken the young Sandhurst graduate into the regiment as a favor to Winston's mother. From the start Winston loved the life in the cavalry: the regiment's barracks comradeship and subaltern antics, the disciplined drill and maneuver on horseback, "the stir of the horses, the clank of their equipment, the thrill of motion, the tossing plumes, the sense of incorporation in a living machine, the suave dignity" of their blue and gold uniforms.[4]

But he also knew something was missing: serving in action. Colonel Brabazon had fought in Africa and Afghanistan in the 1870s and had the chestful of decorations to prove it. But then peace had descended on even the empire's remotest outposts. Randolph Churchill's war with Burma in 1885 barely rippled its tranquil surface. When his son joined the Fourth Hussars, "scarcely a captain, hardly ever a subaltern, could be found throughout Her Majesty's forces who had fought even the smallest kind of war."

Young Winston took more than a professional interest in the experience of battle. "From very early youth," he wrote later, "I had brooded about soldiers and war, and often I had imagined in dreams and daydreams the sensations attendant upon being under fire for the first time."[5] Battle was an ultimate test of manhood for Winston, one that his late father, for all his pride and swagger, had never undergone. In fact, Winston was so desperate for it that one summer he and a friend got leave to go to Cuba, where Spanish troops were fighting guerrilla insurgents. It gave Winston his first chance to observe troops in battle, and he even got shot at "without result," the experience he would later describe as one of life's most exhilarating. But it was still not the real thing. There was one place where he might get the chance. That was India.

So it was with a sense of excitement and expectation that Winston disembarked in Bombay harbor. But his arrival was less than propitious. As Lieutenant Churchill got out of the landing skiff and reached for a handhold on the seawall, he lost his footing and wrenched his shoulder. The injury haunted him for the rest of his life.[6] He refused to let it stop him from performing his regimental duties or anything else, but years later, when he was swimming or taking a book off the shelf or even making a sudden gesture in the House of Commons, it would suddenly go out of joint. The conquest of pain, like the conquest of everything else, became another test of his growing confidence in his own self-will. As he told his fellow officers, when they had playfully tried to hogpile him on shipboard and he triumphantly crawled out, "You can't keep me down like *that*!"[7]

The shoulder gave him a sleepless night when they made camp at Poona. But daylight brought "suave, ceremonious, turbaned applicants for the offices of butler, dressing boy, and head groom," and "after brief formalities and salaams [they] laid hold of one's worldly possessions and assumed absolute responsibility for one's whole domestic life." This was the white man's India, where "obsequious native servants" were "cheap and plentiful," as he told his brother Jack. He saw more of it when they arrived at Bangalore, two hundred miles due west of Madras and three thousand feet above sea level, where even in summer the days were warm with a "not unbearable" sun and evenings "fresh and cool." There he found "flowers, flowering shrubs and creepers" in profusion, and "brilliant butterflies dancing in the sunshine, and nautch-girls by the light of the moon."

Winston and two other subalterns set up in a pink and white stucco bungalow, with a spacious veranda and a large garden tended by two groundskeepers, three water-carriers, and a night watchman. "If you liked to be waited on and relieved of home worries," Churchill would write later, India of the 1890s "was perfection...Princes could live no better than we." After forty-eight hours in country, "I formed a highly favorable opinion of India."[8]

Every day began before dawn with a shave given by yet another servant, followed by parade at six a.m. for an hour and a half before breakfast in the mess, and then a bath. Then came the daily tour of the stables and paperwork in the orderly room until the growing tropical sun sent Winston and his fellow officers back to their bungalow. "Long before eleven o'clock," he remembered, "all white men were in shelter."

After luncheon everyone retired for a two-hour siesta—a habit Churchill would retain for the rest of his life. Dinner was at eight-thirty, "to the strains of the regimental band and the clinking of ice in well-filled glasses," followed by card games or sitting and smoking on the veranda in the moonlight. "Such was the 'long, long Indian day' as I knew it for three years," Churchill would write in his autobiography, "and not such a bad day either."[9]

Nor was it an inactive one, because the hours between four o'clock in the afternoon and dinner were devoted to the sport that almost became an obsession for Churchill: polo.

Polo in India was far more than just excellent extracurricular training for budding cavalry officers, or a favorite sport for Britain's upper classes. India had been one of the original homes of polo. It remained a passion among the Indian princes who had taught the game to the British. It became one of the principal bonds between the Raj and India's traditional ruling class. Churchill had played polo in England but had never seen anything like the enthusiastic crowds who turned out for every match to cheer the native team against their European opponents. "Polo in this country attracts the interest and attention of the whole community," Winston wrote to his mother in November. "The entire population turns out to watch and betting runs not infrequently into thousands of rupees."[10]

Despite his injured shoulder, Churchill became a proficient, even brilliant player. He chased the ball headlong with "complete absorption" past the yelling crowds, "the tents and canopied stand thronged with the British community and the Indian rank and fashion," to the sound of thundering horses and shouts of tumbling riders, with victory celebrated and defeat and injuries soothed in the regimental tent with bumpers of brandy and champagne. The game would fascinate him all his life. It had everything he loved: speed, strategy, aggressive competition, and emotional exhilaration combined with physical danger, as well as ancient rituals and aristocratic tradition. He would dub it "the emperor of games" and play his last match in Malta when he was fifty-two. The young Churchill was as inseparable from his polo mallet as the older Churchill from his whiskey and cigar.

A cousin of Aga Khan who met him in Poona said of all the hussar officers he met, "none had a keener, more discriminating eye, none was a better judge of a horse, than a young subaltern by the name of Winston Churchill." His drive and energy amazed everyone. "Mr. Churchill was a live one," the sergeant-major later remembered. "He was busier than half the others put together... Once when I went into his bungalow I could scarcely get in what with all the books and papers and foolscap all over the place."[11]

Polo at Bangalore represented one kind of education for Winston Churchill; his readings in the hours after luncheon were another. "I began to feel myself wanting in even the vaguest knowledge about many large spheres of thought," he said later. Casual references to history and literature during dinner sailed clear over his head. So "the desire for learning came upon me." Until now he had shown no interest in books. Those he read at school had seemed the dullest his teachers and schoolmasters could find.

Now, over the winter of 1896, Winston set off on a crash reading program. He started with one of his father's favorite books, Edward Gibbon's *Decline and Fall of the Roman Empire*. "All through the long glistening middle hours of the Indian day," he remembered later, "from when we quitted stables till the evening shadows proclaimed the hour of Polo, I devoured Gibbon," frantically scribbling comments in the margins.[12]

What Winston found was a powerful cautionary tale about the fate of empires, ancient or modern. He read how a great empire had been built on "ancient renown and disciplined valour" and had given the world stability, peace, and prosperity, but then was destroyed by barbarians from without and by superstition and fanaticism from within.

He learned how, for one hundred years, the Pax Romana had maintained "the only period of history in which the happiness of a great people was the sole object of government." But unfortunately "this long peace" also introduced "a slow and secret poison into the vitals of the empire," which sapped "a love of independence, a sense of national honor and physical danger...and the habit of command" necessary to maintain it. Eventually, Gibbon concluded, "the fire of genius was extinguished, and even the military spirit evaporated," leaving Rome vulnerable to the barbarian Germanic tribes and a fanatically intolerant Christian Church. Together they dissolved the empire, wiped away ancient civilization, and left the Dark Ages in its place.[13]

From Gibbon he moved on to that paragon of Whig liberalism and elegist of British rule in India, Thomas Babington Macaulay. Winston read Macaulay's *History of England,* which taught him that liberty and self-government like Britain's were an achievement, not a right, as well as Macaulay's brilliant essays on Clive and Hastings. These too had a personal resonance. In the life of Clive he could read how "the valour and genius of an obscure English youth suddenly turned the tide of fortune" at the siege of Arcot, and how Clive's family, especially his father, "seem to have been hardly able to comprehend how their naughty idle Bobby had become so great a man" before he was thirty.[14] "The old gentleman [was] heard to growl out that, after all, the booby had something in him"—words Churchill had yearned to hear from his own father but never did.

Winston could also learn how Clive at Plassey had "scattered an army of near sixty thousand men, and subdued an empire larger and more populous than Great Britain," thanks to Western weapons and discipline. Macaulay described for the young subaltern the steps by which Warren Hastings, for all his ruthlessness, managed to create "a rude and imperfect order" out of an India locked in chaos and anarchy, and set the stage for making "the young minds of Bengal familiar with Milton and

Adam Smith" and the other blessings of Western civilization. And finally Macaulay taught Churchill how the history of India proved that "neither tenfold odds, nor the martial ardor of the boldest Asiatic nations, could avail aught against English science and resolution" or "the unconquerable British courage which is never so sedate and stubborn as towards the close of a doubtful and murderous day."[15]

From Macaulay and history he turned to Adam Smith's *Wealth of Nations,* Henry Hallam's *Constitutional History,* William Lecky's *Rise and Influence of Rationalism,* and Schopenhauer, Plato, Darwin, and Pascal. ("I read three or four books at a time to avoid tedium," he told his astonished family, who had never seen him read even a single book.) Then he picked up a volume that had been recommended by his commanding officer: Winwood Reade's *The Martyrdom of Man.* Its impact, as he remembered later, was intense. Reade's theme reinforced the lessons from Macaulay: history as the story of the triumph of modern progress and science over primitive cruelty and superstition.

Born in 1838, Winwood Reade traveled widely in Africa and had been a correspondent of Charles Darwin as well as a keen proponent of evolution. Indeed, *The Martyrdom of Man* was an early manifesto of what would later be called Social Darwinism. It presented history as a single process of the rise and survival of the fittest, showing how, in Reade's words, "our own prosperity is founded on the agonies of the past."[16]

The book made an indelible impression on the young Churchill. (Another fan was the young H. G. Wells.) He was also struck by *Martyrdom of Man*'s devastating critique of Christianity and of religious faith as reflections of man's most backward tendencies. Reade's unabashed atheism left Winston, by his own admission, with "a predominantly secular view" of life and human nature that lasted until his death. More than half a century later he would querulously ask his doctor how any trained physician could possibly believe in an afterlife.[17]

Reade's bleak picture of the individual as helpless and alone in the universe, an "infant crying in the night," however, was balanced by his optimistic image of man's progress and civilization thanks to the power of science. Civilization would outlast barbarism, Reade explained, because its virtues were of a "higher," less brutishly material type. "We cannot say that a good man will always overcome a knave; but the evolutionist will not hesitate to affirm that the nation with the highest ideals would succeed."[18]

That last quotation comes not from Reade but from Churchill himself.

It is found in the novel he started writing while in Bangalore, entitled *Affairs of State*. (Later he renamed it after the novel's hero, *Savrola*.) "All of my philosophy is put into the mouth of the hero," Winston told his mother, including his new secularist view of man and nature, which was bleakly confirmed by his reading of Darwin's *Origin of Species* and Malthus's *Essay on Population*. Life is "the struggle between vitality and decay," Savrola says at one point, "between energy and indolence; a struggle that always ends in silence."[19]

Later, Churchill's view of life would become softer and more nuanced; the old man would be more forgiving of the world than his twentysomething predecessor. But the rejection of a religious framework remained fundamental to his philosophy of life, and it drew the crucial battle line between himself and Gandhi.

For Gandhi, God is everywhere and the starting point for all things. For Churchill, He is nowhere. In a universe without God, or at least without the immanent presence of divinity, Churchill found redemption in the unfolding of history itself, as the story of man's biological and cultural ascent. If, as Savrola says, "nature never considers the individual; she only looks at the average fitness of the species," then Churchill believed nature had invested the species's best hope in those nations that pushed progress forward, as opposed to those that fought to hold it back—even though it must all end in extinction and oblivion.

Reade's Social Darwinism would also underline Churchill's belief in England's civilizing mission and reinforced Gibbon's verdict that Rome's weakness allowed barbarism and superstition to defeat civilization. Four decades later Churchill would see the new barbarism in figures like Hitler and Stalin, who seemed to him to be, in historian John Lukacs's words, the "reincarnation of an ancient evil" but also something "terribly modern": the face of modern man's slide back into brutish violence and the worship of power.[20]

To Churchill, the figure who most embodied the second threat to civilization, that of superstition and fanaticism, would be Gandhi. By rejecting Western standards of science, law, and civilization, Gandhi rejected what Churchill saw as man's one hope for salvation, just as Gandhi's constant appeal to his religious faith seemed gross hypocrisy. Eventually Churchill would come to see Gandhi as the embodiment of a benighted and hieratic Hinduism, with its "shrines and burning ghats... priests and ascetics," a religion with "mysterious practices and multiform ritual...unchanged through the centuries, untouched by the

West."[21] The barefoot Gandhi, with his *dhoti* and shawl, seemed the modern version of the fanatical Egyptian monks whom Gibbon had described, coming out of the desert to "overspread and darken the Christian world" on the eve of Rome's collapse and destroy the pagan classical tradition. In this way the monks had rendered the Roman Empire demoralized and culturally helpless in facing the marauding German tribes. Gandhi and his supporters must have seemed determined to do the same to the British Empire.

No wonder that Churchill's favorite epithet for Gandhi would be "fakir" and "fanatic." Gandhi was more than just a threat to British rule in India. He became a threat to everything Churchill believed in, and in the end Churchill would fight him with everything he had.

After seven months of reading, on April 6, 1897, the twenty-two-year-old subaltern jotted down his new political credo, which summed up his experiences in Bangalore. Britain's future, he believed, rested on its detachment from world affairs. "Isolated if you like," he blithely wrote, adding, "A mighty navy must keep the seas. The army may be reduced to a training depot for India with one army corps for petty expeditions." Having thus solved the problem of imperial defense, he turned to the empire itself. He saw it dividing into two halves. On one side would be the white colonies like Canada and Australia, with whom Britain must form an imperial federation for joint security.

But "East of Suez Democratic reins are impossible," he wrote. "India must be governed on old principles," meaning the principles of his father and men like General Roberts. In capsule form, it was the credo he would hold for the rest of his life.[22] "Why be apologetic about Anglo-Saxon superiority," he would say during the Second World War. "We *are* superior." Fixed ideas, Prince Metternich once said, are like fixed guns: "They are dangerous for those who stand or move along its line of trajectory." This would be also true of Churchill's view of India. Over the next decades Churchill would deal with, even befriend, men and women of many different political persuasions. He would show remarkable flexibility on key issues of national policy and imperial strategy, including during two world wars.

But on India he would be prepared to wreck friendships and his own career. In the dark days of 1942 he would even consider resigning as prime minister. Almost every other policymaker on India—Sir Edwin Montagu, Stanley Baldwin, Leo Amery, Lord Irwin, Lord Wavell—all would feel the furious fire from Churchill when they dared to cross his line of sight on the subject. "India," wrote Leo Amery, who held the India secretaryship during the Second World War, when the conflict with Indian nationalism and Gandhi reached a climax, "or any form of self-government for coloured peoples, raises in him a wholly uncontrollable complex." Churchill's outbursts were sometimes so intemperate that Amery wondered in his diary if "on the subject of India, he is really quite sane." Certainly there seemed to be "no relation between his manner, physical and intellectual," on India and on the other issues affecting the war, even the gravest and most urgent.[23]

Indeed there was not. Because with India it was not only his own vision of the British Empire and civilization that he had to uphold. Over his shoulder loomed another shadowy figure, a man in a top hat with an exquisite mustache, bulging eyes, and a ferocious contempt for his son's shortcomings. On India, at least, Winston would never let down the father he had barely known, and whose approval he otherwise never hoped to hear.

A month after formulating his credo, Churchill left Bombay for London, "in sweltering heat, rough weather, and fearful seasickness."[24] British officers in India had three months' leave every year, so Churchill decided to spend his at home. He stopped first in Italy and was able to visit Rome for the first time, seeing it through Gibbon's eyes as the seat of vanished imperial power and magnificence. He then arrived in the new seat of imperial power, London, just as it was gearing up to celebrate Queen Victoria's Diamond Jubilee.

Eighteen hundred and ninety-seven was a watershed date for Great Britain. In her sixtieth year as queen, Victoria presided over an empire that was more populous and more extensive than any in world history; it was now more than a third larger than it had been when Winston was born. One in five people on the planet now owed some form of allegiance to her. The parades, pageants, and celebrations that year, including a massive display of the Royal Navy at Spithead on June 26, were emblems of a great historical accomplishment and global responsibility—as well as global risk. Other Western powers, including France, Belgium, Germany, and soon the United States, were busy carving out colonial empires of their own. Britain still occupied the imperial summit. But the winds there were turning colder, and the view was becoming less clear.

On July 26, to mark the Diamond Jubilee, a patriotic association called the Primrose League held a public outdoor meeting in Bath. Their speaker was the freckled and sunburned young officer just returned from India. It was Winston's very first political speech. Already his mind was turning to possibly standing for Parliament, as a Tory like his father. His remarks to the picnickers and onlookers in Bath sounded the first notes of what was to come.

He started with the obvious: "In this Jubilee year, our Empire has reached the height of its glory and power." Some were saying that "now we should begin to decline, as Babylon, Carthage, and Rome had declined." Winston asked his audience not to believe these "croakers," as he called them. It was time for true Britons to show the world that "the vigour and vitality of our race is unimpaired and that our determination is to uphold the Empire that we have inherited from our fathers as Englishmen." He assured them that he and his generation would continue to "carry out our mission of bearing peace, civilization, and good government to the uttermost ends of the earth."[25]

The crowd cheered and the band played. Winston grinned and waved back. Those reassuring words in the warm summer sunshine had conjured up a familiar sense of serene self-satisfaction. But not very far away another man recently back from India was watching the parades and pomp of the Jubilee celebration. The poet Rudyard Kipling had a very different take on what it all meant. Indeed, the words he wrote were almost a warning to the smiling and confident young officer:

> *If drunk with sight of power, we loose*
> *Wild tongues that have not Thee in awe—*
> *Such boastings as the Gentiles use,*
> *Or lesser breeds without the Law—*
> *Lord God of Hosts, be with us yet,*
> *Lest we forget—lest we forget!*
>
> *For heathen heart that puts her trust*
> *In reeking tube and iron shard,*
> *All valiant dust that builds on dust,*
> *And guarding, calls not Thee to guard,*
> *For frantic boast and foolish word—*
> *Thy mercy on Thy People, Lord!*

At the same time, India was suddenly back in Winston's thoughts, thanks to the newspapers. Pathan tribesmen on the frontier between India and Afghanistan were on the warpath, and three brigades from the Indian Army were being sent up into the Malakand Valley under veteran General Bindon Blood to confront them.

Here was a chance to get into some real fighting, Winston thought, the one military experience that still eluded him. Churchill had actually met General Blood the previous summer. As it happened, Blood had been one of Jennie Churchill's ardent suitors, and Winston had extracted from the general the promise that if he ever led troops against the Pathans again, he would bring Winston along with him.

At once Winston fired off a cable to Blood reminding him of his promise. He scrambled to catch the next boat back to India, leaving behind a new stack of books, his polo sticks, and his pet dog Peas.[26] It was August, the worst time of the year for traveling on the Red Sea, and the steamer's crowded and stifling dining saloon reeked of stale food. "But these physical discomforts were nothing beside my mental anxieties," Winston remembered later, certainly nothing beside his fear that the fighting might already be over and that he would arrive too late.[27]

When he reached Bombay, he found a brief reply from General Blood. "Very difficult; no vacancies," it read. "Come up as a correspondent, will try to fit you in. B.B." At Bangalore Churchill browbeat his commanding officer into extending his leave (his second in five months!), while back in England his mother arranged for any dispatches he wrote to be carried by the *Daily Telegraph* at £5 a column. Winston was ready to go to war. Soon he would be bundled on a sweltering train, "deeply-shuttered and blinded from the blistering sun," for the five-day journey to Peshawar, capital of the Northwest Frontier province and jumping-off point for the Khyber Pass and the Malakand Valley.[28]

It was the main theater of operations for the Indian Army and classic Kipling country, the setting for poems like "Gunga Din" and stories like "The Man Who Would Be King." British and Indian troops had skirmished with Afridi and Pathan tribesmen along this rugged range of mountains for decades. The Malakand Pass itself was a deep cleft in a jagged bowl of mountainous ridges, guarded by a typical British garrison of Sikhs, Punjabis, and Bengal Lancers under the command of white officers. Some of those officers had been playing polo in a nearby town when locals warned them of an imminent uprising led by a local

Muslim holy man or fakir, whom Churchill in his colorful dispatches to the *Daily Telegraph* dubbed the Mad Mullah.

The mullah was "a wild enthusiast," as Winston described him, "convinced of his divine mission," while "crafty politicians, hitherto powerless," seized the opportunity of the call for war on the unbeliever to strike a blow against the British.[29] Forty-eight hours later the telegraph wires had been cut and the Malakand garrison surrounded. Calcutta ordered General Blood to organize a relief column of 6,800 infantry and 700 cavalry to break them out.

It was, as Churchill noted, a typical frontier tiff. Inevitably, the British would march to the garrison's rescue. Inevitably, British and Indian soldiers would be killed and wounded, and many more Pathans. And inevitably, the Pathans would withdraw to fight another day. Certainly "the fate of empires does not hang on the result." Yet Winston's dispatches for the *Pioneer* newspaper and the *Daily Telegraph,* and the book he composed out of them called *The Story of the Malakand Field Force,* gave this brief but violent encounter a more powerful significance, especially in light of the Diamond Jubilee and his reading of Gibbon.[30]

Churchill turned the battle into a classic confrontation between superior civilization and primitive barbarism. *The Malakand Field Force* is an epic of vigorous British law and order prevailing over the Mad Mullah and his hordes of screaming Ghazis, although Churchill noted that when the native Guides cavalry overran one of the Pathans' strongholds, "no quarter was asked or given, and every tribesman caught was speared or cut down at once." The dead bodies were "thickly strewed about the fields, spotting with black and white patches, the bright green of the rice crop."[31]

Strategically the Malakand campaign was meaningless. But to young Winston, it was a conflict in which "the spectator may observe and accurately appreciate all grades of human courage." He saw the courage of native Indian soldiers, who up to this time had entered his consciousness only as servants or opponents at polo. The garrison's Sikhs and Punjabis fought and stood guard with cool steadiness for ninety-six hours without a break. Sepoy Prem Singh dodged sniper fire day after day while he sent semaphore signals from the garrison's tower—"an action as brave as any which my pages record," Churchill told his readers.*[32]

---

* Prem Singh's heroism even led Winston to wonder whether awards of the Victoria Cross should not be extended to native soldiers, adding: "In sport, in courage, and in the sight of heaven, all men meet on equal terms." However, that reform had to wait until 1911.

He saw an army doctor stoically hold between his thumb and forefinger the ruptured artery of a wounded man so he did not bleed to death. General Blood had to shoot down a knife-wielding fanatic who treacherously attacked him under a flag of truce: the general coolly dropped his would-be assassin with a single bullet. "It is easy to imagine how delighted everyone in the Field Force, down to the most untouchable sweeper, was at such an event," Churchill wrote.[33]

Last but not least on the scale of courage was Winston himself. In the second week of September, after securing the Malakand garrison, the brigade was sent to suppress rebels in the neighboring Mamund Valley. Churchill had not yet fired a shot, or had a shot fired at him in anger, despite the "rather grim" experience of dividing up the revolver, blanket, boots, and shirts of a dead fellow officer. But when General Jeffreys's column was ordered up the valley to burn out the disobedient Pathans' fields and villages, General Blood told Winston: "If you want to see a fight, you may ride back and join Jeffreys."

"All night long the bullets flew across the camp," Winston remembered years later, "but everyone now had good holes to lie in."[34] At dawn the brigade swung up the valley and fanned out. Winston had attached himself to a party of Sikhs led by a British officer. As they approached a seemingly deserted village, the entire mountainside sprang to life with volleys of rifle fire and sword-waving Pathans dodging from rock to rock.

The Sikhs scrambled for cover, even as "a shrill crying arose from many points." Winston grabbed a rifle and began picking off the blue and white figures as they descended and clustered behind boulders one hundred yards from the tiny party. "We had certainly found the adventure for which we had been looking," he laconically wrote later. The Sikh whose rifle Winston had borrowed got ready to leave, as did the rest of the group. As they turned to retreat, "there was a ragged volley from the rocks: shouts, exclamations, and a scream." Two Sikh soldiers had been killed, and three wounded. "The British officer was spinning around just behind me, his face a mass of blood, his right eye cut out."[35]

Together with another subaltern, the regimental adjutant, and a Sikh *havildar* or sergeant, Winston and his men managed to half-carry, half-drag the wounded down the slope. Pathan bullets continued to whiz around them. One struck the Sikh soldier at Winston's side. "He shouted with pain," Winston later recalled, "his turban fell off; and his long black hair streamed over his shoulders—a tragic golliwog."[36]

Then the adjutant was hit and went down, and a party of Pathans sprang forward to finish the job. The other bearers fled. Only Winston stood between the wounded man and the lead tribesman, who slashed away at the prone figure with his sword. "I forgot everything else at this moment," Churchill remembered, "except a desire to kill this man."

He fired once, twice, three times with his pistol: but with the confusion and pumping adrenaline, he could not be sure he had actually hit his target. Nor could he be sure, after joining the Sikhs at the bottom of the hill, that any of the thirty or forty dodging Pathans he fired at were dead or had even been hit. But when relief came in the form of the Ross-shire Buffs and Bengal cavalry, a single exhilarating thought crossed his mind. He had fought his fight and survived. Whatever else anyone could say about him, Winston Churchill had served in action—although technically only as a newspaper correspondent.[37]

A couple of weeks later Winston would again serve under fire. By then General Blood had appointed him as his orderly, writing to the Fourth Hussars' Brabazon that "if he gets the chance [he] will have the VC or DSO."[38] Winston wrote jubilantly to his mother, "I am still alive and well after another exciting week."

But he was not scoring points with his fellow officers. They felt that his behavior during the campaign had been unseemly; they whispered that he was a medal hunter, a self-advertiser, and an unscrupulous "thruster"—precisely the words antagonists would whisper about him for the rest of his career. The adjutant general in Simla turned down his appointment as Blood's orderly. His mother's urgent letters to her husband's old friend, General Roberts, failed to induce the a.g. to reverse his decision, while the publication of the self-advertising *Malakand Field Force* made him more enemies in the Indian Army than friends.

Yet in his own mind Winston was taking his leave of those antagonists. The losses among white officers in the Malakand and Mamund fighting gave him a temporary posting with the Thirty-first Punjab Infantry. Churchill did not speak a word of Hindi or Urdu. He saw no reason to learn, noting, as he told his brother Jack, that every Indian he met in Bangalore spoke perfect English.[39] However, command forced him to learn at last two words: *maro* (kill) and *chalo* (hurry up). Otherwise, "if you grinned, they grinned. So I grinned industriously." But since the Thirty-first Punjabis were largely out of the fighting, he was getting bored. He had got what he wanted out of India. He had had experience as a cavalry officer, the pleasure of being literally part of a "master race," and the thrill of combat, plus an unanticipated benefit: a self-taught education with the greatest books in the English language. He was already looking around for fresh opportunities.

During the Malakand campaign he had proclaimed to the *Daily Telegraph*'s readers: "Civilization is face to face with militant Mohammedanism." At the close of 1897, however, the storm center of that confrontation was not in India but in Africa, in the Sudan. In January 1885 the armies of the radical Islamic prophet the Mahdi had overrun Khartoum, killing the Egyptian pasha's governor, General Charles George Gordon, and massacring the inhabitants. Twelve years later London was organizing a punitive expedition of 25,000 British and Egyptian troops, to be led by General Herbert Kitchener. Winston decided he wanted to be part of it.

He knew and admired Kitchener as one of the British Army's most dedicated and bravest officers; he also knew Kitchener was, like General Blood, an admirer of his mother.[40] The problem was that Kitchener did not admire him. A stern professional, Kitchener considered the publication of *Malakand Field Force,* with its sometimes caustic comments about Winston's senior officers, bad form and self-serving. The last person he wanted around him was a bumptious, cocksure young busybody who was sure to pass everything he saw on to the newspapers.

So Kitchener remained deaf to Jennie Churchill's pleadings and refused point-blank to take Winston on his staff. However, "No young man should ever take no for an answer," Winston would say later,[41] for the book that had so offended Kitchener and the rest of the army now came to his rescue. The prime minister and his father's old colleague, Lord Salisbury, asked to see him. Salisbury had read *Malakand Field Force* and been deeply impressed by it. "I myself have been able to form a truer picture of the kind of fighting that has been going on in these frontier valleys," he told Winston, "from your writings than from any other documents which it has been my duty to read." In mid-July they met for half an hour at Number 10. When Winston left, Salisbury told him if he ever needed anything to let him know.[42]

It was a heaven-sent opportunity, and Winston seized it. As it happened, Kitchener had absolute authority over all appointments in the Egyptian army, and not even a prime minister's entreaty was going to move him. But Kitchener's British regiments were designated as part of a joint expeditionary force and were thus under the authority of the War Office.[43]

So less than a week later Winston received a telegram appointing him "supernumerary lieutenant" to the Twenty-first Lancers and ordering him to show up at regimental headquarters in Cairo. Six days later he was reporting for duty, with another newspaper contract, this time for the *Morning Post,* jammed in his tunic.

As a participant in the expedition against the Mahdi, Churchill took part in the last major confrontation between a British and a native army in Africa, at Omdurman on September 4, 1898. He also took part in the last great cavalry charge in British history, when Kitchener sent in the Twenty-first Lancers to complete the Dervishes' rout. Winston's chronic shoulder injury kept him from wielding either a lance or a sword, "like a knight in days of old." Instead, he had to make do with a very large and very unchivalric Mauser pistol. But "everyone expected that we were going to make a charge," he wrote years later. "In those days, before the Boer War, the British cavalry did little else."[44]

And so they did. Winston was the first to see what they were charging at: "a long row of blue-black objects, two or three yards apart" advancing on their flank, which turned out to be "men—enemy men—squatting on the ground." At that moment the regimental trumpeter sounded "Trot." In an instant "the whole long column of cavalry began to jingle and clatter across the front of those crouching figures."[45]

For Churchill, the charge was the climax of his military career and his ultimate reward for all those hours on the polo field. He left a long description in his dispatches for the *Morning Post,* which he also turned into a book. Thirty years later he wrote another account for his autobiography. But the most vivid version appears in a letter to one of his senior officers, Sir Ian Hamilton, right after the battle.

"The fire was too hot to allow of second lines," he told Hamilton. "The only order given was Right Wheel into Line, Gallop and Charge were understood." As they flew along, Churchill and the other Lancers assumed that the tribesmen wildly firing at them would break or scatter as the riders plunged into their line, where they were standing or kneeling four deep. But they did not. As the horses reared and plunged, the Dervishes "all fell knocked arse over tip and we passed through without any sort of shock."[46]

Everything was flying confusion and dissolved into one-on-one combat. "I heard none of their bullets," he told Hamilton, "which went Heaven knows where." Winston kept firing his pistol until he ran out of ammunition, "killing several—3 for certain—2 doubtful—one very doubtful." (Later he boasted to his mother that he had killed five for certain.) Then he saw he was alone and that the rest of the squadron had dropped back to regroup. He managed to join them "without a hair of my horse or a stitch of my clothing being touched. Very few," he added, "can say the same."[47]

It had all been over in less than two minutes: "It was I suppose the most dangerous 2 minutes I shall live to see." Out of 310 men, the Twenty-first Lancers had lost five officers killed or wounded, sixty-five troopers, and 120 horses—a quarter of their strength.[48] Winston observed their bodies on the field afterward and was horrified to see that they had been terribly butchered and mutilated. But all around them were the bodies of the enemy, cut down by the rest of the army's rifles and Maxim guns, "scattered like bits of newspaper." In fact, the combined firepower of more than 20,000 British rifles and machine guns had mowed down 11,000 charging Dervish warriors with a loss of only 360 men for the entire army. Winston had had his moment of chivalrous action, "as in days of old," and was lucky to be alive. But it was science and civilization that had decisively defeated the forces of barbarism and fanaticism. "My faith in our race and blood was much strengthened," by the victory, Winston told Hamilton.[49]

By Christmas he was back in Bangalore. Then in February 1899 came his last chance to lead the Fourth Hussars to the polo championship. Despite another fall that nearly permanently crippled his shoulder, he led his team to victory over the Fourth Dragoon Guards, 4 to 3, before a crowd of thousands. It was his final triumphant moment in India. Inside of a month he would be leaving it, and the army, for good.*

Certainly as a stage in his military career, India had been important. But as a stage in his personal development, it had been decisive. For the culture and people, he developed no great sense of respect or warmth, unlike some other British who had served in India. Just before he left, he noted in a letter that the plague had broken out in Bombay and southern India, killing nearly seventy thousand. His only observation was pure Winwood Reade: "Nature applies her own checks to population and a philosopher may watch unmoved the destruction of some superfluous millions, whose life must of necessity be destitute of pleasure."

---

* He also left behind an unpaid bill at the Bangalore Club, which until recently still hung in its frame on the club's wall. The sum is not small.

Nonetheless, British rule there seemed to reveal how a great nation could civilize a foreign people for its own good by introducing good government, law and order, and respect for property and "the fruits of work, enterprise, or thrift." It was nothing less than the mission of the British Empire and the Raj.

He had seen, as he wrote later, "a sedate Government tied up by laws, tangled about with parleys and many intimate relationships" and by "purely Anglo-Indian restraints varying from the grandest conceptions of liberal magnanimity down to the most minute obstructions and inconveniences of red tapes." Yet the system seemed to work. The government "is patient because among other things it knows that if the worst comes to the worst, it can shoot anybody down. Its problem is to avoid such hateful conclusions."

Indeed, in some ways the Raj had seemed to him a model for all governments. "Overwhelming force on the side of the rulers, innumerable objections to the use of any part of it."[50] Yet he also knew that deeper darker passions ran through the ruler as well as the ruled, "the deep-seated instincts of savagery, over which civilization has but cast a veil of doubtful thickness."[51] He had seen it in the slaughter of Pathan tribesmen by the Guides. He saw it again in Kitchener's treatment of the wounded Dervishes at Omdurman, where most were simply shot or bayoneted out of hand. And he would see it again in the actions of General Reginald Dyer in the enclosed square at Amritsar in 1919, which Churchill would describe in a phrase he remembered from his reading of Macaulay: "the most frightful of all spectacles, the strength of civilization without its mercy."[52]

Still, India would remain a precious memory for him. "India is a great trust for which we are responsible," he would say early in his parliamentary career. "The lives, liberties, the progress towards civilization—towards a better and happier life—of nearly 300 million souls are in our hands."[53] The Raj "could not endure—certainly not a month—unless it were founded on the belief which the people of India have acquired that our motives are lofty" and that "British justice is the foundation of British domination." The grave, turbaned servants; the moonlit verandas; the polo-playing maharajas; the grinning Punjabi and the fearless Sikh soldiers—this was the India he remembered and cherished. On January 28, 1944, he was at Chequers with his secretary Marian Holmes. He was "in a reminiscent mood," she recalled years later, and he spoke wistfully of his days fifty years earlier as a young subaltern, of his reading of Gibbon and Macaulay and playing polo, "the other great occupation of his life then."[54]

A year later he was on HMS *Orion* making his way to his fateful meeting with Roosevelt and Stalin at Yalta. His mood was more somber. "I have had for some time a feeling of despair about the British connection with India," he wrote to his wife Clementine, "and still more about what will happen if it is suddenly broken...I see such ugly storms looming up there."[55]

By then his dreams of India had become a nightmare, thanks to Mohandas Gandhi.

Chapter Six

MEN AT WAR
1899–1900

The battle in the end must be to the strong.
WINSTON CHURCHILL, 1899

On December 18, 1897, Gandhi arrived in Durban with his family on the SS *Courland*. The ship was the pride of Dada Abdullah's merchant fleet. Besides Gandhi it carried more than 250 expectant Indian immigrants. The crossing had been rough, with storms and a steady downpour.

After the *Courland* dropped anchor, but before any of the passengers disembarked, the Natal authorities decided to put the ship in quarantine. Their pretext was that there had been an outbreak of plague after the *Courland* left Bombay, but Gandhi knew the real reason: Natal's whites wanted to keep the immigrants out. They also knew Gandhi was on board, and they were determined that he never set foot in South Africa again.[1]

Gandhi was suddenly famous in his chosen home, but not in the way he might have preferred. His Green Pamphlet, published in 1896 during his stay in India, had recited his woes about the treatment that "respectable Indians" suffered in South Africa; how they were forced to use the same lavatories and same entrances to public buildings as African blacks, how they were spat upon and insulted in the street, and so on. The pamphlet had been a sensation in India; it thrilled Natal Indians but outraged Natal whites. Natal's attorney general, Harry Escombe, had been Gandhi's neighbor in exclusive Beach Grove and a Gandhi ally. Now a furious Escombe was the main force behind the quarantine order, which kept the *Courland* laid up in harbor for a total of twenty-three days, including over Christmas and New Year's.

When the quarantine finally ran out, SS *Courland* was permitted to dock. An angry crowd of whites had gathered on the quayside. "I was conscious of my responsibility," Gandhi wrote later. "The lives of the passengers were in danger, and by bringing my family with me I had put them likewise in jeopardy." Gandhi was able to smuggle his family and get the other passengers ashore safely. Kasturbai and their two boys found refuge in the home of one of Gandhi's wealthy Parsi clients, who locked his doors and waited for the worst.

Then Gandhi disembarked, moving swiftly but easily down the gangplank. He made no attempt to disguise his identity. In fact, he got as far as the edge of the harbor when "some youngsters recognized me and shouted, 'Gandhi, Gandhi.' " All at once a mob gathered and descended on him, throwing stones and bricks. "Someone snatched my turban," he wrote, "while others continued to batter and kick me."[2] A white woman, the wife of Durban's police superintendent, finally intervened and shielded the bleeding Gandhi with her parasol. Two policemen carried him to his client's house and to a frightened and sobbing Kasturbai. It was her welcome to South Africa.

That night a howling mob surrounded the house, threatening to burn it down and singing: "Hang old Gandhi on the sour apple tree!" The police superintendent finally convinced Gandhi to escape in disguise and take refuge in the police station. He would spend two days there—his first, but by no means his last, encounter with that institution. He had plenty of time to mull over his situation and his options. Only one thing seemed clear. He would not leave South Africa until he had secured justice both for himself and for his fellow Indians.

In his autobiography, written almost a quarter-century after the event, Gandhi would describe his near-lynching that day in January 1898 as "The Test," without specifying what kind. Certainly it was a test of his loyalty to an empire that, for all its chatter about equal treatment under law for all the queen's subjects, had left him to be treated in this way. Already Gandhi was reaching the reluctant conclusion that Britain's imperial system, and the European civilization that those like Winston Churchill claimed it epitomized, was "superior" only in its projection of coercive force, whether by lawbreakers like the rioters or by law keepers like the police. He had even made a bitter speech to this effect at the New Year's dinner on the *Courland* before they disembarked.[3] It was not what you did, or even who you knew, that seemed to count in

South Africa or anywhere else in the British Empire. It was whom you had the power to hurt.

The incident was a test, also, of the opposite Hindu principle that he had embraced in New Age London and that his recent contacts in India with a Jain thinker named Shrimrad Rajchandra Mehta had reinforced. Later Gandhi listed Raychandbai, as he liked to called him, as one of the three most important personal influences in his life, and the only Indian.* Although a worldly man and brother of one of the Indian National Congress's most powerful politicians, Raychandbhai evoked the principle of nonviolence or *ahimsa* (literally, "not doing harm to others") in all things.

Gandhi would describe Raychandbai as the closest figure to a *guru,* or guiding teacher, he ever encountered.[4] In a world that seemed to tolerate, accept, and on the battlefield even exalt the power to cause pain to others, rejecting violence became for Gandhi a declaration of spiritual independence, much like his rejection of eating meat. "By using violence to subjugate one another," he often said, "we are using violence against our own souls."[5]

In the midst of the battle at Durban wharf, Gandhi had resolutely refused to raise his hand against his attackers. His refusal to pursue the matter in the courts, even when Colonial Secretary Joseph Chamberlain personally urged him to do so, gained the respect even of Natal's whites. Gandhi had shown the power of Jesus' admonition to turn the other cheek and had won, at least in his own mind. It was a powerful lesson for the future.[6]

Finally Gandhi saw the incident as a test for a quality of character that mattered as much to him as it did to the young Churchill: physical courage. Afterward he played the entire sequence over and over in his mind: how he had faced the first murderous mob without flinching but had fled the second in disguise. "Who can say whether I did so because I saw that my life was in jeopardy," he would wonder years later, "or because I did not want to put my friend's life and property or the lives of my wife and children in danger?"

In the end, Gandhi concluded, "it is difficult to say for certain how a particular man would act in a particular set of circumstances."[7] But for the rest of his life acting bravely and boldly *but without violence* would

---

* The other two influences were Leo Tolstoy and John Ruskin.

form the baseline of his own self-respect. Nonviolence "is the supreme virtue of the brave," he declared. "Non-violence is the virtue of the manly." In the midst of a world war, he would even proclaim: "You cannot teach non-violence to a man who cannot kill."[8]

Like Churchill, indeed like other late Victorians, Gandhi was obsessed with standards of manliness and masculinity. Not surprisingly, physical courage was to them both a crucial measure of male character.[9] But in Gandhi's case it had another dimension: he desired to dispel the stereotyped image of Indians, especially Hindus, as unmanly and servile. Physical courage became for Gandhi a powerful measure of equality between Briton and non-Briton, white and nonwhite. Throughout his life Gandhi was determined to live up to that measure wherever he found it.

In the coming South African war, both men would find opportunities to face the supreme test of courage and character.* Indeed, war would bring them together in the danger zone, in the same place but in different ways.

In the meantime, however, Gandhi settled back into his role as lawyer and lobbyist for the organization he had helped to form three years earlier, the Natal Indian Congress. The situation for Indians in South Africa was rapidly deteriorating. The attack on him was only one of a number of anti-immigrant riots that fall and winter. Working-class whites, in particular, were furious that cheap Indian labor was threatening their jobs. "They breed like rabbits," the *Natal Witness* quoted one exasperated demonstrator. "The worst of it is we can't shoot them down."[10] The riots, and the attack on Gandhi in particular, gave the Natal assembly the excuse to put together a harshly restrictive immigration bill in April 1897, limiting new Asian immigrants only to people possessing at least £25 and a working knowledge of English.

This legislation was not just a racial affront, and a challenge to what Gandhi called "the just place of the better class" of Indians, as the Franchise Bill had been.[11] It was a severe economic blow to merchants like Dada Abdullah, who had benefited from mass Indian immigration in their steamship business and moneylending operations. Many white

---

* That respect for masculine virtue made them both admirers of the Boers, and what Gandhi himself called their "pluck, determination, and bravery" and Churchill the Boer farmer's willingness to "fight bravely in defense of the soil on which he lived"—although both men were also repelled by the Boers' rampant racism.

businessmen also relied on that cheap labor to work their sugar plantations and coal mines. The Congress sprang into action again, with petitions and angry newspaper articles, but again to no avail.

The British government in London formally assented to the Franchise Bill, the Immigrant Restriction Bill, and then a Dealers' Licensing Bill, which allowed municipal governments to deny or refuse to renew trading licenses to local Indian merchants (which, under white pressure, they were increasingly doing), without comment. The Crown's approval was a crushing defeat, made more humiliating by the fact that many Indians felt that Gandhi's outspoken efforts had only made whites angrier and guaranteed the bills' passage.[12]

If the situation for Indians was bad in Natal, it was even worse in the Boer Republic of the Transvaal. There no British Colonial Office or viceroy's council in Calcutta had standing to offer even a token defense of Indian rights. The Boers were free to do what they liked. In 1895 they had in effect ordered Indian merchants into separate ghettos or "bazaars" on the edge of cities like Pretoria and Johannesburg. The Indians protested and asked the Colonial Office to intervene, but even their old friend and protector Lord Ripon could do nothing. In August 1898 Gandhi managed to get a Transvaal court to hear an appeal of the bazaar restrictions, only to have the Boer judges resoundingly rule against him.

The blow was particularly bitter for Gandhi, coming at the worst possible time. Inside his beautiful house in Beach Grove, his family life was chaotic. He had had a spectacular quarrel with Kasturbai over a chamber pot. Gandhi had begun simplifying and downsizing his household, part of a growing self-denying puritanism in his personal and professional habits. At age thirty he suddenly decided that he could do many of the menial tasks he usually left to the servants or Kasturbai, like cooking, washing, and even (with hilarious results) cutting his own hair.

Another task was emptying the house's chamber pots, a constant chore in a large house with a wife and three children, including his nephew, twelve servants and staff, and only one indoor toilet. One day, without thinking, he had ordered Kasturbai to carry out his law clerk's chamber pot.

Kasturbai's experiences in South Africa had not been happy ones, to say the least. She found the place totally alien and the people hostile, not to say violent. Gandhi's insistence on running Beach Grove Villa like a European's house meant that she had to give up the Hindu domestic rituals that were precious to her. In addition, Gandhi made her wear Western-style shoes, which pinched her feet, and a sari made in a strange Parsi design, because Gandhi told her the Parsis were "the most civilized" of the Indian immigrant communities.[13]

Now he was commanding her to handle a stranger's filth—an act of pollution fit only for an Indian of the lowest caste.

She exploded in rage. With tears coursing down her cheeks, she screamed at Gandhi: "Keep your house to yourself, and let me go!" Gandhi lost his temper as well; he began yelling and dragging her down to the gate to throw her out, until a sobbing Kasturbai finally persuaded him to let her go.

For Gandhi, it was an extraordinary episode, almost unique. Husband and wife were soon reconciled, but the incident would plague him for years.[14] Certainly some part of him realized it was an explosion of rage not just against Kasturbai's defiance but against his whole situation in Natal.

His efforts on behalf of his countrymen and clients had failed. He had become a lightning rod for criticism in the Indian community and newspapers. His sons were getting no education—Gandhi felt it would be unfair to use special influence to get them enrolled in a Natal school while other Indians lacked that privilege.*

In the summer and autumn of 1899 he was an isolated, unhappy, and increasingly frustrated man living at odds with his own principles. His religious beliefs, his native culture, and his New Age friends must have seemed very far away.

Events, however, were about to shake him out of his confining routine—and transform South Africa and the British Empire in the process.

The summer of 1898 was the last great period of British imperialism, the last glorious iridescence of confidence and unapologetic pride. The Diamond Jubilee of the year before had reminded Victoria's subjects everywhere that they were still part of the greatest empire on earth, extending over ten million square miles. Gandhi and the Natal Congress

---

* By his own admission, his efforts to educate his sons were "inadequate." Harilal and Manilal would deeply resent their father's neglect of their formal schooling. His later excuse would be that he had kept them free from the "shackles" of a formal European education. The truth was that he was too busy to make time for them.

had sent official congratulations to Buckingham Palace, "in token of our joy." They thanked Victoria for "the peace we enjoy in India...and the confidence of security and prosperity which enables us to venture abroad." Gandhi had even taught his children to sing "God Save the Queen" in English.[15]

In 1898 the victor of Omdurman, Herbert Kitchener, secured British hegemony over the Sudan by checkmating French imperial ambitions at Fashoda. In Egypt and Suez Governor-General Lord Cromer had reduced the country's debt, abolished forced labor and the use of the lash, and established a competent Egyptian Civil Service along Indian lines. In the Cape Colony Cecil Rhodes was dreaming of building a great Capetown-to-Cairo railway that would connect Africa north to south and draw the vast interior together under British rule. "We are the first race in the world," he explained, "and the more of the world we [rule], the better it is for the human race." No one, certainly no English speaker, was in the mood to disagree.[16]

Not even Mohandas Gandhi. That same year a new commissioner for Britain's Cape Colony arrived. Alfred Milner was a Cromer protégé and had much the same confident, even arrogant, spirit. Milner wanted to break the power of the Boer republics as a crucial step to confirming British power and making South Africa a civilized country—to his mind, the same thing. As commissioner, he put heavy pressure on the Boers across the border to respect the rights of the British subjects in their midst, including, ironically, Indians living in the Transvaal. For a brief moment Gandhi seemed to have found an ally, if not exactly a champion.[17]

Milner's real focus, however, was securing control of the gold fields of Transvaal, which now provided almost one-third of the world's gold supply. In order to back up his threats against the Boers, Milner threatened to bring in British troops. The Transvaal's president Paul Kruger warned him to desist. When Milner ignored Kruger's ultimatum in October, the situation exploded into war—exactly what Milner and the British government had wanted all along.

Britons assumed it would be an easy win. Many of Gandhi's counterculture friends in London opposed the war as unprovoked aggression against a free people (conveniently ignoring the Boers' own brutal oppression of the Transvaal's black majority). Gandhi, however, did not join them. He saw supporting the war against the Boers both as an obligation and as an opportunity.

In 1899 Gandhi still "vied with Englishmen" in his loyalty to Britain and in support of the axiom that "British rule was on the whole benefi-cial to the ruled," whether in India or Natal or anywhere else. He still believed that the South African color bar was "quite contrary to British traditions" and only temporary. Once the war was won, justice would prevail and Indians would reap the rewards of showing their commit-ment to Queen and Country.

That at least was the gist of Gandhi's proposal to his fellow members of the Natal Indian Congress. "If I demanded rights as a British citizen," he told them, it was also his duty "to participate in the defense of the British Empire."[18] The question was how, especially since the idea of war directly challenged his commitment to nonviolence.

The solution Gandhi arrived at was to organize an ambulance corps. In the past year he had begun volunteering in a Durban free hospital for the poor and indigent run by a white missionary doctor named Lancelot Booth. It had been Gandhi's first real contact with poor Indian laborers, men and women sick with fever or from malnutrition and work-related injuries. He had enjoyed the work; indeed, nursing and tending the sick had become, as he said later, one of the "two passions" of his life. The other was his British patriotism.[19]

Gandhi argued to his fellow Natal Indians that rescuing and tending to British wounded would be a crucial way "to show the Colonists they were worthy subjects of the Queen." Few of them knew anything about firearms: Natal Indians were forbidden to own them by law. But as army medics, they could impress the government with their courage and commitment and build political capital they could use later. So on October 19, 1899, the first group of Indian volunteers gathered to sign up as "ready to do duty for their Sovereign on the battlefield" against the Boers. Gandhi's name headed the list.[20]

Gandhi was not the only person to see war against the Boers as an op-portunity to get into the firing line.

Earlier that month, just as tensions with the Boers were building to a climax, Milner received a letter from Joseph Chamberlain at the Foreign Office in London. "I am sending a line to anticipate a probable visit from Winston Churchill," it read, "who is going as correspondent for the *Morning Post* ... He is a very clever young man with many of his father's qualifications. He had the reputation for being bumptious, but I have not myself found him so, and time will no doubt get rid of the defect if he has it." Chamberlain added, "He is a good writer and full of energy. He hopes to be in Parliament but want of means stands in the way."[21]

In fact, Winston at twenty-four had already tried for a seat in Oldham in Lancashire and lost. The best way to draw votes the next time around, he decided, was to get himself in the middle of another war, especially one that looked like as sure a thing as the one against the Boers. His only worry was that the British Army would wrap things up before he got there, and the fighting would be over. This time certainly he would not be disappointed.

On October 14, 1899, Winston set sail from Southampton on the ship that was carrying the army's new commander in chief for South African operations, General Redvers Buller. A large crowd gathered on the dock to sing "Rule Britannia" and "God Save the Queen."[22] Everything promised an exciting imperial adventure, and Winston had stocked his tropical kit with a plentiful supply of champagne as well as whiskey, for which he had developed an addiction in India.[23]

Another correspondent, J. B. Atkins, spotted him on deck, "slim, slightly reddish-haired, pale, lively, frequently plunging along the deck with neck out-thrust." Winston was battling both seasickness* and his feverish impatience to reach Capetown so that he could get started on his future. "I had not before encountered this sort of ambition," Atkins confessed, "unabashed frankly egotistical . . . It was as though a light was switched on inside him which suddenly shone out through his eyes."[24]

Everyone expected that a war pitting the world's greatest power against a band of outnumbered rednecks like the Boers would proceed swiftly to victory. But the very day Churchill reached Capetown, the British garrison at Ladysmith in Natal had suffered a major reverse. The Boers may have been outnumbered, but they were well armed with modern Mauser rifles and even field artillery, and well led. Acting on the principle that the best defense is a strong offense, they had poured into Natal and swiftly enveloped key strongpoints, including Ladysmith, the railway junction between Durban and the Transvaal.

At Nicholson's Neck, north of Ladysmith, the British to their consternation lost two hundred killed and gave up twelve hundred prisoners to the Afrikaans-speaking cowherds. "We have greatly underestimated the military strength and spirit of the Boers," Winston wrote to his mother after hearing the news. He predicted that "a fierce and bloody

---

* Churchill was a poor sailor, unlike Gandhi, who was never seasick even in the roughest weather.

struggle is before us." In fact, the Boers had started out so well that when Winston presented his introductions to Commissioner Milner, the older man confessed his fears that the Boer insurgency might spread into the Cape Colony.[25]

Winston saw that the heaviest fighting was going to be in Natal and was desperate to get there. He caught a train from Capetown to Port Elizabeth, the last one before the Boers cut the line. From there he boarded a steamer for Durban where, at precisely the same moment, Gandhi was organizing a crash course on medical care for his ambulance corps recruits.[26]

They were going to be needed. In the ship's sick bay Winston had the shock of meeting a fellow officer from the Fourth Hussars, Reggie Barnes. Barnes had been shot through the leg during fierce fighting around Elandslaage. Barnes told him of the Boers' skill with horse and rifle and their bravery and determination. They had proved to be masters of the arid rugged terrain on which the battles of the Boer War were going to be fought.[27] This was not going to be a dashing adventure like Omdurman or the Malakand Valley. It was a grim war of white men killing white men with the latest weapons, firing from trenches and from behind barbed wire—the startling prelude to the slaughter to come in the Great War.

The train from Durban brought Winston as far as Estcourt, thirty miles south of Ladysmith. There he met another former army acquaintance, Captain Aylmer Haldane, and his old school chum Leo Amery, now a correspondent with the London *Times*. They were stuck there because the railway line had been cut. A battalion of Dublin Fusiliers and a handful of Natal volunteer infantry were all that stood between the Boers and Durban. Haldane's commander had ordered him to load up his Dubliners in an armored train and reconnoiter the track ahead. Without hesitation Winston volunteered to go with him.

"Nothing looks more formidable and impressive than an armored train," Winston wrote, "but nothing is in fact more vulnerable and helpless." The long line of armor-plated railway cars with the engine in the middle set out before dawn in a fierce downpour. The weather, however, cleared, and after chugging fourteen miles out of Estcourt they stopped to check the tracks in a narrow defile. Suddenly Churchill and Haldane realized that the hills around and behind them, overlooking the rail line, were swarming with Boers.

The enemy opened fire with rifles and artillery. A shell exploded over

Winston's head—"my first experience with shrapnel," he wrote later laconically, "and almost my last."[28] The train kicked into reverse but had to go back over a blind curve where the Boers had rolled a boulder onto the tracks. The rear armored truck was knocked on its side, and two more went off the rails, blocking any escape. Churchill, Haldane, and their men were trapped.

They had no time to think. Winston jumped down and scrambled back to the engine. The civilian driver had been grazed in the head by flying shrapnel and was not inclined to put himself in danger again, but Winston persuaded him to get back in the cab by repeating the old and transparently untrue army axiom, "No one gets wounded twice in the same day."[29] Then Winston tried to round up men to dislodge the derailed cars and clear the track, even as Boer bullets whizzed and shells exploded all around him.

The Dubliners set down their rifles to push over the disabled cars. "The enemy, relieved of our counter-fire," as Winston described it, "were now plainly visible in large numbers on the face of the hill, firing furiously."[30] At last the track was clear. Winston scrambled back to the train engine, which had filled up with wounded men, and ordered the driver to back up slowly. But the Boers, sensing the train was trying to get away, redoubled their fire, scattering soldiers in all directions. "Order and control vanished...The engine, increasing its pace," raced away and before Winston could get the driver to stop, he had left the Dubliners some three hundred yards behind.

Churchill ordered the driver to wait, while he set out on foot to find Haldane and his men, not knowing they had already surrendered. Suddenly two Boers appeared. Winston turned and ran back for the engine. The Boers' shots flew past his head with a peculiar sound, he remembered, like "two soft kisses sucking in the air." He dropped to the ground but could find no cover in the narrow railway cutting. After dodging a few more bullets, he scrambled up the six-foot bank to escape.

A solitary horseman came from nowhere, cutting him off. Winston reached for his trusty Mauser pistol, but it was gone, left in the engine cab while he was trying to clear the tracks. There was nothing left to do but throw up his hands: "thereupon my captor lowered his rifle and beckoned me across to him." Minutes later he joined Haldane and his fifty-six unwounded men as prisoners of war, wearily trudging away into captivity. Later they even met the Boer commando who had put the boulder on the tracks. He was "a dear old gentleman...[who] hoped we bore no malice. We replied by no means, and that we would do the same for him with pleasure some day."[31]

Winston would spend almost a month in a POW camp, a converted States Model School outside Pretoria, with a host of other British officers, including Haldane. The Boers were fascinated by their prominent young guest. A steady stream of generals, journalists, and dignitaries, including the American consul, came to see and interview him. Yet for Churchill, captivity was "one long boredom from dawn until slumber," and he and his fellow prisoners "thought of nothing else but freedom, and wracked our brains to discover a way to escape."[32]

Winston did try the legal way out, protesting that he was a journalist noncombatant, and Haldane even signed a statement that Winston had taken no part in the battle (which was hardly true). The Boer commander turned him down. Still, Churchill remained upbeat.[33] He was thrilled when newspaper reports of his capture also told of his courage in clearing the track and commandeering the engine. His reputation had been made. Not even spending his twenty-fifth birthday in prison could dampen his spirits, or lessen his impatience to get away.

Finally, on December 12, 1899, the Boer commander relented and signed an order for Churchill's release. Early the next morning a Boer orderly came to Churchill's bunk to rouse him, but there was no response from under the covers.

Finally the man reached down to shake him awake—only to realize the bed had been stuffed with pillows. The very night the release order had been signed, their prominent prisoner had slipped over the fence and escaped.[34]

The plan for escape had been Haldane's, not Churchill's. In fact, if Haldane and his coconspirator, a burly sergeant in the Imperial Light Horse named Brockie, had had their way, he wouldn't have been going along at all. Brockie considered Churchill a serious liability, with his bad shoulder and his face known everywhere from the newspapers. When Winston still insisted they count him in, Haldane persuaded Brockie that Churchill would do all right.

The trio had hoped to jump the fence at an unguarded corner behind the camp latrine on the night of December 11, but the unexpected appearance of a Boer sentry forced them to abandon the attempt. They tried again the next night, but the same thing happened. Brockie and Haldane then retired into the latrine; Winston waited outside. When they returned, the sentry had vanished. So had Winston. When the Boer had turned his back and moved away from the fence, Winston had seen his chance and jumped over, leaving his two comrades behind.

"Your trusted friend," Brockie kept repeating in disgust, "a nice kind of gentleman." Other officers in the camp were furious, too; any other escape plans were useless once Winston's absence was noticed and security tightened.[35] Still, without Brockie, who spoke Afrikaans, Winston would have had no hope of buying food or supplies without detection, and it was nearly three hundred miles to Delagoa Bay in Portuguese East Africa, and safety.

"But when hope had departed," Winston would later write, "fear had gone as well. I formed a plan."[36] Using the cover of night and the stars to guide him, he struck out for a railway line in order to smuggle himself onto a train that would carry him eastward to the port of Lourenço Marques. For almost a week he hid in empty railway cars and in a house belonging to an English employee of the Delagoa Bay Railroad.

Finally, on December 19, even as the Boers were circulating wanted posters looking for "an Englishman, 25 years old, about 5 feet 8 inches tall, average build, walks with a slight stoop...cannot pronounce the letter 's,'" Winston's English protector slipped him onto a train car full of wool bales that carried him across the Portuguese border. Later the next day he strolled into the British consulate at Lourenço Marques and ordered a much-needed bath.[37]

Churchill was an instant celebrity. The story of his daring escape (no one had yet heard Haldane's version) and of life on the lam was something out of a fictional thriller; combined with his heroism on the armored train, it revealed him as a man equipped with audacity, courage, and initiative—along with a strong dose of luck. Winston's heroic story was especially welcome when all the other news out of the war was so glum. On the fifteenth Sir Redvers Buller had suffered a humiliating defeat at Colenso, losing eleven hundred men and ten artillery pieces, making him the first British general to lose a gun in more than a century.[38] Winston Churchill gave the British public something to cheer about, and he was delighted to help lead the cheering.

On December 23, 1899, he arrived by steamer in Durban harbor, not far from where Gandhi had disembarked two years earlier, but to a very different reception. When he stepped forward from the captain's bridge, the crowd that jammed the quayside raised "a rousing cheer," the *Natal Mercury* reported, and everyone recognized "his round boyish face shielded by a large brimmed hat." Winston made an impromptu speech, saying that the Boers' effort to drive the British out of South Africa would fail. When Britain finally prevailed, he concluded, "you will see in this country the beginning of a new era…an era of peace, purity, liberty, equality, and good government in South Africa."[39]

Followed by loud cheers and cries of "God bless you, my boy!" he set off for the town hall and then to the railway station, where a triumphal procession escorted his rickshaw behind a huge Union Jack. The crowd was still cheering when his train at last rolled out of sight. There would be no stopping him now. A couple of months later, during the relief of Ladysmith, a British officer saw a young man in a South African Light Horse uniform talking with an infuriatingly patronizing air to the commanding general, Sir George White.

"Who on earth is that?" the officer said when the young man left. "That's Randolph Churchill's son Winston," White replied. "I don't like the fellow, but he'll be Prime Minister of England one day."[40]

Winston stayed another seven months in South Africa, where he witnessed some of the war's bloodiest fighting. In January a reorganized British Army under General Roberts tried to lift the siege of Ladysmith by breaking through a range of hills to the city's south, at Spion Kop. Churchill, now with the volunteer South African Light Horse but still the *Morning Post*'s star reporter, galloped out to watch Major-General Edward Woodgate's brigade push forward into the Boer trenches and over the summit.

The next morning the Boers counterattacked. "A fierce and furious shelling opened forthwith on the summit," Winston told his readers, causing many casualties and mortally wounding General Woodgate. "No words in these days of extravagant expression," he wrote extravagantly, "can do justice to the glorious endurance which the English regiments—for they were all English—displayed through the long dragging hours of shell fire," which dotted the hillside with chains of smoke and dust.[41] Down the hill came a steady stream of wounded, including General Woodgate on a *dooli* or stretcher. As Winston surveyed the scene with his telescope, he would never know that the slender khaki-clad figure holding the general's dooli was Mohandas Gandhi.

When Gandhi volunteered for ambulance service, the initial reaction had been incredulity, even derision. "You Indians know nothing of war," a Natal legislator told him. "You would have to be taken care of, instead of being a help to us."[42]

It was a standard assumption of British imperialism that Hindus, unlike the Muslim "martial races," were unfit for a manly life of danger and exertion. Part of the reason, it was believed, was their vegetarian diet— mere "slops," as Churchill might have said. In fact, Gandhi could recite a Gujarati ditty from his childhood that used vegetarianism to explain the entire history of the Raj:

> *Behold the mighty Englishman*
> *He rules the Indian small,*
> *Because being a meat-eater*
> *He stands five cubits tall.*

Gandhi was determined to prove the myth wrong. His ambulance drivers and medics were not just going to serve as hospital orderlies. He wanted them on the front line risking their lives alongside Britons, to show they had the same "pluck, determination, and bravery" as the Boers and other white men.[43] He got his volunteers medically certified as fit for service at the front and had Dr. Booth give them a quick training in battlefield medicine.

Gandhi had found eleven hundred Indian volunteers. They were a hodgepodge of ethnicity, religion, and caste. All but three hundred were indentured laborers, and the rest came from similarly humble backgrounds. Gandhi's merchant friends proved generous with their money but found excuses not to risk either their lives or those of their children. Gandhi did not care. The men under his command were born and bred to endure hardship; many of them were Christians, with whom Gandhi had enjoyed working at Booth's hospital.[44] Gandhi believed they would all do him, and the Indian nation, proud.

Their first task was to tend the casualties after the defeat at Colenso on December 15. One of the wounded whom Gandhi personally handled was the only son of General Frederick Roberts, Randolph Churchill's mentor on Indian matters—ironically, the man who, more than any other, had institutionalized the notion of Hindus as the "nonfighting races." Now General Roberts was on his way to assume overall command in South Africa. Lieutenant Roberts would die of his wounds just five days before his father arrived.

Gandhi had been impressed with young Roberts and the other English soldiers, who willingly shared their canteens with their dark-skinned companions. "There was, shall I say, a spirit of brotherhood irrespective of color or creed," he wrote later, as well as the spirit of the *Bhagavad Gita,* in which able men did their duty by cheerfully accepting danger.[45] So while Winston Churchill was enthusing to his *Morning Post* readers about how war brought out the best characteristics of the "strong races," another correspondent found Gandhi, after a day's hard work, crouching beside his ambulance and eating a regulation army biscuit, looking "stoical in his bearing, cheerful, and confident."[46]

The British Army had been at first reluctant to send the Indians into action, for fear of inflaming the Boers' racial feelings.* But the heavy fighting at Spion Kop forced the high command to drop its scruples, and Gandhi and his stretcher-bearers were ordered in.

"We had no hesitation" about going, Gandhi wrote proudly, as ambulances with their fluttering Red Cross flags gathered at the foot of the mountain. Meanwhile, as the dead and wounded were piling up in "a bloody, reeking shambles," Lieutenant Churchill watched from a neighboring hillside.

By four o'clock Churchill could not sit and passively watch any longer. He and a brother officer rode down and through "the village of ambulance wagons" and, leaving their horses behind, climbed up the spur.

"Streams of wounded met us and obstructed our path," he wrote, with men "staggering along alone, or supported by comrades, or crawling on hands and knees, or carried on stretchers." In fact, he and Gandhi must have passed literally within yards of each other, since one of the men Gandhi carried away was indeed the wounded Woodgate—something he would remember with pride more than forty years later.[47]

Gandhi's bearers had to carry the wounded for miles over ground that the rickety ambulances could not traverse, in order to get them to the field hospitals. In some cases they covered as much as twenty-five miles in a single day. Gandhi was delighted when someone said he could think of no European ambulance corpsmen who could have made the trip under the same broiling sun without food or water.[48] General Redvers Buller

---

* There were no Indian regiments in the campaign for the same reason. When General Roberts tried to put an Indian officer on his staff, a nervous colonial government vetoed the idea, in spite of the queen's personal intervention on the officer's behalf.

would mention the Indians' bravery at Spion Kop in his dispatches, and Gandhi and thirty-seven other volunteers were awarded the War Medal. It bore the queen's portrait on one side and a helmeted Britannia on the other, summoning to her aid the men of South Africa. There was even a poem published in praise of their exploits, ending with the refrain: "We are sons of Empire after all."

Some weeks later the Indian ambulance corps was disbanded. "You have shown your patriotism and brought honor to yourself and your country," Gandhi wrote to his fellow corps leaders in April.[49] He could now sit back and wait for the war to end and for the new era of liberty and equality that Churchill and others were promising for South Africa to begin. "Every one believed that the Indians' grievances were now sure to be redressed," Gandhi wrote later.[50]

For the end was finally in sight—or so it seemed. Ladysmith was relieved in March 1, 1900. Johannesburg fell on May 31. Days later the Boers abandoned Pretoria; and on June 5 Lord Roberts and his army entered the Transvaal capital. One of the first to arrive was Lieutenant Churchill, who made a beeline for the Model States School, where his fellow officers were still imprisoned. At half past eight in the morning "suddenly Winston Churchill came galloping over the hill," an astonished prisoner remembered, "and tore down the Boer flag, and hoisted ours to cheers."[51]

Winston would participate in one more firefight, at Diamond Hill, east of Pretoria, on June 11. But with the war almost over and the mission accomplished, he was impatient to leave South Africa. Two days earlier he had written to his mother: "I propose to come home... Politics, Pamela [Pamela Plowden, the daughter of an Indian civil servant whom he had met in Hyderabad and whom he hoped would become his fiancée], finances, and books all need my attention." Among the books was the one he was writing to describe his adventures, entitled *From London to Ladysmith via Pretoria,* which became an instant best seller.

Churchill had had a good war. Several of his friends had been killed or wounded. His own brother Jack had been shot beside him during the relief of Ladysmith.[52] But once again, just as at Omdurman, he had come through without a scratch. And although he would never win the Victoria Cross or marry Pamela Plowden, his celebrity and fame meant he could write his own political ticket.

His boat reached Southampton on July 20, 1900. On September 17

Britain's Tory government, eager to cash in on its success against the Boers, dissolved Parliament and called for a general election for October 1. Winston had less than two weeks to gear up for his campaign to take the seat for Oldham, which he had stood for but lost the year before.

This time things came out right. He came in second at the polls, but Oldham's peculiar electoral rules gave seats to both the first-place and the second-place finishers. Churchill was launched on his father's path at last. A few days later he received a letter from Simla, from India's new viceroy, Lord Curzon, congratulating him on his victory. "It is a great moment," Curzon wrote. "It is the starting point of a career of great possibilities, infinite excitement, and dangerous vicissitudes."[53]

Those words about Churchill's future were truer than even Curzon, one of Britain's most brilliant public men, could know. For despite every obstacle Churchill would reach the goal that eluded Curzon all his distinguished career: Number 10 Downing Street and leadership of the British Empire.

But in the end, India would defeat them both.

Chapter Seven

CONVERGING PATHS
1900–1906

All activity pursued with a pure heart is bound to bear fruit,
whether or not such fruit is visible to us.

M. K. GANDHI

ON OCTOBER 6, 1900, THE BRITISH CROWN annexed the Transvaal and
the Orange Free State. The war would drag on for another year and a
half, its toll brutal. The Boers' continuing guerrilla resistance would
force Britain to launch a ruthless counterinsurgency that cleared tens of
thousands of Boer homesteads and created disease-ridden "concentration camps" to hold the evacuees. Nearly 28,000 Boer prisoners would
die in those camps, including 26,000 women and children and at least
14,000 blacks. But all of South Africa—and its gold fields—was now
under formal British rule.

Through it all, no one had said a word about South Africa's Indians.

The war had launched Winston Churchill's career, but Gandhi's was
left high and dry. The triumphal lifting of discriminatory laws against
Indians that he had expected did not happen. The prospect of returning
to the same thankless and fruitless rounds of protest and petition was
more than Gandhi could stomach, especially given the sense of excitement and purpose that the war had brought him.

He decided it was time to move on. In October 1901 he headed back
to India, "convinced the Congress's cause in Natal was lost."[1]

He remained there a year, struggling to launch himself in Indian nationalist politics. India's leading politician, Gopal K. Gokhale, gave him
his patronage, but Gandhi got nowhere. Then in November 1902 he received a cable from his Natal friends begging him to return. Change was
coming to South Africa, they said, and they would need his help. Later,
in his autobiography, Gandhi suggested that the telegram arrived "just

when I seemed to be settling down as I had intended," as an ordinary Bombay barrister. Some biographers have taken him at his word, but the truth was otherwise. His letters at the time reveal his doubts about his ability to support himself in Bombay (it was a loan from the Natal Congress that had enabled him to move there) either as a lawyer or as a politician. Gandhi realized that if he was going to become a leader of men and inspiration to his fellow Indians, it was going to be in South Africa or nowhere.[2]

The situation there had indeed changed, seemingly for the better. The war and the Boer insurgency were finally over. Lord Milner, the Indians' friend from the Cape, was now in full charge, and another Gandhi sympathizer, Foreign Secretary Joseph Chamberlain, was conducting a personal tour of the region. That December, shortly after he returned to Durban, Gandhi headed an Indian delegation to meet Chamberlain. The Indians reminded Chamberlain of his earlier favorable responses to their petition against the Transvaal "bazaar" laws. Chamberlain's reply was friendly but cautious. "I shall do what I can," he told Gandhi and his fellow delegates, "but you must try your best to placate the Europeans, if you wish to live in their midst."[3]

Later Gandhi remembered how that reply had "cast a chill" over the other members of the delegation. But he was convinced that British rule would do more for Indians in the former Boer republic than it had in Natal. He decided to set up his new law office in Johannesburg, Transvaal's largest city and the very center of the great gold rush. The city was booming, having grown to more than 100,000 settlers with new suburbs springing up on all sides. The pace and pressure were so intense, Gandhi said, that people seemed to run everywhere rather than walk, and the roar of machinery from the mines was incessant from dawn to past dusk. But Gandhi's law practice also thrived, with four Indian clerks, and he soon had to hire a Scottish lady, Miss Dick, because she knew how to type.[4]

Compared to Durban, Johannesburg also had a thriving cultural scene, which enabled Gandhi to resume his New Age counterculture contacts. He made two new European friends, Hermann Kallenbach, a liberal-minded Polish Jew and successful architect, and Henry Solomon Polak. Polak was only twenty-two but a journalist and a devoted follower of Madame Blavatsky, as well as a vegetarian. As a result of meeting Polak, Gandhi would spend most of his evenings at the

Johannesburg Theosophical Society, even as he spent his days trying mobilize Transvaal Indians to assert their political rights.

At first, Gandhi tried to follow Chamberlain's advice. He set up a new lobbying group, the British Indian Association (the name made clear where the members' political loyalties lay), and took over a failing local newspaper, *Indian Opinion,* to serve as the BIA's sounding board.[5] He sought to win support for revoking the harshest anti-Indian laws by convincing whites that the Indian elite of Pretoria and Johannesburg would help to enforce the traditional color bar. Editorials in *Indian Opinion* pushed for a new racial order in which whites and Indians would in effect preside together over South Africa's blacks and coloreds.

"We believe in the purity of race as much as we think" whites do, Gandhi wrote. "If there is one thing which the Indian cherishes more than any other, it is the purity of the [racial] type."[6] Gandhi felt "strongly" that blacks and Indians should not be forced to live in the same Johannesburg suburbs. "I think it is very unfair to the Indian population," he said. In fact, many of Gandhi's proposals in *Indian Opinion* pushing separate facilities for separate races would make him an early architect of apartheid.

Biographers are understandably uncomfortable with or silent on this side of Gandhi. But as historian Maureen Swan has concluded, "Gandhi was a racial purist, and proud of it."[7] He had little or no respect for South Africa's blacks. His goal all along had been, not to overturn the color bar, but to get whites to accept Indians on their side of the line. British Indians, he wrote in June 1903, "admit the British race should be the dominant race in South Africa."[8]

Gandhi was offended not by the system of racial separation per se, but by the "insult" of being legally reduced to the level of the black majority. "In this respect he became a segregationist," Gandhi scholar James Hunt admits, "albeit a liberal one."[9] In fact, his awareness of the importance of race as defining identity would have a huge impact on his thinking about India, once his efforts in South Africa failed.

Because they did fail. Once again the dismally familiar pattern reasserted itself: expectant effort, initial hopes, then crushing disappointment. The truth was that the only imperial minority that Chamberlain and Milner were interested in placating was the Boers. After the long, hard-fought war, the British government was willing to accept as much of the old prewar legislation and racial chauvinism as they needed to win the Boers' acquiescence to the new order. In 1905, when Lord Milner left South Africa, his promise that "respectable British Indians or civilized Asiatics" would never again suffer discrimination was still unfulfilled. In fact, the Cape Colony was now considering its own anti–Indian immigration bill.[10]

Everything Gandhi had done over the past decade had proved useless. Instead of helping South Africa's Indian minority, his campaigns had almost certainly worsened their plight. The pneumonic plague broke out in Johannesburg's indentured laborers' quarters, which heightened the whites' desire to drive the Indians out of the city. Even as he volunteered to work with the sick and dying, and to set up a temporary camp where families could escape the disease and squalor, Gandhi was at his wit's end. He had enough sense to realize that his efforts, indeed his life, needed a radically different direction. It was his new friends Kallenbach and Polak who helped him find it.

Gandhi and Polak already shared a passion for the works of the Russian writer, vegetarian, pacifist, and New Age sage Leo Tolstoy. Tolstoy was a favorite among English-speaking counterculture intellectuals for his rejection of industrial civilization and traditional Christianity, as well as his advocacy of a "return to the land" and nonviolence. Gandhi had read Tolstoy's *The Kingdom of God Is Within You* in the day after his experience on the Maritzburg train platform. He had been "overwhelmed" by its message that God's greatest gift to man was the power of universal love to overcome all conflict and hatred. (Many years later Gandhi would say that it was reading Tolstoy that made him a believer in nonviolence.)[11]

Now, some ten years later, Polak gave him another New Age favorite, John Ruskin's *Unto This Last*. Its effect on him was electric.

First published in 1860, the book was a stinging rejection of the laissez-faire free trade ideology that British liberals had been preaching since Adam Smith. A nation's "true" wealth lay not in its capital or trade or industry, Ruskin proclaimed, but in the simple dignity of self-sacrificing labor.

A true political economy was not about working for profit, but working to benefit others: "Government and cooperation are in all things the Laws of Life; Anarchy and competition the Laws of Death." Mankind's future belonged to those who were willing to give up outward wealth for the sake of inner happiness, and to those who made "the first of possessions, self-possession."

Luxury is indeed possible in the future...luxury for all, and by the help of all; but luxury at present can only be enjoyed by the ignorant; the cruelest man living could not sit at his feast, unless he sat blind-folded...Raise the veil boldly; face the light...until the time come when Christ's gift of bread and bequest of peace shall be Unto this last as unto thee.

Gandhi read this passage on the overnight train from Johannesburg to Durban, just as dawn was coming up over the veldt and filtering through the soot-covered windows. It was the authentic voice of the New Age liberal conscience. Gandhi was so gripped by it that he was unable to sleep. Ruskin's words brought "an instantaneous and practical transformation in my life," he wrote later. Ruskin had led him to con-clude that the only life worth living was that of the simple craftsman or tiller of the soil and that "the good of the individual is contained in the good of all." Certainly, Gandhi realized, he would never be able to change others until he had changed himself. "I arose with the dawn, ready to reduce these principles to practice."[12]

For other readers, *Unto This Last* had been a clarion call to socialism. But Gandhi found in it a different message: a call to a lifetime of selfless labor and service.[13] Together with Leo Tolstoy's notion of the power and truth of universal love, it gave Gandhi a sudden vision of Indians forg-ing a community dedicated to working for others and serving God. "Let us forget all thoughts of 'I a Hindu, you a Muslim' or 'I a Gujarati, you a Madrasi,' " he would write. "Let us sink 'I' and 'mine' in a common Indian nationality" built on love, labor, and truth. By doing so, Indians would find not only God but themselves—and spiritually arm them-selves to defeat their enemies.[14]

In Russia Tolstoy had set up an ideal community dedicated to his reli-gious principles at his farm at Yasnaya Polyana. Now Gandhi would do the same in South Africa. He found what he was looking for near Durban: a patch of land near the railway station and in the heart of sug-arcane country, called Phoenix Farm. It had no lions or jackals, although plenty of snakes hung from the fruit trees during the spring. Phoenix Farm was on some of the most fertile soil in South Africa.[15] With Hermann Kallenbach's money, Gandhi bought Phoenix Farm and, al-though it had no house or even a shed, he began recruiting friends and family to work and live on the land. By the end of the year he had moved *Indian Opinion*'s offices there.

Phoenix Farm set the new pattern of Gandhi's life. From now on he would choose to live in a self-contained community modeled on Tolstoy's farm or a Buddhist ashram, a semimonastic utopia that would embody his values of spiritual purity and hard work. These counterculture communes would be open to visitors (some, like Kasturbai, would say they had too many) but also removed from the world (or, some would say, insulated from reality). Gandhi served as organizer, spiritual teacher, and the driving ego of all the farm's activities. Volunteers like his cousin Chaganlal, his son Harilal, his white secretary Sonja Schlesin (who was also a Theosophist), and for a time even Polak and Hermann Kallenbach came there to learn "the laws of health, and the exercise enjoined by them," as Ruskin had put it. The Phoenix farmers built their own houses, grew their own food, ground their own flour, joined in calisthenics every morning, and read the *Bhagavad Gita* in Edwin Arnold's translation every evening.

Phoenix Farm was a counterculture commune, Edwardian style, and here Gandhi continued to simplify his life, doing his own cooking and cleaning. He experimented with New Age diets of fruits, vegetables, and nuts; preached his opposition to evil Western habits like alcohol and tobacco. (One of his editorials from this period was entitled "On the Evils of Tea.") He carried out his strictures about hygiene and cleanliness, which he felt ordinary Indians neglected. On the farm he also published *Indian Opinion* in four languages,* with the printing press clanging away every evening, and he rode his bicycle to the office every morning, a round-trip of fourteen miles.

Yet Gandhi himself did not live at Phoenix Farm. The change that had begun that night on the train to Durban was neither as sudden nor as drastic as Gandhi's autobiography later implies. He still kept his large house in Johannesburg, and he still needed his substantial income as a lawyer to keep Phoenix Farm and the newspaper going. In 1905 he still wore his suit and tie, even during visits to the farm, which he ruled, as one biographer put it, "as benevolent despot" from a distance.[16]

Gandhi had not completely broken with his past life, but certainly in his own mind he was moving forward to something new, without being exactly sure what it was. A revolution was under way, both in Gandhi's thoughts and in his relationships with others. How it would finally turn

---

* English, Hindi, Gujarati, and Tamil.

out depended on others as much as on himself—and on a world that was itself on the verge of revolution.

In 1905 the old established order was being challenged everywhere and was cracking under the strain. The Boer War had been its prelude. Soon outdated imperial systems were under assault around the world. On January 22, 1905, demonstrators marched on the Russian czar's Winter Palace in St. Petersburg. Soldiers opened fire and killed five hundred, wounding many more. The riots soon spread to other parts of the Russian Empire, including Poland, Lithuania, and Georgia; in March Czar Nicholas II was forced to grant a parliamentary government for the first time in Russia's history.

In Crete protesters demanded independence from the Ottoman Empire. Riots broke out in the Belgian Congo. In June sailors on the Russian battleship *Potemkin* raised the flag of revolt. Japan's crushing victories over Russia at Mukden and Tsushima that spring had challenged conventional racial stereotypes and signaled the rise of the world's first modern nonwhite empire. In China Sun Yat-Sen founded the Chinese Revolutionary League to promote a modernizing nationalist revolt against the Dragon Throne. That November Irish nationalists organized Sinn Fein. The following year clerics and liberals in Persia forced the shah to yield power to an elected assembly, or *majlis*.

The spirit of revolution, and nationalist freedom, also spread to India, with momentous consequences for Gandhi's future. Only two years earlier India had witnessed the most massive display of the Raj's splendor and power in its history. The imperial *durbar* in Delhi, held to celebrate the coronation of King Edward VII, had drawn more than one million spectators. More than 34,000 British and Indian soldiers had paraded to the music of 2,400 bandsmen, while hundreds of maharajas, princes, and lesser chieftains arrived by elephant, camel, and horse to show their loyalty to the King Emperor.

The great spectacle owed its origin to the most brilliant and able viceroy the Raj had ever known, Baron George Curzon of Kedleston. Curzon was attractive and energetic, sharing the same imperial confidence as his fellow Balliol College alumnus, Alfred Milner. Curzon cared deeply about India and its people. He traveled extensively across the subcontinent, as far north as Srinigar and as far west as Afghanistan, and devoted large sums to restoring India's greatest monuments, including the Red Fort of Delhi and the Taj Mahal.[17] He had great contempt for the kind of crude racist stereotypes that had fueled the White Mutiny.

But Curzon also believed that he knew what Indians wanted better than Indians themselves did. That led him to make two fateful decisions. The first was to submit India's universities to government regulation, thereby striking at the very institutions that India's elite revered as their ticket to success.[18] The second was to divide Bengal into two new administrative provinces, partly because the old province and former kingdom was too large and heterogeneous to govern effectively, and partly to give the eastern half's eighteen million Muslims their own civil administration and system of justice.

Bengal was the home of poets and writers and India's Western-educated elite. It was also the epicenter of incipient Indian nationalism. Many jumped to the conclusion that Curzon's partition was a blow against the nationalist movement and another example of the Raj's old policy of divide and conquer, especially since Bengalis would now become a minority in their own province.* A furious backlash broke out in Bengal and quickly spread to other parts of India, particularly Bombay, the other hotbed of nationalist feeling.[19]

Curzon dismissed the protests against partition as an "hysterical outcry" by "a small disloyal faction." But protesters organized an effective boycott of imported British goods as a way to punish Curzon and the British. Crowds made spectacular bonfires of cotton cloth that came from Manchester and Liverpool. Even moderate Indian politicians called for a tax revolt and *swadeshi,* or economic independence from British imports. That soon led to calls for *political* independence, an Indian version of the Irish demand for Home Rule. Overnight Curzon inadvertently transformed the Indian National Congress from a sleepy club of loyalist graybeards into a vehicle for national protest. In August 1905 he left India, his policy and reputation in tatters.[20] The anger aroused by his partition of Bengal, even among non-Bengalis, would outlive him. The bond of trust between the Raj and the educated Hindu elite, which had survived even the White Mutiny, was finally broken. In fact, Indian nationalists had found a new ally, India's urban middle class, and the National Congress an active and growing constituency.

Gandhi observed the partition furor from afar in South Africa. The partition of Bengal had sown the discontent, and created the forms of mass protest, that he would mobilize later on. But for now his attention

---

* The 48 million Bengalis were outnumbered by the inhabitants of Bihar and Orissa, the other parts of the old province.

was diverted by the spread of unrest to this newest addition to the British Empire. The Boers were still protesting the British rule that was being imposed on them, when in February 1906 the Zulu tribes in northeastern Natal exploded in revolt.

"I bore no grudge against the Zulus, they had harmed no Indian," he wrote later. Since they were rebelling against a poll tax they believed to be unjust, Gandhi claimed later that he secretly sympathized with their cause.[21] But he still believed that Indians should support the British Empire against its enemies, including the Zulus, and that military service would be good for his fellow countrymen. "Those who can take care of themselves and lead regular lives at the front can live in health and happiness," he explained in *Indian Opinion*. "A man going to the battle front had to train himself to endure severe hardship" and develop the same toughness and self-sacrifice that Indians would need to build a new future.[22]

This time, in the campaign against the Zulus, Gandhi tried to convince authorities to actually arm his Indian volunteers, but he failed. Instead, he and they went in again as an ambulance unit, in a conflict far uglier than the Boer War. Gandhi watched as Zulus were mowed down by machine guns, flogged and hanged, or wounded and left for dead. White soldiers tried to stop Gandhi from treating them. Gandhi would remember later the constant crackle of gunfire as troops entered Zulu villages and shot anyone they found, including by mistake some black stretcher-bearers who were part of Gandhi's unit. "This was no war but a man-hunt," he said later. It was also a display of imperial power at its most brutal and savage.[23]

For the thirty-seven-year-old Gandhi, the Zulu rebellion marked another personal turning point—although once again he preferred to see things in moral, not political, terms. While he was marching across the bleak Natal landscape carrying a stretcher, or helping to bandage a wounded man, he realized "that I should have more and more occasions for service of the kind I was rendering," but "I should find myself unequal to the task if I were engaged in the pleasures of family life and in the propagation and rearing of children."[24]

Much ink has been spilled about Gandhi's vow of *brahmacharya,* or sexual abstinence, which he announced to Kasturbai when he returned from the Zulu campaign. Certainly sexuality was always for Gandhi a kind of inner demon that had to be tamed or conquered, which he compared to a snake in one's bed. "I vow to flee the serpent I know will bite me," he wrote later. "I do not simply make an effort to flee him."[25] To his mind, formal celibacy marked a further step toward spiritual enlightenment and purity, which is why the traditional Hindu vow, like all forms of renunciation, appealed to him.

Yet his *brahmacharya* was also linked to his very un-Indian concern about clean latrines and drains and his obsessions with diet, even his insistence that Indians be strong and able soldiers. To paraphrase John Ruskin, Gandhi's most important possession had become self-possession. It was an essential part of his belief in manliness. If he and other Indians were ever to control their own political destiny, Gandhi was convinced that they must start by controlling their minds and bodies—including the energies they normally spent on sex.

It was an idiosyncratic twist on the cliché Victorian attitude toward sexuality. Even Gandhi's statement that "*brahmacharya* means control of the senses in thought, word, and deed" contains clear echoes of the Boy Scout creed.[26] But such self-control, he believed, was "impossible to attain by mere human effort." Instead, the truly enlightened would preserve their sexual essences through a kind of spiritual grace, like the celibacy of a monk. Certainly until the end of Gandhi's life *brahmacharya* was his supreme act of personal triumph. The issue constantly intruded into his dealings with women, even into politics. Exactly forty years later, when Gandhi was in his late seventies, he could be overheard grimly muttering, "if I can do this," meaning keep his vow of *brahmacharya*, "I can still beat Jinnah."[27]

But in 1906 "the prospect of the vow brought a certain kind of exultation," he remembered. "Instead of closing the door to real freedom, [it] opened it." Certainly Kasturbai "had no objection." She and Gandhi were already sleeping in separate beds when the family moved to Phoenix Farm. For Gandhi himself, turning his back on sex and normal family life seemed to open "limitless vistas of service."[28] And at that moment the next political bombshell was already exploding.

In August 1906 the Colonial Office announced a new law as part of its racial settlement under the new Transvaal constitution. The law required every Indian resident over eight years of age to be fingerprinted and registered, so that he or she could offer proof of residence if and when new restrictions on Indian immigration were imposed. To the government, it seemed a convenient way to keep track of which Indians were legal residents in the Transvaal and which were not. Prominent Indian politicians in London, including member of Parliament and sometime Gandhi mentor Dadabhai Naoroji, signed off on the idea, saying "the subject was a small one and the real issue to Indians was India."[29]

But Gandhi thought it an outrage. He knew that the British judicial system limited fingerprinting to criminal suspects. He supposed (wrongly) that the law was the first step toward complete expulsion of Indians from the colony. "I have never known legislation of this nature being directed against free men in any part of the world," he would write. South Africa's Indians had to take drastic steps in response.[30]

Gandhi had found a new target for his anger about the treatment of Indians under British colonial rule—but also an unexpected new outlet for his belief in the power of self-sacrifice. All his life Gandhi had the power to make a sudden decision and hold to it with a passion and tenacity that astonished those who thought they knew him. These supreme acts of will could shock, inspire, and sometimes appall or intimidate others. Above all he tolerated no opposition. He had decided to go to London despite the orders of the caste council; and he had refused to sit at the feet of the coach driver at the Maritzburg railway station. His vow of *brahmacharya* was a third such decision.

The announcement of the registration law roused in him the same ferocious, almost reckless intensity.[31] It seemed the perfect opportunity for Indians to show the "pluck and determination," the courage, honor, and self-sacrifice, of soldiers on the battlefield. Gandhi found validation in the fact that he was not alone in his outrage. The Muslim-led Hamidia Islamic Society organized a mass meeting at Johannesburg's Empire Theater on September 11, 1906, to protest the so-called "Black Act." Hamidia's leaders were the meeting's two principal speakers.[32] By the time Gandhi rose to speak, the crowd in the theater had swelled to more than three thousand people. Hindus and Muslims, Gujaratis and Madrasis, wealthy merchants and lawyers, ordinary street hawkers and store clerks, all jammed together to protest this unwarranted attack on their rights and dignity.

Gandhi's speech was in effect a call to arms. He asked every Indian in the Transvaal to pledge that they would never allow their fingerprints to be taken and would never fill out a registration card, even if it meant losing their livelihood and going to prison. "There is only one course open to someone like me—to die, but not to submit to the law!" It was Gandhi's Patrick Henry "Give me liberty or give me death" speech, and it ended with a stirring peroration:

> We may have to go to jail, where we will be insulted...Hard labour may be imposed upon us. We may be flogged by rude warders... Suffering from starvation and similar hardships in jail, some of us may fall ill and die...[But] we shall go on until we succeed, wisdom lies in our understanding that we shall have to suffer things like all that and worse. *Provided the entire community manfully stands the test,* the end will be near.

The British Indian Association's president Haji Habib then led the crowd in taking a vow to go to jail rather than submit to the new law. "I can never forget the scene, which is present before my mind's eye as I write," Gandhi would remember twenty years later.[33] Then everyone raised three thunderous cheers for King-Emperor Edward VII and sang "God Save the King."

Only hours after the crowd dispersed, the building accidentally caught on fire and burned to the ground. But phoenixlike, Gandhi's first campaign to use "passive resistance," as he would call it, to overturn an unjust law and to forge a new muscular Indian identity arose from the ashes of the Empire Theater.

Gandhi, Habib, and the others did agree to a final gesture. They would send Gandhi to London to petition the government in person. An election in Britain that January had brought a Liberal landslide and sweeping change in Parliament. Members like the Labour Party's Keir Hardie and Ramsay MacDonald, and the new Secretary of State for India, Sir John Morley, had a strong sympathetic interest in Indian affairs. In India many were hoping Morley might even reverse the hated Bengal partition.[34] Perhaps the Black Act would meet the same fate.

Here a new opportunity arose to test Gandhi's trust in the British sense of fair play and justice. As his ship RMS *Armadale Castle* slipped out of Capetown on October 3, the issue in his mind boiled down to this: "Is the British constitution going to be revised at Pretoria? Or will justice prevail?"[35]

Gandhi was about to find out. His baggage contained letters of introduction to prominent politicians and a list of planned meetings with the key decision-makers on South Africa. They included Secretary Morley, Prime Minister Henry Campbell-Bannerman, Colonial Secretary Lord Elgin, and the Liberals' bright new hope, Assistant Secretary for the Colonies Winston Churchill.

* * *

For Churchill, the six years that had passed since South Africa had been rocky ones. True, he had the seat in Parliament that he coveted—that tangible link to a dead and adored father. True, also, *From London to Ladysmith* and his public lectures on his experiences in the Boer War (including a speaking tour in the United States) had netted him a "modest fortune" of £10,000.[36] But his political apprenticeship had been full of frustrations and disappointments. None were as severe or as soul-testing as Gandhi's, but they were a prelude to the more difficult ones that would come later.

He had arrived home in 1900 in time for his mother's wedding to a man only nineteen days older than he was. (She was forty-six.)* It was the social scandal of the season; his brother Jack refused to appear at the wedding.[37] The marriage also meant that the energies that Jennie Churchill had hitherto devoted to her eldest son's advancement would be directed elsewhere. For the first time he was truly on his own.

Then his maiden speech in Parliament failed to impress. It had been a convoluted defense of the Tory government's conduct of the war, refuting Liberal critics like David Lloyd George who had accused the government of using "torture" and other barbarous methods to suppress the Boer insurgency. The *Daily Chronicle* had said that Winston seemed "undistinguished-looking" and "lacks force." Everyone was still weighing Winston's speeches in the scales of his father's dramatic performances and generally finding him wanting.[38]

Finally, he had his disagreements with his party's leaders, Arthur Balfour and Joseph Chamberlain. This too was a Churchill tradition. But whereas Randolph had picked fights with the leadership as a political tactic, for Winston the fights reflected his growing belief that the Tories no longer stood for what he believed. They exhibited a pessimism, a lack of confidence in Britain's future, that Winston found infuriating and that surfaced above all on the issue of free trade. That issue led to his final break with the Conservative Party in 1904. At the heart of the divorce, curiously enough, was the question of India.

Joseph Chamberlain—the same Chamberlain who had advised

---

* He was George Cornwallis-West, and they married at St. Paul's Church in Knightsbridge on June 2, 1900. He soon deserted Jennie, who would marry a third time (to another younger man) shortly before her death at age sixty-seven in 1921.

Gandhi to appease white sentiment in South Africa—had triggered the debate. A former manufacturer from Birmingham, he worried that the empire had become too big and expensive. In a speech to the Colonial Conference in 1902 Chamberlain claimed that Britain was becoming "like a weary Titan," who "staggers under the too vast orb of his fate."[39] He proposed solving the problem of imperial overstretch by merging Australia, Canada, South Africa, New Zealand, and the United Kingdom into a vast imperial federation. This quixotic idea went nowhere. Then he tried again, proposing turning the British Empire into a single common market, in which colonies and mother country would share goods and services while high tariff walls around the perimeter preserved jobs and industries.*

Chamberlain's term for his imperial common market was Imperial Preference. For a few years it was debated in newspapers, in learned books, and in Westminster, then vanished into political oblivion. Certainly the proposal flew in the face of the free market orthodoxy that both major political parties had accepted for more than a century. That was why free trade true believers like Winston Churchill reacted so strongly against it, while others, like socialists Sidney and Beatrice Webb, endorsed it (for a time Beatrice entertained marrying Chamberlain). It seems doubtful that Chamberlain ever really thought seriously about the possible economic consequences of his proposal, especially to his home-town of Manchester. To him, Imperial Preference was a political catch-phrase. To other Tories, however, it seemed a call to statism, one that Winston Churchill was furiously eager to rebut.

To a dedicated free trader, to a Whig out of the old school of Adam Smith and Macaulay, or to a Tory like Churchill's father, free market capitalism was an essential part of the British way of life and empire. Churchill was also prepared to argue that free markets were essential to human progress.

"The British Empire is held together by moral not by material forces," he told an audience in Manchester in February 1904. "The greatest triumphs of our race have been won not for Britain only, but for mankind." One such moral principle was constitutional government;

---

* His plan excluded India, just as the proposal for imperial federation had. But Chamberlain's idea was important for India's future nonetheless, because the need for imperial restructuring would spur the granting of Canada's Dominion status to other former colonies, including eventually India.

another was ending the slave trade. The idea of free markets "thrown open to the commerce of all nations freely, to buy and barter as they will," was a third. Free trade, he argued, had created a Britain that was "not inferior in riches, freedom, and contentment to any nation" and that bid fair to do the same for the rest of the world. Churchill's prime exhibit was, strikingly, India.

Like his father, Winston resolutely believed the economic dealings between Britain and India rested not on imperialist domination but the free exchange of raw goods (mostly Indian) for manufactured ones (mostly British). Others, especially Indians like Gandhi, might disagree. But Chamberlain's Imperial Preference left India out in the cold. "That [India's] markets should be free and her people prosperous and contented is absolutely vital to Lancashire trade," Churchill said. Certainly "India is a great trust for which we are responsible... The lives, liberties, the progress towards civilization—towards a better and happier life—of nearly 300 million souls are in our hands." But to impose imperial trade restrictions on India, as Chamberlain was proposing, would destroy that trust and bond forever. "Destroy that," Winston warned, "and the whole stately and stupendous edifice" of the Raj would collapse.[40]

For Britons to turn their backs on India for short-term selfish gain, he said, would betray a maxim that was emblazoned throughout history "in letters of shining gold: 'The victory of Britain means the welfare of the world.' "[41]

Churchill's stirring defense of free trade echoed the optimism buttressed by the arrogance of Lord Curzon, another free trade Tory. "Tolerance and liberty are always more profitable than arbitrary restrictions," Winston confidently asserted. "Large views always triumph over small ideas." Humanity might disagree on where and how free-market capitalism might lead in the future, but "we are not going back—not one inch."[42]

Yet the Conservative Party seemed on the verge of doing just that. Prime Minister Balfour refused to repudiate Imperial Preference, whereupon Churchill intemperately attacked him, outraging the Tory rank and file. Once the mild-mannered Balfour had to rebuke Winston publicly in the House. Churchill's rebellious speeches, "full of scorn and sneer," against Balfour and Chamberlain won him the nickname

"Blenheim Rat." Soon voters in Oldham were clamoring for his recall, and the Hurlingham Polo Club blackballed him. His journalist friend J. B. Atkins noted that Churchill was the hardest-working man in the House of Commons; a Liberal member recalled that he was also the most hated.[43] The relentless attacks took their toll on the twenty-nine-year-old fledgling politician. Some feared they might lead to a Randolph-style breakdown. At one point he did go blank in the middle of a speech and had to sit down, his face buried in his hands.[44]

What sustained Winston in this first serious political trial was what had made him the champion of free trade in the first place: his unquenchable optimistic faith both in history and in himself. He really did believe that large views would triumph over small ideas; that modern progress really would dispel prejudice and barbarism; and that human will and purpose such as his own could overcome every challenge. "Science is better than sleight of hand," he told the Free Trade League, and "truth is stronger than falsehood."

For the rest of his life Churchill never accepted the lazy notion that politics is the art of the possible. Rather, politics became for Churchill a kind of theater, a medieval morality play in which humanity's great dilemmas were acted out and resolved. The House of Commons was an arena where truth, integrity, and freedom were constantly put to the test but would ultimately prevail. This exalted view of politics, even more than his grand historical vision or his vaunted eloquence, was what set him apart from other British statesmen—and what drew him closer to Gandhi than to any other English-speaking politician of his generation. The two came to differ on many, if not most, issues. But the man who would single-handedly defy Hitler in 1940 against all odds bears a striking resemblance to the man who organized the first satyagraha campaign in South Africa. The Winston Churchill who could later endorse Gandhi's notion that "all activity pursued with a pure heart is bound to bear fruit, whether or not such fruit is visible to us" made his first appearance in 1904.

On the last day of May that year, Churchill quietly crossed the aisle in the House of Commons and took his place on the Liberal Party benches. The act cut loose the moorings that bound him to his father's memory. On the Liberal benches he found men with whom he had more in common, like Herbert Asquith, David Lloyd George (their row over the Boer War having been set aside), and John Morley, the Indian policy expert who gave him a book that opened Churchill's eyes on social reform.* Intellectually they seemed head and shoulders above the Tories, whom Churchill accused of a "yearning for mediocrity." He quit his seat in Oldham and stood for another in northeast Manchester, the original home of laissez-faire economics and the free trade tradition, which he won. Now everything depended on how well the opposition Liberals could exploit their opportunities, and how long the Tories could keep themselves in office.

They could not do so for long. By the end of 1905 Joseph Chamberlain's crusade for Imperial Preference had fizzled with the British public but managed to split the Tory party. Balfour's government was finished. So the prime minister tried a desperate poison pill defense: Balfour resigned and called a general election in January 1906, hoping against hope that the opposition would fall out among themselves and that he could return to lead a minority government.

What happened instead was one of the most decisive elections in British history. Liberals patched up their differences over Ireland (which had led to a split between mainstream pro-Irish Home Rule Liberals and Liberal Unionists), struck an alliance with the budding Labour Party, and exploited Tory despondency to achieve a victory so sweeping that even they could not believe their success. They gained control of nearly three-quarters of the seats in the House of Commons, with a government majority of 513.†45

The Liberal triumph was also Winston's. The new prime minister, Henry Campbell-Bannerman, first offered his young colleague a treasury undersecretaryship, but Winston turned it down. He had his eye on a different post, that of undersecretary for the colonies. The new head of the Colonial Office, Lord Elgin, was grandson of the man who had brought the Parthenon marbles to England; he had been viceroy of India when Churchill had been in the Fourth Hussars. Elgin had a sick wife at home in Scotland. He was expected to be frequently away from London, which meant that Winston would have more opportunity to make decisions and shape policy—and shine in the House of Commons.46

Within a few months, his characteristic drive and energy made it

---

* Seebohm Rowntree's *Poverty: A Study of Town Life,* published in 1901, used data on employment, wages, and food and alcohol consumption to argue that laissez-faire capitalism was failing and that new government measures were needed to end poverty. Rowntree had a huge impact on leading Liberals and was later dubbed "the Einstein of the Welfare State." A Quaker, Rowntree's views on temperance and pacifism were strikingly similar to Gandhi's.
† The figure included Labour and Irish MPs.

clear who was really running the Colonial Office. His influence was especially felt on the issue hanging over everyone's head, South Africa.

There Liberals of Churchill's generation faced a policy paradox. The problem lay in their own history of trying to meld social progressivism with classical liberalism. On one hand they wanted to promote racial and social justice in South Africa and protect nonwhites from white oppression. On the other they felt a laissez-faire respect for the right of self-determination (at least for whites) and a sense of moral obligation toward the Boers. Liberal radicals like Churchill's new friend Lloyd George had vigorously opposed the Boer War; their leader Campbell-Bannerman, now prime minister, had denounced its "methods of barbarism," including the use of severe methods of interrogation and concentration camps to defeat the Boer insurgency. The standard Liberal view of the conflict, promoted in books like J. A. Hobson's *Imperialism,* was that the war had been in effect about blood for gold and that Britain had committed an unwarranted attack on the rights of a free people (albeit a racist people). Churchill, who had actually fought in the war, as a Tory had defended those "methods of barbarism" in the House of Commons. His experience had taught him that the Boers had not been fighting for freedom but against a British system of color-blind justice they feared would "place the native on a level with the white man."[47] But he now carefully trimmed his earlier views to fit the course set by his new party. No one wanted to provoke the Boers again. And by making them British allies instead of enemies, Liberals hoped they would ease the burdens of empire in South Africa and solve the problem that Joseph Chamberlain had foreseen, that of imperial overstretch.

So beginning in 1906 steps were taken to return a degree of self-rule to the former Boer republics and to give more of it to the British colonies of Natal and the Cape.* This process gave Churchill some twinges of conscience. Natal's brutal and savage repression of the Zulu rebellion in 1906, which had so horrified Gandhi, horrified Churchill as well. He yearned to step in "to bring this wretched colony—the Hooligans of the British Empire—to its senses."[48] But his support for the principle of self-determination, even if it meant tolerating the intolerable, held him back. When Natal asked for British troops to help to crush the Zulus, he felt he could not refuse. A friend asked if he could not do something about a poor black woman who had had to walk 160 miles to a Natal court to

---

* These measures would end, in 1910, in the merger of all four colonies into the Union of South Africa.

give evidence against her white tormentors. "I am sorry for the poor old lady," he replied, "but she is not of that 'Imperial importance' which would justify our interfering with a self-governing colony."

Instead, he said, her example would have to stand "as an instructive instance of the native treatment in South Africa"—and white misrule.[49] In November 1906 he had to deal with another example, this time against Transvaal's Indians.

Gandhi and his fellow BIA official Haji Ojer Ali arrived at Southampton on Saturday, October 20, 1906. Gandhi told reporters from the *Tribune* and the *Morning Leader* who met them that the central issue in the Transvaal was the Indians' "inability to enjoy the ordinary rights of a British subject or even a human being in a civilized country." His goal in London would be to convince the British Colonial Office to prevent the new registration law from proceeding. Indians accepted the principle of immigration restrictions, he said, and they recognized "the prejudice against color" that ruled across South Africa. But Indians were ready to go to jail, he said, rather than submit to being finger-printed and registered like common criminals.

"If the Colonies persist in this policy," Gandhi later told the London *Times,* "they will force the mother country to confront a serious issue." The mother country in this case was India; in the background were the riots and agitation there aroused by partition. England might not be able to hold India any longer, Gandhi suggested, if its people were "insulted and degraded *as if they belonged to a barbarous race*" (my italics).[50]

For the question in Gandhi's mind was still how to make sure that "respectable" middle-class Indians like himself were considered to be on the right side of the color line. He told the progressive Liberal editor W. T. Stead of his frustration when Transvaal whites instinctively lumped Indians in with blacks as "colored people." The truth was that Indians had "an ancient civilization behind them," Gandhi said, even more ancient than England's, and were perfectly capable of enjoying full rights as citizens.[51]

In short, Gandhi was not seeking an end to racism or class distinctions in South Africa. He wanted instead British justice, what Churchill had said was "the foundation stone of British rule" in India. During that raw November Gandhi was determined to find out how committed Churchill and the Colonial Office were to that exalted standard in South Africa.

Chapter Eight

BRIEF ENCOUNTER
1906–1909

We are in a wholly indefensible position.
WINSTON CHURCHILL, 1906

Blaming the wolf will not help the sheep much. The sheep
must learn not to fall into the clutches of the wolf.
MOHANDAS K. GANDHI, 1907

ON NOVEMBER 7 GANDHI AND H. O. ALI attended a banquet for one hundred members of Parliament in the Grand Committee Room at Westminster. The banquet received lavish coverage in the *Times* and ended with a resolution in support of the repeal of the Black Act. Certainly Gandhi's delegation had powerful friends behind it, white and nonwhite alike. Among them were the two Indian members of Parliament, Dadabhai Naoroji (who sat for the London suburb of Central Finsbury) and Sir Mancherjee Bhownagree. The former was Britain's first Indian Tory MP; the latter was a founding member of the Indian National Congress.

The delegation also included ex-Indian civil servants like Sir Henry Cotton and even Sir Lepel Griffin, who had been Randolph Churchill's mentor on Indian affairs and was a hard-liner opposing Indian self-rule. But the treatment of Indians in the Transvaal, he told everyone, resembled imperial Russia's vicious pogroms against the Jews. Such behavior was "unheard of under the British flag," he said. Indians were "the most orderly, honorable, industrious, temperate race in the world," Griffin added, and since they were descendants of the ancient Aryans, they were "people of our own stock and blood." Surely they deserved better.[1]

Griffin spoke those words when the delegation met Colonial

Secretary Lord Elgin at his Downing Street offices on Thursday, November 8. Naoroji had suggested that the delegation be headed by a white man, Lepel Griffin, rather than an Indian; in fact the delegation consisted of seven whites and five Indians, only one of whom was a Hindu, Gandhi himself.* They were the respectable "civilized" face of India: men in dark frock coats with gold watches, gloves, and canes, flanked by their equally respectable white patrons—protectors, almost. The average age of the delegation members (excluding Gandhi and Ali) was sixty-three. Dignity, wisdom, and self-restraint were engraved in every lined face and gray whisker.[2]

Their plea had earlier won the full support of Secretary of State for India John Morley, although he stressed he had no power over the Colonial Office. It got a much more cautious response from Lord Elgin, who had expressed doubts about meeting the delegation at all.[3] Gandhi nonetheless wrote to Henry Polak that the interview had been "exceedingly good" and that theirs was certainly the biggest and most impressive delegation ever assembled on any Indian cause.

Exactly a week later Gandhi sent a letter to the colonial under-secretary, Winston Churchill:

> Mr Ally and I who have come as a Deputation from the Transvaal on behalf of the British Indians, venture to request an appointment with you in order to enable us to place the British Indian position in the Transvaal before you. We shall be extremely obliged if you could spare a short time to enable us to wait on you.
>
> Your humble servant,
> M. K. Gandhi

The two met on November 28, only a few days before Gandhi had to return to South Africa.[4]

Churchill, two days shy of his thirty-second birthday, gazed across his desk at a slim, urbane man with a low intense voice, dark-skinned from the South African sun, wearing a well-pressed suit and a small mustache. A lawyer trained in the Inner Temple, Gandhi was a Boer War veteran like himself, their paths having crossed only minutes apart on the battlefield at Spion Kop.

---

* The rest were Parsis like Naoroji or Muslims like Ali.

Gandhi and his Muslim companion told Churchill that they were first of all loyal British subjects. They understood that the white man was in charge in the Transvaal. However, "we do feel that we are entitled to all the other ordinary rights as that a British subject should enjoy."

Churchill interrupted them. "If the British government refuses to give its assent to the registration ordinance, what then?" he asked. "Surely the new government in the Transvaal will pass an even more restrictive law."

"No law can be worse than the present law," Gandhi replied, adding, "the future can take care of itself." Churchill promised to do what he could, and the meeting ended on a friendly note.[5]

Churchill would have been impressed, as other observers were, by "Mr. Gandhi's marshaling of the facts" and his "skilled as well as a determined hand" in negotiations.[6] Churchill's warning about what the Transvaal legislature might do under the new constitution that Churchill himself had unveiled to Parliament in March did not trouble Gandhi. The day before a caucus of Liberal MPs had met with Prime Minister Henry Campbell-Bannerman, who said he "did not approve of the ordinance and would speak to Lord Elgin." Surely victory lay within their grasp.

As Gandhi prepared to leave on Friday, December 1, everyone agreed the delegation had been a great success. The *Rand Daily Mail* told readers that Gandhi had "made a deep impression on political and other circles here." He and Mr. Ali "came, saw...and conquered." After his meeting with Churchill, Gandhi told the *Times* that "this week will abide in our memory forever." He sent a letter to the newspaper the day of his departure, adding, "The lesson we have drawn is that we may rely upon the British sense of fair play and justice."[7]

On the way home their ship docked at Madeira, where Gandhi and Ali received cables from both London and Johannesburg. Winston Churchill had announced in the House of Commons that Lord Elgin would refuse his assent to the Black Act. Gandhi was ecstatic. "This [is] more than we hoped for," he exclaimed. "But God's ways are inscrutable. Well-directed efforts yield appropriate fruit."[8] For the rest of the voyage Gandhi and Ali planned their campaign to win the next round of battle over Indian grievances.

The friends who greeted them when they reached Johannesburg, however, were not smiling; their mood was somber and gloomy. Someone pointed out that nowhere in his speech had Churchill said that the Crown would block a registration law passed by a *new* Transvaal legislature under the new British-approved constitution.[9] And in a few months that was exactly what happened. On January 1, 1907, the Transvaal was granted self-government. White legislative candidates assured voters that the British government would now approve the fingerprinting and registering of all Asians. And on March 21, 1907, the Black Act became law in the Transvaal.[10]

"Our disappointment in South Africa was as deep as had been our joy in Madeira," Gandhi later remembered.[11] He and Ali and everyone else assumed they had been tricked by Churchill and the Colonial Office, who wanted to appease white opinion at the expense of the Indians. However, Churchill had told him the truth—it was just not the whole truth.

The fact was that even before he met Gandhi, Churchill and his colleagues had decided they would have to grant the Transvaal the power to force Indians to register, even though they would disallow the old law in order to keep up imperial appearances. When the permanent undersecretary wrote a memo on November 3 describing their predicament, Churchill wrote at the bottom: "I agree entirely. We are in a wholly indefensible position. [Gandhi's] deputation will certainly stir up difficulties in the House of Commons. What can we say, after what we said to Kruger [the Transvaal president]" about the Boers being able to enact their own laws, no matter how offensive.

Churchill concluded, "The new [Transvaal] Parliament may shoulder the burden" of offending British opinion by upholding the Black Act. "Why should we?" When someone asked what to do about the delegation and its supporters, Winston scribbled: "Dawdle."[12]

That was what he did when he met Gandhi, while slyly revealing his hand. The decision to disallow the law had been made almost three weeks before they met. Even the British governor-general of the Transvaal did not know the truth until November 27, and Churchill's speech in the Commons a week later was artfully crafted to evade the storm to come.

To Gandhi, it was a "crooked policy." He added, "I believe it could be given a still harsher name with perfect justice," namely fraud.[13] But to Churchill, it was a sensible compromise. A Liberal government that undercut the Boers' right to self-rule would, Churchill felt, undercut the whole fabric of British rule in South Africa.

Indeed, earlier that spring Churchill had shepherded the new constitutions for the Transvaal and the Orange Free State through Parliament.

Both documents were undeniably liberal in their principles and aspirations. They embodied the principle that the prime minister himself had enunciated: "A good government is no substitute for self-government" (except of course in India).[14] The new constitutions granted universal manhood suffrage for whites, which Britain itself still lacked. Even the question of female suffrage, still a New Ager's pipe dream in England, was left open. "We are prepared," Winston told the Commons, "to make this settlement in the name of the Liberal Party" in order to step forward "into the sunshine of a more gentle and a more generous age."[15] As for Gandhi's Indians, like the poor black Natal woman who had to walk 160 miles for justice, Churchill had to leave them in the shadows. Unlike South Africa's whites, they failed to meet the standard of "Imperial importance" that Churchill had raised in his own mind. It was that standard he adhered to ever after.

To save the British Empire, Churchill would strike deals with South African racists; with Labour radicals; with American isolationists; even with the devil himself, Joseph Stalin. And anyone who dared to stand in Churchill's way would be ruthlessly, even callously, dealt with. Gandhi was the first to learn that lesson in 1906. The world would learn it many times over in the next forty years.

Gandhi, of course, saw things very differently. To his mind Winston Churchill and his Colonial Office colleagues had revealed that "British fair play and justice" was a joke. Gandhi would no longer be interested in promises, only results. The old ways of doing things, with petitions and respectful delegations, had failed. If Indians were going to get what they needed and wanted, Gandhi decided, they must have a new kind of political movement built on new principles. Above all, it would be based on the new idea he had been pushing on his colleagues since September that of passive resistance or, as he preferred to call it, *satyagraha*.

Was satyagraha really new? In retrospect, the 1907 satyagraha campaign that Gandhi launched after his meeting with Churchill was an earth-shaking event. It would have a dramatic impact not only on India and South Africa but on the civil rights movement in the United States and on every other group that would later invoke the term "civil disobedience."[16] Yet Gandhi's autobiography, and even his retrospective account of those years, *Satyagraha in South Africa,* are unclear about how he came up with the idea, almost deliberately so.[17]

Gandhi himself and many Gandhi scholars emphasize satyagraha's roots in Hindu and Jainist traditions of nonviolence or *ahimsa*. Certainly many of the tactics Gandhi employed, like the peaceful collective strikes or *hartals*, had been used to protest the partition of Bengal. One scholar has even seen Gandhi's civil disobedience as having hometown roots, in the traditional Kathiawar practice of "sitting *dharna*," or fasting and sitting outside a ruler's palace in order to rouse his attention and compassion.[18]

Others have stressed the Western influence. A. L. Herman and Martin Green have charted the influence on Gandhi of Leo Tolstoy and Henry David Thoreau.[19] James Hunt has pointed to the 1902 campaign by non-Anglican Protestant churches against the Education Act, which included the mass refusal to pay taxes at the cost of going to prison and which made a strong impression on Gandhi. The campaign's organizers even used the term "passive resistance." Four days after the Empire Theater meeting, Henry Polak even recommended the Education Act resistance campaign to Gandhi as a "historic parallel" for organizing resistance to the Black Act.[20]

Gandhi had also been impressed by Emmeline Pankhurst's suffragette movement, which had been very active in London when he was visiting Churchill in 1906.* The cause appealed to the New Age conscience, and many suffragettes had willingly gone to jail. Their heroic refusal to back down before the awesome power of the law, even in the face of coercion, moved him to write an article for *Indian Opinion* on the movement. It concluded: "If even women display such courage, will the Transvaal Indians fail in their duty and be afraid of jail?"[21]

Gandhi studied the suffragette protests for more than a year before he read Henry David Thoreau's *Civil Disobedience*.[22] However, those protests, like Thoreau's experience of being put in jail in protest of a war he considered unjust, were only examples for Gandhi of *how* passive resistance might work, not the original inspiration. For in the end, whatever blend of Hindu, Nonconformist, and New Age radical ideas were in the air, Gandhi's vision of nonviolent mass action as a moral as well as political force was uniquely his own. To his mind, satyagraha embodied his fundamental belief that spiritual and moral forces, not material or self-interested ones, ruled the world. Churchill's dictum that "larger views must prevail over small ideas" was one that Gandhi whole-

---

* Churchill was viscerally opposed to votes for women and was a frequent target of suffragette protests in Manchester. "I am not going to be henpecked," he stiffly replied, "on a question of such grave importance."

heartedly endorsed. It was the nature of the visions that each man was determined to make prevail that drove them apart.

For Gandhi, nonviolent resistance was a means to a greater end than mere politics. It was the path to man's highest religious truth and embodied the highest spiritual principles. Those who chose that path, therefore, must be disciplined, Gandhi believed. They had to be pure in thought and deed and prepared for self-sacrifice, even death, as his Indian ambulance drivers had been. "The English honor only those who make such sacrifice," he warned his readers even before he left for London. In fighting the Black Act, Indians had a chance "for showing their mettle" just as they had at Spion Kop, but for a higher purpose. On October 6, 1906, the very day he left for London, he had described the decision to go to jail rather than submit to injustice as "a *sacred act,* and only by doing so, can the Indian community maintain its honor" (my italics). Honor, duty, cheerful self-sacrifice: this was the masculine, almost soldierly, ethos that Gandhi wanted his version of passive resistance to express.*

Gandhi always felt uncomfortable with the term *"passive* resistance" because it implied passivity or even weakness—in a word, unmanliness. "If we continue to believe ourselves and let others believe," he wrote later, "that we are weak and helpless and therefore offer passive resistance, our resistance would never make us strong."[23] He even ran a contest in *Indian Opinion* to coin a better term for his movement, offering a prize for the winner. His cousin Maganlal, who was living at Phoenix Farm, suggested *sadagraha,* which in Sanskrit meant "firmness in a good cause." Gandhi amended that to *satyagraha,* or "firmness for truth." "The word 'satya' (Truth)," he would write much later, "is derived from 'sat' which means being. And nothing is or exists in reality except Truth. That is why Sat or Truth is perhaps the most important name of God."[24]

As for *graha,* in Gandhi's mind the word signified much more than just "firmness" or "fortitude." *Satyagraha* or "truth force" (later "soul force") implied bringing manly strength and discipline to a nonviolent cause. By "fostering the idea of strength, we grow stronger and stronger

---

* If Gandhi had any real-life model in mind, it was probably the Salvation Army. Their military discipline, their use of music and banners, their belief in hygiene and the social virtues of soap, and their moral forthrightness (including abstaining from tobacco and drink) were just the kind of qualities he hoped to instill in his own satyagrahis. In 1925 he would remember the Army's courage in entering the sleaziest bars in underworld London to preach their message. And Gandhi's vision of satyagraha as moral uplift closely parallels the movement founded by another admirer of the Salvation Army and Boer War hero: Colonel Robert Baden-Powell's Boy Scouts.

every day."[25] Gandhi saw his campaign as an active spiritual force that would reshape the Indian community in every respect. It would shatter the old bonds of distrust, weakness, and division, fostered by years of colonial domination, and weld Indians together again in love and truth. And every day it would again project this muscular new moral presence onto the political and social landscape. The South African Indian would be someone to be reckoned with, even feared, by his white enemies.

Resistance as spiritual empowerment; spiritual empowerment as a spark for social transformation. That was the formula for success that Gandhi chose for his first satyagraha campaign in 1907 and that he would follow ever after. By joining that movement, he proclaimed, the Transvaal Indian "will be regarded as a hero and acclaimed by all India"—for India was never very far from his thoughts and actions, even in South Africa.[26]

By April Gandhi felt ready to formally launch his campaign against the registration law. Through mass meetings organized over the summer, he tried to summon up again the fiery spirit of the Empire Theater meeting and the sense of expectation and liberation. Posters went up around Johannesburg calling for a boycott of the permit office: "Loyalty to the King of Kings—Indians be Free!" (Gandhi was careful to include Christian imagery in his campaign, even calling Jesus "the first passive resister.") The British Indian Association sponsored marches, pickets, and speeches. One Muslim merchant declared he would rather hang than submit to the new law. Anyone who did submit and allowed himself to be fingerprinted, Gandhi told readers of *Indian Opinion* in July, "will have forsaken his God," and "his honor will have been lost." Again he held up the example of the English suffragettes: "When Women Are Manly, Will Men Be Effeminate?"[27]

The government extended the July 31 registration deadline to October 31, then to November 30. Only eleven Indians out of thirteen thousand submitted registration certificates. Neither the threat of losing their trading licenses, nor the threat of expulsion, could make the Indian merchants of Pretoria and Johannesburg back down.[28] For his campaign really to catch fire, Gandhi felt all he needed was someone willing to go to jail for refusing to register.

He turned to Ram Sandara Pandit, a Hindu priest, thirty years old and married with two children, and one of Gandhi's picket organizers. On November 8 the government arrested him for reentering the Transvaal with an expired registration certificate. Gandhi defended

Sandara in court, saying he had disobeyed the law in order to obey a higher law. The prisoner was sentenced to a month in prison, which led Gandhi to write ecstatically in *Indian Opinion,* "[Ram Sandara] Pandit has opened the gate of our freedom."[29]

Gandhi visited his protégé in prison, interviewed him, and praised him as a hero. He even organized a poetry contest on the theme of satyagraha and self-sacrifice. When Ram Sandara was released in December, Gandhi led a procession through the streets and placed a garland of flowers around the young man's neck. But then two weeks later the government threatened to rearrest Sandara unless he either registered or left the colony. The wretched man took his wife and children and fled to Natal.[30]

Gandhi was furious. The man celebrated as a hero was now denounced as a coward and a traitor. Gandhi warned his other followers: "O God, preserve us from the fate of Ram Sandara!" It was the start of a pattern that would become all too familiar to Gandhi, of followers who embraced his principles in a moment of enthusiasm, then proved unable to summon up the stern moral fiber to sustain them. In fact, over the years all his satyagraha campaigns would exhibit the same dynamic: a sudden explosion of almost hysterical support at the start would quickly dwindle away into inaction, even disillusion and retreat, when the goal failed to materialize. Once those in authority caught on, Gandhi's threat of civil disobedience turned out to be a less powerful weapon than it first appeared.

Meanwhile, with registrations at a standstill, the Transvaal government decided to take tough action. Days after Ram Sandara Pandit fled, it arrested the entire leadership of the British Indian Association and ordered Gandhi to leave in forty-eight hours or face the same fate. Gandhi responded by attending a public meeting in Johannesburg the day the ultimatum ran out. On January 10 he was sentenced to two months in jail. The first of Gandhi's many imprisonments was about to begin.

Prison was a grisly experience.[31] Two other prisoners in his cell, a Chinese and a black, spent the time playing with each other's genitals. More than once Gandhi had to stay awake all night to avoid homosexual rape. What he termed "unnatural vice" was endemic in prison, including among the warders, and the filth and squalor were repulsive. But he had with him a copy of Tolstoy's *The Kingdom of God Is Within You* and comforted himself by reciting some verses by his teacher Raychandbai:

"The sky rings with the name of the Invisible, I sit rapt in the temple, my heart filled with gladness."[32]

Meanwhile, his satyagraha movement was collapsing. More than two thousand of his followers had been arrested. And as imprisonment become a real prospect, not just a theoretical possibility, Pretoria and Johannesburg's merchant elite began to desert. Gandhi learned that Indians were "losing their courage... Those who went to jail lost their nerve in a few days."[33] Before his entire campaign evaporated, he and other leaders agreed to a secret meeting with the Transvaal's colonial secretary, General Jan Christiaan Smuts, to work out a face-saving compromise.

The agreement they reached on January 28 was a strange one for a man who had once argued that the most degrading part of the Black Act had been its use of fingerprinting. Now in exchange for the release of all prisoners, Gandhi promised that all Indians would agree to be fingerprinted—but *voluntarily,* rather than in obedience to the law. When Gandhi was released from jail on the twenty-eighth, he told his followers they had won. "A reasonable man would have no objection to being fingerprinted," he told them. The central issue had been the compulsion, not the fingerprinting itself. Gandhi argued that the government had yielded on that point, so that Indians could now register "with honor."

Some, especially his wealthy friends, breathed a sigh of relief. But others were outraged at what they saw as Gandhi's betrayal. He had given the government precisely what it wanted and called it victory. The angry passions Gandhi had summoned up against the Black Act were now turned on him. Some even said that General Smuts had bought his surrender for £15,000. Gandhi ignored the rumors. The general had said that if anyone still objected to being fingerprinted, they would not be forced to; Gandhi believed him. "A satyagrahi is never afraid of trusting his opponents," he declared. But it was Gandhi's own followers he had to be wary of.[34]

On February 10, 1908, Gandhi took a walk to the Johannesburg registration office in order to be the first to be voluntarily fingerprinted and registered as a resident Asian. A man stopped him, a tall Muslim Pathan named Mir Alam, a mattress maker who had done business with Gandhi and had been active in the satyagraha campaign.

"Where are you going?" he asked Gandhi in a cold tone.

"I am going to take out a registration certificate," Gandhi replied, and offered to take Alam with him. Instead, Alam struck him across the face. Gandhi went sprawling, slicing open his face on the sharp rocks on the ground. Alam started kicking him and was joined by three or four others, cursing and shouting. Finally Gandhi's friends managed to push them away, carried him to a nearby shop, and called for a doctor.

When Henry Polak arrived, Gandhi's face was a bloody pulp—the cuts across his forehead required several stitches. One eye was swelling shut, and his upper lip was split open and bleeding. He had several cracked ribs. Polak and the rest urged him to go to a hospital, but a kindly and sympathetic white minister, Reverend Joseph Doke, took him in as a houseguest instead.

Doke would come to play a key role in Gandhi's life. For the time being, however, Gandhi was too hurt to move. He had to complete his registration in bed, including the fingerprinting, although his arms and hands were swathed in bandages. He had finally done what he saw as his duty as a gentleman.[35]

But his reputation was in tatters, his movement nonexistent. Ironically, Gandhi's effort to unite the Transvaal Indians had worked. In March 1908 it would have been hard to find a man more universally despised than Mohandas Gandhi. On March 5 he was again assaulted in a mass meeting in Durban. The lights went out, a shot was heard, and an irate Pathan charged the platform with a cudgel. The police had to escort Gandhi to safety, "amid much booing and hissing." The next day, when he met with local Pathan leaders, they told Gandhi he had betrayed them. Indeed, many of his former Muslim friends in South Africa never forgave him.[36]

His plans, his efforts, everything had failed. All Gandhi could cling to was his most cherished faith, as he put it, "that all activity pursued with a pure heart is bound to bear fruit, whether or not such fruit is visible to us."[37]

In March 1908 that fruit was not visible to anyone else. Even Gandhi did not know that it was almost in his grasp.

As Mohandas Gandhi nursed his wounds in Johannesburg, Winston Churchill was wallowing in his bath in his bachelor pad in Bolton Street, wondering how to dispel his boredom. It was in his bath that his friend and secretary Edward Marsh found him on that late March afternoon in

1908. Marsh had to remind him they were expected at a dinner party in Portland Place hosted by the woman writer and activist Lady St. Helier. It was on the tip of Churchill's tongue to say no, but at Marsh's urging he finally got dressed and went to the dinner party where he met the woman who would be his wife for the next fifty-five years.[38]

He had actually met Clementine Hozier four years earlier, but the encounter had made little impression on him. Since his breakup with Pamela Plowden and his mother's marriage, women played almost no part in his thoughts. One who did cross his path was Violet Asquith, daughter of the Liberal politician, who first met him a luncheon party in 1906. He lamented to her how old he had become (he was thirty-one) and how lamentably short human life was. "We are all worms," he said finally, after a long diatribe against mortality. "But I do believe I am a glowworm."[39]

Churchill and Violet Asquith (later Violet Bonham Carter) became lifelong friends but never more than that. Clementine Hozier was a different matter. Twenty-three years old, with thick reddish-brown hair and large dark green eyes, she captivated Churchill. She was descended from a Scots family with roots reaching back to the twelfth century. Her parents were divorced. By the standards of the time, she was an ardent feminist and pro-suffragette. Her politics were distinctly to the left of Winston's. Nonetheless "he pursued Clemmie with the same single-mindedness that he did everything else."[40] Not even his defeat in a by-election in April (he soon found another safe Liberal seat, in Dundee in Scotland) could divert him from his courtship. They married in September at Blenheim, then left for an Italian honeymoon. "We have been happy here and Clemmie is very well," he wrote to his mother from Venice. "We have only loitered and loved—a good and serious occupation for which the histories furnish respectable precedents."[41]

For both Churchill and Gandhi, their wives would be the single most important persons in their lives, not excluding their children. Certainly Gandhi's marriage was colored by the male-centered hierarchical rules of his Hindu background, while Churchill's had the more intimate flavor of Late Victorian domesticity. (He and Clementine called each other "Kat" and "Pug.") However, both marriages were deep and abiding lifelong partnerships.

For Churchill, family life would serve as a refuge from the storms of politics and public life. For Gandhi, by contrast, family and marriage became living extensions of his politics. He would subject the long-suffering

Kasturbai to his constant pet experiments and changes of diet and lifestyle as his own thoughts were changing and evolving, sometimes in bizarre directions. Kasturbai learned to put up with his vow of *brahmacharya* as she would everything else, with patient stoicism and unconditional devotion. She willingly joined in his satyagraha campaigns, even going to jail. Over time she became Gandhi's emotional mainstay. When she died in 1944, a disciple noticed "a part of Bapu [Gandhi's nickname] departed" with her.[42]

Yet Kasturbai could never be for Gandhi what "Clemmie" became for Churchill, a true intellectual partner. She would never learn to read or write fluently, while Clementine had been educated at the Sorbonne. Clementine Churchill also helped to nudge Winston's politics in a more leftward direction, into the so-called Radical camp of the Liberal Party. Many of the Radicals were men he respected and befriended in Parliament. Churchill became fast friends with their leading spokesman and fellow free trader David Lloyd George, proclaiming him the greatest political genius he ever met. He also befriended Charles Masterman, who was something of a New Ager: he almost became a Christian Socialist before joining the Liberal Party and lived for a time in a settlement house in the London slums. Masterman had won a seat in the 1906 election at the same time as Winston, and swiftly became Winston's chief political mentor and intellectual confidant. He introduced him to Sidney and Beatrice Webb, who really were socialists. Their friends in turn included the New Age sexologist Havelock Ellis and even his father's old nemesis, Charles Bradlaugh.

And so, ironically, in 1908 Churchill found himself in contact with some of the same counterculture influences that had affected Gandhi so profoundly two decades earlier. His politics took a distinct, even startling, progressive turn. Free trader though he was, he also decided Clemmie and the Webbs were right: it was time to use the power of government to end unemployment and malnutrition and to shape Britain for the better.

In an article in the *Nation* on March 7, 1909, he wrote that there was "little glory in an Empire which can rule the waves and is unable to flush its sewers (a phrase Gandhi might have used)."[43] In Churchill's new Radical mood, government intervention did not contradict free market principles.* Government-legislated social reforms would correct

---

* In fact, free trade had been part of the British Radical tradition dating back to Richard Cobden and John Bright, as a way to batter down social barriers through material prosperity.

"unbridled" capitalism's unanticipated side effects. They would create "a net over the abyss," as he put it, for workers, the sick, and the aged.[44]

In 1909, Churchill moved from the Colonial Office to the Board of Trade, then to the Home Office the following year. Together with David Lloyd George he crafted two of the most socially progressive measures Parliament had ever passed, the Old Age Pensions Act and the National Insurance Act of 1911. In so doing, Churchill laid the foundation for the British welfare state—an astonishing achievement for a man later critics dismissed as a hopeless reactionary.

But there was another darker side to this new progressive Winston Churchill: his growing interest in eugenics and racial science. Eugenics was hardly a reactionary field in 1909. Virtually every progressive social reformer was keen on it, including Havelock Ellis and the Webbs. (In South Africa Gandhi himself endorsed the idea of "the purity of the [racial] type.") An interest in race science was the mark of the "advanced" intellectual. Churchill was hardly alone in worrying that "the unnatural and increasingly rapid growth of the feeble-minded and insane classes...constitutes a national and race danger which it is impossible to exaggerate," or insisting that strong government action was needed to prevent "race suicide."[45] However this worry now haunted his faith in the British Empire.

"If the British people will have a great Empire," Churchill told the National Liberal Club in January 1908, "they will need an imperial race to support the burden."[46] He worried that if the "civilized conditions" of modern society were left on autopilot, they would interrupt the ruthless operations of Darwinian nature that Winwood Reade taught him winnowed out the sick, weak, and mentally infirm from the imperial rank and file. Since history relied on the survival of the fittest, Churchill believed modern society must not be a refuge for the survival of the *un*fittest. Hence the need for government action to prevent the unfit from breeding, and the fear that without "something of the sort the race must decay," and Britain with it.[47] He still believed that under British guidance, humanity was destined to reach the "sunlit uplands," as he would say later. But now he sensed an edge of darkness on the horizon, a darkness that would grow as the twentieth century wore on.

Three years later he would tell Wilfred Blunt that sterilizing "people of weak intellects" should be mandatory. He even drafted a bill for that purpose as home secretary, involving involuntary sterilization of the retarded and insane with Roentgen rays; it never passed into law.*[48] Yet even as Churchill was thinking about how to prevent the unfit from having babies, he and Clementine had one themselves.

Their first child, Dinah, was born July 11, 1909. "The prettiest child ever seen," he told Lloyd George. "Like her mother, I suppose," Lloyd George said. "No, she is exactly like me," Churchill proudly replied.[49]

That was July 11. Just the day before, a passenger had arrived in London by train. It was Gandhi again. He was rather reluctant to be there, on a mission in which he had little faith. But he found to his surprise and chagrin that the British newspapers were all talking about India, and murder.

---

* One eugenics-inspired measure that did pass was his Trade Boards Law of 1909, which included a national minimum wage. This was no gift to the downtrodden. Radicals like the Webbs saw a minimum wage as necessary in order to push "the sick and the crippled," as Sidney Webb described them, "the incorrigibly idle, deficient in strength, speed, and skill," and other "parasites" out of the labor market—thus clearing the way for organized labor.

Chapter Nine

BREAK POINT
1909–1910

The British government in India constitutes a struggle between the Modern Civilization, which is the kingdom of Satan, and the Ancient Civilization which is the kingdom of God. The one is the God of War, the other the God of Love.
MOHANDAS K. GANDHI, *HIND SWARAJ* (1909)

THE IMPERIAL INSTITUTE WAS A VAST brick and stone edifice in London's South Kensington. It had been built in 1887 to commemorate Queen Victoria's Golden Jubilee and "as a monument to the emerging imperial sentiment."* Exhibits, lectures, and scientific conferences from every corner of the empire were hosted there, and every year the Indian National Association, founded by member of Parliament and Gandhi mentor Dadabhai Naoroji, held its annual reception for Indian students in London in the institute's spacious Jehangir Hall.

On the evening of July 1, 1909, guests might have noticed a solitary figure in a sky blue turban coming up the steps. Like the other Indian males in attendance, he wore a suit and necktie. What was strange about his appearance was not the turban but his gold-rimmed green dark glasses. But he was soon circulating with the other guests and students, and no one paid him any further attention. Meanwhile, another guest was leaving. He was Lieutenant Colonel Sir William Curzon Wyllie, aide de camp to the secretary of state for India.

It was almost ten o'clock. Everyone was enjoying the food and champagne and music. As Sir William descended the stairs to say farewell to the other guests, the blue-turbaned figure drew near to his elbow. Wyllie turned and, raising his eyebrows, smiled and said, "Hullo." Even with his dark glasses, the man may have looked vaguely familiar. Curzon Wyllie's last thought might have been, where had he met him before?

---

* Today only the 287-foot tower survives, as part of Imperial College, London.

Suddenly from under his coat the man whipped out a revolver and fired two shots into the civil servant's face. Sir William fell headlong. His wife, watching in horror from the top of the stairs, screamed.

Jehangir Hall dissolved into pandemonium while the man in dark glasses calmly fired shot after shot into the prostrate body. The fifth pierced Curzon Wyllie's right eye, killing him instantly.[1] A Parsi doctor named Cowasji Lalkaka heroically sprang forward to grab the killer's arm. The blue-turbaned figure shot and killed him as well.

It took a few more minutes for bystanders and the police to disarm the assassin. They stripped off his glasses, revealing a young square-jawed Punjabi named Madan Lal Dhingra.[2] He was a student at University College, London, studying mechanical engineering, and the son of a distinguished doctor. But he was also a member of a shadowy group called Abhinav Bharat Sanstha, a Hindu nationalist terrorist cell formed in the aftermath of the Bengal partition by a gaunt twenty-six-year-old fanatic named Vinayak Savarkar.

The Curzon Wyllie and Lalkaka murders took place only nine days before Gandhi arrived in London from Johannesburg. It was still a lead story in the newspapers, with headlines like "Scene After the Murder," "Struggle with Murderer," "Murderer's Career," and "Motive for the Crime." This last issue was most troubling to Gandhi. He did not know Dhingra, but he did know Savarkar. In fact, Savarkar was living in London at that very moment, at India House on Cromwell Avenue near Hampstead Heath. In a few months they would meet face-to-face in a banquet sponsored by India House, or what some were later to call "the House of Terror."[3] For Gandhi, the Wyllie murder was the opening shot in a struggle for the future of Indian nationalism. His goal over the next decade would be to wrest the mantle of nationalist leadership away from men like Savarkar and those he inspired—"stupid young men," as Gandhi called them, in the grip of a "mad idea."[4] But more than that, in Gandhi's mind, this would also be a struggle for the soul of India—a struggle as important as any against Churchill and the British.

At stake was the relationship between nonviolence and India's destiny. "India's freedom must revolutionize the world's outlook on Peace and War," as he put it. The idea of *ahimsa,* he had come to believe, was India's most essential spiritual gift to the rest of humanity. "India has an unbroken tradition of nonviolence from time immemorial," he asserted. However, "if India takes up the doctrine of the sword, then India will cease to be the pride of my heart."[5] That Indians might turn to violence to secure their freedom, and thus unleash the same terrible forces lurking in the human heart that had been unleashed in the Great Mutiny, was a fear that haunted him all his life.

If Gandhi was stunned and horrified by the Wyllie murder, so were Londoners. In one sense, it was nothing new. By 1909 they were used to terror attacks; in 1885 a bomb had even been thrown into the House of Commons. But those acts had been perpetrated by rowdy Irishmen. Indians, especially educated Hindus, were supposed to be the placid and grateful beneficiaries of British rule.

However, the 1905 partition of Bengal had aroused nationalist feelings that defied that racial stereotype. Secret societies like Abhinav Bharat Sanstha sprang up across India, dedicated to murder and assassination. Passionate young men made bombs and collected firearms to use against the hated British occupiers. In December 1907 Hindu terrorists used a bomb to derail a train carrying the viceroy's chief assistant Sir Andrew Fraser. Then on April 30, 1908, another was thrown into a railway carriage that the bombers thought contained a white civil servant. Instead, it killed two English ladies, a Mrs. Kennedy and her daughter.

Britons in India were aghast. Memories of Cawnpore still ran deep, half a century later. There was a furious search for the culprits. At Alipore near Calcutta police stumbled on a bomb-making factory in the garden of a house belonging to a distinguished Bengali family, the Ghoses. Barindra Ghose and his brother Aurobindo were arrested for the Kennedy assassinations, along with twenty-seven other conspirators, including one of India's leading politicians, Bal Gangadhar Tilak.

Their trial lasted almost seven months. By its end, the Raj was as much on trial as the Alipore conspirators. Aurobindo Ghose, the terrorist ringleader, had been a head boy at St. Paul's school in London and graduated from Cambridge. (The chief prosecutor was a former classmate.) His Latin was impeccable, his Greek even better. He and his brother seemed the very model of the "Indian in blood and color, but English in taste and intellect" educated elite that the Raj wanted. But Aurobindo's testimony revealed only his undying hatred of his imperial masters. Eventually he was acquitted, but nineteen others were convicted, and three went to the gallows. One of them, the man who had thrown the bomb that killed the Kennedys, died with a copy of the *Bhagavad Gita* in his hands.[6] Tilak was sentenced to exile in Burma for six years.

Other terrorist cells vowed to hunt down the Alipore conspirators' persecutors one by one. In 1908 they killed a police inspector who had been involved in the Ghoses' arrest. Early in 1909 they killed the trial's public prosecutor. Wyllie had become a prime target because of his involvement in the case. He also happened to be a good friend of the murderer's family, who publicly disowned their son for his terrorist views. The supreme irony was that Curzon Wyllie had the reputation of being deeply pro-Indian, as did his superior, the Liberal Secretary of State for India John Morley. Far from being a hard-liner, "a more kind, genial, unselfish, and helpful creature never existed," Morley wrote of his aide. Morley himself refused to revise his own views on the need for progressive change in India. But after the murder he took care to be followed by three hired detectives.[7]

Madan Lal Dhingra's trial began on July 27, with heavy publicity. It took the court at the Old Bailey less than two days to sentence him to death. Dhingra expressed regret for the death of Dr. Lalkaka but not for Wyllie. His last statement before the court was calm and defiant, with echoes of Nathan Hale. "I believe that a nation held down by foreign bayonets is in a perpetual state of war," he said. "I am proud to lay down my life for my country. But remember we shall have our time in the days to come."

The words impressed many Englishmen both in and out of the courtroom. One of them was the president of the Board of Trade, Winston Churchill. Churchill, in fact, was so impressed that he later could quote Dhingra's words from memory and said they were "the finest ever made in the name of patriotism." Churchill predicted to his friend Wilfred Blunt that Dhingra "will be remembered 2000 years hence, as we remember Regulus and Spartacus and Plutarch's heroes."[8]

It became Gandhi's life task to prove Churchill, and those who used violence in any cause, wrong.

In fact, the murder and trial could not have come at a worse time for Gandhi.[9] He had returned to London to plead the South African Indians' case once more, fresh from his second disastrous satyagraha campaign. And if in the summer of 1909 Winston Churchill's views seemed assured and his future direction plain, Gandhi's were more uncertain than ever.

After his release from prison in January 1908, and the failure of his registration act compromise in March, Gandhi had become distant from ordinary concerns, even from his family. His law practice remained as lucrative as ever, but Gandhi was cheerfully giving the money away or spending it on Phoenix Farm. His eldest son Harilal was now twenty. He still had no formal schooling but was active at Phoenix Farm and in the satyagraha movement. When Harilal was sentenced to jail for resisting registration and his father appeared as his lawyer, Gandhi's main concern was that his son should get the maximum sentence. It was, after all, the kind of self-sacrifice he regularly asked of himself.*[10]

In May 1908 Gandhi decided the government's promises about loosening the registration law were worthless. After his dealings with Churchill and the Colonial Office, he would leave nothing to trust. The registration law was like a collar around a dog's neck, as Gandhi liked to put it. All his efforts would now be devoted to breaking its choke hold.[11]

This time Gandhi spread the campaign into Natal with a missionary zeal that quickly caught fire. All at once he had a movement again. For the first time he was also using the term "satyagraha" to describe what he was doing, and he introduced a new protest tactic: burning the hated registration cards. In August, after Harilal was sentenced to prison, Gandhi organized a mass demonstration outside the Hamidia Mosque to watch more than thirteen hundred certificates being soaked in kerosene, set alight, and burned. The government had just passed a new, stiffer registration law, requiring the reregistration of all Indians, including fingerprinting. Gandhi gave a fierce speech denouncing it and exhorted the crowd "to suffer everything that may be necessary...because I expect this of my countrymen."[12]

In October Gandhi was back in jail. His friend Reverend Doke watched as lines of passive resisters, handcuffed and guarded, were marched up the dusty road to Johannesburg prison. Gandhi himself stumbled along in prison uniform and manacles. "Keep absolutely firm to the end," he wrote on his last day of freedom. "Suffering is our only remedy. Victory is certain."[13]

More than fifteen hundred resisters were in prison as 1908 ended, most of them small traders and street hawkers. But Gandhi was running out of volunteers, and the movement out of steam. Every important resistance organizer was in jail facing three to six months of hard

---

* During his stay in prison he had begun reading Plato and was even writing a Gujarati biography of Socrates, the first philosopher to say that it was preferable to suffer than to wrong others. The title was *The Story of a True Warrior*—precisely the description Gandhi would have liked for himself.

labor, Gandhi and his son included. As the deadline for reregistration neared, and merchants faced the prospect of losing their trading licenses, they began to defect, just as they had a year earlier. With a bitter sense of déjà vu, Gandhi learned in prison that "many [Indians] have given up the fight. Others, it appears, are about to do so."[14]

By February 1909, 97 percent of Transvaal Asians had reregistered under the new law. Gandhi, however, would not quit. When the government released him, he immediately refused to register again and was rearrested. During this third spell in prison in a year, Gandhi learned that the British Indian Association was bankrupt and that "the people have been financially ruined."[15] When a small knot of well-wishers greeted him on his release on May 24, an exhausted Gandhi broke down and wept.

His second satyagraha campaign had been another failure. Other members of the BIA wanted him ousted as leader: in historian Maureen Swan's words, "the vast majority of Transvaal Asians had emphatically repudiated passive resistance." At a tense meeting in June the other BIA leaders discussed how to end the satyagraha campaign and whether to send another deputation to London to try one last time to make the Colonial Office see reason. Gandhi opposed the plan, saying, "The deputation only shows Indians' weakness."[16]

The other leaders insisted, however, and although their effort to make sure the deputation included *no* passive resisters (a blatant repudiation of Gandhi's leadership) was defeated, Gandhi ended up heading the group by default. He was still the formal leader of the Transvaal Indian lobby, but he had virtually no followers and no support in the broader community.

So it was with a bitter sense of frustration that Gandhi arrived in London in July 1909, with little hope of success and even less idea of what would happen next. Oddly enough, the Wyllie murder helped him to get a fix on a new direction. If Gandhi was vague, during the eighteen weeks he spent in London, about what he was now fighting for, he could at least be clear about what and who he was fighting *against*.

The first of these enemies were men like Savarkar and the violent revolutionaries who had inspired Madan Lal Dhingra's terrible deed. The second enemy was the nation that had put Dhingra to death, namely Great Britain. In 1909 Gandhi's years of patient loyalism were finally over. The years of direct, uncompromising confrontation were about to begin.

Gandhi got his opportunity to confront his first enemy at a banquet at the Indian Catering Company in Bayswater in October. The event was a celebration of Dussehra, the festival commemorating Rama's epic rescue of Queen Sita and victory over the demon king Ravana. Most of the guests were from India House, the hotbed of anti-British nationalism. The keynote speaker was Vinayak Savarkar himself.

An air of violence and death seemed to radiate from Savarkar and his gaunt, skull-like visage. He had already turned the backyard of India House into a bomb-making factory, complete with pots of explosive chemicals. Rumor had it that Savarkar had personally given Dhingra the revolver he used to kill Curzon Wyllie, uttering the words, "If you fail, do not show me your face again."[17] His brother Ganesh had just been arrested for sedition in India. In less than two months Savarkar would, not surprisingly, be arrested himself.

His belief in violent revolution and terrorist conspiracy was unapologetic: "Because you deny us a gun, we pick up a pistol...Because you deny us light, we gather in darkness to compass means to knock off the fetters that hold our Mother [India] down." So was his contempt for Gandhi's path of nonviolent resistance. "There can be no substitute for force to achieve complete freedom," he wrote in 1907, "no matter how many little things can be got by other means...[Freedom] can be achieved by physical force alone."[18]

Privately, Gandhi was seething when he arrived at the dinner. He was deeply distressed by Dhingra's murderous act and the responsibility of "the stupid young men" like Savarkar who "seemed to glory in the deed." The notion that murder and terror could bring Indians anything but more terror seemed to Gandhi pure insanity. As he wrote to Hermann Kallenbach, "Even if the British leave in consequence of such murderous acts, who will then rule in their place? The murderers... India can gain nothing from the rule of murderers—no matter whether they are black or white."[19]

But he also admitted, "I have met practically no one who believes India can ever be free without resort to violence." The dinner was his first opportunity to offer publicly an alternative path.

In his Dussehra address Savarkar gave a fiery recital of how Rama slew the demon oppressor in order to establish his own heavenly kingdom on earth (the Rama Raj), and he recounted how the nine-day feast preceding Dussehra honored the bloodstained and terrible ten-armed goddess of vengeance Durga (usually represented riding a lion with a sword in each hand). But Gandhi sounded a very different note. His speech emphasized Rama's role as the symbol of spiritual purity and virtue as well as of war and conquest, of "self restraint, unselfishness, patience, gentleness." These qualities, Gandhi told his audience, "are the flowers which spring beneath the feet of those who accept, but refuse to impose, suffering."

Yes, Indians would one day have to conquer the modern equivalent of the evil King Ravana, namely the unjust rule of the British. But they must do so as followers of Vishnu and his incarnation as the pure and blameless Rama, not as devotees of the bloodsoaked goddess Durga.[20]

It was an understated but crucial moment. By preaching nonviolence to the apostles of armed revolution, Gandhi was staking out his position in the Indian nationalist movement. That movement had begun without him and had grown without his input. In 1909 he was still only a spectator to its debates and controversies. But as Indians' political hopes turned to violence for the first time since the Great Mutiny, Gandhi felt he could no longer sit on the sidelines.

His mother country was entering more and more in his thoughts. "The center of gravity is shifting to India," he wrote to Polak in October, and not only as a way to bring additional pressure to bear on the South Africa problem. Contrary to myth, what prompted Gandhi to make himself a spokesman for the Indian nationalist movement was not disgust with British rule in India. It was his disgust with the growing militancy of Indian nationalism, which he saw as reckless and ultimately un-Indian. On October 8 he had given his first speech on the "Ethics of Passive Resistance," in which he stated, "War with all its glorification of brute force is essentially a degrading thing."[21] In most respects, Gandhi was coming to see South Africa as a staging ground, a rehearsal, for greater things to come.

But first he had to deal with the frustration of petitioning once again a British government that seemed deaf to every reasonable appeal. He still wanted the 1907 registration law, which he had lobbied against the last time he was in London in 1906, repealed. New immigration restrictions, which limited new Indian residents to just six per year, had to go as well. He argued, "There must be legal equality with the whites, *it will not matter then if, in practice, not even a single Indian can get in* [my italics].

We can bear that." This was no longer "a fight for the educated, or the highly educated, but for India's honor, our self-respect."[22]

Even with not one but two ex-viceroys at his side, Lord Ampthill* and Lord Curzon himself, Gandhi got nowhere. He and Ampthill proposed to Colonial Secretary Lord Crewe a reasonable compromise: leave the six-per-year immigration limit up to the Transvaal governor's discretion, instead of inscribing it in law. Crewe made agreeable noises; Gandhi's hopes were briefly aroused. He even cabled back to Johannesburg: "GOVERNMENT AGREE REPEAL."[23]

But then General Smuts, who was also in London, killed the deal. Lord Ampthill urged Gandhi to stay and keep trying. "Yours is a righteous struggle," he kept telling Gandhi, "and you are fighting with clean weapons."[24] They met with the colonial secretary again on September 16. For seven weeks Gandhi waited for a response. On November 3 it arrived. Lord Crewe would do nothing.

Gandhi had reached his limit. To be sure, he had met new and interesting acquaintances during his stay in England. They included members of the London Passive Resistance Society, the suffragette leader Emmeline Pankhurst, and George Allen, a Tolstoyan farmer.[25] He had developed a genuine admiration and affection for Lord Ampthill, who seemed the embodiment of "courtesy and genuine humility."

But as he prepared to leave, the bitterness of defeat spilled over into bitterness against England. He wrote an angry parting letter to the British press: "The only possible justification for holding together the different communities of the Empire under the same Sovereignty is the fact of elementary equality." That principle of equality had been enshrined for Indians for half a century in the Queen's Proclamation of 1858. The Transvaal legislation cut at its very heart. By allowing the law to stand, Gandhi stated, "the Imperial Government are a party to the crime against the Imperial Constitution." As for Indians in India, he wrote in a letter to the Bombay newspaper the *Gujarati,* "If the doctrine of the Transvaal Government be true, the people of India cease to be partners in the empire." The letter ended on a plaintive note: "Will not India come to the rescue?"[26]

---

* Arthur O.V. Russell, Lord Ampthill, had been interim viceroy between Curzon's two terms. Like the late Lepel Griffin, Ampthill was no supporter of either Indian nationalism or the National Congress: he would die fighting the 1935 India Bill alongside Churchill. However, like Griffin he sincerely believed the Indians in South Africa were getting a raw deal. Ampthill recruited Lord Curzon to help Gandhi and wrote the introduction to the first biography of Gandhi when it appeared in 1910.

But how could it? Gandhi asked himself that question as he packed his bags. The next day he would be traveling more than eight thousand miles, back to a movement that was in a state of collapse, and arrive empty-handed. How could Mother India protect her children, when India herself was in the grip of the same regime that denied Indians their rights in South Africa?

Two recently published pieces offered Gandhi tantalizing clues to an answer. One was written by an Englishman. In the wake of the Wyllie murder, the *Illustrated London News* had run a piece on Indian nationalism by G. K. Chesterton. Chesterton was one of Henry Salt's old friends and a fierce critic of modern capitalist civilization, but from the Right not the Left. It took a Roman Catholic self-described reactionary to put Gandhi's fondest thoughts into words. Chesterton suggested that the real problem with revolutionaries like Savarkar was that their view of India's future "is not very Indian." Indian nationalists liked to talk about revolutions, parliaments, constitutions, budgets, and balance of payments. But these were *Western* models of human progress, Chesterton pointed out. (In fact, one of Savarkar's most important role models was the Italian revolutionary Giuseppe Mazzini.) These notions had nothing to do with India's own cultural and spiritual heritage. "If there is such a thing as India," Chesterton said, "it has a right to be Indian"—not an empty vessel to be filled by Western notions.[27]

Reinforcing Chesterton's words was another recent pamphlet by the Russian novelist and Gandhi hero Leo Tolstoy, entitled "Letter to a Hindu."[28] It too was a sharp critique of revolutionary nationalism, but this time from the New Age Left. Tolstoy addressed himself directly to the strange paradox of India, where nearly 300 million people were held in subjection to an evil tyranny run by a "small clique" of white Britons "utterly alien in thought and aspiration and altogether inferior to those whom they enslave."

Just imagine, Tolstoy wrote, if Indians in their millions simply refused to participate in that evil, if they refused to help "in the violent deeds of the administration, of the law courts, the collection of taxes, and what is most important, of the soldiers" who served, both Hindu and Muslim, in the Indian Army. They would not only break the power of the Raj, Tolstoy suggested; they would break the power of violence that enslaved their own hearts. Through passive resistance they would rediscover the law of love, and not only would hundreds of whites be unable to enslave millions of nonwhites, "but millions will be unable to enslave one individual."[29]

As he read the Tolstoy text, Gandhi saw suddenly that that individual was himself. "Life cannot continue in the old ruts as before," Tolstoy continued, in words that must have struck home. "The man must understand that the previous guidance for life is no longer applicable to him." What was needed was to "formulate a new theory of life," Tolstoy concluded, one fit for the individual as he embarks on a "new age."

During his stay in London Gandhi had been reading and rereading the books that mattered most to him, in search of that new theory of life. Tolstoy's *The Kingdom of God Is Within You* and *Confession of Faith;* Henry David Thoreau's *Civil Disobedience;* classics like Ruskin's *Unto This Last* and Edward Carpenter's *Civilization: Its Cause and Cure*. He had picked up R. C. Dutt's *Economic History of India,* which was deeply critical of British rule, and reread a favorite from law school days, Sir Henry Maine's *Village Communities in the East and West,* which argued that India's peasant villages had historically been self-sustaining and self-governing for centuries before the British came.[30]

Ideas were percolating furiously in his brain, and just before he left England, Gandhi drew up his own fifteen-point Confession of Faith. He sent a copy to Henry Polak, to serve as a crucial measure of his personal journey to that point and as the starting point for his next move.

Gandhi's first point was that "there is no impassable barrier between East and West." The second stated that Europeans had "had much in common with the people of the East" before modern civilization killed the West's spiritual values and the simplicity of its rural life. Gandhi worried that the same modern blight was descending on India. "It is not the British who rule India," his fourth point stated, "but modern civilization rules India through its railways, telegraphs, telephone etc." As a result, "Bombay, Calcutta, and other chief cities are the real plague spots of Modern India" because they are the main conduits of civilization's malign influence. Indeed, "if British rule were replaced tomorrow by Indian rule based on modern methods, India would be none the better."

The final world-shattering conclusion came in point number twelve:

> India's salvation consists in unlearning what she has learned during the past fifty years. The railways, telegraphs, hospitals, lawyers, doctors, and such like have all to go, and the so-called upper classes have

to live consciously, religiously, and deliberately the simple peasant life, knowing it to be a life giving true happiness.[31]

In some ways Gandhi's complete rejection of modern medicine was the most shattering of all. "Hospitals are the instruments of the Devil," he wrote. "Medical science is the concentrated essence of Black Magic... If there were no hospitals for venereal diseases, or even for consumptives, we should have less consumption, and less sexual vice amongst us." Gandhi's antipathy to modern comforts, not to mention sexual promiscuity, was nothing new. But his penchant for traditional medicine and his own vegetarian home cures (one experiment nearly killed his son Harilal, while another left Kasturbai ill for weeks even as Gandhi refused to allow her to see doctors), now fitted into a philosophical rejection of all aspects of Western culture, from science and machinery to armies, parliaments, and even laws.

He also wrote a long farewell letter to Lord Ampthill. "An awakening of the national consciousness is inevitable" in India, it read, but "I believe repression will be unavailing...I feel the British rulers will not give liberally and in time." He told Ampthill that "I share in the national spirit" but not in the methods of either extremists or moderates, since each "relies ultimately on violence." He blamed the British for the "blasting effect" of capitalism and materialism in India, the rise of cities like Bombay and Calcutta, and the decline of India's villages. "I do think too much is made of the *Pax Britannica*...I have no quarrel with the rulers. I have every quarrel with their methods."[32] The question uppermost in his mind now was what should replace them.

After booking his passage back to South Africa, Gandhi's mind churned on. "There is no end to the work I have put in on the steamer," Gandhi confessed later in a letter.[33] He began a Gujarati translation of "Letter to a Hindu." But more important, over the course of nine days he composed his own manifesto, which he called *Hind Swaraj,* or "Indian Self-Rule."[34]

It is Gandhi's one original political and moral treatise. Virtually everything else published under his name is either a compilation of his speeches and newspaper articles or, like his autobiography and *Satyagraha in South Africa,* a flow of reminiscence. In a profound sense, everything Gandhi believed or did for the rest of his life sprang from *Hind Swaraj*. It marked the end of a journey that had begun on the Maritzburg rail platform in 1893 and reached a decisive turn in his encounter with Churchill at the Colonial Office in 1906. In every respect, the work signaled Gandhi's point of no return.

Hind Swaraj is a dialogue like the *Bhagavad Gita,* on which it is closely modeled. Its two interlocutors are, significantly, connected to the newspapers, reflecting Gandhi's growing awareness of how the modern media was shaping cultural perceptions and public opinion. The "Reader" is an Indian nationalist, full of fire and confidence, a composite portrait of Savarkar and his followers. He happily describes how the partition of Bengal has transformed Indian nationalist organizations like the Congress from apologists for cooperation with the Raj into advocates of *swaraj* or independence. "For this," he says, "we have to be grateful to Lord Curzon."[35]

Since the British used force to conquer India, the Reader says, it will require force to drive them out. But once that is done, India will be free to organize itself as a modern nation, with an army and navy and an imperial splendor all its own. "Then will India's voice ring through the world," he concludes.[36]

The older wiser man, the Editor, replies along the lines of Chesterton and Tolstoy. "This is English rule without the English," he warns the young Reader. It is "not the Swaraj I want."[37] He predicts that the Reader's path to independence will only turn India into a country like England, full of greedy, dishonest people who cheat and exploit one another, with a Parliament that acts as a "prostitute" to special interests. Its workers in the factories and mines will live lives "worse than that of beasts." Everyone will be ruled by machinery, including inhumane weapons that can kill thousands "at the touch of a trigger." The Editor concludes sardonically, *"This* is civilization," and if India goes that way, "she will be ruined."[38]

However, he says, there is another path to freedom. This path leads backward as well as forward, back to India's roots. It will bring self-rule or *swaraj* not just as political sovereignty but as self-knowledge and self-mastery. Its answers to man's eternal questions, the Editor proclaims, lie in "the ancient civilization of India, which in my opinion, represents the best that the world has ever seen."

India's Hindu ancestors lived without the conveniences of modern life. They remained content with their "ancient villages and peaceful homes" and esteemed their spiritual leaders, their *"rishis* and fakirs," over kings and soldiers, because they realized that wealth and power do not equal happiness.[39] "It was not that we did not know how to invent machinery," the Editor insisted, "but our forefathers knew that, if we set our hearts after such things, we would become slaves and lose our moral fiber."[40]

What doomed this ancient and pure India was not the British conquest, the Editor explains, but Indians' desire to be *like* the British and to cooperate in India's enslavement. "We brought the English [to India]," he says, "and we keep them" there by using British courts and obeying their laws; by using their language and attending their schools; by riding their railways, which, by transporting local produce to distant markets, are "the carriers of plague germs" and of famine; and by turning to Western medicine in defiance of religious law. In all these respects Indians have allied themselves with "the evil nature of man."[41]

Fortunately, India has a way back, Gandhi insists through the words of the Editor: literally a way back to the future. It is satyagraha, combining the ancient Hindu principle of nonviolence with the self-possessed detachment of the "man of steady mind" praised by the *Gita*. Trying to force the British out would be self-defeating, because "brute force is not natural to the Indian soul." Instead, the key is "soul force" or satyagraha, "in other words love conquering hate."[42]

Satyagraha brings its own unique "weapons" to the struggle against British rule, and its weapon of choice is passive resistance. "Passive resistance is a method of securing rights by personal suffering; it is the reverse of resistance by arms. When I refuse to do a thing that is repugnant to my conscience, I use soul force."[43] Through passive resistance, or civil disobedience, nonviolence will become an active principle rippling across the community, like ripples across a pond. The Editor says satyagraha will become an "all-sided sword" that "blesses him that uses it and him against whom it is used," and that will topple unjust laws by making them impossible to enforce.

The Reader, in response, dismisses all this as naïve and, echoing V. B. Savarkar, says that no revolution in history has come without violence. The Editor admonishes him for his cynicism. The belief that what hasn't happened before can't happen now reveals a "disbelief in the dignity of man." Gandhi then lays out a complete nineteen-point program for nonviolence and noncooperation, ranging from refusing to go to school and using English as seldom as possible, to closing Bombay's textile mills and having everyone make their clothes at home.

In short, by refusing to play the cultural game by Western rules, the Editor suggests, Indians can force the British to make a choice. They can either become like the Indians themselves and give up modern civilization in exchange for their own spiritual roots in Christianity and Holy Scripture. Or they can pack up and leave.[44] Whichever choice the British make, India will be finally, completely free. Indians will have true *swaraj,* self-rule, which is rule of the self. By following the path of nonviolence, self-sacrifice, and satyagraha "soul force," they will reach the truth, which is ultimately the kingdom of God.

"The British government in India constitutes a struggle between the Modern Civilization, which is the kingdom of Satan," Gandhi concluded, "and the Ancient Civilization which is the kingdom of God. The one is the God of War, the other the God of Love," and Gandhi no longer had any doubt which would win.

This last passage comes from the preface Gandhi would write for the English translation, when it appeared in Johannesburg in March 1910. The publication of *Hind Swaraj* in the original Gujarati caused consternation and confusion across the political spectrum. Here was a resolute call for expelling the British from India, but also a condemnation of violence in all its forms. Here was a work that condemned Western civilization and all its works, yet quoted from the Bible and called for a reconciliation of Britain and India on a new spiritual basis.

Liberals, including Indian liberals, found Gandhi's ideas hopelessly reactionary. His rejection of Western medicine and education, and his calls for dismantling textile mills and spinning cotton thread at home ("it is no easy task," Gandhi's Editor admits), seemed bizarre, even outrageous.* And the condemnation of Western doctors seemed hypocritical from a man who would consult with doctors all his life (although not always take their advice).

The fact was that *Hind Swaraj* undercut assumptions shared across the spectrum of current Indian opinion, from moderates like his mentor Dadabhai Naoroji to violent extremists like Savarkar who wrote his own angry response.[45] From London to Johannesburg to Madras, it left most readers puzzled, startled, and even amused. All readers, that is, except the British government.

Its censors read *Hind Swaraj* and decided that if it was not actually seditious, it was clearly subversive of British supremacy. If Gandhi's calls

---

* Certainly Gandhi's views on the pernicious effects of railways were wildly off the mark—India's railway system had actually helped to diminish the spread of famine, by quickly moving rice and grain supplies to areas that sorely needed them.

for noncooperation were heeded, the Bombay government's Gujarati translator warned, it would lead to "systematic strikes" in India's public works, railways, and post offices and paralyze the government (exactly what would happen in twenty years). "The sooner [*Hind Swaraj*] is suppressed," he concluded, "the better."[46]

At least one man in England agreed with the censors: Winston Churchill. The man who would become Gandhi's most implacable adversary had already guessed the shape of things to come. On September 5, weeks before Gandhi finished *Hind Swaraj,* the young home secretary predicted with uncanny foresight what would happen if Gandhi's program of noncooperation were ever put in place.

"The game would be up," he frankly told Wilfred Blunt. "If [Indians] could agree to have nothing at all to do with us, the whole thing would collapse," meaning the Raj. Churchill could afford to admire a figure like Dhingra or even Savarkar because they were ultimately powerless. Violence and armed force, even insurrection, were something the British knew how to deal with. Noncooperation on a massive scale was something else again. Even in 1909 Winston Churchill realized that saving the British Empire in India meant halting a visionary like Gandhi in his tracks.[47]

As for Gandhi, he was furious when he learned that his book was banned in India. He still insisted that he was a loyal subject of the empire, except that "my notion of loyalty does not involve acceptance of current rules or government irrespective of its righteousness or otherwise." He was also upset when a South African Theosophist, W. J. Wybergh, spoke out against *Hind Swaraj* as a formula for anarchy. "To destroy" laws and police and government "and put nothing in their place," Wybergh said, "is simply to destroy the possibility of all advance...It is a fatal conclusion to suppose that what is right for the saint is right for everyone else."[48]

But for Gandhi, modern society was already anarchy—spiritual anarchy. Wybergh's argument, he wrote, presupposed that ordinary public life and religious principles could be kept separate: that what was intolerable in one (violence, coercion, greed) should be tolerated in the other: "That is what we see in everyday life under modern conditions." Passive resistance, by contrast, reconnected religion and politics "by testing every one of our actions in the light of ethical principles." It empowered moral persons to end suffering and resist unjust laws. This was why,

General Wheeler's battered entrenchment at Cawnpore, after the Great Mutiny of 1857. The massacre of women and children at Cawnpore, and the brutal retribution that followed, permanently scarred relations between Indians and Britons. (Hulton/Getty Archives)

Lord Randolph Churchill (center) visiting India in 1885, shortly before he became secretary of state for India. "Without India," he argued, "England would cease to be a nation." His son Winston agreed. (Broadwater/Churchill Archives)

Mohandas Gandhi with members
of London's Vegetarian Society,
including his mentor Henry Salt (left,
standing), 1890. It was as a law student
in London that Gandhi first discovered
his Hindu roots.
(V. Jhaveri/Peter Rühe)

Winston Churchill in India in 1896, as
subaltern with the Fourth Hussars. His
experiences there would be the
touchstone for his views on the British
Empire for the rest of his life.
(Broadwater/Churchill Archives)

Gandhi and fellow members of the Indian Ambulance Corps during the Boer War, 1899–1900. "In those days," he later wrote, "I vied with Englishmen in loyalty to the throne." (V. Jhaveri/Peter Rühe)

The *Illustrated Police News*'s heroic version of Churchill's escape from a Boer prison in December 1899 (the truth was somewhat different). Later, at the battle of Spion Kop, Churchill and Gandhi would pass within yards of each other without realizing it. (Broadwater/Churchill Archives)

Gandhi as he appeared when he met Churchill in London in October 1906. (V. Jhaveri/Peter Rühe)

Churchill as secretary of state for the Colonies after his first and only meeting with Gandhi. When asked how to proceed on Gandhi's demand for equal rights for Indians in South Africa, Churchill's response was: "Dawdle." (Broadwater/Churchill Archives)

A rare action photograph of South African police halting Gandhi's dramatic march to the Transvaal, November 1913. It shows Gandhi (center, with stick) in Indian peasant dress, which he adopted after he felt Churchill and the British government had betrayed him. (Local History Museum, Durban/Peter Rühe)

Failure of the Gallipoli campaign in 1915 and the needless death of 200,000 British, Australian, and New Zealand soldiers forced Churchill to resign as first lord of the Admiralty. Yet, ironically, the Gallipoli disaster helped to launch Gandhi's political career in India. (Hulton/Getty Archives)

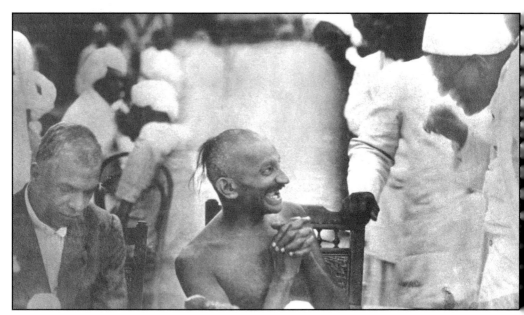

The Mahatma radiant: Gandhi meeting with Indian National Congress stalwarts in September 1921, as his Noncooperation movement got underway. "It amazes me," Churchill told the Indian secretary of state a month later, "that Gandhi should be allowed to go undermining our position month after month and year after year." (V. Jhaveri/Peter Rühe)

Churchill triumphant: the new chancellor of the exchequer on his way to present his first budget to the House of Commons, 1925. As "the smiling Chancellor," Churchill turned Budget Day into a major media event. But the decisions he made on military spending made Britain weaker in the years before World War II.
(Broadwater/Churchill Archives)

Gandhi using his *charkha,* or spinning wheel, at Sabarmati Ashram, 1926. "The spinning wheel is as much a necessity of Indian life as air and water," he wrote, although his belief that it was the key to India's future alienated some of his political allies. (V. Jhaveri/Peter Rühe)

Gandhi believed, "passive resistance, that is soul force, is matchless" and must prevail in the end.[49]

As for the dangers involved in such a radical experiment, Gandhi had already given the answer in *Hind Swaraj*. "I would paraphrase the thought of an English divine and say that anarchy under home rule were better than order under foreign rule"—words that would haunt him later.*

Gandhi sent a copy of *Hind Swaraj* to his new mentor, Leo Tolstoy, who wrote a courteous reply on May 3, 1910. He at least understood Gandhi's New Age message. Now ill and infirm, Tolstoy agreed that passive resistance was "a question of the greatest importance not only for India but for the whole of humanity." Later he added, "Your work in the Transvaal...[is]...most important and fundamental." It was the last long letter Tolstoy ever wrote. Less than two months later he was dead. Gandhi wrote his obituary in *Indian Opinion,* calling Tolstoy "one of the greatest men of our age."[50]

In tribute, Gandhi established a second experimental farm close to Johannesburg that he dubbed Tolstoy Farm. There Gandhi finally made his home, hewing wood, drawing water, doing laundry, and helping to build new houses with gusto. "I am now a farmer," he wrote proudly to Manilal and his other sons, "and I wish you to become farmers." Tolstoy Farm would be the center of his activities for the rest of his stay in South Africa.

Because he was still in South Africa. While *Hind Swaraj* marked a major turning point for Gandhi's life and his theory of nonviolence, the facts on the ground remained unchanged. He had returned from England to a movement devoid of followers and money, even after Henry Polak's money-raising tour of India in 1909–10.[51] Even Governor Smuts and the Transvaal government saw him more as a useful symbol, a canny lawyer willing to cut deals in the name of South Africa's Indians, than as a leader of a movement.

For all of 1910 and the start of 1911 Gandhi's third satyagraha campaign existed in name only. In April he and Smuts reached another agreement on the immigration rules, couched in vague phrases and ambiguities that either man could cast as a victory. "Smuts mistrusted

---

* The English "divine" was John Milton, who has Satan remark in *Paradise Lost*: "Better to rule in hell than to serve in Heaven."

Gandhi," historian Maureen Swan notes, "as much as Gandhi mistrusted Smuts."[52] Neither side was interested in pushing the issue, however. Certainly Gandhi was unwilling to renew the battle until he had found a way to breathe new life into his movement and finally turn soul force into a political force.

Chapter Ten

PARTING OF THE WAYS
1911–1914

What is the destiny of our country to be?
WINSTON CHURCHILL, 1910

How despicable my countrymen are!
MOHANDAS K. GANDHI, 1912

AT 10:45 ON THE MORNING OF January 3, 1911, a Sunday, Winston Churchill was lolling in his bath when the phone rang. Some of the most important moments in Churchill's life seem to have happened when he was either in bed or in the bathtub. This was one of them.

He came to the apparatus "dripping wet and shrouded in a towel."[1] It was the London Metropolitan Police. They had trapped a gang of terrorists in a house in London's East End at Sidney Street. These were not Indian terrorists or even Irishmen but Latvians. They were part of a burglary ring with vague connections to the rising tide of anarchist gangs working in Europe and Russia. They had been hiding out in the slums of Whitechapel, where Jack the Ripper had terrorized London citizenry almost a quarter-century earlier (when Gandhi had been a lonely law student at Inner Temple and Winston a lonely schoolboy at Harrow).

Two weeks earlier the gang had been surprised in a robbery attempt and had shot three constables, killing two. Now on January 3 members of the gang were firing on police from the Sidney Street house. Since Churchill was home secretary, the police needed his permission to call in backup. Churchill told them to call in not only the Scots Guards but the Royal Artillery. He also said he would go down there himself.

Minutes later he was dressed and striding out the door. At thirty-six, he was the Liberals' rising star. In just two years he had gone from being a minor undersecretary to a major player in Prime Minister Herbert Asquith's cabinet. Yet beneath the facade of parliamentary politician, the officer of the Fourth Hussars still lurked. The temptation to see and hear some shots in action, even in the streets of London, was too much for him to resist.

Winston arrived to find the police and Scots Guards blazing away at the house with a large field artillery piece at the ready. He immediately took charge, as a crowd of onlookers gathered.* Later newspaper photos and newsreels would show him, pale and cherubically grim-faced in an astrakhan-collared overcoat and topcoat, directing the gunfire like a general on the battlefield. Soon smoke began to pour from inside the house. The rain of police and army bullets had set the hideout on fire, but Churchill refused to let the fire brigade put out the conflagration, for fear they might be shot at. For over an hour the house was allowed to burn. When the firemen and police finally charged in, they found only two bodies, charred beyond recognition. It was never clear whether they were anarchists or burglars, or even whether their ringleader, the sinister "Peter the Painter," really existed.[2]

The "Siege of Sidney Street," as it became known, drew a firestorm of criticism and ridicule on the home secretary. The Tories found his insistence on personally taking charge and his mock-heroics laughable. His fellow Liberals accused him of using a "steam hammer to crack a nut." A. G. Gardiner in the *Daily News* said it was one more example of Winston's "tendency to exaggerate a situation" and his taste for hysterical dramatics. "He is always unconsciously playing a part, an heroic part," Gardiner wrote. "And he is himself his most astonished spectator."[3]

Churchill was unrepentant. He believed he had struck a blow for public order, even for the British race. "I thought it better to let the house burn," he told Asquith in an explanatory letter, "than spend good British lives in rescuing these ferocious rascals."[4] He believed those "ferocious rascals" represented the new threat to his stable world: socialist revolution.

Churchill may have become a self-declared Radical, but he had no sympathy for socialist ideas, or for the party that claimed to represent

---

* One of them was a young East End social worker named Clement Attlee.

them, the rising Labour Party. "Liberalism is not Socialism, and never will be," he would explain to his constituents. "Socialism seeks to pull down wealth, Liberalism seeks to raise up poverty...Socialism would kill enterprise; liberalism would rescue enterprise from the trammels of privilege and preference."[5] Churchill believed in helping the poor and was willing to do his bit to free them from privilege's trammels, like backing the 1910 bill that had stripped the House of Lords of the power to veto legislation. But the ideas of dictatorship of the proletariat and class warfare horrified him, as well they might horrify the cousin of one of England's greatest peers, the Duke of Marlborough.[6]

Socialist ideas also horrified Gandhi. It is striking that neither man was drawn to them, then or later. Even during his early years in London Gandhi had shown no interest in the radical-left politics of many of his New Age friends. Marx's materialism naturally repelled him. Communists and socialists seemed to want to lead mankind down the same spiritual dead end as capitalism. Socialism on the Marxist model, he believed, "reeked of violence." It seemed to him part of the same disease afflicting Indian nationalism. " 'Kill, kill, kill,' that is all they want," he wrote in *Indian Opinion* in September 1909 in the shadow of the Curzon Wyllie murder. "If this is the way things go on, no one's life will be safe in Europe."[7]

In Churchill's case, however, the repulsion was more visceral, not to mention self-interested. An anarchist like Peter the Painter seemed to him the enemy of decency and order, of the "English way of life," even the basic codes of human conduct. His reaction to anarchists and socialists foreshadowed his hatred of the Russian Revolution and Communism, and his antipathy to revolution of any kind, including Gandhi's kind. The Churchill who would fight Indian independence with all his strength in 1931 and again during the Second World War, first surfaced with "the little general" of the Siege of Sidney Street.

Then over the summer of 1911, as Britain's economy began to turn sour, a bitter seamen and dockworkers' strike broke out. A national railway strike in sympathy seemed certain. The previous year, when a coal workers' strike became ugly and policemen were stoned, the young home secretary had refused to employ troops. After Sidney Street, however, he had no hesitation and not only used troops but gave them powers amounting to martial law. Charles Masterman was appalled as his young friend declared virtual martial law around the country, imperiously directing troops to points on the map. He seriously believed

Winston was longing for bloodshed. When Lloyd George managed to settle the strike, Churchill was disappointed: "I would have been better to have gone on and given these men a good thrashing."[8]

These were callous words in retrospect, but at the time Churchill truly believed that the future of the country was at stake. As the twentieth century entered its second decade, he already had the alarming sense that things were coming unstuck. The liberal optimism that had pushed him to the Radical ranks had curdled. The imperial order of his youth was passing into disorder, from the rise of nationalist violence in Ireland and anarchist violence in Europe to the riots against partition in Bengal. All this was made worse by the growing tensions among the major continental European powers. "A strong tremor of unrest has passed through the gigantic structure of fleets and armies which impress and oppress the civilization of our time," he told his constituents in Dundee in October of that year, when full-scale war between France and Germany over Morocco had narrowly been averted.[9]

Churchill, like other astute observers at the time, was aware of the growing interconnectivity of the world's societies and economies. Globalization and its dangers was as hot a topic then as it is today. The concerns it generated are reflected in best sellers like H. G. Wells's *War of the Worlds* (1898) and *Anticipations* (1901), while G. K. Chesterton's *The Man Who Was Thursday* (1907) and John Buchan's *The Thirty-Nine Steps* (1915) explored the vulnerability of civilization to new internal as well as external threats. A railway strike might bring Britain to the brink of starvation within weeks, Churchill worried, since its great cities all had to feed themselves on rail lines connected by sea to economic networks reaching around the globe. "We are an artificial country," he warned.[10] Britain could not survive without international trade. Nor could the other industrialized countries, yet they were busy arming themselves to the teeth.

Churchill the Free Trader could well argue that interdependence was a basis for peace between nations. Churchill the Imperial Strategist knew that in a global world it might also be a powerful source of conflict, with cataclysmic results. As early as 1901 he had warned that "when mighty populations are impelled against each other" in a modern war, "when the resources of science and civilization sweep away everything that might mitigate their fury," the result would only be "the ruin of the vanquished and the scarcely less fatal commercial dislocation and exhaustion of the conqueror."[11]

Churchill believed that the one institution that might stave off international disaster and defend some semblance of global order was the British Empire. Britain's arrogant hopes of endless imperial expansion were finished, killed off by the Boer War. So was Imperial Preference—the idea of an empire united by formal economic ties had been done in by the British voter. But the idea of an empire as "a moral force," an English-speaking community that might still rally around Britain in a time of crisis but might also sustain the push for "the general happiness and welfare of mankind," became uppermost in Churchill's mind in these years.[12]

He deeply believed that British ideas had had "a healthy and kind influence" upon history, as the driving engine for the spread of human liberty and progress. (Even Gandhi was willing to concede that.) Preserving Britain's overseas empire in its present form, including Egypt and India, would ensure that Britain's benign influence on the world remained powerful.

So while Gandhi in *Hind Swaraj* was wondering how to unravel the political and material bonds that held the empire together for the sake of human freedom, Churchill was looking to preserve and defend the empire for the same purpose. This moment, not their meeting in 1906, marked their true parting of the ways. In the years to come they would clash, but not over personalities or cultures or even (in a strict sense) political ideologies.

They would instead clash over their diametrically opposed views on the relationship between empire and civilization and on man's hope of the future. Everything else, even the fate of India, would fade to secondary importance. For Churchill, the empire he knew and had grown up with offered a clear blueprint for a future global community (framed by the history of the English-speaking peoples). For Gandhi, that empire had become an obstacle to any hope for humanity. "The British people," he would say in 1930, "must realize that the Empire is to come to an end" in order for Britons, as well as Indians, to be truly free.[13] For one man, the end of the British Empire would be the necessary price for the world to live in peace and nonviolence. For the other, preserving that empire was the necessary prerequisite for a world at peace, even *at the price of violence*.

In October 1911 Churchill was given the helm of the military institution that held that empire together: the Royal Navy. As First Lord of the Admiralty, he would direct the fortunes of a fleet larger than its two closest competitors put together. With thirty-eight naval bases and coaling stations scattered around the globe, the Royal Navy's reach extended from the English Channel across the Atlantic to Canada and the British Caribbean, and from Gibraltar and Suez to Capetown and India, and across the Pacific from Singapore to Hong Kong. It defended the world's principal trade routes as well as the possessions of a far-flung empire.[14]

Shortly after his appointment, Churchill visited the fleet at anchor near Portland on the Channel. "A gray afternoon was drawing to a close" as the hulking ships of the British navy emerged out of the haze, row upon row, squadron by squadron. "As night fell," he remembered, "ten thousand lights from sea and shore sprang into being and every masthead twinkled as the ships and squadrons conversed with one another" by signal lamps. He asked, "Who could fail to work for such a service?" Indeed, "Who could fail when the very darkness seemed loaded with the menace of approaching war?"[15]

Churchill then imagined what would happen if "these ships, so vast in themselves, yet so small, so easily lost to sight on the surface of the waters," suddenly disappeared. "The British Empire would dissolve like a dream; each isolated community struggling forward by itself; the central power of union broken; mighty provinces, whole Empires in themselves, drifting hopelessly out of control and falling a prey to others." He told Violet Asquith, "This is...the biggest thing that has ever come my way...I shall pour into it everything I've got."[16]

Like most free trade Liberals, Churchill had once seen large-scale military expenditure as a waste of public money.[17] No longer: with a new sense of mission, he became fascinated, even obsessed, with new military technologies. The bigger and more destructive they were, the better. For example, the navy's new battleships like the *Dreadnought* had ten twelve-inch guns that could demolish a target seven miles away. In Churchill's mind, advanced technological marvels like these were harbingers of the destructive forces that the twentieth century was bound to unleash.

It was the lesson he had first learned in India and had seen reinforced by Omdurman and the Boer War. Modern warfare was going to be more frightful and merciless than its predecessors, and the civilized nations of the world had to prepare for it.[18] The very thing that Gandhi feared most about Western technology, its power to kill "thousands at the touch of a trigger," seemed to Churchill to be more a matter of grim pride than otherwise. The slaughter of Omdurman, after all, had also seemed to him the triumph of "science over barbarism." The moral issue for Churchill boiled down to whose finger was on the trigger. He was determined that it should be British fingers, whether the enemy was the "odious dervishes" or the Pathans or the Boers. Or indeed the new threat, the Germans.

By 1911 the navy was caught up in an arms race with imperial Germany, to determine who would build the biggest, fastest, and most destructive warships. Churchill was determined that the United Kingdom should win. He insisted on growing the navy budget so fast that his own Liberal colleagues howled in protest. He wrote the new charter for the Naval Intelligence Division to discern German intentions and capabilities.* He set out to create a modern professional naval staff, in part to help integrate new technologies, including submarines and dirigible airships, into the strategic equation.

For the same reason, Churchill also became the crucial pioneer of modern naval aviation, as he decided that the Royal Navy's future in the air would be with fixed-wing aircraft. He even took an interest (with disastrous results) in an early helicopter. He became so interested, in fact, that as war clouds gathered on the European horizon, he took flying lessons himself.

In 1913 airplanes were still considered an untried technology and wildly dangerous. His whole family worried about him; Clementine was appalled. Winston, however, refused to be put off, even though it was hard to find willing instructors. "We were all scared stiff," remembered one, "of having a smashed First Lord on our hands." He finally found one willing to risk handing over the controls, Marine Captain Wildman-Lushington. On November 29, 1913, the eve of Winston's thirty-ninth birthday, they went aloft on a bright, clear cold afternoon at the Eastchurch naval flying center.

"He got so bitten by it," the Royal Marine wrote to his fiancée afterward, "I could hardly get him out of the machine...He showed great promise, and is coming down again for further instruction and practice."[19] Churchill invited Wildman-Lushington to join him at his birthday party the next evening. The champagne flowed, and crates of oysters were flown down from Whitstable. Wildman-Lushington sat at

---

* When war came in 1914, its decoding section, known in the Admiralty as Room 40, would crack the German naval code, an inestimable advantage and probably Churchill's single most decisive contribution to winning the First World War.

the head table on the First Lord's right; he even showed Winston a picture of his fiancée.[20]

Two days later, Captain Robert Wildman-Lushington was taking off in the same plane on a wet runway, went into a skid, crashed, and was killed.

The day Winston Churchill was enjoying his flying lesson, Gandhi was sitting in Bloemfontein jail, as Prisoner no. 17339.[21] But his mood was hopeful. His struggle for Indian rights in South Africa was finally reaching its climax.

Gandhi had spent the whole of 1911 vainly trying to get the deal he had worked out with General Smuts on Indian immigration ratified into law. He published the usual stream of articles and editorials in *Indian Opinion*. He wrote the usual letters asking politicians to allow interprovince migration for Asians in the new Union of South Africa, and he made the usual threats of a boycott.

By the time the government introduced its new anti-immigration bill in January 1912, Gandhi had fired all his verbal ammunition without even scratching the target. Satyagraha as he had first conceived it was not working.[22] The white government was too strong, the satyagrahis too few, and the mass of Indians too apathetic. Yet he could not afford to sit still. Unless something was done, the tide of discriminatory legislation would only rise, he feared, until every Indian, Hindu or Muslim, rich or poor, had been driven out of South Africa.

He began planning a "new campaign, and that a big one," he promised the Natal Congress. But in fact he had no idea how to proceed.[23] For nearly a year Gandhi stalled for time. He needed an issue to galvanize opinion, a new approach to satyagraha, and a way to dramatize his inner transformation since writing *Hind Swaraj*.

In December 1912 the grand old man of Indian politics, Gopal Krishna Gokhale, visited South Africa for the first time. The leader of the Indian Congress's moderates, he had been Gandhi's mentor during his stay in India in 1901. A decade later Gandhi and other South African Indians invited him to see their plight firsthand. Even the viceroy, Lord Hardinge, had urged Gokhale to go. Gokhale visited the Transvaal and Natal and spoke at dozens of public meetings and private dinners. He was even graciously received by the white South African government.

The day he left South Africa from Delagoa Bay, Gandhi came to see Gokhale off. For the first time since he was a boy, Gandhi appeared in traditional Indian clothes.[24]

He had reached a crucial decision. He would no longer wear Western attire, only that of his home country. It was a gesture toward *swadeshi,* or self-sufficiency, the rallying cry that had spread across India since the furor over Bengal partition. *Swadeshi,* after all, was an adjunct of *swaraj,* or self-rule. Later Gandhi would claim that the grayish white homespun cotton garments felt softer and friendlier: they bore the intimate feel of nature, including his own nature. And, by "decolonizing" his body,[25] he was also shedding in his own mind the Mohandas Gandhi created by the West and the British Empire.

"*Swadeshi* is reliance on our own strength," he wrote.[26] And Gandhi *was* stronger. The traditional Indian garments revealed a man who was harder and leaner, having gained more endurance from the rounds of hard labor at Tolstoy Farm, not to mention the rigors of prison. Gandhi had come into his own, physically as well as mentally. The Gandhi who would become an international icon, the gaunt figure in homespun cloak and dhoti appearing in photographs and newsreels, made his first appearance at Delagoa Bay in December 1912.

The new look caused no end of trouble. As he tried to disembark after seeing Gokhale off, he was stopped by a white customs official. The official had just let Hermann Kallenbach, who had no identity papers with him, pass through. Gandhi controlled his temper and saved his anger for the ragged Indian immigrants squatting around him, with their miserable bundles and wicker suitcases, some of whom were relieving themselves on deck.

"How despicable my countrymen are!" he confessed in a rare, almost unique outburst in his diary. But then he added: "But why blame the whites...I must share in the benefits and pay the penalties for the impression created by my fellows in South Africa...We are after all like the Indians in India," who deserved some of the white man's scorn for their physical and moral weakness and disgusting habits, Gandhi felt.[27]

"What would be my duty in this case?" Gandhi asked himself. "I must not become or remain selfish. My Indian co-passengers on the deck are living in filth; I must set them an example through my living." Gandhi says he then charged about the deck, urging each family to clean up its rubbish. "They should defer to the simple and reasonable laws of the whites," he explained, like the rules of personal hygiene and courtesy, "and resist their perverse and unreasonable laws with courage and resolution."[28]

It was a strange moment of cultural self-flagellation, rarely to be repeated, but it revealed that Gandhi was once again spoiling for a fight. Three months later the white South African government dropped the excuse into his lap. In fact, it set the pattern that successive British and Indian governments would repeat over the next two decades.

In March 1913 Judge Malcolm Searle of the South African Supreme Court ruled that couples who had married according to religious rites that recognized polygamy, as both Hindus and Muslims did, had no right to emigrate to South Africa, even if their marriage was monogamous. The Searle ruling was, Gandhi felt, a direct attack on every Hindu and Muslim family. Certainly he interpreted it as an attempt to invalidate all Indian marriages in South Africa, and he said so in editorials in *Indian Opinion*.[29]

Since January Gandhi had been planning to leave South Africa for India. He had closed Tolstoy Farm and moved everyone south to Phoenix Farm. He was only waiting for the announcement of a final amnesty for his satyagrahis before he bought the steamship tickets for his family. But then came the marriage ruling. The British Indian Association called a mass meeting on March 30, and Gandhi wrote a stern rebuke to the minister of the interior. On April 9 he saw the final wording of the latest immigration bill, and his worst fears were realized. It tightened rules not only on immigration from India but on immigration from one province of South Africa to another, even for Indians born there. In effect, the law made South Africa's Indians prisoners in their own country.

Gandhi spent May and June preparing the next, his fourth, satyagraha campaign. But this time he had a new approach. On either June 23 or 24, 1913, he wrote to Hermann Kallenbach: "I am resolving in my own mind the idea of doing something for the indentured man."[30]

Indentured workers had come from India since 1860, until the 1911 law closed the door on them. Having signed three-year contracts to provide indentured labor, they worked on the sugar plantations, the upcountry farms, and by the 1890s the factories and mines that drove Natal's economy. Still others worked as servants in the homes of Gandhi's wealthy Indian friends. The "indentured man" made up the bulk of South Africa's Indian population. Gandhi knew next to nothing about

them: even though Phoenix Farm was in the heart of Natal's sugar country, he had never visited any of the plantations or the labor compounds
where indentured Indians lived in appalling filth and squalor.[31]

After all, few of them were Gujaratis. Most were Tamil-speakers, and
almost 60 percent of the agricultural laborers were either *shudras* or untouchables.[32] Gandhi had met some of them as volunteers during his ambulance service and seen something of their lives during his plague relief
efforts in Johannesburg in 1904. Yet as Maureen Swan has recounted,
for years he had convinced himself that they were happy with their lot as
landless laborers and debtors to Natal's Indian merchant elite. Still, the
annual £3 tax imposed on every Indian who had been indentured since
1895, plus the £1 head tax imposed by the white government after the
Boer War, drove many of them back into debt servitude and threatened
their children with the same fate.[33]

If any Indians truly suffered under the white South African regime, it
was not Gandhi's friends but the indentured underclass and their children. But he had ignored them for almost two decades. During his visit
Gokhale had spoken of the need for Indians to rally to oppose the hated
tax. Now Gandhi realized that this might be the issue to mobilize a true
groundswell of support and breathe new life into the movement he had
nearly killed off.

Up until then Gandhi had thought and spoken of satyagraha as an
elite movement, made up of individuals willing to make almost superhuman self-sacrifices, risking their fortunes and lives for their own
honor and that of their fellow "respectable" Indians. In 1913 he began to
think of satyagraha as a *mass* movement, with mass appeal. By mobilizing all Indians, including society's poorest and most vulnerable, Gandhi
realized, he could transform them as well as his movement.

As his campaign got under way in September, he still preferred to use
his satyagrahis, including his own family, as the vanguard. When
President Smuts did not respond to his call to end the tax and overturn
the marriage ruling, he sent a contingent of women from well-to-do
families, including Kasturbai and his white secretary Sonja Schlesin,
along with Gandhi's Tamili friend Thambai Naidu and Hermann
Kallenbach, to break the immigration law by crossing from Natal into
Transvaal. They were all arrested, and Kasturbai and the other women
were sentenced to three months' hard labor.[34]

But when on October 15, 1913, Gandhi called for a strike by indentured laborers against the £3 tax, he was stunned at the response.

Already skeptics in the British Indian Association were calling the confrontational satyagraha campaign a waste of time. Across South Africa the total number of passive resisters came to less than forty. Fistfights broke out at a meeting on October 12, and Gandhi had to promise that he would take a more conciliatory, and conventional, approach to lobbying against the proposed law.[35] The strike call was a "last ditch stand" against his critics, who had seen him fail once too often. It was "a tactic he was so ill-prepared to use that he was uncertain how successful it would be."[36]

Miraculously the next day, October 16, the strike began in the coal fields of northern Natal. The Indian workers there had never struck before. Most had no idea what a strike was. But the rebellion against the £3 tax caught fire in the labor compounds. Within two weeks more than five thousand mine workers had downed tools. Gandhi's success came just in time. On the nineteenth there had been a formal vote of no confidence against him in the BIA, which lost. Gandhi was now poised to capitalize on his unexpected success.

On October 17 Gandhi headed for the mining camps at Newcastle. He wrote excitedly to Kallenbach, "The strike is a real thing. It is now making itself felt."[37] When the mine owners cut off electricity and water, he urged the miners "to go forth like pilgrims" and risk arrest for violating the law for interprovince migration. On October 29 he led the first batch of strikers and their families from Newcastle toward the Transvaal. A day later Thambai Naidu led a second batch; the secretary of a new organization, the Colonial Born Indian Association or CBIA, representing South African–born Indians, led the third.[38]

They established a shanty camp a few miles from the Transvaal border, which a Tamil Christian dubbed Camp Lazarus, after the man whom Christ miraculously raised from the dead—not an inappropriate image for Gandhi's satyagraha movement. As October ended, Gandhi had gathered together more than two thousand men and 180 women and children at Camp Lazarus. All were living on barely a pound and a half of bread and an ounce of sugar a day. After a week Gandhi told them they must decamp and travel light, that they were not to touch any private property, and that if they were arrested as they crossed the border, they were not to resist.[39]

On November 6, on Gandhi's command, they set out at dawn in a long line. Gandhi always liked to think of himself as a general leading his satyagrahi troops into battle: a battle of soul force and *ahimsa* but a battle nonetheless.[40] He had cast himself as a warrior in the tradition of the *Gita* and deeply admired the soldierly ethos. The discipline of regular British Army regiments that he had seen in the Boer War, with their "clockwork regularity" in breaking up camp or going into action, was, he had told the *Times of India,* "wonderful to see." Later he spoke of the "rich experience we gained at the front" and would say of military life, "How many proud, rude, savage spirits has it not broken into gentle creatures of God?"[41]

Nor did he shirk the cost of war, even *his* kind of war, in bloodshed, any more than Winston Churchill did. "I do not know what evil is in me," he confessed in a letter from April 1914. "I have a strain of cruelty in me...such that people force themselves to do things, even to attempt impossible things, in order to please me."[42] Later, English officials would be shocked to hear Gandhi talk coolly of the number of deaths that would result if they did not accede to his demands and riots or communal strife broke out in some Indian city.

"If a man with God's name on his tongue and a sword under his armpit deserved to be called Mahatma," one of his bitterest Indian opponents would say later, "then Gandhi was one."[43] But like an Old Testament Joshua or David, he refused to spare himself in the cost. As he led his "troops" on the march on November 6, he fully expected to be arrested, beaten, and perhaps even shot down as they approached the border.

The police did nothing. Back in Johannesburg, Interior Minister General Smuts was playing a shrewd waiting game. He believed that the coal strike, indeed Gandhi's whole campaign, would collapse without the police having to lift a finger. "Mr. Gandhi appeared to be in a position of much difficulty," Smuts wrote later. "Like Frankenstein he found his monster an uncomfortable creation and he would be glad to be relieved of any further responsibility."[44]

Smuts was almost right. By refusing to arrest the miners as they crossed the border, the South African police put Gandhi in a terrible position. He was responsible for the lives of two thousand people, who had no food or water or shelter. Almost £250 a day were needed to keep them alive, and Gandhi had no funds. By the first week of November, even before they left Camp Lazarus, the government's nonintervention policy "seriously threatened the success of the strike."[45] Now his gesture in leading his people across the border, like Moses leading his people to the promised land, seemed an empty, even ludicrous gesture.

Finally, at Palmford, the police struck—but only by arresting Gandhi. He was livid. He wrote a reproachful letter to Smuts, saying his detention left his marchers "on starvation rations without provision for shelter" or any idea of what they were to do next.[46] Gandhi had been praying to be arrested, but not alone. He had envisioned thousands of martyrs, not just their leader, suffering and even dying for satyagraha. His options were shrinking. Once he was released, he immediately broke the law again, and on November 9 he was rearrested, along with Polak and Kallenbach. Gandhi received a sentence of three months' hard labor. The rest of his bedraggled army, hungry and leaderless, were quietly rounded up and sent back to the mines. Gandhi had lost again.

But then the strikers saved him. Back at the mines the returned Indian miners refused to work and encouraged their coworkers to do the same. Meanwhile the strike was spreading to southern Natal and the coastal sugar plantations. No one organized the miners; most had still never heard of Gandhi. Some indentured laborers left for the cities. Others drifted to Phoenix Farm. Some had heard rumors that a great raja would pay them three pounds not to work. Others said that the great Gokhale would return with a mighty army to abolish the hated tax. But all of them refused to cut cane.[47]

At the end of November more than 50,000 laborers were on strike, and some 7,000 Indians were in jail. The strike paralyzed the Durban and Pietermaritzburg produce markets. Some sugar mills had to close down, and local hotels and resorts had lost all their Indian help.[48] In Ladysmith workers rioted, and mounted police had to charge with batons. Some strikers were shot dead; others were wounded; in the mining camps miners and police battled, and by the second week in December the death toll rose to ten.

The strike was having its effect on opinion overseas, especially British and Indian opinion. Gokhale, who had thought Gandhi was making a mistake in calling the strike, was now demanding a commission of inquiry into the deaths. The Viceroy Lord Hardinge spoke of India's "deep and burning sympathy" for the Indian laborers in South Africa. "This movement of passive resistance has been dealt with by measures which would not for one moment be tolerated by any country that calls itself civilized." The governor of Bombay expressed similar sentiments; the press in Britain and other countries lined up clearly on the side of the Indian strikers.[49]

The turn of public opinion, and the threat of more violence, finally forced General Smuts to the bargaining table. On December 9, 1913, Gandhi was released from prison. He was barefoot, in coolie dress with a homespun white coat and flowing dhoti, and his mustache was shaved off. He was in mourning, he said, for the ten workers killed in the strike. He was asked if he felt responsible for their deaths.

"How glorious," he replied, "it would have been if one of those bullets had struck me!"[50] But Gandhi's death would have left a vacuum, and no one else was up to the task of power negotiations with Jan Christiaan Smuts.

General Smuts, minister of the interior as well as defense, was white South Africa's shrewdest politician. Largely forgotten today, he was for nearly forty years one of the world's most highly regarded statesmen. He was no racist of the Boer stereotype, as Gandhi knew.* When they first met, Smuts had told him, "I could never entertain a dislike for your people. You know I am a barrister. I had some Indian fellow students in my time. But I must do my duty"—precisely the word Gandhi himself might have used, if he had been in the same position.

"You are a simple-living and frugal race, in many respects more intelligent than we are," Smut told Gandhi. "You belong to a civilization that is thousands of years old. Ours, as you say, is but an experiment. Who knows but that the whole damn thing will perish before long. But you see," he added pointedly, "why we do not want you here." As with Gandhi, the issue in Smuts's mind was "simply one of preserving one's own civilization."[51] In Smuts's case, that meant keeping South Africa's Indians down and out, which he had been doing for five years with reasonable success—with Gandhi on the losing end.

But now, as they met in January, Gandhi had more leverage than before. The indentured laborers' strike had revealed his political muscle, including his influence in India, where Calcutta had announced it was launching a full inquiry on the status of Indians in South Africa. "[Gandhi's] activities at that time were very trying to me," Smuts wrote later. While Gandhi had been enjoying "a period of rest and quiet in jail" (Gandhi, who had been pushed to the brink of exhaustion, had to admit that that was true), Smuts had the "odium of carrying out a law which had not strong public support."[52]

---

* In the 1908 satyagraha campaign, the wife of Thambai Naidu had suffered a miscarriage following her husband's arrest. Gandhi had publicly accused Smuts of being "a murderer." The rash remark had hurt the movement, and Gandhi came to regret it—and to revise his opinion of Smuts.

To top it all, for unrelated reasons white railway workers were threatening labor action of their own. In December 1913 South Africa was teetering on economic chaos. Gandhi, however, refused to take advantage of Smuts's dilemma and formally halted the Natal workers' strike, a chivalrous gesture that won Smuts's gratitude and respect.

But Smuts had a strong hand as well. The truth was that the strike was collapsing even before Gandhi called it off. His Natal Indian Association had been too worried about further violence to press ahead and pleaded with workers to remain on their plantations. The strike organizers, and the strikers, were destitute.[53] Gandhi at first resisted the appointment of a commission to hear their grievances because two members were notoriously anti-Indian, but he had no leverage left. As Smuts told him, a renewal of satyagraha and the strike would only bring a "gratuitous infliction of grave suffering on the innocent" and put the onus of any further violence on Gandhi himself.[54]

So with options and time running out, Gandhi signed an agreement to suspend all passive resistance, pending the outcome of the government commission. Smuts, in turn, promised to introduce legislation to address the Indians' concerns, without promising that it would be passed.

In April 1914 the commission recommended that the £3 tax be abolished and that the marriage rights of Muslims and Hindus be recognized. Both measures passed into law. Nothing, however, was said about interprovince emigration, let alone the hated registration law—the infamous Black Act that had launched Gandhi's original passive resistance campaign seven years earlier. The truth, which most biographers prefer to pass over, was that Gandhi had given up on both points in his negotiations with Smuts in January.[55] Natal and Transvaal activists, including his old ally Haji Ojer Ali, subjected Gandhi to a barrage of criticism, complaining about the yawning gap between what he had promised his followers and what he had delivered. It was criticism he would hear again in India, even from his closest followers.

But the deed was done, and Gandhi's days in South Africa were drawing to a close. Thambai Naidu, Henry Polak, Sonja Schlesin, Joseph Doke, and Gandhi's son Harilal would all remain at Phoenix Farm. He said goodbye to them all. After spending more than twenty years in South Africa, Gandhi would never return. To his mind, he had won the victory he wanted. He had proved that passive resistance worked, at least in forcing a reluctant government to the bargaining table. He had shown that satyagraha could unite Indians into a mass movement, although what happened afterward, including the spread of violence, was outside his control. Finally, he had turned the plight of South Africa's Indians into a major cause in India. But Indians in Natal and the Transvaal knew only too well that Gandhi's campaign had done little to change their situation, even that of the indentured underclass that had so unexpectedly come to his rescue.

For a few days he toured South Africa, welcomed by crowds and speaking of their "victory" (which successive white supremacist governments would steadily whittle away until almost nothing was left). As for Smuts, Gandhi asked Sonja Schlesin and Henry Polak to give the general a pair of sandals he had made in prison, as a gift. Smuts was touched by the gesture. He wore them every year at his farm until 1939, when he returned them to their maker as a tribute on Gandhi's seventieth birthday.

"It was my fate to be the protagonist of a man for whom even then I had the highest respect," Smuts would write many years later.[56] In Smuts's long career, only one other politician would win his admiration more: Winston Churchill. But as Gandhi's ship disappeared over the horizon on July 18, 1914, the general's feelings were less sentimental. "The saint has left our shores," he wrote, "I sincerely hope forever."

Ten days later Austria declared war on Serbia, in retaliation for the assassination of Archduke Franz Ferdinand. The terrible world war that Churchill had predicted and dreaded was about to begin. It would burn away the last certainties of the old post-Victorian order and thrust both Gandhi and Churchill into the political inferno.

Chapter Eleven

A BRIDGEHEAD TOO FAR
1914–1915

Winston was often right, but when he was wrong, well, my God.

F. E. SMITH

GANDHI REACHED ENGLAND ON AUGUST 4, 1914. The last time he was there, the London papers had been full of news of India and assassinations. Now they were full of war. That same day Britain declared war on Germany. Germany had done the same to France the day before, and to Russia before that. Vast national armies were being mobilized, and tens of millions of men were on the move, from the Pyrenees to Bombay. "The wars of peoples will be more terrible than the wars of kings," Churchill had predicted back in 1901. History was about to prove him correct.[1]

Gandhi, now forty-five years old, was no longer the sleek and prosperous Indian lawyer. A photograph shows him looking drawn after the years of inner and outer struggle in South Africa. He had regrown his mustache, but the suit, white collar, and tie that he had once again donned were a concession to the English weather, not emblems of his ambition, as they had been when he first arrived as a student in 1888.

The rough cut of his clothes and the stick in his hand (he suffered from bad pleurisy during his stay) gave him a countrified air, like a farmer on a visit to town. And it was as a farmer that he now saw himself. His Confession of Faith had stated that "the simple peasant life" was the life of true happiness, and that "the rude plough" of his ancestors would cut humanity's path to salvation.[2] His visit to London was supposed to be a brief stopover on the way to India, where he was planning to unleash his program of "soul force" and back-to-the-land moral and spiritual uplift—even though in South Africa it had been only a half-success.

The news of war, however, once again galvanized him into action. Certainly no pacifist ever enjoyed preparing for war more than Gandhi. "London in these days was a sight worth seeing," he remembered ten years later. "There was no panic, but all were busy helping to the best of their ability." English sons, brothers, and husbands were enlisting to fight and training for combat; wives and mothers "employed themselves in cutting and making clothes and dressings for the wounded."[3]

Gandhi asked himself a typical Kiplingesque question: "What is my duty?" His conclusion was that he and other Indians must still serve King and Country. "Am I, doing nothing, to continue enjoying myself, eating my food?" was his refrain to friends and family. For Gandhi, the basis of all community, past and future, was sacrifice, including sacrifice in war. He had written in *Hind Swaraj,* "That nation is great which rests its head upon death as a pillow."[4] Now it was time for Indians to rise to the occasion in true warrior spirit.

Gandhi threw himself into organizing another Indian ambulance corps. Lord Crewe, now secretary of state for India, warmly thanked him for his offer of service. The Indian nationalists at India House, however, were scandalized: how could Gandhi possibly advocate helping their British oppressors?

But Gandhi, as usual, weighed his judgment in moral not political terms. "I felt then that it was more the fault of individual British officials," he wrote later, "than of the British system" that Indians were unhappy within the empire.* He conceded that "we were slaves and they were masters." But was it not "the duty of the slave, seeking to be free, to make his master's need his opportunity" by standing beside him in time of peril? "When thousands have come forward to lay down their lives only because they thought it their duty to do so, how could I sit still?" he told his cousin Maganlal. "A rifle in this hand will never fire. And so there only remained nursing the wounded and I took it up."[5]

The first recruits, fifty or so in number, arrived at Eastcote outside

---

* He even wrote this extraordinary passage as he was leaving South Africa: "Though empires have gone and fallen, this Empire may perhaps be an exception...it is an Empire founded not on material but spiritual foundations...the British constitution. Tear away those ideals and you tear away my loyalty to the British constitution; keep those ideals and I am ever a bondsman." In August 1914, despite his *Hind Swaraj* manifesto, the bondsman in Gandhi was still strong.

London on October 2, 1914. Gandhi served them fruit and nut meals, and they met their commanding officer, Lieutenant Colonel Richard Baker, formerly of the Indian Army Medical Service. Already 28,500 Indian Army troops from the Lahore and Meerut divisions, including the Secunderabad Cavalry Brigade, had arrived at Marseilles, headed for the Western front. Gandhi and Baker needed to get the volunteers ready to join them. Some tension arose between Baker and Gandhi over the appointment of noncommissioned officers. Finally Lord Crewe had to remind Gandhi that he was in the army now and thus subject to military discipline.[6]

At the end of October Indian troops were involved in fierce fighting near La Bassée in France, then at Ypres. One of their number, a soldier from the Duke of Connaught's regiment, had already won India's first posthumous Victoria Cross. "What an army!" the American correspondent from the *New York World* enthused, noting that these troops represented "a civilization that was old when Germany was a forest and early Britons stained their naked bodies blue."[7] Gandhi's ambulance men were shipped off to help. The Prince Aga Khan appeared to see the volunteers off. The prince said he envied them and would try to join them later as an interpreter. Gandhi offered to have the entire senior class from his Phoenix Farm School in South Africa come to London to lead the next batch.*

Gandhi wanted to stay longer in London, raising recruits and exhorting Indians to join the cause, but the cold, damp weather had brought on his pleurisy. It must have made Kasturbai miserable as well. Finally a friend from the India Office advised him to go to India to recover. Gandhi embarked on November 18, 1914, after a warm farewell reception at the Westminster Palace Hotel, attended by Indian and English friends. He was in poor health but still full of fire for the "war for civilization," as some would soon term the cataclysm to come. Leaving seemed anti-climactic. On board the SS *Arabia* he plaintively asked a friend: "Having reached [India] what shall I do with myself?"[8]

When he reached India he would continue his war work, in spite of other distractions. It was those distractions, however, that would sweep him to the top of the Indian nationalist movement.

---

* The offer was declined.

* * *

The coming of war had given Winston Churchill the same boost of excitement. The day war was declared, David Lloyd George remembered the First Lord of the Admiralty coming into a cabinet meeting. "Winston dashed into the room radiant," he said, "his face bright, his manner keen...You could see he was really a happy man." As Winston confessed to Clementine, "Is it not horrible to be built like this?"[9]

The apologetic tone was a pretense. In fact, this was the moment he had dreamed of all his life, to lead a great fighting force into battle. Replacing the toy soldiers spread out on the floor of his nursery were the battleships of the Royal Navy, the most sophisticated machines of war ever built, which he watched lined up "squadron by squadron," as they left Portland for Scapa Flow in Scotland just days before war began. "Scores of gigantic castles of steel," he wrote, "wending their way across the misty, shining sea, like giants bowed in anxious thought."[10]

Actually the ships were headed away from battle and away from Europe. Almost from the day he arrived at the Admiralty, Churchill had realized that the navy could not win a war with Germany, only prevent defeat. Everyone assumed the decisive clash would come on land, and in August 1914 Churchill assumed, like everyone else, that that meant in France. The Germans assumed the same thing. At war's outbreak their so-called Schlieffen Plan sent German armies on a massive swing through neutral Belgium, followed by a great wheeling movement south to encircle Paris and entrap the French army. The plan nearly worked. French troops were sent reeling back toward the capital before a single British soldier set foot on French soil. For a crucial week or two it seemed that the British Expeditionary Force might arrive too late to halt German victory, just as the German generals had planned.

But then the German attack ran out of steam. Churchill had predicted this might happen in a memorandum written three years earlier.[11] The French were able to rally at the first Battle of the Marne on September 5. Soldiers from the British Expeditionary Force, which had begun disembarking on French soil on August 15, moved in to fill the gap between the two retreating French armies. The Germans fell back, and on September 14 they halted at the Aisne River, to dig trenches and set up machine guns. A few miles to the west the Allies did the same.

The First World War of stationary trenches, barbed wire, and massive bombardments was about to begin.

Churchill's prediction thirteen years earlier that "the wars of peoples will be more terrible than the wars of kings" would be played out on a scale that few politicians except Churchill could have imagined. For the next four years the Western Front would be the graveyard for millions of British, French, and German soldiers, even as every country from the Urals to the Pyrenees geared up its economy and society to feed the monstrous killing machine.

Few greeted this prospect with any sense of adventure. Churchill was an exception. Apart from Secretary of State for War Lord Kitchener, Churchill was the only member of the War Cabinet to have seen any military action. "Much as war attracts and fascinates my mind," he wrote to Clementine in 1909, "I feel more deeply every year ... what vile and wicked folly and barbarism it all is." Yet despite its horrors, the experience of mobilizing every resource in society for a single purpose aroused the happy warrior in Churchill, much as it did Gandhi during his months in London after the war began.

After a conversation with Churchill, Margot Asquith remarked, "What a strange being! He really likes war."[12] Churchill had to agree. "I think a curse should rest on me because I am so happy," he confessed the following spring, when the British and French armies were making fruitless attacks on the Western Front and the Germans were deploying poison gas for the first time. "I know the war is smashing and shattering the lives of thousands every moment and yet—I cannot help it—I enjoy every second of it."[13]

In September 1914, however, hopes for a decisive breakthrough were still strong. Each side was scrambling to establish a defensive line that eventually ran from the Swiss border to the Channel. But the "race to the sea" had left some important gaps, including south of the Belgian port of Antwerp, which was about to be besieged by a large German army. If Antwerp held, the British and French armies would have time to close the gap. If not, German forces would be poised on their flanks like a deadly sword of Damocles.

From the Admiralty building, Churchill immediately grasped the seriousness of the situation. He fired off a frantic telegram to Prime Minister Asquith, "WE MUST HOLD ANTWERP." The French commander in chief refused to help, as did Lord Kitchener. So Churchill ordered a brigade of Royal Marines and two brigades of scratch naval volunteers across the Channel.* Then for good measure he set off to take command himself.

The three thousand Marines arrived on September 28, 1914, to the ecstatic cheers of the Belgian citizens. "You needn't worry," Churchill told the astonished Antwerp mayor. "We are going to save the city." Winston was everywhere, supervising the construction of defensive works, rounding up workmen and combat teams, scrounging for guns and ammunition, and even siting artillery pieces as the German bombardment got under way. It was the Siege of Sidney Street all over again. This time, however, the lives of thousands, and the course of the war, hung in the balance.

The London correspondent of an Italian newspaper caught sight of him during the bombardment, "enveloped in a cloak and wearing a yachting cap." Churchill "was tranquilly smoking a large cigar and watching the progress of the battle under a rain of shrapnel which I can only call fearful." The reporter mused, "It is not easy to find in all Europe a Minister who would be capable of smoking peacefully under that shell-fire" or coolly planning his counterattack while shells shook the roof over his head and blew out the windows.[14]

As the Germans approached the city, Churchill sent another cable to Asquith. He begged to be allowed to resign from the Cabinet and to be given formal command of the defense of Antwerp. Asquith was as much amused as surprised. When he read the telegram aloud to the other assembled members, the table rocked with laughter.[15] They all looked at one another and shook their heads. What was Winston thinking? But others, especially at the Admiralty, were not amused. They were furious at the First Lord for deserting his official post, arguably the most important in Britain, and for leading the Royal Marines to a foreordained defeat. "It is a tragedy that the Navy should be in such lunatic hands at this time," one officer complained.[16]

Relief for Antwerp proved impossible to provide. Churchill and his men were ordered to return to Dover, and on October 10 the city capitulated, even as the relentless German attack pounded it to ruins. "What a crime!" wrote one eyewitness, the poet Rupert Brooke.† Nearly 2,500

---

* One of the volunteers' officers was Winston's legal father-in-law, George Cornwallis-West. The volunteers also included Brooke and the prime minister's son Arthur.

† Later Brooke would be the most famous fatality of another botched Churchill operation, at Gallipoli.

British Marines and naval volunteers were either taken prisoner or interned, and more than 20,000 Belgians. "Poor Winston is very depressed," Asquith said when Churchill came back. "He feels his mission was in vain."[17]

Many agreed. Newspapers angrily denounced the Antwerp operation as reckless and unnecessary. Even the *Morning Post,* which had carried his dispatches from South Africa, turned against him, calling the First Lord of the Admiralty an "erratic amateur." But the defense of Antwerp had accomplished more than appeared at first glance. Winston had delayed the German advance just long enough for the French to move northward to plug the gap. "Ten days were needed," Churchill would dramatically write later, "and ten days were found."[18]

Others, however, saw in the Antwerp affair a forty-year-old-man with great responsibilities acting impulsively—"like a romantic child," as his friend Violet Asquith admitted—without a single thought about the consequences. Asquith told his wife that the rash adventure made Winston "by far the most disliked man in my Cabinet." Even Lloyd George had to shrug his shoulders in vexation over his friend's impulsiveness. "Winston is like a torpedo," he confessed. "The first you hear of his doings is when you hear the swish of the torpedo dashing through the water."[19]

The Conservative leader Andrew Bonar Law was deeply disturbed by the Antwerp fiasco. "I think [Winston] has very unusual intellectual abilities," he wrote to a fellow Tory MP, "but at the same time he seems to have an entirely unbalanced mind, which is a real danger at a time like this."[20]

Just how dangerous, they were about to find out.

Churchill returned to his duties at the Admiralty and the War Cabinet, but he found little room for the kind of action he craved and few important decisions to make. Nothing decisive was stirring at sea;* not much more on land. As the fighting bogged down in the trenches that winter and British casualties approached the 100,000 mark, Churchill and others wondered if this war was going to be won in France after all.

Winston, back to his usual manic self, fired off ideas and opinions

---

* The challenge of U-boat warfare had not yet begun, despite the sinking of *Cressy, Aboukir,* and *Hogue* by U 23 in August 1914.

with dizzying speed. For example, the prime minister wrote on December 30, 1914, that Churchill had approached him with an idea for equipping soldiers for the next offensive with "armed rollers to crush down barbed wire, bullet proofed shields, and armor," a notion that seemed to Asquith quaintly but pointlessly medieval. Later Winston would take up the idea again with his armored motorized "tank." But for now both he and Maurice Hankey made it clear to the prime minister that something different was needed to break the stalemate in the West. Winston wanted the move to be made "primarily, of course, by means of his Navy," but the Allies needed a way to bypass the dead end in France.[21]

Churchill and Kitchener took turns pondering the map. Perhaps Eastern Europe, they thought, offered a way to get around the German flank. In January 1915 the Russian Grand Duke Nicholas, who was hard-pressed on his front, appealed to them for help. Where could Britain deliver a decisive stroke and possibly join up with her Russian allies? Then one day as he and Kitchener talked and plotted, Churchill's finger slowly traveled down the map—until it stopped at the Dardanelles.

The Dardanelles Straits were the western gateway to Constantinople, capital of the Ottoman or Turkish Empire. They form a narrow passage between the Mediterranean and the landlocked Sea of Marmara, which opens through the Bosporus onto the Black Sea. Since the time of Xerxes and Alexander, these waters had drawn empire-builders from East and West: no less than fifteen decisive battles had been fought nearby.[22] Now there would be another.

For the Dardanelles were hostile territory. Before general hostilities broke out, the Turkish sultan had struck a secret deal with the Germans; the German cruisers *Goeben* and *Breslau* had found shelter from the British navy in Constantinople's harbor. Over the autumn the Turks' ramshackle empire, stretching from the European shore of the Dardanelles through Turkey and Syria and across Mesopotamia to Baghdad, had slowly and painfully mobilized for war. The sultan's armies had launched a disastrous offensive against the British in Egypt through Sinai and another, more successful one against the Russians in the Caucasus. It was that attack that had prompted the plea for help from the Russian commander in chief.

Yet, in the early autumn of 1914 the war in the Middle East had seemed a sideshow, compared to the vital stakes on the Western Front.

And Britain had other reasons for not stirring up the hornets' nest of Turkish politics. Sultan Mehmet V was also caliph or defender of the shrines sacred to Muslims around the world, including Jerusalem, Mecca, and Medina. Millions of Muslims in India considered the sultan caliph (in Urdu, *khalifa*) and nothing less than their spiritual leader. Officials in the India Office worried about where the loyalty of India's Muslims might lie, should the Allies attack the Turks.

Thus, the British tried to avoid any provocation of Indian Muslim feeling. Winston Churchill was told to put off any attack on the *Goeben* and *Breslau* in Constantinople's harbor, for fear that it might trigger trouble.[23] Then in November 1914 the sultan supplemented his declaration of war against the Allies with a declaration of jihad, calling for all Muslims in the British, Russian, and French empires to rise up against their colonial masters.

To the Allied officials' relief, the response across India was minimal. Even in the heavily Muslim Northwest Frontier, the most volatile region of all, where rumors flew over the mountain tops that the German Kaiser had cemented his alliance with the sultan by converting to Islam, things remained quiet. However, there were some flare-ups among Muslim troops in the Indian Army, and soldiers in the Fifth Indian Light Infantry in Singapore besieged their officers in their bungalows and released German internees from prison (who immediately turned around to help suppress the revolt). For several days Singapore lay defenseless. When the mutiny was over, more than forty whites were dead and thirty-six mutineers had been executed. To many at the time, it had looked like Cawnpore all over again.[24] So fears of provoking another Great Mutiny, a remote possibility but still a vivid one,* stayed the British hand when it came to dealing with the Turks.

But as the Western Front bogged down in stalemate, those considerations paled as the British considered using the Dardanelles to stage an end run around the Germans and Austrians, thereby protecting the British Empire's eastern flank. The original idea was certainly not Churchill's—it probably was Kitchener's. It was not even Churchill's first choice as a diversion. His, and First Sea Lord Admiral Jack Fisher's, preference was always for using the navy to cross the Baltic and then land troops in Pomerania, within striking distance of Berlin. The French, however, had earlier proposed a Dardanelles attack. The Admiralty had

---

* Lord Roberts, who had fought in the Mutiny, was still alive until November 14, 1914.

planned for something like it for years.[25] On November 3, after the Turks declared war, Churchill even ordered the navy to bombard the forts guarding the entrance to the Dardanelles, leaving open the option of future operations there. The attack only induced the Turks to reinforce the forts, thus ensuring that any future Allied attack would be more difficult, not less.

But the other members of the British Cabinet's War Council did not know that. At their very first meeting on November 25, the idea of an attack on the Dardanelles began to take shape.[26] By the New Year, it had become Churchill's new obsession. On January 3, 1915, he telegraphed Vice Admiral Sackville Carden, who commanded the fleet in the eastern Mediterranean: "Do you consider the forcing of the Dardanelles by ships alone a practicable operation?"

He was somewhat surprised and perplexed when Carden said no. Carden thought it would require a much larger naval force than he had, as well as a considerable number of troops. On January 21 First Sea Lord Fisher weighed in, saying, "I just abominate the Dardanelles operation, unless a great change is made." The change would be the addition of 200,000 troops in order to conduct landings in support of the fleet.[27]

But Churchill believed the Dardanelles could still be "rushed" by a handful of ships, in the kind of bold strike typical of the Royal Navy. Besides, his growing eagerness for an attack was contagious. On January 13 the War Council set up a subcommittee to study the problem. On the twenty-eighth, Winston reported that the Admiralty, the French, and the Russians had signed on "with enthusiasm."[28] In the end the War Council gave its go-ahead, but with two stipulations. The first was that the expedition had to include an army large enough to land on the narrow Gallipoli peninsula that jutted into the Dardanelles and defeat the Turkish garrison there. The second was that Churchill had to send a force of battleships to start the proceedings with a large naval bombardment.

Thus it was the War Council, including Kitchener, that put together the Dardanelles operation in all its detail and complexity, and hardly Churchill alone.[29] The others had come to see it as he did, as more than just a diversion or an effort to join up with the Russians. They convinced themselves that success in the Dardanelles would bring Greece, Bulgaria, and even Romania into the Allied camp. Kitchener said "the Turkish Army would evacuate Europe altogether." Churchill went further. "A soon as the Dardanelles are open," he enthusiastically predicted on February 23, British forces would be able to occupy Constantinople and "compel the surrender of any Turkish forces in Europe." Its effect on the whole of the Balkans, even perhaps on the war itself, would be "decisive."[30]

A Foreign Office civil servant, Mark Sykes, built an even more elaborate geopolitical castle in the air. On April Fool's Day 1915 he penned a memo predicting that the Dardanelles operation would mean the end of the Ottoman Empire. "Turkey must cease to be," he wrote. "Smyrna shall be Greek...North Syria French, Filistin [Palestine] British, Mesopotamia British and everything else Russian—including Constantinople." It was a wild, outrageous vision that, except for the prediction about the Russians, all came true after the war was over.* In fact, the entire shape of the modern Near East suddenly appeared on the horizon, thanks to Churchill's Dardanelles gambit.[31]

For in the end it was Churchill's gambit. He recognized as much in his own account, published after the war in *The World Crisis*. And the War Council had signed on because they believed Churchill when he said his admirals, as the professional experts, had signed on. What they did not know was that those admirals had far more doubts than they dared to tell Churchill. His keen enthusiasm for the Gallipoli invasion, his swift and fluent reply to any objections or hesitations, had made them reluctant to say what they really thought.[32] That was why Churchill would be surprised and angered when Fisher told him later that he had opposed the plan from the beginning, and why the firestorm of criticism that fell on his head seemed such a betrayal.

This scene would be repeated again and again in Churchill's life, notably in the Second World War and on India. It revealed his crucial weakness as a leader. Churchill always interpreted a lack of objections, whether by admirals or by cabinet members or by the British public, as the equivalent of wholehearted support. He read dissenters' inability to state a contrary conviction as a lack of conviction itself. As he grew older and more self-assured, and as his decisions carried even more weight, Churchill's passion and eloquence in fact became handicaps. They made him deaf and blind to those who were never quite as sure, never quite as optimistic or as staunchly committed on anything, as he was on virtually everything.

The truth was the admirals, including Carden, did not believe the

---

* The Greeks occupied Smyrna briefly after the war, although the Turks forced them to evacuate in 1922. One of the refugees driven out by the Turkish reoccupation was the young Aristotle Onassis.

plan would work. They feared what finally did happen: that the Turks and their canny German advisers would grasp the British plan and use all their resources to turn the narrow strait into a death trap. And in retrospect, it did seem a madcap scheme.

Except for the fact that it almost worked.

On March 18, 1915, Admiral John de Robeck* sailed into the entrance of the Dardanelles with sixteen battleships—twelve British and four French—and a swarm of destroyers, minesweepers, and cruisers, including the new battlecruiser *Inflexible*. It was the biggest naval force ever seen in the eastern Mediterranean. For a time it seemed they might actually force the Dardanelles alone, as Churchill's original plan had suggested. But then the French battleship *Bouvet* and the British *Ocean* and *Irresistible* struck mines that the Turks had laid in the passage, and sank. Furious gunfire from the forts on shore badly damaged the *Suffren* and *Inflexible*. Before long a third of de Robeck's battle fleet was out of action. Under cover of darkness, he withdrew to regroup and refit.

Still, as documents would later show, the weight and power of de Robeck's naval advance had convinced the Turks that they had lost the battle. Orders had gone out to fire off all remaining ammunition (which the Allies mistook for a show of strength) and to abandon all positions the next day. Parties of Marines could have landed freely on beaches that in little more than five weeks would become death traps for entire divisions. If de Robeck had managed to stay in the strait another twenty-four hours, in the judgment of at least one historian, "the fleet could have sailed into Constantinople without opposition."[33] And instead of being Britain's greatest scapegoat in the Great War, Churchill would have been its greatest hero.

But de Robeck did not stay. Instead, he was joined by the army's commander, Sir Ian Hamilton, who ordered the entire expedition back to Alexandria to repack its supply ships and transports. Hamilton, a veteran of the Boer War, had seen the costs of ill-preparation with nonessential supplies stowed on the top and essential ones at the bottom, and he would not allow it to happen on his watch, especially with five infantry divisions under his responsibility.

Unfortunately, what was prudent in 1900 turned out to be foolhardy in 1915. Hamilton wasted an entire month repacking every ship and

---

* The strain of carrying out a plan in which he did not believe forced Carden on the sick list on March 16. He was replaced by his second in command, de Robeck.

making sure everything was safely stowed and secured. All the while the Turks and their German allies poured concrete, strung barbed wire, laid mines, and rebuilt the forts overlooking the narrows and Cape Helles, where they knew the attack would come.

Finally, at dawn on April 25, 1915, soldiers from the Third Australian Brigade of the Australian and New Zealand Army Corps (ANZAC) looked out from their transports through the fading mist and saw the narrow yellow strips of beach on either side of Cape Helles and the headlands towering above. These men were volunteers, sons of the Empire coming to the aid of their mother country, much like Gandhi's Indian volunteers. "To be a New Zealander in 1914 was to be taught that 'The Empire looks to you to be ready in time of need,' " one of them said later. "To be left behind was unthinkable."[34] Their job was to land on the beach at Kaba Tepe and get as far up the bluffs as possible before digging in, despite what promised to be devastating Turkish shelling.

Their British counterparts in the Twenty-ninth Division faced the same daunting challenge. They were battalions from the Lancashire Fusiliers, the Hampshires, and the Munsters, as well as the Dublin Fusiliers—by sheer coincidence, the very same regiment that had been with Churchill on the armored train at Estcourt in the Boer War. These men were to land on the beaches at the tip of Cape Helles, almost directly under the Turkish forts.

Watching it all from the deck of de Robeck's flagship, H.M.S. *Queen Elizabeth,* was Winston's brother Jack, who was attached as a major to Ian Hamilton's staff. Jack had already seen action in France at Ypres. He knew what machine guns and artillery could do to exposed human flesh and how they gave an almost insuperable advantage to defenders in fortified positions like the ones the Turks occupied. But even he would be amazed and then appalled at what was about to unfold that April morning.

The ANZAC landing went badly almost from the start, and soon the Australians and New Zealanders were stuck on the hillside under murderous fire. The Lancashires suffered worse. Their boats became entangled in masses of barbed wire as they landed, while Turkish soldiers opened up from trenches strung out along the beach. "The sea behind was absolutely crimson," one officer, Major Frederick Shaw, remembered, "and you could hear the groans through the rattle of musketry." Shaw tried to order his men to move forward: "I then perceived they were all hit."[35]

More troops landed but could make no headway. The Turks, on the other hand, were not strong enough to drive them back into the sea. For British soldiers, the beach had become a "death trap." Jack Churchill described to his brother how "the Turks dug a series of great caves and from there could shoot anyone on the beach, while guns could not touch them. Forty hundred and fifty four men have already been buried there!"[36]

By May 4, nine days later, more than 10,000 ANZAC troops and 14,000 Turkish troops had been killed or wounded with little or no result. The British assaults had made slightly more gains at a slightly lower cost. The shape of things to come was clear: there would be no breakthrough. The next day Jack Churchill gave his candid assessment of the situation. After four days of almost continuous fighting, he wrote the British troops were holding on, but "we are not very happy about the larger side of the question. Here we are, a comparatively small force clinging on to the end of the Gallipoli peninsula, and having the prospect of fighting the entire Turkish Empire!" Jack did his own tour of the battlefield and was shocked at the filth and carnage. From the side of one hastily dug trench he saw the withered hand of a dead soldier sticking out in a grisly gesture.[37]

Before the month was out Hamilton had lost more than 45,000 men. Instead of providing the Allies a way of escaping the quagmire in the West, Gallipoli had become one itself. By then everyone in the British government realized the Dardanelles campaign had gone hopelessly wrong, and everyone wanted a scapegoat. Every finger would point in the same direction: at the First Lord of the Admiralty, Winston Churchill.

In one sense, blaming Churchill for the fiasco was unfair. It was Kitchener, not Churchill, who had first broached the plan. The entire War Council, including the prime minister, had endorsed the final version and had saddled it with conditions and delays that almost certainly doomed any chance of success.

Yet as Churchill would learn, the power to make great decisions came with equally great responsibility and accountability. He had set out to take the credit if the Gallipoli plan succeeded. Now that it had failed, he could only expect to take the blame.

First Sea Lord Fisher had been his mentor and confidant in naval matters for four years. Now Fisher was the first to turn on him, churning out a bitter memorandum stating that he had thought the Dardanelles diversion was doomed from the start. Fisher resigned as First Sea Lord, hoping this action would prompt Prime Minister Asquith to dismiss Churchill as well. Asquith, however, hesitated, and Churchill might still have kept his office except for another, unrelated event.

In May Asquith agreed to form a coalition National Government with the Tories. They had drawn their sights on Churchill for nearly a decade. The bitterness aroused by his earlier attacks and criticism, not to mention his change of party, had not abated. The failure of the Gallipoli operation gave them an opportunity for revenge that was too delicious to pass up. So it was the Conservatives who finally forced Asquith's hand and made Winston resign from the Admiralty.

He was heartbroken. On May 20 a friend, George Riddell, visited him at his office and found him in a black mood. "I am victim of a political intrigue. I am finished!" Riddell tried to reassure him that he would bounce back. But Winston shook his head. "Yes, finished in respect of all I care for" was his bitter response. "The waging of war; the defeat of the Germans.... This is what I live for."

It was his first experience of true, abject failure in the eyes of his public and himself. Clementine said later she worried he might die of grief. His old friend Violet Asquith, the prime minister's daughter, met him in the House of Commons, "silent, despairing—as I have never seen him." She wept as he brokenly described how he had thought her father might have stuck by him but his head was part of the price of the coalition. "He did not even abuse Fisher," she would write years later, "but simply said, 'I'm finished.' I poured out contradictions, protestations—but he waved them aside. 'No, I'm done.' "[38]

In fact, his career was hardly done. He still had a seat on the War Council, as Chancellor of the Duchy of Lancaster, the sinecure office that Asquith offered him as consolation for losing the Admiralty. And he still believed the Dardanelles campaign could succeed. On June 18 he wrote another hopeful memo. "There can be no doubt that we now possess the means and the power to take Constantinople before the end of the summer," it read. One final great push would do the job; it would save the situation in Russia and Italy "and resound throughout Asia."[39] The government did approve one more landing at Gallipoli, north of Kaba Tepe at Suvla Bay, on August 4. But the new Turkish commander, Mustapha Kemal,* succeeded in blunting the attack, and soon Suvla

---

* Later this brilliant officer would change his name to Kemal Ataturk and become the father of modern Turkey. He would earn the undying enmity of India's Muslims by abolishing the Caliphate in 1924.

Bay became another precarious salient, along with Cape Helles and Anzac Cove, where hundreds of men died daily from Turkish snipers and fever.

Not for another five more months would the Allies decide to cut their losses and evacuate from Gallipoli. By then the coalition government had reorganized the War Council and pointedly left Winston out. On November 11, 1915, Winston formally resigned. He was going to France to serve with the Grenadier Guards. "I have a clear conscience," he wrote to Asquith, "which enables me to bear my responsibility for past events with composure."[40]

That was probably true. But when he reached France in his Guards uniform everyone from his commanding officer (the last survivor from the officers of the original battalion in 1914), to the lowest private gave him the cold shoulder. The reinforcements they needed had been sent to Gallipoli instead, and they knew who was to blame. He arrived at the front in a freezing drizzle on the night of November 20. On his first night the only sleeping quarters he was offered were either an eight-foot square signal office shared with four other men, or a nearby dugout, which he described as "a sort of pit four feet deep containing about one foot of water." It was ten days from his forty-first birthday. A few days later a letter from Clementine informed him that the army was evacuating Gallipoli.[41]

By the second week of January 1916 the beaches at Suvla, Anzac Cove, and Cape Helles were deserted. The sands had been soaked with the blood of more than 265,000 Australians, New Zealanders, Irishmen, Indians, Englishmen, and Frenchmen. (Turkish losses had been higher, close to 300,000.)[42] The battle would leave an indelible impression on the Australian collective memory. The first day of landing, April 25, would forever be a national day of remembrance, and Churchill's name a national curse. For the rest of his life Winston would relentlessly try to justify his decision to attack. He refused point-blank to accept the conclusion by Parliament's own investigative commission that it had been a horrible mistake. "Not to persevere," he would respond, "that was the crime."[43]

Still, the experience had changed him physically, if not in spirit. As photographs show, the eager round-faced cherubic Winston was gone forever. His face was heavier and ruddier, his eyes puffier and sadder. His sandy red hair had almost thinned away. The world-famous face of Winston Churchill appears in the camera lens with qualities that also appear in Gandhi's, at almost the same time.

Both faces were shaped by the experience of, and struggle with, great failure—already more failure, perhaps, than most human beings could have borne. At the close of 1915 Gandhi was forty-six, Churchill forty-one. By now both knew the pain of propelling human beings needlessly to their deaths; in one case for the sake of satyagraha, in the other, for the sake of Empire. It was a burden both would have to carry again before long.

For even as it brought disaster to Churchill, Gallipoli had sounded the death knell of the Turkish Empire. Soon a British-backed Arab revolt would sweep across the Arabian peninsula; the Indian Army would occupy Basra in Mesopotamia. The map of the Middle East predicted in Mark Sykes's rash April Fool's Day memo was about to take shape. And Churchill's madcap scheme had set off a revolution not only in the Middle East but also in India. Indeed, he had inadvertently given Gandhi's political career there a new and decisive boost.

Chapter Twelve

GANDHI'S WAR
1915–1918

You cannot teach non-violence to a man who cannot kill.

MOHANDAS K. GANDHI, 1918

ON JANUARY 9, 1915, WHILE WINSTON Churchill was dreaming of battle-ships steaming up the Dardanelles, Gandhi landed back in India. He had spent almost three-quarters of his life since 1888 outside his mother country, including two decades in South Africa. Except for a short trip to England in 1931, Gandhi would never again leave India. The years of wandering were over. He had returned home.

Gandhi had undergone a major spiritual transformation in the past decade and a half. He had found his life mission, as stated in *Hind Swaraj*: to transform the character of his fellow Indians by bringing them closer to God. By so doing, he intended to undercut the founda-tions of British rule in India and set his people free.

He also believed he had found the tool to achieve both these mam-moth tasks: active nonviolence, or satyagraha. The satyagraha cam-paigns in South Africa, and the government's final capitulation in 1914, had convinced him that through nonviolent mass resistance, the moral or "soul force" inherent in Indian civilization could prevail over the ma-terial force of British civilization. "India is fitted for the religious su-premacy of the world," he told an audience in Indore in 1918, "[and] can conquer all by soul force."[1]

The South African campaigns had made him famous in India. In 1911, when Natal and Transvaal Indians were debating whether Gandhi was a blessing or a curse, India's National Congress seriously considered making him their president.[2] His homecoming in January 1915 was triumphant, almost rapturous. He disembarked in Bombay at the famous Apollo Bunder quay, normally reserved for viceroys and royalty. For the next four months he traversed the country on a speaking tour. Leading Indian intellectuals and politicians hailed him as a conquering hero. Students in Madras pulled his carriage through the streets. Even Viceroy Lord Hardinge publicly thanked him for lightening the legal burden on Indian immigrants in South Africa. Shortly afterward the Nobel Prize–winning poet and philosopher Rabindranath Tagore gave Gandhi the title he would carry forever: that of Mahatma, or "great soul."[3]

Still, Indians were far from ready to follow Gandhi's leadership, especially in politics. Educated Indians knew what Gandhi had done in South Africa, but they had little clue as to how he had done it—satyagraha as an idea and movement meant nothing to them. *Hind Swaraj* had been banned almost immediately after its publication in India and had made little impact.[4] Far from being able to build on his efforts in South Africa, Gandhi had to start over virtually from scratch. His mentor G. K. Gokhale advised him to take a year off to tour the country, to listen and learn. Following Gokhale's suggestion, Gandhi vowed not to get involved in public affairs until he had educated himself about the new Indian scene and the personalities and forces shaping it.

For India was also changing. The subcontinent was entering the modern world. The grip of the past was still firm, especially for the vast rural majority, but new trends and directions had emerged. Gandhi the traditionalist and author of *Hind Swaraj* might deplore them, but Gandhi the aspiring leader could not afford to ignore them.

In 1915 the railroads, which Gandhi in his manifesto had so vociferously condemned, now crisscrossed the country like a great enclosing net. They had become essential to India's economic life as well as to its sense of physical unity. From rice and cotton to British-made industrial goods, freight shipments by rail had almost doubled to more than 80 million tons since his stay fourteen years earlier.[5] Taking a train, like sending a telegram—both exotic rarities in Gandhi's boyhood—had become part of normal everyday life even for poor Indians.

The new mobility allowed almost ten percent of India's population to live and work in towns. Cities like Calcutta (now India's largest city, with a population numbering more than a million), Bombay, Madras, and Ahmedabad had growing industrial centers; smokestacks rose up above the jute and cotton fields and rice paddies. These coal mines, steel mills (the first opened in 1914), and textile factories were not the fruits of colonialism. They were opened and operated by Indians themselves and were becoming as much a part of the scene as temples, maharajas' palaces, and the rural villages inhabited by what Lord Curzon had called India's "voiceless millions." In 1914 India was the eighth largest manufacturing country in the world.[6] No amount of excoriation or execration was going to make the factories, or India's rapidly growing industrial working class, go away.

In addition, a growing profusion of schools and universities had expanded India's educated class, although it still constituted a tiny fraction of India's 280 million people. Nonetheless, in 1915 there were nearly fifteen hundred newspapers in India, reaching perhaps two million readers.[7] Despite the Raj's strict press censorship laws, a vigorous independent Indian public opinion was taking shape and being heard in a variety of languages, including English.

The new media were the sounding board of Indian politics. Indian public opinion had made itself felt in the struggle over the partition of Bengal. It had spoken out on the plight of Indian immigrants in South Africa. Now it would have to take stock of the strange-looking middle-aged man in traditional clothes, whose place in the new India was not very clear, least of all to himself.

India's first impressions of Gandhi were not encouraging. "Queer food he eats," wrote one observer, "only fruit and nuts." The man also noted Gandhi's lack of western clothes: "He had a big sandal mark on his forehead and a *kunkum* dot besides."[8] A correspondent from the *Madras Mail* was stunned when Gandhi told him that "once people make themselves fit by their character and capacity, the grant of privileges [from the British] will follow as a matter of course—in fact there will be no need for people to ask for concessions."[9] Gandhi's vision of India gaining her spiritual independence one person at a time, before political independence, hardly fit the standard agenda of Indian nationalist politics. And that politics meant, above all, the politics of the Indian National Congress.

For the better part of two decades that organization had been dominated by twin competing giants, Gopal Krishna Gokhale and Bal Gangadhar Tilak. Although both men were Chitpavan Brahmins, they were a study in contrasts. Both would influence Gandhi in strikingly different ways. Tilak was tough and acerbic, with a shaven head and bristling mustache, that symbol of masculine virility for traditional Hindus. He championed a militant version of Home Rule for India that looked back to the glory days of the Aryans and Hindu Mahratta princes—even to the Mutiny. Tilak refused to condemn terrorist groups like Abhinav Bharat and even praised their motives. They in turn saw him as their chief inspiration. (It was Tilak's recommendation that had sent his fellow Chitpavan Vinayak Savarkar to England.)[10] Those terrorist links finally led to Tilak's expulsion from the Congress in 1907 and landed him in prison in distant Mandalay the following year, from which he was finally released the year before Gandhi arrived home.

Tilak's downfall left Gokhale and his Bombay associate Pherozeshah Mehta the uncrowned kings of Indian politics. As befitted the leader of the Congress's self-proclaimed Moderates, Gokhale was placid, soft-spoken, and self-effacing, dressed in a Western suit and tie. In contrast to Tilak's Extremists, Gokhale wanted India to gain self-rule in partnership with Britain, along with modern British ideas and institutions. Even as Tilak was going to prison, Gokhale declared, "I want India to take her proper place among the great nations of the world...within the Empire."[11]

For the Raj too had changed with the times. In 1911 Churchill's colleague and Secretary of State for India John Morley decided to reverse the partition of Bengal, thus bringing to an end one of the most contentious issues between Indians and the British government. Two years earlier the Liberal government and Viceroy Lord Minto had permitted the first election of Indian members to provincial councils and the Imperial Legislative Council. The council itself grew from twenty-five to sixty members, with just under half accountable to an Indian electorate.[12] The Morley-Minto reforms, as they were called, included a labyrinth of electoral colleges and indirect voting bodies, to prevent radical nationalists from taking over. But they were the Raj's first real concession to Indian participation in their own governance and helped to deflect nationalist resentment for almost a decade.

Indeed, after the stormy years of partition and terrorism, things seemed to be calming down in India. December 1911 saw another magnificent durbar, presided over in person by the new King-Emperor George V, as well as the new viceroy, Lord Hardinge. There the king announced both the reunification of Bengal and the shift of the capital of the Raj from Calcutta to Delhi, the traditional capital of the Mughals. The move was immediately popular across India (except in Bengal). But to other Indians, "the view that Britain was moving to the heart of

India," as one distinguished historian has explained, "could be read to portend the taking over of the new regime by India."[13]

Only one ominous ripple disturbed the calm. A year after the great durbar, Viceroy Hardinge was making a formal state entry by elephant into Delhi when a Hindu terrorist suddenly threw a bomb into his palanquin. Hardinge suffered a severe back injury, while one of his assistants died in the blast. The police frantically combed the area looking for the killer but never found him. But they did find leaflets scattered on the ground and among the crowd, calling on Hindus and Muslims alike "to kill all the enemies of Motherland, irrespective of caste, creed, or color."[14] Hardinge was not the man to make himself an unpopular target. He was a keen Liberal and committed to good relations with Indians. It was Hardinge who had asked Gokhale to go to South Africa to help Gandhi.[15] But the assassination attempt proved that the forces of discontent had not been dissipated, only submerged.

Still, with the Raj turning over a new leaf, and with Tilak in exile and the radicals in jail (where their notorious ringleader, Aurobindo Ghose, underwent a conversion to Hindu spirituality), Gokhale's Moderates held sway in cooperation with the British. The Congress remained an overwhelmingly Hindu organization, largely Brahmin-led. Its annual meetings, where a new president was chosen every year, rarely showed a single lower-caste or Muslim face. In fact, India's Muslims hardly participated in nationalist politics at all. The Muslim League, which was created on the Congress model in 1906, numbered less than a thousand members, out of a total Muslim population of seventy million.[16] When Muslims did participate, they disagreed bitterly among themselves, much as Hindus did. And India's fifty million or so untouchables were complete nonpersons as far as India's nationalist elite were concerned.

Gandhi's outlook was very different. South Africa's white oppression had taught him to think of all Indians—Hindu and Muslim, Brahmin and untouchable, Bengali and Punjabi—as forming a single nation, even a single race.[17] He had worked with them all and appealed to them all in his satyagraha campaigns. The poisonous splits that festered in Indian national politics in 1915 no longer made sense to him. "I do not recall having ever regarded them as anything but my kith and kin," he wrote of the Hindus and Christians, Gujaratis and Tamils, and others who had frequented his law office in Durban.[18] It was this equalitarian spirit, born paradoxically of race consciousness, that he brought back with him from South Africa and that immediately set him apart from "normal" nationalist politicians.

However, this was not the most important difference. In 1915 Indian nationalists accepted that their path to freedom must be a self-consciously modern path. When they spoke of the future, they sounded very much like Gandhi's Reader in *Hind Swaraj*. When, for example, Gokhale declared, "The greatest work of Western education in the present state of India is...the liberation of the Indian mind from the thralldom of old-world ideas and the assimilation of all that is highest and best in the life and thought of the West," he expressed a consensus view among nationalist activists.[19]

Tilak, the Hindu reactionary, was the exception. His antipathy to Western science and schools matched Gandhi's. But Tilak's aggressive embrace of violence and armed struggle made him an unacceptable model for Gandhi, as did Tilak's disdain for Muslims. Gandhi still looked to Gokhale as his political guru. He always found being with the older man "a joy." In a profound sense, he owed his career to him. It was Gokhale's tour of South Africa, at the viceroy's but also Gandhi's request, that revived Gandhi's standing there, and Gokhale who first proposed using the £3 poll tax issue to reach out to indentured laborers.

Likewise, it was at Gokhale's request that Gandhi had stopped in England in 1914 before returning to India. Later Gandhi said, "The place that Gokhale occupied in my heart...was and is unique."[20] Gokhale's quietism, his sense of humanity and proportion, not to mention his British loyalism, had all appealed to his younger disciple—despite their differences over the modern world. But on February 20, 1915, the Grand Old Man of Indian politics died. Gokhale's death created a vacuum in Indian politics and in Gandhi's life. In July Gandhi spoke about him at a political gathering in Poona, Gokhale's hometown. "Whatever [Gokhale] did, he did with a religious zeal," he declared. "That was the secret of his success. He did not wear his religion on his sleeve; he lived it." Gandhi was still spending his year on the political sidelines, as he promised Gokhale he would. But he did not have to be silent. At Poona he quoted Gokhale's words: " 'We lack in India character, we want religious zeal in the political field.' "[21] Gandhi set out to turn what he saw as Gokhale's last wish into reality.

To do so, he set up his base in the village of Kochrab, outside Ahmedabad in the heart of Gujarat, where a barrister friend lent him his summer bungalow. Here in May 1915 Gandhi launched his Indian version of Tolstoy Farm: an experimental community where he could create the future of India, one soul at a time. But an outbreak of plague forced Gandhi to move four miles north to the west bank of the Sabarmati River, where he established his most famous ashram.

Sabarmati Ashram (which remains a living monument to Gandhi to this day) would be the center of his domestic and political life for the next eighteen years. Ironically, the money to pay for it came from Ahmedabad's well-to-do industrialists, whom Gandhi intended to put out of business in his new India. Their factory smokestacks loomed in plain sight over the Sabarmati compound. Gandhi brought along several refugees from the earlier Tolstoy and Phoenix farms, as well as members of his extended family. He had promised his older brothers that he would look after their families when they died. In the end, no fewer than five of his brothers' widows, and their children, were living under his ashram roof, as well as his sons Manilal and Harilal and their wives.[22]

Kasturbai had to bear the brunt of shame and humiliation when Gandhi announced that he was about to make another addition to the Sabarmati family: an untouchable husband and wife. It set off a domestic pitched battle, and Kasturbai threatened to leave home completely.

However, Gandhi's will prevailed. He had deliberately broken the greatest Hindu taboo of all, the prohibition against any contact with *dalits* or untouchables. It was part of his war against the India he detested most: the India hidebound by ceremony and meaningless tradition, split by ancient religious feuds, festering in its own filth; the India without compassion or pity. His stated goal was make India "a holy land, aye, a purified country," which implied that it was currently not.[23] In 1916, the year of Verdun and the Somme, Gandhi had not forgotten the other larger war raging in Europe or India's place in it. But for now the war at home consumed all his attention. His speech at Benares Hindu University on February 6, 1916, was its opening salvo.

Annie Besant, his erstwhile New Age friend from London, had invited him to speak. Now sixty-seven years old, since her arrival in India in 1892 she had made a steady transition from disciple of Madame Blavatsky to uncompromising advocate of Indian Home Rule.* With her short white hair, piercing eyes, and mellifluous voice ("the most

---

* She even designed a flag for an independent India, which some insist influenced Gandhi's own later design for the Indian Congress.

beautiful voice I have ever heard," Secretary of State Edwin Montagu declared), Besant was a striking figure.[24] She had single-handedly founded Hindu College, to create the kind of modern leaders a free India would need, and when Viceroy Lord Hardinge offered to turn the college into a full-fledged university, she assumed that Gandhi would make a suitable speaker for its opening.

Gandhi arrived without a prepared speech and in a censorious mood. He started with a rambling diatribe against using English for official speeches and expressed his regret that more educated Indians could not speak the myriad vernaculars of their mother country. "If you tell me that our languages are too poor to express our thoughts," he said, "then I say the sooner we are wiped out of existence the better."

The distinguished listeners, including the viceroy and the maharaja of Darbhanga, shifted uneasily in their seats. But Gandhi plunged ahead. "Is it right," he said bitterly, "that the lanes of our sacred temples [in Benares] should be as dirty as they are? The houses around about are built anyhow...If even our temples are not models of cleanliness, what can our self-government be?"

Then Gandhi rounded on his princely audience in their bejeweled splendor and blasted the pomp and ceremony that were hallmarks of the Raj. "I am sure," he said, "it is not the desire of the King-Emperor or Lord Hardinge that in order to show the truest loyalty to our King-Emperor, it is necessary for us to ransack our jewelry boxes." Those jewels might be better used to feed and help India's peasants, Gandhi said. Besides, "is it not better that even Lord Hardinge should die than live a living death" surrounded by bodyguards to protect him from assassination—assassination by men, Gandhi added, whose methods were ignoble but whose aims were not?

Trembling with shame and anger, Besant rose to her feet and asked Gandhi to stop. But Gandhi squeezed in his last words as the audience was scrambling for the exit. He loudly condemned his fellow countrymen for their physical cowardice. Although he deplored violence, he cried out, he deplored his nation's abject surrender to British rule even more: "If we are to receive self-government, we shall have to take it."[25]

Minutes later the dais was empty. The maharaja and other princes left in a rage; the viceroy as well. Annie Besant refused to speak to Gandhi again. He had stirred some in the audience (including a young student and a future disciple, Vinova Bhave).[26] But he had mortally offended many more. Gandhi had wanted to point out the contrast between India's "richly bedecked noblemen" and "the millions of the poor." He had wanted to show how hopeless it was to try to forge a nation where rich and poor felt no sense of shared community, and where no one was prepared to die for his country, as the British were, by the tens of thousands, in the war overseas. For Gandhi, the Benares speech had been a Ruskin moment: speaking truth to power. But it only sidelined Gandhi even more from the growing trend of Indian politics, which involved a sudden upsurge of nationalist sentiment.

In 1914 Tilak was finally released from prison. He and Besant immediately forged an unlikely alliance. They created a series of Home Rule Leagues around the country, to force the British to concede independence as the price for Indian support for the war in Europe. "The moment of England's difficulty is the moment of India's opportunity," the firebrand Besant proclaimed, and Tilak and his supporters fiercely agreed.

In little more than a year their Home Rule Leagues grew to more than sixty thousand full-time members, at a time when the Indian National Congress's annual conference typically drew fewer than twenty thousand.[27] When a Muslim nationalist lawyer named Muhammad Ali Jinnah jumped on board the Home Rule bandwagon, it became the first Indian political movement to cross sectarian lines. By the end of 1916 the league had managed to build an incipient national popular base that reached out beyond the three British presidencies to the Indian heartland, including Gandhi's Gujarat.

To this effort Gandhi had nothing to contribute. He had become yesterday's news. When Indian National Congress delegates gathered at Lucknow in December 1916, all their attention was focused on the Home Rule Leagues and their glamorous rising star, M. A. Jinnah. Tilak was cheered as a triumphant hero. The Congress agreed to the principle of separate electorates for Muslims and Hindus in any future representative Indian body, and Jinnah agreed to a merger of the Muslim League and the Congress, in what became known as the Lucknow Pact.

Muslims and Hindus, everyone assumed, would now present a united front to the British in their demands for independence. "I think I break no secret," Congress president A. C. Mazumdar announced at the end, "when I announce to you that the Hindu-Moslem question has

been settled."[28] Gandhi attended the Lucknow conference, a forlorn figure wearing a large white turban and a long black mustache, but no one
paid him much attention.

No one, that is, except a young man named Raj Kumar Shukla.
Shukla owned an indigo farm in Bihar, the region north of Bengal. He
had tried speaking to several of the VIPs at the Congress, including
Tilak, but they did not have time to listen to his grievances.[29]

Finally in desperation he cornered Gandhi. Gandhi could scarcely
understand the young man's rough dialect, but finally with the help of a
Bihari lawyer named Prasad, Shukla told him his story. It was about indigo farmers, destitute Bihari peasants and their families, and their sufferings at the hands of white landlords. It was a story familiar to Gandhi
from South Africa and his dealings with Indian indentured laborers. All
Shukla wanted Gandhi to do, he said, was to come and see for himself.

"It's very close," the young man said, as Gandhi hesitated and thought
up reasons not to go. "Please spend a day there."

The name of the place, Shukla said, was Champaran.

Champaran was in North Bihar, not far from the Nepalese border. The
original home of both Buddhism and Jainism, it was a backward
province even by Indian standards. Its dismally poor peasants clustered
in tiny hamlets and were almost entirely dependent on the local harvest
for food. In some ways Champaran was also a unique province. Hindu-
Muslim tensions were unknown, although many of the poorest peasants
were Muslim; and there was no trace of a Westernized elite.[30] Shukla's
own tiny village was more than seven miles, along a single dirt track,
from the nearest railway stop. Every major change in India since the
Mutiny seemed to have passed Champaran by.

But it had a visibly oppressive white European presence, thanks to the
planting of indigo. For years Champaran peasants (*raiyats*) had agreed
to grow this important cash crop for the local land leaseholder, under
what was known as the *tinkathia* system. The price planters paid to cultivators was fixed; that meant peasant families never benefited from rising indigo prices. Falling prices, by contrast, led planters to cut back on
production, leaving cultivators in the lurch—even as the coming of war
caused the price of everything else in India to jump.[31]

The majority of Champaran's indigo planters were white. This too
was unusual, but it helped make the local district commissioner reluc-

tant to intervene. Riots broke out in the district in 1908, as more prosperous *raiyats* like Shukla felt the squeeze from the iron law of cash-crop
feudalism, but even after three months of violence the commissioner refused to help.[32] However, the racial component also made the problems
in Champaran a conspicuous symbol of the power imbalance under the
Raj: just what Gandhi needed to get his first satyagraha campaign in
India off the ground.

In the first week of April 1917 Gandhi and Shukla arrived at the railway station at Patna, the capital of Bihar. Thousands of miles away the
United States was entering the war in Europe; Vladimir Lenin had arrived in Petrograd to launch a Bolshevik revolution; in London, a parliamentary commission was about to issue its final report exonerating
Winston Churchill from any blame for the failures of the Gallipoli campaign (public opinion's verdict was another matter); and at Passchendaele
in Flanders the British Army was preparing for the last disastrous Allied
offensive on the Western Front.

Meanwhile, in the dusty windswept streets of Patna, Gandhi felt as if
he had stepped off the edge of the world. He knew no one in the town; it
turned out Shukla did not either. The two men could barely understand
each other, let alone the Bihari dialect of the people in whose sprawling
ancient city they found themselves.

Passersby stared at their peasant clothes and assumed they were beg-
gars. Gandhi and Shukla finally found lodging in a stranger's house, but
since no one knew their caste, even the servants shunned them. The
maids refused to draw water from the garden well when Gandhi used it,
for fear that even a drop of water from Gandhi's bucket might pollute
them.

Later, in his *Experiments with Truth,* Gandhi implied that he took
these indignities in stoic good humor, "for I was inured to such things."[33]
But at the time he concluded that the whole trip was a mistake and that
his host Shukla was an idiot. He wrote a furious letter to Maganlal, complaining, "The man who brought me here doesn't know anything. He
has dumped me in some obscure place...If things go on this way I am
not likely to see Champaran." But Gandhi the good soldier added, "As
for the self, this helps it to grow."[34]

Then Gandhi remembered that a lawyer he knew from his London
days was living nearby in Muzzafarpur, a Muslim named Maulana
Mazharul Haq. Gandhi realized, "I must take the reins in my own
hands," and so the unlikely-looking pair took the train to Muzzafarpur.

There his old friend gave him a rapturous welcome and introduced him to some attorney friends. Mazharul Haq, who had Congress connections, was already active on behalf of the Champaran cultivators. He and his fellow lawyers had taken several cases to court (while charging, Gandhi noted, hefty fees to their impoverished clients).

"When the *ryots [raiyats]* are so crushed and fear ridden, law courts are useless" was his response, according to his own account. "The real relief for them is to be free from fear. We cannot sit still until we have driven the *tinkathia* out of Bihar."[35]

Easier said than done. But Gandhi's approach was simple and time-tested in South Africa. He would meet with the peasants himself, he announced, as many as possible. He would write down their grievances, as part of his own independent inquiry into "the condition of the Champaran agriculturists." Then he would confront the government with the truth. Others immediately volunteered to help, including Haq and a twenty-nine-year-old lawyer named Rajendra Prasad.

Prasad found Gandhi's appearance and behavior bizarre in the extreme. "In those days he was living practically on groundnuts and dates," Prasad remembered later. "Milk of the cow or buffalo was tabooed *[sic]* and even goat's milk," while Gandhi had also vowed not to eat more than five types of food in a single day and to eat no meal after sunset. Although he dressed in homespun peasant clothes, Gandhi spoke not a word of Bihari. He barely understood Hindi.[36] Yet there was something compelling about the strange little man, with his odd habits, his persuasive but pointed banter, and his rapid scuttling walk that made it hard for men two decades his junior to keep up with him.[37]

That compulsion would make Rajendra Prasad go with Gandhi to the poorest and most remote villages in Champaran. He became Gandhi's first intimate disciple outside his home turf. Three decades later Prasad would become India's first president.

Meanwhile local British authorities knew about Gandhi's arrival almost the moment he got off the train. They were deeply alarmed. "His mere presence in Champaran is most undesirable," the district inspector general's special assistant wrote to the provincial police superintendent. Even in remotest Bihar, Raj officials knew of Gandhi's reputation as an agitator, especially on the issue of Indian indentured labor. District Commissioner Morshead had a short interview with Gandhi and concluded that he was keener on stirring up trouble rather than on a serious inquiry.[38] Morshead decided he had to forestall any violence.

On Sunday, April 15, Gandhi and another lawyer named Prasad (not Rajendra but the man he had met at the Lucknow Congress) set off by elephant for the first village in the district, called Chandrahia.[39] Just as they arrived in the dusty, deserted street, a police officer rode up on a bicycle. It was a scene worthy of E. M. Forster, or Paul Scott, with the turbaned khaki-clad officer on his flimsy bicycle standing in the path of the great creaking animal, with its weary and bemused passengers.

They were to stop at once, the policeman said. The district magistrate, W. B. Haycock, had an expulsion order waiting for Gandhi, under the Defense of India Rules. Gandhi returned to Motihari and quietly read the letter. He then informed Haycock that he would disobey the expulsion order and sent a similar letter to the viceroy's private secretary.

Gandhi waited all day Monday to be arrested, even as the news of what was happening spread with torrential speed through neighboring villages. Finally Haycock ordered him to appear on Tuesday at the district court to explain why he should not be put in jail. Gandhi's whole plan, of course, *was* to be put in jail, and he had prepared a statement to that effect.

On Tuesday morning more than two thousand peasants pressed to get into the courtroom. The glass panels of the door broke under the strain, and Haycock had to ask Gandhi to control his followers, which Gandhi gladly did. Gandhi then read his statement, concluding, "I have disregarded the order served upon me not for want of respect for lawful authority, but in obedience to the higher law of our being, the voice of conscience."[40]

Haycock was in a quandary. As Gandhi said later, "He seemed to be a good man, anxious to do justice." Like any British judge in India, he saw his job as defending law and order in his district. Willful disobedience of the law (specifically Section 144 of the Crown Penal Code) called for punishment. But the unexpected and unprecedented outpouring of peasant support for the strange little man standing before his bench unnerved him. Haycock convinced himself more violence would result if he arrested Gandhi than if he left him at liberty. Therefore he announced he would suspend any judgment and adjourned the court. He privately asked Gandhi to put off his village visits (surprisingly, Gandhi agreed), and that night Haycock sent a long telegram to the lieutenant-governor asking, in effect, what he should do.

It was a watershed moment in Gandhi's dealings with British officialdom. In fact, it set the classic pattern of the Raj's response to Gandhi's satyagraha tactics, then and later: first the insistence that the law be obeyed; then surprise at the Mahatma's calm defiance; then confusion at the show of sympathy and support from ordinary Indians; and finally hesitation and inaction and a sheepish letter to superiors asking for further instructions.

So Haycock became the first, but by no means the last, British official in India to be reduced to bumbling helplessness by Gandhi's unorthodox approach. The response to his letter revealed the pressures from the other side. The lieutenant-governor sharply disapproved of the commissioner's action and ordered Haycock to withdraw the expulsion order. Gandhi would be allowed to continue his inquiry, making visits to villages in Champaran. "Mr. Gandhi is doubtless eager to adopt the role of martyr which as you know he has already played in South Africa," the official wrote, and nothing "would suit him better than to undergo a term of imprisonment." The Indian media were already noticing the events in Champaran and were hailing Gandhi as a hero. Better to back down, the lieutenant-governor suggested, than to give Gandhi the publicity he wanted—and possibly set off an even more widespread reaction.[41] Relieved at not having to enforce the law, Haycock dropped the case.

Gandhi had won. Even more important, Champaran's peasantry felt they had won, too. As Gandhi resumed his village visits and continued them for the rest of April and May, men, women, and children poured out of their homes. They followed him everywhere, chanting his name, throwing flowers in his path, and—the most striking part of *darshan,* or sighting of a holy man—gathering the dust from his feet on their fingers. When he finally reached Bettiah and Raj Shukla's home village, the people unhitched the horses from Gandhi's carriage and pulled it through the streets. A local British official watched. The English might think Gandhi a fanatic or even a revolutionary, he noted, but to the peasants "he is their liberator, and they credit him with extraordinary powers."[42]

As for Gandhi himself, he found the outpouring of adulation deeply moving as well as somewhat unexpected. For the first time in his life he saw the deep, inexorable poverty and isolation of the vast majority of his fellow countrymen. "The world outside Champaran was unknown to them," he wrote later. "And yet they received me as though we had been lifelong friends. It is not exaggeration, but the literal truth, to say that in this meeting with the peasants I was face to face with God, Ahimsa, and Truth."[43]

By championing the raiyats of Champaran, historian Judith Brown remarks, "Gandhi began to clothe with flesh and blood the figure which had hitherto been only a shadowy contender" in Indian politics. Brown notes that this first "direct object-lesson in Civil Disobedience," as Gandhi himself described it, "[gave] him an all-India public reputation." He was no longer a figure of fun among educated Indians, most of whom had even less contact with India's rural classes than Gandhi did. Champaran turned him into a man to be respected and admired.[44]

Gandhi also learned a vital lesson in handling the press. He urged newspapers across the country not to send reporters to cover the events unfolding in Bihar. Instead, he explained, he would "send them whatever might be necessary for publication and keep them informed." In effect, he turned the Indian media into his own publicity machine.[45]

In Gandhi's mind, his investigations in Champaran had nothing to do with any future career in politics. On the contrary, he wrote in his autobiography that he fought to "prevent the struggle from becoming political." He was there to fight for the peasants and their rights; his goal was "disinterested service of the people."[46] That goal might be damaged if others perceived his actions as political, or as aimed to draw support from one or another faction in Congress politics.

At the same time it was impossible to keep politics out of Champaran. By the time he completed his survey and the Indian government agreed to launch an official committee of inquiry, he had built his first political following outside his native Gujarat. Its members were Bihar's middle tier: young small-town lawyers like the Prasads, small businessmen from provincial towns, and the occasional prosperous cultivator like Shukla who had a smattering of education and time for social activism.

Devoted to Gandhi, they were a fairly ragtag bunch. Raj officials distrusted them all, but every single British official who had direct contact with Gandhi in the Champaran affair came away with a respect for his sincerity and uprightness. "Mr. Gandhi is a philanthropic enthusiast," was the lieutenant-governor of Bihar's take on him, "but I regard him as perfectly honest; and he was quite reasonable in his discussions with me."[47]

Hence the Raj learned to prefer dealing with Gandhi to dealing with other Indian politicians. He spoke to British officials with the confiding ease of an Inner Temple lawyer, and unlike some of his fellow Congressmen, he seemed to keep his promises. Civil servants, and most politicians, dislike trouble, and all prefer it in small, manageable doses rather than large ones. Hence Champaran laid the seeds of a strange but crucial relationship that grew closer over time. British officials learned that it was better to agree to at least some of Gandhi's demands, no matter how outrageous, than to reject them all and face a mass disturbance.

In turn, Gandhi learned to quietly drop certain grievances that his followers had insisted on, in order not to force New Delhi into a corner. "Why should we blame the government?" he would ask his followers, especially when, in his innermost mind, he believed that Indian weakness had opened the door to British abuses in the first place.[48]

In this way Gandhi and the Raj established a pattern of bilateral negotiation that lasted through to the Salt March and beyond. Other Indian politicians and local officials had to learn to sit on the sidelines when the bargaining began, even as they sometimes fumed with impatience, not to mention envy. Yet this strange alliance would hold the subcontinent together for nearly two decades.

It would take Winston Churchill's rise to power in 1940 to blow it all away.

In May 1917 everyone, Indian and Briton alike, had to agree that Gandhi had won a stunning victory. Gandhi was unhappy that the Committee of Inquiry's final recommendations did little to change the lives of Champaran's cultivators, and the peasant schools he had set up all folded once he left Bihar. Nonetheless, he felt confident enough to try the same thing closer to home, in the province of Kaira, in central Gujarat.

Once again he chose a case that involved farmers' rights, although in Kaira the peasants were more prosperous and wanted tax relief from the Raj. Once again it involved a place where Muslim-Hindu communal strife was nonexistent, making it easier for the peasant community to show a united face.

And once again Gandhi found an enthusiastic band of local activists to help him organize his satyagraha, in this case a pledge from farmers not to pay their land tax at the current onerous rate.[49] One of the activists was Mahadev Desai, who returned with him to Sabarmati as his private secretary. Another was Vallabhbhai Patel, a tough-minded lawyer from a Kaira peasant family who sometimes practiced in Ahmedabad. Patel had been skeptical of Gandhi when he first met him at the Ahmedabad Club. But Gandhi's personal devotion to the plight of the Kaira farmers won him over. He became what Rajendra Prasad was in Bihar, Gandhi's invaluable link to his new rural base.

As in Champaran, the concessions Gandhi eventually won were less than met the eye. The district commissioner agreed to suspend payments for some of Kaira's poorest raiyats, but the central government refused to budge on the overall assessment. Gandhi nonetheless declared victory. He had already moved on to his next cause, the mill workers' strike in Ahmedabad.

This one posed some complications for Gandhi. Two of the mill owners involved, Ambalal and Anasuya Sarabhai, were devout Hindus and generous benefactors of the Sabarmati Ashram. On February 28, 1918, however, the Sarabhai brothers locked out their workers over a wage dispute. Gandhi took up the workers' cause: he was determined to show that satyagraha could work just as well in a factory as in the countryside. When the mill owners and workers failed to reach a deal, Gandhi tried a new tactic: he publicly declared he would starve himself to death, if necessary, to express his disappointment and make the opposing parties see reason.[50]

Thoroughly frightened, everyone gave way. Gandhi won a wage hike (although not the 33 percent increase he had hoped for), and the press carried the glad tidings around India. Gandhi became a hero not only in the villages of Bihar and Gujarat but in factories and sweatshops from Ahmedabad to Calcutta and Bombay.

"There is no mistaking the fact that India is waking up from its long sleep," Gandhi told the editor of the *Bombay Chronicle* on April 15, 1918. To his mind, he had proved that his formula worked: inspire local activists to unite the community around a specific issue or injustice, then confront authority through nonviolent petitions, pledges, demonstrations, and strikes. The events in Kaira and Ahmedabad had inevitable political echoes as well. They proved that "it is impossible to govern men without their consent," he declared. India's peasants had shown that "no Government, no matter how strong, can stand against their will."[51]

Gandhi was a hero to some Indians. Others reacted with resentment, anger, and envy. That local police officials saw him as a troublemaker, even a fraud, is not surprising.* But many Indian politicians also found him aggravating. His unconventional tactics seemed "inopportune and mischievous." Some in the Congress worried that his focus on local

---

* For example, police reports suggested that his Ahmedabad fast was "a typical theatrical finale" and that Gandhi knew all along that the owners and strikers would settle. About this time the Bombay police began keeping track of visitors to and from the Sabarmati Ashram.

grievances detracted from the larger national questions of independence and self-government.

Annie Besant was particularly bitter. She had reason to be. Gandhi's satyagraha in Kaira infringed on turf that she and her Home Rule Leagues had cultivated for a year. She too had tried to reach across caste divisions; she too had stressed organization on the local level in places that elite Congress politicians never touched. The Home Rule Leagues had pioneered what Gandhi was able to carry out with far greater success, at their expense.[52] Only the government's disastrous decision to intern Besant for subverting the war effort in June 1917 restored her waning political fortunes. She would be elected president of the Congress when it met in Calcutta, as Gandhi's star rose across India but the Home Rule Leagues were losing their luster.

Other nationalist politicians were fading in public esteem, too—an ironic development, because events in London were sharply turning in their favor.

As the Great War in Europe dragged on, the Raj found itself walking a thinner and thinner tightrope. Harvests in India had been bad in 1917–18 (one reason for the agitation in Kaira); those of 1918–19 would be worse. At the same time war demand drove up prices, imposing a severe hardship on the average Indian, even as their sons left for war in record numbers. More than 1.1 million Indians went overseas to serve in campaigns in Mesopotamia, Palestine, and France (almost 140,000 fought on the Western Front), as well as in Gallipoli and East Africa—all at the expense of the Indian taxpayer.[53] Indian troops participated in the disasters at Gallipoli and the fall of Kut-al-Amara in 1916, as well as the Battle of the Somme. They saw the indomitable British suddenly stumble and fall. At the same time chaos threatened on the Afghan border. Discontent simmered in India's major cities. The burden of war had broken Russia's back and forced it out of the war. What if India's broke as well?

The government in Westminster felt it needed to do something, fast. Their notion was to throw Indian politicians a bone, something to convince them that their sacrifices for the empire were not in vain. On August 20, 1917, Secretary of State for India Edwin Montagu announced in the House of Commons that His Majesty's Government had a program of action to include more Indians in governing institutions, "with a view to the progressive realization of responsible government in India, as an integral part of the British Empire."[54]

Never have duller words been more ill chosen or set off a longer and more intense controversy. Later, hard-liners like Churchill would blame the liberal Montagu for unreasonably raising Indians' hopes for self-government—even independence. In fact, as historian Penderel Moon has pointed out, the program originated with Montagu's Tory predecessor as secretary of state, Austen Chamberlain; and the words "responsible government" came from the two great hard-liners in the cabinet, Lord Curzon and A. J. Balfour. They had wanted to avoid using the phrase "self-government" and assumed that "responsible government" would be more innocuous and vague.[55]

In fact, the phrase had a distinct political meaning, as Congress's London-trained lawyers (including Mohandas Gandhi) well knew. In the context of British constitutional history, "responsible government" could only mean a governing executive directly responsible to the elected representatives of the people; in other words, an elected Indian parliament. It was the very same formula that Winston Churchill had worked out for the "self-governing" colonies of Natal and Transvaal in 1906 and the South African republic in 1909. Now for the first time, Montagu seemed to suggest, that formula would be applied to a non-white colony, namely India.

Words were important to Indian politicians. In a crucial sense, words were the only thing they had to work with. Verbiage mattered far less to their British counterparts. The British public was neither dismayed nor shocked by Montagu's announcement; it felt that India deserved some reward for its sacrifices and support during the war. In fact, the Montagu declaration revealed something crucial that few Indians realized: that most Britons were perfectly ready to let Indians govern themselves, *as long as they stayed in the empire.*

By 1917 many agreed with the sentiment that Viceroy Lord Minto had expressed ten years earlier, when he and John Morley approved the first elected members for India's legislative councils. "We are mere sojourners" in India, Minto mused. "We are only camping and on the march...How intensely artificial and unnatural is our mighty Raj. And it sets me to wondering whether it can possibly last." With dramatic emphasis he added, "It surely cannot."[56]

Conservatives like Lord Curzon, and Britons with a vested interest in British rule, might deplore this resigned attitude as "defeatism." Later Winston Churchill would try to reverse it. However, it remained a political fact: the British public could not have cared less who governed India or how. And with war still raging in Europe, they had other things to think about. Yet the paradox remained that Montagu's invitation to India self-rule sowed confusion and panic not in England, or even in New Delhi, but among India's political elite.

At first the reaction was rapturous excitement, certainly more than the declaration warranted. Indeed, the only politician to ignore it was Gandhi, just as he ignored the announcement that Montagu would be coming to India in September. Gandhi was unconcerned about when the *British* thought Indians were ready for self-rule—in his view, that was up to the Indians. When he wrote on August 24, "It would seem what we have been fighting for is within our reach," he was talking not about Montagu or independence but about the protests for the release of Annie Besant from her internment.[57]

Gandhi had recently taken up her cause and sent a letter to Viceroy Lord Chelmsford. He confessed, "I myself do not like much in Mrs. Besant's method" and "I have not liked the idea of the political propaganda being carried on in the War. But," he added, "the whole country was against me."[58] She deserved not to be in prison, however wrongheaded her ideas and words were—indeed, Gandhi rejected Besant's entire nationalist vision, along with everyone else's. Formal institutional arrangements like parliaments and local councils meant nothing to him. Later he would write, "The average individual's soul force is any day the most important thing. The political form is but a concrete expression of that soul force."[59]

Home Rule, he told the Gujarat Political Conference, was pointless unless the Indians were fit for it.[60] He had his own ideas about how to bring that about. It led him, in the spring of 1918, in the aftermath of his victory in the Ahmedabad satyagraha, to make one of his most controversial moves.

He had at first refused to attend the Delhi War Conference, organized by Viceroy Lord Chelmsford at the end of April 1918. For one thing, neither Besant or Tilak, vocal opponents of the war but crucial figures in Indian political opinion, had been invited. For another, he had read a rumor that Britain would cede the Turkish capital of Constantinople to the Russians after the war, which would deeply of-fend Indian Muslims.* However, on April 27 he met personally with Chelmsford and decided to go.[61]

In November Gandhi had also met Montagu during the latter's Indian tour. The secretary of state was amazed to find Gandhi "dressed like a coolie" but added that he was a "social reformer" who sincerely wanted "to improve the conditions of his fellow-men." At the same time he saw that Gandhi could be helpful in building support for the empire: "All [Gandhi] wants is to get India on our side."[62]

The war conference showed Gandhi how to do it. In Europe the Western Front was collapsing; German forces were closing on Paris. The fate of the war, and Britain, seemed in doubt. In Kaira Gandhi had worried that "as a responsible citizen of the Empire" he was doing nothing to help Britain win the war. "I feel ashamed that since my arrival in India I can show no war work record in the conventional sense of the term," he said. So he proposed to help recruit soldiers for the war effort. As he told the viceroy's private secretary, "I have an idea that if I became your recruiting agent-in-chief, I might rain men on you."[63] Later he hoped to qualify for a posting to France or Mesopotamia himself.

Gandhi threw himself into the recruiting drive, returning to Kaira in hopes of recruiting twenty men in each village. "Of all my activities," he wrote, " I regard this as the most difficult and the most important."[64] For Gandhi still believed in the ideal, if not the reality, of the British Empire. The English "love justice," he told an audience in Kaira. "The liberty of the individual is very dear to them. They have shielded men against oppression" in India and elsewhere. Now was the time for Indians to step up and show their gratitude—and their courage.[65] It would prove that they were ready to be equal partners in empire. "To sacrifice sons in the war ought to be a cause not of pain but of pleasure to brave men," he announced.[66]

The spectacle of the self-declared pacifist and man of *ahimsa* urging recruits not just to serve as ambulance drivers, as he did in South Africa and London, but to fight at the front startled many. It bewildered his closest supporters like Patel, who refused to help. Opponents like Besant marveled and scoffed at "the Raj's recruiting sergeant." In Congress circles it made him appear even more of an outsider than before.

But Gandhi was unyielding. "I would make India offer all her able-

---

* The rumor was untrue. But it was an example of how Churchill's attack on Gallipoli directly impinged on Indian politics—as Gandhi was quick to realize and exploit.

bodied sons as a sacrifice at this critical moment," he told Lord Chelmsford, "and I know that India, by this very act, would become the most favored partner in the Empire, and racial distinctions would become a thing of the past." To a friend he wrote, "If I succeed, Swaraj is assured."[67]

So Gandhi marched from village to village, sometimes covering twenty miles a day, from May until July. He had hoped for twelve hundred recruits but ended up with fifty. When he spoke of dying for the empire, the crowds of peasants who had hailed him as their savior turned their backs and walked away. Others turned violent. He left some villages to the clatter of thrown rocks and stones.

Few understood Gandhi's motivation, then or later. Certainly he never thought the English might concede self-government out of gratitude—his experience in the Boer War had taught him otherwise. But he did believe war service would restore a strength of will to the Indian character that was critical for Swaraj. He even hoped his sons Ramdas and Harilal would join the army.[68] His English disciple and fellow pacifist Charles Andrews was furious and charged him with abandoning India's heritage of peace and humanity. Gandhi sharply responded, "On the contrary, [Indians] have always been warlike, and the finest hymn composed by Tulsidas in praise of Rama gives the first place to his ability to strike down the enemy." Satyagraha itself required a soldierly instinct, he pointed out. He could state it even more strongly: "You cannot teach *ahimsa* to a man who cannot kill."[69]

Besides, Gandhi added, "I do not say, 'Let us go and kill the Germans.' I say, 'Let us go and die for the sake of India and the Empire.'" To his mind, this was a crucial distinction. As always, Gandhi's focus was on the importance of manly self-sacrifice. Army life would teach that strength of character, just as it would teach the other qualities Indians needed for the future: discipline and teamwork, not to mention hygiene and clean latrines. One reason he cheered the Allied cause in the Great War was that he was convinced its Indian veterans would return home changed men, as "an indomitable army of Home Rulers" ready to reshape India in a new muscular image. "I am absolutely right...in calling upon every Indian to join the army," he told Andrews, not in order to gratify "the lust for blood" but "for the sake of learning not to fear death."[70]

Even years later, when he reflected on this episode, he wrote, "I do not repent of my actions in terms of *ahimsa*. For under Swaraj too, I would not hesitate to advise those who would bear arms to do so and fight for their country." To Andrews he was more direct: "It comes to this. Under exceptional circumstances, war may have to be resorted to as a necessary evil, even as the body is."[71]

No other pacifist would have dared to write such words, and in the context of 1918 India, they won him few converts. He did win the keen appreciations of the Raj, which awarded him the Kaiser-i-Hind gold medal, India's highest award for "important and useful" public service. However, his recruiting drive not only offended some of his closest supporters; it also ruined his health. Gandhi came down with dysentery in late July and was out of action for nearly seven weeks. He refused all medical treatment. Delirium set in. His mill owner friend Ambalal Sarabhai summoned doctors, who said Gandhi was suffering from dysentery and starvation and was on the verge of a nervous breakdown.[72]

If Gandhi had become a physical wreck, his nationalist colleagues were in a political quandary. Montagu's declaration in August had set off a fissiparous scramble within the Congress and across India. Instead of uniting in order to work together, every sect, group, organization, and minority caste across the subcontinent clamored for its rights and claims to be respected under any future constitutional arrangement, whatever that might be.

Muslims and Christians worried that they would be overwhelmed by Hindus; other Hindu castes by Brahmins; rural provinces by the large urban centers. From the start the non-Brahmin paper *Jagrak* sardonically welcomed Montagu's visit to India because "it would enable him to see for himself how sharply divided the several classes of India are." It would also show him that the elite that ran the Indian National Congress "is numerically very small and that its interests clash with those of the majority"—not to mention every other minority in India.[73]

As separate factions bickered over the anticipated spoils of "responsible government," the Lucknow Pact collapsed. Moderates fought with so-called Extremists like Tilak and with one another. Muslim radicals turned against their leaders who had signed the pact. A revived Muslim League witnessed a vicious power struggle. Violent riots broke out between Hindus and Muslims in Arrak in Bihar, consuming 160 villages and taking more than a week to quell.[74]

Chelmsford was horrified. "Our announcement should have rallied" Moderate nationalist opinion, he wrote to the governor of Bombay, "but on the whole this body of moderate opinion...has so far shown itself to be utterly unreliable, inert, and invertebrate." At least one Indian newspaper noted that native opposition to self-government was actually *increasing*, out of fear that it would merely transfer power from the British—who understood power and at least treated Indians impartially—to men who did not and would not.[75]

Chelmsford and Montagu adjusted their sights accordingly. In July they announced their plan for government reform. It expanded both the central and provincial legislative councils and actually transferred power in the provinces to a range of Indian ministers and officials. It grew the Indian electorate to about one in ten adult males (although many of those still could not read or write). But it brought no major change at the center, in New Delhi. Under the Chelmsford-Montagu reforms, or "dyarchy," certain government functions—such as land revenue, justice and police, press censorship and irrigation, and the military—were to be permanently "reserved" to the viceroy and his administration.

The Indian National Congress exploded. They denounced the Chelmsford-Montagu proposals as a farce. Annie Besant bitterly attacked dyarchy as showing that "the bureaucrats...are not prepared to give up materially any fraction of the power which they have enjoyed." But as Judith Brown and others have shown, even as they denounced it, nationalists and local politicians began to jockey for position under the new dispensation. Dyarchy was going to be the only game in town; alternatives were nonexistent. All-India politics, under the Congress model, had proved to be a chimera.

Only one man had the will and the means to pull it back together. Ill and discouraged, Gandhi's deepest desire was to steer clear of the Congress and its cesspool of poisonous factions and frustrated hopes. What finally forced him to return to politics, and take leadership of the nationalist camp, was a series of violent events the following year. Winston Churchill would be at their center.

Chapter Thirteen

BLOODSHED

1919–1920

*Our reign in India or anywhere else has never stood on the basis of
physical force alone, and it would be fatal to the British Empire
if we were to try to base ourselves only upon it.*

WINSTON CHURCHILL, 1920

WHAT SET EVERYTHING OFF WAS THE Rowlatt Acts.

Ironically, they came to pass just as the issue of Indian Home Rule
seemed to have turned a corner. India's magnificent sacrifice in the
Great War had not gone unnoticed. Montagu's pledge in August 1917
and the Chelmsford-Montagu reform package had given birth to the
Government of India Act in May 1919, the British Parliament's stamp of
approval on eventual self-government for India. Elections for the re-
formed legislative councils were already slated for 1920–21. Government
departments like agriculture and education were ready to pass into the
hands of Indian, not British, ministers. The foundations of "real local
self-government" were being laid in many parts of India.[1]

Members of the Indian National Congress and the Home Rule
Leagues were still unsatisfied, but the Swaraj train seemed as if it might
really leave the station this time. Groups and politicians scrambled to
find their seats before it left.

But outside India the atmosphere was stormy. The war ended with
both Germany and Russia engulfed in revolution. Following a bloody
insurrection in Dublin during Easter 1916, Ireland had turned into a
cauldron of violence and sectarian strife. Turkey was in the throes of
revolution as well, and radical Muslim warriors from Afghanistan were
poised along India's border. Winston Churchill told the House of
Commons, "Never has there been a time when people were more disposed to turn to courses of violence or show such scant respect for law
and custom, tradition and procedure."[2] To ally the fears of men like

Churchill, Indian government officials decided to act. What could be simpler, they asked themselves, than for New Delhi to take some preliminary steps to prevent radical revolution from spreading to India?

Consulting with a committee of lawyers, Delhi high court judge Henry Rowlatt drew up two bills to be ready when the Defense of India Act expired six months after the end of the war. The two bills contained two controversial provisions. One allowed judges to convict suspected terrorists or subversives without a jury; the other sanctioned interning those same suspects without trial.

Two members of Rowlatt's committee were Indians. They approved the changes wholeheartedly.[3] But when the bills reached the Imperial Legislative Council in February 1919, an outcry began. Even with every Indian member voting against it, the bill passed in March and became law.[4] In their innocence, officials in New Delhi had never imagined the uproar the new laws would cause.

Gandhi was at the forefront of the agitation. In February 1919, when the Rowlatt bills reached the legislature, he was still recovering from his illness, but from his bed he wrote that the bills were more than just breaches of ordinary law and justice. They were "evidence of a determined policy of repression," he said. As a lawyer, he understood the implications of a law that suspended civil liberties without prior cause. If the government let "such a devilish piece of legislation" stand, Gandhi wrote, "I feel I can no longer render peaceful obedience to the laws." He would invite everyone who felt the same "to join me in the struggle" against such "unjust, subversive laws."[5]

Gandhi was not alone. The proposed laws had offended every quarter of Indian opinion. M. A. Jinnah quit the Legislative Council. Protests filled newspapers like Annie Besant's *Young India,* which accused the Rowlatt Acts of contradicting every promise about eventual self-government. The outrage in newspaper offices, schools and universities, and on the street was palpable. Gandhi suddenly decided he could mobilize it into a force for change. His earlier campaigns in Bihar and Kaira had made him a national figure with a popular following. Here was an opportunity to test its power. At the end of February he announced a formal satyagraha campaign against the Rowlatt Acts, centering on his home turf in Gujarat and the Bombay Presidency.

The hastily organized campaign was a flop. Outside Ahmedabad and Bombay, the response was tepid or nonexistent.[6] Few saw the point of joining Gandhi's pledge to disobey laws that had yet to be implemented.

Besant backed the campaign at first, and her Home Rule League activists joined in. But then she and others asked, not unreasonably, how people could disobey the Rowlatt Acts, directed against subversives, without breaking other laws and becoming subversives themselves—thereby justifying the Rowlatt Acts.* The silver-haired Besant also worried that Gandhi was using the campaign to steal away her followers.[7]

The viceroy, sensing that Gandhi had overreached himself, dismissed the campaign as "a bluff" and refused to be intimidated. The last stage of Gandhi's campaign, the nationwide strike or *hartal* called for April 6, was an abject failure. Besant actively campaigned against it. In Delhi the strike led to violence, and ten people were killed. "Poor Gandhi!" wrote one of his more severe critics, the liberal Srinivasa Sastri. "He [is] on his course unruffled—straight and single-eyed . . . He has some converts but not many."[8]

On April 8, aiming to breathe new life into the hartal, Gandhi left Bombay for Delhi and Amritsar, capital of the Punjab. A huge demonstration was planned in the latter city. Fearful of more violence, the central government ordered Gandhi stopped on the train and sent back to Bombay.† News of this "arrest" triggered a wave of new riots in Bombay and Ahmedabad, where a rampaging mob burned the jail, the telegraph office, and the collector's office, and several people were killed. Violence erupted in cities in the United Provinces as well.

The worst was in Amritsar. On April 10 a mixed mob of Hindus and Muslims burned their way through the city in Gandhi's name, and murdered four Europeans. Troops were ordered in. "Dear me, what a d—d nuisance these saintly fanatics are!" Lord Chelmsford had written even before the riots erupted.[9] The Raj balefully noted that this apostle of nonviolence always managed to inspire violence among his followers.

Certainly the killings in Amritsar shattered Gandhi's credibility as a man of peace. He felt deeply ashamed of his failure. A reporter overheard him describe the Rowlatt satyagraha as a "Himalayan miscalculation." Gandhi called for a national penitential three-day fast to atone for the deaths. Indeed, Amritsar might have been remembered as Gandhi's Waterloo, were it not for what happened next.

---

* In fact, the government never implemented any provisions of the Rowlatt Acts, then or later.

† The governor of the Punjab, Michael O'Dwyer, had wanted Gandhi arrested outright. Delhi worried that that would set off riots and ordered him merely detained and sent home—which set off the riots anyway.

* * *

General Reginald Dyer, C.B., had spent his entire career in the Indian Army. Brave, intelligent, and devoted to his duty, he had been born and bred in India. "Rex" to his friends, Dyer had dedicated his life to service to the Raj. And in a single afternoon he was about to destroy Britain's reputation in India forever.

On April 10 Dyer had marched his brigade of English, Gurkha, Pathan, and Baluchi troops to Amritsar. He found a city in chaos, with crowds burning buildings and tearing up the railway tracks in order to prevent help from arriving. On the thirteenth Dyer entered the city center with a convoy of armored cars, his troops following. With him was Amritsar's town crier. At each street intersection the crier read aloud in English and Urdu Dyer's order banning all large public gatherings, followed by explanations in Punjabi and Hindi. A large bass drum drew the crowds to hear the order. The reaction was derisory. "The Raj is dead," some shouted as the troops marched by. "The British will never shoot," others said.[10]

The troops' march through Amritsar took four and a half hours. When Dyer returned to his temporary headquarters, he learned that a demonstration was under way in the enclosed square adjoining the Sikhs' holiest site, the Golden Temple. Furious at this deliberate violation of his order, Dyer led a detachment of ninety Baluchis and Gurkhas and two armored cars down the narrow street to the square, the Jallianwala Bagh, where a crowd of several thousand had gathered to hear the pro-Gandhi speakers. With Dyer were a lieutenant colonel, his brigade major, and two British bodyguards. Otherwise there were no white soldiers at all.

Dyer was not a racist of the stereotyped Indian Briton mold. He knew Punjabis well. He had commanded a regiment of them, and they had been devoted to him. At Dyer's funeral a Gurkha sergeant who had been with him that day said, "General Dyer was a first-class soldier condemned by people at home who know nothing about India."[11] But Dyer's father and mother had both lived through the Mutiny. He had heard the terrible stories of murders and mob violence. Four Europeans had been killed in Amritsar, and a white woman had been pulled from her bicycle and nearly beaten to death. Memories of Cawnpore and its ghastly well quickened his stride.

As Dyer and his troops arrived at the edge of the Jallianwala Bagh, the densly packed crowd panicked and started running in all directions, some toward his soldiers. At that moment it must have seemed as if 1857 were happening all over again and that Dyer was staring into the abyss.

Dyer barked the order to open fire. One of his men said afterward that "the whole crowd seemed to sink to the ground in a flutter of white garments," as the Gurkhas and Baluchis blazed away.[12] Men, women, and children screamed and scrambled to get away. But they had nowhere to go. The tiny streets leading out became clogged bottlenecks. Almost ten thousand people were trapped in a space, Winston Churchill later pointed out, smaller than Trafalgar Square—while volley after volley rang out.

For ten minutes[13] Dyer encouraged his soldiers to keep shooting, until bodies carpeted the ground. Then he gave the order to cease fire. With military precision he and his men shouldered arms and marched out of the Jallianwala Bagh.

They left behind at least 379 dead and four times that number wounded. Cries of pain and moans rose to the rooftops. Bodies lined the entire wall around the enclosure. In some places, eyewitnesses said, they were ten feet deep. Then for good measure, Dyer ordered every Indian who passed the spot where the woman had been pulled from her bicycle to be forced to crawl on all fours—just as Colonel Neill had done at Cawnpore fifty-six years earlier. He set up a whipping post where any native who refused to crawl would be flogged. He and Governor O'Dwyer then imposed a reign of martial law as harsh as anything since the Mutiny.

The clampdown was so intense that it took several weeks for the news from Amritsar to reach the rest of India. Gandhi did not hear of the massacre until June.[14] At first he could not believe it. Then his first reaction was to blame not the British but the Indians: "I underrated the power of hatred and ill-will."[15] He assumed there must have been some provocation. Massacres like this were precisely the sort of thing the Raj did *not* do. He decided to suspend his satyagraha campaign in hopes that that would defuse the situation. "Both sides had gone mad" was all he could say at first.

Gandhi's incredulity made him slow to react. When he did, again his instinct was to blame his own followers rather than the British.[16] To the vast majority of others, however, the Jallianwala Bagh and the "crawling order" confirmed the worst view of the most extreme radicals: that British rule in India rested on nothing more than race hatred and brutal force.

Gandhi's English friend and clergyman Charlie Andrews said, "English honor has departed." Annie Besant compared the shootings to German war crimes in Belgium. Jinnah called it "physical butchery." Even the Moderate loyalist Srinivasa Sastri called the massacre, and the floggings and arrests that followed, "barbarous."[17] The Congress issued a statement condemning the incident, with understandable exaggeration, as "an act without parallel in modern times." Angry mass meetings took place around the country. The poet Rabindranath Tagore resigned his knighthood in protest.

Nirad Chaudhuri was a young student in Calcutta when the news of what was happening in the Punjab began to trickle out. "It became a torture for us to think of Amritsar," he wrote later. Not just the shootings but the vicious retribution and the arrests of Indians accused of fomenting the riots, while Dyer and his subordinates went free, preyed on every Bengali's mind. One evening at dinner "a young man suddenly recalled that the Punjab leaders were to receive their sentence that day." (Two were in fact executed.) Chaudhuri remembered, "All of us started as if we had been touched by a red-hot iron."[18]

For millions of educated Indians, the Amritsar massacre left a scar that would never heal. The pain united Indians as never before—or after. All around them the British, supposedly their protectors, not only refused to condemn the atrocities but publicly applauded them. Indians seethed as English newspapers cheered Dyer for averting a "second Mutiny" and the shootings as "one more case of a brave man doing his duty." They seethed at the sight of English ladies standing outside men's clubs and hotel doors with collection tins to raise money to give General Dyer a sword of honor.[19] They seethed when the government passed an Indemnity Bill, protecting all officials connected with the shootings or the "crawling order" from lawsuits. (The viceroy did order a halt of the crawling order as soon as he learned of it.)

Then the government offered relatives of the four Europeans murdered in Amritsar 400,000 rupees in compensation, while the relatives of those killed in the Jallianwala Bagh received only 500 rupees per body.*

---

* Few were paid even that. To add insult to injury, O'Dwyer's Punjab government also imposed a 1.85 million–rupee impost on the province to cover the costs of military operations and martial law.

Indians were aghast. More than any other event, Amritsar and its after-math solidified national support for Indian independence. It did so months before Gandhi became involved.

He, like the others, protested against the arrests and trials under mar-tial law. But while even loyalists like Sastri were outspoken in their crit-icism of the government's inaction against Dyer, Gandhi refused to be drawn out, citing insufficient evidence. In fact, his approach was pre-cisely the same as it had been in Champaran. What was needed, he said on May 28, was a government commission to investigate the events in the Punjab. He offered to launch another satyagraha if the government did nothing. Meanwhile the Congress decided to launch an investiga-tion of its own, which excluded Gandhi altogether.[20]

Then the Raj's bureaucratic wheels slowly began to turn. Secretary of State Edwin Montagu convinced New Delhi it had to do something, if only to head the Congress off at the pass. In September the viceroy an-nounced to the Legislative Council that a committee would be set up to investigate the shootings, headed by Judge Lord Hunter, former solici-tor general for Scotland. Indians were skeptical, but Gandhi applauded the inquiry, urging all Indians to cooperate with it and trust to British justice. He cited Champaran as an example of how the Raj could listen and learn. He refused to condemn the Indemnity Bill passed that same session, to the disgust even of his supporters.[21]

But in the early autumn of 1919, as the Hunter Commission began its work, Gandhi's view changed. The commission was swallowing whole Dyer and O'Dwyer's account of a Punjab on the verge of rebellion and their view that the shooting had thwarted a second Mutiny. Like Dyer's military superiors in New Delhi, the commissioners were inclined to be-lieve the "officer on the spot," especially a white one. The commission also refused to meet the Congress's conditions for cooperation, such as releasing activists who had been jailed under O'Dwyer's martial law reign.

In the meantime the Congress's own investigation had become a hopeless muddle. At its head was Motilal Nehru, a distinguished figure in Moderate Congress ranks. He had arrived in Amritsar in June. The scene and smell of death in the Jallianwala Bagh, he told his son Jawaharlal, a young lawyer in Delhi, was "truly gruesome." The scene was like a a strange mirror image of the Bibighar a half-century before. There was even a well in the square, which numerous witnesses said was still filled with dead bodies.[22]

Motilal Nehru, like the rest of the Congress, wanted justice. But very soon he and his fellow committee members were swamped with testimony from some nineteen hundred eyewitnesses, with no clear way to sift through it, let alone a method for producing a report. Everything ground to a halt, as recriminations within the committee began. Finally in October they turned in desperation to the only man who could sort it all out.

Mohandas Gandhi eagerly stepped forward with his usual energy and organizing skill. In a couple of months he turned the tangle of evidence—recorded "in the crudest English," recalled investigator M. R. Jayakar, with "bad typing, incorrect and illegible spelling, misspelt names"—into a carefully crafted piece of lawyerly analysis. The facts, Gandhi the London-trained barrister said, had to fit "like bricks...making a roadway for you to walk to your goal."[23]

The evidence was harrowing. Eyewitnesses who had watched the Jallianwala Bagh killings from the rooftops had seen "blood pouring in profusion...even those who were lying down were shot...Some had their heads cut open, others had eyes shot and nose, chest, arms or legs shattered." Some witnesses had sat all night in the Bagh with dying husbands and brothers. Others remembered the bodies of those who had been shot, but managed to escape, being left in the street for dead—including the bodies of small children.[24]

Still other witnesses described being forced at bayonet point to crawl on their bellies past the point where the white woman had been beaten, then being kicked and beaten by their English tormentors. At one point an entire wedding party had been flogged for failing to follow the crawling order.

All the evidence, all the testimony, all the citation of past law and precedent was pulled together in nearly two hundred tightly argued pages. They led inexorably to Gandhi's conclusion, published in late March 1920, that the events in Punjab were "a calculated piece of inhumanity towards utterly innocent and unarmed men, including children, and unparalleled for its ferocity in the history of modern British administration." He blamed the viceroy for not investigating the events in Punjab himself, for "clothing the officials with indemnity with indecent haste" (Gandhi had reversed his earlier view), and for the "criminal want of imagination" in allowing the death sentences passed under martial law to stand.[25]

When the Congress report was released on March 25, 1920, all India held its breath to see whether the official Hunter Commission would concur. Its own report appeared on May 3. Its tone was very different, although it agreed on many points of fact. The commissioners stated that Dyer had committed "a grave error" in ordering the shootings at Jallianwala Bagh and that his crawling order was "injudicious." But the commission concluded that martial law was fully justified and even blamed "Mr. Gandhi's movement" for undermining the rule of law in the Punjab and elsewhere. Members saw no reason for the government to do anything more than it already had, let alone punish Dyer or O'Dwyer.[26]

The viceroy accepted the Hunter Commission's report, and General Dyer was relieved of command. But across India the reaction was outrage. Gandhi in particular was disappointed. The commission's biggest erstwhile fan blasted the report as "an attempt to condone official lawlessness" and "page after page of thinly disguised official whitewash."[27]

Gandhi had come to another life passage, a moment when the course of events and his place in them had to change. His work with the victims of Amritsar convinced him he had to end what he called his "splendid isolation" and enter the arena of mainstream Indian politics.

In retrospect, this decision seems surprising. The work in Champaran, Kaira, and Ahmedabad, and the Rowlatt satyagraha—weren't they already part of politics? In Gandhi's mind, they were not. He saw himself, and his soul force satyagrahi, as elite shock troops to be mobilized only to correct "a manifest and cruel wrong." Gandhi never meant to use them to pursue the aims of the nationalists, let alone to build a conventional political base.

But in the aftermath of Amritsar, he was poised to strike. Authoring the Congress report moved him to the front rank of Indian politicians, even as he was reconsidering his own loyalty to the British Empire. Like an estranged lover, he felt betrayed by the Hunter report. "I can no longer retain affection," he wrote, "for a Government so evilly-manned as it is nowadays."[28] In April he was asked to replace Annie Besant as president of the All-India Home Rule League. He had already taken editorial control of her newspaper, *Young India,* the previous May. The next month he took a prominent place at the All-India Congress Committee meeting in Benares, which rejected the Hunter report as "tainted by racial bias" and called on the British Parliament to take legal action against Dyer.

"A scandal of this magnitude cannot be tolerated by the [Indian] nation," Gandhi wrote, "if it is to preserve its self-respect and become a full partner in the Empire." Still, even at the end of May 1919, when things seemed so bleak, Gandhi was warning readers of his Navajivan newspaper not to turn their backs on the British government as faithless or to assume that "all the officers in India are autocratic." He still held great love and affection for the British people, he wrote. "They are a brave, un-suspecting and fairly Godfearing people...I believe that no other people, excepting Indians, recognize soul force as quickly as the British do."[29]

But how could the British restore their credibility and honor in India, not only with Gandhi but with its politically active educated elite? That responsibility rested on one man, Dyer's ultimate boss, the secretary of state for war. In June 1920 that man happened to be Winston Churchill.

Four years earlier, in February 1916, Churchill had been a lieutenant colonel in the Royal Scots Fusiliers, shivering and sloshing knee deep in the muddy water that filled the thousand yards of trenches that his battalion had to defend on the Western Front. He was still in disgrace after Gallipoli. A cold, wet, and forlorn figure under his helmet and waterproof, he spent his time encouraging his men and dodging German shell and small-arms fire. Anyone meeting him in his dimly lit dugout would have assumed they were seeing a failed politician at the end of his tether, in Byron's words "half in love with easeful death"—or oblivion.

But in less than two years Churchill was back in Parliament and one of the prime minister's closest advisers. In March 1918, when the Allied front collapsed and all seemed lost, he was the War Cabinet's principal liaison with the French high command. General Douglas Haig dubbed him "a real gun in a crisis." When the armistice with Germany was signed in November, he could count himself among the architects of victory. With indomitable will and astonishing speed Winston Churchill had forged himself a second career, just as Gandhi had in India.

The first step had been the Dardanelles Commission report in May 1917, which fixed some of the blame for the Gallipoli disaster squarely on Asquith and Kitchener (who was conveniently dead). Asquith had resigned the previous December, and the new prime minister was Winston's old friend David Lloyd George. In May 1917 Lloyd George appointed Churchill minister of munitions. It was an enormous and crucial wartime task; the ministry had become in effect the United Kingdom's largest employer.[30] Even his fiercest detractors had to admit that Churchill did well there. He used his position to inspire one of the war's most important new technologies, the land tank.[31]

Even so, he remained frozen out of the center of decision-making, the War Council. Distrust of Churchill, especially among Tories, ran so deep that the other members, including Lord Curzon, threatened to resign if he was let in. Only after victory was won in November 1918 was Winston finally appointed to it as secretary of war. He complained that there was not much point to the post if the war was over. Andrew Bonar Law answered for all of them. "If we thought there was going to be a war," he said pointedly, "we wouldn't appoint you War Secretary."[32]

Nonetheless, it had been an astonishing political rebirth. "None but a first-rate man could survive so many first-rate reverses," wrote the journalist E. T. Raymond. "There has probably been no fall comparable with his which was not final." Yet Churchill had managed to recover and find new outlets for "his courage, his war-like tastes...and his facility for espousing new causes and deserting old ones." Such a Lucifer, Raymond wrote, "should not hope again."[33]

Churchill's second political career looked very different from the first one. Before the war he had enjoyed the reputation of a radical Young Turk. Now, at age forty-five, he was part of the Old Guard. In less than five years he had gone from being fearlessly ahead of his time to being steadfastly behind it. As the 1920s rolled on, he remained self-consciously out of step with the latest public trends.

For if the war had changed India, Britain had changed even more. In 1919 Britons were feeling vulnerable and gun shy. In sheer numbers, Britain's casualties in the Great War (994,000) were actually less than Italy's (1.2 million). But the death toll drew disproportionately from the top rungs of English society, from the generation that was supposed to provide stable leadership for a society with a slowing economy and rising social tensions. The values of the Victorian and Edwardian age seemed gone for good. As a character in a novel of the time put it, "The bottom has been knocked out of everything." Self-confidence was replaced by cynicism, war-weariness, and impatience for change.

Books like John Maynard Keynes's *Economic Consequences of the Peace* taught Britons that the war they had just fought had been for nothing. Pacifist authors like Siegfried Sassoon, Vera Brittain, and the War Poets told them that such a war must never be fought again. Lytton Strachey's *Eminent Victorians* ridiculed the world of their fathers and grandfathers. In the 1920s to be branded as "Victorian" was the equivalent of social death. The future, not the past, was what counted. The war had cleared the way for New Age ideas to enter the cultural mainstream, with a distinctly leftward drift.

The "nonconformist conscience" finally shed its remaining religious clothes and embraced a series of radical causes. Churchill's erstwhile mentors, Sidney and Beatrice Webb, became cheering acolytes of the "worker's paradise" of Lenin's and then Stalin's Soviet Union. Issues of pacifism, vegetarianism, socialism, anti–blood sports, radical ideas about women and sex—all the stuff of Gandhi's counterculture London—were suddenly debated in the mainstream. Bloomsbury intellectuals like Strachey and Virginia Woolf; pacifist activists like Vera Brittain and Goldsworthy Lowes Dickinson; radical churchmen like Hewlett Johnson; writers like D. H. Lawrence; and even Labour politicians like Stafford Cripps and Lord Snowden—all were probably closer in their cultural views and attitudes to Gandhi than to a proud standard-bearer of the past like Winston Churchill.

Politics had changed, too. The Representation of the People Act of 1918 tripled the size of the electorate by giving the vote to men over twenty-one and women over thirty.[34] This meant not only an expanded role for women, whom the war had turned into a workforce and a political presence that could no longer be ignored; it hugely increased the influence of Britain's trade unions, especially in the Labour Party. The Labour Party's share of the vote exploded. Its returns in the 1922 general election were double its tally in 1918–and ten times its returns before the war.[35] Labour's leaders were poised to replace the Liberals as the second party of politics, at a time when they and their trade union supporters were anxious to match the strident militancy of the new self-declared spokesman for the working class, the Communist Party. Indeed, by 1920 Communism too had a presence on British soil and in the political landscape.

Britons felt insecure and uncertain as never before. To a war-weary public, the key to security and peace seemed to be no longer the Royal Navy or the British Army but institutions like the League of Nations. The British Empire itself, it was believed, must eventually give way to something more voluntary and inclusive, the British Commonwealth.[36]

The old idea of British sovereignty was dead, killed in the trenches of the Somme and on the beaches of Gallipoli. Enlightened minds like the Imperial Institute's Lionel Curtis assumed that humanity's future would be multilateral, epitomized by the League of Nations, and that eventually even that body and the British Commonwealth would have to give ground to a single world government. Some took an even longer view, arguing that Western civilization's days as the dominant force on the planet were numbered. In the cynical words of Curtis's protégé Arnold Toynbee, "We will all be Dagos when the world is ruled from China."[37]

Churchill would have none of this historical relativism and self-doubt. "You're not going to get your new world," he told David Lloyd George (who was something of a New Ager himself)* in January 1920. "The old world is a good enough place for me, and there's life in the old dog yet."[38] Churchill had filled his mind with the solid Victorian furniture of his father's generation—the values of the father he had worshipped but never known. He was determined to uphold the very things that Bloomsbury and the New Agers despised. He was determined to uphold the empire that the Victorians had built, the greatest the world had ever seen, as well as the ideals, like the superiority of the British race, that underpinned it. "He cared for the Empire profoundly," his friend Max Aitken remembered, "and he was honestly convinced that only by his advice and methods could it be saved."

"I am an Imperialist," he confessed to his friend Wilfred Blunt.[39] The rejection of "the white man's burden" in books like E. M. Forster's *A Passage to India* and George Orwell's *Burmese Days* seemed to Churchill a profound failure of nerve. As war secretary, Churchill set a defiant, even reactionary tone, launching a one-man battle against the prevailing pessimism of his day.

Even with the war over, his job was daunting. He had to demobilize nearly three million men, while finding money to pay for an army of occupation in Germany and another in Persia, plus 100,000 troops in Mesopotamia, Palestine, and Turkey, not to mention 70,000 British troops in India.† The army budget shrank by more than 70 percent. Mutinies had broken out in several barracks—in one of them nearly five thousand Tommies had demanded their immediate release from military service.[40]

For the first time Britain faced a sharp disconnect between its imperial commitments and its means. After World War II British politicians

---

* As prime minister Lloyd George tried but failed to pass Prohibition in Britain—a cause Gandhi would have wholeheartedly supported. But in 1915, as minister of munitions, he did manage to push through the Licensing Act , which closed Britain's pubs during the afternoons in order to promote sobriety in war industry workplaces. The war ended but the law remained, right down to 2001.

† That figure does not include the more than 400,000 men comprising the Indian Army.

would solve the problem by shedding commitments. In 1919 Churchill's impulse was to keep or increase commitments, while cutting expenditures to the bone.

This policy forced him to continue conscription, while insisting that army and air force planners assume that Britain would not fight a major war in the next ten years. That approach seemed reasonable in 1919, but the so-called Ten Year Rule (which applied to the Admiralty as well) slowed the modernization of Britain's armed forces to a crawl (with disastrous consequences later).[41] Elsewhere Churchill's instinct was to hold the line—and to use force whenever possible. When the cabinet debated cutting back on troops in Persia, he vigorously opposed any rollback, agreeing with Lord Milner that "if we lost Persia we should lose Mesopotamia and then India."[42] As Ireland slid into insurrection and sectarian violence, Churchill ordered hiring ex-veterans on the cheap to reinforce the Royal Ulster Constabulary. These paramilitary squads, the so-called Black and Tans, conducted savage reprisals against the Irish insurgency. It was one of Britain's gravest missteps in that centuries-old conflict. But Churchill preferred deploying the Black and Tans to having to pay for more regular troops, or negotiating a settlement with the IRA.[43]

He was even more belligerent on the issue of Soviet Russia. He pushed hard for Britain to intervene in the Russian Civil War and to back anti-Bolshevik White forces against the Reds, "the armed enemies of the existing civilization of the world." Left to themselves, Churchill insisted, Lenin and Trotsky would unleash their fanatical hordes across Europe and the East, even rampaging to the gates of India. A permanent Soviet Union would be a global disaster, in addition to a threat to the empire. Communism, he warned, was "a ghoul descending from a pile of skulls…It is not a creed; it is a pestilence."[44]

In later years, in the shadow of Stalin, these words would seem prescient. But to Lloyd George and others in the cabinet in 1919, Churchill's view smacked of the Russophobia of Randolph Churchill and the Victorian Raj. They worried their war secretary had "Bolshevism on the brain," while his incessant push for military intervention stood to risk a second Gallipoli. So against Churchill's advice, the cabinet voted to withdraw British troops from the Allied expeditionary force in Archangel and Murmansk. In February 1920 the Reds had largely won the civil war and their armies threatened Warsaw and Constantinople.

It was in the midst of this international turmoil and tension that the Amritsar incident suddenly dropped into Churchill's lap.

As war secretary, it was his duty, not New Delhi's, to decide General Rex Dyer's ultimate fate. For complicated reasons, a formal court-martial was out of the question.* The instinct among the uniformed members of Churchill's Army Council, including Commander in Chief Sir Henry Wilson, was to leave things as they were. They believed the morale of the Indian Army, not to mention the security of India, would suffer if the army took any punitive action against the general, especially at the behest of a band of interfering "baboos."

But Churchill's reaction to the Hunter report was the exact opposite. Ordinarily he was a stickler on law and order in the empire even at the price of blood. His record on Ireland made that clear. But as he read the details of the Jallianwala Bagh massacre, of unarmed civilians mowed down without warning or mercy, his sense of justice was shaken. In private, he said what Dyer had done was nothing less than murder.[45]

In public, he adopted the word used by one of the judges on the Hunter Commission: that Dyer had committed an act of "frightfulness." Translated: the shootings had been a deliberate act of terror, not a defense of empire. In effect, he agreed with Gandhi that Amritsar violated everything British civilization stood for. As he told an audience earlier that year, the British Empire could not and would not survive "if the British name was not held in high repute as being a name associated with fair dealing and ... the general peace and well-being of mankind"— words Gandhi himself might have used ten years earlier.[46]

So Churchill was determined to see Dyer punished or at least removed from the army. But as secretary of war he could take no action without the support of his Army Council, whose sympathies ran quite the other way. In addition, Conservatives and pro-imperialists across the country lauded Dyer's actions. The Punjab's Sikhs, fearful that the mob might have attacked their holiest shrine, the Golden Temple, had even voted to make Dyer an honorary Sikh. Many Britons believed that Dyer had prevented another Cawnpore. "Englishmen decline, and rightly so, to take any chances so far as their wives and daughters are concerned,"

---

* The Army Act allowed for trial for murder or manslaughter by court-martial only for acts committed on active service; strictly speaking, Dyer's actions in Amritsar did not fit this description, since he had gone to Amritsar on his own authority, without specific orders. The other reason for avoiding court-martial was the fear that Dyer might be acquitted and demand reinstatement: that would mean even more public outrage than before.

wrote the *Daily Mail*. "We do not wonder that the name of General Dyer is universally held in honor at the present moment by Englishwomen in Northern India."[47]

Under these political pressures, Churchill and Montagu could not actually fire Dyer, but they could get him forcibly retired. For the next month and a half Churchill tried to bully, cajole, and strong-arm the Army Council into agreeing. Sir Henry Wilson fumed in his diary: "[Churchill] tried again to rush a decision to remove Dyer from the Army saying it was only a matter of form . . . but the more he argued the deeper I put him into the muck heap," by saying it would be unfair to Dyer without a formal hearing, which would take months.[48]

Churchill knew he did not have months. Finally the Army Council agreed to issue a statement that Dyer "cannot be acquitted of an error in judgement" but should not be retired, merely informed that he would no longer be employed in India. The statement was a defeat for Churchill, but the cabinet agreed to accept it.[49] Even this mild step was so controversial that the government agreed to let the decision be debated in the House of Commons.

The crucial confrontation was set for a hot afternoon on July 8, 1920. In the House gallery sat none other than Dyer himself, who had returned to England to try to clear his name. Sitting with him were his wife and the governor of the Punjab, Michael O'Dwyer, along with a row of maharajas. Edward Carson was to take the lead on the floor for the opponents of the Army Council decision, while Secretary Montagu was to speak for the Army Council and the Lloyd George government. Churchill was slated to speak last, or next to last.[50]

A deep feeling of antipathy toward Montagu ran throughout the House, not just because of Dyer. For many Tories, there were really two questions up for debate. "First, Is it English to break a man for doing his duty?" J. L. Maffey wrote afterward. He had been sitting next to Dyer in the sweltering gallery. The second question on everyone's mind, Maffey wrote, was far nastier: "Is a British general to be downed at the bidding of a crooked Jew?"[51]

In truth the race prejudice was steeply against Montagu as he rose to defend Dyer's dismissal. He didn't do much to help his cause. All observers agreed he became unnecessarily emotional and bitter at the constant heckling and interruptions. At one point Montagu angrily blurted out, "Are you going to keep your hold on India by terrorism, racial humiliation, and subordination?" This prompted angry catcalls of "It saved a mutiny" and "What a terrible speech" even from his own benches.

"I have never seen the House so fiercely angry," Austen Chamberlain wrote, "and [Montagu] threw fuel on the flames." Chamberlain could not resist adding his own racial dig—"A Jew rounding on an English-man and throwing him to the wolves—that was the feeling"—as the government's spokesman on Amritsar unexpectedly became its greatest liability.[52]

Finally, exhausted and overwrought, Montagu sat down. He had vir-tually ruined the government's case. Edward Carson then rose and ripped the government, raising shouts of applause as he called Montagu's actions "un-English" (another racial dig). Meanwhile the government's leader of the House, Andrew Bonar Law, did some hard thinking. He had intended for Churchill, who knew the case backward and forward, to sum things up at the end of debate. Bonar Law was no Churchill fan. But now he decided to send Winston in directly after Carson, in hopes he could save the day.

As Carson sat down to raucous cheers, Churchill rose to his feet. The atmosphere was tense, almost explosive. In addition to airing ancient re-sentments over India, the House had just shown the ugly face of anti-Semitism. Privately Churchill must have been horrified. Whatever his views on race, there was not an anti-Semitic bone in his body. Like his father and also like Gandhi, he was happy to count Jews among his clos-est friends and warmest political supporters.[53] Now he needed to quell that antagonism before it boiled over.

"There has not been, I suppose, for many years a case of this kind," he began, "and which has raised so many grave and wide issues."[54] Churchill declared that he wanted to discuss the Dyer case "in a calm spirit, avoiding passion and avoiding attempts to excite prejudice" or race feeling on both sides, because such a case required "a judgement of exceptional seriousness, delicacy and responsibility."

Churchill then took a quarter of an hour[55] to explain that being pushed into retirement was the mildest formal punishment that Dyer could expect, considering what had happened. "This is an episode which appears to me to be without precedent or parallel in the modern history of the British Empire," Churchill said, his voice rising as his eye ranged around the now-silent House, "an extraordinary event, a mon-strous event, an event which stands in singular and sinister isolation."

Every military officer facing a large crowd must make painful decisions, he said, such as whether to fire, not on an enemy, "but on those who are his countrymen, or who are citizens of our common Empire." Even then an officer may be justified in shedding blood in order to save lives or restore order.

But under any circumstance, Churchill said, it was a British officer's duty to avoid anything that smacked of frightfulness: "What I mean by frightfulness is the inflicting of great slaughter or massacre upon a particular crowd of people, with the intention of terrorizing not merely the rest of the crowd, but the whole district or the whole country." Churchill then calmly but remorselessly reviewed the facts.

How Dyer had fired into a crowd that was "not attacking anyone or anything," a crowd trapped in a confined space virtually without exits; a crowd so densely packed that a single bullet was able to pass through and kill or wound three or four people.

How Dyer first ordered his men to fire into the center of the crowd; then when the people fled to the sides, he ordered them to fire on the sides.

How the firing went on for eight to ten minutes, with soldiers loading and reloading until their ammunition ran out. Churchill read aloud the testimony of one of Dyer's subordinates, stating that "if the road had not been so narrow, the machine guns and the armored cars would have" been brought to bear as well.

Churchill paused to let the point sink in. Then he continued: "We have to make it absolutely clear, some way or other, that this is not the British way of doing business." This was the kind of atrocity the Germans had committed in the last war, the kind of "bloody and devastating terrorism" employed by Lenin's Bolsheviks and their "criminal regime."

To fire on an armed crowd was one thing, Churchill said: "Men who take up arms unlawfully cannot expect that the troops will wait until they are quite ready to begin the conflict." But at Amritsar Dyer had violated every principle that Churchill believed Britain stood for: "The august and venerable structure of the British Empire, where lawful authority descends from hand to hand and generation after generation, does not need such aid. Such ideas are absolutely foreign to the British way of doing things."

He then added words that Gandhi supporters would use against him years later. "Our reign in India or anywhere else has never stood on the basis of physical force alone," Churchill declared. The real basis of

British rule was "cooperation and goodwill" between the two races—
which, he added, Montagu's trip to India in 1917 had gone a long way to
restoring. To wreck that cooperation and goodwill by allowing Dyer's
action to go unpunished or unremarked would be "one of the most
melancholy events in the history of the world." What was needed now
was to "to keep alive that spirit of comradeship, that sense of utility and
progress in cooperation, which must ever ally and bind together the
British and Indian peoples."

Churchill sat down. The House sat silent, impressed in spite of itself.
One of the spectators in the gallery, H. A. L. Fisher, called the speech
"excellent, cool, but with imaginative touches."[56] Others agreed. Pro-
Dyer speakers followed. Sir William Joynson-Hicks read aloud a letter
from a British woman in Ahmedabad, saying "the prompt action of
General Dyer in the Punjab saved our lives." Another MP ripped into
Churchill as the man "responsible for the loss of more lives than any
man sitting in this house"—a reference to Gallipoli.*[57]

But Churchill's speech carried the day. The final vote approving the
Army Council's action was 230 to 129. Of the negative votes, 119 came
from members of the government's own coalition.

Dyer left stone-faced, his wife in tears. His career was over. So was
Montagu's. But Churchill had raised himself to a new level. "To me
Winston is by far the most interesting speaker in the House," said
Austen Chamberlain's brother Neville, even before the speech.[58] The
Amritsar debate gave Churchill the reputation for eloquent oratory that
could save an issue—or even a government.

Churchill would make many speeches in his long career, speeches
that are justly celebrated and more famous than the one on July 8, 1920.
Most biographers barely mention the Amritsar debate. But a strong case
can be made that it was in fact his greatest speech. Churchill kept his
usual rhetoric flourishes, which read well in retrospect but often fell flat
with a listening audience, to a minimum. Every paragraph conveyed not
only a cool persuasive power but a depth of moral perception that had
been totally lacking in the younger Churchill (and, some might argue,
that would be lacking in the later one).

Even more strikingly, Churchill had barely mentioned Dyer by
name. He made no effort to tear the general's character down or castigate those who defended him. Instead, he simply and calmly recited the

---

* Ironically, Joynson-Hicks would later be Churchill's ally in fighting the India Bill.

facts. "If we take care of the facts of a case," Gandhi liked to say, "the law will take care of itself."[59] By doing just that, Churchill showed his skeptical audience that what they had assumed was unjust persecution of an officer doing his duty was in fact "a moderate and considered" verdict on a murderous act—an act that, as Churchill put it (quoting Macaulay), exposed "the most frightful of all spectacles, the strength of civilization without its mercy."

In the final analysis, what radiates from the speech is a sense of humanity as well as justice. From Churchill's perspective, that was what made the British Empire different from its successors. On this point he agreed wholeheartedly with Gandhi: that the empire's entire claim to loyalty rested not on its material strength but on its moral authority. "All the world is looking towards this country" for leadership, he told a British audience earlier in February, and "the leading position in the interest and respect of the nations of the world" depended on power devoted to justice and truth.[60]

Gandhi had his own term for it: "soul force." For once, Gandhi and Churchill were on the same side. And if the Amritsar speech was not Churchill's greatest speech, from a moral point of view it was certainly his finest hour.

In India, the effect of Churchill's speech and the House vote was also stunned surprise, but for precisely the opposite reason. A white officer had deliberately ordered more than a thousand unarmed Indians to be shot; he and his superior, Michael O'Dwyer, had beaten, arrested, and humiliated hundreds more. Yet the British government refused to punish Dyer and O'Dwyer, or put them on trial, or even utter a word of public censure. Few if any Indians cared that Churchill had fought hard to carry the case as far as the Parliament was willing to go. In fact, that was precisely the point. For millions of Indians, the Amritsar debate marked the point of no return. In the heat of outraged emotion, any lingering respect for British rule evaporated.

Jawaharlal Nehru was the son of the Congress leader Motilal Nehru and a young lawyer at Delhi's High Court. Educated at Harrow and Cambridge, he barely spoke a word of Hindi. He was the perfect example of Macaulay's "Indian in blood and color but English in taste and intellect." The events at Amritsar shook him deeply. Earlier that December Nehru had crossed paths with Dyer on a train and listened with horror as Dyer boasted to his fellow white officers how he had almost put rebellious Amritsar to the torch "but he took pity on it and refrained."[61]

Later Nehru would recall his rage of hearing the news from Westminster. "This cold-blooded approval of that deed shocked me greatly," he later wrote. "It seemed absolutely immoral, indecent, to use public school language," the Harrow graduate wrote, "it was the height of bad form."[62]

His father was affected even more. Jawaharlal's daughter Indira was only three when she watched her grandfather Motilal, the distinguished loyalist Moderate politician, pile up his British furniture in the garden of his house on a humid August evening and set it alight. As the flames caught and crackled, he began throwing his European clothes into the bonfire. Out of the closet came ties, collars, hats, jackets, trousers, and shoes. A lifetime of conforming to the rules and models of the Raj all went up in smoke. From now on Motilal Nehru would wear only homespun clothes, *khadi,* which had become a symbol of Indian independence—and also of Gandhi's Swaraj movement.[63]

Gandhi was similarly outraged. In *Young India* he wrote of Dyer, "His brutality is unmistakable. His abject and unsoldier-like cowardice is apparent in every line of amazing defence before the Army Council." For Gandhi, Dyer's most unforgivable failing was that his panic, and the resulting massacre, had been "unsoldier-like," a violation of the kind of manly discipline embodied by the traditions of the British Army and the empire.

Gandhi also believed that the greatest crime committed in Amritsar had not even been mentioned by Churchill and the parliamentarians. This was the "slow torture, degradation, and emasculation" of the crawling order and the floggings of innocent passersby. The authors of these deeds "deserve greater condemnation than General Dyer for the Jallianwala Bagh massacre. The latter only destroyed a few bodies but the others tried to kill the soul of a nation."[64]

On August 1, 1920, Bal Gangadhar Tilak died, the last male politician in India who still enjoyed more public prestige than Gandhi.[65] That same day Gandhi returned his South Africa War and Kaisar-I-Hind medals to Viceroy Lord Chelmsford with a note, saying the actions of Parliament and the New Delhi government "have estranged me completely from the present government and have disabled me from tendering, as I have hitherto tendered, my loyal cooperation."

Gandhi sensed the moment to act had come. He had the outrage of an entire subcontinent on his side. In a few days he would launch his largest and most sweeping satyagraha campaign, to force the government to confront its sins. Others still had their doubts about Gandhi's tactics and about his chances of ultimate success. But Gandhi had a secret ally, an alliance spawned, as it happened, on the bloodstained beaches of Gallipoli.

Chapter Fourteen

NONCOOPERATION
1920–1922

*This Empire is guilty of so many crimes that living under
its flag is tantamount to being disloyal to God.*

MOHANDAS K. GANDHI, DECEMBER 1920

*It amazes me that Gandhi should be allowed to go undermining
our position month after month and year after year.*

WINSTON CHURCHILL, OCTOBER 1921

ON AUGUST 1, 1920, GANDHI FORMALLY launched his Noncooperation campaign against the Raj. The issue around which he intended to rally support was neither the Rowlatt Acts nor the Hunter Commission report. It wasn't even the Jallianwala Bagh massacre. Instead, his headline issue was the fate of the caliphate, or *Khilafat,* in far-off Constantinople.

To many it seemed a baffling move. The overwhelming majority of Hindus had never even heard the word, let alone had an opinion on it. Yet the Khilafat question was crucial to India's Muslims, and Gandhi had quietly but publicly embraced it for nearly a year. Turning it into his next major public issue was not only a matter of personal principle but a shrewd political tactic. In fact, it gave him his first nationwide coalition. Churchill's Gallipoli invasion and the ensuing breakup of the Turkish Empire had inadvertently allowed Gandhi to outflank and rout his opponents in the Congress. In less than six months he would stand at the organization's helm.

How could this seemingly recondite issue, one consistently ignored by Gandhi's biographers, have turned him into India's most powerful politician? The answer lies in the history of the Muslim community in India since the Mutiny.

For decades, India's Muslims had felt increasingly vulnerable in an increasingly alien world. They had always been a minority, hardly a fifth of the population.[1] They were devout monotheists among people who practiced a religion that Muslims considered an abomination. The British victory in 1858, by abolishing the Mughal Emperorship, had stripped away their one shred of ancient dignity, the Muslim claim to formal political supremacy over a Hindu majority.[2]

Indian cities like Delhi, Bombay, and Calcutta had large Muslim neighborhoods. Muslims were also a sizable presence in the Punjab, where they lived side by side with Hindus and Sikhs, and they formed the majority in the states of Jammu and Kashmir. But most Indian Muslims lived in the rural areas of eastern Bengal, Bihar, the United Provinces, and the rugged provinces of Baluchistan and the Sind in northwestern India. Everywhere they carried the stamp of poverty and backwardness. In every sector of the new India, from education to business ownership and economic status, not to mention the ability to find jobs in local government and the civil service, they lagged far behind Hindus and minorities like the Parsis.*[3]

As World War I ended, Indian Muslims felt doubly betrayed. On one side, the Allies had waged war on the sultan, the leader of their faith and *Khalifa,* or defender of Islam's holy places, and had systematically dismantled his dominions. "The Indian Mussalman's heart," wrote spokesman Muhammad Ali, "throbs in unison with the Turk of Stamboul, who has to watch an act of shameless brigandage with impotent rage." On the other, Viceroy Lord Chelmsford and Secretary Montagu were giving away concessions to Hindu nationalists that promised to leave Muslims in the dust.[4]

Warnings that Muslim loyalties to Britain were being strained to the breaking point carried little weight in London. The New Delhi government also shrugged off the increasingly pan-Islamic anti-British ideology of men like Abul Kalam Azad, editor of the Urdu journal *al-Hilal,* and Muhammad and Shaukat Ali. As long as life went on normally as before, and Baluchi and Punjabi troops in the Indian Army remained loyal, the Raj was undisturbed by the undercurrent of Islamic resentment.

Only one man understood the desperate Muslim dilemma and offered to help. This was Gandhi. Muslim-Hindu cooperation was the

---

* In the 1880s only four percent of students in Indian colleges were Muslims, even though they were 22 percent of the population. At the start of the new century the literacy rate among Muslim males was half that of Hindus. Among Muslim women it was virtually nonexistent.

hallmark of his South African experience, where he had worked with Gujarati and Bengali Muslims, even Afridis and Pathans, toward a common purpose. It was the same in Champaran, where his old chum Maulana Mazharul Haq was connected to pan-Islamic circles. "We are Indians first," Gandhi liked to say, "and Hindus, Mussulmans, Parsis, Christians after."[5]

By October 1919 Gandhi had become the Muslims' leading advocate in Hindu political circles.[6] That included the Khilafat issue. Azad and the Ali brothers wanted New Delhi to insist that London leave the defeated sultan enough temporal power to discharge his duties as protector of Muslim sanctuaries, above all in Arabia.* Gandhi publicly signed on to their cause in September 1919 and endorsed the first Khilafat Conference the next month, which established October 17 as Khilafat Day, a day of hartals and shop closings.

Gandhi's message to his fellow Hindus was simple: If an issue is important to our Muslim brothers, then it should be important to us. As he always insisted, "The key to success in our fight is unity." Gandhi mobilized his remaining satyagrahi behind the October 17 action and became fast friends with radicals like the Ali brothers. They in turn offered their support and followers to Gandhi, as a reserve army for his future satyagraha campaigns.

Politics makes strange bedfellows, but always between consenting adults. As 1920 dawned, a strange but potentially powerful coalition had taken shape. Gandhi, as usual, saw things in the broadest and most universal terms, with an eye to the future. "I am uniting Hindus and Moslems," Gandhi wrote to his son on May 4, 1920. "I am coming to know one and all and, if non-cooperation goes well, a great power based on brute force will have to submit to a simple-looking thing…My *moksha* lies through them."[7]

The Khilafat satyagraha was to be only one prong of his new offensive. Gandhi decided it was time to aim his campaign directly at the politicians and their principal hangout, the Indian National Congress. That August he traveled with Shaukat Ali around the country, speaking of "the Satanism" of the British government and adding that "this Empire has been guilty of such terrible atrocities" that, if it did not apologize

---

* This wish directly contradicted British support of Prince Faisal's revolt against the Turks, which caused friction between the Foreign Office and India Office. But neither challenged the basic axiom that the future of the Middle East belonged, not to the people who actually lived there, but to the victorious Allies.

to God and the country, "it was the duty of every Indian to destroy it." By betraying the Muslims on the protection of their holy places and slaughtering Hindus at Amritsar, the Raj had lost any claim to loyalty or honor. Gandhi declared that satyagraha was the "only effective remedy" for "healing the wounds" caused by the British betrayal.[8]

Gandhi arrived in Calcutta for a special session of the Indian National Congress scheduled for September 1920, with his forces arrayed behind him.

His key aides were Rajendra Prasad, Vallabhbhai Patel, and a new disciple, thirty-one-year-old Chakravarthi Rajagopalachari. A Brahmin born in a village in Tamil Nadu, in south India, he held a law degree from Madras and had a deep love of English literature. He had been a typical nationalist lawyer, linked first to Tilak and then to Annie Besant—until he met Gandhi. Gandhi, he would say later, saved him from choosing between terrorism and cynicism.[9] Nicknamed Rajaji, he would become the third of Gandhi's Three Musketeers, the Mahatma's closest inner political circle.

Gandhi also had his Muslim advisers, the Ali brothers and Mukhtar Ahmed Ansari, a stalwart of both the Muslim League and Indian Congress, and a former Lucknow Pact enthusiast who now hoped the overthrow of British rule in India would trigger anticolonial movements around the world.[10] Another ally was the Congress's elder statesman, Motilal Nehru. He was older than Gandhi, born in 1861; his father had been a police chief in Delhi when the Mutiny broke out. Nehru belonged to the previous generation of Indian politicians and nationalists, the generation of Tilak and Gokhale. He had been radicalized by the tragedy of Amritsar. Motilal Nehru had been president of the Indian National Congress when it happened and, like his son Jawaharlal, went from being a Gandhi skeptic to a devoted supporter. Dressed in khadi, his white mustache stiff with dignity and outrage, he and another Congress stalwart, the Bengali C .R. Das, would be crucial to guiding Gandhi's ambitious program through the special session of the Congress.

All the same, none of it would have happened without the Muslim activists who flocked to Calcutta from all across India, as well as Hindu and Muslim farmers from Gujarat and Bihar. For most, it was their first entry into mainstream politics and the hallowed sanctuary of the Congress. At Gandhi's behest they took their seats at the special session and simply overwhelmed the more experienced elites. On the program committee, for example, the contingent from Madras (no Islamic stronghold) were almost all Muslims and fiercely pro-Gandhi.[11]

Gandhi announced his plan in open session. It was complete and total noncooperation with the British masters—satyagraha at its most intense. Satyagraha meant no cooperation with evil, Gandhi said, which British rule had become. He outlined an entire campaign of attack, in successive waves, like an army advancing on an enemy stronghold.

First Indians would resign their honorary British titles and positions—knighthoods, society memberships, and the like. At the same time, no one would stand as a candidate in the new legislative elections slated for next year, while students and teachers would stage a mass walkout from schools, colleges, and universities across India.

Then would come a boycott of British courts. Indian lawyers and judges would resign from the High Court in Delhi and other jurisdictions (Motilal Nehru, a leading barrister, had already done so), and government officials would leave their posts. The third wave would be a refusal to buy anything but Indian-made goods. (Some wanted more direct action, so Gandhi added a public boycott of British goods to his swadeshi program.)[12] Finally, once the first three waves had gained momentum, Indians were to withdraw from serving in the police and army, and they would pledge never to pay taxes to the Raj again.

It was precisely the program Gandhi had laid out in Hind Swaraj, broken down into four stages. The goal was the total shutdown of the Raj. The result would be the spiritual liberation of India, from top to bottom. Gandhi now asked the special session to endorse it. The delegates, even the most zealous, stirred nervously. Then Gandhi delivered his punch line. If Indians followed his program, he said, then they would have Swaraj within a year.

Many laughed in disbelief—but others did not. The debate was intense and passionate. Annie Besant was howled down when she tried to speak against the resolution; at one point Shaukat Ali tried to take a punch at Besant's ally Muhammad Jinnah and had to be restrained.[13] But eventually even the scoffers had to shrug and go along. What alternative was there? Old Guard skeptics like Besant had nothing better to propose.

The vote on September 7 was close. One hundred and forty-four voted to support Gandhi's satyagraha; 132 voted against. It was a majority of only twelve. But now Gandhi had the momentum to carry his resolution to the main Congress session in Nagpur. In December more than fourteen thousand delegates showed up in the central Indian town—the largest turnout ever for a Congress meeting (both the Muslim League and Khilafat conference were meeting in Nagpur at the same time). Noncooperation supporters were in charge from the very start; fully 72 percent, or nearly three-quarters, of the delegates were Muslims.[14] Voting by province, the Congress approved the Noncooperation resolution unanimously. The Sind and the United Provinces recorded a single dissenting voice each.

A new era had dawned for the Congress and for the political leadership of India. The group's new constitution, which Gandhi helped to prepare, confirmed the change. It broadened the Congress's base while sharpening its leadership at the top. An executive "working" committee of fifteen members took over running Congress, all fifteen being Gandhi's men. At the same time proportional representation of India's different linguistic areas expanded the number of delegates from obscure provinces, swamping the old Westernized elite who had opposed him. Gandhi completed the Old Guard's rout by insisting that local vernaculars replace English as the language of debate in Congress meetings.

Some old-timers found Gandhi's changes too radical to bear and quit the Congress. Even some supporters balked at what they considered Gandhi's "autocratic" methods. Gandhi didn't care. In the new Congress he had created a truly national movement. In 1918 its district chapters covered barely half of British India; by 1921 it had 212 chapters in every corner of the subcontinent. And every chapter was ready to be mobilized at his behest.[15]

As 1921 dawned, Gandhi threw the chapters into nonviolent battle with the Evil Empire. India's millions of Muslims and Hindus, he wrote on January 2, "are staunch in their faith, have God ever on their lips, and would welcome death in His name."[16] But almost before the campaign began, Winston Churchill had spoiled Gandhi's chances of forcing the British out of India.

Anyone who assumed that Churchill's speech on Amritsar signaled a softening of his views on India would have been badly mistaken.

"I am an Imperialist," he had proudly told Winfred Blunt that fateful autumn of 1909. He agreed with Blunt then that British rule in India had severe problems and that in general the domination of nonwhites by whites was wrong. But his real concern was England and its impover-ished masses. "I would give my life," Churchill said, "to see them put on a right footing in regard to their lives and means of living."[17] Winston in-sisted that that was why the Raj existed in the first place: to provide mar-kets for British industry and job opportunities for Britain's poor. His belief in imperial dominion over India was not a contradiction of his progressive social views but an extension of them.*

India must be kept as part of the British Empire; the Raj must remain in control. "We have not defended our empire all these years," Winston told his Dundee constituents in February 1920, to loud cheers, "in order to surrender it piecemeal at the hysterical dictation of the foolish, the feeble-minded, and the flighty." Britons had to realize that they could not bring "democratic institutions to backward races which had no ca-pacity for self-government." On the contrary, "we must strengthen our position in India."[18] As war secretary and then colonial secretary in the early 1920s, Churchill would do whatever he could to ensure that India remained British, including redrawing the entire map of the Middle East.

The Allied victory in the Great War had shattered the Turkish Empire beyond repair, leaving a hopeless political tangle from the Persian Gulf to Constantinople. Victorious British and French occupiers pushed to reestablish some kind of order, while local populations in places like Arabia, Armenia, Palestine, Syria, and Mesopotamia, along with Kurds and Greeks, pulled for autonomy and self-rule.

On June 10, 1920, Churchill told Lloyd George that matters "are now approaching a climax." This tense tug-of-war could not continue: "We cannot go on sprawled out over these vast regions at ruinous expense and ever-increasing military risk," Churchill told the prime minister.[19]

In Churchill's mind, two priorities were uppermost in the new post-Ottoman Middle East. The first was to protect India and the gateway to India, Suez. The second was to avoid any further costly extension of British responsibilities in the region. The question was how to secure the one without endangering the other.

The answer was the Indian Army. In May 1920, in the former Ottoman region between the Tigris and Euphrates Rivers called

---

* Perhaps for that reason Blunt did not give up hope that Churchill would come around to supporting Home Rule for India. "I should not be surprised if some day he made the Indian cause his own," he wrote. Indeed, Churchill one day would, but not in the way Blunt assumed.

Mesopotamia, the test came. British and Indian troops had occupied Basra on the Persian Gulf in 1914 and marched into Baghdad in 1917. As Turkish authority collapsed, Indian troops had taken on more and more of the duties of maintaining order and preventing civil unrest in the province, much as they were doing in Egypt and Palestine.[20] In April 1920 Britain formally received the League of Nations mandate for control over the region.

The honeymoon between the British and the locals was short. One day in May British troops in the town of Tel Afar arrested a local sheikh for failing to pay his debts. A riot broke out. Locals hurled stones and bricks, and four British soldiers were killed. Reinforcements arrived, including two armored cars. But the rioters, spurred on by radical Islamic clerics, rose up and counterattacked. Two officers and fourteen men were killed; the British commanding officers ordered Tel Afar cleared of all inhabitants.

Instead of quelling the trouble, the order only expanded it. In the nearby town of Mosul, the British crews of a pair of armored cars were lynched by another angry mob, who dragged their bodies through the dirt streets. One hundred and fifty saber-wielding *sowars* from the Eleventh King Edward's Lancers (Probyn's Horse) charged in and, with the help of infantry and an artillery battery, managed to restore order, but only temporarily.[21] By July, as Muslim clerics in Karbala declared a holy war against the British, all of Mesopotamia was in revolt.[22]

It was the nightmare that Americans would come to know in the same place, eighty years later. Churchill responded with his usual furious energy. There could be no question of negotiation. He needed troops to crush the rebellion, but everywhere forces were stretched. Ireland was descending into sectarian civil war; Arab riots had broken out in Jerusalem. British and Indian troops were even fighting Russian-backed insurgents in Persia, while terrorist attacks and bombings took place every day in Egypt.

The only place to get more men was India. At the end of August Winston ordered fourteen Indian battalions and six British to be transferred from India to Mosul, the heart of the revolt. The commanding officer in Mosul, as it happened, was his old cellmate from South Africa, General Aylmer Haldane. "The Cabinet have decided that the rebels must be quelled effectively," he wrote to Haldane, "and I will endeavor to meet all your requirements."[23] Haldane already had 7,000 British and 53,000 Indian troops on the ground, but he complained even twenty new battalions was not enough. Sunnis and Shiites had joined forces and were forcing his men back. He warned Churchill that the conditions were much like fighting the Boers, except in temperatures soaring to 125 degrees. Without more soldiers, he worried he might have to evacuate Baghdad. Churchill told him there were no more soldiers to be had.[24]

There was, however, the Royal Air Force. Churchill immediately ordered its chief, Sir Hugh Trenchard, to mobilize squadrons to attack the desert rebels. Bombs alone might not be enough, Churchill believed. "I think you should certainly proceed with the experimental work on gas bombs," he told Trenchard, "especially mustard gas, which would inflict punishment on recalcitrant natives without inflicting grave injury upon them."[25]

In his Amritsar speech Churchill had condemned the use of murderous force against an *unarmed* crowd as "frightfulness." Such force against an armed one goaded on by radical mullahs was another matter. In the end, the gas was not used. But RAF planes did regularly bomb Arab villages, killing terrorists and civilians alike. In Churchill's mind, it was all about teaching "those Arabs on the Lower Euphrates a good lesson." And his tactics did help to turn the tide. Another 3,000 British and 13,000 Indian troops were soon in country along with Haldane's forces. Some of the fiercest fighting took place west of Baghdad near the town of Fallujah, while around Samawa, to the south, rebels managed to derail a British armored train. Indian troopers from Hodson's Horse had to attack on foot to retake the train, slashing and shooting their way from one carriage to the next until all the insurgents were either dead or had fled.

In October the British reoccupied Mosul. The fighting dragged on until the following February; by then some 450 soldiers, British and Indian, had been killed and 1,600 wounded.[26] But Haldane and Churchill had defeated the Sunni and Shiite insurgency. Baghdad and Basra, which together formed the gateway to the oil fields of Persia and India's western flank, were safe.

But the cost was high enough that no one, least of all Churchill, was willing to pay it again. Already in August the *Times* of London had asked, "How much longer are valuable lives to be sacrificed in the vain endeavour to impose upon the Arab population an elaborate and expensive administration which they never asked for and do not want?"[27] Churchill asked himself the same question. "Pouring armies and treasure into these thankless deserts" could not continue, he wrote to Lloyd

George. "The burden of carrying out the present policy at Constantinople, in Palestine, Egypt, Mesopotamia, and Persia is beyond the strength of the British Army."

It was also producing a backlash in the Indian Army, "upon which we are compelled to rely."[28] The bulk of India's fighting men were Muslims from Sind, Baluchistan, and the Punjab. They resented having to fight and kill fellow Muslims, especially when the fate of their holy places was still up in the air. Roiled by the unrest over the Khilafat question, and by growing nationalist as well as pan-Islamic feeling, the Indian Army was an ideological ticking time bomb.

But, it was more indispensable than ever. Hundreds of thousands of its soldiers had fought in the trenches in France and Flanders; endured the heat and flies of Kut-al-Amara; held down the beaches at Gallipoli and the mountains of Salonika; and marched into Baghdad, all to enable the Allies to win the First World War. Now Indian soldiers were needed to hold on to the peace as well. Churchill's War Office shifted ultimate control of the Indian Army from New Delhi to London—to the fury of Indian nationalists, who resented having to pay for an army so that Britain could play international policeman, but also to the anger of the viceroy and the India Office.

But "the only sound and economical method of imperial defence is to regard the forces of any portion of the Empire as being available for use in any other," the War Office informed the India Office in June 1920.[29] Nonetheless the time had clearly come for a more permanent solution to the problem of keeping order in the Middle East.

As war secretary, Churchill could do little to devise such a solution. That was the task of the colonial secretary. Late in the year he asked Lloyd George for the job, and after much hemming and hawing, the prime minister gave way.

On February 14, 1921, Winston strode into the same neoclassical Colonial Office building in Downing Street where he had begun his career. In 1906, when he met Gandhi, Churchill had been the brash baby-faced young parliamentarian eager to make his mark on the world. Now in 1921 he was the balding red-faced middle-aged statesman, carefully choosing his commitments, as he tried to find a way to save Britain's Middle East empire before it gave way at the seams.

Policy-setting in the Arabian peninsula had always been the prerogative of the viceroy of India, whose representatives in the courts of the Gulf sheikhs were in effect the overseers of Arab affairs.[30] Churchill had taken control of the Indian Army from New Delhi; now he took away its control over the Middle East, with a more lasting impact.

Winston decided he would go and see the situation for himself. He demanded every detailed map of the region and ordered one-page briefings from all his resident experts—almost exactly as he would do when he took over 10 Downing Street in 1940.[31] His principal assistant on Middle East policy, John Evelyn Shuckburgh, was an old India hand. But Churchill had another formidable figure at his elbow, T. E. Lawrence or Lawrence of Arabia himself, whom he made a special assistant secretary.

In early March, together with Lawrence and Air Force chief Trenchard, Churchill set off for Cairo, picking up Clementine in Marseilles on the way. He told her to be sure to bring her tennis racket. But this was hardly to be a vacation. Cairo was in perpetual unrest; placards on cars and taxis read, "Down with Churchill." When he went to the Cairo train station to visit Palestine, a mob of fifteen thousand Arabs, furious about the Balfour Declaration,* screamed "Death to the Jews!" and waved their fists. Churchill understood not a word of Arabic. He smiled and waved back; he thought they were seeing him off.[32]

Churchill and his team then settled into the plush Semiramis Hotel and began deliberations on March 12, 1921. Over the next ten days they redrew the entire map of the Middle East. The most pressing problem was Mesopotamia. Churchill's solution was to lump the disparate ethnic groups living there—Kurds, Shiites, Sunnis, and Jews—into a single country, which was christened Iraq. T. E. Lawrence's comrade in arms, the Arab prince Faisal, was offered the throne of Iraq, even though he had never set foot in the country. Lawrence had told Churchill that Faisal would make a reliable British client. To Churchill's mind, Arab princes were largely interchangeable.[33]

Most important, the creation of a formally independent Iraq allowed British and Indian troops to withdraw, leaving a string of air bases from Cairo to Baghdad to ensure security in the region and to keep Iraq in the British orbit. In March 1922 Churchill was able to boast in the House of Commons that the Iraq garrison had been reduced to four Indian battalions, while eight air force squadrons, one-third of the RAF's total

---

* Promulgated in 1917, the Balfour Declaration pledged British support for an eventual Jewish homeland in Palestine.

strength, were stationed around Baghdad. "There is nothing like it else-where in the British Empire," Churchill said proudly.[34]

Meanwhile, Faisal's brother Abdullah received the throne of an Arab state carved out of Palestine, to be called Transjordan. Jews and Arabs living on the other side of the river were promised their own future states.[35] Churchill never guessed at the trouble he had sown; Jews and Arabs would be at each other's throats for the next eighty years. The same was true in Iraq. By lumping together populations that had noth-ing in common under an alien ruler, Churchill guaranteed eight decades of instability and a cycle of violence that is still going on today. For the region's Kurds, the Cairo Conference brought especially bad news. Churchill had thought about creating an independent Kurdistan as a buffer state between Turkey and Iraq.[36] But instead he left the Kurdish people to suffer under both Turkish and Iraqi masters. The notion of a Kurdish homeland would become only a dream.

The Cairo Conference also resolved the issue of the Khilafat and the Muslim holy places, if only indirectly. Churchill cleared the way for a secular modern Turkish state to emerge under Kemal Atatürk, the same Turkish general who had thwarted Churchill's last gamble at Gallipoli.

On the religious front, the conference wrapped up the issues with dizzying speed. Atatürk, who had deposed the last sultan, also formally renounced the caliphate, while Prince Faisal's father Hussein, as sharif of Mecca and king of Hejaz, took the title himself in 1924. In less than a year he would in turn be driven from power by his rival, Sheikh Ibn Saud. Ibn Saud and his successors never bothered to formally assume the title of caliph. And like Hussein's sons, they would become reliable British and then American clients in the region.[37]

As the guardians of Mecca and Medina, however, the Saudi clan would spread a reactionary version of pan-Islamism, Wahhabism, to the millions of Muslim pilgrims who visited the shrines every year. Without realizing it, Churchill had tipped the ideological scales in favor of an emerging anti-Western Muslim radicalism—one that haunts the Arab-speaking world, the Middle East, and South Asia to this day. Meanwhile, the relatively tame pan-Islamic message of Muslim India's leaders would fade into the background, even as its impact on India it-self would spread and deepen.

Winston Churchill, far from fearing for the future, was profoundly pleased with himself. When he left Cairo at the end of March 1921, he had completed the last great expansion of British imperial power, far greater than anything his father had done. The Raj now served as the eastern flank of a British-dominated Middle East. Its soldiers would be ready to help secure the vital oil fields of Persia and Basra, while serving as garrison troops in Egypt, Palestine, Aden, Singapore, Burma, and (until 1928) Iraq.[38] Thanks to Churchill, India's submission to British rule was now more vital than ever.

For that reason, "it amazes me that Gandhi should be allowed to go undermining our position month after month, and year after year," he wrote to Secretary of State Montagu in October 1921, just as Gandhi's satyagraha was in full swing. "I am sure if he were arrested and deported from India," Churchill went on, "you would meet an immediate reward in Parliamentary support and confidence."[39] In one exasperated moment, he even told Montagu that Gandhi "ought to be laid, bound hand and foot, at the gates of Delhi and then trampled on by an enormous elephant"—the traditional punishment Mughal emperors meted out to traitors.[40]

Montagu declined to take up Churchill's suggestion, but events were about to force his hand. Almost one year later, in 1922, Winston wrote to his old flame, Pamela Plowden, now the Countess of Lytton and wife of the governor of Bengal. He wanted to remind her and her husband to "keep the flag flying" over India and to make sure "the prestige and authority of the white man" remained undiminished. "Our true duty in India," he wrote solemnly, "lies to those 300 millions whose lives and means of existence would be squandered if entrusted to the chatterboxes who are supposed to speak for India today."[41]

The biggest of those "chatterboxes" was Gandhi. Churchill, however, could speak with some confidence. As he wrote those words, Gandhi was in prison serving a six-year sentence for sedition, and his noncooperation movement, on which he and his followers had pinned so much hope twelve months before, was in a shambles.

Most people, including (or especially) historians, tend to read Gandhi and Churchill's lives backward. They assume too easily that both men enjoyed the same public adoration and respect when they were emerging onto their respective national scenes as they did when they left them.

In both cases the truth is very different. In fact, the parallels between Gandhi's assumption of leadership in 1920 and Churchill's in 1940 are striking and instructive.

Both men were accepted as their nation's "man of the hour." Both had political visions that promised victory when others offered only despair. But both were also resented and feared by the establishments of their respective parties. Colleagues and rivals alike branded both as mavericks, headstrong and incorrigibly "impractical." In the end, the Congress went along with Gandhi in 1920, and the Conservatives with Churchill twenty years later, because they had no alternative. But their resentment remained. They would stay on board only so long as their new captain made headway. When he did not, they were all too ready to jump ship.

At Nagpur, Gandhi had forced the Congress leadership into endorsing his campaign of noncooperation as well as its new constitution. But leading Congress politicians worried about the radical changes he had foisted on them and were terrified about what might happen next. Gandhi was undeterred. "The lawyers today lead public opinion and conduct all political activity," he wrote sarcastically. "This they do during the few leisure hours they get for their tennis and billiards." Dividing one's time between politics and billiards, he argued, was not going to bring independence.[42] But mobilizing the masses would. He devoted himself to doing so for the next fourteen months, in a carefully planned campaign that he took to all corners of India.

His schedule carried him everywhere, from Assam in the east to Tamil Nadu in the south. He traveled by the trains he hated, always in third class, although sometimes by car. He often gave several speeches a day to the crowds that flocked to every stop. Peasants lined the tracks for days before his arrival, hoping for a glimpse of the Mahatmaji. "Even in the depth of the night, we could hear cries of *'Mahatma Gandhi ki jai'* in every station where the train had to stop," an eyewitness remembered, as people gathered with torches to see, or even touch the feet of, the man who promised he would deliver them from the "satanic" government of the Raj.[43]

Admirers, and even Gandhi himself, liked to look back on the great Noncooperation campaign of 1921 as a personal triumph. One biographer even enthused that Gandhi revealed himself to be the "greatest general since Napoleon, but with a non-violent army."[44] In fact, the movement sputtered and stalled almost from the start.

Its opponents included India's most articulate and respected voices. The *Bengalee* newspaper warned that "the older provinces which have been the longest in public life," like Bengal, Bombay, and Madras, "are all against non-cooperation." Annie Besant denounced Gandhi's program as dangerously revolutionary; others condemned it as an invitation to chaos. Srinivasa Sastri called the idea of shutting down India "a fantastic notion" and of boycotting the Legislative Council elections "suicidal." Rabindranath Tagore worried that Gandhi's "fierce joy of annihilation" and of obliterating British rule would unloose forces that he and his followers could not control.[45] Noncooperation may have mobilized India's peasants and urban workers in politics for the first time, but those at the top and middle of society soon lost interest, especially when Gandhi's grandiose pronouncement that Swaraj would come within a year proved wildly off the mark.

Many expressed their reservations in subtler ways, even as they paid lip service to the campaign. The call to resign titles and honors drew more than one hundred volunteers by March 1921, but few liked to point out this was out of a total of 5,186 title-holders. One Delhi barrister gave up his Royal Society membership during a public meeting after the crowd turned on him, but in private, he continued to use the "R.S." initials after his name.[46] Most Indian lawyers who quit the royal courts were back in a few months, except true believers like Motilal Nehru and C. R. Das.

At first, schools and universities emptied in response to Gandhi's call. Those in Calcutta had to shut their doors completely. But like the lawyers, the students were soon back in class after a couple of months' unauthorized "vacation." In Bombay, things were back to normal by May.[47] The desire for a Western education, with its promise of honor, office, and material reward, turned out to be greater than loyalty to Gandhi. The same was true in police departments across India (although some Muslims did quit after the Ali brothers were arrested in October) and the armed forces.

Merchants too tended to steer clear of the British goods boycott if it cut into their bottom line, although some imported cloth ended up in spectacular bonfires, including one in Bombay created by Gandhi himself. British exports fell as a result, but not enough to pressure the government. By the end of 1921 Gandhi shifted the focus from boycott to Swadeshi and the production of homespun cloth, in part because he knew the boycott was not working. He made khadi the national uniform for Congress politicians. But such tactics were hardly the way to drive the British out, or to drive capitalist profits away.

Gandhi was wearing his own khadi dhoti and cap when he had an audience with the new viceroy, Lord Reading, in May. "There is nothing striking about his appearance" was how Reading described Gandhi. "I should have passed him by in the street without a second look at him." But "he is direct and expresses himself well in excellent English with a fine appreciation of the value of the words he uses." Lord Reading became convinced that Gandhi's religious views were genuine, "bordering on a fanaticism," and that Gandhi sincerely thought "non-violence and love will give India its independence." But Reading was shrewd enough to realize that in order to get Congress's cooperation, Gandhi had "to accept many with whom he is not in accord, and has to do his best to keep the combination together."[48]

Indeed, Gandhi's national appeal had galvanized people never before involved in Indian politics, largely because no one else had ever asked them. Noncooperation demanded far more volunteers than any of Gandhi's previous campaigns; mill workers, peasants, street hawkers, and small shop owners enthusiastically joined up in towns and villages across India. There were at least eighty thousand volunteers in the United Provinces alone.

As time went on and middle-class Indians began dropping out, the volunteers became "distinctly of a lower class than at first," noted a British official in November. They are also "backed by the riffraff of the town."[49] They were happy to be paid a daily wage for putting up placards, picketing businesses and liquor stores (Noncooperation breathed a whole new life into Gandhi's temperance movement), and harassing cab drivers or street vendors who violated the official hartal days. They adored Gandhi, whom they saw as their savior, but they had no stake in the old political order. As Tagore had predicted, Noncooperation conjured into existence a grassroots political force that its leader could not control, especially among his new Muslim allies.

They were the wild card in the political deck. Thousands of Muslims enthusiastically responded to the Khilafat satyagraha and worked side by side with Gandhi's volunteers, but the Ali brothers were determined to push things in their own pan-Islamic direction. They issued a call for Muslim soldiers and police to quit their jobs—alarming Hindus who worried about chaos if the huge crowds swarming in every city were allowed to run out of control. Some radical Muslim leaders were even muttering about declaring a jihad. This did not happen. But July 1921 saw a national Khilafat conference in Karachi, which at the urging of the Ali brothers approved a resolution that called serving in the Indian Army a sin against the Islamic faith.

Now the government had to act. No one was interested in trying to stop or arrest Gandhi (as Churchill angrily noted), although thousands of his followers were already in jail. New Delhi had learned from the South African experience that Gandhi in prison caused more trouble than Gandhi out of prison. But an open call for soldiers to desert the Indian Army was tantamount to sedition. In October the Ali brothers were arrested and interned.

The anger that had been simmering all summer, and since Amritsar, broke through the flimsy constraints of Gandhi's nonviolent satyagraha. From August to November violence broke out everywhere, from arson in government schools in Orissa, to riots outside courtrooms in Calcutta where Khilafat workers were on trial, to a bloody rural insurrection in Moplal in Malabar, where Muslim peasants murdered their Hindu landlords. British and Indian troops had to be sent in, and some six hundred Hindus were said to have been butchered.[50]

Gandhi was outraged. How, he asked aloud, could he possibly hope for a successful Noncooperation movement if "the masses behave like mobs"?[51] In September he was passing with Rajaji through Madras, where an unruly crowd shouted so much he could not make himself heard. He suddenly decided that he would from now on wear nothing, *absolutely nothing,* except a simple loincloth, like a poor peasant in the field, as an act of penance for his followers' behavior and as an example to others. Rajaji was horrified, but Gandhi was adamant.[52]

What started as a temporary gesture became a permanent badge of honor. His semi-nakedness symbolized Gandhi's solidarity with the lowest of the low, and became part of the essential Gandhi image. However, like his fast after Amritsar, it was his way of protesting not the brutish behavior of the British but of his fellow Indians.

Still, Gandhi was not ready to abandon his Muslim allies, even though some openly embraced violence and the more hard-line ones were already objecting to having infidel Hindus as allies.[53] Gandhi declared that if he had been in Karachi, he would have signed the same resolution—implying he should be in jail as well. In November he proposed for the next Congress session a resolution that for Indians to serve in the Indian Army or the police was "contrary to national dignity."

Gandhi convinced several Congress leaders to sign on as well, and it was published on November 5, 1921.[54]

Twelve days later the Prince of Wales began an official visit to India. Gandhi called for a national hartal. Overnight it turned ugly and violent. In Calcutta the police were overwhelmed by the angry crowds and lost control of the situation. In Bombay, where Gandhi was, mobs roamed the streets and shut down the city. They attacked shops and homes of Parsis or Eurasians who failed to heed the hartal call and beat many more. They set cars and trams on fire; they smashed store windows and carted away what they could find. Swadeshi had become an excuse to loot.

Gandhi found a friend to drive him around the city and tried to quell the violence. He watched in horror and outrage as young men wearing khadi caps stormed stores and beat helpless victims, all the while chanting, *"Mahatma Gandhi ki jai!"* Never, he said later, "has the sound of these words grated so much on my ears."[55]

As the car turned one corner, he came on the bodies of two Indian policemen who had been beaten and stabbed. Gandhi called to bystanders and begged them to help him carry the bleeding men to a hospital. (Both later died.) It was a humiliating disaster. In all, the riots in Bombay left 58 people dead and 381 injured. Gandhi declared a five-day fast to try to restore calm. Yet he still refused to call off the satyagraha, hoping against hope that people would realize that violence would only encourage the British government to strike back.

Certainly his views on the Raj had not changed. "It may be," he told Charlie Andrews, who was having serious doubts about the direction in which Gandhi was taking India, "that the English temperament is not responsive to a status of perfect equality with the black and brown races. Then the English must be made to retire from India."[56] Already an idea was taking root in his mind: If only the British would leave, then perhaps the violence would dissipate and vanish.

Instead, worse was to come. On February 5, 1922, a group of pro-Gandhi marchers in the United Provinces village of Chauri Chaura led a procession past the local police station. The turbaned and khaki-clad policemen, helpless to stop them, taunted some of the demonstrators. The stragglers at the end of the procession responded with rocks and brickbats. Within minutes the situation exploded into a full-scale riot. The police were only twenty-three against several thousand. They fired their pistols into the crowd until the ammunition ran out, then retreated into the Chauri Chaura police station.

Maddened by the gunfire, the crowd became a raging mob. Within minutes they set the besieged station alight with torches and gathered outside, chanting. Eyewitnesses heard screams from inside. Then one by one the desperate Indian policemen ran out, and the mob hacked them to pieces. Body parts—heads, arms, and legs—were thrown back in the fire as the station slowly burned to the ground.[57]

Just a week earlier, Gandhi had made a speech in Surat openly hoping for another Amritsar to help galvanize the movement. "Let some General Dyer stand before us with his troops," he cried. "Let him start firing without warning us." A year before he had predicted that "we have to go probably, possibly, through a sea of blood" to achieve Swaraj. He never imagined the blood would be shed by Indians themselves.[58]

Gandhi immediately decided to hold another penitential fast. He had no doubt who was at fault. "There are certain crimes for which we are directly responsible," he wrote to his cousin Chaganlal. "We have but to atone for these. One such crime is Chauri Chaura." Ten days after the massacre Gandhi decided to bring the Noncooperation satyagraha to a halt.

Many of his closest associates were upset. By now more than thirty thousand of his followers were in jail. They included C. R. Das, Motilal Nehru, and Jawaharlal Nehru. They had sacrificed their freedom, even their careers, in order to secure India's freedom. Now they felt betrayed and accused Gandhi of throwing it all away. Gandhi knew better. "I assure you that if the thing had not been suspended," Gandhi wrote to the imprisoned Jawaharlal, "we would have been leading not a non-violent struggle but a violent struggle." Gandhi noted that the "foetid smell of violence" was in the land, and "it would be unwise to ignore or underrate it." Besides, he added hopefully, "The cause will prosper by this retreat. The movement had unconsciously drifted from the right path. We have come back to our moorings."[59]

But the next time the satyagraha ship left harbor, it would have to sail without the Muslims. Muhammad and Shaukat Ali were particularly bitter over Gandhi's retreat. Many of their followers had felt all along that working with Hindus was a mistake. (One Muslim reporter was particularly outraged when he found pictures being sold on the street that showed Gandhi dressed as Krishna and stamping on an Islamic crescent.) And the horrific Muslim-on-Hindu violence in Moplal had polarized feelings in both communities.

The Alis had always worried that Gandhi might strike a separate deal with the government and leave Muslims, as always, holding the bag. They were not inclined to trust him again. Gandhi's suspension of Noncooperation cost him his Muslim alliance. From this point on, Hindu-Muslim cooperation in Indian politics would a pious hope, not a workable reality.

Meanwhile news of Chauri Chaura hit the British government like a thunderclap. At a Council of Ministers meeting Winston Churchill put the blame squarely on the government's conciliatory attitude toward Gandhi and the nationalists, for acting as though "the British Raj was doomed." He admitted he had once supported the Chelmsford-Montagu reforms, but now "he felt they had received a great setback." Making concessions and introducing democratic reforms only brought demands for more concessions, Churchill declared. Instead of winning Indians' loyalty, liberal reforms only "turned [Indians] against us at every stage." Surely now everyone could see that trying precipitately to turn India over to Indians was a mistake.[60]

Churchill's harsh words horrified Secretary of State Montagu, who had a personal stake in those reforms. To hear them openly denounced in a formal ministers' meeting was chilling. Montagu was so horrified that when he returned to his desk, he penned a note to Prime Minister Lloyd George. He asked whether Churchill's words signified a change in British policy, and if they did not, he wanted the prime minister to reaffirm that His Majesty's Government was committed to "gradually converting India from a dependency into a self-governing partner in the British Empire."[61]

Montagu waited two days for an answer. Lloyd George's reply on February 10 was everything Churchill might have hoped for. "There must be a master in India," Lloyd George said flatly. "Without a master India would relapse into anarchy and chaos. We are now masters in India, and we should let it be understood that we mean to remain so."[62] Disappointed and chagrined, Montagu resigned a month later.

Meanwhile, Gandhi also noted the colonial secretary's remarks about Indians not being ready for self-government. "Mr. Churchill, who understands only the gospel of force," Gandhi wrote in *Young India,* "is quite right in saying that the Irish problem is different in character from the Indian." Having fought for their independence by violence, the Irish would have to keep it by violence as well. "India, on the other hand, if she wins Swaraj by non-violent means, must be able to maintain it chiefly by non-violent means." It was up to Indians to prove Churchill wrong.[63] But privately Gandhi felt that Churchill was probably right. India had not been ready for nonviolence, and if Indians could not control themselves, then (as Gandhi had argued since *Hind Swaraj*) they were not ready to rule themselves, either. A month before he had told his satyagrahi that "human nature in India has advanced so far that the doctrine of non-violence is more natural for the people, than that of violence." Now, in his heart, he knew he had been wrong.[64]

Gandhi had little leisure to ponder his defeat. The next day policemen arrived at Sabarmati Ashram with an order for Gandhi's arrest. Eight days later he was put on trial for trying to foment disaffection in the Indian Army and against "His Majesty's Government established by law in India." Gandhi was upbeat, "festively joyful," as one eyewitness put it. He refused to have any lawyers present and pleaded guilty to all charges.[65]

And he read aloud a lengthy statement, a kind of summary of his life up to that moment. He told how, step by step, he changed from being "a staunch loyalist" to "an uncompromising disaffectionist and noncooperator." How he had learned in South Africa that he had no rights because he was an Indian. How he had tried to change attitudes and the law by volunteering for service in the Boer War, and then the Zulu rebellion, and then the Great War. And how his hopes for "full equality in the Empire for my countrymen" had been dashed first by the Rowlatt Acts, then by the Amritsar massacre and the crawling order.

Gandhi also took full responsibility for "the diabolical crimes of Chauri Chaura" and "the mad outrages of Bombay." But in the end he put the blame for India's disorders and poverty squarely on British shoulders, arguing that the Raj had turned India into an economic dependency, ruining its once-flourishing cotton-weaving industry and spreading famine across the land.

Above all, he said, Britain had broken India's pride. "India is less manly under British rule than she ever was before." To owe loyalty to such a system of government, he said, was impossible. "In my humble opinion, non-cooperation with evil is as much a duty as is co-operation with good." Now, he concluded, it was the judge's duty to throw the book at him and to impose the harshest penalty the law would allow.[66]

On March 22 Gandhi was sentenced to serve six years in the Yeravda jail. Gandhi called the sentence light and "a great honor" and submitted to prison without demur. The government was delighted. It had feared riots and terrible outbreaks across India with Gandhi's incarceration; instead, nothing happened. The Noncooperation program vanished overnight. "Now we are simply routed," one of Gandhi's Punjabi followers, Lajpat Rai, wrote from prison. "The only thing for us to do is to be happy in our prison cells in the consciousness that at least we have not contributed to the collapse of the movement"—unlike their former leader, whose "overconfidence in his judgement" and impetuousness, Lajpat Rai felt, had landed them in this sorry position.[67]

The years in the Yeravda jail would be a time of intellectual reflection and personal reassessment for Gandhi. He had no hard labor to perform; he was allowed a steady flow of visitors. At the end of 1923 he developed dysentery, then appendicitis. The government seriously worried he would die in prison. On February 4, 1924, it ordered his release. Feeble in health and weak in spirit, Gandhi seemed a broken man physically as well as politically. Except for his family and inner circle at Sabarmati, his followers had vanished. The Indian National Congress had reverted to its old ways and the leadership of the Old Guard, dumping Noncooperation on the way. The caliphate had become a nonissue, when the Turks formally abolished the title in 1924.

It was as if the last three years had never happened.

Chapter Fifteen

REVERSAL OF FORTUNES

1922–1929

What a disappointment the twentieth century has been.

WINSTON CHURCHILL, 1922

ON NOVEMBER 15, 1922, TWO WEEKS shy of his forty-eighth birthday, Churchill got the shock of his life.

In the general election that day, Dundee's voters replaced him with a Labour Party pacifist. A guest at a dinner party caught a glimpse of him shortly afterward. "Winston was so down in the dumps he could hardly speak the whole evening," the man remembered. "He thought his world had come to an end—at least his political world. I thought his career was over."[1]

In fact, a new era had begun for British politics, and a decade of turmoil and disappointment for Winston Churchill. He had known the battle for his Dundee seat would be tough. Crowds of socialist-minded young men and women exercising their legal right to vote for the first time heckled him everywhere he went; his reputation as an anti-Bolshevik hard-liner hurt him among Dundee's working-class voters. But he never imagined that when the ballots were counted, he would get less than 14 percent of the votes.

It was a stunning repudiation. T. E. Lawrence wrote to their mutual friend Eddie Marsh: "I'm more sorry about Winston than I can say."[2] The humiliation in Dundee was partly spillover from the shipwreck of Churchill's Middle East policy. In the turmoil that had followed the Turkish Empire's demise, war between Turkey and Greece had threatened to draw in Britain. Churchill and Lloyd George had clashed over what to do and even over which side Britain should take. Voters recoiled from the prospect of Britain entangled in another armed conflict.

Politicians were in no mood for one either, especially in the Middle East. Divided against itself, the Conservative-Liberal coalition that had governed Britain since the Great War crumbled.

India proved a political liability as well. The 1920s saw a sudden rallying to the Raj.* Backbench Tory MPs had felt all along that the Government of India Act of 1919 had gone too far and had helped to provoke the violence not only at Amritsar but at Chauri Chaura. They were angry with their coalition leaders for joining in the "persecution" of General Dyer. The price they demanded was Secretary Montagu's resignation, which came in March 1922. A desperate Lloyd George called for expanding the budget for the Indian Civil Service, the "steel framework," as he termed it, that held India together. One observer called the speech "Kiplingesque" in its imperial overtones, yet it could not save his government.[3] In October the Tories and Andrew Bonar Law walked out, forcing a general election. It brought down the last government that the Liberal Party would ever lead and Churchill with it.

For the first time in twenty-two years, Winston held no elected office. But after his initial shock and despair, he found other outlets for his restless energy.

One of them was painting. Not until he was forty did he discover this "wonderful new world of thought and craft," as he called it. It became a lifelong passion. His friend Violet Asquith was astonished to discover that it was the one activity Churchill could engage in without talking. "When golfing, bathing, rock climbing, building sand castles on the beach," she remembered, "even when playing bezique or bridge he talked"—and talked nonstop.

But while standing or sitting outdoors in front of his canvas, dressed in his white coat and broad hat, Churchill maintained a rapt silence, as he worked away with his brushes, paint tubes, and palette knife. "I felt that I was witnessing a miracle," Violet Asquith said.

She also believed that squeezing the paint tubes, with their bright colors of vermilion, orange, scarlet, and Prussian blue, gave him "a voluptuous kick."[4] Characteristically, Churchill himself compared painting to fighting a battle. It required the same surveying of the terrain and land-

---

* One sign of that resurgence was the large turnout for the funeral of General Reginald Dyer, "the butcher of Amritsar," on July 28, 1927. Rudyard Kipling sent a wreath, as did Dyer's former regiment, the 26th Punjabis. In its obituary the *Morning Post* called Dyer "The Man Who Saved India."

scape, the same devising of a strategy to capture the scene with its variety of objects and colors, "each different in shadow and sunlight." Armed with paintbox, brushes, and paints, he made a forward plunge and finally met with success or defeat on "the pictorial battlefield," meaning he had created either a painting or "a sea of mud."

Painting "is, if anything," he would write, "*more* exciting than fighting if [done] successfully."[5] His pictures, with their sharp vivid colors and quasi-impressionistic landscapes, were soon decorating the rooms of friends and colleagues, as well as the children's nursery.

He also traveled—he now had time for an extended trip to Italy and the Côte d'Azur. He also began working on his war memoirs, the first volume of which appeared in 1923. Rising Tory star Samuel Hoare wrote sardonically to a friend, "I hear that Winston Churchill has written a big book about himself and called it *The World Crisis*." The volumes were in fact the first comprehensive history of the Great War told by a genuine Whitehall insider, and the sale of the serialized rights (plus the death of a cousin who left him several thousand pounds) allowed him to buy a new house, called Chartwell, in Kent.

Churchill fell instantly in love with the place; Clementine's feelings were mixed. But with his enforced leisure, Winston had happy hours to spend redoing the gardens, supervising renovation of the bathrooms, and constructing a new wing, as well as building a tree house for the children. He laid bricks by hand for the garden walls, often in three- and four-hour stretches. Having discovered the pleasures of domesticity, Churchill sensed that, at age forty-eight, he was finally growing up. His mother had died in June 1921; his youngest daughter Marigold in November, of septicemia. Both events severed his ties to the past and sobered his view of the future. Like his Dundee defeat, they reminded him that he had to decide what was really important to him, including his political allegiances.

Winston was still a Liberal and still a leading member of his party. But the party was quickly shrinking into political insignificance, squeezed as it was by the resurgence of Toryism on one side and the rise of Labour on the other. The 1922 election defeat left Liberals sparse on the ground and bitterly divided between the Asquith and Lloyd George wings. Neither considered Churchill a very desirable or reliable asset. And so in his forced retirement Winston found himself being wooed from a very different quarter: the Conservatives.

Clementine resolutely hated the Tories, almost as much as she disliked

Chartwell.[6] She prayed that her husband would remain loyal to his Liberal convictions or at least trade away his loyalty at the highest possible price. Winston had little in common with the Conservative Party. He and they continued to clash over free trade and over "doing something for the poor" through progressive legislation (although thanks to the Labour Party, the recipients of the liberal welfare state's largesse were no longer as grateful and deferential as they had once been).

On the other hand, the Tories were reliable anti-Bolsheviks and dedicated foes of the wild-eyed radicals in the Labour Party. And above all they were "sound" on the empire, including India. In 1920 Lloyd George had half-jokingly called Churchill "the last specimen of a real Tory." In fact, he was not the last Tory but the last Whig. He had made himself into the political heir of the expansive classic liberalism of the Victorian era, of Thomas Macaulay and John Stuart Mill. By 1924 the Conservative Party was the only refuge left for a robust Victorian faith in the healing powers of civilization, science, free trade, and the British way of life—and in taking up "the white man's burden" with enthusiasm. And as Churchill told his wife, the Conservatives' eyes "are fully open to the dangers that lie ahead."[7]

The Conservatives' attitudes toward those dangers, however, were fundamentally different from his. Winston saw the dangers as bracing challenges, as opportunities to put history and Britain on a new course. But the average Conservative politician and backbencher only wanted to make them go away. The failure of Tory nerve in the face of great challenges had led him to leave the party in the first place. Over the next decade, on India and appeasement, they would let him down again. In that sense, nothing had changed. The truth was that Winston Churchill never did fit in with his Tory political brethren, then or later. His return to the Conservative Party was a matter not of homecoming but of finding a port before the impending storm.

Nonetheless, it was the Conservatives' leader Stanley Baldwin who first sought out Churchill. The 1922 election had carried Baldwin into power, but just barely. He believed he could secure his government by hastening the Liberals' demise. He shrewdly grasped that their middle- and upper-middle-class voters would flock to the Conservative standard rather than vote for the "Reds" of Labour. Recruiting Churchill was one way to help pull the Liberals to pieces. Even Winston thought that by joining the Conservatives, he might bring thirty MPs with him.[8]

Baldwin and Churchill met in late February 1923. "He evidently wants very much to secure my return and cooperation," Winston confessed to Clementine. He hesitated to take the plunge, and not only because Clemmie disapproved. Baldwin's Conservatives had embraced protectionism, Winston's bête noir, as their electoral issue for 1923. So when a seat opened up in West Leicester, Winston preferred to run as a Liberal free trader.

He lost to the Labour candidate by four thousand votes. Finally, when enough Liberals joined with Labour to give Britain its first Labour prime minister in Ramsay MacDonald, Churchill realized he had no place left to go except the Tory benches.

In May 1924 he made his first public appearance on a Conservative speakers' rostrum in Liverpool in more than twenty years. The independent Liberal Party no longer had a home, he told his audience. Only the Conservative Party offered a strong enough base for "the successful defeat of Socialism."[9] That October, in another general election, Winston won the seat for Liverpool and joined the Tory victory celebrations (although in his coy way he still preferred to call himself a "Constitutionalist" rather than a full-fledged, official Conservative).

Winston's defection was solitary. Not a single Liberal joined him. But it no longer mattered. The election was a Conservative landslide. Baldwin secured two-thirds of the seats in the House of Commons, while the Liberal membership shrank to just forty.[10]

Baldwin was by no means finished with Churchill. Bringing a brilliant speaker with energy and ambition inside the government made more sense than leaving him out, he realized, where he might be tempted to cause mischief. The cabinet post Baldwin wanted to give Winston was, interestingly enough, his father's first post: secretary of state for India.

But others in the Tory leadership demurred. If Gandhi and his supporters forced the government to take drastic action in India, they warned, the hot-tempered Winston would, as usual, overreact. Baldwin reluctantly agreed, and the post went to Churchill's friend F. E. Smith, Lord Birkenhead, instead.[11]

Churchill expected to become colonial secretary, the last cabinet post he had held before the 1922 election. Instead, Baldwin astonished and thrilled him by offering him the chancellorship of the exchequer. It was the second most influential post in the cabinet next to prime minister. Indeed, it was often the stepping-stone to the premiership itself. It was also the post Randolph Churchill had held before he died. "This fulfills my ambition," Churchill gushed when Baldwin offered the post. "I still have my father's robes as Chancellor. I shall be proud to serve you in this splendid office."[12]

An ambition had been fulfilled. Certainly it must have seemed to Churchill that he was now poised on a new exciting public course, one that would allow him to guide his newly chosen party in a new direction, toward moderate social reform and economic liberalism; one that must eventually take him to 10 Downing Street. He was right—only his timing was off by a decade and a half. In less than six years he would nearly wreck his political career almost beyond repair, even as Gandhi's was scaling to new heights.

"Scaling new heights" would have seemed a bizarre prediction to anyone watching Gandhi shuffle slowly out of the Yeravda prison on February 6, 1924.

His release had come at the order of Ramsay MacDonald's short-lived Labour government. Gandhi had served only two years of his six-year sentence. Frail and ill, he was angry that his poor health had forced an end to his incarceration and placed him under obligation to a government that preferred to have him die out of prison rather than at Yeravda. "I still have much to do," he petulantly told a Gujarati interviewer.[13] In jail he had had some moral leverage. As a free man, he was compelled to sweep up what remained of his movement.

His program of Noncooperation was a shambles. The riots, Chauri Chaura, and his subsequent arrest had sapped away his credibility as a political strategist. He had declared that he wanted "independence inside the Empire, if possible; outside it, if necessary."[14] Old-style liberals like Srinivasa Sastri and M. R. Jayakar thought he had pushed the British too far; fiery radicals like the young Jawaharlal Nehru thought he had not gone far enough. In June Gandhi felt strong enough to attend the All-India Congress Committee (AICC) meeting in Ahmedabad. The same figures who had stood with him in 1920 were there, but they were no longer so deferential.

Gandhi stoutly presented his program one last time. He asked the AICC to renew its endorsement of khadi, including the proposal that all Congress members learn to spin their own cotton thread, and to endorse nonviolence as official Congress policy. The result, in the words of one distinguished Gandhi historian, was "dramatic." At the mention of the spinning wheel, his erstwhile colleagues, Motilal Nehru and C. R. Das, walked out. Others shook their heads in disgust. They, and many others, had had enough of Gandhi putting his own personal obsessions ahead of constructive action. The resolution on nonviolence passed, but with a majority of only ten.[15]

When the votes were counted, Gandhi wept at the rebuke. He confessed to the conference that he was "defeated and humbled" by the hairbreadth measure of the Congress's support. His remaining supporters urged him to continue the fight by creating his own Swarajist party, but he refused. He worried that it would only further divide the Congress and the national movement. "I do not despair," he wrote to Jawaharlal Nehru. "My faith is in God. I know only the moment's duty. It is given to me to know no more. Why then should I worry?"[16] To his mind, and the minds of friends and foes alike, Gandhi's political career was over.

The Raj breathed a deep sigh of relief. "Poor Gandhi has indeed perished!" crowed the new secretary of state for India, Lord Birkenhead. He felt free to dismiss Gandhi as a "pathetic" figure. Certainly he was no one the Raj would have to worry about again.[17]

After a brief recuperation in Poona, Gandhi withdrew to Sabarmati. He was immensely proud of the semimonastic community he had set up there, always calling it "my best creation." Now it would be the setting for a self-imposed period of rest, reflection, and reassessment. This was something new for Gandhi; something he would never have time for again. Out of it would emerge the Mahatma Gandhi that the world has come to respect and revere, one ready to do battle again with the Raj.

In some ways the years from 1924 to 1927 were a continuation of his routine at Yeravda. The truth was Gandhi had enjoyed his time in prison. It had been a chance to read, experiment with his diet (at one point he was living on nothing but goat's milk, oranges, and raisins), and sleep without the interruptions of his usual furious schedule. During his two years at Yeravda he read an estimated 150 books. They included Kipling's *Barrack Room Ballads* and *Second Jungle Book*; Macaulay's *Lays of Ancient Rome* and Goethe's *Faust*; *Dr. Jekyll and Mr. Hyde* and *Ivanhoe*; Buckle's *History of Civilization* and that Churchillian favorite, Gibbon's *Decline and Fall of the Roman Empire,* which Gandhi hugely enjoyed.[18]

He also finally had time to read the entire *Mahabharata* (it took six months) and other Indian classics. And he intensely reread the *Bhagavad Gita,* which inspired him to compose a series of lectures on the *Gita* when he returned to Sabarmati as well as an autobiography, which he dubbed *My Experiments with Truth*. He had tried to start the latter during the months of solitude in prison, but had found no time. But he did manage to write thirty chapters of another autobiographical work, *Satyagraha in South Africa*.

The Yeravda and Sabarmati years form a confluence. They were a time for listening to what Gandhi called his "inner voice" and for reimmersing himself in the principles that motivated his life and thought.

The first of those principles, which he articulated in his *Gita* lectures, was that satyagraha meant nothing without a religious focus. "I believe politics cannot be divorced from religion," he told an American interviewer soon after his release.[19] Gandhi had been so caught up with the day-to day politics of Noncooperation, he realized, that he had lost sight of the movement's spiritual basis; if he lost sight of what he was trying to accomplish through Swaraj, others would, too. Violence and death at Chaura Chauri had been the result.

He had found a new appreciation for the *Gita*'s message of selfless sacrifice and of redemption of the individual through moral action, regardless of consequences. "If one man gains spiritually," he wrote in December 1924, "the whole world gains with him; and if one man fails, the world fails to that extent."[20] That included saving humanity from industrial society. "It is not possible to conceive of gods inhabiting a land which is made hideous by the smoke and din of mill chimneys and factories"—or of men who were spiritually whole.[21]

This was why the *charkha,* the spinning wheel of ancient India, became so important to him. Even when growing up in India, Gandhi had never actually seen one. However, in 1917 a friend discovered a traditional spinning wheel in the neglected storeroom of a house in Vijapur.[22] Gandhi painstakingly learned how to wind threads using its constantly turning spindles and wheel (*charkha* means "wheel"). To him the charkha represented India before the British came: an India at spiritual peace with itself, as well as economically and culturally self-sufficient. For the rest of his life, no day was complete without two or even three hours crouched beside his charkha, with the regular "humming of the wheel serving as the background music of his thoughts."[23]

Gandhi fervently believed that by spinning their own cotton and making their own clothes, Indians would not only free themselves from the "evils" of market capitalism; they would also experience the spiritual regeneration that was essential to Swaraj. "It is my certain conviction," he once told an audience, "that with every thread I draw, I am spinning the destiny of India."[24] Behind his back Congress politicians laughed or became impatient when he sang the charkha's praises. They had walked out on him when he brought it up at the Ahmedabad meeting. Some of them knew, even if Gandhi did not, that far from being a symbol of contented village life, the charkha had always been an unheard of luxury to India's rural masses.*[25]

But they dutifully learned to use the wheel (Jawaharlal Nehru became so proficient that he could turn out 300,000 yards of thread a year), and the homespun khadi cap and dhoti became the de facto uniform of the Indian National Congress. By January 1925 Gandhi could say, "The key to Swaraj lies in fulfilling three conditions alone—the charkha, Hindu-Moslem unity, and in the removal of untouchability." These became Gandhi's program for the future, his blueprint for a spiritual "revolution" in India. But achieving them proved more difficult than ending British rule.

In 1924 the gulf between Hindu and Muslim, which Gandhi had tried to bridge during the Khilafat satyagraha, was wider and deeper than ever. His former allies, the Ali brothers, were mired in pan-Islamic politics and completely estranged from the Congress—and from Gandhi. At Yeravda Gandhi had tried to study Urdu and read histories of Islam, in hopes of understanding the challenges the Muslims faced in a Hindu-dominated society.[26] But neither he nor Congress politicians ever fully came to grips with the unstable combination of pride, hope, vulnerability, and fear that drove India's Islamic minority and its spokesmen. Gandhi could never accept that the same public religious gestures that made the Hindu masses revere him as a *sadhu* (holy man) made Muslims suspicious and uneasy, made them feel that Gandhi too would sell them out in the end. Even his constant invocation of the god Rama and *Rama Raj* (the future rule of Rama across India) seemed to many a virtual declaration of war on their faith.[27]

For all his talk about religious reconciliation, Gandhi could not ignore the fact that like everyone else, he was sitting on a sectarian powder keg. In September 1924 Muslims in Kohat on the Northwest Frontier ran riot, murdering Hindus who fled for their lives until troops arrived. At Sabarmati Gandhi held a five-day fast in protest. But the sporadic

---

* Gandhi belatedly realized this, and by 1931 a team of disciples devised a smaller, portable charkha that would fit into a briefcase. Nicknamed the book or Yeravda Charkha because Gandhi used it during his extended stay at the prison following the Salt March, it became the most popular version of the charkha. It is still sold over the Indian Internet today.

outbursts of communal violence never stopped. In the United Provinces alone there were more than 88 serious outbreaks in four years, killing 81 and injuring 2,300 more. By 1927 Gandhi was admitting, "I dare not touch the problem of Hindu-Moslem unity. It has passed out of human hands and has been transferred to God's hands alone."[28]

Equally disturbing was the status of India's *dalits* or untouchables, and the larger question of India's caste system. There was a time, shortly after his return to India, when Gandhi had been willing to view the role of caste "with guarded approval," as encouraging self-discipline among caste and *jati* members.[29] Untouchability was another matter. Gandhi said it poisoned the Hindu caste system, "as a drop of arsenic would poison an entire tank of milk." His readings of the Hindu classics, like the *Upanishads,* had convinced him that untouchability was an aberration, an excrescence on orthodox Hindu social values and ideals. Gandhi refused to believe that the faith of his fathers could be callously indifferent to the fate, or even existence, of nearly sixty million fellow human beings—so callous that untouchable men could be lynched for wearing their mustaches with points turned up instead of down.[30]

"Untouchability for me," he told an American interviewer, "is more insufferable than British rule. If Hinduism embraces [it], then Hinduism is dead and gone."[31] Instead, Gandhi started preaching a revised ideal vision of caste, called *varnasharmadharma,* in which the ancient fourfold division of Hindu society would represent a division of labor, not claims of superior or inferior status.[32]

Few, however, were willing to be convinced, including (or especially) the *dalits* themselves. They were learning from their Muslim counterparts how to find spokesmen who would represent their interests directly to the Raj and the Hindu majority, rather than rely on the kindness of strangers like Gandhi. On the other side, old-fashioned Hindu nationalists like Tilak and radicals like Vinayak Savarkar saw upholding the age-old taboos as essential to their faith. Popular protests against Gandhi's "heresy" on untouchability broke out in 1925 and 1926. Even at Sabarmati, Gandhi had to give up trying to get Hindu disciples to share food with the untouchables in the ashram.[33]

For Gandhi, it was all part of the same issue. How could he bring peace and unity to a subcontinent where every social identity was built on difference and conflict? At Sabarmati he was willing to take a stab at it.

During his three-year withdrawal from politics, the ashram became his laboratory for spiritually transforming India. Here forty or so men, women, and children grew their own food, spun their own thread, made their own clothes, prayed and sang, and recited the *Bhagavad Gita*. At its core were the disciples who had followed him from Tolstoy Farm in South Africa, including his family. Although close political disciples like Patel and Prasad often visited the ashram, they were never part of it. Instead, its inhabitants formed a special cadre of Gandhi intimates, with whom he shared everything* and who were willing to live by the rules of the Mahatma.

One of them was Mahadev Desai. He had been a lawyer, poet, and collector of local folk songs when Gandhi met him in Ahmedabad in 1917. The slim, sensitive Desai was twenty-five years old; Gandhi forty-eight. "Leave everything else," Gandhi said to him, "and come to me." Mahadevbhai became Gandhi's surrogate son, replacing the errant Harilal, and even closer than Manilal. Although he was married, Desai felt no compunction about moving to the ashram and becoming Gandhi's personal secretary and amanuensis.

Everyone agreed that Mahadev wrote with a strong, beautiful hand; he even had Gandhi's style of expressing himself. In conversation he was known to often finish Gandhi's sentences for him. As personal secretary, Desai brought order and coherence where it had often been lacking. A usual comment after a long meeting with the Mahatma was "We will know what he said when we get Mahadevbhai's notes."[34]

Desai's son Narayan has left a vivid memoir of the ashram and the gallery of personalities who inhabited it in the late 1920s. There was Kasturbai, the busy matriarch who spoiled the children and scolded Gandhi for feeding the guests too much. There was Bhansali, a recluse and former teacher of French who had taken a twelve-year vow of silence. When someone stepped on his foot in the dark, and he cried out involuntarily, he had his lips sewn shut with a copper wire in penance. There was Premabehn Kantak, a twenty-something female disciple who tried to maintain some discipline over the horde of children who were constantly under foot. There was even a police spy, Ismailbhai, who tried to bribe the boys and girls with sweets in order to find out what the adults were talking about.[35]

---

* Including daily inquiries of "How are your bowels today?" Gandhi saw intestinal regularity as a sign of spiritual health and took a keen interest in the results, whether in his case or that of his disciples. Indeed, one of his favorite books in London had been *Constipation and Civilization,* which purported to show a direct link between the corruption of modern life and various gastrointestinal disorders.

And there was Gandhi himself, who often joined the children in the fun; he used his watch to keep time for their relay races and went swimming in the Sabarmati River. He also supervised the young people's plays and musical programs after supper, like a benevolent Victorian patriarch in a London suburb. To Narayan and the other children, he was always "Bapu," or Father—while Narayan's own father was merely "Uncle."

Apart from Bapu himself, the center of life at Sabarmati was its large bronze bell. It tolled out the time for every activity in the community, from rising in the predawn morning to the midday and evening meals, to going to bed at night. One day the children decided to count how many separate rings it made. They counted fifty-six.[36] At mealtimes the great bell would ring once to summon everyone to the dining hall. At the second ring the hall doors shut. At the third ring the diners began their prayers. Entering the hall after the second ring required the forgiveness of the Mahatma himself.[37]

Mealtime was the opportunity for Gandhi to experiment in new diets. He knew his attitude toward food veered very far from the conventional, even for a vegetarian. He even published a column in *Young India* titled "Confessions of a Food Faddist." But like voluntary celibacy and spinning, diet was yet another path to Gandhi's austere version of Swaraj, meaning "rule over the self."

Even the most dedicated ashramites had trouble keeping up. At Tolstoy Farm in South Africa meals had normally consisted of a range of vegetable and lentil dishes, along with nuts, hard-baked whole-meal bread and butter, and green salads. Then Gandhi shifted to eating only fruits and nuts; then only *sun-baked* fruits like raisins.[38]

Gandhi was still avoiding cooked foods when he returned to India in 1915. "No fire should be necessary in the making of food," he told a skeptical Srinivasa Sastri, "fire being unnatural." (One of his favorite books at the time was Adolf Just's *Return to Nature*.)[39] He also felt that cooking food forced women to spend their lives in the kitchen, just as his mother had done. But raw vegetables put an intolerable strain on his digestive system, especially after his bout with dysentery in prison. In August 1929 another flare-up forced him to give up uncooked food. He was soon experimenting with raw but soaked grains instead—hardly a digestive improvement.[40]

Like the meals, the ashram rules for adults were austere and monastically strict, "sometimes harsh as well."[41] Like monks in a Buddhist monastery, entrants, including women, shaved their heads. They took vows to always tell the truth, to eschew all forms of violence, to own no possessions, and to practice celibacy—although Gandhi found celibacy impossible to enforce with all the married couples living under his roof and had to make it voluntary.*

For the children, however, like Narayan Desai and Gandhi's grandchildren, Sabarmati was a nonstop summer camp. Since there was almost no schooling or book learning, life was a series of games. On Gokul Ashtami, Krishna's birthday, the adults and children gathered to chant the *Bhagavad Gita*. The children dressed in the costume Lord Krishna wore when he was a young cowherd and would run out bare-chested in loincloths and red turbans to graze the cattle. On the way home, they would munch on sweets made in the dairy. (Adults, on the other hand, were allowed almost no cows' milk products.)†[42]

The children learned songs like "Don't kill, learn to die—this is what Gandhiji teaches" and "Think of prison as a temple" and "The spinning wheel is an arrow that will pierce the government's heart." And all the ashram's children learned to spin thread "nonstop," although it too became a kind of game. Some boys and girls would work at their charkhas as much as eight hours a day, chanting and laughing. Others organized a twenty-four-hour "charkha-thon," switching off in relays like medieval monks chanting a perpetual mass.[43]

All the while, the smokestacks of Ahmedabad's textile factories loomed above them, clearly visible on the Sabarmati's opposite bank. There the great machines Gandhi so despised churned out textiles to be sold all across India and Asia, the profits of which lined the pockets of Ahmedabad businessmen. These businessmen piously and generously donated the funds without which Sabarmati Ashram could not have survived. Gandhi may not have been blind to the irony, but he took the money. In the immortal words of one observer, the Bengali poetess and Gandhi acolyte Sarojini Naidu, "It cost a great deal of money to keep the Mahatma living in poverty."[44]

Naidu first met Gandhi in 1914. Born into a famous Brahmin family and brilliantly educated, she was only one of the accomplished women

---

* When he found out that some of the older boys had been caught in homosexual practices, he held a six-day fast to admonish them. Homosexuality was a direct reproach to Gandhi's most cherished values, including both *brahmacharya* and "manliness." When the same thing had happened at Tolstoy Farm in 1914, Gandhi wrote some of his most anguished and soul-searching passages.

† Gandhi was a strict vegetarian, but he was no vegan. When he left India for the first time, he had promised his mother to drink no milk, but he considered goat's milk within bounds of his vow.

who found themselves irresistibly drawn to Gandhi and became part of his inner circle, if not part of the ashram itself. Another was Saraladevi Chaudhurani, the niece of Rabindranath Tagore. Headstrong and passionate, fluent in English, French, Farsi, and Sanskrit, she was, like Gandhi, a champion of New Age ideas (her mother had been a Theosophist) and would spend her life fighting for Indian women's rights, including the right to vote.

Saraladevi and her husband never lived at the ashram. But their daughter did, and Saraladevi was a frequent visitor and one of Gandhi's closest confidantes. She accompanied him everywhere on his Noncooperation tour in 1921. She wrote the unofficial anthem of the satyagrahis, "I Bow to India." Indeed, the attraction was not a one-way street. Gandhi's letters to her reveal a warmth, even an eroticism, that no one else ever kindled. When Gandhi met Margaret Sanger in 1935, he confided that Saraladevi was the only woman who ever made him think about leaving his wife.[45]

Then on November 7, 1925, another single woman arrived at the ashram. When Gandhi came to the gates to greet her, she knelt at his feet and addressed him as "Bapu," or father. Gandhi stretched out his hands and raised her up, murmuring, "And you shall be my daughter." The next day she shaved her head, like the other Sabarmati women, and donned the obligatory khadi sari. She would be a fixture at Gandhi's ashram for the next two decades.

The difference was that Madeleine Slade was an Englishwoman, the daughter of a Royal Navy admiral. Admiral Slade commanded the East Indies fleet and even served on the board of Churchill's Anglo-Persian Oil Company.[46] Far more than Gandhi's other white friends, like Charlie Andrews or Henry Polak or his secretary from Johannesburg days, Sonja Schlesin, Madeleine Slade was ready to turn her back on all Western values to prove her allegiance to Gandhi's cause. She even surrendered her identity, changing her name to Mira or Mirabehn, after Gandhi's favorite medieval Indian poet.

Madeleine Slade was the early hint of what would become a cultural tidal wave. Under Gandhi's inspiration, thousands of educated Westerners would soon jettison their own culture to find a new spiritual inspiration in India. What began with Mirabehn (although there were earlier examples of Westerners turning to Indian culture) would finish with the Hare Krishnas and the Beatles. And the book that more than any other set it off (Slade had booked passage to India almost as soon as she finished reading it) had appeared in European bookstores about the time Gandhi left the Yeravda jail. An international best seller, the book made Gandhi famous outside India for the first time and turned him into a New Age icon.

The book was *Mahatma Gandhi: The Man Who Became One with the Universal Being.* Its author was French writer Romain Rolland, a leading contributor to the counterculture magazine *New Age* and later winner of the Nobel Prize for literature. Rolland, a pacifist and a keen admirer of Tolstoy, had always been fascinated by Eastern philosophy.* He had learned about Gandhi while corresponding with the poet Tagore and originally wrote his admiring portrait of Gandhi for the magazine *Europe* without actually visiting India or even meeting Gandhi. Rolland was convinced that Gandhi held not only India's but the world's destiny in his hands. To Rolland, Gandhi was the greatest religious leader since Jesus Christ.

"This is the man who has stirred 300 million people to revolt," Rolland breathlessly wrote, "who has shaken the foundations of the British Empire, and who has introduced into human politics the strongest religious impetus of the last 2,000 years."[47] From the beginning, "Gandhi and India have formed a pact," Rolland explained. "They understand each other without words...and India is prepared to give whatever Gandhi may demand." Gandhi was "the orchestra leader" of India's "oceans of men," who would soon overwhelm the British in a tidal wave of spiritual liberation.[48]

That message of peace and harmony was destined to reach far beyond India. Rolland portrayed Gandhi as the messiah of a New Age of universal enlightenment, whose message embodied "the principle of life and non-violence." The only thing Gandhi's gospel lacked, he gushed at one point, "is the cross."[49]

Rolland put it as plainly as he could: "The Apostle of India is the Apostle of the World...The battle the Mahatma began fighting four years ago is our battle" and "will lead a new humanity on to a new path."[50]

Mahatma Gandhi appeared in 1924, when Gandhi's fortunes were at their lowest. Soon all Europe was buzzing about the Mahatma. Far from being embarrassed by Rolland's exaggerations and distortions, Gandhi was delighted. It was marvelous, he wrote to Rolland in late

---

* His friend Hermann Hesse dedicated his best seller on the life of Buddha, *Siddhartha,* to Rolland.

March that year, how he had managed to interpret Gandhi's message so truly without ever meeting or knowing him. This proved, Gandhi suggested, the essential unity of human nature. From that day forward Gandhi liked to refer to Rolland as his publicity agent.[51]

Romain Rolland created the public myth of Mahatma Gandhi that the Western world has admired ever since. At least once a decade it is reproduced in adulatory biographies and hit movies. It is the myth of Gandhi the universal saint, the gentle apostle of nonviolence and humanitarian goodness who gladly turned his cheek to his enemies and won out by sheer moral example. Rolland's mythmaking deliberately ignored the other sides of Gandhi. It ignored the tough-minded warrior who read Kipling with pleasure and who could write, "You cannot teach non-violence to a man who cannot kill." It omitted the Victorian patriarch who set impossible standards for his children and refused to allow his son Devadas to marry a girl from a different caste.[52] It left out the shrewd organizer and hard bargainer, and the stern uncompromising moralist. Instead, it projected only a soft New Age glow.

Just as important, this saintly image sharply distorted Gandhi's role in Indian politics. By implying that Gandhi spoke for all Indians, Rolland ignored the bitter rivalries and divisions of the subcontinent and discounted the challenges that lay ahead. Nonetheless the book's impact on Western audience was decisive. *Mahatma Gandhi* sharply elevated Gandhi's stature both with admirers and with antagonists, including a succession of viceroys and imperial ministers. If Gandhi was the modern Jesus, no one wanted to end up as his Pontius Pilate.

One man was impervious to the new Gandhi cult. That was Winston Churchill. His public image had also changed in the 1920s, but not in a saintly direction.

At first the newspapers called him the "smiling Chancellor." Ebullient, bubbling with charm and charisma, Churchill made his annual speech on the budget into a major media event—just as it is today. His first budget speech in 1925 was a rhetorical tour de force, as he kept the House of Commons enthralled for two hours and forty minutes, switching from broad humor that had the members rocking with laughter, to emotionally gripping descriptions of the need for pensions for widows and mothers that held them in spellbound silence.

Prime Minister Baldwin told the king that "Mr. Churchill rose magnificently to the occasion" and showed he had not only the skills of a consummate parliamentarian but "the versatility of an actor."[53] Baldwin must have congratulated himself in making the right choice for chancellor.

Yet Baldwin's secretary P. J. Grigg predicted sourly, "Within a year Winston will have committed some irretrievable blunder which, if he does not imperil the government will bring Winston down."[54] Grigg knew his Winston, and his prediction proved correct. Behind the media publicity and hype, and the parties at Chartwell with the rich, smart, and famous, came a series of decisions that can only be described as reckless. Churchill's five years at the Exchequer were disastrous for Britain and sowed much of the trouble that lay ahead.

The first misstep appeared in his first budget. Churchill decided to return Britain to the gold standard, which it had abandoned during the war. Before making the momentous move he consulted with many leading economists (including John Maynard Keynes, later one of the decision's harshest critics). Churchill wanted to send a signal that Britain was returning to the old prewar certainties, including monetary certainties.

Pegging the pound sterling to the price of gold was probably not a bad idea. By itself it might have given Britain's economy the kind of rock-solid monetary stability it needed. But the economists at the Bank of England who advised him set the price of the pound too high, by returning to the old rate. The result made British exports too expensive and stalled the country's industrial recovery. It also put fiscal policy on a collision course with the government's efforts to placate trade unions by raising wages. One of the results would be chronically high unemployment, and the General Strike two years later.[55]

As chancellor, Winston went on a cost-cutting rampage. He targeted the Royal Navy for a special slashing. It was an amazing, even outrageous move from an ex–First Lord of the Admiralty. But the cuts Churchill wanted over the next five years reflected his belief, reinforced by the Washington Naval Treaty,* that the days of a large standing fleet were over. "We cannot have a lot of silly little cruisers," he told Assistant Cabinet Secretary Tom Jones, "which would be of no use anyway." He bullied the Admiralty into accepting reduced budgets until finally First

---

* Signed in 1922, the treaty set British, American, and other nations' capital ship ratios at 5:5:3, which meant the Royal Navy actually had to scrap existing ships while its Italian and Japanese counterparts were free to keep building.

Sea Lord Admiral Bridgeman threatened to resign rather than let Churchill, as he put it, "ruin the Navy."[56]

Churchill's haughty reply was "You know, I do not write about these naval matters without experience." He even tried to convince the cabinet to turn the Ten Year Rule into a twenty-year rule for the Royal Navy, insisting that Germany would need decades to become a naval power again and that "war with Japan is not a possibility which any reasonable government need take into account." As he told Stanley Baldwin in December 1924, "Japan is at the other end of the world. She cannot menace our security in any way."[57]

Acting on this blithe assumption, Churchill oversaw cuts in Royal Navy strength that were staggering and that grew larger when Labour took power in 1929. The navy had had 443 destroyers in 1918; it had barely 120 left in 1931. Its seventy cruisers shrank to fifty. In the fifteen years after the war ended, only two new battleships were built as well as the ill-fated battle cruiser *Hood*. The naval air arm dropped to 159 aircraft. By contrast, Japan's grew to more than four hundred. In 1926 Churchill urged postponing the navy's plans to modernize and fortify its base at Singapore for at least six years. The only power to threaten Singapore would be Japan, and again, "Why should there be a [war] with Japan? The Japanese are our allies. I do not believe there is the slightest chance of [war] in our lifetime."[58]

To his mind, Churchill was not abandoning the empire. Instead, his hope was that saving money on defense would leave more for social spending.[59] But his strategic miscalculations weakened the Royal Navy's ability to patrol the globe, including the Pacific, and left Singapore virtually defenseless, with fatal consequences later. If any single person can be blamed for the collapse of Britain's East Asian empire in 1942, and for allowing Japan to advance to the gates of India, it is Chancellor of the Exchequer Winston Churchill.

At the time, however, nothing adversely affected Churchill's reputation more than his role in the 1926 General Strike.

It began on May Day as a strike by miners in Britain's coal industry, coal being the essential fuel of the island kingdom's economic engine. Other unions belonging to the Trades Union Congress (TUC) threatened to join in. The ostensible issue was the usual one of pay. But the real agenda among TUC radicals, including many Communists, was to use a "general strike" as a weapon for toppling the Conservative government, perhaps even the capitalist system. For ten tense days, from May 3 to May 12, Baldwin's government had to confront the specter of complete economic shutdown as workers in one vital industry after another, from the railways and newspapers to electric plants and dockyards, went on strike in sympathy with British miners.

As chancellor, Churchill was in the forefront of the confrontation. In private, he was actually more conciliatory toward the miners than many of his cabinet colleagues. In public, however, his words were over the top. "We are at war," he declared to the cabinet on May 7, and he urged its fellow members to show no compromise. "Either the country will break the General Strike," he had written the previous day, "or the General Strike will break the country."[60]

In a strict sense, Churchill was correct. But the strident tone and the call to arms horrified the home secretary, Neville Chamberlain. Churchill "simply revels in this affair," he wrote, "which he will continually talk and treat of as if it were 1914." Others saw in Churchill the same "vainglory and excessive excitement" that had led to the Gallipoli disaster. The cabinet had to stop him from printing an article calling for the Territorial Army to march against the strikers.[61]

The prime minister took the prudent step of keeping Churchill away from the sensitive negotiations with the trade unions. Winston had to content himself with setting up and turning out his own newspaper, the *British Gazette,* which was supposed to replace the newspapers the strike had paralyzed. He wrote many of the *Gazette*'s more strident articles, whose unmeasured language made him a lightning rod of criticism. He denounced strikers and organizers as "reckless, violent," and even unmanly—words that made him lifelong enemies in the ranks of the Trades Union Congress and the Labour Party.

By ignoring Churchill's advice but also by adamantly refusing to give in to any demands until the strike was called off, Baldwin brought the General Strike to a halt. The coal miners held out for nearly five more months. To his credit, Churchill tried to work out a compromise to end it, but the coal owners turned it down.[62]

Finally on November 20, 1926, the coal strike collapsed. Capitalism in Britain had survived. Winston celebrated by taking a holiday trip to the Mediterranean. He planned to play a final game of polo on the Island of Malta ("If I expire on the ground, it will at any rate be a worthy end!" he wrote) and to visit Italy. There he met for the first and last time the man who had ruthlessly seized power there in 1922, Benito Mussolini.

Privately, Churchill could be scathing about Italy's dictator. But he believed (wrongly) that he and Mussolini shared a deep antipathy to Soviet Communism. In the aftermath of the General Strike, he embraced the vainglorious mountebank as an ally. After their meeting Winston said, "I could not help being charmed, like so many other people have been, by his gentle and simple bearing." He added that if he were an Italian, he would be a fascist, too. Churchill's final words, telling Mussolini that "your movement has rendered service to the whole world," burned whatever boats he still had left with the British Left.[63]

But to a growing circle of young Tories, Churchill was emerging as a hero. Many of them were dissatisfied with Prime Minister Baldwin, who had exhausted himself in the fight against the General Strike and whose hand was none too strong. They also disliked Baldwin's high-minded but dull-as-dishwater allies like Chamberlain and the Minister of Air Sir Samuel Hoare (whom Lord Birkenhead said looked like he came from a long line of maiden aunts).[64]

By contrast, Churchill offered excitement, intellectual verve, good food and drink, and brilliant conversation. His house at Chartwell became a gathering place for the party's young and not-so-young rebels; Churchill reigned as paterfamilias and general center of attention, much as Gandhi did at Sabarmati. On any given evening in the 1920s and early 1930s, disciples gathered at Chartwell to hear his words, catch his enthusiasm, and consume his whiskey.

Victor Cazalet considered himself a "liberal" Conservative along the lines of "Tory Democracy." He had met Churchill during the war, and as MP for Chippenham Cazalet became a regular fixture at Chartwell. He spoke admiringly of Churchill's "inspiration, courage, affection, vitality, and ability" in those years and of his disarming ability to talk unaffectedly for hours with people twenty or even thirty years his junior.[65]

Duff Cooper was thirty-four when he was elected to Winston's old seat at Oldham. He came to Chartwell often, as did the twenty-four-year-old MP for East Aberdeenshire Robert Boothby, and Harold Macmillan, member for Stockton. Cooper and Boothby would remain Winston's close disciples before and during the Second World War. But none would be closer than Brendan Bracken, a strange young man of no apparent parentage, with granny glasses and a thick thatch of carrot-colored hair whom others dismissed as that "red headed freak" but who made himself at home at Chartwell, and (despite Clementine's hostility) virtually a part of the Churchill family—even Winston's surrogate son.*[66]

At Chartwell, Churchill usually rose at eight, after dictating pages of the last volume of his war memoirs, *The World Crisis,* until the early hours of the morning. His normal breakfast was orange juice, eggs, toast, a steak or chicken leg left over from dinner, and plenty of black cherry jam. After breakfast and a bath, he would glance through newspapers and letters, usually with a whiskey-and-soda, the first of the day, at his elbow as well as the first cigar (always a Havana). Then came more dictation before lunch, followed by work in the garden or on the new house he was building for his butler. Guests were often astonished to watch Winston intently laying bricks, trowel in one hand and cigar in the other, for four-hour stretches.[67]

The lunch guests would arrive. Sometimes they included a celebrity like T. E. Lawrence, who would appear on his motorcycle, or Charlie Chaplin. After lunch Churchill settled in for his daily nap, which often lasted an hour and a half, followed by more yard work until dinner. Then after dinner would come the highlight of the day as Winston would talk and his guests listened, in interlocutory sessions that often lasted past midnight. In compensation for the late hours, he supplied his audience "with unlimited quantities of champagne, cigars, and brandy." And Winston talked, often pacing up and down the room with his thumbs in the armholes of his waistcoat and his head aggressively thrust forward, as the monologue moved effortlessly from the most recent political debates and his experiences in India to Alexander the Great's campaigns and the American Civil War. Many of his observations were profoundly astute; others were wildly off the mark. Almost all were memorable. And if the brilliant flow of observation and reminiscence showed signs of slowing down, one listener remembered, "all you have to do is make some moderately intelligent observation, and off he goes again."[68]

Churchill loved putting his younger guests on the spot, by jocularly comparing their still-meager accomplishments with those of great figures in history like Alexander or Napoleon or indeed Winston himself.

---

* Some even speculated that he really was Winston's natural son, born in adultery. The rumors became so rampant at one point that Clementine confronted Churchill and demanded to know if it was true. "I've looked the matter up," he shamefacedly confessed, "but the dates don't coincide."

Once he asked Alan Lennox-Boyd, later a longtime Conservative MP for Mid-Bedfordshire, how old he was. Lennox-Boyd said, "Nearly twenty-five." Winston promptly replied that Napoleon had taken Toulon before he was twenty-five. He whipped out his watch. "You have just got time to take Toulon before you are twenty-five," he growled goodnaturedly as he gazed at its face. "Quick, quick—go and take Toulon!"[69]

Others in the Chartwell circle were not quite so young. The brilliant and charismatic F. E. Smith, Lord Birkenhead and secretary of state for India, was two years older than Winston and a determined hard-liner on Indian independence. Another hard-liner was fifty-year-old George Lloyd, a graduate of Eton and Cambridge and former colleague of T. E. Lawrence during the Arab Revolt. After the war Lloyd had gone on to become governor of Bombay. He had faced the brunt of Gandhi's Noncooperation campaign and was the one person in Winston's inner circle who had personally dealt with Gandhi (except Churchill himself). In fact, it had been George Lloyd who sent Gandhi to the Yeravda jail.

Their paths had first crossed in March 1919. According to Lloyd, Gandhi's first words were: "I wish to goodness, Sir George, you would arrest me."[70] In the midst of the Rowlatt satyagraha, Lloyd was all too willing to oblige. But Viceroy Reading had vetoed the move. Then came Chauri Chaura. Lloyd described the next encounter with Gandhi to a reporter.[71] "You're preaching non-violence," Lloyd said he told Gandhi, "but that's all theory. In practice it won't work out... You can't control men's passions... You are responsible." Bombay's governor-general then pointed an accusing finger at the barefoot figure sitting in front of him.

According to Lloyd, Gandhi had covered his face with his hands and said, "I know it." Then he murmured, "Put me in gaol, Your Excellency."

"Yes, I will put you in gaol," Lloyd had replied sternly, "but not until I get good and ready." Lloyd had not wanted to make Gandhi a martyr and had to make sure his leading followers were rounded up before arresting him. Although Lloyd considered Gandhi a dangerous menace, he was not unyielding. He had given Gandhi two cells at Yeravda instead of one and allowed him his books and his diet of bread, goat's milk, raisins, and oranges. But Lloyd had also sharply limited the number of visitors, and when Gandhi asked to have certain fellow prisoners transferred to his minimum security section, Lloyd turned him down flat.[72]

Very few British officials had closer dealings with Gandhi than

Lloyd. It is very likely that on at least one evening in the 1920s, the conversation at Chartwell turned to the subject of the strange little Indian nationalist leader, with George Lloyd passing on his advice as he stroked his trim mustache and fingered his whiskey and soda, and Winston listening intently.*

"Just a thin, spindly shrimp of a fellow," Lloyd would say. "He doesn't care for material things, and preaches nothing but the ideals and morals of India."

Then Lloyd would pause and glance at Churchill. "You can't govern a country with ideals," he would declare, "but that was where he got his grip upon the people. He was their god. India must always have its god. First it was [B. G.] Tilak, then Gandhi now."

Remembering, the ex–governor-general would shake his head ruefully. "He gave us a scare," he would admit. "His programme filled our gaols. You can't go on arresting people forever, you know—not when they are 319 million of them."

There would have been a burst of laughter around the room, while Churchill had time to recall his own prediction to Wilfred Blunt years before that if the Indians ever really stopped cooperating with the British, then "the game would be up with us."

Lloyd then went on: "Gandhi's was the most colossal experiment in [the] world's history, and it came within an inch of succeeding. But he couldn't control men's passions. They became violent, and he called off the programme. You know the rest."

Lloyd would then finish his drink, as Winston or F. E. or someone else would ask, "What's your final assessment of him?"

"I am afraid he is really pretty wicked," Lloyd would confess, "as cunning as a fox and at heart bitterly anti-British."[73]

Whether this conversation ever took place is hard to say. But it is a fact that the man who first put Gandhi in an Indian jail would become Churchill's most trusted adviser on India.

Meanwhile Churchill's popularity with the young Tories, and the brilliance of the "Chartwell set," could not disguise his increasingly *un*popularity where it counted, namely with his own leadership.

---

* Although what follows is a reconstruction, every word is George Lloyd's verbatim and is in the historical record.

After the 1926 General Strike his conflicts with his cabinet colleagues redoubled. There were bruising battles over the naval budget and Soviet Russia; Churchill adamantly opposed any formal recognition of the Communist power. When George Lloyd became High Commissioner of Egypt the next year, he and Winston successfully wrecked an attempt to give the Egyptians more control of their country and the Suez Canal, which infuriated the Foreign Office. On the domestic front, Winston's "derating" plan for eliminating taxation on certain industries and municipalities landed him in an ugly scrap with Neville Chamberlain, the man who was his likely rival in any leadership contest to replace the aging Stanley Baldwin.[74]

Meanwhile the next general election approached, set for May 1929. After seven years in power, the Tories seemed to have overstayed their welcome. Some speculated that if the Conservatives managed somehow to win reelection, they would have to find a new chancellor. "An announcement that Neville was going to the Exchequer," Leo Amery pleaded with Baldwin, "would be worth twenty or thirty seats at least." Although Winston was a friend, Amery warned "the fact remains that he is a handicap rather than an asset to us in the eyes of the public."[75]

The next month voters went to the polls. On the night of May 30, as the results came in on a ticker tape, Winston went down to Number 10 to study the results with Baldwin. Sitting at a desk with a large whiskey and soda, he read through the thin slips of paper. An eyewitness watched him "getting redder and redder, rising and going out often to glare at the machine itself, hunching his shoulders, bowing his head like a bull about to charge. As Labour gain after gain was announced... he glared at the figures, tore the sheets and behaved as though if any more Labour gains came along he would smash the entire apparatus." His comments to the staff, the eyewitness added, "were quite unprintable."[76]

Labour had won 288 seats, the Conservatives 260. The Liberals were reduced to just 59 seats—and political irrelevancy. Winston himself had been reelected, but without a majority. His young Tory friends Harold Macmillan and Duff Cooper had both been defeated. Bob Boothby scraped through to a win. Baldwin had no choice but to resign, and he, Churchill, Chamberlain, and the rest handed over their seals of office on June 6.

After five stormy years Churchill was out. The Labour Party, the party he feared and despised more than any other, was back in power, this time with a majority for the foreseeable future. Churchill feared for that future, including for the empire. That fear was confirmed when one of Ramsay MacDonald's earliest acts was to dismiss George Lloyd as High Commissioner of Egypt. Soon afterward riots broke out in Palestine between Jews and Arabs. Churchill warned that they were a "bloody foretaste of what would happen in Egypt and India if the protected and controlling hand of Great Britain were withdrawn."

He trembled to think what Labour had up its sleeve but was powerless to do anything about it. So he bided his time by planning a new book, a biography of his ancestor the Duke of Marlborough, and by taking a trip to Canada and the United States.

The trip put the final seal on his sense of foreboding about the future and reminded him how fragile the civilization he loved and believed in really was. He was in New York the week the stock market crashed. The run started on Monday, October 21. The next day, "Black Tuesday," as prices plunged, an unheard-of sixteen million shares changed hands. On Thursday he attended a dinner party with his friend the financier Bernard Baruch. The mood was somber and uncertain. One dinner guest jocularly raised a toast to his "friends and former millionaires."[77]

On Friday morning, while Churchill was having breakfast at his hotel, the Savoy-Plaza, he heard shrieks on the street outside. He looked out the window. A man had jumped from the fifteenth story of the hotel, the first of eleven suicides that day triggered by the stock market collapse. Winston's own position can hardly have been reassuring. He was heavily invested in the American market; like more than half a million other investors he had been buying on margin "about ten times my usual scale," as he had told Clementine in September.[78]

Later he walked down Wall Street, where someone invited him to look in on the stock exchange floor. Churchill expected to see chaos but saw only subdued resignation. The investors, he later remembered, were "walking to and fro like a slow-motion picture of a disturbed ant heap, offering each other enormous blocks of securities at a third of their old prices and half their present value." Those included Churchill's own shares. When he returned home, he had to tell Clementine that their American investments had been completely wiped out.[79]

It was an experience that would shake anyone's confidence. "What a disappointment the twentieth century has been," Winston declared afterward. Thus far it had been a century of total war on an unimaginable scale, of violent revolution and steady socialist advance, of class conflict and industrial strife. Now came financial collapse. On October 30

Churchill sailed back to England. In a few months the financial panic would spread to Europe; soon Britain would be in the grip of the Great Depression.

"We are entering a period when the struggle for self-preservation is going to present itself with great intenseness to thickly populated countries," Churchill wrote to the viceroy of India, Lord Irwin.[80] The brittle prosperity and stability of the 1920s was coming to an abrupt end. World events, including events in India, were about to rise up like a tsunami around a beleaguered Britain.

Chapter Sixteen

EVE OF BATTLE
1929

Pray to God to relieve us from the curse of disunity.
MOHANDAS K. GANDHI, NOVEMBER 1929

THE 1920S HAD BEEN THE calm before the storm. For a short time the Bolshevik threat to Europe had receded.* The Allies had still been united, and Germany still disarmed. The League of Nations had reigned supreme in international affairs. The bomb of class warfare, which the Great Strike had hoped to detonate, failed to explode. For the first time in more than a generation, British politicians had time to turn their attention to India.

The ground had been prepared in 1925 by Churchill's friend and Chartwell stalwart F. E. Smith, now Lord Birkenhead and secretary of state for India. "F.E." to his friends, his tall ungainly frame and sallow mournful face hid a mordant wit and a restless appetite for power (as well as for alcohol, which eventually killed him). Like Churchill, he loved the reality as well as the ideal of the British Empire, and like Churchill he considered Edwin Montagu's earlier concessions to Indian national sentiment a failure. Birkenhead considered the Raj an important part of the British Empire and saw no one reason to change that. "I am not able," he told the House of Lords in May 1925, "in any discernible future, to discern a moment when we may safely, either to ourselves or to India," give up control over the subcontinent.[1]

With exquisite cunning, Birkenhead decided that the way to cement

---

* In 1925 Joseph Stalin proclaimed that Communism's aim was no longer world revolution but "socialism in one country," namely the Soviet Union. The result would be unimaginable pain for the people of Russia. To the rest of the world, however, it meant a respite from "the Bolshevik menace."

that control was, paradoxically, to speed up the next step toward Indian self-rule. The 1919 Government of India Act had authorized a statutory commission to assess the outlook for self-rule after ten years. Birkenhead had worried that by then a Labour government might be in power, one that was "soft" on India. (Both predictions turned out to be correct.) So four years ahead of schedule, in 1925, Birkenhead moved to assemble the commission. He figured he could appoint enough like-minded members who would blanch at the prospect of devolving power to native Indians and would be happy to slow down the process or even halt it altogether.[2]

The commission, formed in November 1927, was led by a Liberal and old Birkenhead classmate from Oxford, Sir John Simon. The rest of the members were undistinguished: a pair of peers and four backbench MPs. With the same exquisite cunning, Birkenhead even offered their ignorance about India as a selling point to members of Parliament who were more sympathetic to the Indian cause, since most Britons who had any experience there were fiercely opposed to making steps toward self-rule.

It was a brilliant scheme. It had only one flaw: not a single Indian was named to the commission that would decide the fate of India for the next generation. When Indians learned this fact, public opinion erupted in rage. It did not care that by statute members of the commission were supposed to be members of Parliament. (There were two Indians in Parliament, including one in the House of Lords, who could have been invited.)[3] Birkenhead had told Viceroy Lord Irwin that he had "no delusions as to the howls of rage with which our proposals will be received by the Indian Press,"[4] but neither man anticipated the firestorm they set off.

Gandhi, still in semiretirement at Sabarmati, did not join in the gales of protest. Instead, the man of the hour in political terms was Gandhi's sometime disciple, Jawaharlal Nehru. Brilliant, articulate, and educated at Harrow, slim and movie-star handsome, he was part of the rising generation of Congress leadership. Yet even with all his gifts, Nehru might never have succeeded in mobilizing the forces of resentment against the Simon Commission without the unintentional help of an American journalist and author.

Her name was Katherine Mayo, and her book was *Mother India*. The title was meant to be ironic. In fact, the book was a startling exposé of the exploitation of Indian women by Hindu as well as Muslim society. Mayo described in ugly detail the customs of child marriage, of widow murder or suttee, of untouchability and caste prejudice, as well as the rampant disease and poor hygiene of what was, despite the changes since the turn of the century, still a desperately poor country.

The result, Mayo claimed, was that the fate of Indian womanhood was "early to marriage, early to die." More than three million women died in childbirth every year. Thanks to malnutrition, most were "too small-boned, or too internally misshapen and diseased to give normal birth to a child" and were left to the mercies of ignorant midwives or a crude surgeon's knife.[5]

Mayo's picture of the average Indian male was equally damning. He was, she concluded, "a feeble creature at best, bankrupt in bone-stuff and vitality, often venereally poisoned." In addition, he was emotionally corrupted by a cultural atmosphere that worshipped the male phallus (the *lingam* of the god Shiva) and that encouraged sexual incontinence, sodomy, and "ultra indecent" practices of every kind. The result was, she claimed, that seven to eight out of ten Hindu males under thirty were impotent, at the same age when Anglo-Saxon males were "just coming into the full glory of manhood."[6]

According to Mayo, this situation had political consequences. The physically and emotionally inferior Indian male, she wrote, never developed into a real or lasting leader. Those who "from time to time aspire to that rank are able only for a brief interval to hold the flitting minds of their followers." This included Gandhi, whom she had visited at Sabarmati Ashram. She found him to be a not-unsympathetic figure and quoted his criticisms of traditional Hinduism and untouchability at length. However, his solutions promised to be nothing more than a "drag on the wheels of progress," and his vision of a society without modern technology, industry, or medicine would be a disaster for India.[7] "Disease, dirt, and ignorance are the characteristics of my country," she quoted one Indian schoolteacher as saying. Nothing Gandhi proposed, including expulsion of the British, would change that.[8]

Mother India should have been titled *Unmanly India*. It offered a picture of Gandhi and India that was the exact opposite of Romain Rolland's worshipful New Age tract—and just as misleading. However, to British hard-liners it came as confirmation of what they had always believed: that left to themselves, Indians would destroy their own country. Winston Churchill in particular was delighted. He sent copies of *Mother India* to friends, including Birkenhead. In the summer of 1927

Victor Cazalet noted that Churchill "admires the book *Mother India* and would have no mercy with the Hindus who marry little girls aged ten."[9]

Gandhi, reviewing Mayo's book in the pages of *Young India,* dismissed it as "The Drain Inspector's Report" and suggested it had been financed by pro-British interests. Mayo's recitation of his criticisms of his fellow Indians quoted out of context were certainly painful, and her conclusion that India was actually more decadent, materialistic, and "egocentric" than the West must have galled. But he saw the book for what it was, a sensational piece of fluff, and never gave it a second thought.[10]

The outrage among other educated Indians ran deeper. They could tolerate criticism of the caste system (many had doubts themselves); even exposure of India's poverty and its treatment of women and untouchables. But the suggestion that Indian males were unhealthy, oversexed degenerates drove them to fury. More than sixty years later the grand old man of Bengali letters, Nirad Chaudhuri, could write, "Even now it is impossible to say whether it was an infinite capacity for self-deception or brazen hypocrisy which made her maintain her position."[11]

Mother India appeared in July 1927; four months later the all-white Simon Commission was announced. Many Indians suspected this timing was no coincidence. Their paranoia was understandable, given their sense of betrayal over Amritsar and the Hunter Commission. Fear that the British considered Indians physically and emotionally unfit to rule themselves, and were about to reassert their supremacy over India, encouraged the Indian National Congress to take its next step.

A month after the appointment of the Simon Commission, it endorsed a resolution from thirty-eight-year-old Jawaharlal Nehru declaring that India would never accept anything less than "complete independence" from Britain. When the Simon Commission visited India the following spring, even the Congress's Moderates voted to boycott it. The Muslim League, whose members were more fearful of a Hindu Raj than of a British one, split on the issue.[12] Nonetheless the skirmish lines were drawn. The question in everyone's mind was which way Gandhi would lean, and whether the Simon Commission issue would tempt him out of his self-imposed isolation.

Certainly to Gandhi, the all-white Simon Commission was "an organized insult to a whole people."[13] All the same he disliked Congress's resolution rejecting Dominion status in favor of straight independence, and he saw little point to the boycott. He also confessed to the British editor of the Indian edition of the *Statesman* that "neither the [Simon] Statutory Commission nor constitution-making processes interest me very much." He still believed in following his own separate path to Swaraj. He would certainly welcome Sir John if he wanted to visit the ashram, he said. Otherwise, he washed his hands of the whole matter.[14]

Gandhi had learned long ago not to reveal his true feelings to journalists, European journalists above all. He was not as detached from Indian politics as he pretended. Indeed, his long period of intellectual incubation and self-examination was almost over. In January 1928 his beloved son Ramdas married. A month later his cousin Maganlal died, the man who had coined the phrase "satyagraha" and had been Gandhi's intellectual conscience since his earliest days in South Africa. The loss of Maganlal "is well nigh unbearable," he told Jawaharlal Nehru; he said his cousin had been his hands, feet, and eyes for twenty-four years. "However I am putting on a brave front."[15]

Gandhi did not attend the Congress in December 1927 but was in constant contact with its leadership. What he learned alarmed him. Although the British government was steadily losing legitimacy in the eyes of ordinary Indians, the Congress offered no better alternative. It had become a teeming anthill of rivalries and conflicting ideologies. Hindu nationalists, Bengali nationalists, Sikh separatists, old-line loyalists, and cutting-edge socialists all vied for power in its sessions. The Nehru family was split between a father who admired Gandhi and a son who admired the Soviet Union. Muslims were completely estranged from the organization, even as orthodox Hindu organizations like the Mahasabha became furious whenever concessions to Muslim opinion were even mentioned. Gandhi realized that unless he stepped forward to take the helm, the whole Indian nationalist movement would shatter into splinters.

By August 1928 he felt ready for the task. His disciple Vallabhbhai Patel had just completed a highly successful satyagraha campaign in the Bardoli province of Gujarat against a land tax increase. (This was one area where peasants paid the tax directly to the government.) Gandhi did not personally go to Bardoli, but this was his home turf and Patel's organizers constantly invoked his name. For six months the peasants endured arrest, seizure of property, and government intimidation. They remained united across religious and caste lines; when government agents seized land and cattle and put them up for sale, they found no buyers. Bardoli officials finally gave way, and those in other districts canceled planned tax increases. The peasants had won without violence and also drawn national publicity. Gandhi was thrilled. "Bardoli has shown the way and cleared it," he wrote. "Swaraj lies on that route."[16] Bardoli restored his faith in the possibilities of satyagraha and signaled that it was time for him to return to politics.

That month he helped Motilal Nehru and other Moderate Congress officials draft their own plan for self-government in defiance of the Simon Commission. The so-called Nehru plan proposed direct "responsible government" for India, with elected legislatures in New Delhi and in the provinces and a federative constitution to incorporate the princely states. The goal was democratic Indian self-rule, under Dominion status. Muslims would have a guaranteed majority in places where they were a majority, like the Punjab and Sind. Otherwise the Nehru plan was a formula for Hindu majority rule. The Nehru plan offered India less independence from Britain than Gandhi had wanted in 1920, but he felt the time had come to endorse it.[17]

In February Simon and his fellow commissioners arrived in India. They were greeted by a massive national boycott, with demonstrations, shop closings, black flags, and shouts of "Simon Go Back." When they visited again in October, full-scale riots erupted. Policemen waded in with truncheons and lathis, the metal-tipped canes used to control violent crowds. In Lahore, veteran Punjabi leader Lajpat Rai (no admirer of Gandhi) was beaten and died. The policeman responsible was then shot dead by a young revolutionary.[18] In Lucknow police lathis sent Jawaharlal Nehru to the hospital.

As 1928 ended, the mood in India was ugly, but the mood in London was even uglier. Despite the riots Simon got to meet many Indian leaders, including Motilal Nehru, the Muslim League's Muhammad Jinnah, National Liberal Federation leader T. B. Sapru, and even Lajpat Rai before his death. Simon and his colleagues were deeply unimpressed by what they heard. "I cannot imagine any more terrible fate in the world," Lord Birkenhead wrote after hearing their complaints, "than to try to hack out a new constitution with such talkative and incompetent colleagues."[19]

The situation had reached an impasse. Indians of every political stripe believed that the first step toward self-government for India had to be a public grant of independence. Then the Indians could hammer out a constitution with British help, working as equal partners. London, by contrast, believed that self-government was a matter not for Indians but for Parliament to decide.* Once everyone agreed on a constitution (including India's Muslims, who had dismissed the Nehru plan out of hand), steps toward a transfer of power could follow. In short, Indians wanted independence, then a constitution. The British wanted to see a constitution before they granted independence.

Otherwise, Britons asked not unreasonably, to whom could they *give* independence? Not the legislative councils set up in 1919: as creations of the Raj, they were utterly incapable of independent action. Not the Indian National Congress: it was riven by competing interests and factions, as was the Muslim League. In fact, by now every religion and region in India, every class and caste—even the untouchables—had "spokesmen" who were clamoring for attention and demanding to be part of any final deal. Even if the Simon Commission had wanted to include Indian members, the groups left out would have attacked them as unrepresentative.[20]

The problem of identity in India was proving to be a political Gordian knot, too tangled even for Gandhi to unravel. In December the INC assembled once more in Calcutta. The meeting was barely contained chaos. Opposition to the Moderates' last stand, the Nehru plan, was led by Nehru's own son together with a young Bengali radical named Subhas Chandra Bose, who joined forces to demand nothing less than instant and total independence from Britain. Tens of thousands of mill workers occupied the assembly site for two hours and passed a resolution supporting the radicals.[21] For a few days it seemed that the Calcutta Congress might split down the middle.

Gandhi's arrival saved the day. He entered the plenary session to wild applause and to Motilal Nehru's relief. With Gandhi's backing, the Moderates told themselves, their paper plan to convince Britain to grant Dominion status might still succeed. But Gandhi was not in a conciliatory mood. Privately, he was appalled at the Congress's shabby financial state (individuals and entire provinces were deeply in debt) and its decay at the local level.[22] "I shall only lead India when the nation comes to me to be led," he had told supporters in November. And he would answer that call only when the nation agreed to play by his rules.

Gandhi made that clear from the beginning of the Calcutta Congress. He hammered out a compromise resolution with the younger Nehru

---

* Technically London was correct. By law, only Parliament had the statutory authority to devolve the powers that would make India a self-governing part of the empire.

and Bose. If the British refused to grant Dominion status within one year, it stated, then Indians would unite in a massive noncooperative campaign that would not quit until full independence was achieved. The resolution passed the Subjects Committee 118 to 45 (a sign that not everyone was on the Mahatma's bandwagon), and it passed the open Congress with deafening cheers.

Then Gandhi insisted the delegates approve the other planks of his program: banning untouchability; supporting khadi and a boycott of all foreign cloth; even abstention from alcohol and the inclusion of women in new social roles. These planks too passed. Whether anyone thought they would be carried out was a different matter.[23]

Gandhi had infuriated young radicals like Bose with his brusque "take it or leave it" approach, but he felt he had no time to waste. He was nearly sixty. Many in his inner circle worried that his health could not stand another major political campaign, with its endless rounds of speeches, demonstrations, and travel, not to mention the occasional fast. But "no apology is necessary for taking me to Calcutta," he told Motilal Nehru a few days later. "I was quite happy over it...[Now] we have to do battle both within and without."[24]

"The battle within" meant spreading the message of Swaraj and its spiritual principles across India and deep into the ranks of Congress. "The battle without" meant gaining independence from the British.

Gandhi probably hoped to avoid a final confrontation with the government and that London would see the light before the December 1929 deadline. According to historian Judith Brown, for nearly a year Gandhi and the Congress awaited a response but made no plans for what to do if the British said no.[25] After the chaos of the Calcutta Congress, Gandhi wondered whether Indians were ready for a satyagraha showdown with the Raj. "I know well enough how to lead to civil disobedience a people who are prepared to embark upon it on my terms," he wrote in August, as the deadline approached. "I see no such sign on the horizon." However, he added, "I am still hoping [that] a way out of the 'encircling gloom' will be found."[26]

Then a light did break through the gloom, emanating not from London but from New Delhi. The man who lit it would become a crucial figure not only in Gandhi's life but Churchill's as well. In fact, it is no exaggeration to say that for the next dozen years he would hold the fate of both men in his thin, spindly hands.

* * *

His name was Edward Wood, Lord Irwin, later Viscount Halifax. He was everything Churchill was not. Tall, lean, austerely angular, and deceptively soft-spoken, he was deeply religious to the point of sanctimoniousness. He was an easy man to respect but hard to admire. Halifax's name is forever associated with the Neville Chamberlain policy of appeasement, of which he was the main architect. But in 1940 millions of Britons hoped he would become prime minister instead of Winston Churchill. He came within a hairbreadth of succeeding. In 1929 he was viceroy of India, and more than any other man he became Gandhi's partner in shaping the destiny of India—and foiling the plans of Churchill and his hard-line allies.

Irwin was an unexpected choice for viceroy. When Stanley Baldwin approached him about the post in October 1925, the forty-four-year-old son of the Marquis of Halifax was almost unknown in British politics.* Lord Birkenhead, who with his thirst for power had coveted the post, declared that the choice proved that in public life it paid "to be blameless rather than brilliant."[27] Neither Birkenhead nor anyone else could have guessed what a momentous appointment it really was.

Irwin arrived in India in March 1926 to take up a position that had lost some of its pomp since Lord Curzon's day but was still one of the most powerful on earth. Under the new 1919 rules, viceroys were supposed to weigh all decisions with their Imperial Legislative Council and consult with the legislative councils in the provinces. On any truly important matter he was also bound to check with his colleagues, the governors-general of Bombay and Madras.

But in 1926 his word was still largely law. The viceroy of India was the single most powerful man in the British Empire, far more powerful than the prime minister. In Iran, China, and the Arabian peninsula, the influence of New Delhi counted as much as that of Whitehall.[28] Irwin traveled across India in his own private train. He needed two full-time private secretaries and six aides-de-camp to keep track of his empire's paperwork.

His official residence was the most lavish building in India, the still-unfinished Viceroy House. It was the visible monument to two centuries

---

* Interestingly, his grandfather, like Churchill's father, had once been secretary of state for India.

of British rule. Construction had begun two years after Curzon's great 1903 durbar and was still going on in 1931. Bigger than Louis XIV's palace at Versailles, it occupied four and a half acres and had 340 rooms. Viceroy House was topped by an enormous gleaming Taj Mahal-esque dome designed by Britain's most distinguished architect, Sir Edwin Lutyens, while its exterior was made from the same red and buff sandstone that the Mughal emperors had used to build their palaces centuries before. As for the interior, hallways and rooms gleamed with multicolor marble inlays from every part of India: white from Jodhpur, green from Baroda, black from Gaya, pink from Alwar, and yellow from Jaisalmer.[29]

Running Viceroy House required a staff of six thousand plus four hundred gardeners, including fifty whose only job was chasing away the birds.[30] Lady Irwin later estimated that in the cold-weather months they never sat down to a meal requiring fewer than forty-two servants. Many dinner parties required more than 120. Every meal became a ritual ceremony, as the viceroy presided over multiple tables of distinguished civil servants, generals, foreign diplomats and visitors, native princes and maharajas. When he appeared at a formal evening function, the English ladies were expected to curtsy at least seven times, as an official measure of respect.*[31]

Viceroy House was also the hub of a vast bureaucratic wheel whose spokes extended into every corner of the subcontinent. Walking down King's Way, a visitor would pass the other official buildings of the British government in India, the myriad ministries from forestry and the post office to the railways and the Imperial Mint. It was a government built on the assumption that it would do everything that Indians could not do for themselves. On the walls of the viceroy's Secretariat was a bronze plaque that read:

LIBERTY DOES NOT DESCEND TO A PEOPLE.
A PEOPLE MUST RAISE THEMSELVES TO LIBERTY.
IT IS A BLESSING THAT MUST BE EARNED
BEFORE IT CAN BE ENJOYED.

Irwin no longer believed that was true. In 1926 he had been sent out essentially as a peacemaker, a "soft-liner," to succeed hard-liners like his predecessor Lord Reading and Churchill's friend George Lloyd. Irwin

---

* Irwin reduced that to three.

considered himself an idealist, but an idealist without illusions. One of the illusions he rejected was the idea that the Raj could remain in India. He belonged to a high-minded but disillusioned postwar generation who were convinced that national self-determination could not be stopped, either in Europe or elsewhere. "The Congress," Irwin argued, "was a force that had the tide of history behind it."[32] Indians wanted self-government, and the British had no right to deny it to them. Irwin saw his task as viceroy helping the inevitable transfer of power and "to keep our tempers" as well as the peace.[33]

The very day he arrived in India, a riot in Calcutta cost one hundred lives and lasted two weeks. In 1926 alone there were thirty-five Hindu-Muslim clashes that qualified as "serious."[34] Like Gandhi, Irwin was aware that Indians were facing a potential sectarian meltdown. He performed one indispensable service during his tenure in office: he was the very first viceroy to publicly raise the issue of what would happen when the British left India. The answers were not encouraging. Unless the British could help Indians achieve religious and social reconciliation, Irwin concluded, the result would be catastrophe.

A devout Anglo-Catholic, Irwin hoped that his own religious faith might bond a trust with Indians like Gandhi. "It is a change of soul that India needs today," Irwin had told a mixed audience of Indians and Britons in his first public speech in India, at the Chelmsford Club in Simla in July 1926. He hoped (or perhaps assumed) that he was the man to bring it about.[35]

For this reason Irwin bitterly regretted agreeing to have no Indians on the Simon Commission. He had to look for another way to build bridges before the next wave of civil disobedience, or perhaps something worse, struck the Raj. Most Indians, he supposed, felt the same. "In nearly all quarters," he wrote in January 1929, as the Congress's countdown started, "there would be very genuine relief if some face-saving device which afforded an excuse for the introduction of saner counsels could be found."[36]

Although he was a Tory, Irwin saw his chance with the election of a Labour government in July 1929. He and the new secretary of state, William Wedgwood Benn, saw eye to eye on India, as did Prime Minister Ramsay MacDonald. So while the Simon Commission was drafting its report for Parliament, Irwin cleverly arranged for the final version to include a plan for a federal constitution for India and a series of conferences with Indian representatives to hash out the details.

Finally, on October 31, 1929, he issued a wordy but weighty statement from New Delhi. "I am authorized on behalf of His Majesty's Government to state clearly that in their judgement it is implicit in the [Montagu] declaration of 1917 that the natural issue of India's constitutional progress as there contemplated is *the attainment of Dominion Status*." In short, Irwin stated that India was now officially on track for independence on a scale that only former white colonies like Canada and Australia had ever enjoyed.[37]

But was it true? Indians felt they could not be sure. Since Amritsar, few were willing to trust the Raj's word on anything.[38] But Irwin had alerted Indian leaders of his plan beforehand and struck a vein of cautious optimism among Moderates and National Liberals. One of them, M. A. Ansari, met privately with Gandhi and afterwards assured the viceroy that the Mahatma, while not exactly enthusiastic about the announcement, "on the whole" was pleased with Irwin's words.[39] Now, like everyone else, he would wait to see what happened in Britain.

What happened was a political explosion that rocked Whitehall, and especially the Tory party. Most politicians understood that Irwin's words were, after all, only words. The timing, circumstances, and final form that India's Dominion status might take were still open. Prime Minister MacDonald even ventured to say that Irwin's statement represented nothing new in British policy toward India.

However, Lords Birkenhead and Reading, the former secretary and former viceroy, were "horrified." They knew that the term "Dominion status" had a new meaning under the so-called Balfour formula of 1926 (later embodied in the Statute of Westminster); it would give India virtual carte blanche on matters of foreign and defense policy—the very areas where India was so vital to British interests.[40] Sir John Simon was furious at Irwin for in effect trumping his commission's report before it came out. The Liberal leader, Lloyd George, also quietly seethed at the news. As for the Tories, Baldwin at first endorsed Irwin's statement because he assumed it had been cleared with Simon. (It had not.) When he learned the truth, Baldwin realized he had been made to look foolish, and he too lived to regret the whole incident.

But none of this compared with Churchill's reaction, when he landed back in Britain on Guy Fawkes Day, November 5, 1929.

He was already in a belligerent mood. First, he had to confess to Clementine that all their American investments had been wiped out in the Wall Street crash. Now Irwin's announcement made him feel that his worst fears about India were being realized. Just ten days before, on October 26, he had published an article in *Answers* magazine prophetically titled, "Will the British Empire Last?" There he had stated, "The idea that India is a nation, or could ever be fashioned into a nation is known to be a delusion by everyone acquainted with the facts." Unfortunately British officials there had a tendency to believe that "they are merely a rearguard...shuffling continually backwards as part of the final retreat."

It was time to reverse this passive fatalism, Churchill had declared. "Unless the British race has a high confidence in its mission to guide forward these Eastern peoples" to the moral and material advancements of civilization, the empire would be doomed.[41] Already the Labour government had sacked Lloyd George and withdrawn British troops from Egypt to Suez—"an immense blow at our prestige throughout the East." Churchill balefully predicted that the Egyptian capital would soon "sink into an Oriental slum" and the country into chaos.[42] Now India bade fair to end the same way.

The very day he arrived back in London Clementine informed him that a half-dozen worried colleagues were waiting for him in the drawing room. As Winston burst in, they rose and expressed their fears about the Irwin declaration. Baldwin was wrong on India, they believed, but they might face reprisals if they bucked the party leadership. Not to worry, Winston told them. He would speak for everyone who believed India should remain British.[43]

On November 8 Winston went down to the House of Commons for its first debate on the government's policy on India. According to one observer, he was "demented with fury." While Baldwin spoke in support of Irwin's declaration, he sat red-faced and glowering. When Lloyd George attacked it, he raucously cheered. He was not alone in his anger. When Baldwin declared, "If ever the day comes when the Party which I lead ceases to attract men of the calibre of [Lord Irwin], then I have finished with my Party," the rest of his Tory colleagues greeted his words with icy silence.[44]

A battle was brewing—not only for India, but for the heart and soul of the Conservative Party. On one side stood Baldwin, most of the party leadership, and Viceroy Lord Irwin, who certainly had no regrets about his decision or the uproar it had caused. On the contrary, Irwin believed his words would rally "moderate opinion" in both India and Britain, he told his father, and put the "extremists in a quandary."[45] Those "extremists" were Churchill and other Tories determined never to surrender British rule in India, including most former Indian officers and civil servants like George Lloyd.

In between the two sides were the long rows of Tory backbenchers. They were men of neither oppressive intellect nor deep reflection. Few knew much about India; most came from rural constituencies and had no connection to cities like Manchester and Liverpool that had a commercial stake in India's £500 million annual trade with Britain.[46] Baldwin believed that when push came to shove, these men would support him on India. Party loyalty was a Tory tradition; certainly most members in 1929 believed in obeying the leadership. During the war and after they had followed the leadership into a Liberal-led coalition government. They had followed it into giving up Ireland. Later they would follow it in appeasing Nazi Germany.

But India was different. The British presence there was still a palpable legacy inherited from their fathers and grandfathers. Everyone knew someone who had served there, in the army or in the civil service. They had all read verses by Kipling in school about lonely British outposts in the Hindu Kush and the "white man's burden." They had sat in parish churches hung with flags of regiments that had fought and died at Lucknow, Assaye, and Cawnpore.

As boys they had collected cigarette trading cards of "Military Uniforms of the British Overseas," showing the multicolored ceremonial uniforms of Indian troops from regiments with names like the Poona Horse and the Maharaja Holkar's Infantry. They had thrilled to stories in *The Boy's Own Paper* about heroic subalterns, the products of public schools like theirs, fearlessly vanquishing wild-eyed tribesmen on the Northwest Frontier, as loyal *sowars* from the Bengal Lancers helped them foil another evil plot against the Raj.

Now in middle age, these men were prepared to hand India over, if their leaders asked them to. But they would never rid themselves of the feeling that something precious, even romantic, was passing out of their lives—and that it was India that had made Britain great.

Today this view is held in contempt, understandably so. Still, the notion that India existed to gratify the emotional yearnings of white men was not limited to Tory imperialists. It extended to New Agers like Romain Rolland. In a profound way, it even included high-minded figures like Lord Irwin. Deplorable or not, that romantic sentiment was very much alive in 1929, and not only in the Conservative Party. It would give Churchill and his fellow "diehards" an elusive but palpable advantage in the great fight that was to come.

They also enjoyed another advantage: the defeat in July had, paradoxically, increased their influence in the Conservative Party. Instead of numbering 60 out of 400 seats, they now numbered 50 out of 261.[47] In addition, they had a leader of tremendous energy and resolve, namely Winston Churchill, who would make the battle over India the defining moment of his career.

Average middle-class Britons lived the link to India vicariously; Churchill knew it firsthand. He had not just *read* about the intrepid young ensign on the Northwest Frontier: he had *been* that ensign thirty-five years earlier. The Raj was his father's legacy in a very literal sense. No way would he give it up to Irwin or Gandhi, or anyone else, without a fight. And now he would mobilize all his skill and energy to convince the waverers in Tory and Liberal ranks to fight as well.

His declaration of war on the Irwin policy appeared in the *Daily Mail* on November 16. He blasted giving India Dominion status as nothing less than a "crime," and recited all the reasons why British rule had been not only good for India, but essential.

"The rescue of India from ages of barbarism, tyranny, and internecine war, and its slow but ceaseless forward march to civilization constitute upon the whole the finest achievement of our history," he wrote. Thanks to the British, "War has been banished from India; her frontiers have been defended against invasion from the north; famine has been gripped and controlled...Justice has been given—equal between race and race, impartial between man and man. Science, healing or creative, has been harnessed to the service of this immense and, by themselves, helpless population." All this had been achieved "by the willing sacrifices of the best of our race."

But now this legacy was threatened "by a growing lack of confidence at home in the reality of our mission" and the "undermining repercussions of these doubts upon British officials in India," meaning (although Churchill did not say) the viceroy himself. Out of these doubts had come a plan to hand India over to a Hindu elite, with "their veneer of European politics and philosophy,"*[48] so that the subcontinent could

---

* This phrase actually comes from a later Churchill article, but captures his views in both.

become the helpless victim of their "utopian dreams and predatory appetites and subversive movements." This was an unmistakable reference to Gandhi and his supporters.

Churchill finished by declaring that Dominion status must never be given to a society undeserving of it. Certainly that exalted status was not suitable for a society that branded sixty million of its inhabitants as untouchables "whose very presence is pollution"; or one that was "prey to fierce racial and religious dissensions"; or one whose educated political classes were barely a fraction of the "three hundred and fifty millions for whose welfare we are responsible." Rather, this "criminally mischievous plan" demanded "the earnest resistance of the British nation" and the full mobilization of the "sober and resolute forces of the British Empire" in order to safeguard "the life and welfare of all the peoples of Hindustan."[49]

The article set off shock waves across his party. However, it came as no surprise to another Tory colleague, Leo Amery. For a quarter-century he and Churchill had clashed over the future of the British Empire. Amery's view was closer to Irwin's: that it was time for the empire to modernize itself and accommodate the nationalist urges of the peoples living within its orbit. Indeed, Amery foresaw the day when Britain's "imperial mission" existed in name only, as a bond of common heritage and cultural influence and nothing more.[50]

However, "the key to Winston is to realize that he is mid-Victorian," Amery wrote in his diary, and "steeped in the politics of his father's period." Churchill "can only think in phrases, and close argument is really lost on him." Churchill's "verbal exuberance and abounding vitality" managed to disguise that fact from others, Amery admitted. But "on essentials he is still where he was 25 years ago," Amery concluded, including on India.[51]

Other thoughtful Tories felt the same way. That weekend Winston appeared at a country house party in Hertfordshire, "very full of his article in the *Daily Mail*." His host and fellow Conservative, Lord Lytton, called the article "thoroughly mischievous" and sternly warned Churchill that he was only feeding the Indian distrust of Britain that Irwin was trying to dispel. Lytton said there was a crucial difference between a doctor telling a patient that he was definitely on the road to recovery and one telling him that recovery might be slow but sure. The one offered hope; the other just repeated a meaningless cliché.

Winston would have none of it. "It may be legitimate to encourage a sick patient with hope," he replied, "but that is very different from deluding a vain people with false promises."[52]

Lytton never asked which vain people Winston was talking about. Was it the Indians, or perhaps the British themselves? Over the next six years, as the debate over India raged, Churchill never made up his mind. He never could decide who was more self-deluded: the Indians who imagined they could rule themselves without help, or the British public and a Conservative Party who believed they could give up India without dire consequences.

This bleak realization, that Britons might actually hand over their hard-won heritage without a fight, did not come to him immediately. Yet even as he joined in Lord Lytton's party that weekend in Hertfordshire and pontificated at the breakfast table on the need to block Dominion status for India, the seeds of another plan, a larger and bolder one, was taking shape in his mind.

Churchill wanted a showdown on India. Everyone else, it seemed, wanted the opposite. Everyone, that is, except Gandhi.

Gandhi had been strangely silent in the days after Irwin's historic pronouncement on October 29. Historians and biographers all speculate about his state of mind; his own words are of little help. Certainly he felt enormous pressures to go along with Moderates like M. A. Ansari and Gandhi's old friend Motilal Nehru. They sensed a breakthrough was imminent; Irwin seemed to have offered the last best hope for a deal on independence before the radicals won over the "Indian street." If it cooperated, the Indian National Congress could win significant concessions in the first of the so-called Round Table Conferences, scheduled for next year.

Gandhi saw their point, and when he and they met in Delhi in the first two days of November, he worked hard to arrange a compromise statement that he, they, and radicals like Jawaharlal Nehru and S. C. Bose could all sign. The result was the Delhi Declaration of November 2. It was hardly a victory for Lord Irwin or his Indian supporters. It demanded that all political prisoners be released; that full Dominion status be granted *before* the Round Table Conferences; that the Indian National Congress be the main representative of Indian opinion at the conferences; and that all discussions center on framing a suitable "Dominion Constitution for India."[53]

The Moderates thought this statement too truculent but signed on anyway. Bose and the younger Nehru considered it too mild, and Gandhi had to use all his influence to get them to put their names to it. Both resigned from the Congress Working Committee immediately afterward, showing how much they disliked the declaration and disliked being arm-twisted by Gandhi.[54]

The usual Gandhi image is that of a man prepared to walk alone rather than compromise his principles. In fact, the Delhi Declaration reveals him at his negotiating best. Members of his Bania caste had a reputation as keen bargainers. Most Indian observers, and the savvy British ones, attributed Gandhi's skill to his Bania background as well as his breeding in Kathiawar, long considered the home of hard-headed merchants and sharp businessmen.[55] It was a crucial aspect of Gandhi's personality that sentimental admirers like Romain Rolland, as well as modern filmmakers, miss. Gandhi possessed a clear principled mind, a lawyer's skill in verbal distinctions, a sharp empathy for understanding his opponents' position, infinite patience, and an iron will—all the ingredients of a master negotiator.

From that perspective, the November 1929 declaration may be his masterpiece. Certainly Gandhi had managed to pull Indian leaders together on a divisive issue, if only temporarily. Yet it is not at all clear that he thought it mattered. He did not read Churchill's article in the *Daily Mail,* but it would only have fed his growing suspicion that the Labour Party was not strong enough to get Dominion status for India through Parliament. Opposition there would render Irwin's promises, however well meant, worthless: "a piece of waste paper to be thrown into the basket designed for such papers." In the end, Indians would have to take their independence for themselves, just as Gandhi had always intended. "The winning of Swaraj," he reiterated in *Navajivan* on November 10, "depends only on our own strength."[56]

That week Lord Irwin heard from an American visitor to Sabarmati named Sherwood Eddy. It was Eddy's impression that Gandhi would hold out against any further compromise on independence. The Delhi Declaration was his final word on the subject, Eddy told Irwin. If its demands were not met by December 31, Gandhi was ready to start the next wave of civil disobedience, whether his Moderate and Liberal friends were ready or not.[57]

They suspected the same thing. At first, Srinivasa Sastri wrote, "I thought he was genuinely struggling on our side. Now, however, a doubt has begun to cross my mind. Is he not after all thirsting for a great opportunity for his mighty weapon?"—namely, mass *ahimsa*.[58]

The truth was, Gandhi was eager to test his new approach to satyagraha as a national mass movement. The Bardoli experience had bolstered his confidence that its bugs had been worked out; that skilled and motivated local leaders could mobilize local support without violence; and that the discipline of his satyagrahis could extend down to ordinary people by example. Why put off until tomorrow what would work today? Why allow false hopes of compromise to postpone final victory? Gandhi figured the perfect place to stage his next move would be the next Congress, which would be in Lahore over Christmas Week—just as the Calcutta deadline expired.

Viceroy Irwin had thought his declaration would rally moderate men of all shades of opinion. In fact, it was encouraging men to become more extreme: first Churchill, now Gandhi. On the eve of Lahore, in a last ditch effort to forestall disaster, Irwin arranged a meeting with Gandhi and other leaders. The news from Britain was equally discouraging. His friend George Lane-Fox confessed that "Baldwin has gotten himself into rather a tiresome hole" with his support for Irwin and that Churchill's militancy promised an ugly fight in the Commons.[59]

And others were equally eager to get into the picture.

In the predawn hours of December 22, 1929, Lord Irwin boarded his special viceregal train in Hyderabad. He was headed for New Delhi to take up official residence at the new Viceroy House. That very afternoon he would meet Gandhi and the other politicians to discuss his declaration about Dominion status.

The gleaming white train glided through the darkness. As the sun rose, the train approached the station at Delhi, breaking through the thick damp fog that had settled across the railway tracks. It was nearly eight o'clock in the morning. Irwin was comfortably settled in his plush seat and reading the sermons of Richard Challoner, a seventeenth-century bishop who was one of Irwin's favorite authors.

The train slowed to thirty-five miles per hour in order to chug up along a high curved embankment, near the Old Fort or Purana Qila, at the outskirts of Delhi. As he turned the page, Irwin suddenly heard a loud bang.

He set down his book and listened. "That must be a bomb," he told himself. Amid a cacophony of squealing brakes, the acrid smell of cordite wafted down the car corridor. The train ground to a halt. Men and soldiers jumped down onto the track, guns drawn.

They soon found a large hole in the tracks where a dynamite charge had gone off. Terrorists had set the fuse inside the nearby Old Fort, which loomed over the rail line. It had been timed to explode when the engine reached the curve. The plan had been to derail the viceroy's train and send it tumbling down the thirty-foot embankment, crushing him and everyone else on board.

However, the fuse had been badly laid. The engine and the first three cars had already passed before it detonated, and the rest of the train was able to pass over the gap unharmed.

Irwin had calmly returned to reading his Challoner when one of his assistants dropped in to suggest he take a look. He eased his long, slim form down the carriage steps and ambled along the track, as the train's engine hissed and huffed in the background. There he found the stricken car. The blast had yanked the carriage floor upward into an arch of twisted steel, with splintered planking sticking out in all directions. Several yards of the steel tracks had been blown apart. Miraculously the only casualty was an Indian servant who had been slightly injured by the blast. Everyone else on the train was safe. Hindu terrorists had tried to turn the Raj upside down by murdering its viceroy, and failed.[60]

Irwin ruefully surveyed the damage. "It is really astonishing," he wrote to his father later, "that there should be people who think these kinds of things can sincerely benefit them."[61] But part of him was almost pleased by the assassination attempt. He had nearly become a martyr for moderation. Gandhi had always said that nothing unites people like suffering. Halifax had not exactly suffered in the attack, but surely, he thought, this incident must convince Gandhi and his allies that he was sincere and that it was time to reach an agreement.

With characteristic British fortitude, Irwin arrived at his meeting at Viceroy House on time. Gandhi, Motilal Nehru, Liberals T. B. Sapru and V. B. Patel,* along with the Muslim leader Muhammad Jinnah, were all waiting for him. Gandhi congratulated Irwin on his miraculous escape, but thereafter he was, Irwin wrote later, "at his intolerable worst." Irwin's near-martyrdom had not helped him at all.

---

* No relation to Gandhi's disciple, "Sardar" Vallabhbhai Patel.

On the contrary, Gandhi and the others told him there could be no further compromise. If the British government was unprepared to meet the demands of the Delhi Declaration, they would have no choice but to carry out their plan of mass civil disobedience. Gandhi added that he could not attend the Round Table Conference in London as long as the British government refused to let the Indians speak "with a single voice" through the Congress. It was not members of Parliament, but Indians, who should frame India's future. Motilal Nehru agreed. The goal of any conference should be "the transfer of power" from Great Britain to India—and the Indian National Congress.

Finally, Irwin asked point-blank if Gandhi believed the British were being insincere about wanting to give Indians self-government. Gandhi replied he still believed in the sincerity of individuals like Irwin but not in the government as a whole. Jinnah and Sapru tried to be more conciliatory, but it was Gandhi's meeting. After two and a half hours, he and the others left. Irwin's generous gesture, his declaration on Dominion status, had been brusquely brushed aside.[62]

"They really were impossible," Irwin angrily told his secretary of state, Wedgwood Benn, "and left me more than usually depressed about the lack of political sense that extremist politicians naturally betray." But, he shrewdly guessed that Gandhi's truculence arose in part from his fear that a truly open Round Table Conference would only expose Indian rivalries and divisions, which the British could exploit: "It seemed better to their minds to invent a reason not to participate in it." However, if Gandhi and his supporters resorted to noncooperation again, he warned, "we shall lose no time in jumping on their heads"— even though, Irwin added piously, "I am a pacifist by nature."[63]

A week before the New Year the preliminaries for the Lahore Congress got under way. It was the most divisive Congress of Gandhi's career. The Moderates begged him to be more reasonable and to give room for Lord Irwin to negotiate. Gandhi's one concession was a vote congratulating the viceroy on escaping assassination. It barely passed. At the same time, however, S. C. Bose's attempt to get support for forming an independent opposition government also went down to defeat.

This was Gandhi's mood: a rebuff to the Moderates, then a rebuff to the radicals. The only agenda left was Gandhi or nothing. The resolution he proposed and rammed through was that unless the British government gave way on Dominion status by midnight on New Year's Eve, the Congress would mobilize all means to achieve Purana Swaraj:

complete independence. In the final session, the resolution passed over-whelmingly, with passionate cries of *"Mahatma Gandhi ki jai!"*

Gandhi had won. Master of the situation, he looked forward confi-dently to battle—even though a police spy noted that "every point in his program is bitterly distasteful to one important section or another."[64] At almost the same time Winston Churchill was writing his own letter to the viceroy. He had telegrammed Irwin earlier to congratulate him on escaping assassination. Irwin had written back on the twenty-sixth, thanking him and saying he understood Churchill's position on Dominion status. Irwin wryly added, "I am not wholly insane" in be-lieving he could still palliate Indian opinion. He truly believed that "half the problem is psychological and a case of hurt feelings" and that by re-assuring Gandhi and other Indian leaders about British intentions, he could bring about a final settlement.

"I do think," Irwin had written, that "once Edwin Montagu set our feet upon our present road" the British government was bound to see it to the end—"unless we are prepared indefinitely to pursue methods that I don't think British would long tolerate," namely full-scale violent re-pression.[65]

Churchill refused to be ruffled. "I do not think that we need fear any shock in India of violence," he wrote that New Years' Day. "Strength will be given to us in proportion to our need." If Indians rejected rea-sonable reforms, the British should not hesitate to take back direct rule. "Once the evil elements" among Indian nationalists met resolute British will power, "our task will be rendered far less formidable and difficult."

Churchill even told Irwin, "I believe you have a great opportunity on your hands" to show British resolve and to crush any renewal of civil disobedience. Churchill fully expected compromise to fail, with even the so-called Moderates routed and silenced. "It is my conviction," he wrote, "that upon the supreme issue of India the British Empire will arise in its old strength and that those who, like you, are risking their lives to keep the flag flying, may act with growing confidence."[66]

Even as Churchill wrote these lines, however, another flag was being unfurled on the banks of the Ravi River. Midnight had come to Lahore, and the New Year had begun. As the crowd danced and sang, Jawaharlal Nehru, the Congress president, hoisted the new na-tional flag of India. The flag owed its basic tricolor design to Gandhi, with a stripe of saffron for Hindus, green for Muslims, and white for everyone else, and with a charkha represented at its center.

Gandhi had also composed a rousing Declaration of Independence:

> We believe it is the inalienable right of the Indian people, as of any other people, to have freedom and enjoy the fruits of their toil and have the necessities of life... The British Government of India has not only deprived the Indian people of their freedom but has based itself on the exploitation of the masses, and has ruined India economically, politically, culturally, and spiritually. We believe, therefore, that India must sever the British connection and attain *Purana Swaraj,* or Complete Independence.

The battle had begun.

Chapter Seventeen

SALT

1930

This is God's grace, let us remain unmoved and watch His miracles.

MOHANDAS K. GANDHI, APRIL 5, 1930

BATTLE HAD BEEN JOINED, BUT FOR six weeks almost nothing happened.

Many Indian cities celebrated Congress's India Independence Day, which Gandhi had set for January 26, 1930. Some Union Jacks were burned; some new Indian flags were flown. On the thirtieth Subhas Chandra Bose and some companions went to jail for one year. But their crime was not to have committed acts of civil disobedience or noncooperation. The crime was to have organized an unauthorized parade as part of All-Bengal Political Sufferers' Day the previous August.[1]

In fact few visible acts of civil disobedience took place anywhere in India—certainly few that were meaningful. This should have come as no surprise to Gandhi. Very reluctantly he had agreed at Lahore to drop the boycott of schools and universities and courts from his satyagraha program, thus letting India's urban middle class off the civil disobedience hook. Schools, shops, and factories stayed open. Congress members were still supposed to resign from the provincial legislatures, but few did.[2]

Gandhi, meanwhile, was back at Sabarmati, spinning cotton thread by the hour and thinking. At Lahore his Congress supporters had looked more like a disorganized rabble than a strong disciplined elite.[3] He decided he could not expect them to take any initiative or follow complicated orders. Gandhi wanted a satyagraha campaign that would give Indians a sense of unity and moral uplift: Swaraj in the truest sense. But as he freely admitted, he had no idea how to do it. "It may be impossible to offer civil disobedience at this stage," he wrote on January 9. "Just now everything is in the embryonic state."[4]

Gandhi also realized that he must not repeat the mistakes of the past. His hopes in 1920 had perished in the flames of Chauri Chaura. He had to find a different path this time, something that would be both more effective and less likely to spin out of the bounds of ahimsa. On the ninth he told readers of *Young India,* "I am concentrating all my powers on discovering a working formula." Not until mid-February did he find the answer.

There were several reasons why Gandhi finally decided to make abolition of the salt tax into the issue to launch his next (and ultimately most famous) satyagraha campaign. First, the sale of salt had been a government monopoly going back to Mughal times. Robert Clive used the accompanying tax to reward his cronies in Bengal, and in 1878 it became uniform across India and the princely states.[5] The salt tax had been a symbol of sovereignty since the days of Akbar, and since 1878 a symbol of India's subjection to the British.

That meant that everyone in India, rich or poor, paid the tax. It made a clear and unambiguous uncontroversial target for popular action. Even Muslims, who had largely opted out of the January 26 independence celebrations, paid it. Gandhi hoped the protest against the salt tax could unite Hindus and Muslims against the Raj. It might also draw in the peasantry, whom the tax hurt most.[6] India's poorest had rallied to him in his most successful satyagraha campaigns, in Champaran and in Kaira and most recently in Bardoli. Before that they had saved him from humiliation in South Africa. More and more Gandhi saw them as his true constituency. Here was a chance to free them from a tax that pinched their meager incomes, especially as the worldwide depression loomed on the doorstep of India.

Gandhi had also found a new approach to civil disobedience, which he tested at Bardoli. Only trained and committed satyagrahis were to commit overt acts of resistance. As his picked elite, they would lead, while ordinary people would watch and bear witness. Gandhi was determined that if violence broke out, it would not be the satyagrahis' fault, or Gandhi's.

His plan was debated and approved at an AICC meeting at Sabarmati in mid-February. "It is only a wonder," Motilal Nehru confessed to M. A. Ansari on the seventeenth, "that no one else ever thought of it."[7] But Gandhi's real stroke of genius came later. He decided he would walk, *Bhagavad Gita* in hand, from Sabarmati ashram to the town of Dandi, on Gujarat's west coast, and formally break the law himself by making salt from the sea.

No written document tells us how or when he arrived at this extraordinary plan. He certainly knew that Bombay, as well as Madras and the central and southern princely states, all got their salt from government sea salt plants along that coast. It was the same coast where residents had made their own salt for centuries. Gandhi had used the march formula in previous satyagraha campaigns, and Dandi was in the district (Jalalpur) where he had first launched his Bardoli satyagraha. "I still have many sweet memories of my experience of the place," he wrote. The organizational structure for civil disobedience in Jalalpur was still up and working.*[8]

As late as February 27, in an article in *Young India* entitled, "When I Am Arrested," Gandhi brought up the satyagraha without mentioning any march. On March 2 he sent a letter to Lord Irwin. Beginning "Dear Friend," it contained his Eleven Points, or eleven grievances against British rule that, if not corrected, would force him to break the salt law. Even at this point the march to the sea may still only have been a fleeting idea—Gandhi's letter did not mention it—but it did warn Irwin that once he broke the law, it would be the signal for followers across India to do the same.

Setting off a fresh round of civil disobedience meant running a "risk I have dreaded," he admitted, even a "mad risk." However, "the victories of truth have never been won without risks, often of the gravest character." The campaign, he said, would begin on March 12. The letter was a chivalrous heads-up but also a gauntlet tossed at the viceroy's feet. Gandhi was virtually daring him and the entire machinery of the Raj to stop him.[9]

The letter was delivered by a Quaker friend to Viceroy House, where Irwin had just returned from watching polo matches at Meerut.[10] Irwin, sensitive but unresponsive as always, sent a four-line reply. It only expressed regret that Gandhi intended to break the law. Gandhi was crest-

---

* Yet all the evidence suggests that Dandi was not the first choice for ending the march. That seems to have been Badalpur, on the tidal Mahi Sagar River and only eight days' walk from Sabarmati. But one of Gandhi's aides, Kalianji Mehta, proposed extending the march, for the maximum publicity benefit. Gandhi agreed, and an informal committee of Patel, Mehta, Narhari Parikh, and Lakshmidas Asare selected Dandi.

fallen. "On bended knee, I asked for bread," he told followers, "and I received stone instead." On the eleventh he began final preparations for his march. He told the members of the ashram that night, "Our cause is just, our means are strong, and God is with us."[11]

He chose from their ranks seventy-nine companions to make the 240-mile journey, in the middle of the dry season. Those he chose were delighted; the others, including six-year-old Narayan Desai and the other children, were crushed at being left behind. But they all rose before dawn to see him off.

A crowd from town had gathered throughout the night. Before the morning's first light they numbered in the hundreds of thousands. "Beneath the ashram's ancient tamarind tree," Desai remembered fifty years later, "were parked what seemed like all the cars in Ahmedabad."[12] There were correspondents from Indian, European, and American newspapers and news photographers. Because of the crowd, morning prayers could not be held on the usual ground. They moved instead to the dried-up riverbed of the Sabarmati. Pandit Khare, who led the prayers at the ashram every morning, could barely make his voice heard over the throng.

The voices soon joined together in chanting, *"Raghupati Raghave Rajaram."* Just before leaving, Gandhi visited some of the ashram's sick children. Three had just died of smallpox, including Pandit Khare's infant son—a revealing index of the general state of health at the ashram. But Khare, like Sarojini Naidu and Gandhi's secretaries Desai and Pyarelal, was still marching.

They gathered in the courtyard. The marchers had been carefully selected as a rainbow coalition of followers, including Muslims, Sikhs, untouchables, and Christians. They were all men and covered a span of ages. The youngest was sixteen; Gandhi was the oldest, at sixty-one.[13] Vallabhbhai Patel was not among them; he had been arrested four days earlier. Neither were the Nehrus. But each marcher had his copy of the *Gita,* and homespun cotton garlands hung around their necks, like beasts to the sacrifice. Many, including Gandhi, thought the police might gun them down as they left the ashram. Most assumed Gandhi would be arrested before he set out.

Gandhi brought along a long bamboo stick to lean on, with an iron tip. The children's teacher pinned a badge to his shawl and kissed him goodbye. Another woman applied a red paste dot or *bindi* to his forehead, to ward off bad luck. Then as the crowd cried and chanted *"Vaishnav Jan"** and the *Ramanama,* Gandhi set off.[14]

The march to the sea may have been heroic, even saintly. But it was also carefully planned and executed. Besides his seventy-eight fellow pilgrims, an enormous crowd of newspaper reporters, photographers, and other onlookers followed Gandhi everywhere. *Navajivan* and *Young India* had published his proposed route, which wound through Kaira province to Dandi, and the fact that he would travel in the early morning hours and late afternoon. This made it easier for casual spectators and supporters to make the rendezvous and join the throng.[15]

Gandhi's goal was to stop in at least one village during the morning and another at night. He expected no accommodations for himself or his friends. They would sleep in the open. The horde of news media and other hangers-on had to make their own arrangements. Gandhi himself required only a place to wash and water and some uncooked food to eat. He also wanted information: on the village's population and sanitation, on how much alcohol was consumed (Gandhi the New Ager was still determined to make India a teetotal nation), and how much the peasants had to pay in land and salt tax.[16] Like the march across Champaran in 1917, this one was to be a walking lesson on conditions in India, a peripatetic education for himself and his followers as well as the London *Times,* the *Bombay Chronicle,* and other media following in his wake.

The march to the coast was India's introduction to the art of public relations on a massive scale. It proceeded at a leisurely pace and took a month. At each village Gandhi spoke of his vision for satyagraha, gave press interviews, and dictated articles for his *Navajivan* and *Young India,* even as the crowds grew and grew. At Nadiad, Kaira's largest town, he attracted 20,000 people; in Anand, 10,000; in Broach, almost 15,000. Then in Surat, only forty kilometers from Dandi, he drew more than 30,000.[17]

On April 3 he was close to his goal, at Navsari. That evening he spoke to the crowd of 9,000 (organizers claimed 50,000), seated on a raised dais, as electric lights paid for by a local Parsi businessman illuminated the darkness. Gandhi thanked the local Parsis for their support and emphasized the importance of women for this satyagraha campaign, since they were the living "embodiment of renunciation and compassion, i.e. nonviolence." At Vanji he had told his followers to be prepared for a violent crackdown: "We have prepared ourselves for death from cannons and

---

* "Hail to Vishnu."

guns."[18] Indeed, as his march neared its end, Gandhi secretly wondered what the government *was* doing and why Irwin and his police officials hadn't moved in.

The truth was the march caught Irwin by surprise. Privately, he was amazed that a man of sixty-one known to have a tricky heart and a history of high blood pressure was capable of it: "The will power of the man must be enormous." The viceroy's first impulse was not to rise to what he considered Gandhi's bait. He even nursed a hope that Gandhi's health would give out: an incapacitated Gandhi, or even a dead one, would solve everyone's problems.[19] But otherwise Irwin took what one biographer calls "a low key approach" and resisted officials who wanted to disperse the crowd with tear gas and toss Gandhi in jail at once. He had no desire to give Gandhi his "martyr's halo," as he put it, or trigger worse trouble once Indians learned of Gandhi's arrest.

So when Gandhi finally reached Dandi on April 5, not a policeman was in sight.[20] He told the vast crowd that he had been uncertain if the government would let him get this far. But the government was too ashamed to try, he suggested. That sense of shame was proof of the power of nonviolence. "Tomorrow we will break the salt law," Gandhi announced in a clear voice. If the government did not stop him, it meant the salt tax would have to be abolished. If it was not abolished, it did not matter: "This movement is based on the faith that when a whole nation is roused and on the march no leader is necessary."

Gandhi said his goal was for every Indian to make salt at home, "as our ancestors did," until the government's stock became useless. But he reminded the crowd of a greater goal beyond that: of Swaraj, "the goddess." "Our minds will not be at peace till we have her *darshan,* nor will we allow the government any peace."[21]

For Gandhi, Dandi represented the end of a journey in more ways than one. He was saying goodbye once and for all to his British connection, to his "infatuation" with British rule that for half a century had led him to think it could treat its subjects justly. The days of trust and reasonable negotiation were over, he said. It was time for action and Indian unity.

"This is a struggle of not one man, but millions of us," he cried out. "My heart now is as hard as stone. I am in this struggle for Swaraj ready to sacrifice thousands and hundreds of thousands of men if necessary." The hushed crowd listened to he spoke his final words to them: "This is God's grace; let us remain unmoved and watch His miracles."[22]

The next morning Gandhi wandered down to the beach. He had been up as usual since four a.m. Beside him were the poetess Sarojini Naidu as well as Mahadev Desai. Gandhi first waded into the sea to wash himself: April 6 was a traditional day of penance and purification. Besides, Gandhi said, all religious wars begin with a ritual bath. He then waded back, his dhoti dripping wet, and led everyone down to a shallow salt pit. At about six-thirty he stooped down and gingerly gathered up some salt, left by the surf, into a small ball of mud. Naidu exclaimed, "Hail, Deliverer." According to Desai, Gandhi murmured, "With this salt I am shaking the foundations of the empire."[23]

The deed was done. By now others in the crowd were stooping and gathering salt in the palms of their hands, laughing and singing as if on holiday. Gandhi told an interviewer, "Now that a technical or ceremonial breach of the salt law has been committed, it is now open to anyone ...to manufacture whenever he wishes" instead of buying it from the government.

"What if the government doesn't arrest you?" the correspondent from the *Free Press* asked.

"Oh, I shall continue to manufacture illicit salt," Gandhi blithely replied.[24]

In fact, the government did not arrest him for almost another month. They arrested every other satyagrahi they could find, as the salt satyagraha spread across India. On that same day, April 6, his son Ramdas was arrested with a large band of ashramites. Later, so were Devadas Gandhi and Mahadev Desai. So was the mayor of Calcutta, when he urged his fellow citizens to boycott foreign cloth, which cost him a six-month sentence. All told there were more than five thousand separate satyagraha acts across India. It was the biggest and most organized protest movement the subcontinent had ever known.

The Gandhi inner circle led the way. Rajendra Prasad was arrested with a large crowd of satyagrahis when mounted police charged them and they lay down in front of their horses' hooves. Miraculously no one was hurt, but the protesters had to be lifted bodily by constables and thrown onto trucks to be taken to prison.[25] On April 16 Gandhi learned that Jawaharlal Nehru had been arrested for breaking the salt law. He sent an ecstatic telegram to Motilal Nehru, congratulating him and his wife as happy parents: "Jawaharlal has earned his crown of thorns."[26]

Meanwhile, in the village of Aat, Gandhi personally supervised villagers who were gathering illicit salt and refusing to give it up as police moved in to arrest them. That day was his "silence day," but as he told a reporter for the Bombay *Chronicle* afterward, "There was no violence. To them their salt was as dear as their blood." He hoped that by their patience and suffering they would change the hearts even of the police.[27]

Soon even non-Gandhians joined in. Nirad Chaudhuri was an editor of *The Monthly Review* in Calcutta. An educated Bengali intellectual and a liberal, he had always been a Gandhi skeptic. But news of Gandhi's march triggered "a sudden conversion." One afternoon, with birds crying and circling overhead, he wandered down to Calcutta's saltwater marshes. He watched while a Bengali follower of Gandhi, Satis Chandra Das Gupta, boiled a pot of sea water on a mudflat and extracted the salt. Chaudhuri felt compelled to make a donation and take a small packet of salt—but he never used it. "Perhaps," he would write many years later, "it [was] too sacred for consumption."[28]

Another eyewitness watched as satyagrahis boiled sea water on the Esplanade Maidan in Bombay, surrounded by concentric rings of Congress volunteers linked arm in arm. "On one occasion," he remembered, "no less than thirty rings were used, three consisted of Sikhs and three of women." This arrangement forced the police to break through each ring to get at the perpetrator, which involved lots of broken heads and slashing lathis, "so the crowd more often than not became violent and pelted them with stones."[29]

Crowd violence was low-level but widespread, in spite of Gandhi's hopes and warnings. His biographer Louis Fischer's claim that "Chauri Chaura in 1922 had taught India a lesson" is false. On the night of April 17–18 one hundred armed members of the Hindustan Republican Association stormed an army depot at Chittagong in eastern Bengal, killing a British sergeant. Then on April 23 riots broke out in Peshawar. British and Gurkha troops were sent in and opened fire, killing thirty rioters and wounding thirty-five. The Royal Garwhal Rifles were also ordered into the fray; they refused and had to be disarmed by Gurkha troops.

British troops withdrew and Peshawar descended into ten days of riots. As the British left, Pathan and Afridi tribesmen descended from the hills in pursuit of loot. Far off in England, Churchill told colleagues that the whole incident "marked the lowest ebb yet seen of British authority in India."[30] And yet Irwin still refused to have Gandhi arrested.

Finally, even Gandhi became fed up with Lord Irwin's inaction. He was keen to show that his arrest would do nothing to halt the campaign's momentum. So he announced that his satyagrahi would storm the Dharasana Salt Works, some 150 miles north of Bombay. Twenty-five hundred volunteers gathered in the haze of early morning. Leading them was Sarojini Naidu herself, who told the volunteers, "You must not resist; you must not even raise a hand to ward off a blow."

A United Press reporter described what happened next:

"At a word of command, scores of native policemen" rushed in wielding their lathis. "Not one of the marchers even raised an arm to fend off the blows. They went down like nine-pins. From where I stood I heard the sickening whack of the clubs on unprotected skulls." The satyagrahi still advanced, wave after wave. Yet there was "no fight, no struggle; the marchers simply walked forward til struck down." Meanwhile stretcher-bearers carried away a stream of "inert, bleeding bodies." Later, the reporter visited their makeshift aid station. He counted 320 injured; many were still unconscious. Eventually two died.[31]

Meanwhile, as the sun rose in the bright clear sky, the temperature reached 116 degrees. The nonviolent but futile assault, the satyagraha equivalent of the first day of the Somme, subsided. Naidu and Gandhi's son Manilal were both arrested. Gandhi himself was unfazed. As he had said, "In a Satanic Government, innocent persons must suffer." Irwin realized he could not afford to wait to see what Gandhi planned to do next.

On May 5, just a few minutes past midnight, Gandhi was camping comfortably under a mango tree at Karadi, a village near Dandi. There was a rustle in the bushes, and then thirty armed Indian policemen and the British district magistrate slowly approached his lean-to.

Gandhi woke up and gazed at the solemn figures looming out of the blackness. He asked, "Do you want me?"

"Are you Mohandas Karamchand Gandhi?" the magistrate asked for form's sake.[32]

Gandhi admitted he was. He learned that he was to be incarcerated under an obscure 1827 regulation that permitted a state prisoner to be held without trial or even a charge. Irwin had wanted to avoid giving Gandhi his martyr's halo, but circumstances had forced his hand. Unlike the Noncooperation campaign of 1920, Gandhi's salt satyagraha had rocked the Raj to its foundations. Arresting Gandhi seemed the only alternative to losing control of the subcontinent.

Gandhi's arrival at the Yeravda prison was a virtual homecoming. Standing at the gate was a senior police official who remembered

Gandhi from eight years before. They greeted each other like old friends; the officer remarked that Gandhi looked healthier and younger than when he'd seen him last. The outdoor life must agree with you, he joked. He gave Gandhi a bar of Sunlight soap and let him take a much-needed bath.[33] Gandhi and his jailers settled in for a long stay.

If Irwin and his policemen thought Gandhi's arrest might end their troubles, as it had done in 1922, they were sorely mistaken. Noncooperation intensified over the next ten months. The coming of the monsoon effectively ended the salt satyagraha.[34] But other forms of resistance broke out in every province of India, as tens and even hundreds of thousands joined in. By February 1931 the government could count nearly 24,000 resisters in jail. More than 60,000 were imprisoned over the whole course of the campaign. Some estimates run as high as 100,000.[35]

Who they were reveals how extensive Gandhi's activist core had become. Most came from cities like Bombay and the large Hindu provinces. Thanks to Rajaji, the area around Madras had now become a Gandhi stronghold.[36] The resisters also tended to be young, sometimes very young. Almost 700 of the 4,700 prisoners in Bengal prisons were under the age of seventeen. Many were also students. In Calcutta their strike forced the university law school to cancel exams. At the Scottish Church College they held the world's first student sit-in, lying down to form a human blanket in front of the doors so that other students could not go in.[37]

The other large group were women. Gandhi had come to see them as the heart and soul of his campaign: he believed females had a greater instinct for self-sacrifice than males and "greater courage of the right type."[38] He told the village women in Umber, "If this movement is to succeed, yours will have to be as big a share as men's if not greater."[39] In his chivalrous way, Gandhi still did not want the women in "the front line," as it were, where people could get hurt. He wanted male satyagrahis to defend the salt pans and storm the salt works. Instead, he saw women resisters devoting themselves to spinning khadi, boycotting, and picketing. They were to picket liquor stores, among other things, and visit homes of drunkards to plead with them to stop. "I have seen women of the Salvation Army do this," he said. "Why should not the women of India do the same?"[40]

Gandhi made alcohol a target of satyagraha not only for moral reasons but because the government relied on a liquor tax for revenue. Narayan Desai remembered joining hands with the ashram women standing outside the Sabarmati village liquor store and chanting, "Drinking has destroyed everything, oh addict. Give it up!" Other ashram women did make it into the front lines. Desai remembered the elderly Gangabehn Majumdar, who had given Gandhi his first charkha and was reputed to be more than a hundred years of age, coming home from an encounter with police with her homespun sari stained pink with blood.[41] All in all, Gandhi's satyagraha gave Indian women a new activist social role, especially as the campaign shifted focus to the cities and the antiforeign boycotts.

Women regularly picketed shops where British-made cloth was being sold. They would follow other women leaving the stores and try to persuade them to return their purchases. More menacingly, they organized *siapa* or mock mournings, in which the effigies of merchants who refused to take the boycott pledge were cremated in front of their homes.[42]

In Bombay and Gujarat the boycott put Indian businessmen, already hard hit by the world depression, in serious trouble. To the satyagrahis, it didn't seem to matter. A British official confessed, "The Congress really runs Bombay." Gandhi caps filled the streets, and pickets were posted with the efficient regularity of police constables.[43] As Bombay's governor-general told Viceroy Irwin, "the population as a whole seems to have been carried away on a wave of semi-hysterical enthusiasm." Parsis and Christians, women and children, were "all possessed with the mania for martyrdom." Even the most veteran police officials had never known antigovernment feeling to be so strong or so widespread.[44]

In Calcutta, middle-class support for Gandhi was also strong, although Bengali nationalist revolutionaries also raised their heads, and civil disobedience sometimes turned violent. In the weeks after Gandhi's arrest, Nirad Chaudhuri remembered, perpetual throngs of anxious people milled in the streets, breaking like ocean waves as armored cars, with turbaned policemen ready at their machine guns, patrolled the streets.[45] Chaudhuri's fellow editors at the *Monthly Review* were hit hard by Gandhi's arrest. They ran an editorial quoting the Gospel of Saint Matthew: "When they sought to lay hands on him, they feared the multitude, because they took him for a prophet."

Chaudhuri himself collected the pictures of the arrests and beatings that ran day after day in every newspaper. He hoped to run an issue of *Monthly Review* devoted to the shocking pictures, but the government confiscated the copies. He told his wealthy lawyer brother that he wanted to do something more dramatic and be arrested; his brother only laughed and said Nirad was acting like a child.[46] But Chaudhuri's reaction was more typical of India's educated elite; and skeptics like his brother were becoming scarcer. A successful political movement never requires more than a handful with a "mania for martyrdom"; it only needs a silent majority to watch and sympathize. After fifteen years of trying, Gandhi had brought about a seismic shift in Indian politics.

There were, however, limits to that shift. The courts, provincial councils, and legislatures defied the boycott (although many members stayed away out of fear of mob retaliation). Unrest sometimes resulted when Gandhians tried to include untouchables in the protests. And the silence from the Islamic community was ominous: less than one in twenty of the imprisoned resisters was a Muslim.[47]

Still, Gandhi could be satisfied. In Yeravda he was given his old suite of two cells. He was allowed one of his portable spinning wheels, which he worked nearly six hours a day, and a goat for making his milk. He was even allowed a secretary, to keep up with his unceasing correspondence, and newspapers, including the *Times of India,* to follow the progress of events. He was content, even relaxed: "I have been quite happy and making up for arrears in sleep," he told Mirabehn after a week—and he was totally unmoved by the government's discomfiture.[48] As far as he was concerned, he had said his last word on the subject. "This Indian Empire was conceived in immorality," he wrote before his arrest. "There is no way open to the people save to end a system whose very foundations are immoral."[49] Every day the protests seemed to grow bolder and more effective. What better way to help with India's self-purification than to ignore the pleas for compromise and see the campaign to its end?

Because as the dry season gave way to the monsoons, the only disturbance in Gandhi's calm was the steady stream of distinguished visitors sent by Irwin to try to persuade Gandhi to talk to the government. T. B. Sapru, M. Jayakar, the ailing Motilal Nehru, and the newly released Jawaharlal, then Sapru and Jayakar again. All came away empty-handed. The warden of Yeravda understood Gandhi better than Lord Irwin did. "He sticks to his own opinions," he noted, "and does not listen to the advice of others."[50]

Sapru saw Gandhi in early September 1930. A lawyer and pillar of the National Liberal Federation, Sapru considered himself the true keeper of Gokhale's Moderate flame. For years he had distrusted Gandhi's motives and had been skeptical that noncooperation could achieve much. But as the Congress boycotters took over the cities, as legislators were forced to quit by their neighbors, and as even peasants in outlying districts refused to pay their taxes, "I have been compelled by personal experience to revise some of my opinions," he confessed to the viceroy on September 19.

"The Congress has undoubtedly acquired a great hold on popular imaginations," Sapru marveled, including large numbers of people who had never had any political opinions before. "The popular feeling is one of intense excitement, fed from day to day by continuous and persistent" Congress propaganda. However, Sapru worried that this bred not only an enthusiasm for Gandhi and the Congress but a contempt for government as a whole, including fanning "racial feeling." Law-breaking in the name of civil disobedience was becoming a habit. Unless it stopped, the result would be the collapse not just of the Raj but of the India that Sapru and his elite colleagues hoped to rule in its stead.[51]

But there was nothing Irwin could do. The power to shape events in India had shifted to London. And there one man in particular was looking forward to succeeding where Irwin and everyone else had failed.

In January 1930 Harold Nicolson ran into Churchill at Stornoway House, the country estate of press baron Lord Beaverbrook. Winston looked "very changed from when I had last seen him," Harold remarked. He seemed "incredibly aged" with "a great white face like a blister." Nicholson noted that the former *enfant terrible* of British politics had declined into its elder statesman: "His spirits have also declined and he sighs that he has lost his old fighting power."[52]

But as wave after wave of bad news from India hit the papers, Churchill found a new cause to revive his old drive and energy. Before the summer was out, he had become Britain's major spokesman for a policy of no surrender on India. In just over a year he would use the issue to nearly topple the Tory leadership and put himself at his party's head. The coming battle over India would be Churchill's rehearsal for his fight for rearmament in the middle of the decade and against appeasement at its end. And just as the specter of Adolf Hitler haunted

Churchill in 1940, the shadow of the Mahatma fell across everything he said or did about India for the next five years.

At first Churchill thought Gandhi's arrest meant the government was finally cracking down on the nationalist movement. Then came the news of the negotiations at Yeravda. Winston flew into paroxysms of rage. He accused Irwin and the government of allowing "this malevolent fanatic" to hold "cabinet councils with fellow conspirators in jail," while the government "waited cap in hand outside the cell door." Everything the viceroy was doing was sending the wrong signal, that "the government was clearing out of India," merely fighting a rearguard action, and so on. Turmoil and violence were bound to be the natural result.[53]

This attack in August 1930 rang alarm bells in Tory corridors. A member of the Simon Commission, George Lane-Fox, warned Lord Irwin that Churchill was deliberately alienating "Indian opinion" as well as "stampeding the Conservatives by the cry that the Socialists are giving away India." Lane-Fox found Churchill's words inflammatory and utterly reprehensible, "just the very sort of phrases which we did our best in our Report to avoid."[54] Lane-Fox, like T. B. Sapru, sensed that Gandhi and Churchill could between them upset a carefully balanced apple cart. Not for the last time "moderate men of all stripes of opinion" despaired of both of them.

The long-awaited Simon Commission report tried to set out the terms of balance in June and July. On the issue of Indian self-government, it recommended a policy of caution—or, to suspicious Indian eyes, deliberate delay. Nothing was said of Dominion status.[55] Instead, Simon and his colleagues recommended allowing Indians to govern themselves at the provincial level: a major step. But they also argued that the British government should maintain full powers over the army and the police. Even after the provinces and princely states joined together in a future united government, it averred, a strong viceroy should remain in New Delhi with the power of veto.

This formula for a balance or division of powers between an Indian legislature and a British executive, known by the catchphrase "dyarchy," was never meant as a final settlement for India. It was supposed to be just another landmark on the Long March to Independence (which more and more Indians were coming to believe was a journey without end). But as a political formula, it created more problems than it solved.

Indians were no happier with it than were the Churchill conservatives, who saw the whole scheme as a giveaway. Viceroy Irwin, for that matter, called it a "conjuring trick" and a "fraud" and was furious that his concession on the principle of Dominion status had been ignored.[56]

But events had already passed dyarchy by. Shortly after Gandhi's arrest Irwin announced his plan for a Round Table Conference or summit of British and Indian politicians, scheduled for the autumn. Irwin made plain that its agenda would be set by New Delhi, not by the Simon Commission—although Irwin untruthfully reassured the king that its report would be the principal basis of discussion.[57] Simon was humiliated to learn that he was not even invited. The issue had suddenly become not *if* India was to get Dominion status, but *when* and *how*—even as Gandhi's refusal to attend promised to doom the conference before it started.

Meanwhile the ugly flare-ups of violence in India reminded the British public of what was at stake. In Solapur in Maharashtra, just three days after Gandhi's arrest, three Muslim constables were seized by a Hindu mob, tied together, and set ablaze after being soaked in gasoline. Irwin said this "uncomfortable episode" was a reminder what would happen "if ever we lose grip on the situation."[58] But that was exactly what Churchill and his allies feared was happening.

Not until late August were the violent disturbances in Peshawar stamped out. Churchill growled that in his day British troops would have been sent at once to crush the Pathan rebels who had attacked the city, or to hound them back into the hills. Instead, "the spirit of defeatism in high places" had hesitated to use force; the result was chaos. And now Irwin and his Socialist allies, Churchill warned, were about to use this so-called Round Table Conference to hand India over to a clique of "politically minded, highly educated Hindus" who would reduce India "to the deepest depths of Oriental tyranny and despotism."[59]

The leader of Churchill's own party, the party of empire, however, seemed unwilling to do anything to stop it. In October Stanley Baldwin announced there would be a Tory delegation at the conference. So Winston decided he himself had to take the lead in thwarting the defeatists and in saving India.

Chapter Eighteen

ROUND TABLES AND NAKED FAKIRS
1930–1931

The truth is Gandhi-ism, and everything it stands for, will have to be crushed.
WINSTON CHURCHILL, 1930

CHURCHILL'S RESOURCES FOR THE COMING FIGHT were meager but not insubstantial. His ally George Lloyd, who was now Lord Lloyd, was prepared to mobilize support in the House of Lords. Lloyd was a founder of the India Empire Society: made up largely of ex–Indian Army officers and Indian Civil Service men (including several MPs), it hoped to bring public pressure to bear on the issue of "no surrender" and on the stakes involved. In March Lloyd published a series of articles in the *Daily Telegraph* purporting to show how much British rule had improved the lives of ordinary Indians and how minorities like Muslims and untouchables relied on the British to protect them from a Hindu Brahmin elite.

Giving away India would not be progress, Lloyd argued, but a step backward, to the bad old days before the British brought law and order and civilization to the subcontinent. Such a step would be "the height of cowardice." Lloyd's plaintive cry was the same as Churchill's: "What has become of our old genius to rule and our instinct to understand, better than all others, the needs of our Indian Empire?"[1]

One powerful ally whom Churchill had banked on, Lord Birkenhead, died on September 30. But he picked up two Liberal supporters: Sir John Simon, who was miffed at being excluded from the Round Table Conference; and Irwin's immediate predecessor as viceroy, Lord Reading. What these Liberals lacked in numbers they made up in prestige. In addition, many other Liberals feared for India's future without the Raj, including David Lloyd George. When a German envoy,

Prince von Bismarck, arrived in October, he heard both Churchill and Lord Reading express "great anxieties over the forthcoming Indian Round Table Conference." Both put the blame for the disorder in India on Irwin and what they called "his policy of appeasement"—marking the first time that word became part of Churchill's political vocabulary.[2]

Winston also hoped to mobilize Britain's most powerful press lords, Rothermere and Beaverbrook. Rothermere and the imperialist *Daily Mail* were already on board. Then on September 23, Winston approached Beaverbrook to "help our Island out of the rotten state into which it has now fallen." The danger was that after the sacrifices of the Great War "we should now throw away our conquests and our inheritance."[3]

Churchill affirmed that his sole interest now was to prevent such a development and that he needed Beaverbrook's help in launching "a new and strong assertion of Britain's right to live and right to reign with her Empire splendid and united." Churchill and Beaverbrook had their sharp differences over issues of free trade and Imperial Preference, he pointed out, but now "we ought to be all helping each other" in what was for Winston the "supreme issue": India.[4]

He also warned Stanley Baldwin, "The most serious of all our problems is India...I must confess myself to care more about this business than anything else in public life."[5] Meanwhile letters were pouring in from well-wishers. Lord Burnham, former proprietor of the *Daily Telegraph*, told him that surrendering India would be "a crime against civilization." Field Marshal Sir Claud Jacob sent an eyewitness account of how "we are galloping downhill" in Bombay and elsewhere in India. T. E. Lawrence assured him, "You will remain an indispensable part of the early twentieth century." Even his old commanding officer in India, eighty-eight-year-old Sir Bindon Blood, wrote, "I am full of hope that the way to No 10 is clearing for you."[6]

Meanwhile on November 13, 1930, the Round Table Conference began in London. Sixteen British and fifty-six Indian delegates (including sixteen Muslims and sixteen from the princely states) tried to hash out the details of devolving power in a great empire. Hashing out the fate of the Habsburg Empire after World War I, with Czechs, Poles, Hungarians, Slovaks, Slovenians, and Germans all clamoring for self-determination, proved simple by comparison. In this case, Muslims, Hindus, Sikhs, Bengalis, Punjabis, Parsis, Anglo-Indian Eurasians, and representatives of the untouchables or what was coming to be called the

Depressed Classes, not to mention powerful Hindu religious parties like the Mahasabha, were all fighting for a voice within a *single* state—and a decisive voice at that.

As with most such conferences, the delegates soon found a slogan instead of a solution. That slogan was "an All India Federation." What it would look like, no one could guess. But it soon emerged as the "dominant principle" for the entire nine weeks of discussion.[7] The government in India and the British delegates liked the idea of an Indian federation, because it offered a way to preserve the role for a viceroy as an executive figure with "reserve powers." It certainly seemed preferable to a majority-rule democratic India, which might elect an Indian legislature ready to demand full powers, including power over the army.

Indian delegates were equally enthusiastic. T. B. Sapru was staking his entire political career on getting a federation scheme approved. Jinnah and other Muslims indicated they might agree to one. Even India's princes, who were supposed to be a great stumbling block to any constitutional changes, endorsed it with minor qualifications.

Churchill was "in the depths of gloom," Baldwin gleefully wrote, as the conference failed to collapse and the delegates seemed ready to make progress. But the whole exercise was a waste of time, since no Congress delegation—and no Gandhi—was present. As Gandhi himself put it, it was *Hamlet* without the prince. For that reason alone the Mahatma could be expected to oppose any formula that left out the Indian National Congress as the main representative of the Indian people, or any "All-India Federation" that left British power largely intact. He was hardly alone. The protests continuing across India spoke volumes on where their future lay. Even before the month of November was out, the two chief deal-makers, Jinnah and Sapru, "found themselves spurned by many of their respective co-religionists."[8]

Churchill and his supporters weighed in from the other side. On December 11 the India Empire Society held its first major public meeting, at Cannon Street. Winston was the principal speaker.

A sea of faces watched as the portly, balding figure in a black suit and bow tie strode to the microphone to pronounce sentence on a process that was in fact already DOA. "From many quarters we hear statements that opinion in India has advanced with violent speed," he said. "Full Dominion Status with the right to secede from the British Empire" is being clamored for on all sides.

However, he warned, "no agreement reached at the [Round Table]

Conference will be binding" morally or legally, on Parliament. That body, and that body alone, would have final say on the future of India. And "the British nation has we believe no intention whatever of relinquishing effectual control of Indian life and progress."[9]

As the thunderous applause died, Winston defiantly plunged on. "So much for the facts in England! What are the facts in India?" India had not changed since his father's time, he told his audience. The Western-educated elite who aspired to power there bore "no relation whatever to the life and thought of India": its faceless poor, its sixty million untouchables, its Muslim minority who would be left to the mercies of a "Hindu despotism supplied by an army of European mercenaries"—a reference to an offhand remark by Gandhi that the one service whites might still offer a free India would be to train and equip its army.[10] To reinforce his point, Churchill even quoted his father, saying that the British Raj served as "a sheet of oil spread out over and keeping free from storms a vast and profound ocean of humanity." However, if "the British Raj is to be replaced by the Gandhi Raj," then rulers of the native states must expect to be stripped of their powers; Muslims and untouchables of their rights; and Indian police and soldiers of any support from the new government.[11]

Then Churchill brought the cheering throng to his central point. "If Gandhi had been arrested and tried as soon as he broke the law"; if the Lahore Congress, where the Union Jack had been burned, had been broken up and its leaders deported; then three-quarters of the distress now sweeping India could have avoided. Instead, "the shame is that our moral and intellectual guidance should have not been exerted as firmly as our material power." Weakness at the center and "the defeatist tendency of our present politics" had encouraged Gandhi and others to think the British were leaving.

Now Parliament had to make clear its intention to "guide the destinies of the Indian people in faithful loyalty to Indian interest," not to the demands of the political class. "The bold experiment" of Montagu and his reforms, and Irwin's efforts at compromise, had failed. The past ten years, Churchill asserted, "have been years of failure." It was time for Parliament to reclaim its "right and power to restrict Indian constitutional liberties" until new "more intimate, more representative organisms of self-government" had taken root.[12]

How that would happen, Churchill did not specify. But he did conclude with a dire prediction. "The truth is Gandhi-ism and all it stands for will, sooner or later, have to be grappled with and crushed," he declared. "It is no use trying to satisfy a tiger by feeding him cat's meat. The sooner this is realized," the better. The alternative was to accept the downfall of the British Empire:

> That great organism would pass at a stroke out of life into history. From such a catastrophe there could be no recovery...The race and nation which have achieved so many prodigies and have faithfully discharged so many difficult tasks...will [have fallen] a victim to their own lack of self-confidence and moral strength.[13]

The speech received widespread coverage in the media, much of it critical. The *Times* of London's editor Geoffrey Dawson (who had met with and been impressed by Gandhi) deplored Churchill's attack on the search "for a solution of the most difficult and dangerous situation which confronts the British Empire." Churchill's retrograde views, Dawson noted, still strongly reflected his views as a young officer in India in *My Early Life*. "The omniscient subaltern of 1896 is not, after all, so very far removed from the statesman who has nothing to learn in 1930."[14]

Lord Irwin blasted the speech as "monstrous" and speculated on whether Winston was "rather out of heart with politics altogether... with the result that he is rather mad-dogging." He warned that "the day is past when you make nations live in vacuums...[and] when Winston's possessive instinct can be applied to Empires and the like." Practicing Churchill's kind of imperialism was like trying to "fly a balloon that won't hold gas...The thing just won't work."[15]

Perhaps, but Winston and the hard-liners whom Lord Irwin and Dawson dismissed as superannuated Colonel Blimps were moving on to another mass meeting in Manchester. On December 24 Sir Malcolm Hailey warned Irwin that "the influence of Mr. Winston Churchill was strong" in local Tory circles and growing. Stanley Baldwin, he worried, might be underestimating his ability to carry the party with him. Certainly many concurred with former Governor-General of Bombay Lord Sydenham, who loved Churchill's speech and told him the collapse of the Round Table Conference would be the best possible outcome for Britain. Indeed, any federation scheme "would split India to pieces" and by encouraging that kind of thinking, Sydenham said, the government "is playing a very dangerous game."[16]

But the hard-liners' outrage, and Churchill's, was nothing compared to their fury when they learned that Lord Irwin had not only released Gandhi from jail but struck a personal deal with the Mahatma himself.

New Year's Day 1931 broke clear and bright over India. Virtually nothing had changed since the previous summer. Gandhi was still in prison, saying nothing; so were thousands of his followers. The streets of Bombay and other major cities were tranquil but deserted. The failure of the London Round Table Conference had triggered no great surprise or commotion and had done nothing to dispel the sullen atmosphere. It was Lord Irwin, and Lord Irwin alone, who decided to break the impasse, first by setting Gandhi free and then, six weeks later, by agreeing to meet with him at Viceroy House.

Here as usual in Gandhi's career, historical truth and popular legend stand very far apart. Books and films portray Gandhi's meeting with Irwin as a stupendous, even unique event and a singular triumph for Gandhi. The truth was that Gandhi had met several viceroys before, including Irwin. Certainly Irwin seemed different. When the viceroy ordered Gandhi's release from Yeravda on January 26, 1931, which Irwin made clear was not an act of surrender but a gesture of goodwill to reopen negotiations, Gandhi was personally touched.

But Gandhi had dealt with cunning European negotiators previously, including General Smuts. He may have sensed that Lord Irwin was a man with principles but no convictions; a man whose sensitive and intelligent gifts were unaccompanied by any positive agenda. He was, in historian Alan Taylor's words, "fertile with negations" and content to let others take the lead, whether at Viceroy House in 1931 or at Berchtesgaden in 1938.[17] Irwin was the classic product of a ruling class that had lost faith in itself. Gandhi the barrister grasped that this was a man who could be pushed in the direction he wanted.

Another truth was that Gandhi himself was under pressure from his supporters to cut a deal. After the unprecedented success of 1930, the civil disobedience campaign was showing signs of losing momentum. Except in Gujarat, the United Provinces, and Bihar, it had been fading since October.[18] The day after his release Gandhi met with Patel and his business friends in Bombay, who gave him an earful about their business woes thanks to the boycott. He heard the same complaints from supporters in Ahmedabad.[19] Jawaharlal Nehru, also released on the twenty-sixth, and Nehru's ailing father Motilal, both urged Gandhi to remain firm. Gandhi admitted that his inner voice offered no guidance on what to do, but the Bania lawyer sensed the time was ripe for moving forward, not standing still.

On February 7 he sent a letter to Irwin asking for a meeting: "I would like to meet not so much the viceroy of India as the man in you." Irwin agreed, and at half past two on February 17, 1931, the historic meeting took place. At six foot five, Lord Irwin stood almost a full twelve inches taller than his guest, who arrived in his usual dhoti and cloak, looking "small, wizened, rather emaciated, no front teeth," Irwin told King George V later. Gandhi cut a very strange figure in the splendid marble halls of the palace. "And yet," Irwin added, "you cannot help feeling the force of character behind the sharp little eyes and immensely active and acutely working mind."[20]

Srinivasa Sastri had told Irwin that "nothing is impossible" in dealing with Gandhi as long as one hit the right note.[21] As an educated devout Christian, Irwin shared Gandhi's spiritual side; he was also deeply sympathetic with India's nationalist aspirations. At least at a personal level, the two hit it off. As Gandhi left following their first discussion, Irwin saw him to the door and said, "Good night, Mr. Gandhi, and my prayers go with you."[22] It was a graceful personal gesture that Gandhi never forgot.

But striking a final deal required hard bargaining, which took almost two weeks. Gandhi stayed in Delhi at his friend Ansari's house. He met regularly with Irwin's Indian supporters, Sapru, Jayakar, and Sastri. Sapru in particular was desperate to make the negotiations work. The Round Table Conference had blown up in his face as soon as it adjourned on January 13, even while Prime Minister MacDonald was promising responsible government for India. The detonator had been the "communal question," a euphemism for Hindu-Muslim enmity. Sapru returned to India determined to stave off the collapse of all his hopes. He and other Liberals pushed Gandhi hard to find an "honorable settlement," which meant one that Irwin could sell to his party and his superiors in London.[23]

The final result, the so-called Gandhi-Irwin pact, was announced on March 5, 1931. It was hardly a breakthrough; at least one historian has described it an anticlimax. Gandhi agreed to suspend all civil disobedience in exchange for the release of all prisoners, even though village officers who had resigned were to return only if their offices had not been filled. Gandhi also agreed to attend the next Round Table Conference, without insisting on Congress's role as the leading representative. He also dropped his call for investigation of cases of police brutality during the salt satyagraha. Most ironic of all, the government's salt monopoly and salt tax were left intact (although the government did concede that people in coastal areas could gather their own for personal use).

Gandhians around the country were stunned. They had fought hard, gone to jail, and risked everything for one goal: independence. But the agreement said nothing about independence, let alone Purana Swaraj. Far from feeling triumphant, they felt, in Jawaharlal Nehru's words, "a great emptiness as of something precious gone, almost beyond recall." After all the demonstrations and struggle, some feared that Gandhi had lost his way and that, like the Moderates, he was letting the British set the pace for the Long March to Independence.

"You are making a great mistake," Gandhi told them. On March 6 he gave a press interview and answered the question about whether Indians were back where they started on New Year's Eve 1929. "It is not the same position," he insisted. "Today Dominion Status is a certainty and it is within our power to make it as comprehensive as possible so as to mean complete independence," through the next Round Table Conference.[24]

Many in the Congress felt otherwise, but no one was prepared to challenge their leader. The one person who might have, Motilal Nehru, died on January 30. Jawaharlal could only bury his head on Gandhi's shoulder and weep angry tears of disappointment.[25] For the first time Gandhi's most passionate supporters felt their Mahatma had let them down.

If the Indian reaction to the Gandhi-Irwin pact was stunned disappointment, the British reaction was splenetic. Churchill was at the fore.

The tired old man of the previous January had been transformed into a human dynamo. On January 8, 1931, he wrote to his son Randolph a letter marked "secret" that is deeply revealing. First, he told Randolph that he had secured the support of Lord Rothermere's *Daily Mail* for his campaign and that he believed the Labour government would fall in the upcoming election and Baldwin would again be prime minister. But Winston would refuse to join the cabinet. There would be no more pol-

Mohandas and Kasturbai Gandhi after arriving in India in January 1915. When Kasturbai died in 1944, "a part of Bapu departed," a disciple wrote. (V. Jhaveri/Peter Rühe)

Winston and Clementine Churchill on his return to England from America, 1929. A week earlier, he had witnessed the great Wall Street crash in New York. When this picture was taken, he had just learned that the government was planning to give India independence and dominion status. (Hulton/Getty Archives)

The beginning of Gandhi's Salt March at Sabarmati, March 1930. The smokestacks of Ahmedabad can be seen in the distance. (GandhiServe/Peter Rühe)

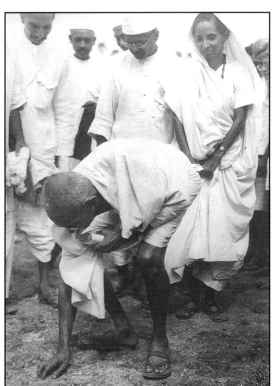

This photograph is usually identified as Gandhi making salt at Dandi at the end of his epic march, on April 6, 1930. In fact, it was taken four days later, at Bhimpur. (V. Jhaveri/Peter Rühe)

Salt satyagraha in Bombay, as dark-clothed Indian police charge with lathis. (*Daily Herald* Archive/Peter Rühe)

Churchill speaks against Indian independence to meeting of the Indian Empire Society, December 10, 1930. "It must be made plain that the British nation has no intention of relinquishing its mission in India or failing in its duty to the Indian masses." (Fox Photos/Getty Archives)

Gandhi (with Prime Minister Ramsay MacDonald [sixth from left] and Sir Samuel Hoare [center] sitting to the Mahatma's right) at second Round Table Conference, London 1931. Discussions there convinced Gandhi that only passive resistance, or *satyagraha,* could give India complete independence. (V. Jhaveri/Peter Rühe)

A left-wing cartoonist's view of Churchill against the Government of India Bill, 1933. Churchill's bitter five-year battle against the bill alienated him from his own Conservative party, and drove him into the political wilderness. (Broadwater/Churchill Archives)

Gandhi with the *enfant terrible* of Indian nationalist politics, Subhas Chandra Bose (center), at the Indian National Congress meeting in 1938. Gandhi feared Bose's radicalism and tried unsuccessfully to keep him from being re-elected president of the INC. Here he tries to put the best face on their relationship. The face of Gandhi's deputy Vallalabhai Patel (right) tells a different story. (Hulton/Getty Archives)

itics as usual. He was more than bitterly disappointed that former viceroy Lord Reading and Lloyd George, whom he thought would be his allies, had signed on to the next Round Table Conference and Indian Federation scheme.

Winston was convinced his position was still strong. "It is a great comfort when one finds a question one cares about more than office or party or friendship," he wrote. "I am going to fight this Indian business *à outrance*." He and the India Empire Society (who "feed out of my hand") were planning another mass rally at the end of the month; together they would rally the nation against the surrender of India and defeat "Irwinism" once and for all.[26]

Lord Irwin, for his part, had worried that Winston might "make mischief" over Gandhi's release; and he was right.[27] On January 26, the very day Gandhi left prison, Churchill rose in the House of Commons.

First he lambasted the recent Round Table Conference and "the hysterical landslide of opinion" that had preceded it. "While all the world wondered," he announced, "the Sovereign Power, which had created modern India and which was its sole support and defense," entered into unprecedented negotiations to hand over "the title deeds of the British position in India." Could there have been a "worse way of dealing with so grave a problem"? No wonder a firestorm of violence and lawlessness had erupted in India. And now that "Mr. Gandhi is again at large, no doubt he will contribute a further gloss upon the Government's proposals" and make Indians of every political stripe believe that the British Raj was about to be replaced by a "Gandhi Raj."[28]

Everyone, Churchill added, expected India to be ready someday for Dominion status, but not in anyone's lifetime. Churchill had been intimately involved in handing over power in South Africa, then in Ireland, "but nothing of the sort is possible in India." Now, however, "the orbs of power have been dangled before the gleaming eyes of excitable millions," in expectation that a handover was only a matter of details.[29]

The result was that the subcontinent teetered on the brink of chaos, and the viceroy was "forced to impose restrictions on civil liberty without precedent in India since the Mutiny." The Indian political elite had became radicalized, and "what had been accepted before was now brushed aside." A legacy of "two centuries of effort and achievement, of lives on a hundred fields, of more lives given and consumed in faithful and devoted service to the Indian people themselves," was about to be thrown away.[30]

"The great liner is sinking," Churchill cried, and it was sinking in a calm sea. As the compartments belowdecks flooded one after the other, Britons were jammed in the saloon dancing to jazz bands. But Churchill refused to believe that "our people will consent to be edged, pushed, talked and cozened out of India." When the British people living there awakened to their peril, with "their individual fellow country men scattered about, with their women and children, throughout this enormous land, in hourly peril amidst the Indian multitudes," Churchill felt sure that Britain's "unmeasured strength will once more be used" and the empire made secure.[31]

The remark about orbs of power being "dangled before gleaming eyes" was certainly racially offensive. So was the reference to European women and children being in peril from Indian multitudes—a deliberate play on race memories of the massacre at Cawnpore and the Mutiny. Churchill also alienated his ex-allies with his cutting references to Lord Reading and Lloyd George selling out by belatedly supporting the Round Table Conference, just as he wildly overestimated the conference's impact.

Nonetheless, the speech did touch on genuine worries about the loss of India within the House of Commons. George Lane-Fox wrote to Irwin that he had been sitting in the back benches "and when Winston began he had not much support." But as the speech went on, other Tories "began to feel this represented their own doubts" about Gandhi's release. "Gradually quite a number first began to purr and then to cheer." When Baldwin rose to respond, he managed to get cheers from Labour MPs but none at all "on our own benches," where there was only an "ominous silence."[32]

Lane-Fox felt frustrated that Baldwin had seemed so "weak and woolly" in the debate. He seemed to defer to Irwin too much and was too cooperative with Labour by half. The passion, the energy, was clearly on the other side. Still Baldwin refused to budge. He even announced that if the Tories did return to power, their "one duty" would be to implement their predecessor's agreements at the next Round Table Conference.[33]

On the twenty-seventh Winston sent his party leader a brief note.

"Now that our divergences of view upon Indian policy have become public," he wrote, "I feel I ought not any longer attend meetings of your Business Committee," which in effect set the agenda for the Conservatives' shadow cabinet.[34] Baldwin accepted the resignation from the committee without demur. The next time Winston Churchill held any official post in his party or the government would be in September 1939.

That was certainly not what he had planned. For as he spoke at another mass rally in Manchester at the Free Trade Hall on January 30, 1931, his mind was already racing ahead. The hall was full to overflowing; Churchill's speech, according to one of the meeting organizers, was "tremendous." It reminded his audience, many of them mill workers, how much their own fortunes depended on India as an outlet for exports. "The declared determination of Gandhi to exclude for ever by boycott or a prohibitive tariff" all foreign piece-goods would mean the ruin of Manchester and the economy of Lancashire as a whole. The loss of India would be "final and fatal" for Britain, Churchill added, but also fatal to India.[35]

This was the other note Churchill was now adding to his campaign against the government: that India's future, as well as Britain's, had to be safeguarded against the likes of Gandhi. Gandhi was "a fanatic and an ascetic of the fakir type well known in the East," Churchill said, whose incarceration had made him "a martyr under very comfortable conditions, and a national hero without running any risk." With his release, "he now emerges on the scene a triumphant victor." A British withdrawal would leave India in his clutches. In a very short time Gandhi and his radical friends would reduce their country to the kind of anarchy in which China now found itself. Churchill avowed, "If, guided by counsels of madness and cowardice disguised as false benevolence, you troop home from India, you will leave behind you what John Morley called 'a bloody chaos,' and you will find famine to greet you on the horizon when you return."[36]

As Churchill returned to London with Manchester's cheers still reverberating in his ears, he sensed that in this hour of peril Britain needed a leader. Others agreed. Even Baldwin's supporters had been complaining for months that his leadership, especially on India, was "uninspiring." Lord Rothermere was now convinced that India would be the issue that would carry Winston to the premiership. Randolph Churchill wrote to his father: "I am so thrilled at your stand on India...Perhaps the Tories will have come to their senses and you will be leader of the party"—which must eventually mean Number 10 itself.[37]

These thoughts had crossed Churchill's mind as well, but he knew he had to proceed step by step. The ultimate question of leadership, he told Rothermere, remained in "the remote distance." First he would have to secure a vote of confidence from his constituents, now that he had turned against his party hierarchy. Then he would have to get the party's India Committee to debate Baldwin's support for the second Round Table Conference. If Baldwin lost there, it would shake Conservative confidence in their leader. Finally, he would step up his speeches and the pressure in the media. He begged Rothermere to promise him the *Daily Mail*'s support: "Otherwise Baldwin with the [London] *Times* at his back is master of the fate of India."[38]

Winston felt sure the plan would work. "As long as I am fighting a cause," he said, "I am not afraid of anything." He was sure many Tory MPs backed him up but were afraid to speak for fear of being labeled disloyal. But loyalty to Baldwin and the party were "mere irrelevancies" compared to the vital issue of India. "Win there," Winston said, "win everywhere."[39] By the time the next general party conference rolled around, Baldwin would be finished as leader—and Winston would be perfectly poised to take his place.

Indeed, for almost a month Baldwin's position grew steadily weaker, as the Tory party teetered on the brink of a major shakeup. As Winston had foreseen, the debate in the India Committee on February 9 went badly for Baldwin. Winston did not attend, but Lord Lloyd gave "a forcible Die-hard speech," Leo Amery recorded in his diary, while others backed up his view that any compromise on India sprang from "cowardice and time serving." No decision was made, but members agreed to hold a special Conservative Members Committee meeting on the subject.

In the hallway Churchill could be heard telling the press that he was not going to let India be betrayed without telling England all about it. "I am afraid we are in real difficulties over the India business," Amery wrote to Baldwin. "Winston has chosen his moment and his excuse for separating with the Party very adroitly."[40]

More fiery speeches followed in Edinburgh and at the West Essex Conservative Association, as Churchill's momentum grew. The India

Committee for the Tory party grew from 80 to 100 members, and all of them Diehards, one of Baldwin's intimates told him. Brendan Bracken assured Randolph that his father had "rallied all the fighters in the Tory Party" and "reestablished himself as a potential leader."[41] The *Daily Mail* and the *Evening News* were, if anything, "overdoing their support," Churchill himself said. Even Sir John Simon agreed to come to the next India Empire Society rally at Albert Hall.

On February 25 Winston wrote to his wife, "It is astonishing looking back over the past six weeks what a change has been brought in my position…Anything may happen now if opinion has time to develop." In private, many MPs were already talking about whether Baldwin should quit, under the terms. "All I need is time," Winston said.[42]

Then quite suddenly time ran out.

On March 5 Irwin's pact with Gandhi was announced. At one blow it wrecked any chance that Churchill would ascend to the leadership, and it ensured that the next Conservative prime minister would be Stanley Baldwin.

At first glance, the pact should have had the opposite effect. Indeed, when news of their first private meetings leaked out, Churchill had heaped scorn on the idea of Irwin striking a private deal with "this malignant subversive fanatic."

"In dealing with Oriental races," he had told the West Essex Conservative Association on February 23, "it is a mistake to try to gloss over grave differences" or "ignore or conceal or put in the background rugged but unpleasant facts." But this was just what Viceroy Irwin was trying to do, Churchill said. Then he shifted his anger to Gandhi, with words that were to become famous, even notorious:

> It is alarming and also nauseating to see Mr. Gandhi, a seditious Middle Temple lawyer now posing as a fakir of a type well-known in the East, striding half-naked up the steps of the Vice-regal palace, while he is still organizing and conducting a campaign of civil disobedience, to parley on equal terms with the representative of the King-Emperor. Such a spectacle can only increase the unrest in India and the danger to which white people there are exposed.[43]

Churchill had certainly said worse things about Gandhi. For his part Gandhi, when he learned what Churchill had said, was more amused than otherwise. Years later Gandhi even mentioned the phrase in the only personal letter he ever sent the British leader.* However, the vehemence sprang from Churchill's mistaken belief that Gandhi was more powerful than he was. It never occurred to Churchill that Gandhi was also under pressure to make a deal. Being largely ignorant of the current Indian scene, he did not realize that Indian politicians suffered from their own version of "Irwinism." They were quite willing to settle for half a loaf in exchange for some peace of mind, while the Conservative rank and file in Parliament were ready to do the same.

Contrary to Churchill's expectations, the Gandhi-Irwin pact did reconcile Baldwin with his party, and it saved the Tory leader from Churchill's clutches. Indeed, evidence suggests Irwin worked the deal with that in mind.[44] Both Geoffrey Dawson and Colonel Herbert Spender-Clay had warned him that Baldwin's resignation could not be postponed any longer. But once the pact was announced, Baldwin's position was much stronger. "Don't think that I imagine that Winston could ever be leader of the Party," Spender-Clay said, yet that was what members had been saying just days before.

Another Irwin supporter was ecstatic. "All the crooks," meaning Churchill and Rothermere, had thought Irwin couldn't reach an agreement with Gandhi. "Now we who had faith in you [i.e., Irwin] have been justified and our leaders—you and Baldwin—are enthroned."[45]

Winston refused to believe it was over but kept swinging with his characteristic verve, even after the bell had rung. He and George Lloyd spoke at the Members Committee meeting on March 9 and tried to compel Baldwin to repudiate the Round Table Conference. Baldwin, however, adroitly parried the blow. Then on March 12 came the final showdown in the House of Commons. The subject for debate was His Majesty's Government's policy on India; the contest was between Baldwin and Churchill for leadership of the Tory party.

As Baldwin entered the chamber, he was still not sure that Churchill might not pull off a triumph. He knew Churchill's pyrotechnic skills as a speaker. He also knew, as he confessed to Thomas Jones, that "no Party is as divided as mine." Old-fashioned Tories who had once loathed Winston were now rallying around him. Baldwin's own allies were weak. "Sam Hoare is a timid rabbit," Baldwin complained. "Oliver Stanley has cold feet...It is a party of fools."[46] But his fellow politicians,

---

* See Chapter 28.

including Churchill, had spent their lives underestimating Stanley Baldwin. He would prove them wrong again.

The atmosphere on the twelfth was tense. The two men sat only a few yards from each other. Churchill, sitting "with flushed features and twitching hands, looked as though he might spring." Baldwin, by contrast, conveyed "the impression of a passion frozen into obedience which is his trump card."[47]

Winston gave a long, stormy speech, raging against the impending Round Table Conference and the invitation extended to Gandhi to attend. "Once it is judged an aim of high policy to persuade the extremists to come to a Conference," he declared, then one could only expect the worst. Gandhi had not called off the civil disobedience campaign and boycotts, only suspended them. "They can be loosed at any moment by the mere lifting of Mr. Gandhi's little finger."[48]

Thanks to Lord Irwin, Churchill said, "Gandhi has become the symbol and the almost godlike champion of all those forces which are now working for our exclusion from India" and a breakdown of law and order across the subcontinent. "When Mr. Gandhi went to the seashore a year ago to make salt he was not looking for salt," Churchill thundered, "he was looking for trouble." Instead of arresting Gandhi when he clearly broke the law, the viceroy had decided to confine him "under some old Statute as a prisoner of State." Then Irwin had tried to negotiate with Gandhi while he was still in the Yeravda jail. Then finally he released him unconditionally and opened negotiations with Gandhi "as if he were the victor in some war-like encounter" instead of a criminal and a miscreant.[49]

It was a good lesson, Churchill said, in how to build up the reputation of a politician or leader of a revolution. Irwin's policy had turned what should have been Gandhi's ignominious defeat into "a trophy of victory" that would be hailed from the Himalayas to Ceylon. The Gandhi-Irwin pact, he said, represented "a victory of lawbreakers," meaning Gandhi, the Congress, and the "circle of wealthy men" who were Gandhi's financial backers, and "who see at their fingertips the acquisition of the resources of an Empire."[50]

He finished with a story from Gibbon, of how in the waning days of the Roman Empire a senator had once bought the imperial throne for a mere £200. "That was fairly cheap," Churchill warned, "but upon my word the terms upon which the Empire is being offered to this group surrounding Mr. Gandhi, are cheaper still."[51]

Churchill's speech was good, but Baldwin's, by everyone's estimate, was better. Indeed, Thomas Jones called it "the speech of his life."[52] Baldwin spoke of how "the unchanging East has changed" and how the world needed to recognize the power of Indian nationalist sentiment. "We have impregnated India ourselves with Western ideas," like national liberty, he pointed out; "for good or for ill, we are reaping the fruits of our own work." The All-India Federation plan, he said, was the best hope for realizing self-government for India "as an integral part of the British Empire"; Lord Irwin had valiantly taken on "the superhuman task" of negotiating an agreement "upon the success or failure of which may well depend the whole future—the prosperity, the very duration—of the British Empire."[53]

But he also spoke of Churchill, and cleverly he quoted the words Churchill had used during his speech a decade earlier condemning the massacre at Amritsar. "Our reign in India or anywhere else has never stood on the basis of physical force alone," Churchill had said then, but on "cooperation and goodwill" between the two races. That cooperation and goodwill, Baldwin now said, was the basis of the Gandhi-Irwin pact. Members smiled and tittered in recognition of the Churchill quotation. Take that away, Baldwin told them, and all that would be left was force— and the terrifying prospect of holding India together by martial law.

Finally, Baldwin spoke of himself. "If there are a majority in my own party who approach the subject in a niggling spirit, who would have reluctant concessions forced from them one after another" instead of embracing self-government for India, "if, I say, they are in a majority, then in God's name let them choose a man to lead them!" Baldwin turned and glared at Churchill. He went on: "If they are in a minority, then let them refrain at least from throwing difficulties in the way."[54]

Churchill spoke after Baldwin, but it was too late. His Tory colleagues had been offered a stark choice: support your leader on India, or get a new leader. Few, even among the Diehards, were ready to choose Churchill over Baldwin. (Indeed, many would be reluctant to do it almost a decade later in a far worse crisis.) Churchill's hopes for replacing Baldwin were dead, as were his hopes for uprooting Irwin's policy on India.

On March 18 at the Albert Hall, in the third great public rally for the India Empire Society, Churchill fired off one last furious bolt. After denouncing Gandhi as an anti-British agitator, and the government for its "hideous act of self-mutilation, astounding to every nation in the world" in inviting him to London, Churchill warned his audience that more sinister forces stood beyond Gandhi. Revolutionaries like Jawaharlal Nehru (whose first name Churchill could barely pronounce), and industrial robber barons like Ambalal Sarabhai, would use Gandhi's victory for their own dark purposes.

Churchill issued a grim warning of terrible events to come, if Indians won Dominion status. A "triumphant Brahmin oligarchy" would drive out the Muslim minority and grind the untouchables into the dust; Gandhi's wealthy backers would extract their fortunes from the sweat of the poor; graft and corruption would become the rule of the day; and the lives of Britons in India would be in gravest peril.

"It is our duty to guard those millions from that fate," Churchill exclaimed. "Our fight is hard. It will also be long...But win or lose, we must do our duty."[55]

But as Baldwin had foretold, Churchill's was now a minority view, even within his own party. After March 12, 1931, he and his Diehard allies could only fight a rearguard action, in hopes of postponing the final bitter day when Parliament would pass its sovereign power into Indian hands. The rest of Westminster looked forward to that day with expectant relief. Labourites, Liberals, and Tories alike scoffed at Winston's wild Cassandra-like prophecies. It never occurred to them that, like Cassandra, he might be right. Or that the process would start in the very city that epitomized the violence and horrors of the imperial past, namely Cawnpore.

On March 24 Hindu businessmen there organized a hartal to mourn the death of a Punjabi revolutionary who had been executed for killing a British policeman. Some Muslim traders declined to join in. A Hindu mob descended on their shops, and an orgy of arson, looting, and murder followed. For the first time in nearly three-quarters of a century, mangled and mutilated bodies lay strewn in Cawnpore's streets. By the end of the month, more than a thousand people were dead.[56]

Churchill balefully warned that "the struggle for power is now beginning between the Moslems and Hindus."[57] Churchill was one of two people who understood the terrible dangers India now faced. The other was Gandhi.

Chapter Nineteen

CONTRA MUNDUM
1931–1932

The loss of India will be the death blow of the British Empire.
WINSTON CHURCHILL, APRIL 1931

ON A CHILLY WET DAY IN mid-September 1931 a small, bald bespectacled man in a dhoti and homespun cloak descended the gangplank at Folkestone Harbour. A crowd of press reporters and admirers greeted him, including members of Parliament and the Dean of Canterbury. They were expecting to meet a New Age Hindu saint, an exotic sentinel from the spiritual East. Mohandas Karamchand Gandhi, the Mahatma, did not disappoint them. For the next two and a half months his bald head, naked legs, and what the press called "his loincloth and shawl" would become a familiar sight in the streets of London.[1]

This was Gandhi's fifth and final visit to London, the city he had once admired as the center of civilization. On the first visit he had been the ambitious law student. On the second, in 1906, he had been the earnest petitioner from South Africa, meeting Undersecretary Winston Churchill in frock coat and stiff collar. He had been a petitioner again in 1909, albeit a disillusioned one. On his last visit, in 1914, hardly anyone even noticed his presence.

But now Gandhi was a world figure. International press coverage of the Salt March and civil disobedience campaign had made him famous. The book by Romain Rolland (he and Gandhi would finally meet on this trip) and admiring biographies like *Gandhi: The Dawn of Indian Freedom* and *"The Naked Fakir,"* along with *Mahatma Gandhi at Work* by Charles Andrews and *Mr. Gandhi: The Man* by Henry Polak's daughter Millie, prepared the way. Hundreds gathered in a driving rain at the reception for him at Friends House in Euston Road.

"I represent, without any fear of contradiction, the dumb, semi-starved millions of my country, India," Gandhi told them. "The Congress wants freedom, demands freedom for India and its starving millions." Another mob of journalists and photographers met him at Kingsley Hall, the pacifist settlement house founded by a former Sabarmati pilgrim, Muriel Lester. It would be home for Gandhi, Sarojini Naidu, and his secretary Desai for the next ten weeks.[2]

To his Western admirers, Gandhi seemed a serenely confident, even triumphant presence. But he was racked by doubts; he sensed from the beginning that this trip would be a failure. Increasingly he was realizing that what he wanted, and what the rest of the world wanted, were two different things. The same was true of the man who had emerged as his fiercest foe, Winston Churchill.

"What if" is a game that historians like to play, but with a serious purpose. Imagining what might have happened but didn't can sometimes reveal how small events or large personalities can suddenly shift the balance of historical forces in a new direction.

If, for example, the Tories had won the 1929 election instead of Labour, Winston Churchill would very probably have become secretary of state for India.[3] The whole tenor of Indian policy for the next two years would have taken an abrupt shift as a result. The moment Gandhi threatened civil disobedience, Churchill would have insisted on his immediate arrest, overruling Viceroy Irwin's objections. In short, there would have been no Salt March, no iconic image of Gandhi at Dandi to galvanize India or broadcast to the world.

Likewise, if Churchill had managed to force Baldwin's resignation in the second week of March 1931, he probably would have emerged not only as the leader of but the dominant personality in his party. No one else was in a position to compete. Austen Chamberlain had retired, and his brother Neville was a rising but still minor star. The spring of 1931 was the closest Winston Churchill ever came to leaving his personal stamp on his Conservative Party—closer even than during the Second World War.

The results would have been momentous. With Churchill at the helm, the Tories of the 1930s would have been the party of empire; the party of rearmament and a tough stance toward rising totalitarian powers in Europe; the party of battling Bolshevism abroad and creeping socialism at home. They might not have won another election, but they would have avoided the tainted legacy of appeasement.

And if politicians and negotiators had used the Gandhi-Irwin pact to rush an India Dominion Bill through Parliament in the summer of 1931, Bangladesh, Pakistan, and India would be one country today. News of the pact had temporarily paralyzed Churchill and his Diehard allies. Everyone else, including Conservatives, would have signed on with relief. In 1931 Muslims were still too divided to thwart an Indian federation with a Hindu majority. Gandhi was still the only nationalist spokesman who mattered.

A day after the pact Gandhi even seemed to endorse the idea of India staying in the empire. In the 1920s he had told a student, "I should be quite satisfied with Dominion Status within the British Empire, if it is a reality and not a sham."[4] Now in 1931 he told journalists that "today Dominion Status is a certainty." Being part of the British Commonwealth did not contradict absolute independence (Purana Swaraj) as long as it meant "absolute equality" between the two powers. Gandhi even predicted that one day Delhi would replace "Downing Street" as the center of the empire.[5]

But this did not happen. The queen of England's face does not grace Indian coins and stamps today, as it does Australian and Canadian ones. No Union Jack appears in the upper left corner of the Indian flag. Two men, in the fall of 1931, prevented that from happening. One was Churchill; the other was Gandhi.

Gandhi arrived for the London talks with a deceptively strong hand. Before leaving he had secured a resolution from a unified Indian National Congress at Karachi, stating that only the Congress could speak for India and that Gandhi spoke for the Congress. But Gandhi knew that unity was an illusion. Only his own force of will and saintly reputation could pull together the sharp divisions within the Congress and across India. The very day he arrived in Karachi, he was met at the train station by a mob of young Marxist protesters who were furious over his Irwin pact "sellout." They angrily chanted "Down with Gandhi!" "Down with the traitor Gandhi!" and waved black flags in his face. One protester nearly brained him with his flagpole.

Then came the worst outbreak of communal violence since the 1857 Mutiny, in of all places Cawnpore. Even as the Karachi Congress met, more than 150 Muslims and 110 Hindus had been killed. When American reporter William Shirer arrived in Cawnpore from Karachi, the bodies of men, women, and children were still putrefying in the streets. "The tales of atrocities on both sides [were] so sickening," that he hesitated to include them in his dispatches.[6] And the very day Gandhi arrived in London, on September 12, fresh riots were breaking out in the Punjab.

Gandhi never felt more divided within himself. Shirer saw him on the eleventh in Marseilles, when he arrived from India on the SS *Rajputana*. The Mahatma briskly set forth his goals for the forthcoming conference. They no longer included Dominion status. He would now accept only complete independence and coequal status with Britain. Only then, he stated, would he and the Congress consider any "reservations and safeguards," a phrase that was London's euphemism for a continuing British presence in India.

Shirer was shocked. No Dominion of India? Gandhi was ruling it out, ironically, on racial grounds, much as Churchill did. Indians belonged to a different race and culture, Gandhi averred. They were different from the white Anglo-Saxons who made up the other Dominion countries and therefore had a different destiny. "The world is sick of bloodletting," he would say later in a CBS radio broadcast from London. "I flatter myself that it will be the privilege of the ancient land of India to show the way out" of the labyrinth of violence as a way of life to a higher truth.[7]

Outwardly Gandhi projected confidence and conciliation. He told the Associated Press that he believed Britain was "faced with such staggering domestic problems" that it would have to give in to his demands. He even told the *Daily Mail* he hoped to meet Winston Churchill "and all those who speak and write against me." But Shirer sensed that Gandhi was actually determined to wreck the conference.[8]

In fact, as historian Judith Brown has pointed out, the second Round Table Conference became a necessary casualty in Gandhi's struggle to stay in charge of the Indian National Congress. His reference to the Congress in his earlier speech at Friends House was calculated. His leadership depended on making the Congress the sole voice of "authentic" Indian nationalism in any and all forums. Gandhi realized that the image of give-and-take discussion of these Round Table Conferences was an illusion. Indians could propose all day, and did, but it was the British and the British alone who would dispose the future of India.

Indians labored under the illusion that they could talk, or at least intrigue, their way to independence. But Gandhi also knew that the British labored under their own illusion, that somehow they could keep

India by agreeing to set it free. "The British people," Gandhi said, "have a faculty for self-delusion as no other people have."[9] It was one of his most profound observations, and he and Churchill were the only ones who understood its implications. What Indians needed to be free, the British could not afford to give up. And what the British were willing to give up, Indians did not want.

Churchill, meanwhile, continued to thunder away at Gandhi in the House of Commons. On July 9 he deplored allowing Gandhi to come to London for meetings "from which nothing but further surrenders of British authority can emerge," instead of keeping him in jail.[10] Once again he branded the Gandhi-Irwin pact a farce. This time he quoted in support of his view "the highest authority of all, Mr. Gandhi." Churchill read from a news report in which the reporter asked the Mahatma if the pact with the viceroy marked a truce or a peace. Gandhi had replied: "It can never be a peace." Churchill looked up from the paper in his hand. "That is Mr. Gandhi," he pointed out. The odd thing was that Churchill had to agree with him.[11]

Then Churchill turned to the atrocities in Cawnpore. He did not scruple to play on racially charged memories of the earlier Cawnpore massacre and described how Muslims and untouchables, but especially Britons in India *and their wives,* were left "quaking with fear or anxiety" at the threats of the Hindu mob. "I do not wonder at it," he said, for the riots in Cawnpore were an "outbreak of primordial fury" and "animal and bestial instincts." They were a bitter foretaste, he implied, of what would happen if Gandhi got his way.[12]

Yet Gandhi still hoped he could arrange to meet Churchill through "common friends."[13] Such a meeting, almost twenty-five years to the day since their last, would have been a splashy news event. Whether it would have changed anyone's mind is doubtful. Churchill, however, declined to descend from his fastness at Chartwell to meet the Mahatma.[14] Others, however, did (including his son Randolph). The flow of visitors into Kingsley Hall and the temporary office that was opened for Gandhi at Knightsbridge, to house his secretaries and staff, became a torrent. "In every corner of the room," a witness remembered, "there were famous sculptors and artists trying to get a model or a picture of this elusive man." In the center of the visitors, with the secretaries murmuring to one another and the floor strewn with letters and telegrams, sat the imperturbable Mahatma, quietly spinning on his portable charkha. When he learned it was time to go to the conference, "he would dart out to his car, followed by panting detectives, and some of his staff clutching the famous spinning wheel and the green rush basket containing his food."[15]

Malcolm Muggeridge covered the conference opening for the *Manchester Guardian*. Muggeridge had been a schoolteacher in Alwaye when Gandhi came to address the college in the 1920s. He remembered Gandhi speaking in a "subtle and discriminating" English, while the students exultantly cried: *"Mahatma Gandhi ki jai!"*—their careful lessons on Ruskin and Dryden instantly forgotten. Now Gandhi seemed changed, "somehow crafty and calculating," as he sat with ministers and maharajas, including an enormously fat Aga Khan representing India's Muslims. There were "knights brown and white, turbans and shining pates," 112 delegates in all. They listened politely to Prime Minister Ramsay MacDonald's droning introductory speech, which included a bizarre appeal for "the lion to lie down with the lamb," although MacDonald frankly admitted he didn't know which was which. From that point on, Muggeridge noted, delegates laboriously took up the metaphor, "with everyone trying to decide to which category he belonged."[16]

All, that is, except Gandhi, who attended all the conference's sessions[17] but seemed barely to be listening. Photographs show him wrapped in his shawl, looking bored and out of place. When he spoke, the reaction from British observers, including the most sympathetic, was one of severe disappointment. They expected to hear a man "of commanding gifts" who would mesmerize his audience with spiritual insight and superior wisdom. That expectation, the *Times* declared, "was not fulfilled. He had no mastery of details... His interventions in discussion... often had little real connexion with the matter at hand... constitutional problems did not interest him."[18] But it was constitutional questions with which they were supposed to deal. Gandhi renewed his call for a partnership of equals between Britain and India, but it was pro forma. His task was to establish beyond appeal that Congress, and Congress alone, knew what was best for India, in order to hold his fragile Congress coalition together. Beyond that, he took little interest in the broader discussion. The other delegates, like Aga Khan and T. B. Sapru, had different agenda. But the ground had shifted under their feet even before the conference met.

On August 24 a general election turned out the Labour government and brought in a multiparty National Government instead. MacDonald

remained prime minister, but he now had a swarm of Tories in his cabinet, including a new secretary of state for India, Sir Samuel Hoare.
Hoare had visited India and had Indian friends. He was much closer to
Irwin than Churchill on Indian independence; he keenly supported
Baldwin's support of the government. And descended from Quakers,
Hoare had emotional roots in Nonconformist social activism, which
should have been another opening to the Mahatma. Instead, Hoare's
first meeting with Gandhi was unsatisfactory and hinted at difficulties
to come.

It was a wet, cold, and blustery day when they met at India House.
Gandhi arrived in his usual costume of cloak and dhoti, totally unsuited
for either the occasion or the weather. Hoare, however, was determined
to be ingratiating. He invited Gandhi to sit near the fire to dry his cloak
and bare legs. "He...looked even smaller and more bent than his pictures showed him," Hoare remembered many years later. "His bony
knees and toothless mouth would have made him ridiculous if they had
not been completely overshadowed by the dominating impression of a
great personality."

As they sat by the hissing coal fire, Hoare tried to get Gandhi to open
up on the most pressing issue. "I believe that if I had been able to say to
him, 'Take Dominion Status at once without any safeguards,' we should
have found him one of our best friends," Hoare wrote, but Gandhi refused to be drawn out. The meeting remained friendly. As he left,
Gandhi warmly shook Hoare's hand and thanked him. But Hoare was
not fooled. He told the new viceroy, Lord Willingdon, "we cannot possibly make an agreement with him." Subsequent meetings, and Gandhi's
conduct in the conference, only confirmed that view.[*][19]

The crux of the matter was the communal problem and the need to
reassure India's multiple minorities that their rights would be respected
in a democratic state dominated by a quarter-billion Hindus. Gandhi
chaired the Committee on Minorities meetings of late September and
early October, where representatives for Muslims, Sikhs, Anglo-
Indians, and untouchables bickered over separate electorates province
by province. It was a tedious and dismal exercise. Elaborate formulas
were proposed for deciding who would vote for how many seats in the

---

* Hoare would one day inadvertently help engineer Gandhi's assassination. A book he wrote on the
  Russian conspiracy to assassinate Grand Duke Sergei, *The Fourth Seal*, proved an invaluable guide to the
  men who plotted the Mahatma's death in 1948. Gandhi himself had read and enjoyed *The Fourth Seal* in
  the Yeravda prison and recommended it to his secretary Desai.

Punjab, the United Provinces, and Bengal.[20] The debate raged for hours, to no avail, over what had become an elaborate game of constitutional musical chairs. No group was willing to give up its claim to reserved seats or votes, not even in exchange for more seats and votes in the future, for fear that someone else might steal their original allotment.

Gandhi himself would consent to separate electorates for only two groups, Muslims and Sikhs. But other minorities insisted on separate representation as well, while Gandhi horrified Hindu delegates by suggesting they should give Muslims "a blank check" on the question of separate voting. The Muslim delegates then demanded that all communal questions be settled before the constitution was drawn up—whereas others, including Gandhi, saw that issue as *part* of drawing up a constitution.[21]

In the end discussion collapsed on what to do about the Punjab, where Hindus, Muslims, and Sikhs all vied for power in a provincial legislature that did not yet exist. On October 8 Gandhi and the Committee on Minorities had to report their failure to the general conference. William Shirer watched with consternation: "Hindus, Moslems, Sikhs, Christians, and untouchables fairly flew at each other's throats."[22] If anything seemed calculated to show the British delegates that Indians were incapable of peaceful self-rule, this was it.

The bitterest words toward Gandhi came from Dr. B. R. Ambedkar. Born in the garrison town of Mhow and the son of an untouchable soldier, Bhimrao Ramji Ambedkar had been educated in America at Columbia University. A Mahar dalit by caste, "the highest of the lowest," he was now the leading spokesman for India's estimated fifty million untouchables.[23] He respected Gandhi's desire to lift the burden of shame and discrimination from India's depressed classes, but he also resented Gandhi's attitude of knowing what was best for them. Ambedkar knew firsthand the hardships of being an untouchable; Gandhi did not. As even Muriel Lester had to point out, "Who was likely to know best where the shoe pinched?"[24]

However, Gandhi claimed that untouchables were an indissoluble part of the Hindu nation and therefore were part of Congress. Special electoral protections were unnecessary. Ambedkar vehemently disagreed, accusing Gandhi of committing a "breach of faith," dealing dishonestly, and handling the whole minorities problem in an "irresponsible" manner. It was a bitter tirade; Gandhi murmured only a sarcastic "Thank you, sir," in reply. But that evening he confessed:

"This has been the most humiliating day of my life."[25] He wrote a note to Lord Irwin: "It does not dismay me. I shall toil on." But he knew it was hopeless.[26]

The impasse was complete. The only possible umpire were the British, but Gandhi rejected that solution at once. He blamed the British for the entire problem of communal strife in India, just as he blamed them for India's poverty, its famines, and its cultural and economic dependency. "I have not a shadow of a doubt," he said on October 8, "that the iceberg of communal differences will melt under the warmth of the sun of freedom." It was a gross oversimplification of history, but it seemed to gain credence when, over the September 18 weekend, the British government without warning had devalued the rupee.[27] Industry, businesses, and pensioners in India all took it on the chin. Even wealthy Indians were left to conclude that the sooner India separated from Britain, the better.

Time for reaching an amicable solution was running out. Less than two weeks after Gandhi had to admit his "failure" to find a solution to the communal tangle, Britain held yet another general election. This one resulted in a Conservative sweep; Labour lost almost 236 seats. Ramsay MacDonald still clung onto his premiership, but of the National Government's 554 members, 473 were now Tories. The election of October 27, 1931, brought "the most Conservative Parliament of the century."[28] Churchill himself had almost doubled his vote in his constituency. Chances that Britain would "give away" India anytime soon seemed to fade.

The Round Table Conference met for another fruitless month. On December 1 Prime Minister MacDonald addressed the final session. His Majesty's Government, he stated, was still committed to the process of granting India "responsible government" and self-rule in an all-India federation, but Britain might have to decide how to handle the Muslims and the minorities by itself.

Gandhi listened stonily, then said, "We have come to the parting of the ways." MacDonald hastily remonstrated, "My dear Mahatma, let us go on in this way; it is the best way, you may find it will be the only way." That night Gandhi returned to Knightsbridge and sat by the fire, spinning with his charkha, hour after hour, saying nothing.[29]

Winston Churchill, by contrast, had a great deal to say. Two days after the conference ended, he made a triumphant speech on the floor of the House of Commons. The gist of it was that Parliament should endorse no part of the Round Table proceedings: not the idea of federation; not the granting of Dominion status (especially since Parliament had just extended the autonomy of existing Dominions in the Statute of Westminster to include foreign and defense matters); not even the promise of further negotiations. For nearly an hour Churchill reviewed the history of Britain's attempt to give India self-rule since Montagu's first momentous statement in 1917. Each time Britain made a concession, Churchill thundered, the Indians had demanded more; and each time India became more unstable and ungovernable.

Then he came to Gandhi. "We saw the spectacle of Mr. Gandhi and some of his leading lieutenants negotiating almost on equal terms with the Viceroy" to arrive at the Gandhi-Irwin pact. This was a "most profoundly injurious blow at British authority, not only in India, but throughout the globe." Churchill even blamed the recent plunge in the pound on it: "all the world could see...an apparent complete absence of backbone in our Imperial affairs."[30] The government had said that unless the Indians were promised the same rights as New Zealanders and white South Africans, India would dissolve into bloody chaos. Now the government had done so. The result was—bloody chaos.

Churchill returned once again to the massacres at Cawnpore with an almost hideous relish. He described the corpses of men, women, and children rotting in the streets, the atrocities, the aftermath of bestial fury. "Not for a hundred years," he said, "have the relations between Hindus and Moslems been so poisoned as they have been since England was deemed to be losing its grip and was believed to be ready to quit the scene if told to go." Now the government was asking the House of Commons to endorse its shoddy dealings with Gandhi and his coconspirators. Only by scaling back on the plans for Indian Dominion, Churchill warned, would Parliament be able to "uphold the rights of Britons and tell the truth to India," namely, that self-government was still a long way off.[31]

It was Churchill's most powerful attack on Gandhi yet, lasting nearly an hour and a half. But the reaction in the House was less than overwhelming. Samuel Hoare slipped into the corridor to pen a note to the viceroy. He had been "very nervous" going into the debate, he confessed, but now even before it was over he was convinced that "three quarters of the House at least will accept our position."[32]

He was right. Tory members may have fidgeted in their seats as Churchill railed away at their leaders' submission to Labour's lead on

India. They may have agreed with him that the plan to create "450 road-less constituencies as large as Scotland, each containing half-a-million illiterate voters," in a subcontinent "with more national, racial and religious divisions than Europe," and to forge a United States of India with no plan on how to merge the princely states, with no plan to protect untouchables and other minorities or to preserve law and order, was an invitation to disaster.[33] They shuddered over the memories of Cawnpore. They may even have felt that by letting India go, they would be surrendering something powerful and significant and would be undermining what Churchill called "the great historical position of Britain" in the East.

But in the end it was not worth defying their party leadership to side with Churchill. Once again Baldwin prevailed. Churchill's effort to amend the resolution drew exactly forty-six votes. George Lloyd's effort to stop it in the House of Lords lost by almost two to one. Just four days earlier Churchill had completed an article for *The Strand* magazine entitled "Great Fighters for Lost Causes."[34] Now he had an inkling he might be joining them. He nursed his disappointment the next day by leaving for America on the liner *Europa*.

Gandhi was leaving, too. On December 5, after a final meeting with Hoare and Prime Minister MacDonald, he took the train to Folkestone. The weather was bright and warm, "summer in December." He told an interviewer, "My last words to England must be: Farewell and beware! I came a seeker after peace. I return fearful of war."[35]

In personal terms, his final visit to London had been a public relations success. He had traveled to Lancashire to meet with the textile workers whom Churchill had said would be out of work if Gandhi got his way. They had greeted him with warmth, even affection. He had met with Quakers and New Age admirers; he had met Charlie Chaplin. He had even had tea with the king at Buckingham Palace.* He had talked with

---

* It was Sir Samuel Hoare who achieved this feat, as part of the official reception for the Round Table Conference. At first the king refused to meet a man he considered a "rebel fakir" (echoes of Churchill). Gandhi, in turn, refused to meet the king-emperor in anything but dhoti and shawl. In the end, however, Hoare prevailed on His Majesty, and the meeting went well, although Hoare claimed he heard George V mutter something about "the little man" with "no proper clothes on."

    The king could not resist a final jab as they parted: "Remember, Mr. Gandhi, I won't have any attacks on my empire!" Gandhi smiled and replied, "I must not be drawn into a political argument in Your Majesty's Palace after Your Majesty's hospitality." All observers, including Hoare, thought the encounter a success. The feelings of Churchill and other India hard-liners can be imagined. George Lloyd called it "tea with treason."

left-leaning intellectuals at Oxford like Gilbert Murray and Edward Thompson, dismissing their worries that India might not be ready for self-government. "Give us the liberty to make mistakes," he told them. "Trust us to ourselves."[36]

On the way home he had a chance to finally meet Romain Rolland and visited Rome for an uneasy meeting with Benito Mussolini. Gandhi's praise of Mussolini was only slightly less effusive than Churchill's six years earlier. He noted that the dictator was "a great personality" and patriot and that Mussolini "never interferes with voluntary activities for the betterment of the country"—unlike the British with the Indian National Congress.[37]

However, Gandhi's troubles began when he docked in Bombay. Irwin was gone, having departed the previous October. The new viceroy, Lord Willingdon, was a very different figure. Unlike Irwin, he had long official experience in India as governor-general of both Bombay and Madras. Although he had been a Liberal MP and opposed the Churchill hard line on self-rule, he was in no mood to put up with "any nonsense" from native politicians, least of all Gandhi.

They had met at Simla the previous April, before Gandhi went to London. Willingdon had refused to change municipal rules that banned all cars in Simla except for those of the viceroy and the commander in chief. Since Gandhi refused to ride a rickshaw—"I shall never allow my brother men to become beasts of burden for me," he said—he had had to walk the six miles to the viceregal lodge every day and back, often in a cold drenching rain.[38]

Indians were furious, but Willingdon had made his point. He had respect for Gandhi. "He may be a saint," he told Sir Samuel Hoare, "he may be a holy man." But "I am perfectly certain that he is one of the most astute politically minded and bargaining little gentleman I [have] ever come across." Willingdon was determined not to give him the upper hand.[39] The days of the Mahatma's soulful give and take with Irwin, a fellow "man of God," were over.

The other problem was that violence was spreading. Terrorist attacks were becoming common in Bengal. On the Northwest Frontier groups of nationalist Red Shirts clashed with police. In the United Provinces Jawaharlal Nehru was leading a protest against farm taxes, which set off pitched battles with authorities. Willingdon cracked down on the violence and even prepared for war if need be. On December 17 he had drawn up an order-in-council in case Gandhi and his supporters resisted. The order included a general police roundup and invoked the Emergency Powers Ordinance. There was also a decree that any meeting of the Congress's leadership would be deemed an unlawful assembly, and that Gandhi himself was to be immediately jailed. In fact, when Gandhi disembarked in Bombay, his cell at Yeravda was already waiting for him.[40]

Gandhi, of course, knew nothing of this. He was unhappy with the disturbances and with Nehru's role in fomenting them. But he felt bound to stand by his wayward lieutenant, especially when Nehru was seized on his way to see Gandhi. The strains of holding together the Congress were showing; after the disaster of the second Round Table Conference Gandhi could not afford another setback. On December 29 he wrote to Viceroy Lord Willingdon, hoping to open a dialogue. But Willingdon's council had made him swear he would not meet with the Mahatma while riots were still going on in the United Provinces; Willingdon in turn told Gandhi there could be no meeting unless Gandhi immediately denounced the violence. Nor would he discuss the emergency measures already in place.[41]

Gandhi felt he had no choice. On New Year's Day he and the Congress Working Committee passed a resolution authorizing a renewal of civil disobedience until the government revoked its Emergency Power ordinances. "My conscience is clear," Gandhi told Sapru.[42] The government, however, moved first. Just before dawn on January 4, 1932, police swooped down on his quarters in the Mani Buvan building in Bombay. Arrest of the other Working Committee members soon followed.

Others started up the noncooperation campaign without them, with the usual flag-waving processions, boycotts, and pickets. Nearly 15,000 went to jail the first month, and another 17,000 in February. But in March the number fell to 7,000.[43] Without Gandhi's leadership, the campaign fizzled. By mid-1932 the entire movement was at a standstill.

The Round Table Conference, too, was a shambles. The Gandhi-Irwin pact was officially "dead" (Willingdon's word). Civil disobedience had been crushed, and virtual martial law was the order of the day; the Mahatma was back in prison for the second time in less than a year. If anyone was the loser in this struggle, it was Gandhi. And if anyone was the winner, it should have been Winston Churchill.

But once again appearances deceived. In the 1920s, their respective fortunes had undergone a strange and sudden reversal; now it happened again. Gandhi would leave the Yeravda prison more politically potent than ever, while Churchill was descending into a parliamentary oblivion from which many thought he would never emerge.

Certainly the months of January and February 1932 were triumphant ones for Churchill. Ironically he almost did not live to see them.

On December 13 he was in New York City, planning to visit his friend the millionaire Bernard Baruch after dinner. Churchill called a taxi to the Waldorf Astoria and ordered the driver to take him to Baruch's house, farther up Fifth Avenue. But Churchill could not remember the house number or its cross street. Like most visitors to New York, he found that one cross street looked very much like another, especially in the dark. So for nearly an hour, he and the cab driver drove fruitlessly up and down Fifth Avenue.

"Drop me here," Churchill finally barked. He got out on the Central Park side, under the dark overhanging trees. He had decided he would simply walk up Fifth Avenue until he recognized Baruch's house. He only hoped the millionaire and his guests would still be waiting for him.

As Winston crossed Fifth Avenue, he knew enough to glance left for oncoming traffic. (The instinct of most Britons would have been to glance right.) But in doing so he failed to notice a driver headed the opposite way, who in turn failed to see the portly figure emerging from the gloom until it was too late. The car struck Churchill at thirty-five miles an hour and sent him skittering across the pavement.

A crowd instantly gathered. Churchill was badly hurt but still conscious. He mumbled to the first policeman who came to his side that the accident was entirely his own fault.* Finally a taxi driver took him to Lenox Hill Hospital, where he spent nearly a week recuperating from two cracked ribs, general bruising, and a badly cut scalp and another two weeks laid up at the Waldorf Astoria.

Churchill, unperturbed, dismissed the accident as "a bad bump" and even wrote an account for the *Daily Mail* that was syndicated around the world and earned him £600.[44] Lying in his bed, he could read in the English newspapers about events in India that seemed to justify his

---

* The driver, Mario Constasino, became an acquaintance and even attended Winston's first lecture in New York.

earlier warnings. "It is obvious the Government must either shoot up or shut up Gandhi" had been Lord Beaverbrook's prediction on January 2. Two days later it came true.

Greatly relieved, Churchill penned a note to his son: "What troubles [the government] have brought upon themselves, the Indians and all of us!" Now "a strong united Conservative Parliament will soon expose the hollowness" of the claim that suppressing Gandhi and the Congress would take entire divisions of troops from England. "As I have always said, an effort at will-power was the main need." Churchill's mood became warm and conciliatory. Now that MacDonald, Baldwin, Hoare, and the rest had done the right thing, "there seems to be nothing to quarrel with them now."[45]

A month later he wrote another note from the Waldorf Astoria: "It seems to me that the Government have been forced by the march of events to take exactly the line in India we always advocated. Now that they are maintaining law and order," he assured Sir James Hankey, "the Constitutional issue is, for the time being, in the background."[46] Not until he returned to England on March 17 did he realize how wrong he was.

In India, the arrests continued and emergency powers remained in effect. But by the end of the month Ramsay MacDonald was plaintively asking how much longer they would have to continue locking up Congress members, and how long Gandhi would have to stay in prison, before "Mr. Gandhi will be allowed to enter into political conversations for the purpose of reaching an agreement."[47] Secretary Hoare thought he had the answer: by pushing ahead his plan for a constitution, in consultation with a committee of non-Congress Moderates like Sapru and Jayakar, the British could do an end run around the Indian National Congress and its jailed leader. Hoare craftily suggested baiting the hook by offering to hand over certain responsibilities from New Delhi to Indians in the provinces. Then the British could reel in the Indian princes, minorities, and leading business interests with a full-fledged Government of India act. Meanwhile the government would also announce its plan to present a settlement of the communal question. This would be further bait to Muslims and other non-Hindus to join hands with the British as they planned "the transfer of power"—the new phrase for giving India back to the Indians.

In short, Gandhi's arrest had changed nothing. India would be handed over to Indians, with or without him. The only question was whether it would be done with one or two parliamentary bills. (In the end, it was one.) From the other side of the Atlantic, Churchill had misread the mood. He and his hard-line troops would have to fight an uphill battle alone.

The first part of his campaign had been to arouse the media and public. To do so, Churchill increasingly concentrated his attacks on Gandhi, as the evil genius behind the handover. This was unfair and untrue. On the other hand, Gandhi made an irresistible and useful target. Many Tories and ordinary Britons had been shocked at Irwin's direct dealings with Gandhi, a man "seditious in aim and in practice, and directly responsible for the loss of hundreds of lives."[48] They were equally shocked by the sight of Gandhi wandering at will in the streets of London in his strange costume ("Cover your Nudity!" was the angry note one retired British colonel passed to Gandhi) and even having tea with the king—"tea with treason," as George Lloyd called it.[49]

Winston no longer limited himself to calling Gandhi the "seditious Middle Temple lawyer" and "half-naked...fakir." The Mahatma had became a protean enemy, a multiform menace. In one speech Gandhi appeared as the cunning huckster, scheming to replace the Raj with his Brahmin cronies and exploiting the ignorance of India's masses for his own selfish gain. In another Churchill accused Gandhi of using "Moscow methods," portraying him as a kind of dhoti-clad commissar who after every concession simply made more demands.[50] Yet Churchill could also paint Gandhi as the atavistic spokesman of a pagan Hinduism, with its "shrines and burning ghats, its priests and ascetics, its mysterious practices and multiform ritual...unchanged through the centuries, untouched by the West."[51]

In still other forums, he played on Gandhi's links to leading Indian industrialists, the "Bombay merchants and mill owners" who were "the power behind" Gandhi's hartals and boycotts. "No class of capitalists in the world, in this present year of depression, has made such vast profits," Churchill charged. These hard-faced men in turbans had built their fortunes on the backs of India's poor and would profit even more from tariffs on British goods once "the swindle" of independence was achieved. "Superstition and greed," he concluded, "are marching hand in hand to the spoliation of millions of people."[52]

Finally, Churchill painted Gandhi as the aspiring dictator of India, a

Hindu Mussolini who spouted nonviolence out of one side of his mouth and who spoke of hiring white Europeans (white janissaries as Churchill called them) to train a new Swaraj Indian army, out of the other. He even accused Gandhi of wanting to foment a race war, in which whites and Indians would either "exhaust or destroy the other."

"This is the man," Churchill scornfully concluded, "that you have by your policy made the one outstanding figure with whom you are now to negotiate the future." But what future could India indeed have without the British? he asked. "India is a geographic term," he told the Constitutional Club. "It is no more a united nation than the Equator." Yet by pretending that it was, Britain would be delivering 300 million people to the tender mercies of an out-of-touch Hindu elite and their monstrous ringleader.[53]

Rousing the nation was one thing; actually blocking or delaying independence was another. Churchill's parliamentary lieutenants were few but eager. They were determined to fight for India "to the last ditch," as one of them, Alfred Knox, phrased it, and fervently believed Britain's silent majority would rally to their cause. On May 25, 1932, Winston kicked off his campaign with a speech to the India Empire Society at the Carleton Club. He reminded his followers that back in 1930 he had said, "Sooner or later we shall have to crush Gandhi and the Congress, and all that they stand for." He had been abused for saying so at the time, but now that Gandhi was in prison and order restored, everyone realized he had been right. All that was needed was the willpower to act, Churchill affirmed, and a willingness to face the fact that India would be helpless without the British.

"I can assure you that Parliament will stand no nonsense about India," he said as his audience cheered. "When this Parliament acts, [the] Government will obey, and India will be saved."[54]

Even as members were finishing their port and Winston lit his second cigar, the government's plans for granting Dominion status to India ground on. Although he said nothing to anyone, this was Churchill's greatest fear. He did not worry about Gandhi, or the industrialists, or the fiery ghats and Brahmin priests. Despite the rhetoric, he was not even concerned that the Indians might rise up in a second Mutiny and drive the British out.

His real anxiety was that the British themselves would simply give up, out of a combination of weakness, pacifism, fear, and misplaced conscience. Reading Gibbon on the veranda in Bangalore had taught him that such defeatism was "the slow and secret poison" that doomed the Roman Empire and sapped the Romans' "sense of national honor" and "habit of command." If it had happened to Rome, it could happen to Britain as well.

"What is the disease we are suffering from now in this island?" he had plaintively asked the crowd in Liverpool's Philharmonic Hall back in February 1931. "It is a disease of the willpower." Churchill found it incredible that "the British lion, so fierce and valiant in bygone days… can now be chased by rabbits from the fields and forests of his former glory"—or that Britons could forget their duty to remain in India.[55]

Churchill knew if that happened, and Gandhi won, it would be the end of his Great Britain.

Forever.

Chapter Twenty

LAST DITCH

1932–1935

When a man fasts, it is not the gallons of water
he drinks that sustains him, but God.

MOHANDAS K. GANDHI

IF CHURCHILL FELT A GROWING DISENCHANTMENT with events, so did
Gandhi. Life in the Yeravda prison followed the usual pattern of praying, reading, and spinning. He had the company of a fellow satyagrahi
prisoner, Vallabhbhai Patel. Patel liked to prepare Gandhi's morning
"cocktail" of honey and lemon water and peel his fruit for him. It
amused him that Gandhi spent so much time brushing his teeth (sometimes two hours a day) when he had only two teeth left. Patel also offered advice for answering the myriad letters Gandhi received, many
from complete strangers. One man asked what he could do about his
unattractive wife. "Tell him to keep his eyes shut" was Patel's response.[1]

Gandhi's own mood was far from jovial or serene. With his satyagraha
campaign crushed and his followers either in jail or sharply divided,
events seemed to be spinning out of his control. He sent a regular stream
of complaints to the warden and to the warden's superiors in Bombay
and New Delhi. Patel sensed that he did so "lest they think he is a spent
force." Yeravda was looking less like an inspiring beacon and more like a
gilded cage. Gandhi realized he was losing his ability to influence Indian
politics—exactly what the government had hoped would happen.

This reality came home to him in August 1932, when the MacDonald
government announced its Communal Award, or plan for minority representation in India's future constitution. Drawn up by Secretary of
State Hoare in consultation with various Indian Liberals, the plan was
dense and detailed and varied from province to province. Muslims
proved the biggest winners: Punjabi Sikhs and Hindus, along with

Bengal's Hindus, were stunned to learn that Muslims would outnumber them in their own provincial legislatures. (Of 250 seats in Bengal, Muslims would get 111 and Hindus only 88, with another 25 reserved for the province's Europeans.)[2]

But the most startling part of the plan was its creation of a separate electorate for India's untouchables—they gained the right to contest seats even at the national level. It signaled a cultural as well as a political revolution for India. Gandhi for one was going to have no part of it.

Others shared his anger. What to the British was a matter of political gerrymandering to gratify political interests (and to groom potential allies for keeping India securely within the empire) was to Hindus a question of vital religious identity. Giving untouchables a separate status meant in effect splitting the Hindu nation across the bow. For better or worse, the existence of the dalit, the beggar, and other low castes served to remind other Hindus of the inexorable law of karma and their own benefit from its workings. Besides, granting the so-called Depressed Classes *political* rights opened the possibility that they might demand other rights in a new Dominion India as well, such as equal employment, education, and housing.

For Gandhi, the issue was particularly tricky. He considered untouchability an abomination, and its eradication was essential to his own dream of Swaraj. "I would far rather that Hinduism died," he had said during the second Round Table Conference, "than that untouchability lived." More than once he had said, "To remove untouchability is a penance that caste Hindus owe to Hinduism and to themselves."[3] But solving the problem was up to Hindus, he had told the conference, not constitutional lawyers. "Those who speak about political rights of the Untouchables, do not know India and do not know how Indian society is today constructed." Accepting separate electorates would be a disaster for India, Gandhi felt. Moreover it would probably shatter the Congress's alliance with the ultra-orthodox Hindu Mahasabha brotherhood, which had a history of supporting violent extremists like Savarkar but that was now headed by Gandhi's friend Madan Mohan Malaviya.[4]

In March Gandhi had warned Sir Samuel Hoare that he would resist any concession of separate electorate with a "fast unto death," claiming that the award would "vivisect and disrupt" Hinduism.[5] The day after the award was announced, Gandhi began composing his own announcement: on September 20 he would begin a fast to convince the British authorities to change their minds. "It may be that my judgement is warped," he wrote to MacDonald, "and that I am wholly in error in regarding separate electorates for Depressed Classes as harmful to them or to Hinduism." In that case, he said simply, "my death by fasting will be at once a penance for my error."[6]

It was a bizarre letter, even by Gandhi's standards, and when he leaked it to the public in advance of the fast, the government was livid, as it allowed public alarm and pressure on the government to mount. Hoare, MacDonald, and even Viceroy Willingdon were at a loss about what to do. There was talk of trying to move Gandhi out of Yeravda, in case he fell ill or even died. But no one doubted for a moment Gandhi's resolve, even those who did not understand why he was doing it. Young Nehru, in particular, was angry that Gandhi was wasting his energy, perhaps even killing himself, on what seemed a peripheral issue. Nehru was getting fed up with what he called Gandhi's "religious and sentimental approach to a political question." He sent the Mahatma a note explaining his "mental agony and confusion" at Gandhi's decision but that he now waited with peace of mind.[7] In private he worried that the beloved leader had lost his way.

But Gandhi had never changed paths. After forty years he remained true to his New Age quest. To his mind, political questions were always subordinate to moral and religious ones. Issues of independence, constitutions, empires, and wars all fitted into his unique perspective like shards of glass in a kaleidoscope, which he turned and turned until they made an image that suited him. That image sometimes inspired others, but just as often it confused everyone except his most unquestioning followers.

The fast against the Communal Award was a good example. From his jail cell Gandhi told anyone who would listen that its real object was to sway not the British but his fellow Hindus, to convince them to shake off "the age-long superstition" of untouchability. His declared hope was that by suffering, perhaps even dying, he might change the minds of tens of millions of Hindus "and sting the Hindu conscience into right action."[8] It was disinterested self-sacrifice, as he understood it from the *Gita*: perhaps the final act of service to his country.

Others, perhaps understandably, viewed it as an overtly political act, even political grandstanding. No one expected that the British government would yield. To back off in the face of Gandhi's threat would throw the whole constitutional process into confusion and bring down a rain of thunderbolts from the likes of Churchill and George Lloyd.

Ramsay MacDonald wrote a last letter, asking Gandhi to reconsider. Gandhi thanked him but said he would stick to his decision. Many other aspects to the Communal Award, he warned, were also open to "very grave objection," but none warranted "self immolation as my conscience has prompted me in the matter of the Depressed Classes."[9]

On September 15 he wrote a touching letter to Kasturbai, who was at Sabarmati. "You have probably heard about my fast," it read. "Do not get frightened in the slightest degree by the news and also do not let the other women get frightened." He hoped she would understand that he had decided to fast for the sake of what was right, or *dharma*: "If, however, I have to carry it on till the end, you should indeed thank God. Only one in a million meets [the] death for which he has prayed. What good fortune it would be if I met that fate!" After fifty years of living together, she above all should understand his will and his need to do this "service."[10]

On the twentieth Gandhi rose as usual before dawn. The fast was to begin at noon. The night before he ate his usual meal as he described it to Mirabehn—"brown bread, milk, a vegetable, some dates (not bad),—and *musambis*."[11] He prayed and sang with his companions his favorite Hindu hymn, *"Vaishnava Jana,"* and from six to eight-thirty they recited the *Bhagavad Gita* together. Gandhi also received a telegram from Rabindranath Tagore, who supported his fast for the sake of "India's unity and her social integrity." Half an hour before noon Patel prepared his last glass of honey and lemon juice. Then Gandhi lay down on his cot and awaited his destiny.

All across India there were expressions of fear and dread. Tagore told his students at Santiniketan that a shadow had fallen across the sun.[12] British doctors checked on Gandhi's condition every day. Gandhi had predicted that he might last two weeks. Given his frail body and blood pressure, most gave him only a few days, a week at most.

The next day a group of worried men gathered in the prison office. They included Sapru, Gandhi's friend G. D. Birla, Rajagopalachari, Patel, and Mahadev Desai. Gandhi sat quietly on the table and listened as they proposed offering terms to the one man who might break the impasse: the untouchable leader Dr. Ambedkar. If he and Gandhi could reach some agreement by sorting through the complexities of reserved seats and weighted electorates, perhaps the government might relent, and the fast could be over.

Gandhi listened but said nothing to encourage them. On the other hand, he did not rule out a compromise, so the group hurried to catch the train for Bombay. Gandhi moved out into the courtyard (the warden had graciously allowed him to set up his cot under a mango tree) and sat down, occasionally sipping a glass of water and not speaking, since it exhausted him too much. Desai, Patel, and Sarojini Naidu sat with him, as the fierce sun passed overhead.

The next day came and went, and then the next. Gandhi grew progressively weaker and could no longer sit up. Fearing the worst, the authorities had Kasturbai brought from Sabarmati to Poona to be near her husband. The following day the gates of the prison opened, and Dr. Ambedkar stepped through.

Portly, broad-shouldered, and bespectacled, Dr. Ambedkar was there against his will. If he hated any man living, it was Mahatma Gandhi. Indeed, along with Jinnah and S. C. Bose, he formed part of the trio of Indian leaders who would hinder and harass Gandhi in his last decade like angry furies. He was also the first openly to challenge Gandhi's New Age vision of India.

Bhimrao Ambedkar was as resolutely modern as Gandhi was deliberately reactionary. He had little choice. As an untouchable, the India that Gandhi revered had rendered him a nonperson. Instead, he had found Christian patrons who had paid his way to the nondenominational Elphinstone College in Bombay and then to Columbia University, where he had earned a Ph.D. as an expert on Indian finance.

Ambedkar was convinced that the problem of caste in India was neither religious nor philosophical but sociological.[13] For centuries, Ambedkar argued, traditional India had maintained itself by a system of exploitation disguised as spiritual hierarchy, "a progressive order of reverence and a graded order of contempt." That system relegated those who did the hard menial work that kept society alive, the dalits and sudras, to the bottom, and those who reaped the benefits, the Brahmins, to the top.

With his transatlantic perspective, Ambedkar saw a strong analogy between untouchability in India and slavery in the American South. The political figure he revered more than any other was Abraham Lincoln. He fervently believed that India's untouchables needed the equivalent of an Emancipation Proclamation to free them from servitude to traditional Hinduism. The formation of a separate electorate would be a crucial first step.

Gandhi's position seemed to Ambedkar delusional at best, and self-serving hypocrisy at worst. The notion that somehow untouchables would lose out by being cut off from other Hindu castes made him choke. He could remember how, when he was a child, people had recoiled from him in horror and stepped five paces back when they learned his caste, and how at school he had been forced to sit on the floor so that he did not pollute the chairs. His teachers and fellow students refused to give him a drink of water unless they could pour it into his mouth without his lips touching the glass.[14] Ambedkar was determined to force on Hindus a robust series of protections for those they had abused for centuries. He was furious that Gandhi now chose to stand in his way.

He had heard the request to save Gandhi's life when he was attending a convention of other untouchable spokesmen in Bombay. His first inclination was to do nothing. Who did the Mahatma think he was? "If he wants to eat," he said contemptuously, "let him dine with me." It was another dalit leader, M. C. Rajah of Madras, who had brought him around.

"For thousands of years," Rajah told him, "we have been downtrodden, insulted, despised. The Mahatma is staking his life for our sake, and if he dies, for the next thousands of years we shall be where we have been, if not worse." The Hindus would blame the untouchables for Gandhi's death; it could be a catastrophe for the untouchable cause. Ambedkar listened and finally said, "I am willing to compromise."[15]

So Ambedkar went to Poona, and on the fifth day of the fast he met with Gandhi. The Columbia graduate was in a grim mood. "I want my compensation," he said to the prone figure on the cot. Gandhi looked up at him, and his eyes glinted.

"You say you are interested in my life?" he murmured, with the faintest hint of sarcasm. He knew Ambedkar was not, but Gandhi had dealt him no choice. Sitting together in his prison cell they worked out a formula that became known as the Poona Pact. It raised the reserved seats for untouchables in the future Legislative Council to 148, instead of the 71 in MacDonald's Communal Award; and reserved them seats in the Federal Council. But it abolished the principle of a separate electorate once and for all. Only Muslims, and Sikhs in the Punjab, would have that distinction.

Gandhi had won. "In accepting the Poona Pact," he told Ambedkar, "you accept the position that you are Hindus." Ambedkar (who became a Buddhist afterward) only said, "Mahatmas have come and Mahatmas have gone, but Untouchables have remained Untouchables," and headed back to Bombay.[16]

On September 26 Gandhi received word that the British Cabinet had accepted the pact. An hour later Gandhi and two hundred people gathered in the courtyard to watch him break his fast. Rabindranath Tagore arrived to lead the prayers and then the singing of *"Vaishnava Jana."* Gandhi drank a single glass of orange juice. The six-day fast was over. He told his Quaker friend Horace Alexander, "God was never nearer to me than during the fast."[17]

Yet Gandhi had hurt himself as much as he had helped his cause. To this day his admirers like to celebrate the "fast unto death" as a heroic event. His adoring secretary Pyarelal devoted an entire book to it, entitled *The Great Fast,* in which he, like other Gandhians, cast Ambedkar in a deeply sinister light. Even a sober historian like R. J. Moore has called Gandhi's fast "a successful experiment in satyagraha for the sake of Indian unity."[18] But that unity was an illusion, and even Gandhi's admirers had to admit that the fast had been nothing less than blackmail. Fasting in order to stop people from killing one another, as in 1922, was one thing. Fasting to keep them beholden to a system that denied their very personhood was another.

Gandhi's intentions were noble—they always were. Once he recovered his health, he devoted himself to an elaborate one-year campaign to eradicate untouchability. He even came up with a new term for its victims, *Harijans* or Children of God, and founded a journal with that name to carry on the campaign. But the effort proved hollow. During his fast and for some weeks afterward Hindus opened their temples and wells to dalits, publicly embraced untouchable men, women, and children, and even hosted intercaste dinners. But then the habits of three thousand years reasserted themselves. The moment untouchables left, the temples were repurified; soon they would be closed again. Gandhi's All-India Anti-Untouchability League, headed by his friend G. D. Birla, raised huge sums of money but changed no one's mind. The euphoria of reconciliation and forgiveness soon passed.

The damage went further. Gandhi's arm-twisting made a bitter lifelong enemy of Ambedkar: the title of Ambedkar's 1945 book, *What Gandhi and the National Congress Have Done to Untouchables,* reveals the intensity of that bitterness. At the same time orthodox upper-caste Hindus like V. Savarkar and others seethed over what they felt had been an abject compromise. They, too, plotted their revenge.

Jawaharlal Nehru was furious over the whole episode for different reasons. "As I watched the emotional upheaval during the fast," he confessed to his diary, "I wondered more and more if this was the right method of politics...All India, or most of it, stares reverently at the Mahatma and expects him to perform miracle after miracle and put an end to untouchability and get Swaraj and so on—and does nothing itself!" He added, that Gandhi's "continual references to God irritate me exceedingly." The problem was that neither he nor any of Gandhi's closest allies could ever guess where Gandhi was going, or where he intended to lead them. His leadership was a mystery. And, Nehru asked himself, has Gandhi "thought out what the objective, the ideal should be?" The disturbing answer was: "Very probably not."[19]

None of the doubts, the scratching of heads, or even Ambedkar's impotent rage disturbed the Mahatma. The fact remained that his Harijan campaign of 1933–34 was a welcome distraction from his fading influence on political events. A third and final Round Table Conference met in November. Then in March 1933 came a government White Paper that provided a complete plan for an Indian constitution. And the Indian National Congress, thanks to Gandhi's intransigence, played no part in either.

This omission puzzled and distressed Congress members. Why was Gandhi holding them back, they asked, even as other groups and politicians in India were lining up their futures in the post-Raj Dominion? To prove he was still in charge, Gandhi announced another fast in April. Then without warning the government released him, and he found himself back on the street—physically weak and politically impotent.

At long last New Delhi had found a way to neutralize the redoubtable Mahatma. If he tried to organize another civil disobedience campaign, as he would in August 1933, the government would pounce and put him in jail, depriving his troops of his inspiration and leadership. If he then tried to kick-start things from jail by fasting or performing some other dramatic gesture, as he would two weeks after his August arrest, they set him free. Whichever way he turned, it seemed, Viceroy Willingdon and Secretary Hoare were there ahead of him.

It was a time of unceasing frustration for Gandhi, like his time in South Africa during the Black Act agitation. In January 1934 an earthquake struck northern Bihar, affecting thirty thousand square miles and leaving thousands of people dead or homeless. Villages he had visited during his Champaran campaign were obliterated. Gandhi announced that it was God's punishment for the Hindu sin of untouchability. The remark set off a furious reaction. Crowds began to shout him down when he traveled around India and angrily waved black flags as his car passed. In Jassidi in South Bihar orthodox Hindus threw rocks through the car's back window. When he stopped in Poona, the site of his Communal Award fast, someone even threw a bomb.[20]

Congress members, meanwhile, were growing more impatient. They desperately wanted to assume a significant role in the new dispensation. At the Bombay Congress in October 1934 Gandhi finally had to yield: he allowed Congress members to stand for the coming assembly elections, the last under the old Indian constitution. The ostensible reason was to allow Congress to express its official opposition to the government's awards of special status to minorities. The real reason was that men who had waited a long time to hold political office could wait no longer. Men like Patel, Bengal's B. C. Roy, and the Congress's leading Muslim M. A. Azad found themselves in the position of Tammany Hall's George Washington Plunkett: they saw their opportunity, and the time had come to take it.

It was an impulse that Gandhi could neither understand nor withstand. In the end he decided to quit the Congress altogether. "I feel sure that it will do good to the Congress and to me," he wrote. It was his way of swallowing his disappointment.[21] The Mahatma began his Wilderness Years almost a year before Winston Churchill did and for the same reason: public opinion and events were passing him by.

Meanwhile Churchill spent the end of August and early September 1932 on the Continent, touring the battlefields of his ancestor the Duke of Marlborough. He had begun a two-volume biography of his illustrious predecessor in 1929 for the British publisher Hoddard. The project involved everything he loved: military history, family pride, and the story of redoubtable Englishmen defeating Britain's enemies. In a large comfortable touring car Winston visited the key battlefields where the Duke of Marlborough had not only built his reputation as the greatest general of the age but laid the foundations of the British Empire: Ramillies, Malplaquet, Blenheim.

It was a personal as well as historical revelation. Winston walked across the spreading green fields where his ancestor had commanded armies and where cannon shot the size of cricket balls could still be dug up.[22] He gained a renewed sense of Britain's destiny and of how that destiny relied on generations of Churchills, first on the battlefield and now in the House of Commons. He returned to England just as the fight over India was entering its last, critical phase.

In July it had become crystal clear that the government was going to push through Parliament a final settlement of self-government for India. Churchill appeared for the first debate with "sheets of typewritten invective against everybody and everything," according to Stanley Baldwin. But not even Winston could fault the government on one crucial point: Parliament, and no one else, would have the final say over India's future. In fact, Hoare and the government would submit their plan to a joint select committee of members of both the Commons and the Peers *before* presenting a bill to the full Parliament—a procedure that Churchill told his ally Lord Salisbury "is most advantageous from our point of view."[23]

To Churchill's relief, Gandhi no longer had any voice in the matter; his antics over the Communal Award had cost him any further role. Churchill's hope now was to rally the Tories behind him and tear up the government's plan before it left Hoare's desk.

The crucial moment came at the Conservative Party Conference in Blackpool in October 1932. Churchill had desperately hoped to be there, but a sudden flare-up of paratyphoid fever left him laid up at Chartwell. So it was George Lloyd who led the opening salvo against the government's India policy, with a resounding speech that drew "an ovation so prolonged and enthusiastic as clearly to indicate that he and his convictions had the support of the great majority," as a reporter for the *Morning Post* put it.[24] "There was no doubt about it that the sentiment of the meeting was on one side," Secretary Hoare confessed in a letter to Viceroy Willingdon. "When he sat down most people would have said he would carry Winston's resolution with a big majority."

But then Hoare and a young MP for Saffron Walden named Richard A. Butler produced a counterblast of their own. Despite their support for Lloyd, the Conservatives who gathered in the hotel's great ballroom could not ignore the fact that their leadership was now completely wedded to a National Government plan for "giving away" India. Hoare in fact was its principal architect. To abandon the plan would be to abandon their leadership. That would leave the party to Churchill, a step that few older Tories were willing to take. Besides, Hoare intimated to his fellow Conservatives, without actually saying so, that if they turned down a Government of India bill now, a Labour government would come up with a far bigger giveaway plan down the road.

Politics is not always the art of the possible. It is sometimes the art of choosing between the distasteful and the disastrous. So it was in Blackpool: the Conservative Party Conference reluctantly backed Baldwin and the government, and for the first time Churchill saw the handwriting on the wall.

As New Year 1933 came and went, an alarmed Churchill worried that "creeping Irwinism" had "rotted the soul of the Tory Party." He knew Baldwin and Hoare had mobilized the whole machinery of the Conservative Party and the National Government to squelch opposition to any India bill—they even got the BBC to shut off its microphones to him.[25] With the Tory leaders pulling, and their whips prodding from behind, he feared Conservative MPs "will vote for any measure however disastrous."

"Still it is our duty to fight with every scrap of strength we can command," he told his loyal retinue.[26] Secretary of State Hoare was just as firm. "My course is set," he told Baldwin on January 9. "Neither Winston or George Lloyd will deflect it." Some of his confidence sprang from the fact that he and Lord Willingdon had at last gotten Gandhi muzzled; if they could only get Winston muzzled, they would be home free.[27]

Churchill's Diehard lieutenant Alfred Knox had promised they would fight Indian Dominion to "the last ditch." But one by one the ditches began to fall.

The House first debated a motion to limit Indian government reform to the provinces only. Churchill could muster only forty-two votes in support. Then in late February came a meeting of the National Union of Conservative Associations, where "the Winston crowd have been very active with meetings, lunches, and propaganda of every kind," Hoare told Willingdon. "Winston is out to make the maximum of trouble. He is determined to smash the National Government and believes India is a good battering ram." Winston gave what Hoare conceded was one of his best speeches yet, but when the votes were counted, the Diehards had lost again, albeit by only a twenty-five-vote margin.[28]

In March the government issued its White Paper, recommending that a joint select committee draw up an Indian constitution. Churchill launched a tirade, attacking not just the idea of eventual Indian self-government but also the timing. Gandhi was in jail; India was at peace—what was the rush to hand over the subcontinent? "It is a tragedy that the greatest gift which Britain has given to India was not the fight that India needed most," he concluded. "You cannot desert them, you cannot abandon them," he said of India's toiling faceless masses. "They are as much our children as any children can be...It is impossible that you should hand them over to the oppressor and to the spoiler, and disinterest yourself in their future." But that was what the House of Commons did. At the end of a three-day debate, the vote was overwhelmingly in favor of the recommendation, 475 to 42.[29]

Winston was undeterred. "I shall fight this business to the end," he wrote on March 31. "You may be quite sure that any check or disappointment only makes me fight harder." But the disappointments were coming faster; and a new menace had appeared on the horizon. On January 30, 1933, Adolf Hitler became Chancellor of Germany, the youngest in its history. Within two weeks Hitler established special emergency measures that made him absolute Führer. Dictatorship had taken root in Germany and Italy as well as in Poland, Yugoslavia, and Austria. Indeed, Churchill noted, "three-quarters of the peoples of Europe are under dictatorships."[30] Civic unrest was breaking out in France and Spain. And now the end of the Raj was in sight. To Churchill, the light of enlightened civilization seemed to be guttering like a candle.

Then came an even more wounding blow. On February 17 the Oxford Union, the training ground for the next generation of Britain's leaders, passed a resolution that its members would "not fight for King and Country." This "abject, squalid, shameless avowal," as Churchill called it, came even as powers like Germany and Italy were "eagerly seeking the most terrible weapons of war."[31] What would the world think now if Britain compounded this unmanliness by "divesting itself gratuitously, wantonly, without any need or compulsion," of its empire in India and "the title-deeds of its power and fame?"[32]

Everything seemed to be unraveling. Churchill realized that he could not halt the disintegration of the national character by himself, but he at least could make a clear stand against a Government of India bill that handed over India to the Indians—and to Gandhi.

On June 28, 1933, he carried his fight to the Conservative Central Council, which had been called upon to pass a resolution approving the coming India bill. He told the delegates that surrender on India meant surrender everywhere. "The way in which this question is handled by the British nation will be proof of their resolve to defend their rights and uphold their interests in every quarter of the globe." The final vote was 838 yes to 316 no. It was the biggest repudiation yet of Baldwin by his own party. Hoare declared the no votes "the high water mark of

Winston's influence."[33] But it was a defeat nonetheless. Churchill's options were slipping away.

Even his supporters admitted that many of his wounds were self-inflicted. His gift for alienating supporters while failing to convert old enemies remained remarkably unimpaired.[34] His speech in the March debate had included a gratuitous attack on the Indian Civil Service: "the path of promotion has tended to be more easy for those who readily throw themselves into what are regarded as the irresistible moods of the British nation." He meant it as criticism of those at the top, including Lord Irwin. But the remark made many an ex–civil service man's mustache bristle, and even the chairman of the Conservative India Committee was outraged.[35]

Then both he and Lloyd had refused to serve on the Joint Select Committee to draw up the bill, fearing that their minority view would simply be set aside in any final report. It was a severe tactical blunder. Instead of helping to shape a future bill, Churchill was reduced to attacking it from outside. It convinced many, including the committee's chair Lord Linlithgow, that Churchill's critics were right all along: Churchill was interested only in bashing the government with the idea of taking over himself. "I believe that at the back of his mind he thinks that he will not only smash the Government but that England is going Fascist," Hoare venomously wrote, "and that he, or someone like him, will eventually be able to rule India as Mussolini governs north Africa."[36]

The charge was unfair but understandable. Churchill's old reputation as an unprincipled thruster, someone who did not care where he went as long as he was in the driver's seat, had come back to haunt him.

So did his past record as a Liberal reformer who had brought self-government to South Africa and Ireland a decade before. So why not India? opponents asked. Churchill's answer was that India was "unsuited to democracy" because of its cultural backwardness and widespread illiteracy. But many suspected the real reason for his resistance was racial. The man who declaimed that "it is never possible to make concessions to Orientals" and shamelessly evoked memories of the 1857 Cawnpore massacre and the Mutiny seemed to use race-baiting in ways that disgusted many in his own party.[37] Privately, they may have agreed, but the days were gone when publicly playing the race card could win an argument over India.

"We are in for a long hard fight," Churchill admitted to Captain Diggle of the India Defense League in April 1933. Victor Cazalet dined with him and found him shrouded in gloom. "He was passionate on India, though I think his arguments are very weak," his young disciple confessed. Winston admitted he felt like cutting people and hated them "as he had never hated in his life." He foretold a "very nationalist world—a world of armaments and self-contained nations." The empire would be more necessary than ever, yet it was slipping away.[38] Winston even told Linlithgow he was ready to quit public life were it not for the fight over India.

One more huge stink broke out over the Joint Select Committee, when it declined to hear a delegation from Manchester manufacturers. Winston smelled a rat: he accused the committee and Samuel Hoare of denying the manufacturers a voice because they were bound to oppose any scheme that would allow India to impose tariffs on British goods. The long, tiresome, and pointless battle dragged on well into 1934 and ended up in front of Parliament's Committee of Privileges. Churchill lost again, then launched a bitter attack on the committee, accusing it of a cover-up and accusing Hoare and Lord Derby, a highly respected Tory stalwart, of lying.

Even his supporters were aghast. Leo Amery, who was not one of them, spoke after Churchill and said it was Winston's "unique achievement" to stir up a hornet's nest where there were no hornets. Churchill's whole aim, he insinuated, was to force Hoare's resignation as secretary for India and "shatter the Conservative Party." It was, Amery said, the application of Winston's favorite motto, *"Fiat justitia ruat coelum"* (Let justice be done even if the heavens fall).

Churchill jumped up. "Translate it!" he called out, trying to score a rhetorical point.

Absolutely deadpan, Amery turned and said, " 'If I can trip up Sam, the government's bust.' "

The House of Commons dissolved in raucous, derisive laughter. Winston's whole campaign to awaken his fellow members to the dangers of surrendering India to Gandhi and the Congress was blown away in a gust of ridicule. All he could do now was prepare for the final hopeless battle, when the Government of India Bill itself was introduced.

Before he started, he received an unexpected female visitor. It was Madeleine Slade, or Mirabehn, the admiral's daughter, direct from Gandhi's ashram.

After reaching London on September 10, she had written a letter to Churchill. "You will wonder who this is writing to you," she started diffidently. She explained that she had spent the last nine years with Gandhi, and "I should like to share that experience with you... You may say, 'Why—our points of view are poles asunder.' That may be so, but we have one great thing in common, a deep interest in India." She hoped she might be able to meet Churchill before she left.[39]

It was the kind of thing Gandhi himself might have done, and Churchill was moved to see her. When they met at the House of Commons, he "greeted me very affably," she remembered later, and they talked of India. "The Indian nation does not exist," he told her emphatically. "There is no such thing." Mirabehn laughed and assured him that there was a more unifying culture throughout the land than appeared from outside, and that "from North to South and East to West, wherever you go, you find the yearning for freedom." Churchill grunted skeptically but said nothing.

Then they spoke of Gandhi. Churchill said he admired Gandhi for his "work for the moral and social uplift" and admired him as a religious leader; "but I would not choose him for flying the latest airship"— meaning he doubted Gandhi's political leadership. Mirabehn told him that, on the contrary, "Bapu was one of the most practical people in the world, and loved to call himself a practical idealist," although he was in his true element when he was "unfettered by any political ties." Churchill, she wrote, "caught on to this thought rather keenly."

They discussed the constitutional bill, which would soon be before the House. "It is a ridiculous, useless thing," Churchill declared. "It neither pleases us nor you. It falls between two stools, and what is the use of a constitution... if it is not backed by the people of the country for which it is meant?" Churchill said he would have liked something different, "a kind of fellowship of Hindus, Moslems, and Christians, with a strong rule to hold it together. The Orient needs a different kind of government," he added dogmatically. "You need a strong rule for the good of the people."

Mirabehn pressed him for details, but he had none to give, any more than Gandhi did. All he knew was that his vision for India was falling apart. "Who knows what will happen?" he said, referring to the bill. "I have done my best, now we shall see." He muttered a phrase in Hindustani that she could not catch. Mirabehn had him translate it into English so that she could render it again in Hindi. It was "Whatever will be, will be." Churchill proudly said, "I have been in India, you know," and smiled.

As she left, he asked her to convey his kind regards to Gandhi and to say he was sorry they had not met during Gandhi's visit for the Round Table Conference, "but politically it would not have done." Mirabehn left the Parliament building. A phrase of Churchill's kept running through her head, which he had repeated over and over: "I believe in truth, pure truth." It stuck with her, simply because it was exactly what Gandhi would have said.[40]

In January 1935 the government introduced its Government of India Bill. It was tremendously long—the longest bill Parliament would ever pass—and profoundly complicated. Over the next six months it would be subject to countless amendments and many hours of tedious debate. But its basic form never altered.

First, it provided India with Dominion status through an All-India Federation that excluded Burma but included the princely states. Those states' rulers would pick their representatives for the federation legislature, while Hindus and Muslims in British India, as well as Sikhs in the Punjab, voted for theirs.

Second, the bill set up an entirely autonomous provincial administration and governance for British India, with ministers and legislators all chosen by Indian voters—almost a sixth of the population (a huge advance over previous electorates). The British governors-general would still preside, along with the Indian Civil Service. A British viceroy would remain with certain "reserve" powers at the center, such as over the army and the police. He would also be able to raise taxes to finance them.* But otherwise India would be governed by Indians themselves. The bill signaled the end of the Raj and the beginning of the self-governing Dominion of India.

Or so the government hoped. For three long years Churchill and his allies had fought a delaying action against the bill. All they could do now was amend the bill, such as by offering some protection for Lancashire's textile industry and for religious minorities under a constitution that gave India's Hindu majority its first taste of real power. "There is a very stern fight before us," Winston warned his dwindling troops. He was long past any reconciliation with his party or his leadership. In a radio speech he denounced the measure as "a monstrous Bill erected by pygmies" and foretold that its passage would be "a catastrophe which will shake the world."[41]

---

* Including, ironically, the salt tax.

No one believed him anymore. As the bill faced its second reading on February 6, the House's impatience to finish, and the anger at Churchill for delaying it, became palpable. Hoare's opening speech was scathing in its denunciation of Churchill's tactics. Labour's Herbert Samuel said that if Churchill had been born an Indian, "he would have been a Congress man of a type compared to which Mr. Gandhi would be as a dove to a tiger." Winston's son Randolph had tried to add one more vote to his father's column by standing in the by-election in Wavertree as a self-declared anti–India Bill candidate. He managed only to split the Conservative vote, and the Labour candidate won instead.

On February 11 Churchill made one last speech to try to halt the end of an epoch. "We are now at the beginning of these long debates on India," he declared. "How shall we come out? ...No one can tell." In fact, everyone could and did. He received wild cheers as he finished. But the vote was 404 votes in favor of the bill and only 133 against, including 84 Tories. (The rest of the naysayers were radical Labourites who felt the reforms did not go far enough.)

The bill's passage was certain now. On the twenty-first a Churchill amendment was defeated 308 to 50. Even when the Indian princes took a belated hand and met in Bombay to denounce the federal constitution scheme, they could not halt the Government of India Bill freight train. Hoare and R. A. Butler told the princes it was too late, they would have to accept what was offered and negotiate the details later. Winston's motion to suspend the bill went down to defeat, and what Churchill called "one of the most melancholy, one of the most perverse, one of the unnecessary chapters in the whole history of the British people" was about to become law.[42]

The third and final reading did not come until June 4. In the last tally the government enjoyed a majority of 264; even with Labour's support Churchill could muster only 122 votes.

Churchill saved his last bitter words for Sir Samuel Hoare: "He has won his victory, he has won the victory for which he has fought hard, and long and adroitly; but it is not a victory in our opinion for the interests of the country nor a victory for the welfare of the peoples of India." He only hoped it did not sound the death "knell of the British Empire in the East."[43]

As always with Churchill, the bitterness did not last. "We must now look forward and not back," he told a supporter on July 2. He sent an open letter to his constituents, thanking them for their support through the long, arduous process: "We have done our best and we have done our duty. We cannot do more." He recalled the words of his father's old chief, Lord Salisbury: " 'It is the duty of every Englishman, and of every English party to accept a political defeat cordially, and to lend their best endeavors to secure the success, or to neutralize the evil, of the principles to which they have been forced to succumb.' We have no wish," Churchill added, "to be unfaithful to so wholesome a tradition."[44] Whatever his feelings toward Baldwin, Irwin, Butler, and the rest, Winston was willing to forgive and forget.*

His sense of magnanimity extended to his opponents on the other side of the world and to the man who he thought, more than any other, had thwarted his will. So he invited one of Gandhi's closest Indian associates, G. D. Birla, to lunch at Chartwell.

Ghanshyam Das Birla was typical of the new men who would take over India from the British. His grandfather, Seth Shivnarain Birla, had been born into the Marwari merchant caste and had been an accountant in a Hyderabad banking house. In 1862 Seth Birla had traveled by camel to Bombay to venture out on his own as a wholesale broker in the seed and gold bullion trade—and in opium. The fortune he built grew more substantial under his sons. His grandson was barely out of his teens when he decided to expand the house of Birla from the brokerage business into industry and set up the first Indian-owned jute processing mill.[45]

The stiff fibers of the jute plant were the indispensable material for the world's gunny sacks. No industry or business, from South American coffee plantations to European gunpowder plants, could function without them. Indian farmers had grown jute for centuries, but until G. D. Birla, jute processing had been considered a British preserve. The hostility and prejudice Birla faced from his white competitors led him to become interested in politics and the nationalist movement. By his own account, he even had to go underground for a time because of his overly close associations with a Hindu terrorist cell.[46]

Then in 1916 he met Gandhi, and as with so many other Indians, the meeting changed his life. When they became friends and correspondents, Birla was only thirty years old but already one of the richest men in India. He loved the Mahatma as much as he loved any man. "In all my actions," he wrote later, "I felt he was close beside me, and I was his

---

* With one exception, namely Samuel Hoare. Later, when Prime Minister Churchill was repeatedly urged to send Hoare to India as viceroy. Churchill refused to consider him. Not then. Not ever.

shadow."[47] Although he was a faithful Hindu, at Gandhi's request Birla became president of the All-India Anti-Untouchability League. It was in Birla's mansion in Delhi that Gandhi would live his last days, and in the garden where he would draw his last breath.

So Birla accepted Churchill's invitation to lunch with some trepidation. They had never met. As Birla's car drew past Chartwell's stone gates and he unpacked his long lanky form from the backseat to stand in the gravel drive, he may have wondered if he was going to have to deal once again with the arrogance and racial prejudice of Britons who considered themselves experts on India.

Instead, Birla had a wonderful time. He found Churchill working in the garden, wearing an enormous hat with a feather in it and a workingman's apron that he continued to wear during lunch. Churchill gave him a tour of Chartwell, showing him the garden, the heated pool, and the buildings and brick walls he had built with his own hands. He also set out some of the pictures he had painted.

They were at lunch for two hours. Churchill "did 75 percent of the talking." Almost all of it was about India and Gandhi. Birla was polite but astonished at how little Churchill really knew about modern India. He knew nothing about its extensive rail networks and believed that India's villages still lived in isolation from the towns. Birla had to explain that his factory employed 25,000 men, all of whom went home to their village at least twice a year. "He thought motor cars had not reached the villages. Again I corrected him."[48]

On the whole Birla found Churchill's views on India "most peculiar." At the same time, his talk was "never boring" and "as eloquent in private as it is in a public speech."

Churchill asked about Gandhi. Birla told him at length about the Mahatma's Harijan campaign. Churchill was impressed. "Mr. Gandhi has gone very high in my esteem since he stood up for the Untouchables," he said. He asked about Gandhi's village work. Was Gandhi inclined to wreck the new constitution? Birla told him no, Gandhi was indifferent to constitutions. What mattered to him was liberty, and Gandhi firmly believed that India's future had to depend on the Indians themselves.

Churchill completely agreed. "My test is improvement in the lot of the masses," he declared, "morally as well as materially." Gandhi would doubtless have said the same thing, and Birla must have been startled when Churchill added, "I do not care whether you are more or less loyal to Great Britain. I do not mind about education, but give the masses more butter. I stand for butter."

As the lunch ended, Winston seemed to soften, even to grow wistful. "Tell Mr. Gandhi to use the powers that are offered and make the thing a success, " he said. He repeated how sorry he was that he did not meet Gandhi when he was in London. "I should like to meet him now. I would love to go to India before I die." Would he be well received? Birla assured him he would be.

Churchill's last words, however, were full of foreboding—not for India but for Britain.

"India, I fear, is a burden to us," he confessed. "We have to maintain an army and for the sake of India we have to maintain Singapore and Near East strength. If India could look after herself we would be delighted." He said he genuinely hoped the reforms worked. "Make it a success," he told Birla, "and if you do I will advocate your getting much more."[49]

It was a kind and unexpectedly sympathetic statement. But as he left, the astute Birla must have realized there was little Churchill could do for anyone. For the sake of preserving the Raj, Winston had burned his last boats with his party leadership, with his party's rank and file, and with British public opinion.

The Wilderness Years had begun. Churchill's defeat over the India Bill confirmed what shrewd and knowledgeable observers like Lady Astor had known three years earlier. She had led a delegation to Moscow to meet with Joseph Stalin. Stalin had asked about British politicians. Lady Astor told him the rising man was Neville Chamberlain. Stalin then asked: "What about Winston Churchill?"

"Churchill?!" she laughed in wide-eyed astonishment. "Oh, he's finished!"[50]

Chapter Twenty-one

AGAINST THE CURRENT

1936–1938

We are really in great danger.

WINSTON CHURCHILL, 1936

G. D. BIRLA RETURNED TO INDIA IN September 1935 and went to see Gandhi. He told him about his meeting with Churchill. The Mahatma was pleased and keenly interested. He even brought up his own encounter with Churchill almost thirty years before. "I have got a good recollection of Mr. Churchill when he was in the Colonial Office," Gandhi told Birla, "and somehow or other since then I have held the opinion that I can always rely on his sympathy and goodwill." It was a courteous, if guarded compliment. He must have known it would get back to Churchill. (It did.)[1]

As 1935 drew to a close, Churchill found himself isolated and alone. He had taken his stand on India and lost. His reward was almost four years of political ostracism. Gandhi too had taken his stand—and won, or so it seemed. His reward was national veneration, almost sainthood. But it left him just as isolated and unhappy.

To an ordinary man, the passage of the Government of India Bill would have seemed an incredible victory. Thanks to his tireless efforts and acts of satyagraha, even risking his life, the Mahatma had forced the British to do what they had never seriously imagined they would do. Against their will, they had put 300 million Indians on the road to self-rule.

But was it Gandhi's victory? Gandhi was not so sure. He had the sense to realize that the British had given in not because they were swayed by his gospel of nonviolence but because they feared *more* violence if they did not. The Irish had won their freedom from Britain because they were willing to fight a bloody civil war. The Indians had won theirs (at least in a technical sense) because the British had wanted to avoid something similar.

This was not what Gandhi had wanted. No British politician, not even Lord Irwin, had truly grasped Gandhi's fundamental message. They had marked him down as a clever bargainer with a gift for mesmerizing the masses; they would soon be saying much the same about Adolf Hitler. The dream that Gandhi had offered up twenty-six years before in *Hind Swaraj,* of Britons and Indians finding common spiritual ground through satyagraha, remained unfulfilled.

Equally uncomprehending of his message, he was realizing to his sorrow, were the Indians themselves. The rising generation of Indian leaders did not share his late Victorian New Age outlook. Their priorities were very different. His former inner circle, onetime disciples like Rajendra Prasad, V. Patel, and lean, hook-nosed Rajagopalachari or "Rajaji," were now political powers in their own right, with their own regional bases and often sycophantic followers.

The journalist Nirad Chaudhuri met them all when Gandhi came to Calcutta for a meeting of the All-India Congress Committee in 1937. Later Chaudhuri described the anxious hustle and bustle before Gandhi's arrival at his employer Sarat Bose's house: the "formidably long" list of foods Gandhi needed to have on hand at all times of day or night, the search for a goat in order to provide the Mahatma with his milk, and the ceaseless stream of visitors and the throngs of ordinary Indians in the streets around the house hoping for a glance of the great man. Meanwhile middle-class Anglo-Indians in the block of flats opposite peered out of their windows "with clearly discernible expressions of disgust and anger."[2]

But above all Chaudhuri remembered the physical appearance of the men in Gandhi's inner circle and the heavyweights on the Working Committee. "I had never before seen such impassive hardness of countenance," Chaudhuri wrote, "nor such cold hauteur on the faces of men." They had "an overweening expression of arrogance" that exceeded even that of the most hidebound British officials; it "coated their faces and seemed to lie like make-up on their cheeks and foreheads." Gandhi's expression, by contrast, "was one of extraordinary innocence and benignity, with two soft beams streaming out of his eyes ... I must say I looked on spellbound in spite of my dislike for Gandhi's ideas." As for his followers, "all of them were silent, husky, and dry men, with eyes of steel."[3]

Even the man who groomed himself as Gandhi's newest protégé and presumptive successor, Jawaharlal Nehru, remained impervious to Gandhi's message. Nehru saw India's future more in terms of Western-style socialism and industrial planning than renunciation and the spinning wheel. Winston Churchill had warned about Nehru: "Already he is planning to supersede [Gandhi] the moment he has squeezed the last drop from the British lemon."[4] This harsh prediction was largely correct.

In 1935 Gandhi's dream of Swaraj faced two more immediate challenges. Muhammad Ali Jinnah of the Muslim League had been in politics longer than Gandhi and was a former ally. But every step in the process toward self-government fortified Jinnah's belief that India's Muslims could find justice only in their own separate state. No issue filled Gandhi with more anguish than the danger of a Hindu-Muslim split: "My whole soul rebels at the idea that Hinduism and Islam represent two antagonistic cultures and doctrines."[5] But by insisting that the Congress he had created was the sole voice for all Indians, and by embracing his role as a Hindu religious figure as well as political sage, Gandhi was alienating Jinnah and other Muslim nationalists even as the goal they had worked for together since 1916 drew near.

The Bengali nationalist Subhas Chandra Bose fought Gandhi from the opposite direction. Young, outspoken, and charismatic, he would twice be elected president of the Indian National Congress—the second time against Gandhi's wishes. He was Hotspur to Nehru's Prince Hal: the hot-tempered rival for the mantle of Gandhi's successor. Along with Jinnah and the untouchable leader Ambedkar, Bose made the 1930s into a torment for the Mahatma, as his vision of a spiritually free and politically united India threatened to dissolve before his eyes.

But probably no one caused Gandhi more disappointment than his own followers in the Indian National Congress. The salt satyagraha and previous campaigns had brought literally thousands of men and women into the public scene for the first time. They found participating in civil disobedience an exhilarating and unifying experience, but few outside his ashram circle saw Gandhi's satyagraha as a form of self-purification or as the path to the truth.[6] Most saw it in purely utilitarian terms. If it worked in forcing the British to make concessions, they would join in and organize their neighbors to help. If it did not, they would stop.

The Government of India Act seemed to prove it *had* worked. Now Congressmen wanted to reap the rewards of political activism: offices, status, influence, the ability to help friends and injure enemies—in a word, power. Especially after the India Act these rewards became the primary focus of discussion for successive Congresses. In the spring of 1934 Gandhi had had to accept a compromise whereby Congress members could stand for office in the upcoming legislative elections. Their ostensible reason was to better express their opposition to the government's Communal Award. The truth was they just wanted to win seats.[7]

Over the next four years Gandhi would learn to his sorrow that Indian politicians, even his hand-picked disciples, were much like politicians everywhere. He gave way in part because he was too tired to fight anymore. After fourteen years he felt it was time to take his leave of the Indian National Congress. In October 1934 he formally severed his ties in order to continue his work alone. "I shall better influence the Congress being outside," he insisted to his worried disciples. He had worked outside in 1919 and again in 1928. But this time he knew that he and India's politicians had reached the fork in the road.

The surest sign that Gandhi was looking for a new path was his creation in 1936 of a new ashram, outside Wardha in the heart of the Central Provinces. Sabarmati remained up and running, and Gandhi remained Sabarmati's spiritual guide, firing off memos and directives that sometimes bewildered his disciples. But he had vowed in 1931 that he would not return there until India had independence.[8] After his release from prison he stayed with relatives and friends. But he still needed a place where he could think, spin, meditate, and conduct business, including his new organization, the All-India Village Industries Association; and where Kasturbai and his inner circle could join him. So at the end of April 1936 he and Mirabehn strolled through some barren fields north of Segaon village and picked out building sites for a new ashram that he called Sevagram or "Service Village."[9]

Sevagram was a real village, or at least Segaon was, in one of the poorest parts of India. Gandhi was launching a campaign of what he called village work, to uplift the lives of India's destitute rural masses hamlet by hamlet. It was a natural extension of his Harijan campaign: India's poorest came almost exclusively from its lowest castes. It also meshed with his hopes that the charkha would remake India's political economy, since he saw the production of khadi as essential to making villages strong and self-sufficient.

By 1936 the peasant village had become the focus of all Gandhi's hopes for India—one could even say his last hope. "India lives in her seven hundred thousand villages," Gandhi told his followers. "You cannot build non-violence on a factory civilization, but it can be built on self-contained villages."[10] Therefore he decided, at age sixty-six, like Tolstoy before him, to live like a peasant. His first house at Sevagram was only a mud-wall hut, 14 by 29 feet. The compound soon grew, however, as devotees and family members moved in, including Kasturbai (who was appalled by the lack of privacy and insisted that Gandhi's patron, cotton merchant Jamnalal Bajaj, build her a separate house).[11] Eventually there was a road and even telegraph wires.

But Sevagram never brought the spiritual serenity of Sabarmati to its founder or his followers. Virtually everyone, including Gandhi, came down with malaria or dysentery. The thick grass around the compound was infested with kraits, whose bite was sixteen times deadlier than a cobra's. Gandhi's own bout with malaria put him in Wardha's hospital, while his high blood pressure made any sustained physical labor almost impossible. A visitor told Nehru he found the Mahatma looking tired and depressed.[12] In fact, these were years of personal as well as physical pain.

The personal pain started with the unexpected reappearance of his eldest son Harilal, now forty-seven. For three decades Harilal had tried by turns to either please or horrify his father into noticing him. He had almost destroyed his physical health with bouts in prison during the South Africa satyagrahas. The sudden death of his wife in 1918 and then the death of his son of typhoid fever at Sabarmati in 1929 helped to wreck what was left of Harilal's mental health. He became a shambling alcoholic, with a reputation for consorting with loose women and embezzling from employers. He wrote ugly letters to his brothers Manilal, Devadas, and Ramdas, denouncing them as charlatans for trying to emulate their father.

In 1934 he appeared on Gandhi's doorstep like the Prodigal Son. Despite the years of bitterness, Gandhi was pleased to have him back. He blamed himself for Harilal's failures. The boy had been conceived when Gandhi was at his most self-indulgent, he confessed to others. Clearly his own sinfulness had made Harilal the way he was. But even in his father's presence Harilal refused to change. He became a living reproach to Gandhi's temperance campaign. "He goes about drunk and begs from people," Gandhi wrote matter-of-factly. He hoped his eldest son might remarry, but the one likely prospect, an alliance with European Gandhi devotee Margarette Spiegel, soon fell through.[13]

Eventually Harilal wandered back to Rajkot, where he tried selling wristwatches for a living. Gandhi strongly disapproved but was most concerned about his son's drinking, which became steadily worse. Finally Harilal wrote a string of angry reproachful letters to his father. None survive, but Gandhi himself wrote: "This chapter is becoming more and more painful." Soon afterward Harilal dropped out of sight. Gandhi wrote to his cousin Narandas: "Leave him to his fate." Occasionally news reached him that Harilal was destitute and homeless, traveling from one big city to another in third-class rail carriages.[14]

Almost two years later Gandhi and Kasturbai were passing through the town of Katni in their usual third-class railway compartment. A toothless figure in rags with matted hair hanging down to his shoulders halted them on the train platform. They suddenly realized it was Harilal—looking for all the world like a caricature of the Hindu *sadhu* his father had become. Harilal gave a trembling greeting to Kasturbai but not his father. From a tattered dirty pocket he pulled out an orange, which he presented to his mother.

"Have you nothing for me?" Gandhi asked.

"No, I have brought the orange only for Ba," Harilal stammered. "I have only one thing to say to you. If you are so great, you owe it to Ba." A tearful Kasturbai begged Harilal to come back with them, but he refused. As they pulled out of the station, they heard him calling in a high-pitched voice: *"Mata Kasturbai ki jai!"*

She never saw their son again.[15]

Less than a month after he founded Sevagram, Gandhi received the bitterest blow. On May 29, 1936, Harilal stood in one of Delhi's major mosques, the Jamma Masjid, and formally converted to Islam. He took a new name, Abdullah, and made a speech to a large cheering crowd. A Muslim brotherhood sent the story to Gandhi and mockingly asked him whether he was thinking of converting as well.[16]

Gandhi was deeply wounded, but not because Harilal had become a Muslim. Harilal had told his father he owed money to Muslim creditors and that missionaries of various faiths were hounding him to convert. He had openly said he considered yielding to the highest bidder.[17] To Gandhi, for whom nothing mattered as much as religious faith, the news of his son's sellout was a personal humiliation.

"I must confess that all this has hurt me," he wrote in a long letter. "Conversion without cleanness of heart can only be a matter for sorrow, not joy, to a godly person."[18] True to form, Harilal did not remain a Muslim for very long. But the incident helped to strain Gandhi's relations not only with his wayward son, but with India's largest minority community. Those relations were already tense, thanks to the man who would emerge as Gandhi's Muslim nemesis, Muhammad Ali Jinnah.

A stranger might have taken Jinnah for Gandhi's taller younger brother. They had much in common. Lean and long-boned, like Gandhi he came from Gujarat, although he had been born in Karachi. His grandfather and grandmother had lived only thirty miles from Gandhi's home in Rajkot. Like the Mahatma, Jinnah was a London-trained barrister and protégé of both D. Naoroji and G. K. Gokhale. Ironically, he had even been a champion of Muslim-Hindu unity. His membership in the Indian National Congress (he joined in 1896) and support for the 1916 Lucknow Pact had earned Jinnah many enemies in more radical pan-Islamic circles.

But as the Indian Muslim movement changed over the 1920s and 1930s, Jinnah changed with it. Jinnah could say with many other politicians: There go my followers, I must lead them. And by 1930 they were leading not just to a separate Muslim electorate but a separate Muslim nation.

The idea of a Muslim nation was not entirely new—it had even crossed the minds of some Hindus.[19] For Muslims, however, it became more and more attractive as the British seemed ready to abandon India, leaving them to the mercies of a large Hindu majority. The focus of this fear and resentment was Jinnah's Muslim League. With his elegant suits, stiff collars, and even a monocle, Jinnah cut an unsympathetic, even pompous figure beside Gandhi. Gandhians and Gandhi himself found him an easy target for ridicule. Later during partition, Indian historians would make him appear sinister, even satanic.

But Muhammad Jinnah was also a passionate man, and he was passionate about protecting the interests of Muslims across the subcontinent once the British left. At every stage, he felt, Gandhi and the Congress had crossed him. He had walked out of the 1920 Nagpur Congress after he had been shouted down, saying, "I have *no* voice or *power*."[20] His counterproposal to Motilal Nehru's plan for a Hindu-majority Dominion had been ignored. He had become so upset at the pointless wrangling at the Round Table Conferences that he left India in disgust in 1931.

It was Kashmiri poet Muhammad Iqbal who first drew Jinnah to the idea of forging a separate Muslim state out of India's four northwestern provinces. Iqbal had grown up in the Punjab, where Muslims treated

British rule as a gift from God that freed them from the tyranny of the Sikhs.[21] At a Muslim League meeting in 1930, as the possibility of the British leaving loomed, Iqbal broached the idea of creating two nations in India, Hindu and Muslim. Three years later a Muslim student at Cambridge, Chaudhuri Rahmat Ali, came up with the name for this putative state. He chose the letter P for the Punjab, A for the New West Frontier Province or Afghania, K for Kashmir, S for Sind, and TAN for Baluchistan. Taken together they formed the word Pakistan, which meant in Urdu "Land of the Pure." The name became both "a symbol and a slogan" for India's politically active Muslims, who realized that if Pakistan really were formed, it would be the largest Islamic nation in the world.[22]

One of those whom Iqbal managed to convince was Jinnah. "Why should not the Moslems of Northwestern India and Bengal," he asked Jinnah in a crucial letter in June 1937, "be considered as nations entitled to self-determination" just like other nations and peoples were?[23] Such a question, it seemed to Jinnah, had only one answer. Paradoxically, this also led him to a view of India and the Congress similar to Churchill's. India was not a single nation and never would be. Talk of Indian unity was a "myth," a cloak for a Hindu power grab or worse. Indeed, many Hindu nationalists considered Muslims on the subcontinent to be lapsed Hindus. Some spoke openly of reconversion by force or otherwise, or at least expulsion. One ideologue, Madhav Golwalkar, even recommended dealing with the Muslims of India as Hitler dealt with Germany's Jews: "a good lesson for us to learn and profit by."[24]

There was another problem with the settlement the British had arranged. Jinnah realized (as had Dr. Ambedkar) that "separate electorates" set not only a minimum but also a maximum political influence, for minorities and their representatives. Under the All-India Federation scheme, no Muslim would ever become prime minister of India, no matter how agreeable his principles or revered his person. This prospect did not appeal to Muhammad Ali Jinnah, and so he returned to India in 1934 to become the Muslim League's president and to prepare for battle.

The battleground would be the first round of legislative elections under the new constitution, slated for 1937. Shortly before he died that year, Iqbal wrote to Jinnah: "You are the only Moslem in India today to whom the community has a right to look up for safe guidance through the storm that is coming."[25] In just two and a half years Jinnah had managed to reorganize the Muslim League into an effective political machine. His model, ironically, was Gandhi's Congress. Jinnah set up provincial parliamentary boards and a Central Parliamentary Board modeled on the Congress Working Committee. He strove to achieve the same dedication and party discipline. Jinnah even remade himself. He dropped the stiff collars and Savile Row suits and donned close-fitting black Punjabi *sherwani* coats that fell below the knees and that had once been the court dress of the Mughal Empire. There was even a Persian lamb Jinnah cap, to match the khadi Gandhi cap of the Congress. Muslims went into the 1937 election campaign prepared and organized as never before.[26]

The 1937 elections were a watershed for the Indian National Congress as well. The organization found itself in an odd position. Officially it still opposed the Government of India Act, but it also allowed its members to run for office in the act's first legislative elections. The men who had been Gandhi's closest disciples, "the Mahatmaji circle"—Prasad, Patel, Rajagopalachari, and J. B. Kripalani—mobilized their local "ward heelers" and got out the vote with the skill and aplomb of Tammany Hall bosses. Even the fiercest opponent of the 1935 Act, Jawaharlal Nehru, deemed it prudent to hit the campaign trail.

The Congress had scored well in the last Pre-Act elections in 1934, winning 44 of 88 seats. They could smell success in the upcoming round and defeat for the Muslim League upstarts. And so as Gandhi watched silently from the sidelines, the Indian National Congress made its first serious bid for electoral success.

The bosses were proved right. Out of 1,585 total seats, the Congress took 716, with clear majorities in five provinces: Madras, Bihar, Orissa, United Provinces, and Central Provinces. In three others they had strong showings.[27] The Muslim League, by contrast, did badly. Only one in twenty Muslims across India circled its crescent and star symbol on their ballots. (Congress's symbol was, of course, the charkha.) The League won only 109 of the 482 seats reserved for Muslims, and nowhere did it secure power, not even in Jinnah's home province of Sind.[28]

Paradoxically, the League's failure worked to its long-term favor. Seeing the election results, many Muslims became more frightened than ever that their rights and identities would be crushed by the Congress juggernaut. When Nehru announced, "There are only two forces in India today, British imperialism and Indian nationalism as represented by the Congress," Jinnah's retort was swift and furious. "There is a third party in this country," he countered, "and that is the

Moslems."[29] Many politically minded Muslims now saw supporting his party as their last resort. Jinnah's goal was clear: to make the Muslim League the sole voice of India's Muslims, just as Congress claimed to speak for all Hindus.

To Nehru, now the Congress president, Jinnah proposed a power-sharing plan, with the League and the Congress divvying up the spoils once India achieved independence. Nehru rejected his blandishments at once. On this subject his view was the same as Gandhi's. Congress represented all Indians, not just Hindus (and by extension dalits and other Scheduled castes) but Muslims, Christians, and all the rest. To the secular-minded socialist Nehru, his disagreement with Jinnah was a simple conflict "between those who wanted a free, united, and democratic India and certain reactionary and feudal elements" who were exploiting religious difference to protect their privileges.[30]

Yet Jinnah knew that Muslims in the Congress were hard to find. Only one, Gandhi's friend Maulan Abul Kalam Azad, sat in the Congress leadership; and the only reason Congress had scored well in Muslim provinces like the Northwest Frontier was that the Muslim vote had been split. So Jinnah took Nehru's rejection philosophically. "Eighty millions of Musulmans have nothing to fear," he told his followers. "They have their destiny in their hands." In any case, there was only one person whose view really mattered in the Congress, he believed, and that was Gandhi. After the New Year he aimed to cut a private deal with the Mahatma, just as Viceroy Irwin had done after the Salt March.

But the Gandhi of 1938 was a different man from the one who had climbed the steps of Viceroy House seven years before. He was preoccupied with his village work; his high blood pressure made him tire easily and his attention wander. He was weary of politics. But the Congress would not let him go. His Congress followers turned to him for help on the question of whether they should *accept* the offices to which they had just been elected. Nehru and his more radical friends said no: they had wanted the elections to be a show of Congress force, nothing more. Prasad and the Mahatmaji circle took the opposite view: they naturally wanted to reward their followers for their loyalty and hard work. Gandhi was forced to work out a compromise. In the end, he arrived at a plan with the new viceroy, Lord Linlithgow, to allow Congress members to take their offices without having to comply with the government's emergency measures.[31] The episode had been a tedious distraction for Gandhi, who considered the whole business irrelevant. And now his old nemesis Jinnah wanted to bypass Nehru to talk to him directly.

Gandhi felt an obligation to defer to his younger disciple, who was almost his son. But in late February 1938 he wrote to Jinnah: "I am at your disposal." A month later, on April 28, Gandhi took the train to Bombay and arrived at Jinnah's magnificent house on Malabar Hill. (Jinnah had married a rich Parsi heiress.) They sat down for a three-and-half-hour discussion. If Jinnah had expected an Irwin-style breakthrough, he was disappointed. Gandhi made some notes but was too tired and depressed to decide anything. He confessed to Nehru afterward: "I have lost the self-confidence that I possessed only a month ago." He would leave any final decision to Nehru. That ensured that the answer to Jinnah's offer of a League-Congress compact was no.[32]

There would be another fruitless summit meeting in May, but Jinnah's mind was made up. Gandhi had let him down for the last time. Now India's Muslims had to take matters into their own hands. He told his followers: "We must stand on our own inherent strength, and build up our own power." For the first time he talked to Muslims of achieving their "national goal": the first sign that he believed that when the British left India, there would be two nations, not one.[33]

On October 9, 1938, the Sind Muslim League met in Karachi, Jinnah's birthplace. The Sind District Board and city fathers presented Jinnah with the key to the city on an engraved silver tray. Over their heads flew the Muslim League flag, green with a silver crescent and star in the center. At that meeting the League would pass a formal resolution rejecting the All-India Federation and calling a united Indian nation "impossible of realization."[34]

The League flag was not yet a national flag. But a week earlier, on the other side of the world, an event took place that would, improbably enough, bring that a step closer to reality.

On the last day of September a large crowd gathered at the edge of the grassy airfield in Heston, ten miles west of London. They lifted their heads expectantly at the sound as an airplane made its final approach and landed. A swarm of photographers and reporters dashed onto the field to set up their microphones and newsreel cameras, including the very first television camera.[35] The crowd watched with rapt expectation as the plane door opened and a thin man with spectacles and a small mustache descended the ramp. As he stepped to the radio microphones, he pulled from his pocket a single sheet of paper that fluttered in the autumn breeze.

"I've got it," he said with a smile. The crowd went wild with joy.

Prime Minister Arthur Neville Chamberlain had achieved what everyone had desired but thought impossible. He had reached a final agreement signed by Adolf Hitler's own hand, to prevent the growing crisis over Czech Sudetenland from triggering a general European war. As the crowd settled down, Chamberlain completed his statement: "My good friends, for the second time in our history a British prime minister has returned from Germany bringing peace with honor. I believe it is peace for our time."

The crowd continued to cheer as he climbed into a waiting car. Then "London's ovation to Mr. Chamberlain," reported the *Illustrated London News,* "reached its climax when he went straight from Heston Airdrome to Buckingham Palace." There "he was shown to Their Majesties' private apartments, where [Mrs. Chamberlain] was already present, and received the Royal congratulations." The king had wanted to meet Chamberlain personally at Heston, to welcome him after his diplomatic triumph.[36] But he had been persuaded to let the prime minister come to Buckingham Palace instead, where Chamberlain received an honor unprecedented for a commoner. He was allowed to stand beside his monarch and the queen on the palace balcony, while an immense throng pressed underneath and cheered.

Later at 10 Downing Street Chamberlain repeated the phrase he had used in his statement at Heston: "I believe it is peace for our time." Then he told the crowd, "Go home and get a nice sleep." Both his foreign secretary, the former Lord Irwin and now Viscount Halifax, and Chancellor of the Exchequer Sir John Simon, gave him fulsome congratulations. No one particularly cared that the Munich agreement meant the partition of Czechoslovakia and the transfer of the Sudetenland to the Third Reich. The agreement was applauded by every newspaper in Britain except *Reynolds News.*[37] The *Times* of London even sold Christmas cards showing Chamberlain with a smiling king and queen.

The one sour note was sounded by Winston Churchill. That evening he stopped with a friend at a restaurant near the Savoy Hotel. The crowd inside was delighted, even ecstatic, that Chamberlain and Hitler had agreed there would be no need for war. The pair stood watching for a moment in the doorway. "I was acutely conscious of the brooding figure beside me," his companion noted later. "As we turned away, [Churchill] muttered, 'Those poor people! They little know what they will have to face.' "[38]

Churchill's gloom was matched only by his frustration. For almost five years he had fought a single-minded campaign against the idea that Hitler's ambitions could be satisfied by negotiation and concession—the policy called, then and now, "appeasement." The Munich agreement was appeasement's masterpiece.[39] It also marked appeasement's end.

"This is only the beginning of the reckoning," Churchill thundered in the House of Commons on October 6. "This is only the first sip, the first foretaste of a bitter cup which will be proffered to us year by year." Many were already realizing the enormity of what had happened, and that despite Hitler's declaration—"This marks the end of Germany's territorial demands"—the agreement was worthless the moment it was signed.

Permanent Foreign Undersecretary Oliver Harvey noted the "vast crowds" and "hysterical enthusiasm" but also saw that "many feel it to be a great humiliation." Almost a week earlier Leo Amery, no Churchill fan, wrote to Lord Halifax: "Almost everyone I have met has been horrified by the so-called 'peace' we have forced upon the Czechs."[40] Chamberlain himself realized that the emotional tide was about to turn even as he made his way from Heston airport. "All this will be over in three months," he said as he gazed at the smiling throngs.

Indeed, the next six months would see a reversal of public opinion so sweeping and stunning that it would turn Chamberlain from a shining hero into a discredited scapegoat, and turn Winston Churchill from political pariah into national savior.

Those bitter years before Munich have passed into Churchillian legend as the Wilderness Years, with Churchill as a prophet without honor in his own country. Certainly the sequence of totalitarian advance and democratic retreat during that time is all too familiar.

It began in 1935 with Mussolini's invasion of Abyssinia, which the League of Nations and the Western powers opposed but could not decide how to stop. In 1936 came the outbreak of civil war in Spain, with Fascist Italy, Nazi Germany, and the Soviet Union all pulling the strings and encouraging the slaughter. That same year Hitler broke the Versailles treaty by remilitarizing the Rhineland and Germany's frontier with France, while Britain and France did nothing. The year before Hitler had repudiated all treaty restrictions on German armaments. Britain's only response was to sign a naval agreement with Hitler, vainly hoping to limit the size of any future German fleet by treaty with a man who had manifestly shown that treaties meant nothing to him. "Such a view seems to be the acme of gullibility" was Churchill's choleric comment.[41]

The following year, in July 1937, shortly after Neville Chamberlain became prime minister, Japan declared war on China. In March 1938 Hitler occupied Austria while the Western powers sat idly by; and on September 30 he and they signed the Munich agreement partitioning Czechoslovakia. At each step, with every negotiation and conference, British prime ministers Baldwin and Chamberlain and their French counterparts made every accommodation and bent every principle in order to avoid being sucked into war. And at each step the appetite of the dictators grew more insatiable, and their demands bolder—just as Churchill and a handful of followers predicted.

For four long years Churchill trudged day after day into the House of Commons to voice his warnings about Hitler, Mussolini, and the need for Britain to rearm. Usually he spoke to an empty chamber, with only Brendan Bracken or Bob Boothby sitting loyally nearby. At other times the chamber might be full, but only with Conservatives who came to hoot derisively at Churchill's impotent fury, or to hear Prime Minister Chamberlain or Secretary of War Leslie Hore-Belisha deliver some withering counterblast, which would set them cheering. The king and queen considered Churchill's speeches dangerous and hateful. By the time of Munich a movement had developed among formerly loyal supporters to oust him from his parliamentary seat.[42]

In retrospect Churchill's dogged persistence has an irresistible heroic quality. Kipling's "If" (Gandhi's favorite poem) contains the lines:

> *If you can trust yourself when all men doubt you . . .*
> *If you can wait and not be tired by waiting . . .*
> *Or being hated, don't give way to hating . . .*
> *If you can fill the unforgiving minute*
> *With sixty seconds' worth of distance run,*
> *Yours is the Earth and everything that's in it,*
> *And—which is more—you'll be a Man, my son!*

By that measure these were the years when Churchill the man first rose to greatness.

He may have exaggerated German air strength and the speed and size of Hitler's rearmament.[43] Undeniably his own policies at the Exchequer in the 1920s had critically weakened the British navy and army.* It is also true that his lingering regard for Mussolini led him to dodge the question of how to halt Italian aggression in Abyssinia, and that his sympathy for the Nationalist leader General Francisco Franco made him wobbly on Spain, instead of insisting that Britain oppose intervention there by all foreign powers, including the Soviet Union.

But the fact remains that Churchill's basic argument against appeasement was correct. No amount of accommodation or compromise was going to gratify the appetite for territory and power on the part of the world's rising totalitarian states, especially Germany. As a student of history, Churchill saw in Hitler a peculiarly sinister force that others missed. Even in 1930, when Hitler was still a second-rate politician, Churchill warned a German Foreign Office emissary that Hitler wanted far more than just to remedy the "injustices" of Versailles.[44] In November 1932, after Hitler had gained a majority in the German Reichstag and was invited into the government, Churchill foretold, "Do not believe that all that Germany is asking for is equal status ... All these bands of sturdy Teutonic youths, marching through the streets and roads of Germany...are not looking for status. They are looking for weapons...and when they have those will demand lost territories and colonies, and shatter the foundations of Europe."[45] By 1934 he was warning that the German people are "the most powerful and most dangerous nation in the western world."[46]

The problem was that no one believed him. When he warned of a terrible looming "conflict of spiritual and moral ideas," Britons only wanted to be left alone. When he argued that only the threat of armed force could stop Hitler—"we must arm ourselves so that the good cause may not find itself at a hopeless disadvantage against the aggressor"— others heard needless warmongering. Even as late as 1938 most people found Churchill's rhetoric overblown and his warnings against the Nazis exaggerated. (A few historians still do.)[47]

This skepticism was especially prevalent among his fellow Conservatives. "W. C. they regard with complete mistrust," Nancy Dugdale, wife of a leading Tory, wrote in summing up the feelings of her husband's colleagues. "W. C. is really the counterpart of Goering in

---

* Only the Japanese invasion of Manchuria in 1932 finally forced the cabinet to rescind the Ten Year Rule regarding future conflicts, which Churchill had so foolishly extended.

England...bloated with ego and over-feeding, the same treachery running through his veins, punctuated by heroics and hot air." Those words were written on May 12, 1940, just four days after Churchill had become prime minister.[48]

Contrary to myth, the distrust of and disbelief in Churchill did *not* spring from a cavalier disregard of the German threat. Many people, especially in the armed services, were worried about German war preparations and British weakness, although few were willing to speak out as forthrightly as Churchill. Major Desmond Morton of the Industrial Intelligence Center passed him confidential estimates of growing German air strength. The general in charge of Britain's mobile armored forces personally gave him a detailed account of how obsolete and outclassed his tanks were. A steady stream of "leaks" like these from reliable sources gave Churchill valuable ammunition for his thunderous speeches in the House of Commons.*[49]

Nor did the British political establishment turn against Churchill because they were somehow sympathetic with the Nazis. The idea that appeasement was driven by "guilty men" who were willing to sell out Britain and bolster Hitler in order to protect themselves against the Left is a myth. A handful, notably Oswald Mosley and the Duke of Windsor, openly approved of Hitler, but none had any direct influence on policy. More thought that if they had no choice, they could accept a Nazi-dominated Eastern Europe as a useful bulwark against Bolshevism. (Churchill, the ultimate anti-Bolshevik, was not among them.) But no one, least of all Neville Chamberlain, was willing to accept that dominance without putting up a struggle, or would deliberately betray British interests.

The truth is that Churchill's exclusion from influence and power was the direct result of his conduct in the India debates. He had cried wolf for nearly five years, forecasting doom and destruction if the Government of India Bill passed: "a catastrophe that will shake the world," he had called it. Then the bill passed, and nothing happened. Rarely had a politician been proved so hopelessly wrong, after nearly wrecking his own political party in the process. When he forecast doom again, over Germany, few were inclined to believe him, least of all Conservatives.

---

* There is even evidence that Baldwin and his secretary for war knew of the leaks, and approved. They may have seen Winston's "warmongering" as a usefully oblique way to prepare the British public for the need for more defense spending: hardly proof that Churchill had become a permanent political pariah.

Also contrary to myth, he was never a complete political pariah. More than once his name appeared on lists for prospective cabinet posts. He came closest in 1935, when the post of minister for coordination of defense was created. (It went to Thomas Inskip instead.) As late as March 1938 he was under consideration for air minister or even a return to the Admiralty.[50]

But the appointments never came. Years later, when Stanley Baldwin's biographer G. M. Young asked the former prime minister what had kept Churchill out of the running for any cabinet office and alienated him from his party, Baldwin answered in one word: "India."[51]

Churchill's long battle against Dominion status for India had crippled his effectiveness when it was most needed. At the same time it safeguarded the reputation of the men he had attacked. The champions of the Government of India Act—Baldwin, Sir Samuel Hoare, and Lord Irwin—became the principal architects of appeasement. Tories who battled Churchill in the rancorous debates over India, rising young politicians like R. A. Butler, fought him just as hard over how to deal with Hitler.

Their principles also remained the same. Nationalism, they believed, whether among Indians or Irishmen or Germans, was the trend of the future. It could not be resisted. Using repression or threatening armed force only inflamed passions and aroused more anger and discontent. The only solution was face-to-face negotiation and give-and-take compromise. The success of the new constitution in India seemed to prove that "nations became calm and pacified when their just claims were met."[52] In this sense, the final fruit of the Gandhi-Irwin pact was the Hitler-Chamberlain agreement in Munich.

Certainly Lord Halifax made his experiences in dealing with Gandhi into his touchstone for dealing with Hitler. In July 1936, right after German troops reentered the Rhineland, Sir John Simon's former private secretary Thomas Stopford put the question to him. "Is there not a certain similarity" between Hitler and Gandhi? he asked.

Halifax enthusiastically agreed. Both men had the same "strong inferiority complex, the same idealism, the belief in the divine mission to lead his people and the same difficulty with unruly lieutenants"—as if Nehru and Prasad were khadi versions of Herman Göring and Ernst Röhm. Halifax told another friend that Hitler "reminded him of Gandhi in that he has a message to deliver...a prophetic message."

Having cut through the rhetoric of an obstreperous man like Gandhi to strike a deal, surely he could do the same with a "very nasty" but "inspired" man like Hitler.[53]

Even two years later, as one disappointment followed another, Halifax's basic view did not change. He wrote to the governor of Madras, Lord Erskine: "I cannot help contrasting my period at the India Office with the work I do now," in arranging a deal with Hitler. To Halifax they involved addressing the same set of problems, assuaging the same hurt feelings. "The main difference between the two nations is that a mild Hindu is probably less alarming than the vigorous Prussian."[54]

To Halifax and his appeasement allies, establishing peace in Europe seemed no different from drawing up the Communal Award. In dividing up the spoils of power, they had to make sure no one felt excluded. And if one could shape a more just settlement in India by splitting Muslim Sind from Hindu Bombay, or Orissa from Bihar, as was done in 1935, then why not do the same for the German Sudetens in Czechoslovakia? For years critics had deplored the subjection of three million Germans to an alien Czech and Slovak majority. One of those critics had been a leading socialist, H. N. Brailsford. From that perspective, as historian A. J. P. Taylor noted, Munich had been "a triumph for those who had preached equal justice between peoples."[55] The same was certainly true of the India Act.

By the same token, Churchill's opposition to appeasement was the logical extension of his fight against Gandhi and the India Act. He even used the same term for it. His friend Lord Birkenhead had first used "appeasement" in a disparaging political sense on November 5, 1929, when he spoke in the House of Lords against "the appeasers of Gandhi."[56] Churchill had borrowed the word when he discussed the government's "policy of appeasement" on India with a sympathetic German diplomat in 1930. In 1933 he was already using it to describe British policy toward Hitler.

For Churchill also saw parallels between Gandhi and Hitler, but very different ones. What scared him about all mass national movements of the twentieth century, including Gandhi's, was that they lacked moorings in any pre-established social or political order. Churchill rejected the conventional wisdom that movements for "national self-determination," were voices for freedom. Since the Versailles treaty, he believed, they had proven rather to be a formula for chaos. The path to peace was to preserve empires, the historical accretions of centuries of legitimate rule and stability; not to break them up. But instead Britain was planning to break up one empire in India just as it was performing last rites for another in Central Europe, the old Habsburg Empire. In both cases the result was a terrible new barbarism unleashed on a helpless humanity.

Churchill sensed something chillingly new and modern, but also frighteningly ancient and familiar, about the Nazi movement. In an article in October 1935 he wrote that Hitler's "triumphant career has been borne onwards, not by a passionate love of Germany, but by currents of hatred so intense as to sear the souls of those who swim upon them."[57] Hitler had turned Germany into "an armed camp," where "concentration camps pock-marked the German soil." Absolute power had been entrusted to a single ruthless man. Nothing was new about this "odious, pernicious, and degrading" form of one-man rule, Churchill said: "it can be seen in the history of every despot." He had even seen it in Gandhi and his "almost god-like" status among Indian nationalists.[58]

But the angry marching crowds; the vicious anti-Semitic measures applied against every Jew from famous scientists to "wrecked little Jewish children"; the trampling of innocence and the conventions of mercy, tolerance, and decency; above all, the thirst for weapons and war: all suggested a resurgence of the barbarism that had once destroyed civilization in Europe. Now armed with modern weapons and "the irresistible power of the Totalitarian State," that barbarism was threatening to do it again.

Churchill believed the only antidote was "the great theories of government which the British race devised" and that reflected the essential English character. Constitutional democracy was, he concluded, "the foundation on which [modern] civilization rests and without which it will fall." Britons needed to value "these treasures—glories I call them—as we do our lives; and there should be no sacrifice we would not make...to hand them over unmutilated and unbesmirched to our children."[59] He confessed to George Bernard Shaw, "I hope I shall die" before those glories were "overturned."[60]

Those glories of civilization had seemed to sound their death knell in India. Gandhi explicitly turned his back on them. Churchill feared the same was happening in Europe. Years ago in India Edward Gibbon had taught him that the twin destroyers of the Roman Empire had been barbarism and fanaticism. Just as Churchill had seen himself trying to save the British Empire from Gandhi's fanaticism, now he had to rally England against Hitler's barbarism.

Just as he finished his multivolume biography of Marlborough in 1934, he chose as his next historical project an epic saga on the rise of Anglo-Saxon civilization. It would be entitled *The History of the English-Speaking Peoples*.[61] For Churchill, "those institutions, laws and customs and national characteristics which are the common inheritance, or supposed to be, of the English-speaking world," which he had believed were the last hope for India, would now become the last ray of hope for the rest of the world.[62]

His absorption in historical work, and the constant stream of magazine articles, essays, and travel pieces he wrote, were a welcome distraction in these years. "It is a comfort to me," he confessed to historian Mortimer Wheeler, as he began work on *English-Speaking Peoples*, "to put a thousand years between my thoughts and the twentieth century."[63] For in addition to his political isolation, he experienced personal disappointment.

On November 30, 1935, he celebrated his sixty-first birthday. Like Gandhi, he had a distinct feeling that the current generation was passing him by. Old friends were dying, not to be replaced. The death of "F.E.," Lord Birkenhead, in September 1930, had hit him especially hard. Austen Chamberlain, one of his few prominent allies in the fight against appeasement, suffered a stroke and died in March 1937. T. E. Lawrence was killed in a motorcycle accident in 1935. Earlier Churchill's beloved cousin "Sunny" Marlborough suddenly died of cancer. "It was only a month ago," Churchill wrote wistfully, "that he was riding out to watch his horses at Newmarket or preparing a speech for the House of Lords." They had been friends since childhood; his death only reminded Winston that he too belonged to a vanished "bygone age." He went into one of his notorious "black dog" depressions and spoke of his own obsolescence. "Please do not talk of yourself as a very old man," a friend had to tell him. "You are letting us all down by doing so."[64]

The chairs at the dinner table at Chartwell were empty for other reasons. "Thank God I am not a vindictive man," he said after the India debates.[65] But even former friends could feel the sting of his rage and bitterness if they supported a foreign policy he considered an invitation to catastrophe. Patrick Donner had loyally supported Churchill on India, but they fell out over appeasement. "I was no longer 'Patrick' after ten years," Donner said years later. The happy frequent visits to Chartwell came to an end. "If somebody took an action which in [Churchill's] judgement was contrary to the national interest," Donner remembered, "he would have absolutely nothing further to do with that person . . . He was prosecution counsel and judge combined."[66]

But Winston's biggest disappointment was his son, Randolph. Randolph was no Harilal (although ironically he too would eventually succumb to alcoholism). Outwardly Randolph was devoted to his father, perhaps too devoted. (His accusations against Chamberlain and the appeasers were sometimes unbalanced and made Winston's look mild.) Randolph had many gifts. He was slim and stunningly handsome, and he was verbally articulate to the point of glibness. However, he had more enthusiasm than ability, and more passion than energy. He tried desperately to follow in his father's footsteps, but the result was almost always a bad stumble.

His independent run for the Wavertree parliamentary seat in January 1935 was "a most rash and unconsidered plunge," Winston told Clementine, predicting exactly what did happen: Randolph split the Tory vote and a Labourite won.[67] The next month Randolph put up an anti-India Act candidate for a contest in Norwood, against his father's expressed wishes. The man turned out to be a British fascist; later during the war he had to be interned. He not only lost abysmally; the press used him to smear Churchill's entire campaign against the bill.[68] Later father and son had a knock-down, drag-out verbal fight at the dinner table. Randolph stormed out in a rage. It was the first of many such fights, often in the presence of eminent guests.

Randolph's drinking, gambling, and womanizing landed him in the scandal sheets, causing embarrassment to his family. His drinking bouts often ended in physical violence, even against his father's friends. Once he threw Brendan Bracken's glasses into the sea.[69]

Clementine believed Winston spoiled Randolph, and he sheepishly agreed.[70] He regularly paid the debts Randolph ran up with his extravagant lifestyle. Randolph had a lavish flat in Westminster Gardens, threw champagne parties at Claridge's, and took yacht cruises in the Caribbean and the Mediterranean. In 1933 Winston set up a trust fund for Randolph of £10,000 (the equivalent of one million dollars in today's money.) A little more than a year later Randolph had to ask his father and his uncle Jack to advance him £6,000 to cover his gambling debts, including almost £2,000 owed to a casino in Cannes. Both men made him sign an agreement never to gamble beyond his means again. Yet later he and his father could be seen together at the baccarat tables along the Riviera.[71]

The understanding was that if Randolph married and had children, Chartwell would be his. But Randolph's busy social agenda in the 1930s did not allow for marriage, let alone character-building adventures like Winston's in India and the Boer War.[72] It did not occur to Winston that their relationship reproduced his own with *his* father—or that whereas Lord Randolph had mercifully died before Winston was twenty, Randolph Junior could never hope to escape the aura of his famous dad.

Others, even enemies, recognized the difficult relationship and sympathized. If many found Winston arrogant, they found his son odious. When Randolph had to have a benign tumor removed from his alimentary canal, Evelyn Waugh's reaction was typical. "Trust those damn fool doctors," he said, "to cut out of Randolph the only part of him that is not malignant."[73]

The kindest analysis came from a political opponent, Lord Londonderry. He warned Winston that Randolph was "so like you" in his "enterprise, courage, and forcefulness" but was clearly unlike his father "because he does not seem to recognize that knowledge is the secret of power."[74] Someone once asked Winston how long it took him to prepare a forty-five-minute speech for the House of Commons. "Eighteen hours," he said.[75] That kind of application was beyond Randolph (and most people). It doomed any relationship between a son and a father who was still, after half a century, "a young man in a hurry."

But if some old friends and guests were no longer in Winston's orbit, his battle against appeasement brought him new ones. The last myth is that in the Wilderness Years Churchill stood alone against appeasement. The truth was that his name, reputation, and fearless speeches made him the standard-bearer for a growing number of people who were convinced, with Churchill, that "surely it is worth a supreme effort…to control the hideous drift and arrest calamity upon the threshold… NOW is the time to stop it!"[76]

Chartwell and Morpeth Mansions (where Winston and Clementine kept their London flat) became this group's gathering places. One gatheree was Desmond Morton, the Industrial Intelligence Center number-cruncher who sweated German military preparations as much as Churchill. Two others were Sir Robert Vansittart and Ralph Wigram of the Foreign Office. Wigram, whom Churchill called "the departmental volcano," was a victim of infantile paralysis but still came out to Chartwell to supply Churchill with full texts of all Hitler's speeches until his own untimely death in 1936.

Another visitor in those years was G. D. Birla. In fact, even as Hitler's shadow lengthened across Europe, India was never far from Churchill's mind. He worried about the rise of Japan in Asia and the possible threat to India. The days when he had blithely claimed that "there was not slightest chance" of war with Japan were long gone. "One must consider" Germany and Japan, he told his wife in January 1936, "as working in accord." (He made this remark fully four years before Japan, Germany, and Italy signed their Axis Pact.)[77]

The following April he confided similar fears to Birla. "You should certainly consider the present state of the world," he wrote. "If Great Britain were persuaded or forced for any cause, Indian or European, to withdraw her protection from India, it would continuously become the prey of Fascist dictator nations, Italy, Germany, or Japan," and suffer under a tyranny "even worse than any experienced in bygone ages."[78] Churchill thought this a powerful argument for Indians to stick close to Britain. Birla knew Indians had other things to worry about, but in July 1937 he did agree to go out for another lunch at Chartwell.

They spoke for two hours. "Well, a big experiment has begun," Churchill asserted, meaning the new Indian constitution. Birla agreed but added that it needed "all your sympathy and good wishes."

Churchill swore that Indians had them, adding that he had not said a word against the India Act since the king had signed it. He hoped for the best for India. "You know how democracy is attacked around the world," Churchill said ominously. "It is only Great Britain that has preserved democracy, and if you can show by your actions that you can make democracy a success, you will have no difficulty in advancing further."

Again Birla urged him to come to India and see for himself. Churchill conceded that the viceroy, Lord Linlithgow, had invited him. "But if Mr. Gandhi also desires it," he said lightly, "I will go." He certainly had great respect for Gandhi, he told Birla: "Tell him that I wish him all success."

Then they spoke of Europe, and Churchill's mood darkened. "For one more year he did not expect war," Birla told Gandhi later, "but he would not say about the far future."[79]

Contributing to Churchill's gloom that spring was the fate of Philip Cunliffe-Lister, Lord Swinton. He was minister of air and had shared valuable data with Churchill about Germany's growing air force. Swinton had fought hard, if in vain, to compel Britain to close the widening gap with the Luftwaffe. Finally in March 1938 Chamberlain again vetoed Swinton's plans for expanding the Royal Air Force, whereupon the peer announced he had no choice but to resign. The one remaining cabinet voice for rearmament had been silenced. He joined Churchill's growing band of dissidents in the House of Commons.[80]

The most spectacular resignation, and the most important conversion to Churchill's cause, came a month before that. Anthony Eden bore a superficial resemblance to Randolph: he was slim and handsome, with a broad forehead and a full head of hair. But he was also graceful, cool, and poised with a keen intelligence. He might have been the son that Winston wished for (and later he would address Eden as if he were his son). Certainly Eden was the glamorous rising star of the Tory party in the 1930s.

He had become foreign secretary at only thirty-eight, standing firm with his party against Churchill on India and supporting its policy toward Germany and Italy. He had even been an early user of the term "appeasement" in a *positive* sense—conceding dictators' reasonable claims in hopes that they would abandon their unreasonable ones.[81] But year by year Eden watched the opposite happen. Hesitant to conclude that Churchill had been right, he could no longer escape the fact that Chamberlain, Halifax, and the rest had been wrong.

The critical moment came not over Hitler but over Mussolini. In early 1938 Prime Minister Neville Chamberlain was eager to reopen negotiations with Italy in hopes that Mussolini might provide some counterweight against Hitler. Given the dictator's previous betrayal of promises to Britain—over Abyssinia and Italian troops in Spain—the gambit was ignoble if not entirely unpromising. Eden, however, had been at the receiving end of those worthless promises. He told the cabinet in Chamberlain's presence that he could not support such a policy in the House of Commons. The cabinet voted to support Chamberlain, and on February 21 Anthony Eden resigned as foreign secretary.

It was a serious step, the first major break in the appeasement phalanx. Churchill hurried down to the House of Commons to deliver a speech. "This has been a good week for dictators," Winston declared. "It is one of the best they have ever had." Not only was Hitler consolidating his power over Austria, but Mussolini had seen his fiercest foe removed from the Chamberlain cabinet. "What price have we all to pay for this?" Churchill asked.[82]

The answer came at the end of April. It was Czechoslovakia.

Chapter Twenty-two

EDGE OF DARKNESS
1938–1939

Non-violence to be worth anything has to work in the face of hostile forces.
MOHANDAS K. GANDHI, JANUARY 1937

CZECHOSLOVAKIA IN 1938 WAS PROBABLY THE optimal place to finally put the brakes on Hitler's ambitions. It had a formal defense treaty with France and Russia. It had an effective army—perhaps even better than Germany's. Except for its three million Sudeten Germans, it had no nationalist sympathies with Germany as Austria did. And unlike Austria before the Anschluss, it was still a democracy. Czech president Edvard Beneš was also prepared to mobilize for war rather than allow Hitler to grab an inch of Czech territory.

But if the Czechs were prepared to fight, the French and British governments were not. Prime Minister Chamberlain was neither a weakling nor a dupe. He possessed a stronger streak of realism than Lord Halifax, who replaced Eden as foreign secretary.[1] But if Halifax was the architect of appeasement, Chamberlain was its buyer. Like anyone who has paid a high price for a dubious commodity, Chamberlain had set aside all doubts about its value. And by the end of summer in 1938 even Halifax was having his misgivings about a policy of endless accommodation. He had learned that what worked with Gandhi bred only disaster with a man like Hitler.[2]

But Chamberlain was still a believer. It was he who had resolutely stood in the way of Churchill entering the cabinet—precisely because Churchill had lambasted the principles that Chamberlain still hoped would bring peace. It was Chamberlain who insisted on going to Germany to see Hitler "as the best means of reaching agreement" over

Czechoslovakia, even though many in his cabinet, including Halifax, thought it a bad idea.[3]

It was Chamberlain who convinced the French to abandon their alliance with the Czechs (not, it must be admitted, a difficult task). It was Chamberlain, not Hitler, who strong-armed President Beneš into allowing his country to be dismantled. And it was Chamberlain who put his signature to a final agreement on September 30 that would bring shame to Great Britain and, instead of creating "peace for our time" as Chamberlain promised on the field at Heston, move the world one major step closer to war.

All this became clear when the Munich agreement was debated in Parliament on October 3. Labour's leader Clement Attlee called it a "humiliation" and "a victory for brute force." The Liberals' Archibald Sinclair called it a "surrender." Anthony Eden, now sitting on Churchill's side of the Tory benches, warned, "Successive surrenders bring only successive humiliation."[4]

But Churchill's speech on October 5 surpassed them all. It was a towering masterpiece of deconstruction. Just the day before he had written in the *Daily Telegraph,* "It is a crime to despair ... It is the hour, not for despair, but for courage and re-building." His speech on the floor of the House spared no one.

"We are in the presence of a disaster of the first magnitude," he proclaimed. "Do not let us blind ourselves to that." Blame for an unbroken decade of retreat sat squarely on the shoulders of Baldwin, Chamberlain, and the other leaders of the National Government. "They neither prevented Germany from rearming, nor did they rearm ourselves in time," he said. Now "the system of alliances in Central Europe upon which France has relied for her safety has been swept away ... The road down the Danube Valley to the Black Sea, the resources of corn and oil, the road which leads as far as Turkey, has been opened." He might have added: even the road to India.

He had noted the jubilant celebrations and did not begrudge the British people "the natural, spontaneous outburst of joy and relief." But they "should know that we have sustained a defeat without a war, the consequences of which will travel far with us along our road; they should know we have passed an awful milestone in our history." Churchill warned with solemn emphasis that "the terrible words have for the time being been pronounced against the Western democracies: *Thou art weighed in the balance and found wanting.*"[5]

Six months before, a speech like this from Churchill would have drawn jeers and catcalls. This one did not. For the first time in nearly a decade his words had the weight of credibility. He did not yet realize it, but Churchill was on his way back, although for now, he could only focus on the magnitude of the setback. The day Chamberlain left for Munich, Churchill and Harold Nicolson had met at the elevator at Morpeth Mansions.

"This is hell," Nicolson remarked, referring to the news that Chamberlain would beg for one more deal.

Churchill's response was: "This is the end of the British Empire."[6]

The news from Munich hit two men in India like a thunderclap, but they reacted in very different ways.

One was Gandhi. "Peace has been preserved but at the price of honor," he wrote from Delhi on October 4. He had been on his way to the Northwest Frontier to meet with the Pathan followers of Khan Abdul Ghaffar Khan when he learned what Chamberlain had done. "Europe has sold her soul for the sake of a seven days' earthly existence," he wrote sadly.[7]

Forty-one-year-old Subhas Chandra Bose, by contrast, heard the news with grim satisfaction. "This abject surrender to Nazi Germany on the part of the Western Powers, France and Great Britain," he realized, had given Hitler control of Europe "without a shot being fired." Thanks to Munich and a host of other setbacks around the world, British and French imperialisms "have received a considerable setback." The time had come, he announced, for Indians to take advantage of it.[8]

Bose was no ordinary observer: he was now president of the Indian National Congress. He had lived in Europe, including in Vienna, and knew the players and stakes involved. Strikingly, he agreed with Churchill. The Western democracies *had* been found wanting. A great new force *was* stalking the world. But it was Bose's aim to make India part of it.

S. C. Bose—Netaji to his followers—was born the same year as Anthony Eden, in 1897. Intellectually precocious, he enjoyed academic success both at the Scottish Church College in Calcutta and at Cambridge. In 1920 he scored fourth in the examinations for the Indian Civil Service and was poised for a brilliant career there, perhaps the most brilliant of all. But he renounced it all to take up Indian nationalist politics, which by then meant Gandhi's politics.

The fiery, articulate Bose had chafed under Gandhi's leadership from the start. Their first meeting in Bombay was a disaster; then Bose came to resent that Gandhi and his inner circle sidelined his mentor, C. R. Das, the standard-bearer of the nationalist movement in Bengal.[9] Like Virginians in the early American republic, Bengalis saw themselves as the natural leaders of their nation. Thanks to the international renown of poet Rabindranath Tagore, they even claimed to be the leaders of Indian civilization. The presence of the Gujarati upstart* chafed their sense of innate superiority.[10] It certainly chafed Bose. Paradoxically, he also resented the close relations between the Mahatma and the heir presumptive, J. Nehru, even though he was actually closer ideologically to Nehru than Gandhi ever was. For a time in the early 1930s, Bose and Nehru had even been allies in trying to push the Congress in a more modern radical direction.

Both Nehru and Bose felt that India had no choice but to move forward into the industrial world, rather than back to Gandhi's idealized India of small villages and delicate handcrafts, so remote from the trends sweeping the rest of the world. Nehru believed that India's future lay in the Soviet Union. A four-day visit there in 1927 was all he needed to confirm his faith in Marxism as the solution to India's ills.[11] For Bose, the future lay with the emerging dictatorships of Germany and Italy. What Churchill feared most, the power of the totalitarian state, held a irresistible fascination for the young Bose.

Bose never thought of himself as a fascist. Instead, the term he used to describe himself when his book *The Indian Struggle* was published in 1934, was "left-wing nationalist."[12] Certain aspects of Nazism, such as its racial policies, repelled him. Nazis like Heinrich Himmler were fascinated by the ancient Indo-European link between India's Aryans and Germanic Europe. Even Gandhi had once appealed to it; it meant nothing to Bose. Nonetheless, his first visit to Germany came in 1933, when Hitler had begun his transformation of Germany from a broken bankrupt shell into the most feared nation in Europe. Bose met numerous German intellectuals; he met officials in the German Foreign Office. He

---

* Nirad Chaudhuri would remember that Bengali nationalists of his acquaintance dismissed Gandhi as a *napumsaka,* a Bengali word for an unmanly schmuck: "a dud, in fact."

even met Hitler's right-hand man Hermann Göring. Those encounters left an aura that years of disappointment and disillusionment never quite dispelled. They also opened a tantalizing window on a future alliance against the British Empire.

A little later someone asked Bose how he could contemplate forging a connection with thugs like the Nazis, but he only shrugged. "It is dreadful but it must be done," he replied. If that was the only way to get rid of the British, he was prepared to pay any price. Even "the collapse of Europe," he said, was fine with him: "It is a rotten Europe and therefore does not concern me." Two years later he horrified Romain Rolland by saying that for nonwhite peoples seeking their freedom, war between the European powers would be not an unmixed evil.[13]

Bose made a second trip to Europe from November 1937 to January 1938, meeting Mussolini as well as German and Austrian politicians. He came back to India determined to set the nation alight. His vision was of mobilizing the masses for the "complete political and economic liberation" of India. His encounters with Europe's new leaders had revealed to him the path to the future, as he described it in *The Indian Struggle*.

According to Bose, a truly free India would be able to use a "strong Central government with dictatorial powers" to reorganize its social and economic structure. It would reject "democracy in the mid-Victorian sense of the term" and instead allow itself to be led by "a strong party bound together by military discipline, as the only means of holding India together and preventing chaos." Bose condemned Gandhi's hopes for a self-sufficient Swaraj India as hopelessly parochial and out-of-date. "The next phase of world history will produce a synthesis of Communism and Fascism," Bose predicted, and he wanted India to be part of it.[14]

The Indian Struggle was Bose's *Mein Kampf*. The British banned it the moment it hit the streets in India, but it made Bose an instant hero with young Indian radicals who resented the leadership of Gandhi's aging inner circle. Bose had boldly stated that "Congress has no role to play" in India's future because it lacked a coherent ideology or revolutionary program. Like Gandhi himself, it was part of the late Victorian clutter that the coming clash of world forces would sweep aside.

Yet Gandhi had also made the Congress the principal vehicle of political power in India. Bose could do nothing without it—or indeed without Gandhi's support. And so with the help of his fellow Bengali nationalists, he made himself a candidate for its presidency in 1938.

The Old Guard had deep doubts about Bose; then and later R. Prasad and others worried about his Nazi connections. But Gandhi overrode them. Officially, he was out of Congress politics, but the tradition was that he nominate the next president of the Congress, who was then elected by unanimous vote.[15] He had nominated Nehru as president in 1936 and 1937 to be the voice of the next generation. At the Haripuri Congress in February 1938 he did the same for Bose.

Bose's first presidential speech might have forced Gandhi to wonder if he had made a mistake. The thousands of delegates from across India heard Bose speak of a law of empires that governed the rise, expansion, and decline of great powers. Such a law had brought doom to Rome, he said, and then to Turkey and Russia in 1917. Now that moment of doom, he averred, hovered over the British Empire.

"The British Empire at the present moment is suffering strain at a number of points," Bose pointed out, and not only in India. It was February 1938: Palestine, Egypt, Iraq, and the Far East were all in turmoil. "How long can the British Empire withstand the cumulative effect of this pressure and strain?" he asked the assembled delegates. The answer was, not long. "The clay feet of a gigantic empire now stand exposed as they never have before."

"This interplay of world forces" worked to India's advantage, Bose argued. "Ours is a vast country" with a huge population; it was on the verge of doing great things. But it could fulfill that destiny only by severing its connection to a crumbling Britain, which still tried to impose its atrophying will over 300 million human beings through its scheme for Dominion and Federation. "The ultimate stage in our progress," Bose stated, "will be the severance of the British connection." Bose wanted Congress to be more than the party of Swaraj. He saw it as the party of power in the future. A new disciplined Congress would take over the administration and the economy and launch a program of social reconstruction. "Only then will it fulfill its role."

He urged the Congress to look to Europe, where the only countries that saw "orderly and continuous progress" were those "where the party which seized power" undertook the task of governing. What the Brown Shirts were in Germany, and the Black Shirts in Italy, Bose saw Congress becoming in India.[16]

It was a forlorn hope; Bose would be as disappointed by the sheer normality of his fellow Congressmen as Gandhi was, and for some of the same reasons. Congress politicians were no more interested in Bose's version of mass party discipline than they had been in Gandhi's. They desired office and influence. They were getting both under the new constitution. The year of Bose's presidency saw a strange disconnection between the leaders and the led. In the provinces and cities Congress members settled into their roles as councilors and administrators. They began pushing (with Gandhi's encouragement) India's princely states to open the corridors of power to Congress methods and candidates. A quiet revolution was taking place, as Indians assumed more and more control over their country, with the Congress taking the lead.

But at the center, inside the Working Committee, a battle royal of wills and personalities was being fought. Bose wanted the Congress to pull out of any and all constitutional arrangements and force the British to an ultimatum. The Old Guard Gandhians on the committee did not. At the end of the year Gandhi was forced to step in.

Privately, Bose's ideological program appalled him, although he did not challenge Bose in public. It contained painful echoes of the arrogant ultra-nationalist Reader in *Hind Swaraj*. Gandhi was also upset that the Bengali Bose was trying to force out the elected Muslim government in his home province. The loss of Bengal to the forces of Islam had been a bitter pill for Bengali Hindus.[17] Gandhi saw Bose creating more trouble for Congress's already strained relations with India's Muslims.

In 1938 Gandhi also sharply disapproved of Bose's push for a showdown with the British. "I do not like your constant threats about Federation and ultimatum," Gandhi wrote to him. "The idea of ultimatum is in my opinion premature." But Gandhi added self-effacingly, "It is the voice of a dying man who speaks," and "responsibility is not mine but yours for shaping the national destiny."[18] When the time came for nominating the next president, some thought Bose would be the best choice, but instead Gandhi named Dr. Pattabhi Sitaramayya, a relative newcomer.[19]

The Bose forces exploded. Bose learned that several provinces had already renominated him for the presidency. He saw no reason why he should not run for reelection. "It is no use having a democratic constitution for the Congress," he said, "if the delegates do not have the freedom to think and vote as they like."[20] His public defiance of Gandhi was unprecedented. A bruising contest of wills unfolded at the Congress meeting at the end of January 1939, with angry speeches, shouting, and shoves and insulting gestures. Gandhi mobilized all his supporters, including a reluctant Nehru, to line up against Bose's reelection. Bose struck back, accusing both Gandhi and Nehru of bad faith. It was a crisis of the first magnitude. Never since 1924 had Gandhi's personal prestige been so much on the line.

The final tally came on January 29. Delegates on both sides were stunned when Bose emerged the winner. Gandhi's handpicked candidate lost by more than two thousand votes. The Mahatma acknowledged that his enemies had won a "decisive victory" not only over Sitaramayya but over himself. "The defeat," as he put it, "is more mine than his."

Nonetheless, he courteously if coldly congratulated Bose on his success; "after all, Subhas Babu is not an enemy of the country." He added that those who could not fully support Bose and his program should probably leave the Congress. Then he picked up his parcel of belongings and left.[21]

To many of the delegates, it seemed a gesture of surrender. In fact, it proved Bose's undoing. Bose had won the election but had lost any support from the Working Committee, most of whose members were Gandhi supporters. Bose did not help matters by accusing them of striking a secret deal with the British to accept the Government of India Bill.[22] On February 22 twelve out of fifteen members of the Working Committee quit, saying they would work with Bose no longer.

To his fury, Bose found himself outmaneuvered by the old man he underestimated as a relic of the past. Gandhi "has done me more harm than the activities of the 12 stalwarts" on the Working Committee, Bose raged to a relative.[23] He and his Bengali supporters set off for the Congress session at Tripuri in March for a final stand.

For a week they sparred with opponents, as Jawaharlal Nehru assumed more and more the role of Gandhi's champion against Bose. In the end the Bengalis realized that their position was hopeless. Nirad Chaudhuri remembered Subhas's brother Sarat returning to Calcutta afterward, looking ill and haggard: "I could see what he had gone through for the sake of his brother."[24] Subhas really did become ill. His health broke down, as it frequently did in a crisis, and he left Tripur for a month to nurse his body—and his anger.

At the end of April 1939 Bose resigned as Congress president. Gandhi had won. But like Jinnah, Bose was now resolved to take unilateral action. Within days he announced the formation of his own political party, the Forward Bloc, to carry on his struggle. "Give me blood, and I will give you freedom," he would later tell his followers. "The latest phase of Gandhism with its sanctimonious hypocrisy," he would also write, "its outrage on democracy...is sickening. One is forced to wonder which is a greater menace to India's political future—the British bureaucracy or Gandhian hierarchy."[25] Bose's struggle against both Gandhi and the British was just beginning.

Gandhi, however, remained aloof and unconcerned. He had already moved on to his next cause. In late February he went to Rajkot for his "princely satyagraha." V. Patel had convinced him that integrating India's remaining princely states with their movement would be a crucial way to expand the Congress's political base—and to thwart Bose's chances of doing the same.

Five hundred and thirty-two separate principalities still governed nearly a third of India. From the biggest (like Hyderabad and Kashmir) to the tiniest (some no larger than a few square miles), they had posed no threat to the Raj since the Mutiny. But they did threaten Indian nationalism, since without their rulers' cooperation no federation, no true Indian unity, was possible.

Thus far the princely states had been untouched by the larger currents of Indian politics. But "if the [princely] States persist in their obstinacy and hug their ignorance of the awakening that has taken place throughout India," Gandhi warned the previous September, "they are courting disaster."[26] Now he arrived in his former home state of Rajkot to try to bring them on board.

More than sixty years earlier Gandhi's father had come to Rajkot to serve its ruler as diwan. Now the son came to dictate terms to the ruler. Unless its prince or *thakur* permitted Congress members to take up posts as local officials, Gandhi said, he would conduct a fast. The decision was an entirely spiritual one, he claimed, but shrewdly warned the viceroy what was about to happen.

In 1939 Lord Linlithgow could no more afford a dead Gandhi than he could an India in full revolt. So with the help of the Chief Justice of India, the viceroy arranged a compromise with the wretched prince. Gandhi called off his fast, although many followers felt betrayed and that once again he had accepted a compromise that ignored their months-long efforts.[27]

It was Gandhi's second victory in three months as well as his last prewar satyagraha. Both victories revealed a new impatience, even ruthlessness, in a man approaching his seventieth birthday. After fending off the

Bose threat, he had come back into politics with a vengeance. Later he admitted that the threat of a "fast unto death" had been coercive and had not been conducted with the true satyagraha goal of converting his opponent.

But at seventy, his time was running out, as was his patience. "I have become old, I lose my temper," he confessed to an old friend exactly a year before. "I am not prepared to listen to anyone on anything." Jinnah, Bose, and Churchill: henceforth they would take him on at their own risk.[28]

On March 7, 1939, Gandhi formally broke his fast. One week later German tanks rolled into Prague.

Winston Churchill was sitting in the smoking room of the House of Commons with Anthony Eden when the evening papers brought them the news from the Czech capital. It was just six months after Hitler had signed his agreement with Chamberlain, pledging that Germany had no more territorial demands. "Even those who, like us, had no illusions," Churchill wrote afterward in his *Gathering Storm,* "were surprised at the sudden violence of this outrage."[29]

In Prague sullen, silent crowds watched as German troops marched through the streets, while church bells tolled the death of their country. Within days the Republic of Czechoslovakia, the last self-governing republic in Eastern Europe, was replaced by a Nazi protectorate. The rounding up of Jews would begin shortly afterward, just as it had in Austria.

Finally and much too late Chamberlain seemed to awaken from the fog of appeasement. "Who can fail to feel his heart go out in sympathy to the proud, brave people who have suddenly been subjected to this invasion," he told a crowd in Birmingham on March 17. "Is this in fact a step in the direction of an attempt to dominate the world by force?" Chamberlain asked. If so, he concluded, then it was "one which the Democracies must resist."[30]

The government took the first tentative steps to show it meant business. It recalled the British ambassador from Berlin. At the end of April it introduced a limited draft for the army. However, if Chamberlain wanted to make his new defiant stand more credible, the person he needed at his side was Winston Churchill.

For the past five months Churchill had been steadily hammering away at the government without effect. After the fall of Prague the public finally began to listen. "British opinion was stirred as it had not been by the absorption of Austria or the capitulation at Munich," historian Alan Taylor has written. Churchill and his stalwarts had warned that Hitler's ambitions were insatiable and could not be stopped except by threat of armed force. "Like water dropping on a stone, their words suddenly broke through the crust of credulity."[31]

Churchill received telegrams of support, as if he had won a great victory. A Liberal candidate for North Cornwall told him that in every one of his speeches he was saying that the man Britain needed for prime minister was Winston Churchill. It took a few minutes "for the idea to sink in," T. L. Horabin wrote, and then invariably "there was an outburst of applause."[32]

Very slowly and steadily over the spring and summer, a wave of public sentiment began to gather. It carried one message: Bring Winston into the cabinet. On April 22 the *Evening News* suggested him for either the Admiralty or secretary of state for air. When the new Military Training Act resulted in a minor cabinet shakeup, "There was much disappointment on both sides of the House," the *British Weekly* reported, "that the changes in the Cabinet did not include such outstanding figures as Mr. Winston Churchill and Mr. Anthony Eden."[33]

In May the *News Chronicle* reported that 56 percent of poll respondents wanted Churchill in the cabinet. By June it became clear that the next confrontation with Hitler was coming, this time over Poland and Danzig. The clamor to bring Churchill on board became almost deafening, with the *Evening Standard,* the *Daily Mail,* and *The Spectator* all joining in.

No one, with the possible exception of Mr Horabin, had seen Churchill as a potential war leader, let alone prime minister. Conventional wisdom had simply crystallized around the notion that putting Churchill in the Admiralty or the Air Ministry would show Hitler that Britons were finally, really serious about halting aggression. It would "send a message" that could not be missed—or so people hoped. A leading German minister in Hitler's cabinet wanted the same message and secretly communicated that wish to an official in the Foreign Office. "Churchill is the only Englishman Hitler is afraid of," the German was reported to say. "The mere fact of giving him a leading ministerial post would convince Hitler that [the English] really meant to stand up to him."[34]

Most still hoped that Britain might avoid war somehow, by making the right statements or sending the right signals. If Churchill was aware of such hopes, however, he did not care. He predicted that Poland would be the next hot spot (not a difficult guess) and was furiously trying to assess the state of British readiness as if he were already in the cabinet. Harold Nicolson caught him buttonholing the Russian ambassador in the Commons smoking room and heard him growl, "Now look here, Mr. Ambassador, if we are to make a success of this new policy, we require the help of Russia."[35] Meanwhile old friends like Reggie Barnes from the Boer War days were sending him letters and telegrams, stating baldly, "England owes you many apologies."[36]

Winston, sensing that the capricious winds of public opinion were shifting in his direction, wanted to communicate to the men he had excoriated as spineless appeasers that he was willing to let bygones be bygones. That magnanimity even extended as far as India, as Churchill himself hinted in a speech at the 1900 Club on June 21. The guest of honor was Lord Halifax, and Churchill was happy to speak on the exviceroy's behalf. "If differences remain," he told the assembled members, gesturing toward the former viceroy, "they will only be upon emphasis and method, upon timing and degree." He might have been referring to dealing with the Indian Congress or to Hitler; in Churchill's forgiving mind, it no longer mattered.[37]

The threat of war drew closer. By July 1939 even cabinet members, especially the younger ones, were urging Chamberlain to bring Churchill on board. But he still refused. "Winston Churchill's nomination to the Cabinet," he told friends as early as April, "would send a message of open warfare to Berlin." Chamberlain had served with Churchill since the 1920s; he had seen his bold, reckless plans go awry at the Exchequer and during the General Strike. "If you did not agree with him," Chamberlain confessed to Lord Camrose on July 3, "he was liable to lose his temper and a number of his colleagues had found that the easier way was not to oppose him," with disastrous results. Chamberlain was determined not to repeat earlier mistakes. Besides, Chamberlain told Camrose, "I have not yet given up hopes of peace."[38] Chamberlain clung to that forlorn hope even after Hitler and Stalin signed their nonaggression pact on August 26, securing Germany's eastern flank, and even as German panzers massed on the Polish frontier on August 31.

Churchill, meanwhile, was feverishly preparing for war more conscientiously than the government was. To clear the decks, in a prodigious feat of concentration and endurance, he virtually finished his *History of the English-Speaking Peoples*. Over the tense summer its theme had bucked him up: "the growth of freedom and law, of the rights of the individual, of the subordination of the State to the fundamental and moral conceptions of an ever-comprehending community." They were the principles at stake in the coming fight, Churchill felt. And "of these ideas the English-speaking peoples were the authors, then the trustees, and must now become the armed champions," as he wrote to his assistant Maurice Ashley.[39]

In August he made a final visit to France, to inspect its Maginot Line defenses and meet various French commanders in chief. He and a friend took a break to do some painting at Dreux. That same day 375 members of the staff of every British university signed an appeal to the *Times* asking Chamberlain to put Churchill in the government.

On the other side of the Channel, Winston and his friend Paul Maze painted silently side by side. The sun was bright and warm, the air breathtakingly clear. In Europe the summer of 1939 was one of the most beautiful in years. Churchill remarked, "This is the last picture we shall paint in peace for a very long time."

He made some more brushstrokes, squinting with his usual concentration. Then he said, "They are strong, I tell you, they are strong," referring to the Germans. A few more brushstrokes, and then Churchill's jaw clenched in determination, his cigar bristling. "Ah," he said in a deep growl, "with it all, we shall have them."[40]

Churchill returned to England a couple of days later. At eight-thirty on the morning of September 1 the Polish ambassador phoned Chartwell to tell Winston that the German invasion had begun. At ten Churchill phoned General Edmund Ironside at the War Office. "They've started," Churchill said. "Warsaw and Cracow are being bombed now." That afternoon he drove down to London.

There the War Office had ordered full mobilization starting at two o'clock. The House of Commons was to meet at six. At Chamberlain's request Churchill stopped at Number 10 for a quick meeting. Chamberlain said: "The die is cast." He intended, he said, to create a War Cabinet of Ministers without departments; he asked Winston to join it. Winston instantly agreed and hurried off to the House of Commons.[41]

All that night and the next day Churchill waited for the final summons, pacing back and forth in the Commons smoking room. Sir Maurice Hankey caught sight of him holding forth in a circle of his cronies. "He was brimful of ideas, some good, others not so good," Hankey wrote the next day. "I only wish he didn't give one the impression that he does himself too well!" But even Hankey admitted that Churchill's presence was "heartening and big."

Hour by hour Churchill paced back and forth, "like a lion in a cage," his secretary Mrs. Hill remembered. He was expecting a call; but the call never came.[42]

At the last minute Chamberlain had lost his nerve. Even as German Stukas were pounding Polish airfields and German panzers were driving deep into Poland, Chamberlain announced to the House of Commons that night that "if the German Government should agree to withdraw their forces, then His Majesty's Government would be willing to regard the position as being the same" as if no attack had occurred at all.

Appeasement was making its last stand. The House was appalled. "There was no doubt that the temper of the House was for war," Churchill remembered later. "I deemed it even more resolute and united than in the similar scene on August 3, 1914, in which I had also taken part."[43] Everyone sat in disbelief that Chamberlain was making one last futile gesture to halt the inevitable.

Then a single figure sprang to his feet. It was not Churchill but his old antagonist over India, Leopold Amery. They had been to school together, and in South Africa. They had clashed over free trade (Amery was a devout imperial protectionist) and over the Empire and India— and they would clash again. Privately, Amery considered Churchill a reckless anachronism, a relic from a defunct Whiggish past who would do Britain more harm than good.

But Amery had also stood foursquare against appeasement and, in spite of himself, had even cheered some of Churchill's furious antigovernment speeches. Now, listening to Chamberlain's diffident droning voice explain once again why it was best to do nothing, Amery could stand it no longer. As Arthur Greenwood rose to speak for the Labour Opposition, Amery suddenly burst out:

"Speak for England!"

A stunned silence, then deafening cheers broke out on all sides. With three simple words Amery had saved the situation—and saved Winston Churchill's career. Just before midnight Chamberlain met with his cabinet again. "I never heard the Prime Minister so disturbed," Halifax recalled. The cabinet agreed, including Halifax and Sir John Simon, that there could be no more equivocation.[44] Britain issued one final ultimatum (the last of three) to Germany asking it to stop the attack on Poland. When it became clear that Germany would not, at eleven-fifteen on September 3 a reluctant and dispirited Chamberlain announced to the British nation that they were at war.

After his speech air raid sirens sounded all across London—the first of many for the next five years. Churchill went up onto the roof of Morpeth Mansions to see "what was going on," as he wrote later. To his pleasure and surprise, thirty or forty antiaircraft barrage balloons were already lifting their heads up "in the clear, cool September sunlight." Then, "armed with a bottle of brandy and other appropriate medical comforts," he and Clementine headed for the bomb shelter down the street.[45]

"A very strong sense of calm came over me," he said as he sat in the House of Commons later that evening. Chamberlain announced to resounding cheers, "I hope I may live to see the day when Hitlerism is destroyed."* Then, after Labour and Liberal leaders had their turn, Churchill spoke.

"We must not underrate the gravity of the task which lies before us," he said, "or the severity of the ordeal, to which we shall not be found unequal.

> This is not a question of fighting for Danzig or fighting for Poland. We fight to save the whole world from the pestilence of Nazi tyranny and in defense of all that is most sacred in man. This is no war of domination or imperial aggrandizement or material gain; no war to shut any country out of its sunlight and means of progress. It is a war...to establish on impregnable rocks, the rights of the individual, and it is a war to establish and revive the stature of man.

Afterward, Leo Amery admitted to his diary: "I think I see Winston emerging as PM out of it all by the end of the year."[46]

By now Churchill knew what his post in Chamberlain's cabinet would be: First Lord of the Admiralty, the same as in 1914. That afternoon the signal went out to the entire British fleet: "Winston's back."

---

* He did not live to see it. He died a broken man on November 9, 1940, in the darkest hours of the Blitz.

Duff Cooper's wife Diana accompanied him as he drove down to Admiralty House in the early evening.

As they turned the corner at the Horse Guards Parade, they came upon roll after roll of concertina barbed wire in front of the Admiralty. The instant war was declared, the wire had gone up all around Whitehall as a security precaution. The sight, however, startled Churchill's companion.

"Great God!" Diana Cooper exclaimed. "What's *that* for?"

Churchill smiled and then growled, "That's to keep me out."[47]

Then the sentries recognized their new first lord, saluted, and waved them through. In a moment the car pulled up at the front door, where his secretary Kathleen Hill was waiting for him. She went with him as he strode into the First Lord's Room and watched as he eased himself into the same chair he had last occupied twenty-four years before.

In the paneling behind the desk was a cupboard. Winston suddenly stood up and flung the door open with a dramatic gesture. There behind the paneling was a large map still showing the location of all German ships in the North Sea on the day he left the Admiralty in 1915—as if frozen in time.

"Once again we must fight for life and honor against all the might and fury of the valiant, disciplined, and ruthless German race," he thought to himself. "Once again! So be it."[48]

He was wrong. This war would be very different from its predecessor, far more complicated and destructive. Unlike the last one it would reach to the farthest ends of the British Empire, even to India. In fact, at almost that very moment, at the Viceregal Lodge in Simla, a man was signing his name to a document that would hurl that side of the world into turmoil and trigger a chain of events that sent Churchill into his final confrontation with his old adversary, Mahatma Gandhi.

Chapter Twenty-three

COLLISION COURSE
1939–1940

The word "defeat" is not in my vocabulary.

MOHANDAS K. GANDHI, 1940

VICTOR ALEXANDER JOHN HOPE, SECOND MARQUESS of Linlithgow, did not look like a man who was about to change history. A shy, tall, and lean Scot, he had suffered from polio as a child.* He was in India not to open a dialogue with Indian nationalists, as Lord Irwin had done, nor to preserve the status quo, as Lord Willingdon had done. Rather, he had been sent out in April 1936 to make the new Indian constitution work.

In a sense, the constitution was his brainchild. As chairman of the Select Committee, he had painted its broader strokes—and in the process fought fiercely with Churchill. Far from being a hard-liner, Linlithgow saw a British-sponsored federation as the last best hope of keeping India in the empire. For three tiresome years he had struggled with the problems that the Government of India Act had not addressed: the communal problem; the issue of what to do about the princely states; and the battle over whether the Indian National Congress should accept offices in the various provinces and if so under what conditions. Gandhi had helped him solve the last one. Their discussions had led Linlithgow to take a liking to the Mahatma, whom he found "attractive and extremely shrewd," even though "I judge him to be implacable in his hostility to British rule in India."[1]

But the other issues seemed almost beyond human solution, or at least a British solution. "The more I reflect upon the political situation as a

---

* Later he would point out that he and fellow polio sufferer Franklin D. Roosevelt were responsible for the lives of more human beings than any other leaders on earth.

whole," he confessed to his secretary of state, Lord Zetland, "the more impressed I am by the importance of achieving Federation as early as possible." He was the first, but not the last, viceroy to sense that the Raj had become a ticking time bomb and that, except for Gandhi, all the principal parties—Jinnah, Nehru, Bose, even leading princes—were only waiting for an excuse to set it off, in hopes of building their own order out of the rubble.[2] He certainly never imagined that on September 3, 1939, he would be the one to give them that opportunity.

He had agreed with Zetland that if war in Europe came, he would issue a statement to the Legislative Assembly in New Delhi that a state of war also existed between India and Germany. There was no question of prior consultation with the various party leaders or a parliamentary vote. By law, if Britain went to war, so did India—automatically. Dominions like Australia (which declared war on the same day, September 3) and South Africa (on September 6) had a mechanism for consultation with elected ministers, but that would not exist in India until full federation, at least two years away.

Besides, Linlithgow knew that if he did ask for a vote, the Indian National Congress, which now governed eight of India's eleven provinces, would likely turn him down.[3] So the first notion Indians had that they were at war was when they heard the king speak on the BBC Overseas Service, followed by the viceroy's announcement that a state of war emergency now existed in India.

The accusation is often made that Linlithgow dragged Indians into war without their consent and that this "humiliation" poisoned British-Indian relations in the last years of the Raj. Some even suggest that Linlithgow's decision was a "fatal mistake."[4] In fact, there was no decision to make. Indeed, if anyone was to blame, it was Winston Churchill. For almost four years he had dragged out the battle over the India Act, delaying its implementation until 1937. Its first phase, that of handing over power in the provinces, had hardly been tested when war broke out. The Assembly had no consultative role because there was still no Indian federation. And with a war on, that situation was unlikely to change. Churchill had laid the grim foundations for what was to come—along with Gandhi.

Unlike other Indian leaders, in September 1939 Gandhi was very much "in the loop" on the issue of going to war. The day before Britain made its formal declaration, Linlithgow had sent a message to the Mahatma at Sevagram, who wrote back from the telegraph office at

Wardha. "SORRY TERRIBLE NEWS," Gandhi wired. "TAKING EARLIEST TRAIN. ARRIVING SIMLA FOURTH MORNING." That night he was hurtling along the tracks en route for the Viceregal Lodge.

"Terrible news." From Sevagram, Gandhi had watched the approach of war in Europe with deep foreboding. The rise of fascism had only confirmed his gloomy assessment of the terrible fate awaiting Western materialism. According to biographer Robert Payne, the betrayal at Munich had led him to the edge of a complete breakdown.[5] The one reed of hope that Gandhi clung to was that Europeans might discover the power of nonviolence before it was too late.

In 1938 he had urged the Czechs to use nonviolence against the Germans instead of bullets. He urged German Jews to do the same. "The Jews of Germany can offer Satyagraha under infinitely better auspices than Indians in South Africa," he wrote in *Harijan* on November 11, 1938. "They are more gifted than the Indians of South Africa." A "calm and determined stand offered by unarmed men and women" would turn their "winter of despair" into "a summer of hope," Gandhi felt. It would win the world's admiration and perhaps even that of the German people: "The German Jews will score a lasting victory over the German gentiles, in the sense that they will have converted the latter to an appreciation of human dignity."[6]

Gandhi even urged Jews to disarm their persecutors by praying for Hitler. "If even one Jew acted thus," he said confidently, "he would save his self-respect and leave an example which, if it became infectious, would save the whole of Jewry." Even his old friend Hermann Kallenbach had to demur. "[Hermann] wants to be non-violent" was Gandhi's explanation for their disagreement, "but the sufferings of his fellow Jews are too much to bear." Gandhi added, "I do not quarrel with him over his anger," but then he repeated the aphorism that "revenge is sweet, [but] forgiveness is divine."[7]

Even after the war, when the full extent of the Holocaust became known, Gandhi still felt that "the Jews should have offered themselves to the butcher's knife...They should have thrown themselves into the sea from cliffs...It would have aroused the world and the people of Germany...As it is they succumbed anyway in their millions."[8]

In the shadow of Treblinka and Auschwitz or even Kristallnacht, Gandhi's remarks seem extraordinary, even obscenely naïve. In the same vein, his ambivalent views on Hitler shocked even his supporters. On July 23, 1939, he had written an open letter to Hitler begging him to renounce violence. "It is clear that you are today the one person in the world who can prevent a war which may reduce humanity to the savage state," it read. "Will you listen to the appeal of one who has deliberately shunned the method of war?"[9]

Hitler, of course, did not. But that did not stop Gandhi from sending the dictator more letters in May and June 1940, or from telling Linlithgow that same month, "Hitler is not a bad man." As Hitler's panzers roared across France, Gandhi wrote that future generations of Germans would "honor Herr Hitler as a genius, as a brave man, as a matchless organizer and much more."[10] In his last missive to Hitler, written the day before Christmas 1941, Gandhi praised "your bravery [and] devotion to your fatherland...Nor do we believe that you are the monster described by your opponents"—one of the most vocal being Winston Churchill.

What could critics expect? At seventy, Gandhi was not about to change his mind on the moral imperative of ahimsa and the spiritual power of nonviolence. "Man may shed his own blood for establishing what he considers to be his 'right,'" Gandhi would write, but "he may not shed the blood of his opponent" for the same thing. For Gandhi, this was a cardinal rule.[11] This idea led him to one of his most famous maxims, uttered to a group of American clergymen: "To be truly nonviolent, I must love [my adversary] and pray for him even when he hits me." To Gandhi, this was not a formula for passivity or cowardice but the sublime expression of the highest form of courage. To others, however, it seemed an invitation to surrender.

A group of American Methodist missionaries met with Gandhi at Sevagram in December 1938, in the aftermath of Munich and the anti-Jewish riots of Kristallnacht. In Abyssinia the Italian army was using poison gas against recalcitrant tribesmen. Like other New Age Christians, the Americans deeply admired Gandhi but begged him to understand that nonviolence would be useless against ruthless dictators like Hitler and Mussolini and would actually play into their hands. "They are incapable of any moral response," one of them said. "They have no conscience and have made themselves impervious to world opinion."

In response, Gandhi was dismissive, almost contemptuous: "Your argument presupposes that men like Hitler and Mussolini are beyond redemption."[12] Gandhi never could accept such a final judgment against his fellow men, not even the worst of them. But what seemed reasonable and humane to Gandhi seemed daylight madness to others, and vice versa.

And of course in a sense, until now he had been lucky. He had never had to deal with a truly fanatical enemy like a Hitler or a Himmler, one for whom mass murder was a means to an end, and mass terror an end in itself. Had his own adversary been more ideologically driven, more fanatical, Gandhi's claim that "under non-violence only those would have been killed who had trained themselves to be killed" would have been reduced to vicious nonsense.

The truth was that the British in India, and even whites in South Africa, at least professed a set of consistent moral principles and an objective standard of justice to which Gandhi could effectively appeal. He had done so for more than forty years. What he himself had termed the "British sense of fair play" had saved him more than once. Whatever they thought of the Mahatma, Willingdon, Irwin, Reading, and Gandhi's other viceregal adversaries had lived according to the Christian-based moral temper of Churchill's "English-speaking peoples." Even General Dyer had been dismissed after Amritsar, not promoted as Stalin or Hitler might have done, and Yeravda was no gulag. Without this implicit moral contract between ruler and ruled, Gandhi's career as a nationalist leader would have been nasty, brutish, and short.*[13]

Paradoxically, Gandhi's spiritual strength was also his intellectual blind spot. A world without God was unimaginable to Gandhi, yet it was all around him. From his vantage point, Gandhi could see no fundamental difference between the values of the Raj and those of Hitler. Both in his mind were founded on violence or *himsa*.

Churchill, on the other hand, could and did. In a godless world Churchill clung to Western civilization as man's best hope because he took full measure of its alternatives both past and present. If Hitler won and Britain lost, he would say in his "Finest Hour" speech, "then the whole world, including the United States, including all we have known and cared for, will sink into the abyss of a new Dark Age, made more sinister, and more protracted, by the lights of perverted science."[14] He could perceive the disaster of totalitarian victory and democratic defeat in historical terms, not just moral ones. That perception gave him the

---

* Hitler had proposed a final solution for Britain's India problem to Lord Halifax when they met in 1938. "Shoot Gandhi," he told the startled ex-viceroy.

spiritual energy to summon an entire nation to oppose evil, much as Gandhi had summoned an entire nation to oppose the Raj.

Gandhi and Churchill had one other startling difference that biographers and historians often miss. Gandhi had the gift to see the goodness in all human beings, even in a Hitler. Churchill had the gift to see the evil, because he recognized that quality in himself. The man who denounced Hitler as dictator and murderer was also the one who ordered the firebombing of German cities. He was the prime minister who would order doctors to let Gandhi die in prison and allow millions of Indians to die of famine in 1943 rather than risk diverting the war effort.

At the same time however, Gandhi had no illusions about what Hitler represented, or the consequences of his triumph. His same Christmas letter in 1941 that praised Hitler's "bravery or devotion" said also that there "was no room for doubt that many of your acts are monstrous and unbecoming of human dignity." Nazism itself, Gandhi told his followers, was "naked, ruthless force reduced to an exact science and worked with scientific precision"—a startling echo of Churchill's words about National Socialism as "perverted science."[15] And on September 4, 1939, during his meeting with Viceroy Linlithgow, he and Churchill were on the same wavelength at last.

He and the viceroy spoke for two hours. The Mahatma stressed that he could speak only for himself and not for the Indian National Congress, but he pledged unconditional support to the British cause. "It almost seems as if Herr Hitler knows no God but brute force," Gandhi said, "and, as Mr. Chamberlain says, he will listen to nothing else."

Then Gandhi confessed that he contemplated war "with an English heart" and could not think of the destruction of London "without being stirred to the very depths" of his being. As the Mahatma conjured up the picture of Westminster Abbey and the Parliament buildings destroyed by German bombs, an astonished Linlithgow watched Gandhi drop his head and weep.[16]

It was an extraordinary moment. But like Gandhi's stand on nonviolence against the dictators, the emotion was consistent with a forty-year history. Gandhi had stood by the empire in 1899 and again in 1914. Despite a lifetime of disappointments, he was ready to do it a third time in 1939. His were tears that Winston Churchill, who himself wept easily and unashamedly, would have understood. If at that moment Churchill had been prime minister and could have summoned Gandhi to London, they might have struck an alliance as far-reaching and meaningful as anything later arranged with de Gaulle or Roosevelt. A great catastrophe could have been avoided, and perhaps a final friendship made.

But Churchill was not prime minister in 1939, and Linlithgow was no Churchill. He did not know how to respond, and the moment passed. So Gandhi wiped his eyes and again stressed that he had no right to speak for the nation. He left. Afterward he told the press that the final decision on India's support for the war, "this terrible drama," was up to the Congress, which meant Jawaharlal Nehru.[17]

Nehru had groomed himself as Gandhi's heir apparent for more than a decade. Their relationship was undeniably close, even intimate, especially after the death of Nehru's father in 1931. Nehru was always careful to be seen beside the Mahatma and to have his picture taken with him. In fact, they were very different men, even opposites. Their deepest differences would not appear until it was too late, when Gandhi's legacy for India had turned to tragedy.

Like Churchill, Nehru had been educated at Harrow. Like Bose, he was a graduate of Cambridge. But while Bose (despite his classical education) had remained an Indian and a Bengali, Nehru was undeniably a man of the British Left. Gandhi himself said that Nehru was "more English than Indian in his thoughts and make-up" and that he was "more at home with Englishmen than with his own countrymen,"[18] especially Englishmen who read left-leaning journals like the *New Statesman* and the *Guardian* and voted for the Labour Party.* Nehru made their enthusiasms *his* enthusiasms: for the nationalization of industries, for socialist planning, and for the defeat of capitalism and colonialism.

One of those enthusiasms was also for Stalin's Soviet Union. A host of European and English socialists in the 1930s, including Churchill's old mentors the Webbs, had deluded themselves into believing that Russia was the model of social perfection. So it became nirvana for Nehru as well. Nehru, like other British leftists, would accept the mendacious Moscow show trials at face value. It is in Stalin's Russia, he wrote in April 1936, that "we find the essentials of democracy present in far greater degree among the masses there than anywhere else." This was in the aftermath of the Great Famine and just before Stalin's purges got into high gear.[19]

---

* Nirad Chaudhuri noticed a revealing snobbery about Nehru's spoken English. In any discussion Nehru would listen carefully to his interlocutor's accent, then carefully calibrate his own so that it would sound at least one social cut above.

Nehru never became a Communist, although he did cooperate with India's fledgling Communist Party. But he did see the world, including India, through simplistic Marxist stereotypes of imperialism, capitalism, and "socialist democracy," a code phrase for Soviet-style, top-down dictatorship. If S. C. Bose saw Germany and Italy as the blueprint for his country's future, Nehru's blueprint was the "workers' paradise" of Soviet Russia.

So while Nehru strongly endorsed Gandhi's diagnosis of India's ills as the result of "British imperialism," he rejected Gandhi's solutions. Certainly he paid lip service to the principles of civil disobedience and satyagraha, but he saw them purely in terms of political leverage, and he privately fumed over their overt religious dimension. If Gandhi believed in the law of ahimsa, Nehru believed in the law of class conflict. The Mahatma's "continual references to God irritate me exceedingly," Nehru confessed as early as 1933, and he was just as upset over Gandhi's pro-British feelings now.[20]

At once Nehru saw that the war offered an opportunity to hold Britain's feet to the fire over independence, just as Annie Besant had tried to do during World War I. It took Nehru four days of adroit negotiation to craft the statement he and Congress leaders released on September 14. It was full of platitudes about democracy and fighting oppression, and condemnations of Nazism and fascism. But it also put the blame for the crisis squarely on the British and the French and denounced their colonial empires. "The true measure of democracy is the ending of imperialism and fascism alike," the statement read; "the horror has to be checked in Europe and China, but it will not end until its root causes, fascism and imperialism, are removed" and until India was finally free.[21]

The September 14 statement (or September Manifesto, as Nehru preferred to call it) offered the British a choice, or rather an ultimatum. Congress would support the war effort in exchange for a declaration that India would be granted full and complete independence. Unless Congress got the latter, it would take specific steps to ensure Britain never got the former.

Neither the thinking nor the ultimatum reflected Gandhi's view. He had hoped to convince the Congress to endorse his own plan for unconditional, but also nonviolent, support of the British, but the Congress turned him down. He felt he had no choice but to go along. "Of all the organizations of the world," he wrote in *Harijan,* "the Congress is the

best fitted to show it the better way, indeed the only way, to the true life."
To break publicly with Nehru and the leadership now, he felt, would
only expose just how divided the Congress was over the war and much
else.[22]

Indeed the Indian National Congress truly *was* divided, perhaps
more than at any time in a decade. If the British government refused his
ultimatum, Nehru's next step was to have all Congress officials quit
their elected offices in the provincial legislatures. But in truth they were
quite happy with their jobs and their success in governing. In the words
of one historian, the British experiment in cooperating with the
Congress in the late 1930s had "paid off spectacularly."[23]

At first, British officials were skeptical about Congress's ability to govern. But the disciplined Congress cadres provided more stable governments in their eight provinces than non-INC governments in the other
three. Linlithgow himself called it "a distinguished record of public
achievement." Indeed, two governors of Congress-dominated provinces,
Madras and the United Provinces, published articles about their extraordinary success to serve as blueprints for Indian government in the future.
They revealed how maintaining law and order, organizing public works,
and maintaining sanitation were all easier with the help of a popularly
elected legislature. Veteran Indian Civil Service men learned to respect
and like their Indian counterparts in the field. For the first time, thanks
to the new constitution, Indians exercised a "very real influence over government." Meanwhile the recruitment of Englishmen for the civil service, instead of declining after the India Act as Churchill and others had
forecast, remained strong.[24]

The September Manifesto threatened to overturn this happy state of
affairs and to prove the critics right: the Indian National Congress really
was ready to stab Britain in the back. Just as the self-government experiment was getting under way, Winston Churchill had expressed misgivings to Linlithgow about cooperating with enemies of Britain like the
Congress, but Linlithgow had demurred. "My strong impression is that
these men are sincere in what they say," he wrote. Trends pointed to
more cooperation, even in the princely states. "Take it from me," he told
Churchill, "the old order...is dying fast." But Linlithgow had also
warned that Nehru might still endanger any new order and that legislators "are very hard hunted by their left wing."[25] Now what Linlithgow
had feared seemed to be coming to pass.

Anxious to find a way to answer the September Manifesto, Linlithgow met with no less than fifty-two different Indian politicians, including Nehru, Gandhi, R. Prasad, and Muhammad Jinnah. The result was fifty-two different opinions about what to do next. Linlithgow believed Gandhi was willing to arrange a compromise, perhaps even accept the All-India Federation plan. But the pressure from Nehru was too strong. "Whatever his hesitations as to the soundness of Nehru's policy," Linlithgow wrote to Lord Zetland, Gandhi felt duty bound to support him even in things "which would never have commended themselves to the old man himself had he still been in sole and effective charge."[26]

On October 17 Linlithgow felt he had no choice but to publicly and finally turn the Congress down. Gandhi's reaction was angry and swift. "The Viceregal declaration is profoundly disappointing," he told the press. He dismissed Linlithgow's offer to summon an All Parties Conference to sort out their difference as "the old policy of divide and rule." He wrote on October 30 for *Harijan*: "The Congress support would have put the British cause on an unassailable moral basis...But God has willed otherwise."[27] Meanwhile every Congress official, most very reluctantly, had resigned from provincial office. Nehru achieved what he had secretly wanted to do six months earlier: force a showdown with the Raj. The declaration of war had been a useful pretext. But at the same time the "potentially fruitful experiment" in Indian self-government under British supervision collapsed.[28]

Only one other person was actually pleased with this result: Muhammad Ali Jinnah. When he learned Congress officials were quitting all their posts, Jinnah's gaunt face broke into one of his rare smiles, and he officially declared December 22, 1939, a day of thanksgiving for Muslims. He had ignored appeals from Nehru and Gandhi to join them in the September Manifesto. He knew Congress had made a serious, possibly fatal error. The demise of the Indian National Congress was a new opportunity for the Muslim League and a new dawn for the idea of a separate Islamic state.

There could be no grounds for reconciliation, he was now fully convinced. "The Hindus and Moslems belong to two different civilizations which are based mainly on conflicting ideas and conceptions," he was telling followers.[29] He no longer had any reason to pretend otherwise. So as the dry season came and Gandhi retired to Sevagram and

Nehru and other Congress officials debated their next step, Jinnah made his move.

On March 22, 1940, more than sixty thousand men gathered in Lahore and occupied a gigantic tent in Minto (now Allama Iqbal) Park for a meeting of the Muslim League. The next day—as Germany was preparing to invade Norway and Japan to install a puppet regime in Nanking—Jinnah and the league passed a public resolution calling for a separate Islamic state.

The Lahore Resolution came as a surprise to the viceroy, a bitter defeat to Nehru, and a personal wound to Gandhi. But Gandhi more than anyone had helped to prepare the way for it. His emergence as the Mahatma had solidified his support among Hindus and step by step made him the spiritual authority of an entire nation. But step by step it had also alienated Muslims. When Gandhi described himself as a Hindu of Hindus, Muslims seethed. "Everything about him, his dietary habits, his clothes, his sexual abstinence, his prayers, his ashrams," all highlighted his status as a holy man to the Hindu masses but anathematized him among Muslims.[30]

To Jinnah's mind, the instigator for creating two nations, Hindu and Muslim, was neither the British nor himself but Gandhi. Now Jinnah was only waiting for the British to take their leave to put the final touches on the process. The war barely entered into the Muslim leader's calculations.[31] Any declaration of an independent "India" would now be a dead letter and bring harsh recriminations, or worse, from the followers of the Muslim League.

Jinnah's hard line left the Indian National Congress stranded. Foiled by the British, betrayed by the Muslims, hopelessly divided over what to do next, the Congress turned in desperation to the one man who still might save them.

He had retreated back to Sevagram. "I have become disconsolate," Gandhi had admitted when the war broke out. "In the secret of my heart I am in perpetual quarrel with God that He should allow such things to go on. My non-violence seems almost impotent." Still, he realized that it was not God or even nonviolence that was helpless but man. "I must try [to go] on," he concluded, "without losing faith even though I may break in the attempt."[32] The clashes over the September Manifesto only served to deepen Gandhi's gloom.

But he never allowed the war news, the storms over resignations, or the bitter Congress rivalries to dominate his mind. Over the new year Gandhi returned to the work he considered most meaningful: to encourage khadi and home spinning, to support the campaign for the Harijans, and to preach the message of ahimsa.

He found time to advise a high school in Baroda, when he learned the students were not using the charkha. He wrote about communal violence in Sukkur and Shikarpur in the Sind; he took up the cause of using unadulterated ghee or clarified butter. He sent a reproachful memo to the members of the ashram: "Everyone must observe restraint in eating. Eight ounces of greens at a time should be deemed sufficient."

He arranged for someone to go with a friend to have his teeth extracted, and he advised another on how to relax. "Don't devote more than twenty minutes to massage," he warned. "You should read, rest, or spin during the rest of the time."[33] His push for khadi remained unrelenting, and he organized a large handcraft fair to be part of the next Congress meeting when delegates assembled at Ramargh in late March.

Gandhi spoke at Ramargh in open session, for the first time since 1934. The Congress needed leadership; he wanted followers. But he arrived full of misgivings about the Congress members: "There is no doubt that many are corrupt," he had said a year earlier.[34] He was also worried about the future of nonviolence and not just because of events in Europe. He told Nehru that he had heard people were displaying placards around India "asking people to cut wires and tear rails." He said, "If people take the law into their own hands, I must give up all command of [the] civil disobedience movement."[35] On March 13 a Punjabi student studying in London murdered former governor Michael O'Dwyer and wounded Secretary Zetland and two others.* As Gandhi mounted the dais at Ramargh, he sensed that satyagraha might be making its last stand.

His opening quotation from the Gospel of Saint Matthew—"Not Everyone that sayeth to me Lord, Lord, shall enter into the Kingdom of Heaven"—puzzled the delegates, but they responded with a tremendous cheer. Gandhi cut them short. "I do not need your cheers," he said reproachfully. "I want to win your hearts and intellects, and your cheers stand in the way of winning them."

The multitude fell silent as he continued. "I feel you are not pre-

---

* It was a last revenge for the Amritsar massacre twenty-one years earlier, which O'Dwyer had sanctioned and then followed up with harsh martial law measures across the Punjab.

pared" for "civil disobedience properly launched and conducted," he told them. "We all realize that we will have to fight for freedom." The delegates cheered, but again he angrily stopped them.

"Your claps only demonstrate that you do not understand what this preparation means," he scolded them. "Your General finds that you are not ready, that you are not real soldiers and...that we are bound to be defeated." Then Gandhi read them their marching orders. The Indian National Congress, he said, would have to follow his formula for satyagraha exactly and without question. Every member of the Congress must be personally committed to khadi and using the spinning wheel daily—"no one who does not believe in the charkha can be a soldier under me," he sternly told them. They must uphold an absolute standard of ahimsa: "With me there is no other alternative to non-violence." Above all, every member of the Congress must have love, not hatred, in their hearts.

"All the sermons you heard today against British imperialism," he warned, will not help. "They will only make you angry." But "we have no quarrel with the British people...We want to be their friends and retain their goodwill, not on the basis of their domination, but on the basis of a free and equal India."

If the Congress followed his formula exactly, like a patient obeying a doctor, he said, "I shall march forth and then I shall have no doubts about victory." But "if you are not prepared to follow this path," he added with words that tolled out across the crowd, "please leave me alone." He told the astonished delegates that he would not look on such an outcome as a defeat; "the word 'defeat' is not in my dictionary." But "I am not prepared to do anything for which I will have to repent."[36]

The members of Congress could cheer him. They revered him. But they could no longer follow him. They wanted and needed him to lead a civil disobedience campaign, but only as political leverage, not as a prelude to a national moral transformation. His stern summons to action, so reminiscent of Churchill, fell on deaf ears. Instead of accepting Gandhi's program, they chose to hold out for a compromise. Three days later the Muslim League announced its Lahore Resolution. Gandhi watched helplessly as two more months of debate and equivocation finally, in the first week of July 1940, yielded an offer to the British government.

Rajagopalachari, Nehru, and the Congress pledged full support for the war effort in exchange for Britain's declaration that India would be free at the war's end and creation of a National Government of Indian ministry. Gandhi said, "If Rajaji's draft reflects the Congress's mind, it must be accepted." Characteristically, Nehru at the last minute changed "war effort" to "defense of the country"—a much narrower offer. But Gandhi still said, "I feel [it] will be accepted by the Government."[37]

It was too late. If the offer had come two months earlier, Neville Chamberlain and Lord Zetland at the India Office might have considered it. But with the new prime minister who had taken office on May 10, it had no chance. He was none other than Gandhi's nemesis, Winston Churchill.

Chapter Twenty-four

FROM NARVIK TO BARDOLI

April 1940–December 1941

Even if Nazi legions stood triumphant on the Black Sea, or indeed the Caspian,
even if Hitler were at the gates of India, it would profit him nothing.

WINSTON CHURCHILL, 1940

WHEN HE FINALLY PUSHED OPEN THE door of 10 Downing Street as prime minister in May 1940 at age sixty-five, Churchill was already facing a major crisis in the war in Europe. Ironically, it was a crisis largely of his own making.

In September the previous year, when the war was not yet five hours old, he had taken his post in Chamberlain's War Cabinet. Sitting with him were his old opponents from the India Act. Sir John Simon was now secretary of the Treasury, and Sir Samuel Hoare was now Lord Privy Seal. Also at the table were Sir Kingsley Wood (minister of air), Leslie Hore-Belisha (war), and Maurice Hankey, not to mention Neville Chamberlain: men he had publicly excoriated for their stand on appeasement, first in India and then in Europe. They in turn viewed him with deep distrust, if not real hatred. "I shall never forgive Winston," Hoare had written after their battle over India. "He and his friends are completely unscrupulous. They stick at nothing."[1] Winston, for his part, was willing to let bygones be bygones for sake of the war effort.

The new First Lord of the Admiralty arrived ready for action. Unfortunately, there was little action to take. The only fighting was in Poland, where the Germans were already making massive headway. Britain's French ally resisted making a strong demonstration against the Germans on its western border, out of fear the Allies would do as badly as the Poles.

In a matter of three weeks Poland collapsed. France and Britain settled into the so-called "phony war," with no discernible activity on either side of the western frontier. As the stalemate dragged on for weeks and then months, Churchill (not surprisingly) grew restless.

At the Admiralty, Churchill kept busy organizing the largest fleet in the world for war. But "I could not rest content with the policy of 'convoy and blockade,' " he wrote later. "I sought earnestly for a way to attack Germany by naval means." In fact, he was looking for his next Gallipoli moment. What others had thought the First World War's biggest disaster, he still considered a missed opportunity and a model of how to "make the enemy wonder where he is going to [be] hit next."[2] Winston was not willing to let the opportunity slip away again.

This time the thumb and cigar moved northward across the Admiralty maps, to Norway. The cabinet already had a plan afoot for sending troops to reinforce the Finns in their life-or-death struggle against Hitler's ally, Stalin. Churchill pushed to expand the operation to include mining the major Norwegian ports, especially Narvik, in order to sever German access to iron ore from Sweden. The Finns surrendered before the relief expedition could leave, but the Norway plan remained an idée fixe in Churchill's mind.

What Chamberlain had always feared would happen if Churchill joined the cabinet, happened. His brisk arguments swept aside the doubts of Hore-Belisha, Wood, and the rest. When the German fleet came out to Narvik to clear the mines, he confidently predicted, the Royal Navy could pounce. British and French troops could occupy the principal Norwegian ports, and Hitler's fate in the north would be sealed. He even convinced Chamberlain to appoint him head of the Military Coordinating Committee, so he could oversee every detail of what would become Plan R-4: the mining of Norwegian waters, then the deployment of troops to occupy Narvik and Trondheim once Germans violated Norwegian neutrality. The cabinet set the date for the operation to begin on April 8, 1940.

In fact, it was Gallipoli all over again. What the cabinet did not know, and could not have known, was that the Germans were planning on doing exactly the same thing. Hitler had shrewdly guessed that Norway's deep fjords and snug protected harbors would attract Churchill's wandering eye.[3] So he organized his own Norway invasion force, which sailed on April 9—a day before the British. The two expeditions, with their fleets of destroyers, cruisers, and transports, missed each other in the North Sea, although both suspected the presence of the other. The Germans, however, reached the Norwegian coast first.

They suffered some initial setbacks. Alert Norwegian shore guns knocked out the German heavy cruiser *Blücher,* which sank, carrying two thousand soldiers and sailors to their deaths. A British submarine sank another German cruiser and aircraft crippled a pocket battleship, the *Lützow.* Royal Navy Captain Henry Warburton-Lee led a gallant dash with his destroyer flotilla to keep the Germans out of Narvik, which cost him his life but sank two German destroyers and damaged five more. British and French troops were poised to begin their landings.

Then everything began to go wrong. The Germans got their troops ashore first and took Norway's principal cities; at the same time they occupied Denmark. Twenty-five-year-old John Colville was Chamberlain's cabinet secretary that blustery April when the Narvik campaign was announced. He, like every one else in Downing Street, watched the huge map of Scandinavia that hung in the prime minister's office with obsessive attention, hungry for any news. As early as the ninth he was learning that "we, who started the whole business, seem to have lost the initiative." Of course, "if we can secure a naval victory the balance will be redressed in our favor." However, "bad visibility and a heavy sea" were hampering British vessels. According to the government's chief whip, "The whole thing seems to be 'rather a fog.' "[4]

The fog would get worse, in every sense. Over the next several days Colville learned that the landing of British and French troops had been botched from the start, that the Germans had managed to recover and retake key positions, and that the Supreme War Council was finally forced to consider pulling out of Norway with its tail between its legs.

On April 24, as Colville watched, a disillusioned Chamberlain stood before the great map, where colored pins were being moved from point to point. Chamberlain was "depressed more by Winston's rampages" than by the growing problems in Norway. "I have an uneasy feeling," Colville wrote, "that all is not being as competently handled as it might be." If a full-scale evacuation became necessary, "I think the psychological cost would be considerable."[5]

Colville was right. The evacuation began. The colored pins came off the map and were put away. The public, and Parliament, demanded that someone pay for the botched expedition. Churchill could already feel the fingers pointing at him, just as after Gallipoli. "I certainly bore an exceptional measure of responsibility for the brief and disastrous Norwegian campaign," he wrote after the war, "if campaign it can be called."[6] It had resulted in far fewer casualties than had Gallipoli and no losses large enough to poison relations with a Dominion like Australia. Nonetheless, Churchill braced himself for the inevitable onslaught in the press and on the floor of the House of Commons.

But this time the fingers pointed not at him but at Chamberlain. The public saw the Norway campaign, far from being too bold, as smacking of the hesitancy and half-hearted measures typical of the man forever branded as Hitler's appeaser. In the opinion of Colville (no Churchill admirer), "The country believes that Winston is the man of action who is winning the war." Colville disagreed, but in the end the country was right.[7] Churchill at least had a thirst, if not yet the right strategy, for victory. Chamberlain had a yearning only for peace and it showed in the Norway debacle.

So on May 3, as the reality of failure sank in, the leaders of the opposition parties asked for a debate on the Norway campaign and its leadership. Churchill thought giving in to their demands would be a mistake. But Chamberlain said "it was out of the question to cancel the public debate" on so momentous an issue and agreed to it—thus sealing his own fate.[8] On Tuesday, May 7, a steady rain of accusations fell on his head from all sides, even from his own party. The Labour deputy leader Arthur Greenwood admitted, "I have never known the House in graver mood."

The next day the debate took on the atmosphere of a vote of censure or no confidence. In a dramatic gesture Admiral Roger Keyes, member for North Portsmouth, appeared in his naval uniform and decorations to castigate the government for throwing away "a priceless chance" by its procrastination and timidity.[9] To his credit, Churchill tried to take some of the blame for what happened. "I take the fullest responsibility," he said, for listening to the advice of the experts on the Norway incursion. "I thought they were right at the time...and I have seen no reason to alter my view by what I have learned since."[10]

But the anger of the House was directed not at him but squarely at Chamberlain. Once again it was Churchill's old acquaintance Leo Amery whose intervention proved decisive. He dismissed Chamberlain's careful explanations of why the Norway campaign had failed: "It is always possible to do that after every failure. Making a case and winning a war are not the same thing." Then he finished by quoting Oliver Cromwell, who had said, when the Rump Parliament was dismissed in 1653: "You have sat too long here for any good you have been doing. Depart I say, and let us have done with you. In the name of God, go!"

It was what everyone was thinking. "I had driven the nail home," Amery realized, and the next day Chamberlain was fighting for his political life.[11] Churchill finished the debate with an eloquent forty-five-minute defense of Chamberlain and again tried to place the blame on his own shoulders. But the other members would have none of it. Duff Cooper, who had resigned in protest after Munich, said Churchill was "defending with his eloquence those who have so long refused to listen to his counsel, who treated his warnings with contempt"—meaning not only Norway but Munich and before.

After Churchill spoke, members filed into the corridor as the division for a vote of no confidence took place. When they returned, the atmosphere was electric. Ears and heads strained as the government's chief whip read out the result in a faltering voice. Chamberlain had won, but by only eighty-one votes. Experts had estimated he needed at least one hundred to stay in office. Thirty-three Tories had voted against their own party leader, and another sixty had deliberately abstained.

There was a tremendous gasp, and then shouts of "resign, resign." Chamberlain stood up—"erect, unyielding, sardonic," Leo Amery remembered—and walked out without a word. All around him the House was in chaos, as Labour members chanted over and over: "Go, in God's name go!"[12]

Chamberlain was finished. The morning of the ninth he tried without success to convince Labour to join him in a National Government. Labour flatly refused: they would serve with someone else but not him. Afterward Chamberlain confessed to Churchill that he might have to resign.[13] The question on his and everyone else's mind was, who would take his place?

Chamberlain and many other Conservatives had their candidate: Lord Halifax. Not only was he foreign minister, but his reputation, unaccountably, had survived the shipwreck of Munich. He was popularly viewed as a rock of integrity and diplomatic wisdom—in sharp contrast to the man many feared was the other leading candidate, Winston Churchill. "One can't speak of them in the same breath," Lady Alexandra Metcalfe, a Halifax friend and daughter of Lord Curzon, wrote. "I am terrified of Winston."[14] Many patriotic people agreed, including the king and queen of England.

One who did not was Kingsley Wood, the minister of air. Drab and unprepossessing, one of the worst speakers in the House of Commons, his chief qualification for office had been his loyalty first to Baldwin and then to Chamberlain. He knew almost nothing about war or airplanes. But the morning of May 9 he sat down to lunch with Churchill and Anthony Eden and announced that if Chamberlain had to go, then Winston must take his place.[15] It was an extraordinary admission, an indication that the conventional wisdom was starting to turn. It must have echoed in Churchill's mind when he received the summons that afternoon to meet Chamberlain in the Cabinet Room.

Chamberlain and Lord Halifax were both present when he arrived. The prime minister said there was no hope of forming a National Government; he would have to resign. His "demeanor was cool, unruffled, and seemingly quite detached from the personal aspect of the affair," Churchill remembered later. The only question was who should replace him as prime minister.

Chamberlain looked at both men across the table. Then he asked with a sharp glance, "Can you see any reason, Winston, why in these days a peer should not be prime minister?"

Churchill realized at once that this was a subtle trap.* If he answered no, then the mantle of power would almost certainly fall on Halifax. The man who had bested him over India still enjoyed the full faith and confidence of the Tory party, but he would be as disastrous a war leader as Chamberlain had been. On the other hand, if Winston answered yes, it would reveal his ambition for the post himself—while seeming to use a minor constitutional point to secure it.

It was a no-win situation. So Churchill decided to say nothing. For a full two minutes the room was silent—"it certainly seemed longer than the two minutes which one observes in the commemorations of Armistice Day," Churchill remembered. He gazed out the window at the Horse Guards Parade and waited for someone else to break the spell.[16]

Finally Halifax cleared his throat. For the second time in his life, he performed a purely selfless act to protect his country. The first had propelled Gandhi to national leadership; the second would do the same for Winston.

"It would be a hopeless position," Halifax said, for him to accept the prime ministership. "If I am not in charge of the war operations, and if I

---

* Britain had had no prime minister from the House of Lords since Lord Rosebery in 1892. Since then the tradition, but not the rule, had been that a seat in the House of Commons was the prerequisite for anyone occupying Number 10.

didn't lead the House [of Commons], I should be a cipher. I think Winston is a better choice."

Churchill, as Halifax sardonically put it in his notes after the historic discussion, "did *not* demur."[17] A few minutes later the Tory chief whip entered, and the four men settled down to the business of planning the next government. At around six that afternoon Chamberlain went to Buckingham Palace to submit his resignation. An hour later Winston Leonard Spencer Churchill went to the palace, where King George VI (no doubt with some misgivings) spoke the fateful words, "I want you to form a government."[18]

Churchill was prime minister. Many were horrified; some despaired. Chamberlain and Halifax had "weakly surrendered to a half-breed American,*" R. A. Butler railed to John Colville. Another parliamentarian wrote in his diary, "Perhaps the darkest day in English history...I sat numb with misery."[19] Perhaps no one was more surprised than Churchill himself. "It was a marvel," as he remarked later. By engineering a major military disaster, he had managed to propel himself to the leadership of his country.

Yet in a sense his entire life had been preparation for this moment. At sixty-five years of age, he was the one member of the government who had personally served in *both* of Britain's previous full-scale wars: the conflict with the Boers and the Great War. He was the only figure who had served in a War Cabinet twice against the German foe, once in 1914 and again in 1939. Even as he drew up the list for cabinet posts and decided which Labour and Liberal figures would be invited to join his National Government, his mind was already tackling the immense task of deciding on his war strategy and its twin objectives.

The first aim was to defeat Hitler—at whatever cost. On May 10 this aim was not only a strategic goal but an imperative. That same day Hitler had hurled his forces into Holland and Belgium. The war in the west had begun; and even while, under steady German air attack, the Royal Navy was extracting the last of the Norway expedition, German panzers were executing their breakthrough in France.

Churchill spent his first weeks in office in a cyclone of disasters. By May 27 it was clear that France was doomed. The French army, which Winston only four years earlier had thanked God for serving as a bulwark against Hitler, collapsed. The British Expeditionary Force had to

---

* Since Winston's mother, Jennie Jerome Churchill, had been an American.

withdraw to the beaches at Dunkirk to be evacuated. With a huge heroic effort, the Royal Navy managed to save the British Army; but as Winston noted in his speech afterward, "Wars are not won by evacuations."[20]

By the third week of June 1940 the war was very close to being lost. The French sued for an armistice. Britain and Churchill found themselves standing alone against the Nazi war machine. Churchill's goal of defeating Hitler had to take a dramatic detour to achieve a new goal: saving Great Britain itself.

Even at this hour Churchill did not forget the imperative to protect Britain's empire: in his later famous phrase, "I have not become the King's First Minister in order to preside over the liquidation of the British Empire." To his mind, this goal was not separate from that of defeating Hitler. They were part and parcel of the same thing. Just as Hitler represented the forces of darkness, so the British Empire represented the forces of light, even in India. The peoples of the empire held "the title deeds of progress" and of "Christian civilization," which to Churchill meant the moral standards that governed modern life.[21]

"The British Empire stands invincible," he told a jammed House of Commons on August 20 after the most intense attack yet on British airfields by German bombers. By standing firm against Hitler, he proclaimed, the empire "will kindle again the spark of hope in the breasts of hundreds of millions of down-trodden or despairing men and women throughout Europe," which will "presently [become a] cleansing and devouring flame." Countries "bred under institutions of freedom" will "prove more enduring and resilient than anything that can be got out of the most efficiently enforced mechanical discipline."[22] Gandhi had a term for such spiritual power: satyagraha. To Churchill, the British Empire was not the negation of soul force but its living embodiment.

He never doubted its ultimate victory. He spoke of the empire as an irresistible force, almost a force of nature, and it was encapsulated in his notion of the English-speaking peoples. It included the Dominions; it included America, where President Franklin Roosevelt had made the first tentative gestures toward support of Britain in its most desperate hour. He had concluded his August 20 speech with a reference to future Anglo-American cooperation as a mighty river like the Mississippi: "Let it roll on!" he boomed. In the drive back to Number 10 afterward, John Colville could hear him singing "Old Man River" from the backseat.[23]

Churchill also believed in the empire in narrower terms, "Imperial England, beribboned and bestarred and splendid, living in majestic profusion up till the very moment of war."[24] Maintaining that empire intact was also a crucial goal for Churchill, albeit a far more precarious one. His fear was that Britain's momentary weakness might have ripple effects across the Dominions, across the Middle East, and into the very heart of that empire in India.

India was never far from his thoughts, even in the worst moments. His second wartime broadcast on November 12, 1939, when he was still First Lord of the Admiralty, had mentioned that "the hundreds of millions of people in India and China, whatever their other feelings, would regard with undisguised dread a Nazi triumph, well knowing what their fate would be." After Dunkirk, the Indian Army was crucial to his plans for rebuilding the British Army—Indian units would replace British forces in Palestine. Even in that famous speech of August 20, 1940, while the Battle of Britain raged in the skies overhead and he paid tribute to the Royal Air Force by saying "never in the field of human endeavor was so much owed by so many to so few," he added, "Even if Hitler were at the gates of India, it would profit him nothing," as long as Great Britain stood firm.[25]

Three weeks earlier he had made his first major decision as prime minister regarding India. On July 22 he learned of the Congress's September offer. The earlier news of conflict between the Congress and the Muslim League had been music to his ears. Sir John Simon reported that Churchill's "masculine and simple view" was that the conflict worked to keep Britain in charge in India, and said "[Churchill] hoped it would be bitter and bloody and was glad that we had made the suggestion of Dominion status which was acting as a cat among the pigeons."[26] Lord Zetland had resigned as secretary of state for India as soon as he learned Winston was to be prime minister: he knew his moderate and conciliatory approach would no longer find favor at Number 10. Linlithgow and the new secretary of state, Leo Amery, would soon find out the same thing.

That month was one of the tensest yet. On July 3 Churchill risked all-out war with France's new Vichy government when he decided to order British warships to fire on the fleet of his former ally at Mers-el-Kebir. On July 10 the British and Italian fleets clashed in the Mediterranean, and on the seventeenth Winston went down to Portsmouth to visit the coastal defenses, as military experts tried to guess where and when a German invasion would come. Having to deal with unwelcome news from India angered him. He told his secretary that

Congress's offer was "long-winded as ever and a piece of hypocrisy from beginning to end."[27] Even more infuriating, Linlithgow and Amery had been talking behind his back.

Leo Amery was as much an imperialist as Winston, perhaps even more of one. For years he had dreamed of transforming the empire from an agglomeration of separate territories into "an arch of British influence stretching...from Egypt through the Middle East to India through Southeast Asia," with the Dominions (South Africa, Australia, New Zealand) as its foundation.[28] Bereft of racial prejudice, he saw no reason why India should not join them.* But he found Churchill's views on the subject "romantic, false and dangerous," and they had fought bitterly over the India Bill. Amery realized that the attachment to the Raj was one of Winston's "deepest and sincerest emotions." But "I am by no means sure whether on this subject of India he is quite sane," and he speculated that "India, or any form of self-government for colored peoples, raises in him an uncontrollable complex."[29]

This suspicion was confirmed on July 26. Amery had been pushing Linlithgow to make some encouraging statement about Indian independence one year after the war, in order to meet the Congress demands halfway. As secretary of state for India, Amery no more consulted with the cabinet on this matter than Winston's father might have done. When he learned of it, however, Churchill exploded. John Colville noted in his diary that there was "a bloody row" between the two Old Harrovians, and he worried that Amery might have to resign. (He did not.) Churchill, meanwhile, sent a furious signal to Linlithgow.[30]

"[Amery] has shown me the telegrams which have been passed," it said, "and for the first time I realize what has been going on." Churchill asked that he be allowed to show all the cables to the rest of the cabinet: "It does not seem to me possible to withhold the facts from my colleagues." In the meantime, he said, the cabinet was committed to the policy of the past: it would make no promise about postwar independence and no promise (as Amery wanted) of a constitutional assembly for India. He wound up his telegram by pleading that the war precluded any decisions about India. "You must remember that we are here facing constant threat of invasion," he wrote. "In these circumstances immense constitutional departures cannot be effectively discussed in Parliament and only by the Cabinet to the detriment of matters touching the final

---

* Or the Jews and Arabs in Palestine. Amery had been a major author of the Balfour Declaration.

life and safety of the State." Churchill had John Colville hand-carry the message over to the India Office so that Amery would not see it. "[I] had to suborn one of the men in the telegram dispatch room," Colville confided in his diary, "and cypher the telegram with him."[31]

And so, without anyone except Amery and Linlithgow noticing it, another road was left untaken—while events moved closer to a final collision between Churchill and Gandhi. The government would not budge; Congress's offer to support the war effort had been rejected. Certainly one cannot blame Churchill too much—he had other things on his mind. The outcome of the Battle of Britain still hung in the balance. He now firmly believed Hitler could be defeated only with the help of the United States and Russia, but he still had no idea how.

He had another difficulty that summer: despite his national popularity, the majority of his Tory colleagues still distrusted him and even despised him. One member wrote at the end of May that Churchill was "fighting a war on two fronts, against Hitler and against enemies much nearer at home," meaning his own party. Ill feeling from the battle over India, a sense that Churchill had "betrayed" Chamberlain, hope that Halifax might still replace him, lingered in Tory ranks and leadership (as historian Andrew Roberts argues) until well into the following summer. Ironically, Churchill's staunchest supporters sat on the Labour and Liberal benches.[32]

Under these pressures Churchill was more reluctant than ever to let India go. "The crown jewel" of the empire, as he called it, had become the embossed seal of British greatness. Seven years earlier he had told the viceroy that with the rise of dictatorships and the retreat of democracies around the globe, the "crux" of England's position in the world "will be not only the retention of India but a much stronger assertion of [our] commercial rights [there]." As long as Britons were acting in the Indians' best interests, "we are justified in using our undoubted power for their welfare and for our own."[33] What had been true in 1933 was even more so in 1940.

Besides, Churchill fought bitterly against the fatalistic view that the loss of India to Gandhi and the nationalists was inevitable. As he told Linlithgow, "I think we differ principally in this, that you assume the future is a mere extension of the past, whereas I find history full of unexpected turns and retrogressions." He put it slightly differently to Anthony Eden during one of the war's darkest periods: "No one can foresee how the balance of power will lie or where the winning armies will stand at the end of the war."[34] He was determined to make sure that when the war did end and the dust cleared, India would still be British.

In the summer of 1940 Churchill and Gandhi shared one conviction: that they could shape the destiny of their respective nations by sheer willpower. In Churchill's case, it was the will to resist Hitler's aggression, as well as the naysayers in his own government.* In Gandhi's case, it was the will to use satyagraha to finally force the British out.

On August 8 Gandhi and the Indian National Congress learned of Churchill's negative response to their overture. "I have carefully read over your pronouncement," the Mahatma told Linlithgow in a note from Sevagram. "It has made me sad." The implications of the government's refusal to budge "frighten me, I cannot help feeling that a profound mistake has been made."[35]

India's politicians, shattered by Churchill's rebuff, turned to Gandhi in desperation once more. In mid-September 1940 they summoned him to reassume leadership of the Congress and lead another civil disobedience campaign—even though they doubted that it would be effective. Distrust of Gandhi, especially among younger members and on the Left, was palpable. But in an important sense the Congress had nowhere else to turn. The parallels with Churchill's elevation to the premiership are striking. Like Churchill, Gandhi had come to symbolize the will to resist the common enemy, in this case the British. And like Churchill, Gandhi agreed to take charge because he was anxious to try his own method of winning this "war"—the one he had been waging in one form or another for twenty years.

Before he started the new satyagraha campaign, Gandhi asked for a final interview with Linlithgow. He told the viceroy he and the Congress no longer disagreed on opposition to the war, and he revealed his strategy. He would encourage every Indian to refuse to support the war effort, Gandhi said, just as conscientious objectors in Britain were allowed to forgo serving in the armed services or working in war industries. This time there would be no mass demonstrations, no dramatic gesture of defiance. Every Indian would simply listen to his or her "in-

---

* At the end of May 1940 Halifax raised the possibility of trying to reach terms with Hitler. (He believed Britain could not go on with France defeated.) It took Churchill four days to convince the cabinet finally and unambiguously to refuse. On June 26 he had to remind Halifax that it was the government's position to "fight on to death"—even in the shadow of Dunkirk.

ner voice" and freely choose the path of nonviolence. It was "an experiment never before tried in the political field," he said, and he was eager to start.[36]

The campaign began in October 1940. German bombs were raining down on St. Paul's Cathedral, just as Gandhi had once feared they might. But now "it is wrong to help the British war effort with men or money," Gandhi was telling his followers. "The only worthy effort is to resist all war effort."[37] He still insisted his new stance was consistent with support for Britain. "I said I would not embarrass Britain," he emphatically told an English reporter. "I do not wish disaster to British arms."[38]

If the war was about ending fascism and imperialism, Gandhi believed, then his new campaign would strike a blow against the latter. By avoiding collective action, the Mahatma hoped that "individual" satyagraha would prevent rioting or any Muslim-Hindu confrontation. Above all, he saw this "individual" satyagraha as crucial to the spiritual awakening of India, as each person's inner conscience put them on the path to ahimsa and righteousness. He oversaw every step of its organization and even personally scrutinized the list of individuals who were to make public acts of civil disobedience, throwing out the names of those he considered insufficiently committed.[39]

Seen from that perspective, the October 1940 campaign was the most personal of all his satyagraha efforts. It was also the most disastrous. It became Gandhi's Narvik: a strategic and tactical blunder. Far from refusing to participate in the war effort, Indians joined the army and navy in record numbers—more than 2.5 million before the war's end. The government reported that the civil disobedience campaign had almost no support; the Indian public quickly lost interest. At its final stage, in May 1941, only fourteen thousand satyagrahi were in jail—less than .001 percent of India's population. In August the old liberal T. B. Sapru crowed, "A good many Congress leaders are fed up with the barren program of the Mahatma."[40] With leading members of the Working Committee in jail, including Nehru, the Congress was left rudderless.

Gandhi refused to be discouraged. Where others saw quixotic failure, he saw great opportunity. At Sevagram he settled in for a long campaign—five years if need be, he said.[41] Meanwhile, great events were taking place in Europe and around the world. British and Indian troops were clashing with Rommel's panzers in North Africa. Muslim insurgents had risen up in Iraq in support of the Nazis. On June 22 Hitler invaded the Soviet Union, while the United States was taking the first steps toward entering the war on Britain's behalf.

India was far from everyone's thoughts. But when Rajendra Prasad visited his old mentor at Sevagram in October 1941, he found him in excellent health and "thoroughly satisfied. I have never seen him so optimistic about the future." Certainly there was no one left to push a strategy to reenter negotiations with the British. Gandhi told others that any suggestion of compromise might provoke more rancor and disharmony. Secretly, he preferred nonactivity to any move that might bring about Congress's complete collapse.[42]

In early December the government began releasing its satyagraha prisoners from jail—a sure sign that it no longer considered the campaign a threat. That month Gandhi traveled by train from Wardha to Bardoli to attend the next Congress session. Train travel always seemed to have a catalytic effect on Gandhi's mind. His first great spiritual breakthrough had come at the Maritzburg railway platform. His reading of Ruskin on a train from Durban to Johannesburg had inspired him to create Phoenix Farm. Now, as the miles clicked monotonously by, he began to write out a document that in its way was more revealing than *My Experiments with Truth* and as significant as *Hind Swaraj*.

He called it his Constructive Program. It was a complete blueprint of how a nationwide campaign could achieve "complete independence through truth and non-violence." The book was organized into eighteen sections, among them "Communal Unity," "Removal of Untouchability," "Khadi," "Village Sanitation," "Basic Education" (intended to transform children into model villagers), and "Students." ("Students must not participate in party politics. They are students, learners, searchers, not masters" and "they will be scrupulously correct and chivalrous in their behavior toward female students.")[43]

What is striking is how little Gandhi's basic ideas had changed since *Hind Swaraj* thirty years earlier. Nonviolence was still more powerful than violence; sanitation and clean drains were still essential ("instead of graceful hamlets dotting the land, we have dung-heaps"); and machines were still evil. Parliaments were a waste of time: civil disobedience was the true source of power: "It has been my effort in the last twenty-one years to convince the people of this truth." Echoes of Tolstoy ("imagine a whole people unwilling to conform to the laws of the legislature... They would bring the entire legislative and executive machinery to a standstill") intermingled with newer themes, like the liberation of women and the empowerment of the peasantry.[44]

But his version of nonviolence and civil disobedience, he perceived, might be going out of date. Gandhi admitted that his notion of villages holding their possessions together in trusteeship had been ridiculed; his plan for village cooperatives might be "impossible in a country like ours." The reader might even "make the mistake of laughing" at all the elements he insisted be included in a civil disobedience campaign. Again and again he hearkened back to the Champaran satyagraha with nostalgia, as his touchstone of success—even though the intervening two decades had seen at least eight other satyagraha campaigns.

The last paragraph is the most revealing:

> Such at least is my view. It may be that of a mad man. If it makes no appeal to the Congressman, I must be rejected. For my handling of civil disobedience without the constructive program will be like a paralyzed hand attempting to lift a spoon.[45]

When the train reached Bardoli, Gandhi put down his pen. He sent a short note to Mirabehn: "I was immersed in writing work which I have just finished."[46] Lost in his thoughts, he must have felt the war was very far away. But in fact events were about to bring it right to India's doorstep.

Chapter Twenty-five

DEBACLE

1941–1942

Is there any man who does not bungle? What else is
Churchill doing? And what am I doing?

MOHANDAS K. GANDHI, APRIL 25, 1941

ON DECEMBER 10, 1941, CHURCHILL'S WORKDAY began as usual in bed, as he was opening his dispatch boxes. The telephone rang. It was Sir Dudley Pound, First Sea Lord. He and Churchill had an uneasy relationship. Many in the Admiralty felt that Pound should have been doing more, over the past two years, to rein in Churchill's more extravagant strategic notions, which often resulted in setback and even disaster. *

But this morning Pound could barely speak—Churchill had trouble understanding him. The gist of the story was that the two great ships Churchill had sent to Singapore in November, the *Prince of Wales* and *Repulse,* had both been sunk by Japanese air attack in the Gulf of Siam. The commanding admiral, Tom Phillips, a Churchill favorite, was dead.

"Are you sure this is true?" Churchill asked.

"There is no doubt at all," said the subdued voice on the other end.

Churchill let the phone drop back into its cradle. "I was grateful to be alone," he wrote later. "In all the war I never received a more direct shock."[1]

Three days earlier he and the rest of the world had learned of the Japanese attack on Pearl Harbor. The War Cabinet had immediately declared war on Japan in support of America, which was now Britain's formal ally against the Axis.† Churchill told Parliament they should not

---

* These setbacks included not only Norway but the invasion of Greece in March 1941, which had led to the bloody evacuation of Crete and serious Royal Navy losses.

† On December 11, Hitler declared war on the United States.

underrate "the gravity of the new dangers we have to meet, either here or in the United States."

But the sinking of the *Repulse* and *Prince of Wales* was more earth-shaking than Pearl Harbor, not only for Britain but for the world. For more than a century Great Britain had been the dominant power in Asia. The Royal Navy's supremacy in the Pacific had secured an empire that stretched from Hong Kong and Singapore to Australia and New Zealand. At one stroke under a clear December sky, Japanese dive bombers and torpedo planes had stripped that empire of its principal defense: "All over this vast expanse of waters Japan was supreme, and we everywhere were weak and naked."[2]

Nowhere was the empire more naked than in Malaya, where at that moment Japanese army units were landing. In less than a month they would close on the British fortress at Singapore. In less than three months they would be at the gates of India. "The full horror" of the news of *Repulse* and *Prince of Wales* in December 1941, as Churchill described it, was not just that a whole new war front had opened, a war against Asia's most dynamic rising power. The British Empire suddenly found itself staring into the abyss. In 1942 Churchill and Gandhi would battle for the highest stakes of all: the fate of the empire itself.

Ironically the sinking of the *Prince of Wales* and *Repulse* came at the end of what had been, after a wobbly beginning, a very good year. After a humiliating retreat from Greece and Crete, the eastern Mediterranean had stabilized. Erwin Rommel's drive for Egypt and Suez, the gateway to India, had been contained. The Battle of the Atlantic to get convoys past the German U-boat wolf pack continued, but with diminishing losses: only 35 ships were lost in November, compared with 109 in June.[3] Defeat of a pro-Nazi revolt in Iraq in May had closed the door to any German incursion into the oil-rich Persian Gulf.*

---

* The revolt was led by the anti-British and pro-German Rashid Ali, who staged a coup d'état in April 1941. The Indian Tenth Infantry Division landed at Basra on April 18 in response. Rashid's ultimatum to the British led to a counterultimatum. On May 2 British bombs fell on Iraqi troops surrounding the RAF base at Habbaniya. After several days of fierce fighting the city of Fallujah fell to British and Indian forces, even though the German Luftwaffe sent planes from a base in Mosul to hit British installations. The British took Baghdad soon afterward, and on June 1, 1941, Rashid Ali fled first to Iran, then to Germany. His associate Yunis el-Sabawi, who had translated *Mein Kampf* into Arabic, was captured and hanged. Another young officer who fought for Rashid Ali was Khairallah Talfah. He escaped but would pass the lessons of the Iraq war, and of the Nazi cause, on to his four-year-old nephew, Saddam Hussein.

Then on June 22 Hitler launched his fateful and fatal attack on the Soviet Union. With a sigh of relief, Churchill realized that Hitler would not invade England. The German army's panzer divisions would be diverted into an unwinnable war in Russia. Churchill pledged his full support to Russia. "Any man or state who fights on against Nazism will have our aid," he told a national radio audience that night. "We shall give whatever help we can to Russia and the Russian people."

John Colville asked how Churchill felt, after a lifetime of anti-Bolshevism, siding with a man like Stalin. "If Hitler invaded Hell," Churchill answered, "I would make at least a favorable reference to the Devil in the House of Commons."[4] The invasion represented a turning point in the war at home as well: the British Communist Party and trade unions sympathetic to the Soviet cause, not to mention the Communist Party in India, would now be fully on Britain's side.

But Churchill's biggest accomplishment that spring was to cement the close bond of trust and cooperation between himself and the American president, Franklin Roosevelt. It began with the Lend-Lease program, which Churchill in March 1941 described to the House of Commons as "a second Magna Carta" guaranteeing Britain's freedom, and it grew with their meeting on board HMS *Prince of Wales* that same month when they signed the Atlantic Charter promising to extend that freedom to the peoples oppressed by the Axis powers. Ironically, just nine months later that same *Prince of Wales* would be lying on the bottom of the Gulf of Siam.

Like any alliance, the "special relationship" between Britain and the United States, and the bond between Roosevelt and Churchill, had its shaky moments. Almost all of them came over India. The clash began with the Atlantic Charter itself, which included a joint declaration calling for "the right of all peoples to choose the form of government under which they live" and the restoration of self-government for those who had been deprived of it. Churchill assumed that this declaration applied to European nations conquered by Hitler and Stalin. But other officials, including Leo Amery, feared that the wording was a Pearl Harbor–style sneak attack on the foundations of the British Empire.[5] They knew Americans considered European overseas empires to be iniquitous relics of a discredited colonial past (unlike their own holdings such as Puerto Rico and Guam). Churchill seemed to have been tricked into endorsing the breakup of the Empire on which the Sun Never Set. On August 16 the newspaper *Daily Herald* seemed to confirm that assumption when it ran the headline: "The Atlantic Charter: It Means Dark Races As Well."

The Colonial Office became officially upset. Leo Amery said the declaration "let loose a lot of questions about its application to the Empire," particularly to India, and he suggested that the India and Colonial Offices file a joint memorandum.[6] For once Churchill agreed with Amery. He spoke to the matter in the House of Commons on September 9, reassuring members that the declaration had nothing to do with the British Empire or India. "We are pledged," he announced, "to help India, to obtain free and equal partnership in the British Commonwealth with ourselves, subject of course," he added, "to the fulfilment of obligations arising from our long connection with India and our responsibilities to its many creeds, races, and interests."[7] In short, nothing about the American alliance had changed Churchill's mind about either India or self-government for "the darker races."

In fact, his mood that autumn was distinctly upbeat. The war seemed to have turned a significant corner—although, as he presciently told John Colville, "we cannot afford military failures."[8] In October he visited his old school, Harrow, and gave one of his most celebrated and inspiring speeches.

He reminded his audience that they had sat together in the same seats a year earlier, during the darkest days of the Blitz. "Can anyone sitting here today," he said, "this October day, not be thankful for the time that has past and the improved condition in which our country finds itself?" He told the assembled boys and masters and other onlookers, "Surely from this period of ten months this is the lesson: never give in, never give in, *never, never, never, never* ... never give in except to convictions of honor and good sense ... We have only to persevere to conquer."[9] Just six weeks later a great naval disaster would put that self-confidence and resolution to the test and give the issue of India a spectacular new urgency.

Gandhi too had thought Britain's tribulations were fewer than met the eye. The conventional wisdom among India's intellectual and political elite in 1940 was that Hitler would win and Britain was doomed.[10] In 1941 that view had been quietly but steadily reversed. Churchill's iron resolve had impressed, and dismayed, nationalists who had seen Britain's defeat as their ticket to independence. When Hitler attacked Russia in June, India's Communists and other radicals turned overnight from opponents to outspoken supporters of the war. Communist leaders even attempted to persuade Gandhi to change his mind and back what had become "the war against Fascism," but Gandhi refused to budge.[11]

Meanwhile, the crackdown on the Congress and other dissidents continued. "India is being ground down under the British heel," Gandhi complained to the press in late April, but to little avail. Nehru and other Congress leaders remained in prison until early December, while the Muslim League remained as intractably opposed as ever to any cooperation with its Hindu counterpart. Gandhi as always blamed this intransigence not on Jinnah but the British: " 'Divide and rule' has been Great Britain's proud and ill-conceived rule," he told the press.[12] Yet he could not deny that, as the year wore on, divide and rule seemed to be working. He and the Congress languished in irrelevancy.

The sinking of the *Prince of Wales* and *Repulse* changed everything. In Madras the prices of grain and other essential commodities shot through the roof.[13] In Calcutta Nirad Chaudhuri was sitting in his office at the *Monthly Review* when his personal assistant told him the ships were gone. "At first I could not believe it, but he said he had heard the names clearly on the radio." Chaudhuri felt "dazed," and "I felt again the pain in my chest which I had suffered after the French defeat of 1940"—a harbinger of disaster to come.[14]

He was right. On December 8 the first Japanese bombs fell on Singapore. On the eleventh their planes attacked Penang, on Malaya's northwest coast. No one in Malaya had seen a war in generations. Europeans, Malays, Chinese, and Indians turned out to watch, as if they were attending an air show display. Curiosity turned to horror as the Japanese began strafing the crowds and spectators died by the hundreds. An English doctor recorded in his diary that it was like H. G. Wells's *War of the Worlds* come to life.[15]

Across the British Empire in Asia, white and nonwhite alike were swept up in an incomprehensible wave of destruction, as the Japanese tsunami smashed into their world. The whites of Penang evacuated in a panic (on ships manned by sailors rescued from the *Prince of Wales*), leaving their servants, employees, and tenants to their fate. "The white man's burden" was forgotten. It was left to the Tamil editor of the *Straits Echo,* Penang's English-language newspaper, to lower the last Union Jack. After a century and a half British rule in Malaya had come to an end.[16]

Indians living in other Asian outposts realized that the empire that they may have hated but that they also relied on for a living and for protection was dissolving before their eyes. On December 16 Japanese bombers hit Rangoon, capital of Burma. Meanwhile Japanese soldiers equipped with six thousand bicycles swarmed down both sides of the Malay peninsula, converging on Singapore. On Christmas Day Hong Kong fell. In Bangkok the head of the Indian Independence League called on all overseas Indians to join the Japanese in driving "the Anglo-Saxon from the whole of Asia." On New Year's Eve a Japanese intelligence official began recruiting collaborators from Indian POWs, thus forming the core of what would become the Indian National Army.[17]

Meanwhile other Indian soldiers were fighting and dying in the hopeless effort to keep the Japanese out of Singapore. Like the rest of the British forces in Malaya, they were poorly prepared and poorly led. In the end they and their British and Australian comrades had to abandon the mainland to the enemy and withdraw for a final stand on Singapore Island—ironically, the site of the last Indian Army mutiny twenty-seven years earlier.[18]

On January 27, 1942, engineers blew up the causeway connecting the island to the mainland. The English principal at Raffles College asked some passing boys what the noise was. One of them promptly answered, "That is the end of the British Empire."*[19]

Churchill was still determined to save it. On December 26 he was visiting Roosevelt in Washington, D.C. That afternoon he had addressed a joint session of Congress, dissolving his audience into helpless laughter when he observed, "I cannot help reflecting that if my father had been an American, and my mother British, instead of the other way around, I might have gotten here on my own."

That night in his White House bedroom Winston got up to open a window. As he threw up the sash, he felt a dull pain over his heart that passed down to his left arm. He had his doctor, Sir Charles Wilson (later Lord Moran), summoned. Wilson whipped out his stethoscope and confirmed Churchill's suspicion. It had been a heart attack: fruit of the worst two weeks of his premiership, from the sinking of the *Repulse* and *Prince of Wales* to the abandonment of Malaya. The prime minister, however, swore his doctor to secrecy. Even Roosevelt must not know

---

* The boy was Lee Kuan Yew, future president of the Republic of Singapore.

what happened. (In fact, no one knew about the heart attack until after Churchill's death, when Lord Moran's wartime journal was released.) "No one else can do this job," he told his doubtful doctor. "I must." Churchill was terrified that he might be replaced even as his empire was teetering on collapse.[20]

It was not the Japanese alone who were causing the pain. Before Churchill left for Washington, he had received a telegram from Linlithgow. Given the magnitude of the crisis, the viceroy wanted to re-open negotiations with Gandhi and the Congress. Churchill angrily refused, using the Muslim League's opposition as his excuse. "Personally, I would rather accord India independence than that we should have to keep an army there to hold down the fighting races [i.e., Muslims] for the benefit of the Hindu priesthood and caucus," he sputtered. In January he was still fuming and reiterated that there would be no consti-tutional change for India "at a moment when the enemy is upon the frontier."[21]

But defiant words could not stop the rising Japanese tide. By February 9 their troops had landed on Singapore Island itself and were widening their bridgehead. Churchill frantically demanded a last-ditch stand. "There must be no thought of saving troops or sparing the popu-lation," he told Archibald Wavell, the commander in chief. With the Americans and Russians watching, "the whole reputation of our coun-try and our race is involved." He assured FDR, whose troops were sim-ilarly engaged in the Philippines, "The battle must be fought to the bitter end."[22]

But British resistance was already crumbling. General Arthur Percival, with 85,000 men and strong defensive positions, faced an army that had been reduced to nearly a third the size of his and that was running low on ammunition. But during the pell-mell retreat Percival had lost heart as well as honor, as one of his own officers angrily pointed out. In his mis-guided but civilized way, Percival had no wish to prolong the bloodshed, especially among civilians. It never occurred to him that after the surren-der the Japanese would murder thousands, especially Singapore's over-seas Chinese. Percival's soldiers, shaken and demoralized, summed up the situation in a quatrain that mocked Churchill's own words:

> *Never before have so many*
> *been buggered about by so few*

And neither the few nor the many
Have bugger all idea what to do.[23]

Just four days after Churchill's last frantic order, Singapore surrendered. In a radio broadcast, the prime minister put the best face on it. "This," he said, "is one of the moments when the British race and nation can show their quality and their genius...So far we have not failed. We shall not fail now. Let us move forward steadfastly together into the storm."[24] But in private he was more candid, pronouncing it the worst disaster in the history of British arms.

It was also the worst disaster in the history of the Indian Army. For literally thousands of Indian POWs, their world had collapsed. One British officer simply told his men, "Now you belong to the Japanese army"— words that would later haunt Churchill and the Raj.[25] Interestingly, Japanese soldiers had been told to sort out their Indian prisoners by asking them a single question: "Gandhi?" Those who gave a nod of recognition were shunted aside. Some were recruited to join the puppet Indian National Army. Others, including their officers, were shot.

One Indian captain told his captors that his father was a friend of Gandhi; he was spared. He watched as his British second in command was beheaded with a samurai sword. But Captain Prem Sehgal felt no regret. "The fall of Singapore finally convinced me of the degeneration of the British people," he wrote later, "and I thought the last days of the British Empire had come."[26]

Burma was the next to collapse. On February 27 the new head of the British Army or CIGS (Chief of the Imperial General Staff) General Alan Brooke, confided to his diary, "I cannot see how we are going to go on holding Rangoon much longer."[27] Through Burma spread a very real fear that at this pace the Japanese might reach eastern Bengal before the monsoon. Tens of thousands of Indians who had been living and working in Burma, some for generations, seemed to have no choice but to pack their belongings and run. The retreat from Burma turned into a rout and a human disaster: as many as eighty thousand died en route of hunger and exposure, most of them poor ordinary Indians who "trailed like herds of animals before a forest fire," an eyewitness said.[28] Once again British colonials fled in a panic, leaving chaos behind them. Randolph Churchill's proudest boast, that he had added Upper Burma to the empire, became Britain's greatest shame.

The war that had seemed so far away was now on India's doorstep. The question was whether India would fight, and on whose side. Many Indians wondered seriously if there would still be a British side left to fight for. Gandhi was asking himself that question as well. On January 22 he told a Congress worker, "Jawaharlal [Nehru] believes the British Empire is finished. We all wish it to be finished, but I do not think it is finished." He knew from experience what Churchill was made of: "Mr. Churchill has said that [the British] are not 'sugar candies,' and that they can meet rough with rough. Therefore it will be long before the Empire is finished."[29]

Still, the speed and squalor of the East Asian collapse impressed even Gandhi. When Singapore surrendered, he had felt compelled to issue a statement calling for public calm. "The recent British reverses ought not to create panic in the land," he wrote as he rode a train to Calcutta on February 17, in an editorial that appeared in *Harijan*. "Failures do not dismay or demoralize [the English]. They take them with calmness... Wars for them are like a game of football. The defeated team heartily congratulates the successful one almost as if it was a joint victory, and drowns the sorrows of defeat in a glass of whisky."[30]

Gandhi overestimated British fortitude: the trauma of war triggered in far too many British colonials a moral collapse. Gandhi's view of the British at war, like Churchill's, still had a Victorian frame, made up of memories of the Boer War. But both were right in that the British people themselves were prepared to fight and endure. With uncanny instinct, Churchill had managed to channel their feelings of determination into a war policy that defied defeat and disappointment before, and would do so again. Gandhi could admire that resolve, even as he sensed a deeper tragedy: that India could not participate in it. "We are a house divided against itself and there is no living bond between ruler and ruled," he lamented. "The tragedy is deepened by the knowledge that all parties feel so helpless."[31]

Would ordinary Indians help the British cause? That was the critical question for Churchill and his War Cabinet during the headlong flight from Burma. For the even more frightening possibility was that Indians would not only allow their country to be overrun but would rise up against their British masters and join the Japanese. One man was already working to make that happen: Subhas Chandra Bose.

Bose had been imprisoned during Gandhi's "personal" satyagraha, then was released under house arrest. Furious at being sidelined while world events were unfolding, on January 17, 1941, Bose gave his guards the slip. Like a character in a Kipling or John Buchan novel, he traveled incognito across India and headed for Kabul. There he met first with the Russian legation (at that time Stalin was still Hitler's ally) and then with the Italians, who gave him a Sicilian passport under the name Orlando Mazzota, along with a Russian visa.

On April 2, 1941, Bose landed in Berlin. His plan was to make India the second front in the Nazi war on Britain. "For the sake of my country, I have risked my neck to come to Germany, " he told his hosts. "I am confident that India will win its freedom in this war." He wanted German help to do it.[32]

German intelligence officials listened politely, but their plans to put Bose to work hung fire for months. They did allow him to set up a Hindi propaganda station in Berlin, Azad Hind Radio, which broadcast news of German victories and British disasters into India.* In time the Germans gave Bose money, uniforms, and military equipment to form his own Free India Corps with ex-Indian Army volunteers.[33]

The news of the Japanese attack and fall of Singapore seized Bose's imagination and gave him a new resolve. "The fall of Singapore means the collapse of the British Empire," he ecstatically proclaimed, "and the dawn of a new era in Indian history."[34] When he learned that the Japanese were actively recruiting Indian troops from POWs and overseas Indians, he became frantic to get to Malaya. He told the Japanese ambassador in Berlin that "a new order in greater East Asia will be accomplished only with the cooperation of 350 million people in India." To build that order, the Japanese would need Bose.

They, at least, were nothing loathsome—their Indian recruits in Singapore "worshiped Bose like a God." As they made plans to get Bose back into Asia, their Indian National Army (INA) was growing into a genuine force. Its members were divided into three regiments, each named after an Indian nationalist: Gandhi, Nehru, and Azad.† The INA held its first parade in Singapore on October 2, 1942.

That date was chosen because it was Gandhi's birthday.[35]

---

* The purpose was to counteract the pro-British perspective being broadcast on the BBC with the help of the Ministry of Information. The man who composed the scripts for the BBC (which Azad Hind said stood for the "Bluff and Bluster Corporation"), and later read some of them over the air himself, was former Burma policeman Eric Blair, better known under his pen name, George Orwell.
† Maulana Abul Kalam Azad, the most prominent Muslim member of the Congress.

* * *

In London that spring, as the Japanese were racing to the Indian border, as Gandhi's name was being invoked by Britain's enemies, and as Bose was summoning German and Japanese help for an armed insurrection, everyone realized something urgent had to be done. "India is vital to our existence," General Claude Auchinleck, now commander of British forces in the Western Desert, told Churchill. "We could still hold India without the Middle East, but we cannot hold the Middle East without India."[36]

Churchill had little choice but to agree. In February he also had a new cabinet. Halifax was now in Washington as British ambassador; Anthony Eden took his place at the Foreign Office. The leader of the Labour opposition, Clement Attlee, became deputy prime minister, and another Labour stalwart, Sir Stafford Cripps, was officially leader of the House of Commons as well as Lord Privy Seal. Together with their colleague Ernest Bevin, they began to pressure Churchill to give way on India.

Now "is the time for an act of statesmanship," Attlee told the cabinet on February 2, even before Singapore fell. "A renewed effort must be made to get the leaders of the Indian political parties to unite." Viceroy Linlithgow was not the man for the job, Attlee felt; nor was the Indian secretary Leo Amery. Amery and Linlithgow were stalemated over what to do, terrified that any move might jeopardize the original 1935 settlement. Even an offer from the Liberal politician T. B. Sapru and twelve other non-Congress leaders in early January 1942, promising to support the war if Britain gave India immediate par status with the other Dominions and formed a national government, met with hesitation from New Delhi and London and finally a negative response.[37]

Attlee felt it was time to cut the Gordian knot by sending a single representative from the cabinet with full powers to negotiate a final settlement with all parties, including the Muslim League. "There is a precedent for such action," he wrote in his memorandum. "Lord Durham saved Canada to the British Empire.* We need a man to do in India what Durham did in Canada." Attlee had in mind Stafford Cripps, who was deeply sympathetic to the Indian cause and had been

---

* John Lambton, Lord Durham, was sent to Canada as governor-general in 1838. He returned five months later to recommend union and responsible government for Canada.

Labour's point man on the India Bill. Cripps was a socialist like Nehru, and like Nehru he believed India's problems were about not religion or ethnicity but class. He had met and dealt with Jinnah in talks in December 1939. He was even a vegetarian like Gandhi. To his party's leader, Cripps seemed the perfect man to bring Indians of all shades of opinion together and rally them in the fight against fascism, in exchange for their freedom.

Churchill's feelings when he read this proposal can be imagined, but Attlee's memorandum proved decisive.[38] After Singapore's fall Churchill's hand was weaker than at any time since he had assumed the premiership. He had insisted on a vote of confidence immediately afterward, which he won overwhelmingly, but for the first time since the war began, his inner confidence was shaken. John Colville, now serving in Pretoria with the Royal Air Force, noticed it at once when he heard his former boss announce Singapore's surrender on the radio. "All the mastery of his oratory was there," Colville noted in his diary, "but also a new note of appeal lacking the usual confidence of support." A few days before, Churchill had run into his friend from days past, Violet Bonham Carter. She had never seen him so depressed, worse even than after Gallipoli. He confessed to her his fear that the British soldier of the day was not as good as his predecessors. "We have so many men in Singapore," he said over and over, "so many men—they should have done better." It seemed an epitaph for an empire as well as an army.[39]

Churchill was also feeling inexorable pressure from the Americans and Roosevelt. "India," wrote the editor of the American magazine *Foreign Affairs,* "had become a touchstone" of the Anglo-American alliance. The issue was no longer American anti-imperialist feelings or even admiration for Gandhi as "a man of peace," as it had been in April 1941. India was becoming a vital supply base for the U.S. reinforcement of Chiang Kai-shek's forces in China. If the two-thousand-mile long Burma Road became permanently shut, or if India dropped out of the war, Chiang's struggle against the occupying Japanese would be doomed.

Chiang himself realized this, and in the second week of February the Generalissimo made a sudden visit to India to try to rally public opinion. The meetings, including a four-hour chat with Gandhi, were not promising. A thoroughly depressed Chiang reported back to Churchill and to FDR that "if the Japanese should know of the real situation and attack India, they would be virtually unopposed."[40]

On February 25 Roosevelt sat at his desk and composed a long letter to Churchill. "I feel that there is real danger in India now" and "too much suspicion and dissatisfaction in too many places." Roosevelt continued, "I have been for many years interested in the problem of the relations between Europeans and Americans on the one side [and] varieties of races in eastern and southern Asia and the Indians on the other. There is no question in my mind that the old relationship ceased to exist 10 or 20 years ago, and that no substitute has yet been worked out except the American policy of eventual freedom." From that standpoint, Roosevelt worried that Indian resistance against the Japanese would falter unless Britain made some firm offer of a new constitutional arrangement.[41]

In the end Roosevelt decided not to send the letter. But he did go forward with a plan of his own for India—he was neither the first nor the last statesman who felt he knew what Indians needed better than Indians did. It involved forming a "temporary government" along the lines of America's Articles of Confederation, led by "a small, representative group covering different castes, occupations, religions and geographies" who would act as a temporary Dominion government until they could call an assembly to draft a final constitution. "Perhaps the analogy of some such method to the travails and problems of the United States from 1783 to 1789 might give a new slant in India itself," Roosevelt concluded, "and it might cause the people there to forget hard feelings, to feel more loyal to the British Empire, and to stress the danger of Japanese domination."[42]

It was a plan breathtaking in its boldness—and in its simplemindedness. It reflected the general American consensus that Churchill and the British were responsible for the discontent in India, because of their "unwillingness to concede the right of self-government to the Indians."[43] That consensus, like Roosevelt's plan, ignored the realities of the past ten years, as well as two hundred years of the Raj, not to mention thousands of years of Indian history. But it was a sincere attempt to break the logjam. Churchill's doctor had noticed that disagreements with FDR "took more out of him than any major disaster in the field."[44] But if Churchill was unwilling to accept the American plan, he would have to accept someone's before India became the next battleground.

On March 6, 1942, General Harold Alexander ordered the evacuation of Rangoon. Churchill wrote to FDR, "The weight of the war is very heavy now, and I must expect it to get steadily worse for some time to come." On the tenth he received FDR's Articles of Confederation–style proposal for India. But he and the cabinet had already decided to act.

Characteristically, Churchill's first instinct was to go to India himself. He announced to the cabinet that he would personally hammer out an understanding with Gandhi and other leaders on a national assembly, which would create a constitution for India after the war. Alexander Cadogan of the Foreign Office thought the idea "brilliantly imaginative and bold." Eden and his private secretary Oliver Harvey agreed. Churchill was "the only person who could do it all ... What a decision to take, and how gallant of the old boy himself."[45]

But then they joined the sixty-seven-year-old prime minister for lunch. They watched him consume his usual pre-luncheon whiskeys, several bottles of beer, three glasses of port, and three brandies afterward.[46] The bizarre image of Churchill sitting down to a meal of lentils and goat's milk at Sevagram while Gandhi twirled his charkha must have crossed their minds. Was Churchill really up to the challenges of thrashing out the future of the subcontinent with the likes of Gandhi and Nehru and Muhammad Ali Jinnah, arguing at length day after day, with the future of the empire—not to mention Churchill's own reputation and the course of the war—on the line?

Given Churchill's failing heart, his doctor opposed the trip, but Churchill was adamant. Only the fall of Singapore forced Churchill first to postpone, then finally to cancel, the trip that would have brought him and the Mahatma face-to-face for the first time in thirty-five years.[47]

So in the end it was Cripps who went. On March 3 Oliver Harvey noted in his diary, "The Cabinet are about to take an immense step [on India], an offer of complete independence like a Dominion after the war." Drafts of the declaration were batted back and forth in the cabinet's India Committee for a week; Churchill and Leo Amery held out against the more radical proposals of Attlee and Cripps. Linlithgow threatened to resign at the usurpation of what he saw as his constitutional role. It took all of Churchill's powers of persuasion to get him to back down.[48]

On March 7 Churchill told Roosevelt, "We are still persevering to find some conciliatory and inspiring process." In the end the hard-liners gave more than they got. The result was the so-called Cripps offer, which promised Indians immediate independence after the war and freedom to draw up their own constitution. In a nod to the Muslim

League, provinces that refused to abide by a new constitution were free to secede on their own. Even the princely states would be allowed to bow out. The old formula that Indians must come together in unity before final independence, a key assumption behind the 1935 Government of India Act and reaching back to Edwin Montagu, died a swift and necessary death.

Literally everything would now be on the table, as long as India was willing to fight Japan. Churchill was not at all happy, realizing it would be nearly impossible to rescind an offer of independence, even if it were turned down.[49] But he had no choice. The Americans, and Gandhi's gloomy meeting with Chiang Kai-shek, had left him no room to maneuver.

It was with this proposal in his pocket that a hopeful Stafford Cripps left for India on March 14, 1942. He arrived on the twenty-second. Days later an American representative, Colonel Louis Johnson, arrived to help massage the deal. It was the nadir of Britain's fortunes in Asia. The Japanese had entered Rangoon. Within days they closed the Burma Road, isolating Chiang's army in China. The day after Cripps arrived Japanese troops occupied the Andaman Islands in the Bay of Bengal. The Japanese navy freely roamed the Indian coast, sinking Indian and neutral shipping.

Indians had always been taught that rule by Britain, whatever its shortcomings, at least kept them safe from any foreign invader. That assumption, which had propped up the Raj for the better part of a century, collapsed ignominiously overnight. Thousands of people fled Madras, fearing an imminent Japanese attack. Thousands of others arrived from Ceylon as refugees. Churchill and the Admiralty made grim plans for a last-ditch battle there to hold Trincomalee, Ceylon's vital naval base. Then on April 5 five Japanese aircraft carriers made their way toward the island. Japanese bombers took to the air and sank the heavy cruisers *Dorsetshire* and *Cornwall* along with two other British warships. The next day the Japanese also sank the carrier *Hermes*. "Our naval forces are not strong enough to oppose this," a weary Churchill told FDR. Disaster in India loomed, just as it had loomed over Singapore the previous December.[50]

If ever there was a time to finally settle India's outstanding issues, this was it. But to his astonishment, Cripps found he could make no headway. The Congress was furious that the offer included the right of individual provinces to secede—a clear invitation to the creation of a separate Pakistan. The Muslim League was furious that the Congress was furious. The viceroy was furious that he had no role in negotiations that were taking place not just behind his back but in front of his face. Meanwhile Commander in Chief General Wavell worried that time would run out with nothing accomplished and that once they had digested their conquests in Burma and Malaya the Japanese would spring across the border into Assam.

Despite these immense difficulties and pressures, Cripps, Johnson, and the Congress managed to pull together a preliminary deal. It involved complicated arrangements for native ministers to take office, and even to supervise India's defense, as part of a genuine Indian national government thinly disguised as a new executive council for the viceroy.

This was on April 9. That same afternoon the Congress negotiators had a long telephone conversation with Gandhi at Wardha. They came back to the negotiating table and announced they had to reject the entire offer. Cripps was crushed—and enraged at Gandhi, whom he assumed had sabotaged the deal. He left India on April 12, his friendship with Nehru in tatters and his trust in the good faith of Indians destroyed.

Six days earlier the first Japanese bombs had fallen near Calcutta.[51] It seemed only a miracle could stop Japan's conquest of India now.

Chapter Twenty-six

QUIT INDIA
1942

I have not become the King's First Minister in order to
preside over the liquidation of the British Empire.

WINSTON CHURCHILL, 1942

SOME STILL DOUBTED THAT THE JAPANESE could pull it off. Nirad
Chaudhuri, for example, was now working for All-India Radio in
Delhi, as part of the Allied propaganda effort. "Before I left Calcutta I
felt sure that the Japanese would not attempt an invasion of eastern
India from Burma," he wrote years later.* Even the news of the disastrous sinkings of British ships in the Indian Ocean, which delighted his
anti-British Bengali friends, did not faze him. He sensed that a Japanese
landing would bring not a massive uprising against the Raj but only
more fleeing refugees.[1]

Since 1940 Chaudhuri had come to admire Winston Churchill for his
single-minded and single-handed struggle against the Nazis, whom
Chaudhuri saw as genuinely evil compared to India's British masters,
with their relatively mild flaws. But even Chaudhuri had to wonder. "It
is not easy," Churchill had written to FDR, "to assign limits to the
Japanese aggression."[2] If the Japanese were free to roam the Indian
Ocean at will, how long would it be before the British would have to
abandon India in order to protect their interests elsewhere?

Others in London had a different worry. Why had Gandhi undermined the Cripps mission? The consensus among scholars today is that
he did not. Gandhi did meet Cripps, but he was adamant that he would

---

* He was correct. The Japanese had badly overextended themselves with the speed of their advance. The
early monsoon in April 1942 also put an end to any thoughts of an invasion. Besides, India played no real
part in their imperial ambitions. They craved the oil from Burma and the Dutch East Indies, not the
headache of being the Raj's successor.

leave all negotiations to the Congress's official representatives, Nehru and Azad. Gandhi himself denied he ever had any contact with members of the Congress Working Committee after he left Delhi on April 5.

But others believed he did.[3] In fact, two people were actually relieved that the Cripps mission had failed. One was Churchill, who believed that the collapse of the talks would ultimately have a "beneficial" impact on his relations with the Americans and hence the war. The Americans had wanted the British to offer Indians independence. Now the British had done so, and the Indians had turned them down. Churchill could echo Cripps's words to him in his last communication on April 11: "Now we get on with the job of defending India."[4]

The other man who wanted the mission to fail was certainly Gandhi. He may have had no hand in sabotaging it, but he considered the Cripps offer a "post-dated cheque on a failing bank"—too little too late. Days after Cripps left, another plan was taking shape in Gandhi's mind. It came to him on his silence day, with the kind of intuitive stroke that had inspired his campaign against the salt tax. This plan, however, was far bolder. He confessed to his friend Horace Alexander that it "would mean courage of a higher order"—perhaps higher than India herself could achieve. But like Churchill, Gandhi had reached a point where he felt there were no choices left.[5]

His idea was that the British should leave India. Now. Completely, immediately, and for good. "Britain cannot defend India, much less herself on Indian soil with any strength," he told Alexander. "The best thing she can do is leave India to her fate. I feel somehow India will not do badly then."[6]

It was a breathtaking idea. Even if the British agreed, the logistics alone would be appalling. But the British—and Winston Churchill—would never agree. Still, Gandhi felt it was the next logical step in the campaign to finally lift the British incubus from India's shoulders. Demonstrations of loyalty had failed, noncooperation had failed, negotiation with viceroys and even members of the British cabinet had failed. What indeed was left except forcing the British to pack up and leave—especially in the face of an irresistible Japanese advance? For by the spring of 1942 Gandhi was convinced that the Axis could no longer be resisted. (He was not alone.) Bose and his supporters seemed right: the British were going to lose. And they would bring India down with them unless he, and the Indian people, acted first.

Nor did Gandhi believe the British departure would leave India helpless before the Japanese enemy. He had actually weighed this possibility during his very first noncooperation campaign. Back in December 1920 some had said that if the British left, India would fall under foreign domination. "Imagine the worst," Gandhi had argued against them, with uncanny prescience, *the Japanese overwhelming us from the Bay of Bengal,* the Gurkhas from the hills, and the Pathans from the Northwest." India would have to defend itself, Gandhi said, and nonviolently resist the invader—which was exactly what they should do against the British. What if the enemy refused to turn back? Then the Indians would have to resort to arms to drive them out. Either way, Gandhi believed, it "will be a more manly course than a helpless submission" to the Raj.[7]

But in 1942 Gandhi had convinced himself that the Japanese did not want to conquer India. Once the British left, the reasons for the Japanese to attack would disappear. He even foresaw a free India negotiating a formal nonaggression treaty with imperial Japan.[8]

He also rejected the notion that the withdrawal of British troops and command of the police would lead to anarchy and chaos. "Our ahimsa will remain lame as long as we do not get rid of the fear of anarchy," he impatiently responded. "We have to take the risk of violence to shake off the great calamity of slavery." India needed to have "unflinching faith" in nonviolence and to expect the best instead of fearing the worst: "This is the time to prove that there is no power stronger than ahimsa in the world."[9]

Far from turning India upside down, Gandhi expected that a concerted move to force the British out would unify the Indian National Congress, which had been shattered by the failure of the Cripps mission and desperately needed a cause to rally around. It was also the kind of satyagraha that he believed might open the door to Hindu-Muslim reconciliation. Indeed, one of his deepest worries about the Cripps offer had been that if Congress did endorse the war effort, it might trigger a fresh wave of communal violence. Once the British left, Gandhi kept telling himself, everything would work out. As he told the press, "I shall expect nonviolence to arise out of chaos."[10]

There was still one more reason why Gandhi decided on this bold, even quixotic course. In his heart he wanted to prove to Churchill and the British that Indians were not "sugar candies." Churchill had rallied a people and a nation to fight a war for freedom that others had said could not be won. (Indeed some, including Gandhi, still believed it could not be won.) Gandhi was determined to show that he could rally a people and nation to gain their freedom *without a war*.

That previous October he had composed an editorial that is deeply revealing of his state of mind. "My faith in human nature is progressively growing," he wrote. "I have concluded, on the basis of my experiments, that human nature can be easily molded." At the moment "Churchill and Hitler are striving to change the nature of their countrymen by forcing and hammering violent methods on them," Gandhi sought to prove that "ahimsa...can change human nature and *sooner than men like Churchill and Hitler can*."[11]

Contrary to Churchill, it was humanity not history that constantly changed for the better. In effect, the Quit India movement would be Gandhi's final attempt to prove that Churchill, and those who thought like him, were wrong. Now at seventy-three, it would be his last throw of the dice—a final test of his faith in his fellow man.

By June 1942 he had formulated his resolution, and in July he submitted it to the Congress Working Committee. The reactions were mixed, to say the least. Rajagopalachari was horrified—a sudden and total British withdrawal might mean "the dissolution of the State and society itself." He begged the Mahatma to call the whole thing off.[12] Nehru too was deeply uneasy. Gandhi was being hopelessly naïve, he understood, in assuming that the Japanese would leave India alone once the British left. Moreover such a campaign might brand the Congress members as seditionists, perhaps even fifth columnists. S. C. Bose's brother Sarat had been arrested in December and locked up under suspicion of having had contacts with Japanese. How would the British react to such a direct and massive threat to the war effort?

In answer to these objections, Gandhi made a concession: he would allow British forces to remain in India during hostilities, although not the British government. He also conceded that a free India might enter the war on the side of the Allies. India turned into an armed camp would be distressing, but he still did not want Britain to lose. "I am more interested than the British in keeping the Japanese out," he told the American journalist Louis Fischer. However, "I am sure Britain cannot win unless the Indian people become free." He broadly hinted that a new government, grateful for its freedom, would gladly permit British and American soldiers to remain on Indian soil. But for now "it is not at India's request or with India's consent that they are here."[13]

In fact, Gandhi implied that leaving India would work to Britain's advantage, both strategically and morally: "If British rule ends, that moral act will save Britain." In any case, it was not up to Churchill or Amery or anyone else to tell the Indians how to run their lives: "Let them entrust India to God or in modern parlance anarchy."[14]

God or anarchy. Gandhi envisioned a campaign whose scale was far greater than that of the salt satyagraha. It would involve mass noncoop- eration at every level of society and government, with hartals, strikes, pickets, and student walk outs and sit-ins, all under the direction of Congress and all under Gandhi's direct orders. He grimly expected trouble, even violence: "I want to guard against a sudden outburst of an- archy or a state of things that may be calculated to invite the Japanese ag- gression." And the British would undoubtedly resist by any means necessary, including violence. But "I have made up my mind that it would be a good thing if a million people were shot in a brave and non- violent resistance against the British rule."

He was just as casual (or callous) about India's post-British future. "All the parties will fight one another like dogs," he conceded. It "may take us years before we can evolve order out of chaos." But out of it must eventually come "a reasonable agreement" and an India worth living and dying for.[15]

In his imperious way Gandhi beat down the objections and hesita- tions, one by one. Watching uneasily from the sidelines, Viceroy Linlithgow admitted that "the old man has lost none of his political skill with age."

Like Churchill, Gandhi's power of persuasion could carry everything before them—even reasonable precaution. Linlithgow warned London that Gandhi would almost certainly get what he wanted out of Congress, even though if the campaign failed, the blow to Congress's prestige would be immense.[16] Britain and the Raj would be faced with the equivalent of mass albeit unarmed rebellion, at the war's most cru- cial juncture. As the All-India Congress Committee met in Bombay to consider Gandhi's Quit India resolution, Linlithgow and his executive council made feverish preparations.

Debate in Bombay was short, even subdued. The Congress had nowhere else to turn and no one else to follow. On August 7 the AICC passed a resolution calling on the British to immediately leave India "for the vindication of India's inalienable right to freedom and indepen- dence" and sanctioning "the starting of a mass struggle on non-violent lines on the widest possible scale" if they did not. Out of 250 delegates, only thirteen cast negative votes. The delegates then asked Gandhi to lead and direct the Indian nation (although the resolution envisaged the formation of a new national government by all parties, including Muslims, once the British were gone).

The next day Gandhi returned to the dais. His speech on August 8 was one of his most riveting—his "Few" or "Finest Hour" speech. He first congratulated the delegates on passing his resolution. Then he called on all parties, including Jinnah's Muslim League, to join with the Congress in the Quit India campaign. Finally he addressed the question of what the campaign meant.

"It is not a make believe that I am suggesting to you," he assured them. "It is the very essence of freedom. The bond of the slave is snapped the moment he considers himself to be a free being." Congress would not try to bargain with the viceroys this time, he promised, or negotiate concessions. If Lord Linlithgow asked Gandhi what he wanted, "I will say, 'Nothing less than freedom.'"

As the wild cheers died down, Gandhi's eyes flashed behind his glasses. "Here is a mantra, a short one, that I give you," he said. "You may imprint it in your hearts and let every breath of yours give expression to it. The mantra is: 'Do or Die.' We shall either free India or die in the attempt." This campaign, he added, was "open rebellion."[17]

Even as the AICC met, Mirabehn made a quiet journey to New Delhi. She begged to see the viceroy, but he refused. She did meet with his private secretary for more than an hour, telling him, "Gandhiji is in deadly earnest. This time it will be impossible for you to hold him. No jail will contain him, no crushing force will silence him." The government was faced with two alternatives, she said: declaring India's independence or killing Gandhi. "And once you kill him you kill forever all hope of friendship between India and England."

She let her words sink in, then asked, "What are you going to do about it?"[18]

The secretary knew all too well but said nothing. That afternoon Mirabehn caught the train to Bombay. The truth was that despite his defiant words, Gandhi hoped he could meet the viceroy before a nationwide hartal began, to convince him to convince Churchill and the cabinet to give up before "the rebellion burst." From Mirabehn, however, Gandhi learned that such a meeting was out of the question. It was after midnight. As the banners were furled and the delegates left, he and the other Working Committee members congratulated themselves.

Tomorrow they would draw up plans, write letters, and mobilize satya-grahi around the country.

Gandhi was calm but excited. The Tennyson quotation—"Do or die"—was much on his mind. "Believe me, friends, I do not wish to die," he told them. "I want to live a full span of life. According to me, it is 120 years at least," he joked. But "by that time India will be free, the world will be free." As he had told the delegates, "What you think you be-come."[19] He went to bed full of hope for the future and for the battle to come.

He never saw the battle. At four o'clock in the morning, while Gandhi, Mirabehn, Nehru, and a dozen other Congress Working Committee members were still asleep, British police barged in and ar-rested them all. This time they were taken not to Yeravda but to the summer palace of the Aga Khan in Poona, lent for the purpose, where a double row of barbed wire and soldiers with machine guns guarded the perimeter. Gandhi had assumed it would take two or even three weeks for the government to act.[20] But this was wartime. This time Winston Churchill, not Lord Irwin and Stanley Baldwin, was in charge. In one swift stroke, the government had decapitated the Quit India movement before it got started.

Meanwhile India erupted. News of Gandhi's arrest set off a tidal wave of agitation and violence. There were two weeks of angry hartals in India's major cities. Gandhi cheered them on with a message from the Aga Khan's palace: "Everyone is free to go to the fullest length under *ahimsa,*" he wrote. "Let every non-violent soldier of freedom write out the slogan 'do or die' on a piece of paper or cloth and stick it on his clothes, so that in case he died in the course of offering satyagraha, he might be distinguished by that sign from other elements who do not subscribe to non-violence."[21] He expected that his incarceration would trigger violence on an even more massive scale.

The news of the Quit India resolution and Gandhi's arrest had caught Nirad Chaudhuri by surprise. It rocked Delhi. At one point someone burst into the office and announced that the Railway Accounts Office was on fire. Chaudhuri rushed down and joined the throng watching as flames sprang out of the windows. Beyond it he could see other build-ings on fire. Standing beside him were some of his Bengali friends who worked in the Railway Accounts Office. They had smiles on their faces—"I could guess they were not wholly uninvolved." They watched silently as the building burned to its foundations. Their deed "not only satisfied their patriotic anger, but also spared them a lot of work."[22]

The next day Delhi was back to normal, however, even as riots exploded in other parts of India, especially Bihar, Bombay, and the United Provinces. At one point two Canadian RAF officers were dragged from a train and murdered by a mob in Fatwah in Bihar. But otherwise, to almost everyone's surprise, the Quit India insurrection committed almost no violence against whites, let alone British or American soldiers. Instead, the mounting wave of vandalism, sabotage, and arson was directed against government offices and the railways. Organized gangs removed railway tracks and sleepers; smashed signals and signal boxes; and cut telegraph wires and toppled telephone poles. At one point the Bihar Flying Club had to fly messages to the remoter parts of the district, since all other communication had become impossible.

Mobs also stormed police stations and post offices. All together 208 police stations were burned to the ground. Nearly 750 other government buildings were destroyed, including 50 post offices and 250 railway stations. Police and soldiers had to fire hundreds of times, killing and wounding some 2,500 people. At the height of the disorder Linlithgow and Wavell were forced to employ more than fifty battalions of British and Indian troops to impose order.[23]

On August 31 Linlithgow sent a tense wire to Churchill. "I am engaged here in meeting by far the most serious rebellion since 1857," it read, "the gravity and extent of which we have so far concealed from the world for reasons of military security." What Linlithgow did not say was that some Indian Army officers had refused to confront the demonstrators. As a result the British feared that they might be facing a full-scale mutiny in Indian Army ranks—the first in India in eighty-five years.[24]

Even as Linlithgow sent his telegram, however, the worst riots were already over. Within a month the British managed to disperse the mobs, reopen the rail lines, and reconnect the telephone wires. Except in Bihar, everything had returned almost to normal by September 21. Trains again ran on time; government officials and ministers returned to their offices—or found new ones to replace the ones burned to the ground. Linlithgow told Secretary Amery that things were "pretty comfortable." In just six weeks the Quit India movement, and the specter of a second Mutiny, had been crushed.

In his diary Amery wrote that Gandhi's actions had been "dictated by the conviction that [the British] were down and out" in Asia and would leave India to cut their losses.[25] Working together, Churchill, Amery, and Linlithgow had proved him wrong. Thousands would remain in prison, as many as 60,000 (although some insist the total was closer to 100,000). Yet ten months later in June 1943 Amery could write to Linlithgow, "It looks as if India had never been so quiet politically as at this moment."[26]

As the last mass riots died away, Gandhi was still in the Aga Khan's gilded cage. He had seen Quit India as the decisive campaign of his life. In fact, it was among his most fruitless. From the beginning violence, not nonviolence, was its hallmark. As an exercise in satyagraha, it had proved a miserable failure.

It had also been, in the words of Gandhi scholar Judith Brown, "patchy" and "uncoordinated." The truth was that Gandhi had grossly underestimated the forces arrayed against him. He failed to anticipate not only the speed and ruthlessness of the British response but the Muslims' opposition to the campaign—they were still outraged by the sabotaging of the Cripps mission.[27] Gandhi had also misread the mood of the Indian public—not a difficult feat from the fastness of Sevagram. Few shared his delicate understanding of the moral stakes involved in the Second World War. Many, perhaps most Indian intellectuals, were openly pro-Axis. The Bombay and Calcutta students who joined in the riots looked to Subhas Chandra Bose, not Gandhi, as their role model and inspiration.

Most Indians living in cities, on the other hand, recognized that for them the war represented an economic opportunity. The British and American military were buying foodstuffs and equipment in unprecedented quantities. Their personnel required a range of services, from barbers and rickshaws to transport ships and tankers, as well as leather boots and cotton uniforms. Every day the Allies flew tons of supplies from India over the Himalayas (or "the Hump") to Chiang Kai-shek's forces. Almost all the cargo was supplied by Indian merchants and manufacturers. Over the course of the war India provided £286.5 million worth of supplies.[28] India's middle class may not have loved the Raj, but it loved the money that a wartime Raj put in their wallets.

Nor did the Indian Civil Service respond to Gandhi's call. In 1940, for the first time, the civil service had more Indian than British members (614 versus 587). Whatever their feelings about the British or independence, the overwhelming majority remained at their posts during the Quit India days. So did the Indian Army. In its quiet way, in the 1920s and 1930s, it had undergone a steady "Indianization." Native VCOs, or viceroy's commissioned officers, had been present in the Indian Army for decades. But beginning in 1920 a new class of native officer, the king's commissioned Indian officer or KCIO, had appeared. Officially indistinguishable from his English counterpart, the KCIO shared the mess with British officers, enjoyed similar precedence and promotion, and some even underwent the same training at Sandhurst.

KCIOs became the backbone of the Indian Army in World War II. They were the last soldiers of the Raj as well as "the advance guard of the new Indian nation." For every disgruntled or discouraged subaltern who joined Japan's puppet Indian National Army, a dozen KCIOs and VCOs served with distinction on every front in the British war effort, from Burma and Eritrea to North Africa and Italy.[29]

And the minister of war who created the KCIOs in 1920 had been Winston Churchill. Without realizing it, he had at the stroke of a pen secured India as part of the future Allied cause and created independent India's military legacy. Churchill never grasped the full magnitude of what he had done, but Gandhi nearly did. Many times over the years he had spoken of brave Indian soldiers who would defend their country and then return home to carry the future burden of freedom. "There is a new ferment and a new awakening among all the ranks today," Gandhi later would say about the Indian Army.[30] And the KCIOs were the core of it.*

One of them was Ajit "Jick"Rudra, who came from a Bengali professional family. His father was the man who had sponsored Gandhi's trip from England to India in 1915, and he and the Mahatma had remained friends ever since. Ajit entered the army, served with distinction in the First World War, and won a king's commission. But he had then been appalled by the slaughter at Amritsar. He consulted with Gandhi. Should he stay in the army? Gandhi refused to give a direct answer but said that one day India would be free and would need an army of strong able men and officers like Rudra.[31] Gandhi never guessed it was Churchill who gave those officers to India.

---

* When war broke out in 1939 First Lord of the Admiralty Churchill extended the same procedure to the Indian Navy. He told Tom Phillips that Indian officers were to be treated to the same recognition and promotion as white officers—even to the rank of admiral. "But," he added characteristically, "not too many of them, please."

Churchill himself later acknowledged the debt that he and Britain owed to the Indian Army during the Second World War. Depending on his mood, he could be cynical about where its loyalties ultimately lay. But even he recognized that the army was indispensable to his strategic vision. When Indian regiments scored a major success in driving the Italians out of East Africa, he sent a personal telegram to Linlithgow. "The whole Empire has been stirred by the achievement," he wrote. The Indians' "ardor and perseverance recalled memories of the Northwest Frontier of long years ago." As one "who has had the honor to serve in the field with Indian soldiers from all parts of Hindustan," he felt it a privilege to pass on "the pride and admiration with which we have followed their heroic exploits."[32]

After the war Churchill paid the Indians an even more elaborate tribute. "The loyalty of the Indian Army to the King-Emperor," the "glorious heroism" of its soldiers on campaigns from Abyssinia and North Africa to Burma and Italy, and "the unsurpassed bravery of Indian soldiers and officers, Moslem and Hindu alike, shine forever in the annals of war." He noted with pride that 2.5 million men had volunteered for the army, at a rate of fifty thousand a month—even while Gandhi maintained that "India should remain passive and neutral in the world conflict."[33]

Certainly Churchill took a grim satisfaction at the news of Gandhi's arrest and the defeat of the Quit India insurrection. The India issue had been a sore spot since the spring. Even after the failure of the Cripps mission, the Americans had leaned on Churchill to assure the world that Britain was serious about giving India its independence after the war. The pressure led to a full-scale row between Roosevelt and Churchill. Indeed, the vaunted "special relationship" threatened to run aground over the quesion of what to do next about India.

What nearly put it on the rocks was Roosevelt's suggestion that Cripps should not be allowed to leave India until some sort of national government had been formed. This innocent but incendiary message came to Churchill at three o'clock one morning while he was meeting with Roosevelt's special adviser Harry Hopkins. Churchill was trying to explain to Hopkins the importance of retaining India, even while America and Britain were focusing their forces on the main enemy, Hitler. "We could not possibly face the loss of an army of 600,000 men and the whole manpower of India," he kept saying.[34]

Roosevelt's intrusion, with what Anthony Eden called "a meandering amateurishness lit by discursive flashes," into what Churchill considered internal imperial affairs was too much. First he had had to endure the impromptu lesson in American history in March. Now he was being told that Cripps must do the impossible.

Churchill immediately tried to reach FDR but failed, then sent a frank telegram. "You know the weight which I attach to everything you say to me," it read, "but I did not feel I could take responsibility for the defense of India if everything had again to be thrown into the melting pot at this critical juncture." He promised he would keep Roosevelt's telegram private. "I do not propose to bring it before the Cabinet officially unless you tell me you wish this done. Anything like a serious difference between you and me would break my heart" and would damage the alliance "at the height of this terrible struggle."[35]

Roosevelt quickly realized his mistake and, at Hopkins's urging, backed down. But the outburst was indicative of how sensitive Churchill had become on the India issue and on challenges from outsiders who he felt knew nothing of the stakes involved. In fact, as historian Christopher Thorne has pointed out, Churchill's original response to Roosevelt had been even more pointed and menacing.

"I cannot feel that the common cause would benefit," Churchill had written, if it became known that "we were conforming to US public opinion in a matter that concerns the British Empire." If Roosevelt insisted on consulting with the cabinet, Churchill warned, he himself would have to resign. "I should personally make no objection at all to retiring to private life," he added, "and I have explained all this to Harry [Hopkins] just now." Yet even if he quit, Churchill felt confident that the cabinet would still turn Roosevelt down.[36]

It was the one time during the war when Churchill actually threatened to quit as prime minister. Whether he was bluffing, no one can know. Certainly Hopkins got the message and passed it on to Roosevelt. No more would be said about India, at least for now. But the incident was proof that on the issue of India, Churchill was adamant. No one—not the Germans or the Japanese; not Leo Amery or Clement Attlee; not Franklin Roosevelt or Harry Hopkins—was going to make him surrender the Raj.

And certainly not Gandhi. Churchill had learned of Gandhi's Quit India resolution on June 14, 1942, even as news was coming in of the great sea battle between American and Japanese forces at Midway, and as the ferocious tank battles between Rommel and the British Eighth

Army in the Libyan Desert were drawing to a climax. India's Commander in Chief General Wavell still worried about Japanese attacks on the Indian coast. So Churchill told Amery, "If Gandhi tries to start a really hostile movement against us in this case, I am of the opinion he should be arrested, and that both British and US opinion would support such a step. If he likes to starve himself to death," the prime minister added sardonically, "we cannot help that"—words that were uncannily prophetic.[37]

News of Gandhi's arrest came as Churchill was leaving Moscow after his first meeting with Stalin to decide war strategy. "We have clapped Gandhi into jail," Churchill gleefully told his doctor.[38] In Cairo he got news about the growing riots in India. He told Linlithgow, "My own conclusion is that if this situation is handled with the poise and strength which the Government of India is showing under your guidance it will soon demonstrate the very slender hold which the Congress have both upon the Indian masses and upon the dominant forces in Indian society." The next day his doctor could hear "the PM singing in his bath."[39]

Back in London, Churchill reported to the House of Commons: "Mr. Gandhi and other principal leaders have been interned under conditions of the highest comfort and consideration, and will be kept out of harm's way till the troubles subside." Gandhi's followers had abandoned their leader's theories of nonviolence and revealed themselves to be "a revolutionary movement" designed to "promote disorder" and hamper the war effort by disrupting rail and communication links, looting shops, and attacking police—probably with the help of pro-Axis fifth columnists.

Fortunately, the Congress party and its followers did "not represent all India," Churchill maintained. Above all, Congress had "no influence with the martial races" in the Indian Army, who remained firmly loyal. What emerged most clearly from the riots, Churchill averred, was how little influence Congress really had, "and their powerlessness to throw into confusion the normal peaceful life of India."[40]

Churchill's strong stand had been vindicated. All shades of opinion in Britain, and even in America, were appalled when they learned of Gandhi's quixotic resolution and the bloodshed that followed. Political pressure on the British to make more concessions evaporated, even after stories circulated that British officials had had rioters flogged (shades of Amritsar) and that British soldiers had burned down Bihari villages that backed the insurrection.[41] As October began, the crisis appeared to be over. With the Quit India movement crushed, Gandhi still incarcerated, and things returning to normal, Churchill could get on with the main task of winning the war.

And by November 1942 the Allies were winning it. Erwin Rommel's Afrika Korps was decisively beaten at El Alamein; Anglo-American landings in North Africa with Operation Torch had guaranteed his defeat. German armies in the East were bogged down in front of Leningrad and Stalingrad. German U-boats were on the defensive in the North Atlantic, as Allied convoy losses fell.

Thanks to American naval victories at Coral Sea and Midway, the situation in the Pacific had also stabilized. British and Australian forces turned back a Japanese thrust at Port Moresby in New Guinea in mid-September and the monsoon had damped any chances of a Japanese incursion from Burma into India during the Quit India uprising. The Big Three had agreed to open a second front against Hitler. The Allies were on the verge of turning the war around.

Churchill could also weigh the successes of 1942 in imperial terms. Rommel's defeat preserved British control over Suez. It kept the Germans from reaching the oil-rich empire that Churchill had built in Iran and Iraq in the 1920s—and thereby secured the western border of India. Stalin's army, not just Hitler's, was embroiled in battles east of the Dnieper, far from the heart of Europe. And with Japan on the defensive and Gandhi in jail, India was safe. For the first time Churchill could lay plans for recovering Britain's lost territories farther east, including Burma.

East Asia was the "second front" that really mattered to Churchill. As early as May he had been contemplating this move, talking of a Burma offensive slated for the autumn or winter of 1942.[42] When he arrived at Cairo, he spoke to Generals Bernard Montgomery and Harold Alexander about carrying off "a decisive strike" before the Americans arrived in North Africa. And so September 21, the very day railway lines were reopening in India, saw the opening moves in what would be the first Arakan offensive into Burma. British, Indian, and East African troops massed along the Assam border. As they began their attacks in December, Churchill's mood was epitomized by his defiant words: "I have not become the King's First Minister in order to preside over the liquidation of the British Empire."

Any military operation in that rough terrain along a seven-hundred-mile front would be difficult, Churchill knew. "You might as well eat a porcupine one quill at a time," he told CIGS Alan Brooke.[43] Burma was a world of thick jungles, forbidding hills and mountains, and a tough and deadly adversary. The first Arakan offensive, from December 1942 to February 1943, would be a fiasco, but its failure would provide the British with powerful lessons on how to fight and win a modern land war in Asia. It would also usher in a new generation of British military leadership and a trio of men who would become national heroes: Generals William Slim and Orde Wingate, and Lord Louis Mountbatten, Supreme Commander in Southeast Asia.

Still, even as weary British and Indian troops were trooping back across the Indian border, Gandhi made one more attempt to shift the world's attention from war to nonviolence.

Chapter Twenty-seven

SHOWDOWN
1943

Never give in!

WINSTON CHURCHILL, 1941

IN PHYSICAL TERMS, GANDHI'S CONFINEMENT AT the palace of Aga Khan was hardly arduous. The rooms were spacious and well ventilated, with extensive grounds and gardens—even with the barbed wire. Gandhi had all the food and books he wanted (but no access to interviewers or visitors, which was frustrating). He received a massage twice a day and had around-the-clock medical attention. Even Kasturbai was there, joining her husband on her own volition.

But in mental and spiritual terms, Gandhi found his confinement a torment. For ninety-one hours after his arrest he refused to speak—a clear sign that the government's action had been a shock and humiliation. Gandhi had been positively convinced that the viceroy would ask to speak to him before the Quit India movement started. Even if he could not get Linlithgow to somehow convince Churchill to begin a British evacuation of India, he could at least explain his position in greater detail. "The Government of India should have waited at least till the time I inaugurated mass action," he complained in a letter to Linlithgow on the fourteenth.[1]

Instead, the police had pounced, and his movement had been left leaderless and rudderless. If the government had waited, he said, "the reported deplorable destruction would have most certainly been avoided." For Gandhi was tortured by the constant news of violence, vandalism, and mayhem going on outside—exactly what he had hoped and planned to avoid. He importuned Linlithgow to stop its repressive measures, to release the Congress leaders, and to allow the Congress to calm the country down. On September 26 he sent an emotional letter detailing his proposal. All he got back was a brief dry note acknowledging its receipt.

Even as he tried to maintain his regular routine of spinning, praying, and reading newspapers, someone crucial to that routine was missing. Mahadev Desai had been arrested along with Gandhi and the others and imprisoned with them. But just six days later he had suddenly suffered a seizure and died. "Jail doctors did all they could," Gandhi wrote to a friend, "but God had willed otherwise." Kasturbai lamented, "Bapu has lost his right *and* his left hand."[2] Desai's place as secretary would be taken by others, but as a calm and calming presence, he had helped to keep Gandhi anchored in the real world. Some of the difficulties to come might have been avoided if Desai had been alive and at his side.

Disturbing stories of the mistreatment of prisoners, rioters and satyagrahi alike in various Indian prisons, reached Gandhi. Another detainee, a Professor Bhansali, had launched a hunger strike to protest the beatings at a prison in Chimur. Gandhi asked Linlithgow for permission to meet Bhansali to dissuade him from continuing. The government refused. Then on New Year's Eve Gandhi told the viceroy he might have to go on a hunger strike himself. "I do not want to use it if I can avoid it," he wrote. "This is the way to avoid it: convince me of my error or errors, and I shall make ample amends."[3]

Gandhi was desperate to open some kind of dialogue, to find a way to become relevant again as India slid into apathy under British wartime rule. Linlithgow had made it clear that the government held Gandhi personally responsible for the violence and death in the Quit India riots, an idea that tormented Gandhi. "I seem to be the *fons et origo* of all the evil imputed to the Congress," he wrote sarcastically. "You throw in my face the facts of murders by persons reputed to be Congressmen...My answer is that the Government goaded the people to the point of madness."[4]

Linlithgow replied that the government might relent if Gandhi renounced the Quit India resolution. This Gandhi would not and could not do. So on January 29, 1943, Gandhi said he would undertake a fast of twenty-one days, to end on March 2.

Even his closest supporters could not understand why he was doing it. He explicitly said it was not a "fast unto death," like the one he had used to wreck the Communal Award in 1932. But with his failing heart and high blood pressure, no one believed he could survive a fast of ten days, let alone twenty-one. Linlithgow angrily wrote back, accusing Gandhi of using blackmail. This accusation was probably just. Gandhi told the viceroy he was fasting because "I cannot get soothing balm for my pain," an ambiguous phrase that he chose not to clarify.[5] Certainly he meant the pain of seeing India still in subjection to the British, and of learning of new outbreaks of violence and fresh arrests. But he also likely meant the pain of being isolated in his easeful prison, unable to guide events to the triumphant denouement he envisioned.

Behind the decision to fast was another careful calculation. Gandhi's previous fasts had triggered his immediate release from prison. He assumed the same would happen this time. But he did not reckon on the intransigence of Linlithgow—or Winston Churchill.

In fact, two days before Gandhi's fast was to begin, the government did offer to let him go, but only for the duration of fast itself. He could go anywhere, and with anyone he wanted, the viceroy told him, as long as he was fasting. But afterward he would have to be back in Poona. Not surprisingly, Gandhi refused. "You have left me no loophole for escaping the ordeal I have set before myself," he complained. Linlithgow then said in effect: Whatever happens, let it be on your head. In the meantime Gandhi would be allowed to see any doctors and any visitors he chose. On February 10, one day later than originally planned, Gandhi began the fast.[6]

Churchill was informed of what Gandhi was up to while he was in Casablanca, attending another Allied summit conference.* He now faced the challenge that successive British governments had faced from Gandhi. Churchill was determined to show resolution where they (in his view) had shown weakness. He was convinced that the fast was meaningless street theater by the man whom Indians revered for his "saintly qualities," but whom Churchill thought a fakir and spiritual quack.

One man decided to set him straight on that last matter. It was General Jan Christiaan Smuts, now Field Marshal Smuts and president of South Africa. He and Churchill had met in London in August 1942, shortly after Gandhi was arrested. Churchill admired Smuts more than any other Dominion leader, perhaps more than any other living man. They had been opponents in the Boer War; they had been cabinet col-

---

* This was the conference at which Roosevelt and Churchill agreed on a policy of unconditional surrender to end the war against the Axis.

leagues during the First World War. They shared many values, including a deep repugnance for Nazism and fascism, and the desire to see the commonwealth safe and the war ended.

They did not, however, share the same view of Gandhi. Smuts had dealt with the Mahatma firsthand, and had felt the impact of his penetrating mind and negotiating skill as well as his passionate single-mindedness. He frankly cautioned Churchill against underestimating him.

"He is a man of God," the South African president said. "You and I are mundane people. Gandhi has appealed to religious motives. You never have. That is *where you have failed*."

It was an extraordinary remark to make in August 1942. Thanks to Churchill, Britain had just survived the threat of invasion and the devastation of the Blitz. Many saw the war turning around, again thanks to Churchill. But clearly Smuts was referring not to the war but to Britain's future in India.

Churchill chose to take Smuts's remark as a joke. "I have made more bishops than anyone since St. Augustine," he said with a grin. But Smuts was not joking.

"There is a pattern in history," Smuts added, "but it is not easy to follow," meaning for any mortal man to follow.[7] After years of effort Smuts had finally grasped the secret of Gandhi's continuing resolve and the fact that, although he was in prison, Gandhi was still the single most powerful man in India.

What Smuts the philosopher could see, and Churchill could not, was the Mahatma's supreme spirituality, which had made him revered across India and even in the West. It was a power that few others understood. Most in Gandhi's own inner circle had given up trying. Instead, they had learned to obey it as a matter of principle. Others followed simply as a matter of instinct, as if in obedience to a natural leader.

It was this power that Churchill had never before confronted head-on. During their forty years of encounters and conflicts, he had never understood Gandhi, any more than Gandhi had understood *him*. The reason was simple. The confrontation in February 1943 was not just between two willful men, or between imperialism and freedom, or between what Louis Fischer later called "the past of England and the future of India." It was no longer even between two different conceptions of empire.

The confrontation, rather, was between two different conceptions of life. One rested on secular and humanistic traditions that had been tested by history and centuries of human conflict. The other rested on a vision of spiritual purity in which history and material things (including Gandhi's own body) counted for nothing. Churchill valued human liberty as the product of struggle, as man's supreme achievement. Gandhi, by contrast, valued liberty as *God's* supreme achievement. It was man's duty to live up to that standard. Without it, Gandhi believed, life was meaningless, including his own. "I would far rather that India perished," he once remarked, "than that she won freedom at the price of truth"—meaning God's truth.[8]

In short, both men loved freedom and liberty, but of two fundamentally different kinds. Both were capable of great ruthlessness in pursuit of their goals precisely because of their confidence in those twin but opposite visions, which had sustained them through defeats and disappointments that would have destroyed weaker human beings. Together they might have complemented each other's strengths and bolstered each other's weaknesses. Instead, in February 1943 they went head to head in a final contest of wills, with the fate of India and the Second World War at stake.

Churchill still refused to believe Gandhi was in earnest. He wrote to Linlithgow on February 13: "I have heard that Gandhi usually has glucose in his water when doing his various fasting antics. Would it be possible to verify this." Linlithgow verified that it was *not* true.[9] He knew Gandhi was all too serious, and that if Gandhi died, it would set off a cataclysmic reaction around India.

For the first three days of the fast Gandhi's spirits were up. He greeted friends and even went for morning and evening walks around the palace grounds, although he was living on nothing but water with a few drops of lemon juice. Then he began to slow down. After a while he found it tiring and difficult to speak.

On February 16 six British doctors examined him and pronounced that his condition had "further deteriorated." Linlithgow passed the news on to London. He and his council agreed that Gandhi should not be allowed to die in prison.[10] But could they convince Churchill of the same thing?

By an extraordinary coincidence, at the very moment when Gandhi's health was becoming grave, so was Winston Churchill's. A week after returning from Algiers, on February 1, the prime minister had come down with a bad head cold. On the evening of February 16 his temperature suddenly shot up. His doctor examined his chest and told his patient he had found a "patch" at the base of his left lung.

"What do you mean by 'patch,' " Churchill angrily demanded. "Have I got pneumonia?"[11]

X-rays the next morning confirmed the diagnosis. For a man approaching seventy, pneumonia was a very grave matter. It carried the real possibility of death, just as a prolonged fast did for a man of seventy-three. And for the prime minister of a great country in the midst of a world war, it might mean disaster.

Churchill was sent to bed, where his temperature continued to climb. Although he insisted on working, he was clearly not up to his regular routine. Finally his assistants made him agree to look at only the most important and urgent bulletins. The only other thing he was allowed to read was a novel.* For almost two weeks Churchill and Gandhi spent their duel of wills flat on their backs, surrounded by doctors and officials who were fearful of the worst.

Gandhi's condition, meanwhile, continued to slide. On the seventeenth the Indian members of the viceroy's executive council all walked out in protest of Gandhi's condition. The Central Legislature held a major debate on the fast and passed a resolution calling for Gandhi's immediate release. But Linlithgow could do nothing. He had Churchill's instructions: Gandhi was going to stay where he was.

From February 19 until February 25 Churchill himself was almost completely out of action. He ran a high fever and felt as ill as he had ever been. But he was still not too ill to send a message to Linlithgow, thanking him "for your steadfast and unflinching action…as the Gandhi episode approaches its climax. It is a great comfort to me."[12] Churchill also had news from Lord Halifax, now ambassador in Washington, D.C.: Roosevelt was concerned about Gandhi's condition and strongly felt that the Mahatma should not be allowed to die in prison.

Despite his fever Churchill fired off a furious reply. There was no way the British government "will in any circumstances alter the course it is pursuing about Gandhi." Churchill angrily warned that any interference "would make a great embarrassment between the two Governments."[13] Once again the Americans got the message. "We can-

---

* He chose Daniel Defoe's *Moll Flanders*.

not have a serious breach, personal or political, with [Churchill] now," Secretary of State Cordell Hull concluded, "even if we were disposed to do so."[14] He, Roosevelt, and everyone else around the world could only wait and see if Gandhi survived his self-imposed ordeal.

Crowds of people gathered around the palace at Poona. Hundreds of telegrams bombarded the viceroy, beseeching or demanding that Gandhi be released. Meanwhile British doctors examined Gandhi's almost inert form. He was now taking only water. He was almost continually nauseated. The doctors urged that he be given immediate intravenous feeding. Gandhi's Indian physicians refused. It would kill him, they said. Gandhi regarded any form of injection—even to save his life—as a form of violence. They could not give their consent. The British doctors finally gave up.[15] Linlithgow allowed the crowd outside to enter the palace and file one by one past Gandhi's bed. His sons Devadas and Ramdas arrived. Kasturbai sat in his room day and night. She at least was convinced that Bapu was going to die.

On February 23, the thirteenth day of the fast, Gandhi's kidneys began to fail. His pulse was so feeble the doctors could barely feel it, and his skin felt cold and moist. Kasturbai knelt to pray. She was bidding farewell to her husband.

On the other side of the world, Churchill was still in the grip of a high fever. His daughter Mary came to see him on the twenty-first and was shocked at his condition. "He looked so old and tired—lying back in bed," she told her diary. Work had become all but impossible. Oliver Harvey noted: "He is taking no papers." But Churchill still followed the progress of Gandhi's fast with a manic intensity. One question burned in his mind: When would the man die? On February 22 Churchill was strong enough to dictate a long letter to the king, which ended: "The old humbug Gandhi is lasting much longer than we were assured was possible...One wonders whether his fast is bona fide."[16]

Once more the rumors about secret glucose infusions began.* The surgeon-general of the Bombay Presidency, who was in constant attendance, began to suspect that the Mahatma really had been given some glucose, secretly and unwittingly, by one of his Indian doctors.[17] In any case Gandhi recovered enough to agree to take some extra fruit juice with his water. Overnight on the twenty-third he pulled back from the brink of death. Across India, soldiers and policemen who had been on

---

* Later Lord Linlithgow told his successor General Wavell that he believed the rumors were true.

alert in case "the old zealot should die," as one worried official put it, once more relaxed.

Then on February 24 Churchill's fever finally broke. His wife told their daughter: "I can see for myself that he is better. His face looks quite different. He has lost that weary look." Churchill wrote to Harry Hopkins: "Am feeling definitely better now. So is Gandhi." Then: "Once he saw his antics would have no effect he took a marked turn for the better. I am so glad you did not get drawn in."[18]

He also wrote a note to Linlithgow: "Bulletins look as if he might get through." There was a distinct note of disappointment. Surely one of those Hindu doctors must have slipped him some glucose or something like it![19] To General Smuts on February 26 Churchill almost sounded triumphant: "I do not think Gandhi had the slightest intention of dying, and he has been eating better meals than I have for the last week" (that is, if glasses of water flavored with lime juice counted as a meal). "It looks now highly probable that he will see the fast through." Churchill gave vent to a final angry thought: "What fools we should have been to flinch before all this bluff and sob stuff."[20]

In fact, Gandhi was recovering, but his health remained precarious and he was extremely weak. He had lost almost twenty pounds. "I had to choose between death on the one hand and sweet lime juice on the other" was his explanation for why he had given in to his doctors. "I had promised to live; I must try to live." The next day, February 27, doctors found him in a cheerful mood when they visited at ten o'clock. He spent the day sitting on the eastern veranda of the palace, sunning himself. His daughter-in-law and his surviving secretary Pyarelal sat on a carpet nearby and read the *Gita* aloud.

"This fast was taken solely for service of God and in His presence," he told Mirabehn. "Other people may believe or not, that does not worry me." To Gandhi's mind, it had been a success. However, he knew others considered it a failure. He had neither procured his release nor forced Churchill and the British to back down. The original pretext for the fast—the alleged mistreatment of his fellow prisoners—had been all but forgotten. But Gandhi refused to care. "No fast of mine has ever had such a wonderful ending as this one is having. I do not mean what is going on in the outside world," he hastened to add, "but what is going on inside me. There is a heavenly peace."[21]

On March 3 Kasturbai handed him a glass containing six ounces of orange juice diluted with water. Gandhi sipped it and immediately broke down in tears. He sipped the glass for another twenty minutes, while thanking his doctors, British and Indian, for their attention. His fast was over. Over the next four days he lived on orange juice, then was ready for goat's milk, more fruit juice, and his first solid food in nearly a month: orange and lemon pulp.[22]

Not surprisingly, Churchill was uncharitable in his triumph. "It seems the old rascal will emerge all the better from his so-called fast," he cabled Linlithgow, thanking him once again for "your own strong, cool, sagacious handling of the matter." Linlithgow told Churchill that Britain had won "an important victory, which will help to discredit a wicked system of blackmail and terror, and I am much obliged to you for your staunch support."[23]

Later Churchill would remember the entire crisis as one that "caused me at the time much anxiety," since Gandhi's death "could have produced a profound impression throughout India." But in the end, "convinced of our obduracy, [Gandhi] abandoned his fast, and his health, though he was very weak, was not seriously affected." Churchill and the viceroy "had judged the situation rightly," and a major crisis had been averted. India and the empire were safe.[24]

But Churchill was wrong. The British were back to where they started. At first Gandhi's gesture did indeed seem to backfire. Nirad Chaudhuri remembered that in Delhi the news of the fast left "a strange tenseness on the faces of my colleagues, which was like the restlessness of the tigers and lions in zoos when their feeding time approached." For two weeks the reports of Gandhi's condition had been alarming. People reacted with indignation and fury when told that Churchill had said the Mahatma was given glucose with his water.* Chaudhuri even took the precaution of drawing up Gandhi's obituary for the Indian Information Office.

Then came news that the fast was over. "There was no anger at all," he recalled, "only blank disappointment at the evaporation of a great hope...There was not even any expression of relief." Instead "nobody spoke about Gandhi anymore." Everyone's attention was on the war and the mounting series of Allied victories. Chaudhuri spoke to an elderly Bengali living in Delhi, a nationalist who had confidently awaited Britain's defeat. Chaudhuri asked him what he thought now if Britain won. "I shall believe there is no God," the disappointed old man said.[25]

---

* Chaudhuri, like Linlithgow, came to believe it was true.

If God and Gandhi had disappointed the Indians, other events would make Churchill's triumph seem short-lived.

The Great Bengal Famine, one of the great human catastrophes of the twentieth century, did as much, perhaps more, to undermine Indian confidence in the Raj than anything Gandhi had done. Ironically, while Gandhi flirted with death by voluntarily starving himself, thousands—even tens of thousands—were starving to death through no fault of their own.

In mid-October 1942 a devastating cyclone ripped through the coastal regions of East Bengal, or what is today Bangladesh. The storm killed thousands and devastated the autumn rice crop up to forty miles inland. Bengali peasants ate the rice that should have been planted that winter. When the hot weather came in May 1943, the rice crop would be a fraction of what it should have been to feed Bengal's peasantry.

Making matters worse, the British Empire had lost Burma, the main source of India's rice imports. Within a month starvation was staring all of southeastern India in the face. The government of Bengal was unprepared; too much rice had already been shipped off to feed troops in the Middle East and Ceylon. As the hot weather came, people began to die. By September relief centers were overwhelmed with "rickety babies with arms and legs like sticks; nursing mothers with wrinkled faces; children with swollen faces and hollow-eyed... Walking skeletons all of them."[26] In mid-October the death rate in Calcutta reached more than two thousand a month. British and American soldiers were horrified to step out of a Calcutta cinema and find people literally dying in the street, while vultures, crows, and kites circled overhead.

It was the greatest humanitarian crisis the Raj had faced in more than half a century. But either because officials were too distracted (Bengal's governor fell ill and died during the crisis, leaving an administrative vacuum at the top) or were too slow to react, or simply did not care, the magnitude of what was happening did not reach the attention of London until it was too late.*

Secretary of State Leo Amery at first took a lofty Malthusian view of the crisis, arguing that India was "overpopulated" and that the best

---

* White and Indian officials were equally to blame. Bengal's Muslim League majority ministry failed miserably, while many of its Hindu members made huge profits trading in rice during the shortage.

strategy was to do nothing. But by early summer even Amery was concerned and urged the War Cabinet to take drastic action to prevent mass starvation—and a collapse of the Indian home front.

For his part, Churchill proved callously indifferent. Since Gandhi's fast his mood about India had progressively darkened. Despite what he imagined as the Mahatma's crushing defeat, the British were left with the same problems as before. Linlithgow saw little hope of arriving at a political settlement before or after the war ended, regardless of Gandhi.[27] Churchill's doubts about the Indian Army's loyalty again bubbled to the surface. In May Churchill ripped into Amery, accusing him of "creating a Frankenstein by putting modern weapons in the hands of sepoys." He even spoke of the horrors of the 1857 Mutiny, Amery noted, "and was really almost childish about it."[28]

Churchill proved just as irrational over the famine issue: he was resolutely opposed to any food shipments. Ships were desperately needed for the landings in Italy, which was slated for September even though the Americans opposed the invasion. Sending food to India would mean a loss of valuable transport. Besides, Churchill felt it would do no good. Famine or no famine, Indians will "breed like rabbits." Amery remembered, "Naturally I lost patience and couldn't help telling him that I didn't see much difference between his outlook and Hitler's, which annoyed him no little."[29]

But unwittingly, Churchill did break the famine. Amery prevailed on him to send some relief, albeit only a quarter what was needed.[30] But then in October 1943 Churchill's handpicked new viceroy arrived, General Archibald Wavell.

Until now Wavell had been best known for his willingness to accept responsibility for the failures of others, an indispensable skill in politics and in the military. Having been head of Britain's Middle East command when the war broke out, he had watched while, over his protests, large numbers of his troops were transferred to the abortive campaign in Greece. The result was the collapse of British forces in North Africa under Rommel's assault. That led to Wavell's transfer from the Middle East to commander in chief in India, where he arrived in time to oversee the fall of Singapore and the rout from Burma, events he had not caused and had been helpless to prevent.

Wavell had been raised in India, the son of a major-general, then was educated at Winchester and Sandhurst and joined the Black Watch regiment in 1900. Most recently he had managed to pull India's defenses together, despite slender resources, and crushed the Quit India rebellion before it jeopardized Britain's strategic position or opened the door to any Japanese incursion. Wavell had a shrewd, penetrating mind and an immunity to cant and conventional wisdom. It was Wavell who had first labeled the Versailles treaty, ending the First World War, as "the peace to end all peace." He understood that politicians invariably found ways to create disasters, which soldiers, like himself, had to clean up.

Churchill appointed him viceroy on the assumption that the general would endorse his own hard line. In fact, Wavell would emerge as the best viceroy India ever had. He would chart a new path for its future, one that avoided the pitfalls left by Winston and the Mahatma, his fellow Boer War veterans.

Certainly Wavell found his conversations with his predecessors and colleagues no help. In August he met with Halifax and "got nothing particularly fresh from him," although the former viceroy said he "did not find Gandhi a practical person to deal with...and thinks he is probably worse now." He soon realized that Amery and Churchill were at loggerheads over what to do about India: at a meeting of the cabinet's India Committee on October 7 Amery talked too long and Churchill "waved the bogey of Gandhi at everyone." Oddly, the best advice Wavell got was from Winston's son Randolph, whom he met en route to India in Gibraltar. "He said I went to India with one great advantage over the last few Viceroys," Wavell wrote in his diary. "They had to decide whether and when to lock up Gandhi, I should find him already locked up."[31]

The formalities of his installation as viceroy were a far more stripped-down affair than in Curzon's or even Linlithgow's time. This was wartime, and India was an armed camp. Thousands of British, American, Australian, and East African soldiers were arriving daily. Twenty-five thousand Chinese troops were training in Ramgarh. Orde Wingate's Chindits long-range guerrilla group had recently returned from its second successful raid into Burma, which proved beyond doubt that British and Indian soldiers could beat the Japanese in jungle conditions. After a conversation with Linlithgow, Wavell concluded that the Bengal famine could put the entire war effort in peril and that it would end only if the military stepped in. Wavell branded it "one of the worst disasters that had befallen any people living under British rule." Yet no one had thought to ask the army for help.

His first trip after his swearing-in ceremony was to Calcutta, where he and his wife visited a relief center and spoke to the starving victims. Wavell turned his forces loose to transport rice and food supplies from places where it was actually in surplus, like the Punjab, to areas that needed it most. (In a terrible irony the rice harvest of the autumn of 1943 was one of the biggest in India's history.)[32] He had to bully Churchill into agreeing to send more food. The prime minister "seemed to regard sending food to India as an 'appeasement' of Congress," Wavell realized in disgust. Only his direct threat to resign finally compelled Churchill to back down.[33] Within a few months Wavell brought India back from the brink of demographic disaster. Still, as many as three million Indians had died, and food shortages continued until the end of the Raj.[34]

Wavell also realized that a political solution for India could not wait until after the war. He was going to have to find a way around the current impasse. In July the Congress stubbornly refused to abandon its stance on Quit India. Without Gandhi's sanction, they could not move, but unable to move, they could not help to find a solution. Linlithgow had shown Wavell Gandhi's final bitter letter to him* and told Wavell there would be no real progress in India as long as Gandhi lived.[35]

So Wavell in his soldierlike way decided to take the dilemma by the horns. He asked London to give him the power to summon an all-party coalition government made up of any leaders who were willing to support the war effort and to work under the existing 1935 constitution. His hope was that Congress leaders and Liberals alike, in addition to Jinnah's Muslim League, would succumb to the temptation of real power and real cooperation. Perhaps even Gandhi himself would relent when faced with a concrete offer.

Wavell had put precisely this proposal before the cabinet's India Committee on October 7, even before he left for India. Amery supported it, but Churchill exploded. He launched into an extended tirade "against Congress and all its works," Wavell noted, while Anthony Eden spoke "as if I was proposing to enthrone Gandhi." Most of the

---

* It read in part: "Of all the high functionaries I have had the honor of knowing, none has been the cause of such deep sorrow to me as you have been. It has cut me to the quick to have to think of you as having countenanced untruth...I hope and pray that God will some day put it into your heart to realize that you, as the representative of a great nation, have been led into grievous error."

other cabinet members also balked, including its Labour members, who were likewise frightened by the "Gandhi bogey." (Attlee was an exception.) The whole meeting was "worse than I expected," Wavell wrote afterward, "not because of opposition, but because of spinelessness, lack of interest, opportunism."

Wavell's disgust was complete the next day, when Churchill canceled the India Committee meeting and summoned Wavell to his office alone. Winston was "menacing and unpleasant" and indicated that "only over his dead body would any approach to Gandhi take place." His instructions to Wavell were succinct. Concentrate on winning the war, make peace between the Hindus and Muslims, and utter some vague hints about political progress after the war but offer nothing concrete.[36]

It was General Smuts who explained Churchill's position best to Wavell: "The [prime minister] is not thinking beyond the end of the war—[not] about India or anything else." Churchill still hoped that after the final victory the situation might be turned around—and that all the delays and Fabian retreats over India would ultimately prove worthwhile.

But Wavell saw things more clearly. The war had changed India, for better or worse. The problems it would face, and the solutions needed to address them, had moved beyond the two men who still insisted on clutching its destiny to their hearts: Gandhi and Churchill.

Chapter Twenty-eight

TRIUMPH AND TRAGEDY
1943–1945

A warrior lives on his wars...And he suffers a collapse if
he finds that his warring capacity is no longer wanted.

MOHANDAS K. GANDHI

ON APRIL 21, 1943, THE GERMAN submarine *U-180* broke surface in stormy waters off the tip of Africa. The first officer's charts told him they were four hundred miles south-southwest of Madagascar, exactly as planned. German sailors in foul-weather gear kept watch on the conning tower, straining to see through their binoculars while squall after squall swept across the *U-180*'s streaming deck.

Then one of the sailors cried out and pointed. There out of the dawn mist another submarine was emerging from the depths: the Japanese *I-29*. Their prearranged rendezvous had to wait another forty-eight hours, until the storms subsided, to take place. As the weather finally cleared, both German and Japanese lookouts anxiously watched the skies for any stray passing Allied aircraft.

On the twenty-third, despite the heavy swell, the *I-29* was able to launch a small motor-powered dinghy toward the German U-boat. The *U-180*'s hatch opened, and a stout young man in glasses and civilian clothes climbed out. The Japanese sailors unloaded their cargo—fifty bars of gold, each weighing forty kilograms—which the German crew stowed below while the civilian and Captain Werner Müsenberg watched. After receiving a farewell salute from Captain Müsenberg, the man descended into the dinghy. He and the two escorting Japanese sailors rode the rough waves back to the *I-29*, becoming soaked to the skin. Within minutes the two submarines disappeared from sight, their mission accomplished.[1]

Ten days later the Japanese submarine reached Sabang, on the coast of Sumatra. There Japanese sailors brought their guest to shore. Waiting for them was Colonel Satoshi Yamamoto of Japan's Hikari Kikan, the special intelligence agency set up to recruit Indians and other South Asians in Malaya and Singapore for the war effort against the Allies.

Colonel Yamamoto smiled at his latest and most distinguished recruit and bowed deeply as he muttered words of greeting. Subhas Chandra Bose smiled back. He was back in Asia and ready to get to work.

Bose had left Germany bitterly disappointed. The Germans had offered money and weapons for his Azad Hind or Free India Legion, created in September 1942. But when it failed to draw more than two thousand volunteers, the Germans lost interest.[2] It played no significant role in the war. Bose tried to revive German interest in his cause at a personal meeting with Hitler in March 1942, but he soon realized that the Nazis did not take even a peripheral interest in Indian independence, especially as the tide of war was turning against them.* He left Europe "with his trust in Germany's victory substantially shaken."[3] Now Bose was staking his career on the Japanese.

"Japan has done great things for herself and for Asia," he had proclaimed back in 1937. "Japan has shattered the White Man's prestige in the Far East."[4] Now he saw Japan's war with Britain and America as opening the door to India's independence—or at least *his* kind of independence, with himself and his followers at the helm. As for the Japanese, they hoped Bose would be able to unite the various anti-British Indian factions headquartered in Tokyo and breathe new life into its moribund puppet, the Indian National Army, which was suffering from a lack of volunteers and morale.

Bose made his formal entry into Singapore on July 2, 1943, with General Hideki Tojo himself at his side. Indians across East Asia were electrified. For the first time some three million overseas Indians heard someone speaking directly to them, an energetic, charismatic figure in a buff uniform who promised a brighter future for India once the British were finally gone. "It was really the first speech...I had heard in my life," one young Indian confessed after hearing Bose address a rally in Singapore that also drew Chinese and Malay listeners. The speech was

---

* On the contrary, Hitler admired the British Raj's skill in subduing and ruling hundreds of millions of what Hitler considered subhumans. He particularly liked the Hollywood movie *Lives of the Bengal Lancers* and made it compulsory viewing for his SS, as a model of how to rule an empire of inferior races with a handful of men.

"like magnetic power." When Bose proclaimed, "When I say war I mean WAR—War to the finish—a war that can only end in the freedom of India," millions of Indians believed him.[5]

In the end Bose's INA would draw forty thousand volunteers—a small number compared to the 2.5 million Indians who served in the British Indian Army. Historians of the Second World War, even some historians of the war in Burma, tend to treat Bose and his Free India movement as a minor distraction, even a farce, but its impact on India was incalculable. From mid-1943 onward Bose provided a new model for militant action among young Indians, especially his fellow Bengalis. To them, Gandhi was a revered but also a remote figure, just as ahimsa seemed an outdated formula from the past.

Although Bose was no soldier, he insisted, like Adolf Hitler, on appearing everywhere in uniform. He was India's first genuine war leader for Indians on *both* sides of the battle line. As one of his INA officers said, "He was like a god to us." In many ways, he was a dark amalgam of both Gandhi and Churchill, a figure out of their deepest nightmares yet drawing from the same moral resources.

Like Gandhi, Bose spoke the language of Indian manhood and heroic self-sacrifice. His speeches often quoted Gandhi. He stressed to his soldiers and followers that his vision of Azad Hind marked the final stage of the struggle for Indian independence that Gandhi had launched. Gandhi was waging the struggle from inside India, Bose liked to say, but he was conducting it from outside.[6]

Like Churchill, Bose was committed to waging war to the hilt to win that struggle. "I want total mobilization and nothing less," he proclaimed. "Total mobilization for total war!"[7] Everything else, "however noble, is of secondary value." His determination and eloquence paralleled the British prime minister's: even his most famous maxim, "Give me blood and I will give you independence," contains more than an echo of "I have nothing to offer but blood, toil, tears, and sweat."* And his ultimate message was also directed at the man in Number 10. "Churchill will soon realize," he said in a radio broadcast from Germany even as the Cripps mission was falling apart, "that it is no longer possible to keep Indians on their side by a piece of bread they are going to throw to the Indian people." Indian independence required

---

* Likewise his remark on the battle for Imphal: "a story written with our blood and more so with our sweat."

nothing less than the complete destruction of the empire. "From the ashes of Britain," Bose proclaimed, "will emerge a unified India."[8]

Bose's appeals to join his side fell largely on deaf ears. Few Indians were convinced that they would be truly better off with a Japanese rather than a British victory. As many disillusioned INA volunteers discovered, Japan's empire was far more virulently racist than England's.[9] Yet Bose's offer to send food shipments to an India in the grip of famine, which the British ignored, won popular respect. Even soldiers in the British Indian Army came to admire Bose as a role model for the future, if not necessarily for the present.

Indians would fight the Japanese, even Bose's INA, with unparalleled courage: they would win twenty of the twenty-seven Victoria Crosses awarded in the Burma campaign.[10] But they fought with their eyes fixed firmly not on their king-emperor, as Churchill liked to imagine, but on independence. The arrival of Bose could not change the course of the war, but like the Bengal famine, it signaled the severing of India's last ties of loyalty to Britain. It also signaled the doom of Gandhi's and Churchill's plans for India's future.

In the autumn of 1943 a final Allied victory both in Europe and in the Pacific beckoned, but Churchill was deeply unhappy. Even as his side was winning the war, his hope of preserving or even expanding the British Empire in its wake was vanishing. His own voice mattered less and less in places where he wanted it to count.

In September American and commonwealth troops landed in Italy. The invasion of Italy had been Churchill's idea. The Americans had at first strenuously opposed it but then relented. Churchill argued that Italy was the "soft underbelly" of the Axis and that toppling Mussolini would turn Hitler's flank. But this was only one part of Churchill's grand strategic vision. Knocking Italy out of the war, he hoped, might bring neutral Turkey into it. The Dardanelles would open to convoys of supplies to Russia, and the British Mediterranean fleet would be free to pass through Suez and into the Bay of Bengal in time to launch the liberation of Burma.[11]

It was the old Gallipoli plan again, but this time in reverse. If Istanbul declared war on the Axis, the Allies would be able to drive a wedge northward, slicing Hitler's empire in half and cutting off his armies in Russia. Churchill's "Mediterranean strategy" also had another purpose:

by opening a new war front in Turkey and the eastern Mediterranean, he would make sure the Middle East remained part of the British Empire. It would also interpose British and American forces between the Russians and Eastern Europe.

Above all, it would finally secure the great arc of British influence across the Eastern Hemisphere, from Cape Town to East Africa and Suez, from Iran and Iraq to Burma, Singapore, and Hong Kong, of which India was the mighty keystone. Preserving that arc of empire, and British India, remained a vital part of Churchill's world strategy. Victory in the Mediterranean was the means to secure it.

At Tehran in December 1943, however, Roosevelt and Stalin refused to go along. Here Churchill discovered that Roosevelt no longer considered the Anglo-American alliance to be vital to victory and the postwar era, as Churchill did. To his mind, Roosevelt was trimming the Big Three down to the Big Two, himself and Stalin. Throughout the meeting "Roosevelt tended to side with Stalin at Churchill's expense"—including on India.[*][12] Churchill wanted to pressure Turkey into declaring war within six weeks, but Roosevelt ignored him. Instead, the Americans and Russians pushed a May or June 1944 date for an Allied landing in northern France, code-named Operation Overlord, as well as a second one in southern France.

Churchill had serious doubts about the former and was passionately opposed to the latter. He saw the invasion of France as potentially a repetition of the fruitless battles on the Western Front in the First World War. He believed (wrongly) that the Allies would get bogged down and never break out. He also believed (rightly) that the operation would leave no resources for his Turkey plan or for a major British-led offensive in Asia. He bargained hard with Roosevelt to leave him sixty-eight troop transports to execute his grand Mediterranean strategy, and not divert them for Overlord, but lost.

Still, Churchill clung to hope that his plan would come together. "I am not prepared at the stage to the abandonment of the operation [i.e., Operation Hercules, involving the capture of the island of Rhodes as a

---

* At Tehran both men held an extraordinary discussion of India behind Churchill's back. Roosevelt in effect endorsed Nehru's view and thought the best solution to India's problems "would be reform from the bottom, somewhat on the Soviet line." Stalin, who knew a lot more than Roosevelt about how the Soviet system really worked, disagreed. He said "reform from the bottom would mean revolution" and that the interactions of caste and class made the Indian question "a complicated one." But both men agreed it was best not to raise the issue with Churchill.

prelude for Turkey's entry in the war]," he told his chiefs of staff on December 22, 1943. "To abandon Hercules is to abandon the prize for which all our efforts are directed upon Turkey." But without Russian and American support, his plan was a pipedream.[13] The days when Britain could wage a major offensive on its own were gone.

Still, Churchill hoped for such an offensive in the Far East. There Churchill had brought on board as supreme commander a man of youthful dynamism and drive, forty-three-year-old Louis Mountbatten. By the beginning of 1944 Mountbatten had assembled nearly a million men at arms in India and a large fleet of ships. Churchill wanted him to launch a major push to retake Rangoon. Retaking Singapore and Malaya, possibly by moving through Sumatra, was also high on his list.

Mountbatten had to point out, however, that India, still recovering from the famine the previous year, could not support anything like such an effort. Clearly the Americans would not provide help for any campaign to reestablish the British Empire in Asia. Without American help, no campaign could take place. And unless Churchill reached some resolution over India, American help would not be forthcoming.

In Cairo the previous November Mountbatten had made the mistake of bringing up the realities of the Indian situation with Churchill. He endorsed Viceroy Wavell's view on how to break the impasse through a new political dialogue. "The Prime Minister blew up," Wavell learned, "and damned not only [Mountbatten] but me and all my works."[14]

In April 1944, however, all speculation about mounting a fresh Allied drive into Burma ceased. The Japanese struck first, in a desperate bid to reverse their fortunes in Asia. S. C. Bose had encouraged them to believe that once they sent an army across the Assamese border into India, they would find millions of collaborators. The Indians in the British Army would desert, Bose said, the moment they faced free Indians in arms. He told a huge crowd of supporters in Singapore that before the year's end, they would be standing together on Indian soil.[15]

After a year's preparation, the Japanese attacked India. One thrust ran south toward Imphal, less than fifty kilometers west of the Burmese border. The other stretched north to Kohima, as thousands of Japanese infantry poured through the thick jungle hoping to encircle the massive British base being built at Dimapur. Meanwhile Bose arrived in Rangoon with forty thousand volunteers of his Indian National Army, flying Gandhi's tricolor flag—but with a raging tiger instead of a charkha. With cries of *"Chalo Delhi!"* (On to Delhi!) and *"Azad Hind!"*

Bose's troops boarded trains to head west. Bose himself carried on his lap a small silver casket. It contained earth from the grave of the last Mughal emperor, Bahadur Shah II, who had died in Rangoon after the Great Mutiny and who would now be returned ceremonially to his native land.[16] Bose also had reams of Free India paper currency and his own governor-general, to take charge once Imphal and Kohima fell.

And on April 17 Kohima nearly did fall. Its British and Indian garrison fought with desperate courage. Churchill telegraphed Mountbatten: "Let nothing go from the battle that you need for victory. I will not accept denial of this from any quarter, and will back you to the full." He even ordered Chief of Staff Hastings Ismay to divert supplies and transports that were being stockpiled for his beloved Mediterranean offensive to go at once to Burma: "We cannot on any account throw away this battle."[17]

The fighting in Kohima was hand to hand, with bayonet charges; grenades were tossed through windows or into foxholes. At one point the front line ran on either side of the Kohima Club tennis court.[18] But bit by bit Punjabi and Gurkha units from General Slim's Fifth, Seventeenth, and Twenty-third Indian divisions pushed to their rescue.

Armed with tanks and backed by British air power, this was a new model Indian Army. Its troops were mostly Hindu, not Muslim, as the war emergency forced the government to give up the old Churchillesque clichés about the "martial races." It was also fiercely disciplined and motivated, with a strong spine of VCOs and KCIOs who were the equal of their British counterparts. In fact, as the fighting dragged on through May and June, General Slim began to use Indian troops to stiffen the morale of weary *British* units—reversing a tradition dating back to the Mutiny.[19]

It was the Indian Army's finest hour. Back in London, "we watched their progress with tense feelings," Churchill wrote later.[20] Finally in June, Japanese resistance began to crumble, and in late June after savage fighting Imphal was saved. The Japanese army fled headlong back across the border into Burma. Lost in the jungle, many Japanese soldiers, realizing they had been abandoned by their own high command, chose to fight to the death or commit suicide. "Quarter was never asked," General Slim grimly wrote, "and none was given." All through July and August Sikh and Gurkha fighters waded through jungle streams choked with the bodies of Japanese who died of starvation or exposure. Ultimately, less than half the Japanese soldiers who set out for

India returned. Perhaps as many as eighty thousand lost their lives—the worst military defeat in Japanese history.[21]

As for the INA, it had not even been a factor in the fighting. Of 6,000 men who actually went into action during the invasion, only 400 died in battle. Another 1,500 died of disease or hunger. Almost all of them suffered from abuse and neglect by their supposed allies—Japanese officers had treated them like coolies or worse, even refusing to salute their INA counterparts. Not surprisingly, more than 800 INA volunteers handed themselves over to British-Indian troops while another 750 simply took to their heels and disappeared into the jungle.[22]

Bose, choosing to ignore reality, told Indian supporters in Burma that "neither the INA nor he was in the least disenheartened."[23] But in fact he had shot his bolt. There had been no general Indian uprising in his support. Just the opposite: even the most skeptical anti-British nationalists now realized that the Allies were going to win the war. On July 17, 1944, Bose's biggest Japanese supporter, General Tojo, resigned as prime minister. In a few months Bose would be planning his escape to the Soviet Union, hoping against hope that Stalin could do for his dream of Hind Azad what the Germans and Japanese could not.

The battle for India was over. The battle for Burma was about to begin. And through it all, through the savage jungle fighting and the pounding of artillery and bombs, hardly anyone noticed that Gandhi was finally free.

Wavell had ordered his release on May 6, 1944. The viceroy had heard from doctors that Gandhi had had a severe attack of malaria and "might die any minute." In addition, he was anemic, had continuing high blood pressure, and suffered from hookworm and amoebic dysentery. His doctors thought his kidney failures might trigger cerebral or coronary thrombosis.[24] Given his health, they concluded, he would "not be a factor in active politics again."[25]

With the Bombay government, its Home Department, and other agencies all pushing for Gandhi's release, Wavell turned to Churchill, who finally gave in. On May 24 Churchill explained in a telegram to Wavell: "I assented to letting Gandhi out on the grounds of his grievous state of health." He had been convinced Gandhi really would die—an event he was prepared to accept with equanimity. But now that Gandhi was out, Churchill wanted no further contact with him. For the first time, he expressed his feelings about Gandhi with genuine venom:

> He is a thoroughly evil force, hostile to us in every fiber, largely in the hands of the native vested interests and frozen to his idea of the hand spinning wheel and inefficient cultivation methods for the over-crowded population of India. I look forward to a day when it may be possible to come to an understanding with the real forces that control India.[26]

It was Churchill's tragedy to assume those "real forces" actually existed. Like Gandhi, in fact, he still had not learned that no one controlled India, least of all the British. Churchill had convinced himself that the root of India's problems was its wealthy Hindu landlords and "oppressive industrialists." Those same people, he believed, were bankrolling Gandhi. For an old anti-Bolshevik, Churchill had come to a strangely Marxist view of India's affairs, in which economic interest determined every other consideration, including religion, caste, and culture.

Nor could a decade of experience and advice from every quarter shake Churchill's view. This intransigence meant there could be no serious solution to the "India issue" as long as Churchill remained in office—something Viceroy Wavell understood. In fact, Churchill still liked to pretend there was still no issue at all, only Gandhi and the agitators on one side, and the Raj on the other.

For the time being Churchill worried that Gandhi might recover not only his health but his "political vitality."[27] He need not have worried. Gandhi emerged from Poona a physical and political wreck. However, the illness was not only physical. Something else had happened that affected Gandhi's vitality, and even made him lose his sense of understanding God.

Unlike her husband, Kasturbai had disliked life in prison.[28] She preferred the ashram routine, with lots of children and grandchildren, the comings and goings of visitors, and the constant clamor of the kitchen; at Poona she felt shut in and deprived of inner life. The sudden death of Mahadev Desai shocked her deeply. Desai had been a Brahmin, and she became convinced that his death was in some respect Gandhi's fault. "The sin rests on our shoulders," she told one of Gandhi's young female aides, Sushila Nayyar. "Bapu launched the struggle, and as a result

Mahadev came to jail and died here." She reverted to the Vaishnava faith of her childhood. For hours at a time she worshipped at a tiny altar dedicated to the infant Krishna, and the *samadhi* where Mahadev had been cremated became a virtual shrine for her.

Her health grew worse. In December 1943 it became alarming. She complained of pains in her chest; at times her lips turned blue as she struggled to breathe. Attempts to give her an oxygen catheter failed, and Gandhi quarrelled fiercely with his jailers about nurses and doctors. In January Kasturbai asked to see her sons. Even Harilal made a final appearance, although he was too drunk and had to be sent away. Devadas begged his father to allow their mother to be given penicillin, but Gandhi declined. "Why don't you trust God?" he said. "Why do you wish to drug your mother even on her death bed?" He added, "If God wills it, He will pull her through."[29] But even Gandhi trembled at the thought that Kasturbai might be leaving him forever.

On February 22 Devadas brought her holy water from the Ganges and *tulasi* leaves. Kasturbai drank the water and bade everyone goodbye. That evening Gandhi was about to go for his usual walk when she called out: "Bapu!" He rushed to her room and held her in his arms. "I am going now," she said. "No one should cry after I have gone. I am at peace." She died while Gandhi and everyone else in the room sang the hymn *Ramadhun*.

The next morning she was laid on her funeral pyre in the palace grounds. Gandhi had prepared a prayer drawn from the *Gita,* the Koran, the New Testament, and the *Zend-Avesta* of the Parsis.[30] Afterward Gandhi said, "Ba is ever with me though her body has been consigned to the flames." She had never been fully part of his world, either spiritually or intellectually. After sixty-two years of marriage, she had remained the simple girl he married in Porbandar. Yet she had been the irreplaceable partner of a lifetime, from South Africa days through his fast at Poona. Viceroy Wavell sent a note of condolence. "We were a couple outside the ordinary," Gandhi wrote in reply.[31] To others he simply said, "I cannot imagine life without her." As Mirabehn noted afterward: "With Ba it was as if a part of Bapu departed."[32]

Six weeks later Gandhi had his attack of malaria, which triggered his release. He went to Juhu, a seaside resort near Bombay, to recover. He gave himself two weeks of silence. Then began a long, slow, and tedious recovery both physically and spiritually. "But how God has tested my faith!" he told Pyarelal's sister, thinking not only of Kasturbai's death but of all the events of the past year.[33] Not until early August 1944 did he feel strong enough to return to Sevagram, after almost a two-year absence. Even there he found it hard to concentrate. Any kind of daily routine became a strain for his frail body. No wonder his doctors pronounced him unfit to ever engage in politics again.

But Gandhi could not stay out, even if he had wanted to. And he did not want to. He had left the Indian National Congress in a state of acute crisis. He felt an obligation to somehow bring it back to national relevance. Even with the war reaching its climax, he felt compelled to show that nonviolence was still the answer for India. In his heart he refused to concede that the Quit India movement had been a failure; but it had left a stalemate that he was now anxious to break. So in June he asked Viceroy Wavell, whom he still had not met, for a conference. Wavell had other things on his mind. A few days earlier he had visited his only son, a major in the Black Watch, who had lost a hand in the fierce fighting around Mogaung and was recuperating in a hospital in Assam. Nor did Wavell trust Gandhi, considering the old man "verbose, petty-minded, and quite devoid of any constructive statesmanship" and "bent only on his own self-justification."[34]

But as the viceroy repeatedly tried to explain to Churchill, India was as vital as ever to winning the war. Almost 100 percent of its production of shoes and textiles, and 75 percent of its steel production, were devoted to the Allied armies. Without India's material support, no defeat of the Japanese in Burma or Malaya or even China was possible. Yet unless 750,000 tons of grain arrived to relieve the ongoing famine, India would face a major catastrophe: "a hungry India" might give the Japanese a second chance.[35] Wavell realized that the Mahatma, despite his fading powers and fading reputation, still held at least part of the solution to India's problems. Following Churchill's strict instructions, however, Wavell refused to meet him.

So Gandhi tried sending a personal note. It was his usual way of trying to open a fruitful dialogue with the powers that be, to see what kind of man Wavell was and what might be possible.[36] Wavell still refused, saying they could meet only if Gandhi had a concrete and constructive plan to present. Gandhi immediately responded by offering Congress's support for the war effort in exchange for an immediate declaration of independence—the offer the Congress Working Committee had wanted back in 1942 and that Gandhi had refused.

Wavell realized this was a possible opening, but when Churchill learned of it, he exploded in a towering rage, accusing Wavell of entering negotiations with Gandhi, Britain's "bitter enemy." Wavell had to withdraw. Churchill "sent me a peevish telegram," Wavell noted on July 5, "to ask why Gandhi hadn't died yet!" The prime minister never responded to the viceroy's request for more food aid. "I wonder, " Wavell mused to his diary, "if we shall ever have any chance of a solution till the three intransigent, obstinate, uncompromising principals are out of the way: Gandhi (just over 75), Jinnah (68), and Winston (nearing 70)."[37]

For Jinnah too was still a player, and Gandhi's current anxiety was not just about nonviolence and Congress. The Hindu-Muslim split remained as much a gaping wound as it had been before he was arrested. Gandhi feared the war might end with the Lahore resolution of four years before still in effect. The notion of an India-Pakistan division was anathema to him: he called it a "vivisection." The idea that it could come as a result of religion—"which binds man to God and man to man," Gandhi protested—was even more repellent.[38]

Yet except for some token Muslims in the Congress like his friend Dr. Abul Kalam Azad, Muslims had stayed aloof from the Quit India movement. The Muslim League had not endorsed the British war effort but had hardly opposed it. Just as Churchill believed some mysterious clique controlled the Indian independence movement, so Gandhi was convinced that the British were the "third power" behind the communal issue and the resolution to break India apart. As with Churchill, no amount of argumentation or evidence could budge him, not even the forceful words of Jinnah himself.

Gandhi decided that a direct dialogue with Jinnah might open the way to reconciliation. The businessmen G. D. Birla and Sir P. Thakurdas had hoped for such a meeting since 1940: such was the power that the Mahatma's words and presence were assumed to have on the obstreperous Muslim leader.[39] In September Gandhi felt strong enough to start the talks and set off for Bombay.

"I am going in hope but without expectation," he told T. B. Sapru. For three weeks he and Jinnah discussed a range of issues. Jinnah remained unmoving on his central demand, that an independent Pakistan be accepted and declared before the British left. Gandhi reached for a compromise but in vain. When Gandhi suggested that they wait to see what happened when the British left, Jinnah rejected the notion as prevarication and a waste of time. "The question of the division of India, as Pakistan and Hindustan, is only on your lips and does not come from your heart," he angrily told Gandhi. Gandhi had no reply. Jinnah knew Gandhi was out of touch after nearly two years in prison, and he played on this weakness. "I hope to convert you to the realities and actual conditions prevailing in India today," he said, which were that the Hindu and Muslim communities were headed in divergent directions. "By all the canons of international law, we [Muslims] are a nation," Jinnah insisted. It was not the British who were at fault; it was a thousand years of history. This Gandhi could not accept, and so he and Jinnah parted ways.[40]

The meetings broke up without agreement on September 27. Viceroy Wavell, who had hoped for some kind of compromise, was bitterly disappointed. "I must say I expected better," he wrote. "Two great mountains have met and not even a ridiculous mouse has emerged." He saw it as a failure of Gandhi's leadership and worried about its effect on Churchill and the cabinet. "I am afraid it will increase their dislike of any attempt at a move."[41]

A tired and discouraged Gandhi returned to Sevagram. It was clear to Patel and others that he was exhausted, and in late November he agreed to undergo a full month's rest. Wavell meanwhile was staring at the calendar. With New Year 1945 approaching, the war in Asia was nearing a climax. American troops had landed in the Philippines, while their bombers were attacking Japanese cities. The U.S. Navy and Marines were gearing up for the assault on Iwo Jima. The Japanese soldiers remaining in Burma were hopelessly trapped, even as the new overland route for supplies to China opened: the Ledo Road.

In Europe the war was going so well that the British chiefs of staffs hoped to move 370,000 men and their equipment to India for a full-scale offensive on Singapore. But the failure of Operation Market Garden to drive the Germans out of Holland, and then Hitler's offensive in the Ardennes two months later, halted any such ambitious plan.[42] But the December offensive was the Third Reich's final gasp, while Japan was on the road to certain defeat.

Ironically, the faster the war rushed to a victorious end, the worse the situation looked for India's future. With the war on, all issues and all parties existed in a kind of suspended animation. Once the war was over, they would start up again—and Wavell was deeply worried about the result. Almost alone among the participants, Wavell sensed that something had to be done before the war ended, not after—that is, before the catastrophe everyone feared but tried to ignore actually happened.

Churchill remained deaf to his pleas. As the winter of 1945 turned into spring, his mood was bleaker and blacker than before. On the bright side Germany was collapsing. The Russians were closing on Berlin; Burma was about to fall, and his old nemesis Gandhi had been rendered a political cipher, perhaps permanently.

But Churchill could only feel growing frustration and anger. Not for nothing was the final volume of his history of the Second World War entitled "Triumph and Tragedy." Britain had endured and even triumphed. Churchill had knitted together the greatest alliance of nations ever seen. But Britain was exhausted. One quarter of its national wealth was gone, and its manpower had about run out. Most of its weapons, its planes and tanks, its ships and transports, were now American made. All around him were reminders that Great Britain had lost its force and credibility in the world.

Mountbatten's Southeast Asia Command, which Churchill had seen as a means to restore British rule in the region,* was now officially committed to doing the opposite. Once the Japanese were driven out, southeast Asia, beginning with Burma, would cease to be part of the British Empire. The Americans also refused to relent on their pressure on India. At one point, at the conference in Quebec in September 1944, Churchill finally blew up. "I will give the United States half of India to administer," he said in disgust, "and we will take the other half, and we will see who does better with each other's half."[43] It was meant in jest, but the frustration was real. His half-jocular remark could not disguise the fact that the issue of India, and the empire generally, was driving a stake through the heart of the Anglo-American alliance.

In February 1945 the Big Three met for the last time at Yalta. His doctor Lord Moran, traveling with him, saw Churchill emerge from the meetings in something close to despair. Roosevelt was ill, terminally so. The old trust and familiarity between the two leaders was gone. Churchill still referred to their friendship as "the rock on which I build the world," but the ailing president increasingly saw Churchill "as being wholly out of touch with the times and an obstacle to peace and progress," particularly on colonial issues.[44]

Instead, Roosevelt was staking the future on America's relationship with the Soviet Union. Winston knew that Roosevelt, like most American liberals, had a naïvely sanguine view of Stalin and the Soviet

---

* When the Southeast Asian Command was formed in 1943, Americans derisively said its initials SEAC stood for "Save England's Asian Colonies."

Winston Churchill and Viscount Halifax, 1940. As foreign secretary, former Viceroy of India Halifax used his experience of dealing with Gandhi to justify his course of appeasing Hitler and opposing Churchill. (Getty Images)

Churchill visits the bombed ruins of Coventry Cathedral, 1940. Churchill's skill in rallying the British people against Nazi tyranny deeply impressed Gandhi. (Broadwater/Churchill Archives)

Gandhi hoped to stir the hearts of his own countrymen when he announced his Quit India movement at the Bombay Congress in August 1942 (Gandhi, shown here with his longtime secretary, Mahadev Desai). (V. Jhaveri/Peter Rühe)

Churchill and President Franklin Roosevelt at Sunday services on the HMS *Prince of Wales,* August 1941. Disagreement over India and Gandhi became the major source of tension in their otherwise close wartime alliance. After one exchange, Churchill even threatened to quit as prime minister. (Imperial War Museum)

(Below) Just four months later, Japanese planes would sink the *Prince of Wales* off Singapore, as Britain's empire in Asia tottered and Japanese troops drove to the borders of India. (Imperial War Museum)

Insurgent India: Quit India riot in Bombay, October 1942. The woman in the man's arms has just been overcome by tear gas. (Kanu Gandhi/Peter Rühe)

Loyalist India in World War II: Sikh soldiers in Cairo present a gift to Winston Churchill on his 69th birthday, November 1943. (Imperial War Museum)

Churchill with jubilant crowd on V-E Day, May 8, 1945. He assumed victory in World War II would save British rule in India. The British voters had other ideas. (Imperial War Museum)

General Archibald Wavell, viceroy of India 1943–1946. As he tried to find a solution to India's political stalemate during the war and after, he found Gandhi and Churchill equally frustrating to deal with.
(Time & Life Pictures/Getty Images)

Aftermath of massacres in Calcutta, 1946. British withdrawal and the partition into Moslem Pakistan and Hindu India triggered violence on a scale not seen since the Mutiny of 1857—much as Churchill had predicted. (photo by Margaret Bourke White; Hulton/Getty Archives)

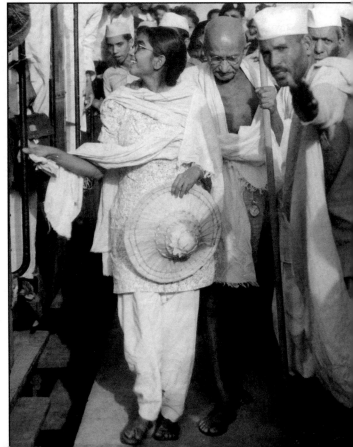

Gandhi arriving with his grandniece Manubehn (with glasses, left) at Delhi train station, March 1947. The Mahatma traveled across India to try to stop the violence, without success. Yet a year earlier he had told Viceroy Wavell: "If India is to have her bloodbath, let her have it." Ironically, the last victim would be Gandhi himself. (V. Jhaveri/P. Rühe)

Gandhi's funeral, January 31, 1948. (V. Jhaveri/Peter Rühe)

Churchill's funeral, January 30, 1965. (Hulton/Getty Archives)

Union. But at Yalta Roosevelt's credulity stretched all limits. As Lord Moran put it, the president "does not see that he has invented a Russia which does not exist."[45]

Later Churchill would be blamed for Yalta's decision to hand over most of Eastern Europe to Stalin, along a boundary line that roughly followed the future Iron Curtain. Critics point to a list that Churchill compiled for Stalin while in Moscow in October, dividing Europe into percentages of Russian and British influence.[46] But what this so-called "naughty document" and the concessions at Yalta over Poland really show was that Churchill was desperate to recover what he could of Europe for the democratic world. He deeply feared that, left to their own devices, Roosevelt and Hopkins would let Stalin's armies devour it all.

On imperial questions, the tension was even worse. Churchill was not the only Briton to feel that Americans were directly hostile to their interests. Moran's own view was that Americans thought they were "back in the War of Independence, fighting their English oppressors at Yorktown." But he admitted that Winston did not help matters: "When the British Empire is mentioned, he indulges in histrionics, which do no good."[47]

When one of the Yalta delegates raised the question of appointing trustees to "former colonies," the phrase inspired a particularly savage outburst. Winston's head jerked upright, his eyes grew wide, and he began to shout, barking out sentences so quickly that some in the room could not make out what he was saying.

But the gist of it was clear. Churchill raged that he "would not have the British Empire run by a bunch of bunglers. He refused point blank to countenance such folly." The stunned American and British delegates tried to calm him down. The American secretary of state Edward Stettinius was "thoroughly rattled" and hastened to say that no one was talking about British colonies. The trustees were for former *enemy* colonies. Winston realized his mistake but refused to be mollified. He calmed down but continued to mutter to himself, "Never, never, never."[48]

His doctor realized that the Americans thought Winston's intransigence over the empire was mostly bluff, but Lord Moran knew better: "He was affirming a faith for which he was prepared to give his life." Churchill was only belatedly realizing that others, even in his own party, no longer shared that faith.

In private Churchill also shared more of Wavell's fears about the future of the Raj than he let on in public. On the way to Yalta he had read a new book on the subcontinent, entitled *Verdict on India.* He told Clementine, "Reading about India has depressed me for I see such ugly storms looming up." Britain, he believed, was "losing confidence in our mission," confidence that had sustained the Raj for two centuries and that Churchill had hoped would sustain it again after the war. But he no longer felt it would.

"I have had for some time a feeling of despair about the British connection with India," he confessed to his wife, "and still more about what will happen if it is suddenly broken. Meanwhile we are holding on to this vast Empire, from which we get nothing, amid the increasing criticism and abuses of the world and our own people." But Churchill refused to give up—or give in. "Out of my shadows has come a renewed resolve to go fighting on as long as possible," he wrote, "and to make sure the Flag is not let down while I am at the wheel."[49]

More unwelcome news awaited when he returned home to Number 10. Wavell was mounting one last effort to make a breakthrough on an Indian constitution. His idea was to summon a conference of all the principal leaders, all Indians except himself and the commander in chief, General Auchinleck. He hoped they could agree on a transitional government now, before war's end, made up of six Hindu representatives, six Muslims, one Sikh, and one member of the Depressed Classes (almost certainly Gandhi's old antagonist, Dr. Ambedkar) acting as his executive council. Together with the viceroy they would assume the full administration of India, including defense, and set up plans for a constituent assembly and an Indian constitution after the war.

Wavell hoped that British sincerity about handing over power, and British insistence that Indians work out their own problems, would force a final breakthrough. His proposal arrived in London in September 1944. In December he still had no response. Amery explained to him that the cabinet was waiting for the war to end in order to dissolve, and then Churchill and Clement Attlee, leader of the Labour Party, would battle it out in the next election. No one, least of all Churchill, was prepared to do anything definite on India until the postwar political scene was sorted out.

Amery knew what he was talking about. That same month he submitted his own plan for full and unqualified independence for India when the war ended in either Asia or Europe. He gave the India

Committee a six-thousand-word proposal. Cripps was the only one to support it. Churchill and Amery then had their biggest fight yet. The prime minister lambasted both Amery and Wavell "for betraying this country's interests in order to curry favor with the Indians." Amery told him sharply to "stop talking nonsense" as the two bellowed at each other.

After a few minutes of this angry spectacle Sir John Simon passed Amery a note: "You had better drop it, Leo." Later Amery apologized to Churchill for his "strong language" but complained to his diary, "I wish he would talk to me about these matters and find out how they really stood." Indeed, he doubted that Winston had even bothered to read the proposal.[50] He sensed that Wavell's proposal would get the same response, or worse.

The viceroy refused to be put off. He pleaded for a personal meeting with the cabinet; he was willing to leave for London at once. In January he was told that late March would be the earliest Churchill could see him. A few weeks later he was told mid-June. Wavell finally blew up and told Churchill he was going to resign. That finally worked, and the next day the cabinet gave him permission to leave for England.[51]

Wavell arrived in late March 1945 and would spend nearly two months in London waiting for a final reply. Day after day the India Committee of the cabinet bandied the issue back and forth. Churchill as usual "indulged in wild and indeed scarcely sane tirades," according to Amery, and was "more hopelessly garrulous and time wasting than ever." He poured scorn on "that ass Wavell and that traitor Auchinleck" for dreaming up such a conference and then "talked rubbish about abolishing landlords and money-lenders," and returning the land to the peasants—a bizarrely Gandhi-like theme which had become a virtual obsession with him.[52]

Amery again felt the heavy hand of Winston's scorn. The prime minister had convinced himself that Amery had put Wavell up to the plan whereas, as Amery admitted a year earlier, "it is rather Wavell who had insisted on pushing forward his view."[53] The wearisome tussle dragged on week after week. Finally in mid-April the India Committee agreed to let the full cabinet hear the viceroy's proposal.

On the last day of May, Wavell was summoned to the Cabinet Room. The entire cabinet was there, including Foreign Secretary Anthony Eden, who had told Wavell the day before that he thought everyone was inclined to back his proposal. All except Churchill, of course, who opened the meeting with a fiercely negative rant. He warned Wavell that his proposal would doom India and the Indians.

"You will lose a good [Executive] Council and get a bad one," he said, adding that the new government would have no democratic foundation. "The workers would be victimized by the capitalists, the agriculturalists by the money-lenders, the Untouchables would remain untouchables, etc. etc.," Wavell remembered. Then he invited Wavell to speak.

Wavell did. "The P.M. gave me a good run and did not interrupt," although Leo Amery interjected his own views on the subject at length until Churchill finally had to cut him off.[54] Then Churchill said, somewhat surprisingly after his first negative sally, that he was prepared to agree to the conference if the India Committee amended parts of Wavell's draft that afternoon.

"The climax of my visit was an extraordinary one," Wavell noted in his journal. He met with the prime minister and the full cabinet again at ten-thirty that evening. Churchill gave a speech in favor of the proposal that was as forceful as the one against it that morning. Wavell exclaimed to himself, "What an extraordinary man he is!"[55] Churchill then said Wavell could summon his conference and meet with any leaders he chose, including Gandhi. The only condition the cabinet was going to impose was that it be put on a take-it-or-leave-it basis. There could be no further negotiations or discussions.

And so finally, at eleven-thirty p.m., just twelve hours before his train was scheduled to leave, Wavell got everything he wanted after eight months of waiting. "It all ended in an atmosphere of good will and congratulations—only temporary, I fear."[56]

Wavell was right. Certainly Churchill was in an ebullient mood. On May 7 Germany had at last surrendered. Hitler was dead, having taken his own life in the ruins of Berlin. The long struggle that Churchill had pursued for four years, with every ounce of his energy and passion, was finally over. On May 8 a vast crowd gathered at Whitehall to celebrate what was dubbed V-E Day, or Victory in Europe Day. Winston, Eden, Attlee, and his other colleagues appeared on the balcony of the Ministry of Health and waved. The crowd yelled its approval.

Winston stepped to the microphone and spoke.

"God bless you all," he said. "This is your victory!"

With one voice, the immense crowd roared back, "No—it is *yours*!" It was the British people's spontaneous and unforgettable tribute to the man whose spirit had pulled them through the war, from the darkest days of the Blitz to the fall of Germany.

Churchill paused and went on. "We were the first, in this ancient land, to draw the sword against tyranny. We were all alone for a whole year...Did anyone want to give in?"

The crowd shouted back, *"No!"*

"Were we down-hearted?"

"No!" came the answer.

"The lights went out and the bombs came down," Churchill said. "But every man, woman, and child in the country had no thought of quitting the struggle...So we came back after long months from the jaws of death, out of the mouth of hell, while all the world wondered...

"Now we have emerged from one deadly struggle," Winston told his ecstatic audience. "But there is another foe who occupies large portions of the British Empire, a foe stained with cruelty and greed—the Japanese." Russia had pledged to enter the fight against the last remaining Axis power, he told them, joining forces with Britain and America. "We will go hand in hand with them. Even if it is a hard struggle we will not be the ones who will fail."[57]

It was an unforgettable moment. "And yet," Churchill's doctor noted, "the PM does not seem at all excited about the end of the war." Perhaps it was because Churchill knew the struggle was just beginning, and not against Japan. In the aftermath of V-E Day his coalition cabinet had broken up. Clement Attlee and Ernest Bevin had hoped to win the Labour Party's endorsement of keeping it together at least until Japan's defeat, but the party refused. They were, Churchill said, "boiling with hate." They were looking forward to the general election in July; they saw the war's end as an opportunity to launch a new social order in Britain— ironically, part of what Churchill had fought the war to prevent.

Churchill's relationship with his own people had reached a turning point. As his doctor told him, "There are two opposing ideas in the country. There's pretty universal gratitude to you, [but] there's a notion about that you aren't very keen on this brave-new-world business."

"The desire for a new world is nothing like universal" was Churchill's dismissive response. "The gratitude is."[58]

Churchill confidently assumed that that gratitude would carry him and his party over the threshold in the coming July election. John Colville had returned to England after active service with the RAF. He visited his old boss on Whitsunday, May 20, and found that "the PM can't get the political prospect out of his head and all day the conversation was on [the] coming election."[59] Churchill also believed that victory in that election would absolve him for any failure to reach a political settlement in India. That was why Churchill had been so willing to agree to Wavell's summit conference proposal, as he told the viceroy himself later.[60] Other members of the India Committee had assured him that no agreement *was* possible. Offering the impossible proposal, Churchill believed, would conclude the matter, at least until the war was over—or even perhaps for good.

On May 2 the British Fourteenth Army entered Rangoon. Almost 70 percent of its soldiers were nonwhites, Indians or Gurkhas or Burmese or Africans.[61] Their pre-monsoon offensive had been faster and more devastating than Hitler's vaunted Blitzkrieg into France in 1940. Novelist John Masters, serving as major with a Gurkha regiment in the Seventeenth Indian Division, watched them advance. "The dust thickened under the trees lining the road" to Rangoon, he later wrote, "until the column was motoring into a thunderous yellow tunnel, first the tanks, infantry all over them, then trucks filled with men," Gurkhas and Punjabis, Kachins and Burmese, Hindus and Muslims, "a dozen religions, a score of languages passed in those trucks and tanks." Masters himself was of mixed English and Indian parentage, as William Shepherd had been.

Masters thought to himself: "This was the old Indian Army going down to the attack, for the last time in history, exactly two hundred and fifty years after the Honorable East India Company enlisted its first ten sepoys on the Coromandel Coast." The difference was that these soldiers were soon to be part of a new future, not returning to an imperial past.[62] A month later Mountbatten staged an elaborate victory parade through Rangoon, a final display of British triumph in the colony that Randolph Churchill had made part of the empire.

But the old order was already dying. Plans were under way to grant Burma Dominion status, even though when and to whom were still unclear. It was precisely the situation that Wavell was hoping he could resolve in India, when he called Muhammad Jinnah, Abul Kalam Azad, Chakravarthi Rajagopalachari, G. S. Motilal, and eighteen other delegates to assemble at the Viceregal Lodge in Simla on June 25.

At the last minute Gandhi agreed to go. When he appeared in Simla, crowds flocked to get a glimpse of him. On the train up, thousands stood along every station cheering wildly as his train, the Frontier Mail, roared past.[63] It was Wavell's first meeting with the Mahatma, and he was deeply curious about him. On June 24 they spoke after lunch for nearly two hours.[64] Wavell found him pleasant and "friendly for the time being" but also "rather vague and discursive." Wavell wanted the delegates at Simla "to pull together for the sake of India and not in a party spirit," and Gandhi agreed.[65]

"Mr. Gandhi then made a long, torturous, and prolix statement" that lasted more than an hour, Wavell remembered. It covered the history of the Indian National Congress as well as the British in India, the British character, and "the qualities of a good soldier." Gandhi reminisced about carrying the wounded General Woodgate down from Spion Kop in 1900, and he expressed regret that he was not permitted to address the Indian Army and that its soldiers had had to come to see him "in mufti and at night."

The army was clearly much on Gandhi's mind, but Wavell stressed that it was important to keep that body nonpolitical. He said they had a commander in chief whom they fully trusted (General Auchinleck) and "that their reputation never stood higher." Wavell wanted to keep it that way. Gandhi again assented.

On one point, however, Wavell could not move him. Gandhi had said he felt it was a bad idea for him to attend the conference, but if Wavell wished him to, he would come "and sit in a corner." But he would represent "nobody except himself." All negotiations he would leave in the hands of the Congress president, Dr. Azad.

That was a mistake, as Jinnah immediately realized when he heard the news.[66] Azad was a hardworking and loyal Gandhi follower. But in a crucial meeting like this he was in over his head. Azad and fellow Congress members hoped they could make headway, and they were pleased that Wavell was willing to work with them and let bygones be bygones about Quit India. But assigning a Muslim to speak for the Congress, as if to prove its shopworn contention that it spoke for all India, could not have been more calculated to arouse Jinnah's suspicion and ire.

His position on partition remained unchanged, and in four years he never suggested otherwise. But if there was going to be a new executive council, he insisted, it could have no Muslim members who were not also members of the Muslim League. Wavell could not agree to that demand without infuriating the Congress, and so after three weeks of fruitless discussion, the Simla conference ended—like so many others— a signal failure.

Wavell blamed himself for the breakdown. "Whether I have done more good or harm by trying," he wrote in his journal, "only time will show."[67] Gandhi took the news of the conference failure "calmly." Like Churchill, he had expected little else. Afterward he sent a gracious note to Wavell: "You have taken the blame [for Simla's failure] on your own shoulders. But the world will think otherwise. India certainly does." He agreed that some would say that the London government was reluctant to pass power "into the hands of their erstwhile prisoners." But "what a pity that the moral height which the British, if not even the Allied Powers, would have occupied by the success of this conference" was not to be.[68]

Gandhi boarded his train with serene resignation. To his mind, the Simla conference would be his last performance on the political stage. Its failure confirmed what he had always believed: the futility of constitutional debates. He withdrew to Poona to begin work on his latest brainchild, a nature-cure clinic for the poor.

The conference had a strange postscript—or rather, prescript. On June 15, just before he left for Simla, Gandhi had released to the press the text of a letter he had written to Winston Churchill nearly a year earlier, on July 17, 1944.

It had been written when Gandhi's spirits were at their lowest, and it read:

> Dear Prime Minister,
>
> You are reported to have a desire to crush the simple "Naked Fakir" as you are said to have described me. I have been long trying to be a Fakir and that naked—a more difficult task. I therefore regard the expression as a compliment, however unintended. I approach you then as such and ask you to trust and use me for the sake of your people and mine and through them those of the world.
>
> Your sincere friend,
> M. K. Gandhi

This strange, jocular note was classic Gandhi. It was his effort to reach out to Churchill in the aftermath of their epic battle. It was the only direct communication between the two men in nearly forty years. But Churchill never received it. After waiting for nearly two months for an answer or at least an acknowledgment, Gandhi contacted the viceroy's private secretary. He learned that the missive never reached London; Gandhi politely asked that it be resent—although in mid-September 1944, "the psychological moment had passed."[69]

On the eve of the Simla summit Gandhi saw again an opportunity to try to open a dialogue with Churchill, and he decided to make the original letter's text public. Its contents, he said, were of "a sacred character and not meant for the public eye." In hopes of establishing a common ground that had eluded them in crisis after crisis, in a last stab at opening a path to friendship and peace, he was finally publishing it for the world to read.[70]

But it was too late for both men, and for India and Britain. Churchill never answered Gandhi's letter. Even if he had wanted to, he was helpless to do anything. To the astonishment of the world, on July 26, 1945, the British voters turned Winston Churchill out of office.

Chapter Twenty-nine

WALK ALONE

1945–1947

The great ship is sinking in the calm sea.
WINSTON CHURCHILL, 1946

If India wants her blood bath she shall have it.
MOHANDAS K. GANDHI, 1946

No ONE WAS MORE SURPRISED THAN Churchill. In June Jock Colville had
returned to his post as the prime minister's secretary and found his old
boss looking forward to the coming election. After his government officially resigned in May, Churchill had as a courtesy allowed his Labour
opponent Clement Attlee to join him at Yalta to meet Stalin and
Truman. But Churchill refused to accept the possibility that the pipe-
smoking former social worker, whom he privately dubbed "a sheep in
sheep's clothing," could ever be prime minister, or that the British public
would ever choose someone other than himself to lead them to final
victory.

It was a severe, if understandable, misreading of the nation's mood.
The British people had clung to Churchill in their worst hours. They
revered his indomitable spirit and refusal to give in. But as victory approached, they saw a different vision on the horizon. After two world
wars in thirty years, Britons had lost their taste for risks and sacrifice.
Labour's vision of the future had been spelled out in the celebrated
Beveridge Report* of 1942: free national health care, social security pen-

---

* Written for the Ministry of Labor by William Beveridge, left-leaning Liberal Party stalwart and later vice
chancellor of London University.

sions, and guaranteed full employment. The cradle-to-grave welfare state, the foundations of which Churchill himself had laid in 1911 with his National Insurance Act, was about to replace the old social and economic order that he had taken for granted.

Even his wife knew Churchill was out of touch with the realities of twentieth-century Britain. He had never ridden a motorbus; he had never had to buy a ticket for a train. He rarely traveled anywhere without a valet and at least sixteen pieces of matched luggage.[1] The truth was the old Victorian certainties around which both he and Gandhi had constructed their lives, including their leadership, had vanished. Churchill had hoped against hope that victory over Hitler might bring a resurgence of the old imperial spirit, especially in regard to India. Instead, victory brought a sense of relief mingled with exhaustion, and a desire to "get on with things." That included shedding India as part of the empire.

Few realized at the time how crucial India had been to the war effort. Its soldiers had preserved Britain's empire in the Middle East and Africa. Two and a half million of them had served in the armed services. Another eight million Indians pitched in with wartime work. But as an imperial possession, India's value to Britain had shrunk. Its surging industries meant that by 1938–39 Lancashire textile mills supplied only four percent of India's demand for cotton goods, while India was nearly 86 percent self-sufficient.[2] The days when an imperialist like Churchill could threaten Britons with economic ruin if India went independent were over.

Now it was more the other way around. For two decades a growing Indian economy had drawn huge sums from British investors. While Britain had expended a quarter of its national wealth to fight the war, India had emerged with its industrial sector strong and thriving. The war also made India one of Britain's biggest creditors. In November 1939 London had agreed to let India pay its normal peacetime military budget plus a supplement for the cost of troops serving overseas, while London paid for virtually everything else, including modernizing India's defense industries. The result was that by the end of the war Britain owed India nearly £1.5 billion, more than a third of Britain's entire overseas liabilities.[3]

That sum was a source of near despair for Churchill.[4] He realized that as Britain's economic fortunes dwindled, India's would only grow brighter. But it also meant India's economic and financial ties to Britain would continue, whether India was independent or not. Without realizing it, Churchill and his Tory colleagues in 1939 had laid the financial foundations for India's economic takeoff at the end of the twentieth century.

In the two months after Germany's surrender, however, Churchill's mind had been entirely focused on defeating Labour—perhaps too focused. On June 4 Churchill made an infamous radio broadcast suggesting that if Attlee and Labour won, they would introduce a socialist police state in Britain. Jock Colville remembered being amused by Churchill's theatrical hand gestures in front of the microphone, as if he had been speaking to a hall full of people.[5] The British public, however, was not amused. Winston's attempt to compare Labour with the Axis powers that had devastated Europe, and with the Soviets who were overrunning what was left, backfired.

Before election day Churchill and Clementine went to France for the first time since 1940. Churchill swam at the beach at Biarritz like "a benevolent hippo," as French police in bathing suits formed a protective cordon. He and Clemmie then returned to England to watch a Labour landslide smash Churchill's plans as well as his personal pride.

The ejection of a national hero from office shocked those closest to him. The Duke of Chandos, who was minister of production, went down to the cabinet office that night to watch the increasingly gloomy returns. He saw Churchill surrounded by a circle of glum faces. Bracken, Macmillan, Beaverbrook, Eden: all were now out of power. Despite the shock Churchill was determined to put a good face on Labour's success. "They won't last forever," he declared. "Pray God they don't do too much damage before we get back at them."[6]

That evening Lord Moran ran into Jock Colville, who told him that the Labour landslide was as decisive as the Liberal landslide of 1906. The vote from the armed services was most humiliating: it had gone solidly Labour, including the British Fourteenth Army, which had so brilliantly fought the war in Burma.[7] Lord Moran went to the Number 10 Annex and found Churchill sitting in a small room adjoining the secretaries' office, staring morosely into space.

"Well, you know what has happened?" Churchill finally growled.

His doctor said he did and mentioned something about ingratitude.

"Oh no," Churchill answered, "I wouldn't call it that. They," meaning the British people, "have had a very hard time."

But then he pointed to the red box full of papers and dispatches. "I have made all my plans," Churchill confessed sadly. "I feel I could have dealt with things better than anyone else. This is Labour's opportunity to bring in Socialism, and they will take it."

He paused and added, "They will go very far." He might have been thinking about India.[8]

Another person shocked by the election's outcome was Clement Attlee. Later he confessed to Colville, who was now his secretary, that he had expected to whittle Churchill's Tory majority down to forty. He never imagined he would take 393 out of 640 seats.[9] As the new prime minister, Attlee faced huge problems. Europe was in ruins. Every major capital except Prague and Paris had been bombed or shattered by war, while Russian armies occupied Berlin and Vienna. Chaos reigned in Asia's capitals as well. On August 6 and 8 atomic bombs were dropped on Hiroshima and Nagasaki, forcing Japan's surrender, the largest capitulation by a standing army in history (nearly 1.2 million Japanese soldiers). In addition to the question of cleaning up the mess that Japan's aggression had created in the Far East, the question of what to do about India once again raised its inconvenient head.

Churchill had stood alone against Hitler but also alone against Gandhi—he believed for many of the same reasons. Now he was gone. Attlee and his Labour colleagues were now free to do in India what Churchill had refused to contemplate: hand over power.

Attlee's own record was clear. He had always been sympathetic to Gandhi and Indian nationalism. He had even opposed the 1935 India constitution because it did not go far enough to accommodate "the living forces of India," by which he meant the left wing of the Indian National Congress.[10] Like his colleague Cripps, whose mission in 1942 had been Attlee's idea, he saw Nehru as a kindred socialist, someone with whom a Labour government could do business. Attlee hoped that by handing over power to Nehru and his colleagues, he could reestablish Britain's relations with an independent India on a progressive, nonimperial basis.

Like Nehru, Attlee saw India's problems as social and economic in nature, and he was inclined to discount the reality of sectarian hatreds.

Like Gandhi, Attlee was convinced that the Hindu-Muslim split would fade once the British left and inconvenient agitators like Muhammad Ali Jinnah, whom Muslims now hailed as Quaid-e-Azam or "Great Leader," were firmly put in their place.

In short, Attlee and his new Secretary of State for India Frederick Pethick-Lawrence, believed it was time to quit India, just as Gandhi had always wanted. If Congress had been waiting for a sympathetic British government with which to finally strike a deal, this was it.

Viceroy Wavell too sensed that the election had brought a major sea change. "I think Labour is likely to take more interest in and be more sympathetic towards India," he wrote in his journal, but added privately, "they will have some weird ideas about it," especially about how easy it was going to be to leave. He recognized that war-weariness, as much as a burst of anti-imperialism, underlay the desire to cut India loose.[11] He also knew Attlee and his colleagues underestimated the scope of the Muslim problem and the necessity of bringing Jinnah along in any final settlement if India were to escape partition or something even worse.

Wavell spent nearly three weeks in London over July and August 1945. He watched the transfer of power in London with optimism mingled with foreboding. Attlee eagerly agreed that India's next round of legislative elections should be held and prisoners who had been detained during the Quit India campaign released; he agreed to lifting the ban on all Congress organizations. On August 14 Japan surrendered. The war was over. Perhaps now the original Cripps offer, extended by a sympathetic Labour government rather than by a reluctant Churchill, would meet approval. Still, Wavell warned that good intentions alone would not solve the Indian problem.[12]

The viceroy had a farewell meeting with Churchill on September 2 at Morpeth Mansions. The two men had been at loggerheads over India for almost two years, and they had exchanged angry words more than once. Wavell realized that overall, Churchill considered him "more a liability than an asset." But he had sent Winston a gracious note to thank him for the opportunity to serve "with so great a man," and Churchill invited him to lunch.

Churchill talked of his plans now that he was out of power, mentioning a trip to Italy's Lake Como to paint. But when the subject of India came up, Winston launched into what Wavell called his "usual jeremiad."

"The anchor is now gone," Churchill warned, meaning himself. "You are on a lee shore with rash pilots," meaning Attlee and the Labour Party. He also confessed to Wavell that he had agreed to the Simla conference the previous June only because he was convinced it would fail.

Nonetheless, the meeting ended on a friendly note. Wavell asked if Churchill meant to write a history of this world war, as he had of the last. Churchill said no, he was too old now. (In fact he did, in five large volumes that would win the Nobel Prize for literature.) But as the former prime minister escorted the viceroy to the lift, he had one final request. Just as the lift door closed, Churchill said with a wry smile: "Keep a bit of India."[13]

It was the final benediction of the subaltern of '96 on the subcontinent he professed to love but never understood. The empire builder knew independence was coming. He knew that his day, and his India, were done.

"I dreamed that life was over," Churchill had confessed to his doctor a few weeks earlier. "I saw—it was very vivid—my dead body under a white sheet on a table in an empty room. I recognized my bare feet projecting from under the sheet. It was very life-like...Perhaps this is the end."[14]

Wavell returned to India, where the news of Churchill's fall was greeted less with joy than with uneasy foreboding about what would happen next.

"I was shocked," Nirad Chaudhuri confessed years later. He could not believe the British people would throw out the man "who had led them to victory from so hopeless a situation." He felt it did not bode well, not for Britain or for India. Churchill had been "the most hated man in India," but he had symbolized the strength and resolution of the Raj, a force for British domination but also for civil order in times of crisis. By throwing Churchill out, the British had surrendered their last claim to respect as well as power. "The Indian people knew that so far as they were concerned they had men of straw to deal with," albeit accommodating ones. Chaudhuri and others realized that when the next crisis came, Indians would be on their own, for better or worse.[15]

Gandhi saw Churchill's defeat as nothing less than a miracle. "To me it is a sufficient miracle," he said, "that in spite of his oratory and brilliance, Churchill should cease to be the idol of the British people who til yesterday hung on his lips and listened to him in awe." The election had bolstered his faith in God, Gandhi told a British interviewer.[16] But otherwise his reaction was muted. Since Simla he had been retiring into himself more and more and taking his leave of politics. He told the press he was deferring all matters regarding India's future to the members of the Working Committee, including Nehru, the Congress's new president.

He did tell the committee that Churchill's election loss "in spite of his unique victories and achievements" was a warning of what could happen when politicians "ceased to reflect the nation's mind."[17] But then Gandhi told reporters it was no good asking him about Indian politics because "my advice, independently given, may be in conflict with their opinion" and only "confuse the public mind."[18] He preferred to pour his remaining energies into his Constructive Program, meaning pushing the use of khadi and the spinning wheel and working with India's sixty million untouchables.

The untouchables were part of the ineluctable reality that was India. Gandhi's term for them, *Harijans* or Children of God, had never caught on. Wavell and other officials despaired of their future if the British left. Churchill had invoked their welfare as an argument for staying in India. Their chief spokesman, Dr. Ambedkar, believed that only built-in constitutional safeguards could save them from oblivion in a Hindu majority state. But Gandhi still believed that moral purity, not legislation, was the true path to achieving Harijan freedom and redemption. At one point he even resolved to live among untouchables in order to be a living example for other Hindus and to bring his Constructive Program to the very lowest rungs of Indian society.

Indeed, on August 14, the very day Japan surrendered, Gandhi was more concerned about his ongoing clash with Dr. Ambedkar, who was now on the viceroy's council. "He wants to destroy Hinduism" was Gandhi's complaint. He hoped the so-called Depressed Classes would abandon their self-declared leader and embrace the Congress instead— even though Gandhi was the only Congress figure who ever expressed any interest in their welfare.[19]

Japan's surrender prompted no remark from Gandhi. He made no acknowledgment that the most destructive war in Asia's history was over, or that India had played a vital role in it. Even the atom bomb, which so impressed Nehru, seemed to Gandhi only one more symptom of the West's sick worship of technology and one more reason for India to remain on its path of spiritual truth. "If India wants to survive in a world of atom bombs," he later told an audience, "she must be disciplined and united first, and untouchability and caste distinctions must go."[20]

October 2, 1945, marked Gandhi's seventy-sixth birthday. To his mind, he was entering the last stage of his life. He liked to say, "God has tied me with a cotton thread," quoting a Mirabai poem. "Whichever way he pulls, I am His."[21] But then as always, events pulled him back into the political arena with a jolt.

The first event was Wavell's announcement on September 18 over Indian radio of the new Labour government's plans for India. In the wake of new elections, he would meet with members of the provincial legislative assemblies to discuss independence and a future constitution. He would form a new executive council out of India's leading political parties, including Congress and the Muslim League. Wavell's announcement had "a favorable reception" in Indian political circles. He hoped that Congress realists like Vallabhbhai Patel would use the new atmosphere of goodwill to guide India to a peaceful transition of power. Reflecting the new mood, Nehru looked forward to Britain quietly leaving India within two to five years.[22]

But then Wavell and the Indian government made a major, even a fatal, mistake. In November the trial of former members of Bose's Indian National Army opened at the Red Fort in Delhi. Bose himself had died in an air crash, while trying to flee Japan for Russia after the war.[23] His hapless followers had been caught up in the aftermath of the Japanese surrender. Some twenty thousand of them were technically army deserters. Wavell knew retaliation would be risky, but Indian Army Commander in Chief Auchinleck fiercely argued that if they did not at least try former INA officers for their crimes (including murdering Indian POWs), it would cripple army discipline.

The first trial opened in Delhi in the full glare of national publicity on November 2. Wavell and Auchinleck had anticipated trouble, but what they got was a national tidal wave of anger and outrage. When Gandhi heard rumors about the trial in July, he at first refused to believe the British could be so vindictive—or so short-sighted. He urged the Congress to use its own funds to find the INA men defense lawyers. Indeed, since the first three defendants were a Muslim, a Hindu, and a Sikh, the Muslim League, the Congress, and Sikh political parties all scrambled to their defense. Even the aging Liberal stalwart T. B. Sapru joined the defense committee, standing shoulder to shoulder with Nehru. The trial boiled everything down to "the old contest, England v. India."[24]

Even the choice of the Red Fort as the trial site was a blunder. This was where the last Mughal emperor had been tried in 1858 at the end of the Great Mutiny—or what more and more Indian nationalists were calling the War of Indian Independence. The setting made the defendants as much a symbol of Indian identity as anything that had happened since the Salt March. As INA prisoners were moved by train to Delhi, crowds gathered at the tracks to cheer and wave pictures of "Netaji" Bose, much as they once had done of Gandhi.[25] All at once, Bose's INA proved to be a more powerful force in defeat than it had ever been on the battlefield.

Anti-British demonstrations broke out around the country, much larger than any in the Quit India campaign. Every political party and all shades of political opinion joined in. In Calcutta members of Bose's old Forward Bloc, Communist students, and Congress radicals combined forces to organize scenes reminiscent of the French Revolution, with huge street demonstrations under enormous banners and speeches praising the INA men as martyrs and heroes.[26] In Calcutta protesters clashed with police. More than thirty people were killed and several hundred injured, while cars and police vehicles were overturned and set on fire across the city. When the viceroy held the official V-J Day parade in Delhi, rioters burned down Delhi's town hall, and the police opened fire, killing many.[27] By then the court had added fuel to the firestorm by acquitting two of the three INA officers. The verdict made the whole proceeding look like pure vindictive spite.

Gandhi was sympathetic but aloof and as usual condemned the violence. Ironically, the one Indian mass protest movement that he did *not* start did the most long-lasting damage to British rule, including to the Indian Army. Even the KCIOs, the bedrock of the officer corps, split on the issue, while the Indian Air Force was "100 percent" in support of the INA defendants. Then in February 1946 the Indian Navy erupted into full-scale mutiny in Bombay and Karachi. Fresh outbreaks of urban violence followed. In Calcutta police stations, post offices, and the YMCA were set on fire. Even Indians wearing Western dress found themselves under attack. In Bombay crowds smashed shops, police *chowkis,* and twelve hundred streetlamps.[28] By the twenty-fifth the violence had spread to Madras.

Wavell realized the situation was spinning out of control. "Every day that passes now brings more and more well-disposed Indians into the anti-British camp," the governor of the Northwest Frontier province wrote. "I dislike saying this intensely," he added, but "the best thing to do is to cut our losses" and stop the trials. Wavell finally had to agree, and by May the prosecution of former INA soldiers ceased. However, Royal Navy ships still had to be sent in to suppress the mutinies in Bombay and Karachi. More than two hundred civilians died in riots in Bombay and another thousand were injured.[29]

Very suddenly the whole dynamic of British-Indian relations had changed. As 1946 dawned, the Indian street controlled the pace of events, and militancy was the order of the day. British rule had shed its last shred of credibility, even among the British. For a decade and a half the British had held a long, careful debate and deliberation about India's future once the Raj ended. Tens of thousands of pages of government reports and White Papers and Blue Books had been issued, more than for any political issue since Irish Home Rule.[30] Now the British began looking for the closest exit. A stampede seemed to be gathering, not just among British officials and Britons in India but among Indians themselves. With the Red Fort trials, lightning had struck close to an already nervous herd. No one panicked, but everyone began edging away from the danger.

In an uneasy London the response was to dispatch a new Cripps delegation to work out final details on an offer of independence. The so-called Cabinet Mission arrived in March 1946. The question was no longer whether the British were pulling out of India, as in the 1930s, or when or under what conditions, as during the war. Now the question was how soon the British could hand over everything, including the administration and army, to someone else—*anyone* else. It was the victory Indian nationalists, among them Gandhi, had dreamed of. But at the same time the various political parties and personalities realized an important albeit ugly truth. The battle against the British was over, but the battle over who would succeed them was about to begin.

The two principal protagonists were now Nehru and Jinnah. Each headed a large, but by no means monolithic, political movement. They deeply despised each other; neither believed the other was capable of acting in good faith. Nehru assumed that the end of the war and Churchill's political demise had made the creation of a Pakistan unnecessary. He had always believed the Muslim League was an artificial creation of the British, as part of a divide-and-rule policy. When the British left, the majority of Muslims would surely come flocking back to the Congress. "We will all march together and ask for independence together," he said confidently in January. "There will be a united India and there will be no problem at all."[31] For his part, Jinnah called Nehru "Peter Pan," the boy who had never grown up. He saw Nehru's program as simply a blind for establishing a Hindu majority dictatorship.[32]

Viceroy Wavell correctly saw his job, and the job of the British, as getting these two contentious personalities to agree on a final settlement. To his disgust, however, the Cabinet Mission insisted on meeting with Gandhi instead. They still believed the international public relations image of Gandhi as India's leader and national savior, the man who could somehow perform magic and unite 350 million people around his charismatic presence.

Wavell knew better. He had met with Gandhi after the Calcutta riots in mid-December 1945. He knew Gandhi was still mentally sharp and in surprisingly good health for a man of seventy-six who had abused his body through fasts, food fads, and overwork, and who was still bitter over what he saw as British intransigence and broken promises. But the grand old man of Indian politics was now detached from events and impotent to affect them. Nonetheless, Wavell agreed to let the Cabinet Mission meet with Gandhi one more time.

The meeting on April 3 fulfilled Wavell's worst expectations. Gandhi arrived wearing nothing but his customary dhoti and greeted Cripps, Pethick-Lawrence, and First Lord of the Admiralty A. V. Alexander with his usual evasive humility. When Gandhi asked for a glass of water, the secretary of state ran to fetch it himself, instead of sending a servant. When Pethick-Lawrence failed to return, Cripps bounded up and ran out the door, as if he and the state secretary were waiters trying to please a demanding guest rather than representatives of a ruling power.

"I was frankly horrified," Wavell wrote in his journal, and more horrified by Gandhi's proposals. They included release of all detainees, meaning the INA prisoners, abolition of the salt tax (still a sore spot for Gandhi after fifteen years), and dismissal of Dr. Ambedkar from the viceroy's executive council. At the same time Gandhi floored everyone by proposing that Jinnah be made prime minister of India, although he also insisted that Jinnah would have to answer to the Hindu majority in the Central Assembly.

"As usual, G. refused to be pinned down to details," Wavell noted. This was what came, the viceroy thought to himself, "of all this slopping good-will all over the place." Then to Wavell's further horror, Pethick-Lawrence closed the meeting with a long rambling speech that expressed "penitence" for British rule. Wavell thought it sent precisely the wrong message, just as meeting with Gandhi was precisely the wrong approach to constitution-making.[33]

When Gandhi left, Wavell and the Labour delegation finally settled down to business. In the growing Delhi heat, they met with virtually every Indian leader who had a national following, including Ambedkar ("sincere, honest, and courageous, but an unattractive personality," Wavell admitted) and leading Sikhs.[34] At the end of two months of complex negotiations they arrived at a plan. Dominion India would finally get its independence, but in a strange and complicated three-tier system. At the top would be the Union of India, forged from British India and the princely states, with overarching power to run foreign affairs, defense, and communications. Below them, individual provinces and princely states would run their own affairs.

Sandwiched in between would be three new regional blocs in the Constituent Assembly. Section A would comprise Muslim-majority Baluchistan, the Sind, the Punjab, and the Northwest Frontier. Section B would contain the six Hindu-majority central and south India provinces. Finally Bengal and Assam, where the Hindu-Muslim split was most contentious, would form Section C. Each of these blocs would hold veto power over legislation emanating from the top, forcing the central government to recognize regional and sectional interests, especially where Muslim and Hindu interests clashed.[35]

The Cabinet Mission hoped that this plan would give Indians the best of both worlds. Hindus and Congress would get their united India, while Muslims would get recognition of their minority status and the power to veto moves they considered threatening. And the provinces and princely states would be free to run their own affairs with minimal interference from above.

Historians, especially Indian historians, have often cast Muhammad Jinnah as the great wrecker of Indian unity. But it is worth noting that he and the Muslim League formally agreed to the Cabinet plan on June 6, even though it made no provision for Jinnah's greatest dream, an independent Pakistan.[36] The Congress balked at full endorsement but did agree to join an interim government in which it and the Muslim League would share key cabinet posts. Nehru opposed making any concession to Jinnah, but the majority of Congress were more realistic. They were willing to accept a half, or more precisely a three-quarters loaf, if it meant an end to British rule and an end to communal strife. With the League and Congress for once in agreement, India's other political parties were prepared to grumble but not back out. By the evening of June 19, 1946, the second Cripps mission seemed to have achieved the impossible, reaching a deal not only for a future constitution but for a fourteen-man interim Indian government.

It was Gandhi, and Gandhi alone, who wrecked everything.

He had learned about the three-tier arrangement on May 16 and soon reduced it to ruins. Its complicated house-of-cards architecture seemed to sum up everything he despised about constitution-making and politics. So he pretended it was not a formal plan at all but "an appeal and an advice" that a future constituent assembly could alter at will. He said individual provinces should be free to opt out of the regional blocs at the outset—which meant the three groupings would actually have no power at all. Other than that, he said, "it is the best document the British Government could have produced in the circumstances." But he predicted that the Congress, and the Indian people, would have nothing to do with it. In the end, Gandhi told Cripps, "you will have to choose between the two—the Moslem League or Congress, both your creations," he added sarcastically.[37] Gandhi refused to endorse any British plan that gave the two organizations equal constitutional footing. So following his wishes, the Congress refused its endorsement as well.

Wavell still had time, however, to organize an interim government. On June 19 he believed they had reached agreement on fourteen people to assume office. Then on the twentieth "the situation seems to have gone haywire again, thanks to Gandhi."[38] At the last minute Rajagopalachari told the viceroy that, at Gandhi's insistence, the Parsi named to the interim council was not acceptable and that the Muslim contingent would have to include Dr. Azad, a Congress member. Wavell realized at once that this change would prompt Jinnah's refusal and doom the deal.

Cripps met with Gandhi for nearly three-quarters of an hour to try to persuade him to change his mind. Gandhi absolutely refused to budge. After almost three months of negotiation in sweltering heat, the deal was dead. Cripps and his fellow cabinet members went home, disappointed and baffled.

Wavell was filled with rage and disgust at the Mahatma. "Gandhi ran true to form and was the real wrecker," he wrote bitterly in his final summary of the mission on July 1. "I am depressed at the future prospect." But he still found room for some rough humor and penned a few lines parodying Lewis Carroll's "Jabberwocky":

> Beware the Gandhiji, my son,
> the satyagraha, the bogy-fast . . .
> The Gandhiji, on wrecking bent,
> Came trippling down the bangi ways,
> And woffled as he went.[39]

Why had Gandhi been so intransigent? His many statements to the press at the time were evasive, if not deliberately misleading. Allowing Jinnah to exclude Azad would certainly have reinforced the Muslim League's claim to speak for all Muslims, a principle Gandhi had never accepted—it had led to a breach between the two men before. But Gandhi's intransigence also marked the beginning of a breach with his closest colleagues, including Rajaji and Patel. It rested on his belief that no British-made constitution could work, or should be allowed to work. It was up to Indians, he believed, to discover the key to their own self-rule, to Swaraj in a proper sense, whatever the risks might be.

In these years his secretary Pyarelal was closer to Gandhi than virtually anyone. But even he was startled by Gandhi's fierce "readiness to face chaos and anarchy in preference to peace imposed by British arms" or even by British methods. Gandhi had convinced himself that only he could "settle directly with the Moslem League after the British had quitted, even if it meant civil war."[40] The apostle of nonviolence had said more than once that he preferred anarchy to slavery; his sabotaging of the Cabinet Mission plan was about to fulfill that wish.

Many individuals and institutions would be responsible for the tragedy that followed in the next year and a half. The Raj heads the list, for its unwillingness to face the reality of Indian independence until it was too late. Politicians like Nehru and Jinnah bear the blame for their willingness to tear India apart unless they got the power they wanted. The Attlee government and the last viceroy, Lord Mountbatten, let it all happen.

Winston Churchill also shares the blame.[41] For more than a decade he had fought to delay the inevitable transfer of power, sowing distrust and allowing bitter resentments to fester. If the 1935 India Bill had passed three or even two years earlier, or if Churchill had offered postwar independence in 1940 instead of in 1942, India might have had breathing space to work out a suitable framework for either a unified constitution or a peaceful India-Pakistan split. Instead, Churchill gambled that delay would force the British people to rise to the challenge of once again being an imperial power, and compel Indians to sink back under their customary fate as a subordinate "Asiatic race." Churchill lost his gamble. Millions of India's poorest and most vulnerable—the very people whose welfare Churchill said was his primary concern and the Raj's mandate for rule—paid the price.

However, the other person who must bear blame is Gandhi. For the sake of an unrealizable ideal, he had undermined the last chance at a peaceful settlement to India's freedom. Indeed, Gandhi's responsibility may run even deeper. His decade and a half of defiance of the law through civil disobedience had bred an atmosphere of contempt for social order, a celebration of recklessness and militancy. This contempt had horrified Liberals like T. B. Sapru in 1930, but by 1946 it had sunk deep into the Indian consciousness. The sad paradox was that the apostle of nonviolence had consistently, if unintentionally, inspired violence by others.[42] His fasts became potent weapons not because of his moral stature but because of fear that his death would set off riots across India. It was violence, not nonviolence, that forced the British first to change course, then to seek Gandhi's approval, and then finally to leave India. However, by encouraging others to see themselves in his exalted image, Gandhi helped to spread the dangerous fiction that all street action was soul force and vice versa.

The first horrific indication of this came six weeks later. Jinnah was the first to take a page from Gandhi's book. He believed that the collapse of the Cabinet Mission proved "beyond a shadow of a doubt that the only solution of Indian's problem is Pakistan." He told the Muslim League Council when they met in Bombay, "I feel we have exhausted all reasons... There is no tribunal to which we can go." The Muslim League had won majorities in key provinces in the recent elections; but Jinnah saw no reward in joining Wavell's interim government. Instead, the Quaid-e-Azam and the council declared August 16 a day of "direct action to achieve Pakistan and to organize the Moslems for the coming struggle."[43]

Jinnah had envisioned the Day of Action as a series of Congress-style protests, boycotts, and hartals. Instead, August 16 set off three days of massacres in Calcutta, where Muslim and Hindu mobs clashed in a bloodbath. More than 5,000 were murdered and another 15,000 were injured, while 100,000 were made homeless, the majority of them Muslims. Four battalions of British troops spent days carrying away the mutilated bodies, many of them women and children.

What Churchill had warned would happen if the British left seemed to have already started. A few people tried to stop the slaughter. A friend of Nirad Chaudhuri was saved by his Muslim neighbors from a mob that besieged his house. But Chaudhuri's brother could not prevent the murder of an elderly Muslim fruit-seller in the Bhowanipore district, who was dragged away even as he pleaded for his life. Bloodlust infused people of all ages and education levels, across religious lines. Calcutta's Sikh population contributed some of the coldest stone killers. One man saw a Muslim boy of fourteen caught by a Hindu mob, stripped naked to see if he was circumcised, then thrown into a pond and forced under water with bamboo poles; a well-known Bengali engineer with a British university degree used his Rolex wristwatch to note how long it took for the boy to drown.[44]

From far away in Delhi Wavell watched the death toll rise, helpless to do anything. On the evening of the eighteenth he begged Nehru to consider joining Jinnah in a coalition government, in order to quell the sectarian violence and restore order. But it was hopeless. Nehru needed the support of the ultra-orthodox Hindu Mahasabha in order to maintain his stature in the Congress; so no compromise with Muslims was possible. On the twentieth Wavell spoke to his deputy private secretary, who was normally upbeat about India's future. "Our only course is to get out of India as soon as possible and leave her to her fate," Ian Scott gloomily said, "which will be civil war."[45]

Wavell, refusing to give in to despair, drew up a plan for a graduated British withdrawal in anticipation of a massive and violent Muslim-Hindu split. He journeyed to Calcutta himself to see the devastation, then returned to push Nehru into reassuring the Muslim League about the future before it was too late. On August 28 he even enlisted Gandhi in the effort, but that only made things worse. The discussion turned heated, until finally (according to Wavell) Gandhi thumped the table with his gnarled fist and said, "If India wants her bloodbath she shall have it."

It was a stunning moment. Wavell said he was shocked to hear such language from the Mahatma.* The following evening Gandhi wrote a highly revealing letter to Wavell. "I write this as a friend and after deep thought," he said.

> If British arms are kept here for internal peace and order your Interim Government would be reduced to farce. The Congress cannot afford to impose its will on warring elements in India through the use of British arms. Nor can the Congress be expected to bend itself and adopt what it considers a wrong course over the brutal exhibition recently witnessed in Bengal. Such submissions would itself lead to an encouragement and repetition of such tragedies... And all this will be chiefly due to the continued presence in India of a foreign power.

After reading it, Wavell thought, "It looked like a declaration of war." But on September 2 he still swore in Jawaharlal Nehru as vice president of the new government. After taking his oath of office, Nehru muttered, *"Jai Hind"* under his breath, but Wavell pretended not to notice.† In late October a formula was finally found to allow Jinnah to enter the government, but it was too late to stop the next major wave of violence of East Bengal, in the remote and lushly green district of Noakhali.

The massacres began on October 10. Muslim gangs murdered Hindus in every village through which they passed, slaughtering the men like animals and raping and killing the women, then throwing the bodies down the wells. Nearly fifty thousand terrified Hindu villagers, who had lived peacefully with their Muslim neighbors for centuries, fled for their lives to neighboring Bihar, where Hindus were a majority. (There Hindu gangs, learning of the horrors in Noakhali, began hunting down and killing Muslims in retaliation.) The district's remoteness and junglelike terrain made restoring order by force almost impossible. It was five days before Gandhi learned what was happening.

The first reports reached him in Delhi, where he was staying in an untouchable neighborhood. Only days before he had been fatalistic

---

* In fact, he was not shocked. The bloodbath remark only confirmed Wavell's view that "Gandhi's professions of non-violence and saintliness are political weapons against the British rather than natural attributes." He was right, but not in the way he thought.

† This phrase was particularly ironic, since it had also been the battle cry of Subhas Chandra Bose, the man Nehru had helped oust from the Indian National Congress.

about communal violence. "Man is born to die," he told a prayer meeting. "So whether God sent [people] a natural death or whether they were killed by an assassin's knife, they must go smiling to their end."[46] His New Age instinct was to blame earlier violence on the evil influence of cities: hadn't he been saying that the Indian village was a peaceful haven that needed no policemen? Now, however, he realized he had to make a more pertinent response.

"Ever since he had heard the news from Noakhali," the *Hindustani Times* reported him telling his fellow worshippers, "indeed ever since the bloodbath of Calcutta, he has been wondering where his duty lay." Nonviolence, not just against the British but against everyone, "was the creed of the Congress. It had brought them this far" and would sustain them now.[47]

Biographers often imply that Gandhi left for Noakhali almost as soon as he heard the news, in order "to dry the tear in every eye." This is false. Gandhi fully knew what was happening by October 15. His greatest concern, however, was that people learn to die without killing others: it was the duty of himself and others in the Congress "to teach people this supreme act." On the seventeenth he spoke again of the massacres but only to say that "women must learn to die" before they are raped or converted to Islam. (Refugees had spread rumors that many were being forcibly converted.) It was better to commit suicide than to submit. He also spoke of the sins of gambling and black-marketing. As for Noakhali, "There is no inner call. When it comes, nothing will hold me back."[48]

By now Hindu retaliation had begun in Bihar, while police and soldiers in Noakhali and nearby Tippera were trying to restore order and count the bodies. On the nineteenth Gandhi was back in Sevagram. He still had no plan to leave. He did send a telegram saying he might go to Bengal on October 23 or 24. There was no need to rush. He told a friend who was horrified by the latest news: "I have no information...Go to Bengal if you want to." As late as the twenty-first he told another Bengali contact, Hemprabha Das Gupta, "You should be calm. Hope [to] come soon."[49] He preferred to wait until Nehru returned to India after his visit to London, and Gandhi could discuss the matter with the Congress Working Committee, before doing anything.

Not until October 25, two weeks after the killings had begun, did Gandhi finally leave—not for Noakhali but for Calcutta, to confer with Nehru about how to "still the fury." In fact, the police and army had already done that. But when Gandhi arrived in Noakhali on November 6 on a special train provided by the Bengali government, there were still burned bodies scattered in the courtyards of Hindu homes and bloodstains on the walls and floorboards. He visited a camp where six thousand refugees had taken shelter. He told them they should be ashamed for running away. "Men should fear only God," he said, and should either fight off their attackers or submit bravely to their martyrdom.

Despite his stern facade, the truth of what was happening finally seemed to sink in. "Ahimsa is indeed put to the test now," Gandhi would write from Noakhali. His Bengali interpreter was a professor from Calcutta University named Nirmal Kumar Bose. Bose was a nationalist and a believer in nonviolence but was hardly an unqualified Gandhi admirer.[50] He was shocked and disappointed when Gandhi told widows of men killed, "I have not come to bring you consolation. I have come to bring you courage." But then he heard Gandhi muttering to himself as he toured the devastation, "What shall I do? What shall I do?" The Mahatma began to wonder if his life's work had all been in vain. "I don't want to die a failure, but as a successful man," he confessed to Nirmal. "But it may be that I am a failure." He spoke for the first time of his own death, even assassination.[51]

"I am groping for light," Gandhi told Nirmal, but "I am surrounded by darkness." Finally he decided there was nothing for him to do but live in Noakhali himself. Together he and Nirmal found a simple hut in the village of Srirampur, and in the second week in December Gandhi's grandniece Manubehn joined them. She did the daily cooking, preparing Gandhi's meals while Nirmal tended to Gandhi's daily massages. As January 1947 began, Gandhi set off on foot to tour Noakhali's villages. With bamboo staff in hand, he set out at dawn every morning, visiting villagers and preaching reconciliation and singing to himself a poem called "Walk Alone" by Rabindranath Tagore:

> *If they answer not thy call, walk alone;*
> *If they are afraid and cower mutely facing the wall;*
> *O thou of evil luck,*
> *Open thy mind and speak out alone.*
>
> *If they turn away and desert you when crossing the wilderness,*
> *O thou of evil luck,*

Trample the thorns under thy tread,
And along the blood-soaked track walk alone.

Meanwhile the violence was still spreading. In the village of Garmuktesar in the United Provinces, Hindus turned on their Muslim neighbors and virtually wiped them out.[52] An AP reporter asked Gandhi if the riots would end. "You may be certain that they will end," he replied archly. "If the British influence were withdrawn, they would end much quicker."[53] Meanwhile Nehru had returned from London, where the discussions had concerned how to withdraw that influence.

On the last day of 1946 Viceroy Wavell prepared to unfurl his plan for terminating British control of India. Bearing the unfortunate and misleading nickname "the Breakdown Plan," it was a plan to prevent chaos, not merely to stem its horrible flow. Wavell envisaged a British withdrawal in three separate stages: first from the southern provinces, which were still fairly secure; then from Bihar and the United Provinces in central India, once the violence had been stopped; and finally from the rest of the subcontinent. Wavell had consulted with the army and Auchinleck, as well as the heads of the Indian Civil Service. The idea was to keep British administration intact in religiously divided provinces and states as long as possible, until everyone had worked out a political settlement that might, but did not necessarily, include creation of an independent Pakistan. Wavell felt it was a plan for all contingencies and even set a date for complete withdrawal: March 31, 1948. But his own head of the civil service predicted that de facto British control would end well before that date.[54] The alternative, in any case, would be full-out civil war.

When the cabinet first got word of the Breakdown Plan, they were aghast.[55] None of them had any idea that conditions in India were so bad. They had faith in Gandhi and Nehru's reassurances that taking concrete steps for British withdrawal would diminish the violence, not exacerbate it, and that the Hindu-Muslim issue would resolve itself once Indians took over. They worried the plan would make the British look pro-Muslim and encourage Muslim separatism.

Above all, they felt the plan made the British appear to be less in control of the situation than Attlee and the Labour government liked to think they were.[56] To Attlee, the Breakdown Plan seemed "evidence of decline in British power and resolution," even "the beginning of the liquidation of the British Empire"—ironically echoing Churchill. The Labour government wanted the withdrawal from India to look like a triumph of British statesmanship, not a headlong flight.

So on January 8, 1947, Attlee told Wavell that the cabinet could not endorse the Breakdown Plan.[57] In his diary Wavell described the letter as "cold, ungracious and indefinite." But unknown to him, Wavell was already on his way out. A month earlier Attlee had secretly approached the man he wanted to replace Wavell as viceroy: Louis Prince Mountbatten. Attlee believed that the man who had overseen the fate of 120 million people in Southeast Asia after the Japanese surrender was just the man to oversee the fate of 400 million now and to find a way for Britain to leave India with honor. Labour politicians also figured Mountbatten's aristocratic charm and royal lineage might awe Indian politicians into compliance, especially its independent princes and maharajas, the last remaining barrier to a handover of power.

Besides, Mountbatten, despite (or perhaps because of) his exalted status, was also a man of the Left. When his troops marched back into Malaya and Burma, he had strongly endorsed local nationalist movements and set both those countries on the path to independence. His wife, Lady Edwina, was a keen Congress supporter. "Of course we think that Gandhi and his friends are absolutely right," she told her friends. "We must try to fit in with what they want us to do."[58] Mountbatten had had no qualms about winding up the British Empire in East Asia; he certainly would have none about doing the same in India.

"Dickie" Mountbatten had one other inestimable advantage: he was a Churchill protégé and a personal favorite. Churchill had appointed him Southeast Asia supreme commander over the heads of older, more experienced men, because he had had the dash and reputation for bold action that Churchill liked. At this crucial juncture Attlee felt the need for some cover on his right flank. Back in October 1946 Churchill had launched a slashing attack on the government over the growing violence in India.

"On the morrow of our victory [in 1945]," he growled in that familiar voice, "and of our services, without which human freedom would not have survived, we are divesting ourselves of the mighty and wonderful empire which had been built up in India by two hundred years of effort and sacrifice." The Labour government had placed the fate of 400 million human beings "into the hands of men who have good reason to be bitterly hostile to the British connection." Churchill added, "I fear that calamity impends upon this mighty sub-Continent...No one can measure the misery and bloodshed which will overtake these enormous masses of humble helpless millions."

"All this is happening every day, every hour," Churchill warned, even as news of Noakhali spread across British newspapers. "The great ship is sinking in the calm sea," he cried. "Those who should have devoted their utmost efforts to keep her afloat have instead opened the sea-cocks... Sometimes in the past I have not been wrong. I pray that I may be wrong now."[59] Attlee counted on Mountbatten's appointment to convince Churchill that the India ship of state was still afloat, although set on a course very different from the one Churchill would have chosen.

The plan worked. Churchill sent his congratulations to the government on its choice of the new viceroy—a gesture he would later regret. Not until February 20, 1947, did he learn the awful truth: Mountbatten's job was not only to extinguish the Raj forever but to do it before June 1, 1948, regardless of the situation on the ground.

Churchill was beside himself.* He rose in the House on March 6 to rip into the government for its "premature hurried scuttle" of its imperial responsibilities in India.

The whole principle that Hindus and Muslims had to agree on a communal solution before the British left, he complained, had been thrown overboard. "One thing seems to me absolutely certain," he said. "The Government, by their 14 months' time limit, have put an end to all prospect of Indian unity." India was about to be subjected "not merely to partition, but fragmentation." Those fourteen months "will not be used for the melting of hearts and the union of Muslim and Hindu all over India. They will be used in preparation for civil war." The scene unfolding now, "with the corpses of men, women, and children littering the ground in thousands," will be repeated in every part of India, if Attlee's plan was allowed to go through.

The only explanation, for this situation, Churchill said, had to be that the government had adopted "one of Mr. Gandhi's most scatterbrained observations," made after the Cripps mission of 1942 had failed. *Leave India in God's hands,* Gandhi had said, *in modern parlance, to anarchy... From [this] a true India will arise in place of the false one we see.*

---

* He did not realize that Wavell had proposed wrapping things up even sooner.

By setting its arbitrary deadline,* Churchill implied, the government had endorsed that hope. He begged Attlee to reconsider.

"Let us not add to the pangs of sorrow many of us feel" over the loss of India, Churchill concluded, "the taint and smear of shame" for handing over the former empire to Gandhi and the forces of chaos.[60] Still, Churchill had one more card to play. He had mentioned it in his letter to Clementine back in January 1945: "Pakistan." Through his secret support for Jinnah and India's Muslims, Churchill still hoped he could deny Gandhi his ultimate victory.

---

* It is not really clear who dreamed up the June 1 date. Mountbatten later claimed he did, but according to R. J. Moore, the idea of setting a "date certain" for British withdrawal, in hopes it would concentrate the minds of Indian politicians, was already in Attlee's thinking when he made Mountbatten's appointment.

Chapter Thirty

DEATH IN THE GARDEN

1947–1948

Mark my words. I prophesied the present war and [now] I prophesy the bloodbath.
WINSTON CHURCHILL, MAY 1943

Alas, do all living creatures kill one another?
GAUTAMA BUDDHA

IN FACT, MOUNTBATTEN'S ARRIVAL WAS HARDLY a victory for Gandhi—it spelled the end of his fondest hopes: "From the moment Mountbatten landed in Delhi, partition became inevitable."[1] No other solution to a possible Hindu-Muslim civil war seemed possible.

Even as Mountbatten's plane touched down on the tarmac, disorder and violence were commonplace in every major city. Most provincial governors, finding the police no longer reliable, had to rely on the army to try to keep armed mobs apart and to count the dead. However, Mountbatten stoutly maintained the fiction that everything was going according to plan. The forty-six-year-old new viceroy, resplendent in a gleaming white uniform bedecked with medals and the Order of India, seemed brimming with vitality. He was greeted by maharajas, rows of soldiers, flags, and ceremonial salutes. The last viceroy was also the first viceroy to have the ceremony recorded on camera and broadcast on an international radio hookup.[2]

Mountbatten's message was as upbeat as Neville Chamberlain's had been when he stepped off the plane at Heston in 1938. "This is not a normal Viceroyalty," he said to the nation. "I believe that every political leader in India feels as I do the urgency of the task before us." The task was the full and complete transfer of power by June 1948.[3] "Lord Louis," as he was called, confidently believed he could succeed where others had failed. He saw opening discussions with the Mahatma at once as a crucial part of his strategy.

That was not going to be easy. Gandhi was many miles away in Bihar, still trying to stop the killing, this time of Muslims by Hindus. Every day he passed through villages where disemboweled corpses lay strewn in dense bamboo thickets, while vultures fed on the remains.[4] When the viceroy's summons came, he reluctantly agreed to take a train to Delhi. But when Mirabehn unthinkingly reserved a double compartment instead of his usual third-class seat, Gandhi's frustration and anger boiled over. How dare she put the government to this extra expense? His rage left her in tears, as the train slowly wound its way through the angry heat-ridden countryside.

The historic meeting with Mountbatten came on March 31. The photograph of the occasion shows Lord and Lady Mountbatten looking friendly but ill at ease, and the Mahatma detached and distant. Having personally dealt with nearly four decades of viceroys, he had watched them come and go. There had been sympathetic Ampthill; well-meaning Hardinge; helpful Minto; colorless Reading; sanctimonious Irwin; contemptuous Willingdon; unresponsive Linlithgow; sensible but unwavering Wavell.

Now there was Mountbatten: much younger than the others and outspokenly pro-Congress. But he also was impatient and infinitely vain.* Gandhi had few expectations about what the British could offer for the future, which seemed to grow darker each day, viceroy or no viceroy.

Gandhi talked to Lord Louis for more than two hours, mostly about his life and his endless battle with the Raj. The next day, April Fool's Day, Gandhi repeated the extraordinary proposal that had so stunned Wavell and the Cabinet Mission. Let Jinnah be India's prime minister, he urged; let him choose his ministers, whether Hindu or Muslim; and let the viceroy's veto power be the only restraint. Gandhi was convinced this was the only way to win the Muslim League's trust and keep India intact. The Congress would complain but would give way if Gandhi got them to see the light.

---

* According to Andrew Roberts, as events and the violence built to a climax that July, Lord Louis spent several days personally designing the flag he would carry as the new governor-general of India and Pakistan and worrying about how to get his Buick limousine flown into Karachi for the installation ceremony.

Mountbatten smiled and said he found the plan attractive. "But I need not say that this solution coming at this time staggered me," he confessed in his official report.[5] He pretended that he would discuss the matter with Nehru. But in fact he had already decided how to proceed.

He and Nehru had spoken on March 24. They knew each other from Singapore after the war, when Nehru had joined the British victory parade and rescued Mountbatten's wife Edwina from the roaring crowds of overseas Indians anxious to shake the Pandit's hand. Now that both men were in Delhi, the intimacy between Nehru and Mountbatten increased—as did Nehru's intimacy with the viceroy's wife. "When Nehru began to call Edwina and me 'his dear friends,'" Mountbatten remembered later, "I began to get the feeling that we were halfway home." From that moment, he became a shameless Nehru partisan, an advantage Nehru did not scruple to exploit.[6]

It was a natural meeting of minds. The Pandit and Dickie shared the same socialist sympathies and elitist public school attitudes. They also shared a friend, V. P. Menon, who would become Mountbatten's closest Indian adviser. Working together, Mountbatten, Nehru, and Menon proceeded to work out India's future and their own. No Muslim was allowed to attend their meetings.[7]

Their plan was simple and brutal. Jinnah and the Muslims would be forced to accept a truncated Pakistan, shorn of Bengal and the Punjab. Nehru would become prime minister of the rest of India, including the princely states, with Menon as his personal representative in London. Mountbatten would serve as governor-general of both countries. Nehru offered Mountbatten another inducement for agreeing to partition: the newly independent India, he vowed, would join the British Commonwealth, the post-imperial gathering of former colonies that Mountbatten and others hoped would be the future face of the British Empire.[8]

Mountbatten did not need persuading. His first meeting with Jinnah on April 5 was a disaster. The viceroy found the Quaid-e-Azam "most frigid, haughty, and disdainful"—mild stuff compared to his later descriptions of Jinnah as "a psychopathic case" and "bastard," once the bitterness of memory settled in.[9] Mountbatten dedicated himself to securing the most he could for Nehru and the Congress as future rulers of India and giving as little to Jinnah and the Muslim League as possible.

Since Gandhi (unbeknownst to Jinnah) was the Muslim leader's strongest ally in Delhi circles, that also meant ignoring Gandhi. "This is no time for idealistic gestures," Mountbatten would say. "This is the time for action." Within two weeks of his arrival Mountbatten had eliminated the Mahatma from any significant contribution to designing the new India. Neither Nehru nor Patel nor any of the other leading Congress politicians ever noticed or complained.[10]

Gandhi was crushed but hardly surprised. Once again the British had disappointed him, even as the Congress informed him that it could never endorse his quixotic plan—the last hope for a unified India. So Gandhi informed the Congress that he would take no part in any further negotiations with the viceroy and left again for Bihar. He would accept partition and do his best to keep as much of India intact as possible. But never again woud he see the Indian National Congress or Nehru as his allies, let alone disciples.

"No one listens to me any more," he sadly confessed. "I am a small man. True there was a time when mine was a big voice... Now neither the Congress nor the Hindus nor the Moslems will listen... I am crying in the wilderness."[11]

Like Churchill, he instinctively understood that the violence was just beginning. In Bihar the killing flared up again, as well as in Noakhali. Violence soon spread to the Punjab, as the reality sank in that either the Muslims *or* the Hindus *or* the Sikhs would rule that province but never all three. The same would happen in Bengal. Those lucky enough not to be murdered set out on the road. At one point five to six million people were in motion across India, the greatest human migration in history.[12]

In Muslim-majority Kashmir the maharaja arrested the local Muslim leader, which promised trouble there. Meanwhile the date for a final deal on partition arrived. Jinnah has been retrospectively cast as the villain of the piece, but in fact his back was to the wall. It is not entirely clear that he ever wanted full and complete partition.[13] Then Gandhi's old protégé Vallabhbhai Patel put the final seal on the plan by insisting on the division of Bengal and the Punjab. Ostensibly this was to give the future Muslim state more territory. In fact, it was to secure as much of those provinces as possible for India. Jinnah realized that far from having to force the issue of partition, it was being forced on him, with the viceroy applying the maximum pressure.

The final meeting between Mountbatten and Jinnah came on June 2 at midnight. Mountbatten's military adviser, General Ismay, sat in. Ismay was an old India officer and another Churchill favorite. Unlike Mountbatten, he was deeply dismayed by what he saw happening around him. In typical Indian officer fashion, he summed up the situation in polo terms: "We are in the last chukka, and down twelve goals." The British could no longer keep order in the subcontinent they had governed for 250 years. "There was slaughter everywhere," he remembered. "The British had all the responsibility and none of the power."[14] Ismay was convinced in spite of himself that partition was the only way out. Mountbatten's aide had said the task of drawing up the boundaries would take two years, but the viceroy had given him just forty days.

At first the meeting with Jinnah seemed hopeless, as the older man dug in. Jinnah refused to give way on the viceroy's plan to split the Punjab and Bengal into Indian and Pakistani halves. His anger was understandable. If the issue were left to a referendum, he knew, the vote would be overwhelmingly on his side. A Greater Pakistan would become a reality, not the "moth eaten" one the viceroy was offering. But then Mountbatten played his trump card. He had a secret message from the one man who could sway the Quaid-e-Azam's mind: Winston Churchill.

Churchill's contacts with Jinnah had begun before the war, and when Jinnah visited London in 1946, he and the opposition leader had lunch at Chartwell. The issue was the fate of India's Muslims under a Hindu majority government. To Churchill, the creation of a Muslim Pakistan with ties to the empire seemed the one way to "save a bit of India" for Britain and to snatch a victory from Gandhi, the Congress, and Attlee.

"I greatly valued our talk the other day," Churchill told Jinnah on December 11. He sent a postal address where Jinnah could send him secret messages "without attracting attention in India. I shall always sign myself 'Gilliatt' "—the name of Churchill's secretary. He urged Jinnah to use a similar pseudonym.[15] In that secret correspondence Churchill assured Jinnah that Pakistan would have a strong protector in the British and would never be expelled from the British commonwealth. "If Jinnah is regarded as the father of Pakistan," remarks one recent historian, "Churchill must qualify as its uncle."[16]

Churchill revealed his bond with Jinnah in a crucial meeting with Mountbatten in May 1947.

The opposition leader had been in bed recovering from a hernia operation when Mountbatten stopped by before departing for India. Mountbatten was trying to build political support for his partition plan. He assured Churchill that he had a letter from Nehru stating that if partition took place in 1947 instead of 1948, India would accept full Dominion status and not cut its ties to Britain. On that basis Churchill was reluctantly willing to accept a transfer-of-power bill that summer. "If you can achieve Dominion status for both Hindustan and Pakistan," he said, "the whole country will be behind you."

Then, leaning forward from his pillows, he asked, "Do you foresee any difficulties with Mr. Gandhi?"

"Gandhi is unpredictable," Mountbatten replied, "but I doubt whether he can create any difficulties which Nehru or Patel cannot handle." The real problem, he said, would be Jinnah.

"By God, he is the one man who cannot do without British help!" the former prime minister exploded. If Jinnah refused to accept Dominion status, Churchill said, "you must threaten [him]." He waved his cigar. "Take away all British officers. Give them military units without British officers. Make it clear to them how impossible it would be to run Pakistan without British help."

If all else failed, Churchill said, "give Jinnah a personal message from me. Tell him this is a matter of life or death for Pakistan, if he does not accept this offer with both hands!"[17]

That was the message Mountbatten now passed on to the Quaid-e-Azam. Jinnah admired Churchill more than any man alive.[18] On hearing the message, Jinnah sat stunned and silent. He could not speak, only give a brief nod of assent. Churchill had done what neither Mountbatten or Gandhi in meetings in the spring could do: get the immovable Jinnah to change his mind. Thanks to Churchill, the last barrier to partition was gone.

Only Gandhi could still wreck everything. But he chose not to. The day Mountbatten asked his opinion was his day of silence. On a scrap of paper Gandhi wrote: "You really don't want to say anything, do you?" But the next day in his bath, he said he felt as if they were not just dividing India but dismembering his own body.[19]

On the morning of June 3, 1947, the leaders of the various parties, including Jinnah, gathered to put their signatures to the agreement. Nehru was alarmed by the growing violence across India—it was far more extensive than he anticipated. Partition was the price he had been willing to pay to be rid of Jinnah and the Muslims and to assume power himself; now for the first time he expressed doubts about the speed with which everything was happening. Mountbatten alone remained confident, almost cheerful. His reputation as the man who gave India its independence and got the British out was assured, whatever else might happen.[20]

That night Nehru, the Sikh leader Baldev Singh, and Jinnah made the announcement of partition to their respective followers over national radio. Jinnah was unable even to utter the words but only grimly nodded to the others when his assent was mentioned. Mountbatten then gave them the thirty-page document his staff had prepared, *Administrative Consequences of Partition.*

"It was clear from the reactions at the meeting," Mountbatten wrote afterward, "that none of the leaders present had even begun to think of the complications with which we are all going to be faced."[21] He saw a row of stunned faces as the reality sank in. India was no more. Ninety million Muslims, 250 million Hindus, 10 million Christians, and 5 million Sikhs were to be divided into two independent countries, both with a single governor-general.* Mountbatten added his own final touch the next day. He calmly announced that independence would not come next June, as originally promised, but in little more than nine weeks, at midnight on August 14—the anniversary of the Japanese surrender.[22] Even Attlee was caught off guard. After 250 years the British had less than seventy-four days to pack their bags and get out.

Mountbatten always claimed he sped up the timetable in order to enhance British prestige and to make sure India stuck to its promise to remain in the commonwealth. But in truth he sensed that he and the British were sitting on the edge of a volcano. They had to leave before it erupted. But when the British were finally quitting India, would there be anything left of India after they did?

The announcement of partition only increased the violence, including in Kashmir. When Gandhi learned of the riots there, he left Bihar for the capital, Srinagar. "You must not expect much of me," he told the crowds when he arrived in the strife-torn city. He visited a women's hospital in a refugee camp in Jammu and had to brush the flies away from festering knife wounds. "Repeat the name of Rama," he told each victim. "That alone will help you."[23] He had tea with the beleaguered maharaja, a man very much in over his head. He spoke to delegations of Hindu workers who were worried about their future if Kashmir became part of Pakistan. He also stopped briefly in the Punjab and its

---

* Jinnah did get his revenge: he steadfastly refused to accept Mountbatten as Pakistan's governor-general and instead appointed himself, thus denying the former viceroy the one title he really wanted.

capital, whose name was forever linked to Gandhi's career and the history of India: Amritsar.

When his train drew up in the railway station, throngs of young Hindu men were standing on the platform. Gandhi moved to the window to greet them. Instead, with one angry voice they shouted out in English, "Go back, Gandhi!" They were furious about the partition, which they saw as Gandhi's betrayal of the dream of Rama Raj. Gandhi had to stop his ears to keep out the deafening chants until the train could pull away.

The latent violence of his fellow Hindus, which the impending British pullout had unleashed, frightened him. Earlier, when he had tried to include a passage from the Koran in his Hindu prayer meeting, a man had exploded in anger and created such a commotion that Gandhi had had to stop. "I see nothing but evil in this partition plan," he told his secretary Pyarelal.[24] He began to speak of going to live in Pakistan, either in East Bengal or in perhaps the Northwest Frontier.[25] In many ways India was becoming a country he no longer recognized.

Gandhi was in a hurry to return to Noakhali by August 15, the day independence would become official. He refused to participate in any of the independence events or celebrations. "India has accepted partition at the point of a bayonet," he said on the train to Kashmir.[26] August 15 should be a day of fasting and spinning and praying as India faced its supreme trial, he argued, not a day of parades or celebrations.

He never reached Noakhali. When the train stopped in Calcutta, members of the city council were waiting for him on the platform. Their drawn anxious faces told the story. Calcutta had seen almost continuous riots since the Day of Action a year ago. Now the city fathers feared that the splitting of Bengal into Hindu and Muslim halves would make them even worse. A former mayor, Muhammad Usman, said he feared the fifteenth might trigger a general massacre of the city's Muslim minority.[27]

Gandhi agreed to stay, but only if Calcutta's Muslim leaders would tell their followers in Noakhali to stop murdering Hindus. (They did as Gandhi asked, with no tangible effect.) Then he and Shaheed Suhrawardy, the Muslim League leader who had organized the original Direct Action Day but now feared Hindu retaliation, agreed to take a stand together. They found a looted house belonging to an elderly Muslim lady in the predominantly Hindu Beliaghata section. Not far away Hindu gangs armed with Sten guns and hand grenades had ethnically cleansed a Muslim working-class neighborhood, leaving no one alive.[28] Together Gandhi and Suhrawardy took rooms in the house, its floors strewn with filth and broken glass, and awaited the coming storm.

On the morning of August 15, 1947, Jawaharlal Nehru raised the Indian flag over Delhi's Red Fort. "The free flag of India is the symbol of freedom and democracy not only for India, but for the whole world," he told the cheering throngs. "If credit is due to any man today it is to Gandhiji."[29] But Gandhi was not present to receive the plaudits. He spent the days leading up to independence in Calcutta literally under siege from an angry Hindu mob. They had demanded to know why he came to Calcutta to defend Muslims but stayed away when Hindus were being killed.

"I have not come for the good of the Moslems alone," he finally told the furious crowd. "If I am to be killed, it is you who can kill me." Those words had a curious tonic effect, as did Suhrawardy's public acceptance of responsibility for the murders during Direct Action. In fact, Independence Day in Calcutta passed better than Gandhi or anyone could have expected. On the fourteenth Hindus and Muslims marched together in a procession through the city, and at dawn cries of *"Hindu Muslim bhai bhai!"** filled the streets. Gandhi found himself surrounded by cheering throngs who showered him with incense and rose petals, as the new national flag flew overhead.

Mountbatten wrote him a congratulatory letter, calling him "my one-man Boundary Force," referring to the 23,000-man force that was supposed to keep order during the partition and was failing virtually everywhere. But Gandhi was deeply unhappy.

"Is there something wrong with me?" he wrote to his disciple Amrit Kaur, now Nehru's health minister. "Or are things really going wrong?" Even the national flag was a disappointment. To his sorrow, Nehru and the Congress had removed his charkha as the national symbol and substituted the wheel of Emperor Ashoka. In effect, the symbol of Swadeshi and Swaraj had been replaced by a symbol of Indian imperial grandeur.

Gandhi felt like a prisoner in Calcutta, terrified that if he left, the killings would start again. In fact, Calcutta had become an oasis of peace in a subcontinent awash in turmoil and bloodshed. Virtually every-

---

* "Hindus and Muslims are brothers!"

where else hundreds of thousands of panicked people were fleeing their homes and businesses to escape from the neighbors with whom they had lived for centuries, Hindus fleeing east and Muslims west. At one point the line of refugees fleeing West Punjab stretched fifty-seven miles. Meanwhile gangs of thugs dogged their heels, killing and raping as many refugees as they could.

An Indian journalist, D. F. Karaka, was taken to inspect a train that had been carrying Muslims out of the Punjab; it had been ambushed by Sikhs at Amritsar station. More than two thousand bodies were still on the train, ten to fifteen per compartment. Their clothes had been ripped off, and "many a head and hand lay dismembered from the rest of the body...Heads lay cracked as if with a huge nut-cracker. Stomachs were ripped open or pierced...The platform and the railway carriages dripped with blood." Karaka bitterly realized there were more people killed on that single train than General Dyer had killed in his notorious massacre twenty-eight years before—ironically in the same city. "Their only crime was that they happened to belong to a different religion from those who butchered them."[30]

Even Nehru realized things were falling apart. He wrote to Gandhi, "All this killing business has reached a stage of complete madness, and vast populations are deserting their habitations and trekking to the west or to the east." He had sent his daughter Indira and her little son Rajiv to the hill station retreat of Mussoorie as soon as Independence Day celebrations ended, in order to escape the tide of violence. At the end of August he flew to the Punjab and was overwhelmed by what he saw. "I am sick with horror," he told Mountbatten. "What we saw was bad, what we heard was worse...There was an odor of death, a smell of blood and burning human flesh...Hundreds of thousands...on the move."[31]

Gandhi had also heard of the killings in the Punjab and was determined to go there. The communal peace in Calcutta had proved artificial. Roving gangs began killing again, and Hindu mobs roamed the streets. This time the object of their rage was Gandhi as much as it was terrified Muslims.

If Jinnah and Muslims distrusted Gandhi as a Hindu partisan, millions of Hindus, especially higher-caste Hindus, saw him as not partisan enough. They had welcomed Indian independence as signifying a resurgence of Hindu greatness. The creation of Pakistan seemed an insult, something contrary to history and nature. Many in ultranationalist groups like Mahasabha and the Vishva Hindu Parishad, and paramilitary militias associated with the RSS,* blamed Gandhi, although he more than anyone else had tried to hold the country together.

A wounded Muslim was brought to Gandhi for shelter. A Hindu mob followed and tried to break into the house. They threatened the Mahatma's life and shouted insults. Someone even tried to hit him with a lathi but missed. A brick aimed at his head struck a Muslim at his side. Two terrified girls who had traveled to Calcutta with him, his grandnieces Manubehn and Abhabehn, had to hold him back from rushing into the crowd as he screamed, "Kill me kill me, I say, why don't you kill me?!" Later, Gandhi conducted a sad tour through the city's smashed streets to view the carnage. He returned looking small and shriveled and in a state of shock. He wrote to Patel, "I feel totally lost."[32]

Gandhi had one last nonviolent remedy to try. He announced he would hold a "fast unto death" unless the killings stopped. For four days he refused all food and drank only soda water, until Calcutta's city fathers, terrified that they might be held responsible if the Mahatma died, agreed to try to stop the mayhem. The next day Gandhi left on the night train for Delhi.

Even from the train platform, he could see the smoke hovering over the city. The very day he ended his fast, September 4, the Indian capital had exploded in bloodshed. Martial law had been declared, the hospitals were full of wounded, and the streets full of dead bodies as crowds looted Muslim shops and set fire to cars and police stations. Nirad Chaudhuri witnessed the violence firsthand that Sunday and returned home in tears.

"I had seen the political riots of August 1942," he wrote later, "but I had never before had the feeling of a breakdown in government," as looting, arson, and murder continued unchecked in India's capital. "I seemed to feel that, figuratively speaking, the ground was slipping from under my feet...I seemed to see the anarchy cooped up within the bowels of Indian society."[33]

So did Nehru, and it drove him into a frenzy. He made repeated radio appeals to stop the pogroms; when they failed, he took up a lathi (ironically, the symbol of hated British rule) to try to disperse the rioters, but to no avail. He told R. Prasad that the violence had shaken "my faith in my people. I could not conceive of the gross brutality and sadistic

* Rashtriya Swayamsevak Sangh, the ancestor of today's Bharatiya Janata Party.

cruelty that people have indulged in...Little children have been butchered in the streets. The houses in many parts of Delhi are still full of corpses...I am fairly thick skinned, but I find this kind of thing more than I can bear."[34]

Only Gandhi remained calm and defiant. The massacres were precisely what he had feared would happen if his people turned away from nonviolence: he knew only too well that there was a fine line between soul force and brute force. Lord Mountbatten congratulated him on "the miracle of Calcutta," but Gandhi was in no mood for congratulations.[35] "I must apply the formula of 'Do or Die' to the capital of India," he said. Despite the threats to his life, he visited the hospitals to offer prayers and consolation. When he was driven to visit a refugee center where some 75,000 Muslims were waiting to be evacuated to Pakistan, a mob of Muslim youths, half-demented by their ordeal, surrounded his car.

His driver panicked, but Gandhi calmly dismounted and spoke to them of the need for Hindu-Muslim unity, even though his terrified companions could hear mutterings of *"Gandhi mordabad!"* or "Death to Gandhi!" all around them. The crowd finally dispersed; Gandhi and the car drove on. It was perhaps as close as Gandhi came to being lynched that summer. Despite his calm demeanor and unrelenting steadfastness, inside he was spiritually dying. The senseless violence even spread into Viceroy House, where several of the viceroy's own servants were murdered. Lady Mountbatten escorted the corpses to the mortuary. Gandhi told her, "Such a happening is unparalleled in the history of the world, and makes me hang my head in shame."[36] For him, that summer in Delhi marked the end of the dream of satyagraha.

The truth was, it had been a dream all along. The truth was, his power over the Indian masses had lasted only as long as he kept them on the path to independence. Now that independence had arrived, he seemed more an obstacle than a help. Like Churchill in 1945, Gandhi became an inconvenience to the very people whom he had led to freedom.

This was true of his closest followers as well. Vallabhbhai Patel had been his most indispensable apostle, almost his Saint Peter. But, years of power-seeking had turned the progenitor of the Salt March into a callous *Realpolitik* nationalist, "silent, husky...with eyes of steel."[37] As home minister, "Sardar" Patel repeatedly told Gandhi that stories of mass murder, even genocide, against Muslims were exaggerated (even though Gandhi had seen the evidence with his own eyes).[38] Privately, Patel had no problems with expelling Muslims from the Punjab and

United Provinces. To his mind, they were all potential traitors. He even boasted that Congress had acceded to partition only as a temporary expedient: once the British left, he said, Indian troops would put an end to Pakistan by military force.[39]

Even as he spoke, the British Indian Army was being divided in two, as its units now swore homage either to Pakistan or to India. Mountbatten had made sure that the bulk of resources and equipment went to India.[40] In the midst of the chaos Patel and Nehru realized that in the military they had a formidable tool not only for reimposing civil order but for "revising" partition's boundaries at will.

The test case was Kashmir. On July 26 Mountbatten had cajoled and persuaded the remaining Indian princes to accept the reality of partition and incorporation into one or the other of the new sovereign states. Only two princely states held out. One was Hyderabad, the largest state in India's south, whose prince insisted on outright independence.* The other was Kashmir. Tucked deep in the mountains between Chinese Turkestan and the Northwest Frontier, Kashmir's population was more than two-thirds Muslim. Its ruler, however, was Hindu and could not decide which state to join. In October 1947 Nehru and Patel decided to make the decision for him.

As early as June Nehru had said that the normal and obvious course was for Kashmir to join the Constituent Assembly for India: "It is absurd to think that Pakistan would create trouble if this happens."[41] After all, the new Pakistani government had its hands full. Jinnah and his ministers were busy setting up their new capital in Karachi, handling the floods of refugees from East Punjab and central India, and trying to establish order in their most distant province, East Bengal, where Hindus and Muslims were at one another's throats. They had little time and few resources to worry about Kashmir.

However, Jinnah could not ignore this flagrant *Anschluss.* By the end of September talk of war between India and Pakistan was widespread. Nehru convinced himself that if he did not move on Kashmir, Jinnah would beat him to the finish line. On October 25 he ordered the First Sikh Battalion to be airlifted into Srinagar, claiming falsely that Afridi tribesmen were crossing the border and massacring non-Muslims.[42] It

---

* He never got it. Once they settled the fate of Kashmir, in September 1948 Nehru and Menon dispatched troops to force Hyderabad to accept union with India, on the grounds that while the ruler was Muslim, its population was overwhelmingly Hindu—ironically, the opposite of the rationale they used to intervene in Kashmir.

was the Great Game all over again, except that the enemy was not Russia anymore but Pakistan's Muslims. The Indian Army's first independent military operation got under way. The first war between Pakistan and India over Kashmir began.

Gandhi was horrified. Just that month he had crossed verbal swords with his old opponent, Winston Churchill, one last time over whether India could ever live at peace. In a thundering speech on September 27 Churchill had delivered his verdict on partition. "The fearful massacres which are occurring in India are no surprise to me," he told an audience at the Royal Wanstead School. "I shall always remember with gratitude how my constituents here supported me...when for four years between 1931 and 1935, we fought against the India Constitution Bill." His predictions then of terrible carnage and chaos were being fulfilled.

"We are of course only at the beginning of these horrors and butcheries," he declared, "perpetrated upon one another, men, women, and children, with the ferocity of cannibals, by races gifted with the capacities for the highest culture and who had for generations dwelt side by side in general peace under the broad, tolerant, and impartial rule of the British Crown and Parliament." India's descent into chaos was, Churchill said, "one of the most melancholy tragedies Asia has ever known."[43]

Gandhi knew those horrors firsthand, but he could not let this judgment go unchallenged. He brought up Churchill and his speech at his daily prayer meeting the next day. The result was a final drawing of the battle lines between them, and a final tribute by Gandhi to his old antagonist.

"You are aware that Mr. Churchill is a great man," he told his listeners. "He belongs to the blue blood of England. [The] Marlborough family is very famous in British history. He says it is folly that Britain should have lost India," and warns the same will now happen in Burma.

Gandhi paused. "But how can I tell Mr. Churchill that we are all too familiar with British history, how they acquired Burma and how they consolidated their power in India. I do not think anyone can be proud of such a history."[44]

Gandhi was more than willing to concede the importance of Churchill's leadership in the recent war. "No doubt he saved the British Empire from a great danger," Gandhi said. "Who else except a man of Mr. Churchill's sharp political diplomacy could have brought all the [Allies] together" in order to defeat the Axis powers? But then at war's end the British people chose a Labour government. "It is the working class that is ruling Britain today," not Winston Churchill. And the British people decided "to end the Empire and establish instead an unseen and more glorious empire of hearts."[45]

Gandhi confessed that this selfless act of renunciation touched him deeply: "In modern history there is no instance that can be compared with the transfer of power by the British." Gandhi could compare it only to Ashoka's act of renunciation of empire in favor of his Buddhist faith. And Gandhi pointed out that Churchill and his party had consented to that transfer of power.

Now, however, "by his speech Mr. Churchill has harmed his country which he greatly served." If tragedy had struck once India became free, did Churchill not consider the possibility that the blame lay with the builders of that empire, not with those who were subjected to it?

"In my view, Mr. Churchill has been too hasty," Gandhi concluded, in calling the transfer of power a failure. He invited Churchill to put "honor before party" and work to make partition succeed, instead of rejoicing at its failure.[46]

To Gandhi's mind, Churchill was more interested in regaining power in Westminster than in saving lives in the Punjab—or in saving Britain's reputation. But Gandhi had to concede that his own former allies, including Nehru, were putting party before honor as well.

"If the people of Kashmir are in favor of opting for Pakistan," he said at a prayer meeting, "no power on earth can stop them from doing so. But they should be left free to decide for themselves." Meanwhile Pakistani troops in British Army trucks were crossing the border. Jinnah declared that India had seized Kashmir by "fraud and violence" and informed Mountbatten (who was secretly orchestrating the entire Indian operation) that Pakistan would never accept the coup. As the fighting escalated, a reporter asked Gandhi if he supported Nehru's deployment of troops to Kashmir. Gandhi replied softly and sadly: "If I could have my way of non-violence and everybody listened to me, we would not send our army as we are doing now...People say that the Sardar is my man and Panditji [i.e., Nehru] also is mine." In fact, Gandhi said with infinite sadness in his voice, "I am a nobody and no one listens to me."[47]

As the fighting dragged on and Mountbatten tried in vain to convince both Pakistan and India to submit the case to a plebiscite under United Nations supervision, Gandhi passed December and the New Year in a kind of internal exile in his residence in Delhi, lent by his businessman friend G. D. Birla. According to Pyarelal, "He was the saddest man one could picture."[48] His mood was indeed gloomy but not despondent. He told an audience on the evening of December 11, "My eyes have now been opened ... Today, everyone in the Congress is running after power. That presages grave danger."[49]

To prevent the collapse of all hopes for India's future Gandhi resolved on what would be his final fast. On January 12, 1948, he held a tense meeting with Nehru and Patel. They tried to explain why it was impossible to stop the continued lynching of Muslims in Delhi, and why they could not pay Pakistan its share of the cash reserve balances in the Reserve Bank of India—nearly 550 million rupees. It would bankrupt the country, they insisted. Pakistan and the Muslims were to blame for all the violence, anyway.

Gandhi said nothing. It was his day of silence. But he had told the loyal Manubehn that he was contemplating a major change in his life, a change connected with the ongoing violence and hopes for peace. On January 9 he said of the massacres in the Punjab, Calcutta, and elsewhere: "I am responsible for all this." Perhaps God had deliberately blinded him to the consequences of his actions, he said, but now at the end of his life he had awakened to his mistake. That afternoon, on January 12, he drew up a long statement on why he was embarking on another fast. If Hindus and Muslims could come together to pledge to live in peace instead of at war, he would break it. If they could not, he would not. "I ask you all to bless the effort and to pray for me and with me."[50]

That evening his son Devadas asked him if the fast was directed against Pakistan.

"No," Gandhi answered, "it is directed against everybody."[51]

The fast began at noon on January 13. Gandhi said on national radio, "I shall terminate the fast only when peace has returned to Delhi."[52] On the fourteenth the seventy-eight-year-old was still strong enough to walk to his evening prayer meeting, then to meet with Nehru and the cabinet at Birla House at nine o'clock. As the ministers left, Gandhi heard a commotion out in the street. He asked what it was. They were Sikhs from West Punjab, made homeless by their Muslim neighbors as the Pakistani portion of the province was ethnically cleansed.

"What are they shouting?" Gandhi asked.

"They are shouting, 'Death to Gandhi,' " he was told.

Gandhi sighed and began reciting the *Ramanama*.

The next day he became weak and complained of pains in his stomach and chills. His doctor noted that his kidneys were failing. Gandhi could barely sit up, but he still managed to speak into a radio microphone hooked up to his bed. He told listeners that the Indian government had finally agreed to transfer the 550 million rupees to Pakistan. Nonetheless he would not stop the fast until India and Pakistan were at peace.

The following evening a vast procession of Hindus and Muslims marched up Albuquerque Road in an emotional display of communal unity. They chanted: *"Bhai! Bhai!"* (Brother! Brother!) and *"Mahatma Gandhi ki jai"* although Manubehn could hear cries of *"Gandhi mordabad!"* on the crowd's fringes.[53] On the seventeenth 130 representatives of India's various communities met at the house of Rajendra Prasad to discuss a resolution calling for reconciliation. Some key members were missing; Prasad urged that they be rounded up in a hurry.

Even if they passed the resolution, it was not clear that Gandhi would know it. Doctors were reporting that he had become delirious.

The Mahatma was dying.

Early that same morning, on January 17, a taxicab pulled off the main road in Bombay and parked along a narrow side street. Three men jumped out and walked to the door of the office of Hindu Sangathan, an ultra-nationalist group. They rang the doorbell. The new national flag of India flew overhead.

A man answered. He was elderly and thin, the skin of his face stretched tight against the skull. He beckoned the three young men inside and, after checking down the street, shut the door.

The man was Vinayak Savarkar. He was former president of the Hindu Mahasabha, now retired. He was revered in orthodox Hindu circles, even more than Gandhi. He and Gandhi knew each other well. They had met at the famous Dussehra dinner in London in 1909, when Gandhi had spoken of the patience and compassion of Krishna while the twenty-six-year-old Savarkar spoke of the awesome power of Durga, the Mother Goddess.* The two had met only once after that, but Savarkar had nursed a burning hatred of the Mahatma ever since.

---

* See Chapter 9.

Since independence he had carefully disguised his feelings. He had praised Nehru as prime minister; he officially adopted the new flag of India. But inwardly he had seethed at the fact of partition. Now he was planning to strike back.

Savarkar warmly greeted the young men. Like Savarkar, Nathuram Godse and Narayan Apte were Chitpavan Brahmins, serious high-caste Hindus and members of Mahasabha. The third young man, Digambar Badge, was told to wait downstairs as the other three went upstairs.

Godse, at thirty-eight, had been a fervent Savarkar disciple since meeting him in 1929. At one time he had been Savarkar's secretary. Godse was puritanical, an intellectual who shunned all contact with women. By contrast, Apte was a ladies' man who drank whiskey and wore fashionable British clothes. Together they edited the Hindu nationalist newspaper *Agrani,* which preached that everyone except Hindus should leave India.[54] Godse and Apte both believed partition was a national calamity, and the man they blamed for it was Gandhi. In an issue published earlier that year, Godse blatantly called for Gandhi's assassination. Now he and Apte were meeting the man who would help make that appeal a reality.

Since his meeting with Gandhi decades earlier Savarkar had continued his course as the leading exponent of terror and violence in the nationalist cause. The night they met in 1909 he had been a hunted man, moving from house to house to evade the London police. After his arrest he had been sentenced to imprisonment for life in the Andaman Islands for his role in the Curzon-Wyllie murder. He had still been there when Gandhi launched his Noncooperation campaign and George Lloyd locked the Mahatma up in the Yeravda jail.

Then in 1924 the new Labour-led government had come in, hoping to make bygones be bygones. It released Savarkar as well as Gandhi. Five years later, when Godse met him, Savarkar still had his prison pallor and was deeply bitter. If anything, his hatred of Gandhi had intensified. He had been outraged by Gandhi's appeal for Muslim help and by his refusal to accept Hindu exclusivism as the basis of nationhood. To Savarkar's mind, nonviolence was the philosophy of cowardice and an invitation to tyranny. "Because every evil doer has his avenger," he once averred, "there is still some hope in the heart of the world that injustice cannot last."[55] Now in the wake of partition, he was determined that Durga would have her final say.

Many Hindus agreed with him. The elite Mahasabha boasted one million members, and its sympathizers numbered many more. The organization was a powerhouse in Congress politics, while the paramilitary RSS had been a major player in the recent violence. To many high-caste Hindus, Gandhi's evangelical version of their religion seemed vulgar and weak-willed.[56] They believed Indian independence should mean a reassertion of Hindu power, after centuries of British but also Mughal imperial domination. Gandhi's appeal for Hindu-Muslim unity and for an end to untouchability seemed baffling, almost blasphemous.

This militant, even militaristic streak in Hindu culture was embedded in India's great epics and its bloodstained history. An educated elite among Chitpavans and Bengalis had nurtured it and kept it alive. It had inspired B. G. Tilak at the beginning of the century and S.C. Bose in the middle. In 1947 it was embodied in the gun-toting bravos of the RSS and Savarkar's own Hindu Rastra Dal, a secret society of Chitpavan Brahmins who were committed to achieving independence through terror. Their leader Savarkar and members like Godse called Gandhi "the father of Pakistan"—an unforgivable sin. Jinnah and the Muslims may have feared and distrusted Gandhi, but Savarkar and his followers truly despised him.

Many threats had been made against Gandhi's life before. In 1934 a bomb was thrown at him. RSS militiamen chanted "Death to Gandhi" on a regular basis; many bystanders found it alarming, but few took it seriously. After all, when Gandhi arrived in Delhi, the crowds that at first had screamed *"Gandhi mordabad!"* then fell weeping at his feet. Godse and Apte realized that if Gandhi was to be punished for his betrayal of his faith, they would have to do it themselves. They discussed their plans in detail with Savarkar. The old man's last words to Dhingra in 1909, as he had handed him his revolver, had been: "Don't show me your face if you fail this time." To Apte and Godse, he said only, "Be successful and come back."

The pair headed downstairs. Later in the taxi they told Badge, "Gandhi's hundred years are over." Badge owned a store that sold guns, as well as steel tiger's claws and knives—everything they would need. If Gandhi survived his fast, they would strike.[57]

Gandhi did survive. On the eighteenth, after the heads of the various faiths and communities signed a statement pledging to "once again live in Delhi like brothers in perfect amity," Gandhi consented to break the fast in his usual way, with a glass of orange juice. The girls sang his favorite hymn, "When I Survey the Wondrous Cross." Gandhi's weight had fallen to just under 107 pounds. The next day he was so frail he could not get out of bed, but he still spoke over the radio about his last remaining hope for India: reconciliation.

"I cannot forecast the future," he said, "but God has endowed me with intellect and a sincere heart...If for one reason or another, we fail to maintain friendly relations with one another, with not only the Moslems of India but the Moslems of Pakistan and the whole world, we should know—and I have no doubt—that India will cease to be ours... We shall become slaves, Pakistan will go into slavery, the Union [of India] will go into slavery, and we shall lose our hard-won freedom."[58]

Gandhi's dream of satyagraha and nonviolence was over. "Today I am the only one left who has faith in ahimsa," he remarked. "I mistook the non-violence of the weak—which I now see is a misnomer and contradiction in terms—for true non-violence."[59] Moreover the clash over Kashmir and the massacres still taking place across India seemed to mark the doom of his other great dream: of Indian Swaraj, self-rule in the moral sense. Would Indians be governed by their love of truth, or would they be slaves to their passion for power and revenge? Gandhi wanted the former; but he made it clear he had no desire to remain alive, if it turned out to be the latter. "If India has no more use for non-violence," he told Pyarelal, "can she have any for me?"

The morning of the twentieth dawned bright and clear. Although Gandhi was still weak, he insisted on attending his daily prayer meeting in the Birla House garden, with his grandniece Manubehn as always by his side. About three hundred people gathered to hear him, while All-India Radio set up microphones to broadcast his message. As Gandhi began speaking in a low croaking voice, there was a sudden explosion.

People turned startled toward the back of the garden. A small section of the wall had been blown out by a slab of guncotton. Police were wrestling a young man to the ground while four others, unnoticed by the crowd, fled. Manubehn had been terrified by the blast, but Gandhi was unshaken. "Why are you frightened?" he asked her as she threw herself at his feet. "What would you do if they really tried to shoot at you and me?" He resumed the prayer meeting as if nothing had happened.[60]

The police, however, knew better. After questioning the arrested man, a Punjabi, they realized that there was a conspiracy afoot to kill Gandhi. As they began issuing bulletins, the other would-be killers, including Godse and Apte, scattered. News of the attack reached a teacher of some of the plotters, Dr. Jain, who frantically alerted police. However, the bureaucratic wheels turned as slowly in the Union of India as they had under the Raj, especially when the police included in their ranks members of RSS.[61] No other arrests were made. After the attack on the twentieth, Patel ordered more guards to be put around Gandhi, but otherwise he remained unconcerned. Still, evidence was mounting that at least fifty people knew of the plot and that the main perpetrators, Apte and Godse, were still on the loose.

As for Gandhi, "it is Rama who protects me," he said. "I become more and more convinced everything else is futile." He refused to have any bodyguards. He sensed that the day he had been preparing for all his life was coming. Two days later he went for a walk with Manubehn and told her, "The explosion was brought about by Him," meaning God. "I wish I might face the assassin's bullets while lying in your lap and repeating the name of Rama with a smile on my face."

He turned to her tenderly. "But whether the world says it or not—for the world has a double face—I tell you that you should regard me as your true mother. I am a true Mahatma."[62] It was the one time Gandhi acknowledged his formal title and revealed how he preferred to die.

Eight days later he got his wish.

Under the heat of the police search, the number of conspirators still at large had shriveled down to three. Apte and Godse had fled to Bombay in hopes of getting a revolver—which, with the help of an elderly member of the Mahasabha, they managed to do. Then they managed to catch a plane back to Delhi, under assumed names, and met the third remaining member, Vishnu Karkare. At noon on January 29 the trio gathered at the Birla Temple to pray and plot under the plaque that read, "He who is known as Vishnu the Preserver is verily Rudra the Destroyer, and He who is Rudra is Brahma the Creator."[63]

Gandhi began the next day as he always did, rising at 3:30 a.m. He woke up Manubehn in his usual way, by tweaking her ear. That morning he was querulous and fussy. During his fast he had developed a deep disturbing cough, which grew worse in the evenings. Manubehn offered to prepare him some clove lozenges. "Who knows what is going to happen before nightfall or whether I shall be alive? If at night I am still alive, you can easily prepare them."[64]

Gandhi was unhappy too because he had to face the usual stream of visitors, thirty on this day alone. One wanted to discuss opening of a nursing home and orphanage; one to discuss publishing the late Mahadev Desai's diary; another had come all the way from Ceylon to get an autograph (the last Gandhi ever wrote). A male French photographer came, and an American female one, Margaret Bourke-White. She had met and photographed Gandhi before. This time she asked him how he would deal with an atomic bomb attack.

"Ah," he said with a smile. "How shall I answer." He gave two or three turns of his charkha and then said enigmatically, "I would meet it with *prayerful action*."

This prompted a discussion of the postwar world. With considerable prescience, Gandhi said, "It is a question now whether the victors are really victorious or victims." Then in a slow, low voice he went on: "Because the world is not at peace. It is still more dreadful."[65]

At four o'clock his most important visitor arrived: Patel, now deputy prime minister, who wanted to discuss his growing rivalry with Nehru and his fear that it would split the government. Gandhi listened politely to his oldest and closest disciple but with disappointment in his heart. This was what he had feared most about politics: that it inevitably boiled down to power and the clash of personalities. "Everyone who goes into politics gets contaminated," he had declared in December. "Let us keep out of it altogether."[66] Now it was too late. As they talked, Gandhi worked at his charkha and then ate soup, goat's milk, and three oranges until Patel's daughter told him he was late for the prayer meeting.

Patel left, and Gandhi strolled into the garden. The grandnieces Manubehn and Abhabehn, his "walking sticks," stood on either side. Manubehn carried his notebook, spectacle case, and bead bracelet for saying his prayers. It was a crisp and clear evening. The crowd parted to let him pass, and Gandhi bowed with his hands folded in *namaskar* fashion and smiled.

Suddenly a man in a bright green pullover darted forward, nearly knocking Manubehn to the ground. She thought he was going to touch Gandhi's feet, as many people did in the moment of *darshan,* and started to scold him. Instead, he pulled out a revolver and fired three quick shots. Nathuram Godse would have fired more if Indian Air Force Sergeant Devraj Singh hadn't been standing nearby and snatched the gun from him.

One of Godse's bullets went into Gandhi's stomach, the two others into his chest. As Gandhi fell, his hands still folded, he was already dying. Manubehn fell sobbing and gathered him in her lap. *"Hai Rama! Hai Rama!"* They were Gandhi's last words. He died as he had wished, with his two young girls at his side.

The news electrified India. Nirad Chaudhuri was sitting at his typewriter when his eldest son burst in and cried: "They have killed Gandhi!" Chaudhuri did not have to ask who "they" were. He had many acquaintances who considered Gandhi a disaster for the nationalist cause, including the now-dead Subhas Bose and his brother Sarat. Chaudhuri knew also that "although the people of India venerated Gandhi for his moral role, they followed him only in so far as he stood for their hatred of British rule." Even his closest Congress followers had heeded "his direction and advice only when that suited them, and totally disregarded them otherwise."[67]

Those followers had joined elections for India's legislature in 1924, when Gandhi had told them not to. They had forced him to give way on holding office under the new constitution in 1937. Finally they had ignored his plea to support the war effort in 1939. Even on partition, he had fought against it, then been forced to surrender. His great campaigns to foist the British out nonviolently, from the Noncooperation campaign of 1920–21 to Quit India in 1942, had been failures. It was the trial of Bose's INA officers, not the Salt March, that broke the back of British rule. It was fear of more violence, not respect for nonviolence, that finally made them leave.

Even so, Chaudhuri had to recognize, "In India the masses make a god of a great man collectively and unconsciously, and succeed in giving to his memory a permanence... There will be no time in the future history of the Hindus in which Mahatma Gandhi will not be remembered in this way. He *has* taken his place in our Pantheon."[68]

The man who had been the intermediary between Gandhi and Churchill in the 1930s, G. D. Birla, was in Pilani and heard the news from college students who were listening to the BBC. Gandhi had been staying at Birla's home for nearly four months. "I immediately felt like dashing to Delhi by car," he recalled, but friends persuaded him to stay until morning. That night he had a dream in which Gandhiji appeared to him and said, "Don't worry about me... I am going to dance with joy as my mission is now over." The next day Birla returned to his home and gazed on the dead face of the man who had been his mentor for thirty-two years: "Alas, we would now be missing that face aglow with human warmth and kindliness."[69]

Dr. Ambedkar was less charitable. When he heard the news, he was silent and then said, "My real enemy is gone; thank goodness the eclipse is over now." If any man can be said to have truly hated Gandhi, it was the untouchable leader. Gandhi's ideas he dismissed as a spurious brew of Tolstoy, Ruskin, and Rousseau: "There is always some simpleton to preach them." Remembering their battle over the Communal Award in 1932, he considered Gandhi's reputation as a saint to be a lie. "I've a feeling I know him better than most people," he confided to a BBC television interviewer years later, "because he opened his fangs to me, you see, and I could see inside the man."[70]

Gandhi's other great opponent, Jinnah, only said, "He was one of the greatest men produced by the Hindu community," and little else. Jinnah himself was dying of cancer; he would pass away on September 11, 1948, reduced to a skeleton weighing less than seventy pounds.*

Jawaharlal Nehru was supposed to see Gandhi that evening after the prayer meeting. Although Nehru and Gandhi had been at odds many times and foresaw India moving on different paths, he felt the assassination as a fierce personal blow. Mountbatten was shocked to see Nehru's swollen, tear-stained face when he arrived at Birla House. "Friends and comrades, the light has gone out of our lives," Nehru said in a radio broadcast that evening, "and there is darkness everywhere." Mountbatten wanted the body embalmed to preserve as a permanent memorial but finally relented to Gandhi's wish to be cremated according to Hindu custom.

Manubehn and the other disciples gave Gandhi's body its ritual purification bath, much as his mother had washed him when he was born. Some sang verses from the *Bhagavad Gita*. Others quietly wept.† The body was laid out for public viewing, a last *darshan,* with a garland of homespun cotton strands and a string of beads. Devadas insisted that his father's chest be laid bare. "No soldier had a finer chest than Bapu's," he said proudly.[71]

---

* His country would lose its debate at the United Nations over Kashmir; Pakistan and India would fight two more wars over the disputed province. A war of terror there is still going on today. The Islamic nation that Quaid-e-Azam had fought Gandhi so hard to found would go through decades of turmoil and instability, even dismemberment. In 1971, with India's connivance, its eastern province would break away and form an independent state, Bangladesh.

† Ironically, Gandhi's murderers would also quote from the *Gita* at their trial, which began in Delhi's Red

The funeral was delayed until noon so that Ramdas could fly in from Nagpur. The cortege extended over two miles, inching along from Birla House to the banks of the Jamnu River. The crowd numbered more than a million and a half people: "It was not so much a great sea of people as an immense glutinous mass clogging the arteries of the city, shapeless and diffuse."[72] A million more watched from roofs and housetops.

The cortege included the exalted—Nehru, Patel, Minister of Education Maulana Abul Kalam Azad—and the humble. It included Hindus, Muslims, Sikhs, Parsis, whites, and untouchables all walking together. The news of Gandhi's death had stopped the violence around India like the throwing of a switch. What Gandhi had failed to achieve in life—the peace and unity of India—he managed to achieve in death: "Gandhi martyred proved even more powerful a bond for Indians than he had been alive."[73]

Ironically, the vehicle that bore the great pacifist's bier was an Indian Army truck, pulled by hand through the streets by two hundred men from the army, navy, and air force. Three air force C-47 Dakota cargo planes dumped hundreds of thousands of rose petals on the cortege as it reached the river. A small funeral pyre had been built along the bank, a brick platform two feet high and twelve feet square. Ramdas lit the pyre, which burned for fourteen hours. The crowd chanted *"Mahatma Gandhi ki jai!"* as the Mahatma's body was reduced to smoke and ash.

That night the smoldering remains had a final visitor. Gandhi's eldest son Harilal, stricken by tuberculosis, returned to pay tribute to the father he never knew. Harilal spent that night at Devadas's house.

He would die in a Bombay hospital less than five months later.[74]

Fort on May 27, 1948. "My respect for the Mahatma was deep and deathless," Godse said in his final statement. "It therefore gave me no pleasure to kill him. Indeed my feelings were like those of Arjuna when he killed Dronacharya, his Guru at whose feet he had learned the art of war." But Godse could not forgive Gandhi for his pro-Muslim bias. Speaking in English, Godse said: "I felt convinced that such a man was the greatest enemy, not only of the Hindus, but of the whole nation." The trial lasted more than a year, with more than 149 prosecution witnesses. Godse and Apte were found guilty and sentenced to death; they were hanged side by side on November 15, 1949, nearly two years after Gandhi's assassination. Vinayak Savarkar, the man most responsible for what had happened, was acquitted on all charges. He lived as a free man until his death in 1966.

Chapter Thirty-one

LION IN TWILIGHT
1948–1965

We have thrown away our glorious Empire,
our wonderful Indian Empire.

WINSTON CHURCHILL, APRIL 1954

TRIBUTES TO GANDHI POURED IN from every country. The pope, the Dalai Lama, President Harry Truman, Chiang Kai-shek, Prime Minister Clement Attlee, and King George VI all spoke of his virtues and his legacy. Albert Einstein said that "in our time of utter moral decadence he was the only statesman to stand for a higher human relationship in the political sphere." Even Douglas MacArthur felt it necessary to praise Gandhi's greatness, as did American Supreme Court justice Felix Frankfurter. Novelist Pearl Buck called his assassination "another crucifixion." Sir Stafford Cripps, more than anyone in the British cabinet, had shared Gandhi's New Age outlook, despite constant disappointments at the hands of the Indians. "I know of no other man of any time or indeed of recent history," Cripps wrote, "who so forcefully and convincingly demonstrated the power of spirit over material things."[1]

There was one public man, however, who did not publish a tribute. Neither then nor later did Winston Churchill ever express any regret at the passing of his longtime rival for India and empire. For Churchill, Gandhi's death was just one more killing in the slaughter that had been going on since 1946. "An awful tragedy has already occurred," he told the House of Commons. "At least 400,000 men and women have slaughtered each other in the Punjab alone." This was more, he pointed out, than all the losses of the British Empire in World War II.

"Many millions more are fugitives, wanderers, or exiles from their place of birth…We can only be thankful that no such catastrophe or anything which approached one twentieth part of its magnitude, fell upon the helpless Indian people during the long years they dwelt in peace and safety under the British Raj and Imperial Crown."*[2]

Churchill was in no mood to pay tribute to the man he still believed had triggered this enormous tragedy. Nor did he feel he had the time. Since assuming the role of leader of the opposition in Parliament, he found himself on the front line of yet another war, the Cold War.

"I am often asked, 'Will there be war,'" he had told the House of Commons just the week before Gandhi's death. "This is a question I have often asked myself."[3] Less than a month later Communists seized power in Czechoslovakia. In June the Soviets blockaded Berlin. These were events Churchill had predicted in his heralded speech on the "Iron Curtain" on March 5, 1946, in Fulton, Missouri. To Churchill's mind, here was another war for civilization. Here was another summons to frustrate "the designs of wicked men." That autumn of 1948 he sounded the first great call for European unity to repel the growing Soviet tide— a speech that in turn inspired the American Marshall Plan for European reconstruction.[4]

This bout of furious activity shook him out of the mental depression that had swept over him after his defeat in July 1945. Churchill's shock and chagrin at being rejected by the British people had been more profound than even his friends had realized. It had triggered one of his famous "black dog" moods, which his doctor Lord Moran diagnosed as melancholia.

These moods, so suggestive of a bipolar personality, came on without warning and could last for months. One had hit when Winston had been home secretary under Asquith, when very suddenly, as Churchill himself described it, "the light faded out of the picture." He said it had led to days when he preferred not to stand too close to the rails of a train or the side of a ship as it passed through the water, moments when "a second's action would end everything."[5]

A similar depression had struck in 1943, when it became clear he was losing Roosevelt's trust and confidence and when his victory over Gandhi was proving to be only temporary. A third came in the aftermath of the 1945 election. One morning that August his doctor came to see him in an upper-story room at a London hotel. Churchill had airily

---

* An angry Labour MP rose to point out, correctly, that millions had died during the 1943 famine under Churchill's watch. Churchill replied, also correctly, that under British rule India's population rose by 100 million and that there was a difference between failing to prevent food shortages and deliberate murder.

waved a hand to indicate the balcony outside his window. "I don't like sleeping near a precipice like that," he declared. "I've no desire to quit the world, but thoughts, desperate thoughts come into the head."[6]

Years later Churchill admitted that there had been one and only one bright spot in his defeat: he did not have to sit as prime minister in 1947 while India got its independence. For the man who had declared just five years before that "we mean to hold our own...and remain effective rulers in India for a long and indefinite period," that would have been the supreme humiliation.[7]

At the time, however, Churchill resigned himself to the transfer of power. On May 21, 1947, he wrote his fateful letter to Prime Minister Attlee, pledging Conservative Party support for "Dominion Status for the several parts of a divided India."[8] But the reality of partition annoyed him almost as much as it did Gandhi. Unifying India had been the one great achievement of the Raj, he always believed; the dissolution of the first seemed to underline the futility of the second. But Churchill chose not to fight the Attlee government over the empire's crown jewel. Mountbatten had pledged to him that both India and Pakistan would become part of the commonwealth and would keep their ties to the British Crown as Dominions, a pledge that turned out to be false.

The one concession to pride that Churchill had asked for was that the final bill for Parliament be called "the India Bill" or "the India Self-Government Bill"—anything but "the India Independence Bill." But Attlee had remained adamant.[9] A few months later Churchill realized that Mountbatten had betrayed him: both India and Pakistan threw off Dominion status as soon as they could; Pakistan even refused to join the commonwealth. Winston was also angry that Mountbatten had sent British-trained troops and RAF planes to support Nehru over Kashmir. "He accused me of having planned and organized the first victory of Hindustan (he refused to call it India) against Pakistan," Mountbatten later confessed, and Churchill demanded that Mountbatten "not involve the King and my country in further backing traitors."[10]

Above all, Churchill was angry that Mountbatten had tried to hide the reality of the massacres from him and the government. Through General Ismay, however, Churchill learned the truth.[11] As a result, his description of the death toll in House of Commons speeches in 1947 and 1948 was far more accurate than the sanitized version Mountbatten offered to the British public. Churchill chose to apply the word "holocaust" to what was happening in India, with good reason. Although he never publicly blamed his former protégé for what had happened, he gave vent to his feelings at a dinner party where his and the former viceroy and governor-general's path crossed in 1951. Churchill said Mountbatten's policy in India had needlessly cost more than a million lives. What Mountbatten had done, Churchill raged, had been a "lash across the face." It would be years before they spoke again.[12]

Churchill did speak out again on India in June 1948, five months after Gandhi's death, when King George VI had to formally renounce his title as King-Emperor. "This melancholy event," Winston said, "is only typical of what is happening to our Empire and Commonwealth in so many parts of the world." That October, when the new Indian government was about to seize the last independent state, Hyderabad, by force, he repeated his warning of two years earlier that the end of British rule would mean only misery and bloodshed: "Alas I was not wrong...Blood, murder and disintegration ride triumphant over that unhappy land."[13]

However, he added with an air of finality, "Our Imperial mission in India is at an end—we must recognize that. Some day justice will be done by world opinion to our record there, but the chapter is closed and

> *The Moving Finger writes; and, having writ,*
> *Moves on; nor all your Piety nor Wit*
> *Shall lure it back to cancel half a Line,*
> *Nor all your tears blot out a word of it."*[14]

By then Churchill could also sense another sign, besides "these horrors and butcheries" in India, of the "retrogression of civilization." Just three years after the war in which he had struggled so hard to save Britain and its empire, Britain's position in the world was slowly but steadily sinking away.

Just as Gandhi, from the confines of Birla House, saw his life's work come unraveled before his eyes, so Churchill saw much the same thing happening from his stronghold at Chartwell. His five-and-a-half-year-old grandson remembered visiting him there in the mornings: "I would find him there tucked up in bed with a mountain of pillows behind him and a bedtable, cut out to accommodate the shape of his belly, piled high with papers in front of him." A soggy cigar would already be in his mouth, and a secretary would be taking notes on a speech or letter. In those years Churchill had had a cinema built in the house, with two huge 35mm projectors, where he and visitors could watch favorites such as *Oliver Twist, Lady Hamilton,* and *Gone With the Wind,* while taking fifteen-minute breaks to refill their brandy glasses and "pump ship," as Winston put it.[15]

But underneath the visits and the fun lay a growing sense of darkness. More and more shadows were falling over the postwar world. Gandhi's last words had been a warning: "It is a question whether the victors are really victors or victims."[16] He might have been speaking directly about Great Britain. Once the most affluent nation in Europe, war had reduced it to an economic basket case, living on bread and potato rationing and loans from the Americans. Its people seemed to be sliding into apathy, and resentment at the cost of Britain's global responsibilities, including its navy and empire.[17]

Churchill had saved England from the Nazis, but he could not save it from itself. And out of the gathering shadows came familiar voices full of reproach and scorn, reminding him of how much he had fallen short.

One afternoon in late November 1947 Churchill was painting in his studio. On an easel was a portrait of his father done in 1886 for the Belfast Conservative Club; it had recently passed into his hands. Winston was working on making a copy, when he suddenly felt a strange sensation.* "I turned around with my palette in my hand," Churchill says, "and there, sitting in my red leather upright chair, was my father."

Looking fit and in his prime, with the familiar exquisite mustache and tall silk hat, the former chancellor of the exchequer and secretary of state for India asked his son what he was doing. He was astonished to learn what year it was. "So more than fifty years have passed," Randolph mused. "A lot must have happened."

"Oh yes indeed," his son answered. He proceeded to give his father's ghost a vivid account of the half-century since his death. He began with the Boer War and General Roberts. ("I appointed him Commander-in-Chief in India when I was Secretary of State," the ghost exclaimed, adding proudly, "That was the year I annexed Burma.") Then Winston summarized the rest: two terrifying world wars, the rise of democracy and the decline of civility, socialist governments and women voters, bombed cities and death camps that were "human slaughter pens like the Chicago stockyards," an American partnership and a renewed

---

* What follows is related by Churchill himself, in a document not released until after his death.

Russian menace. He threw in the latest news of horse racing and the monarchy, along with the creation of a free Ireland.

"And India, is that all right? And Burma?" the ghost asked.

"Alas," Winston had to answer, "they have gone down the drain."

Randolph groaned. "To relieve his consternation," Winston recounted, "I said, 'But perhaps they will come back and join the English speaking world.' "

Otherwise, he had to admit, "Far gone are the days of Queen Victoria, and a settled world order. But, having gone through so much, we do not despair." In the end the will of the people still prevailed, as Churchill believed it should. "You brought me up to that," he told his father.

This, however, brought on an outburst. "I never brought you up to anything!" the ghost exploded. "I was not going to talk politics with a boy like you ever. Bottom of the school! Never passed any examinations, except for the Cavalry! Wrote stilted letters... You were very fond of playing soldiers, so I settled for the Army. I hope you had a successful military career."

"I was a major in the Yeomanry," Churchill answered proudly. His father was less than impressed.

The ghost had to leave but had some final words.

"Winston, you have told me a terrible tale. I would never have believed that such things could happen. I am glad I did not live to see them." Then he added, "Of course you are too old now to think about such things, but when I hear you talk I really wonder you didn't go into politics. You might have done a lot to help. You might even have made a name for yourself." Then the ghost struck a match for his cigar and vanished.

"The chair was empty," Churchill remembered. "The illusion had passed." Only the disapproval of a long-dead father, and the sense of inward failure in the midst of outward triumph, remained.[18]

For six long years Churchill labored in the vineyards of parliamentary opposition. Then suddenly in October 1951 the voters returned him and the Conservatives to office. He had become bitterly critical of the direction Labour was leading the country: nationalizing Britain's steel and coal and transport industries, creating a National Health Service, raising union wages and expanding the welfare state. "Socialism is the philosophy of failure, the creed of ignorance, and the gospel of envy," he told an

audience in 1948. "Unless we can free our country while time remains...
our place in the world will be lost forever."[19]

Millions felt otherwise. After the hardships and suffering of total war,
Britain's decline, like the loss of India, meant little to them. They saw
Churchill and the Tories as shades of a discredited past, men determined
to turn back the clock and snatch away what little they still had—which,
after six years of Labour's command economy, continued rationing, and
high unemployment, was little enough.

On election eve Churchill's grandson Winston went with him to
Devonport to campaign for Randolph, who was standing as a
Conservative candidate. They appeared that night at Plymouth Hoe,
where Francis Drake had once stood to await the coming of the Spanish
Armada, and where now "a seething mass of people" came to cheer their
candidate, the future Labour leader Michael Foot, and boo the Tory
leader and his son.

Years later young Winston would remember how "the mob was filled
with such rage and hatred" of the Churchills that they were "howling
like a pack of hyenas baying for blood." Ten policemen had to escort the
Churchills past the crowd, who spat and kicked their shins and even
pulled Randolph's wife's hair.[20] Needless to say, Randolph lost the seat.

Although Randolph lost, the Conservatives managed to win. And
Winston Churchill was suddenly back at Number 10. With old stalwarts like Anthony Eden, Harold Macmillan, and "Pug" Ismay in his
cabinet, Churchill believed he was poised to renew "the glories of our island home." Ironically, however, the next decade of Tory rule would
only speed up Britain's decline, with Churchill reluctantly but helplessly
leading the way.

The explanation was bitter but simple. The debacle of 1945 had broken the Tories' nerve and to a degree Churchill's. Nothing must be done
to rile a fickle and disgruntled British public, they decided, least of all
Britain's trade unions. Men who had made their names fighting appeasement abroad in the 1930s became enthusiastic appeasers at home in
the 1950s.

Churchill's agenda as prime minister was depressingly limited:
"housing, red meat,* and not getting scuppered."[21] Public spending continued to grow faster than the British economy, especially on subsidized
housing. Apart from reversing Labour's nationalization of the iron and

---

* Which was still being rationed as late as 1956.

steel industries, the new Tory government did nothing to loosen the commanding grip of the State on the national economy—or even to scrutinize the public corporations set up to do the commanding. The so-called Tory "Middle Way" was born, which meant trying to maintain a compromise between embracing American-style capitalism and surrendering to outright socialism. The "Middle Way" would dominate British conservative thinking for the next decade and beyond, until the advent of Margaret Thatcher.

This approach suited Churchill. Although an economic liberal, he was no libertarian either. As president of the Board of Trade in 1909 he had been, after all, the original father of the welfare state. He had no more admiration for (or understanding of) "unfettered capitalism" than Attlee and the Labourites did. But in the 1950s it was the Trades Union Congress, with its eleven million members, that most worried him. Minister of Labor Walter Monckton "had direct orders from Churchill to appease the unions," his private secretary Sir David Hunt recalled.[22] This meant conceding wage hikes regardless of productivity. It meant permitting closed union shops; collective bargaining so that strikes against one company could force a settlement on others; and union members vetoing any major technological change that might mean loss of jobs. All these would become the ugly hallmarks of British industrial policy, and nearly all began during Churchill's premiership. They would also doom Britain to a steady slide into economic obsolescence and social discontent.

The disintegration of Churchill's national policy was matched by the disintegration of his family life. Both his son Randolph and his daughter Sarah had become hopeless alcoholics, victims of what Clementine secretly considered "the drink gene" from her side of the family (although their father's prodigious example certainly did not help). Randolph became prematurely aged, gray and haggard, bitter about his own political failure and two failed marriages, facing the fact that he would never inherit Chartwell.*

Sarah had looks, brains, and the ambition to build a career for herself on the stage. But she "was petrified before [her father's] greatness," remembered a friend, the actress Judy Campbell. "That was why she longed to be a star, and when she failed, everything collapsed around

---

* Knowing that Winston was having troubles maintaining his house, a group of wealthy businessmen bought it for him after the war as a donation to the National Trust. After Churchill's death the heir to the house would be the Trust, not Randolph.

her."[23] Meanwhile Churchill's manic-depressive "black dog" moods became the permanent possession of his other daughter, Diana, who suffered a nervous breakdown in 1953 and would spend the rest of her life in and out of mental clinics, undergoing electroshock therapy. In 1963 she would take her own life with an overdose of sleeping pills.

The only bright spots in Winston's life were his continuing love for Clemmie—"It would have been impossible for any ordinary man to go through what I have had to get through in peace and war without her devoted aid," he liked to say in later years—and his grandson Winston Spencer Churchill. Young Winston spent part of most summer and winter vacations at Chartwell, helping his grandfather lay the brick walls he was still building around the house, visiting the Landrace pigs Churchill kept as part of the farm ("A dog looks up to a man," Churchill would tell him, "a cat looks down on man, but a pig will look you in the eye and see his equal!"), and joining him in the swimming pool.

"Well do I remember," the grandson would write later, "the tremendous splash when Grandpapa, already seventy-six years of age, plunged into the swimming pool from the diving board," or seeing him in the summer evenings, "beneath the great cedar that stands on the lawn below the house, wrapped in a rug on a *chaise-longue* bathed in the evening sun, gazing out over the distant view or dozing peacefully with an extinct and soggy cigar still firmly in his mouth."[24]

None of this outward vitality could quite disguise the fact that Churchill's health was failing. More than a year after the end of the war, Churchill told his doctor he could still work all day without tiring.[25] But then one morning in February 1947 Churchill called to complain of feeling "wheezy." That December Moran visited him in Marrakesh, and "I could see then he was sliding, almost imperceptibly into old age." The years of exuberant eating and drinking, and arteries hardening, were finally taking their toll.

The first stroke hit on August 23, 1949—characteristically, as he was playing cards at two o'clock in the morning at Monte Carlo. Afterward he told his doctor, "There seems to be a veil between me and things," and he described a cramping sensation across his shoulder blades. Otherwise he remained in good spirits, his memory unimpaired.

Moran told him it had been a stroke. "Will I have another?" Churchill asked anxiously. "There may be an election...I may have to take over again." Then he grinned. "It feels like being balanced between the Treasury bench and death. But I don't worry. Fate must take its course."[26]

He seemed to recover, and fate carried him to the Treasury bench one more time. Returning to power, and the accession of a young new monarch, Queen Elizabeth II in 1952, served to revive his spirits. "I, whose youth was passed in the August, unchallenged, and tranquil glories of the Victorian Age," he declared, "may well feel a thrill in invoking, once more, the prayer and Anthem, 'God save the queen!' "[27]

Then on June 24, 1953, Churchill was speaking at a dinner for Italian prime minister Alcide de Gasperi. As the guests left, Churchill suddenly stopped and slumped into a chair. The wife of art historian Kenneth Clark, who was sitting beside him, held his hand as he mumbled, "I want a friend. They put too much on me. Foreign affairs..." until his voice trailed off.[28] Clementine learned what had happened and said he must immediately go to bed. Jock Colville sent the waiters away so that Churchill could be helped out of the room. "I think they thought he had had too much to drink," Colville remembered later.

In fact, it had been a massive stroke, far worse than the earlier one. For months Churchill made a slow recovery, while the cabinet, terrified that his incapacity might mean the loss of their offices and power, did their best to keep the truth hidden from the public. A small team of intimates, including Jock Colville and Churchill's son-in-law Christopher Soames, read state papers and made decisions for him, even though only Soames was an actual member of the government. Meanwhile news of Churchill's stroke was hushed up or downplayed. For almost two months "neither Queen nor Parliament nor people was allowed to know that Britain was without an effective, legally constituted leader."[29]

To his doctor Lord Moran Winston spoke of death. "He did not believe in another world; only in black velvet—eternal sleep." He also admitted that "talking tires me." But by August he had recovered enough to continue working on his history of the Second World War and to meet with the cabinet. In September he was ready to fly down again to Monte Carlo. But the stroke had shaken his confidence and slowed his faculties. When he made a trip in November 1953 to Bermuda to meet with President Eisenhower, his energy noticeably flagged. "Sometimes at meals," Colville told the doctor, "Winston is very apathetic. Then Clemmie gives him a rebuke, he'll pull himself together and be quite normal."[30]

On November 30, 1954, Churchill and the nation celebrated his eightieth birthday. His doctor was able to draw up a grim count of the illnesses that this remarkable man had suffered and endured since he had known him. Two strokes, one of them massive; a heart attack in 1941 after the sinking of the *Prince of Wales* and *Repulse;* three bouts of pneumonia, including the one during Gandhi's hunger strike in 1943.[31] All but twenty-six members of Parliament from all parties signed a birthday greeting, and Clement Attlee gave a graceful speech in the House recalling Churchill's fifty-year career.

Attlee felt free to call Churchill's Dardanelles conception "the only imaginative strategic idea of the war" and described how in 1940 he had been "the daring pilot in extremity...whom Britain had required." Attlee described how time and again people had said, "Churchill is finished," only to have him return to prominence, return to power, and wind up "the most distinguished member of the Parliamentary family."

Churchill rose to thank Attlee and the members. "This is to me the most memorable public occasion of my life," he told them. He thanked them also for their comments about his essential role in the war. However, "I have never accepted what many people have kindly said," he added, "that I inspired the nation...It was the nation and the race dwelling around the globe that had the lion's heart. I had the luck to be called on to give the roar."[32] Now the roar was fading—even as the national heart was fading, too.

No debate about who would succeed him took place, as Foreign Secretary Anthony Eden had been his heir apparent since 1940. "I am now nearing the end of the journey," Churchill told the Commons on his eightieth birthday. Yet he resisted the inevitable transfer of power. The truth was, he was terrified about what his successors might do once he stepped down. Britain's army and navy were steadily shrinking; so was the empire; yet the world seemed more full of menace than ever.

The first test of the hydrogen bomb in 1954 deeply depressed him. "The greatest menace to civilization since the Mongols," he called it. But it was also a sign that the future belonged to the wielders of this massive destructive power, the Soviet Union and the United States. "[The Americans] will make the big decisions now," Winston confided to Eden in July. "Without their help, England would be isolated; she might become, like France, a satellite of Russia." Then his voice broke, and his eyes filled with tears.[33]

Finally Eden decided fourteen years of waiting was long enough. By the spring of 1955 it was clear that Churchill could not go on. The Tories used his name once more to secure their reelection. Then on March 1 Winston gave his last major speech in the House of Commons. It was almost half a century from the day that he had crossed the gangway from the Tory benches to the party of Asquith and Lloyd George. Now he spoke of the bomb, and the division of the world into free and Communist camps. The partnership between Britain and the United States, he said, must never be injured or retarded as long as the forces of darkness continued to stalk the planet.

"Mercifully, there is time and hope if we combine patience and courage," he concluded. "Meanwhile, never flinch, never weary, never despair."[34] It was his farewell message to the British people. A little more than a month later he formally handed over the reins of office.

Jock Colville had been his faithful secretary when he first became prime minister in 1940. He had been with him during the darkest days of the war and in the dark days after the 1945 elections. Colville had been present during his massive stroke. Now he was with him at the farewell dinner at Number 10, including all the members of the cabinet, the successor prime minister Anthony Eden, and even the queen and Prince Philip. Afterward Churchill retired upstairs and sat half-undressed on the bed, silent and deep in thought.

Colville was about to leave when Churchill suddenly looked up and, with real vehemence but also resigned despair, said, "I don't believe that Anthony can do it."[35]

It was his first openly expressed fear that Eden could not keep Britain strong and influential in the world, as Churchill would have wanted. Indeed, the Great Imperial Unraveling was about to begin.

"If Winston has believed in anything at all in the course of his long life," Lord Moran noted in his diary, "it has been the British Empire and all that it stands for." British India had represented his youth. Now India was gone.[36] The end of India in turn meant just what Winston had always feared: the end of the rest of the empire. The Raj had been the keystone of the great arc of empire from South Africa and Egypt to Singapore, Rangoon, and Hong Kong. Without it the pieces no longer fit together, and the design no longer made sense.

Palestine was the first to go, in 1947. Then Burma in 1948. In 1954 Churchill presided over the withdrawal of British troops from Egypt after seventy-two years, which the *Daily Express* blasted as "the greatest surrender ... since the Socialists and Mountbatten engineered the scuttle from India." Churchill was chagrined to be the target of this Churchillian rhetorical assault. "Fancy my ending my career with clearing out of Egypt," he murmured.[37]

Suez was next. Even Churchill had to admit, "Now that we no longer hold India the canal means little to us."[38] Even after British troops left Egypt, Churchill had been adamant about keeping them in the canal zone. But in June 1955 Eden reversed that policy and ordered the evacuation of the last British garrison from Suez. A month later Egypt's dictator Gamal Abdel Nasser seized the vital water route for himself. Eden tried in vain to take it back by force with the help of French tanks and paratroops. When the Americans protested, Eden hesitated and finally pulled the plug on Operation Musketeer. It was an international humiliation for both the British and French. It also cost Eden his health and his job.

Churchill was horrified by the Suez debacle. Nasser he considered a blackguard and "malicious swine," but he was equally disappointed in Eden's vacillation and weakness. In a few short months Eden had destroyed the one imperial legacy Churchill had left, Britain's credibility in the Middle East. Anthony Eden, the reliable son he always wanted* but never had, had in the end betrayed him.

So did Eden's replacement, Harold Macmillan—another old Churchill crony. Macmillan's aristocratic accents, ramrod-stiff manner, and drooping walrus mustache made him seem a Victorian survival, a throwback to palmier imperial days. In fact, it was Macmillan who would extend the Great Unraveling to Africa. Ghana (the former Gold Coast) became independent in 1957, then Nigeria in 1960. Both joined the commonwealth, but the principle was now established that British Africa would be ruled by native, not imperial, priorities.

Indeed, as the Conference of Commonwealth Ministers met every year, the number of black and brown faces grew. Macmillan, always a popular figure at these conferences, made this development seem more a matter of celebration than regret. "The processes which gave birth to the nation-States of Europe have been repeated all over the world," he told an audience in a tour of Africa in 1960. "We have seen the awakening of a national consciousness in people who lived for centuries in dependence upon some other Power." In short, what Gandhi had started in India had

---

* To forge the familial bond, Eden had even married Winston's niece Clarissa.

been, not the extraordinary dream of a living saint or (alternately) a seditious fakir, but part of a historically inevitable process; part of what Macmillan called the "wind of change." This shift in perspective truly marked, as one chronicler has put it, "the end of the imperial ideal."[39]

It also signaled the death, at least in public, of the assumptions about race and culture that had governed Churchill's and Gandhi's generation. Racism and racial ideologies were now seen as uniquely evil. Even Gandhi's own remarks about preserving India's "racial purity" would by 1960 have caused embarrassment, if not quite outrage. And far from assuming that nonwhites were unfit to rule themselves, the new view was that they must rule themselves immediately, whether they were prepared for the task or not.[40]

British decolonization would trigger many problems and crises, particularly in Africa. The bloody scenes that ended British rule in India would be repeated in Nigeria, Uganda, the Congo, and other former European colonies. But the battle Gandhi had fought all his life, to end the color bar within the empire and the commonwealth, had finally been won.*

Not surprisingly, Churchill was unhappy with this development. He realized his views were outdated. "When you learn to think of a race as inferior beings it is difficult to get rid of that way of thinking," Churchill confided to his doctor in 1952. But he also told Clementine that he believed Macmillan had made a mistake in going to Africa "to encourage the black men."[41] Churchill's once-standard view of Empire and the white man's burden no longer found purchase in his Conservative Party. As he had said several autumns before: "I am now merely a retired, and tired old reactionary."

He was also losing his power to focus on events. As he entered his late eighties, Churchill's awareness of the outside world was coming and going, and he became a fading shadow of his former self. But, there could still be small unexpected flashes of the old Winston, as one day in April

---

* Everywhere, that is, except where he had started the fight, in South Africa. The last living link to the South Africa of Gandhi and Churchill, Field Marshal Jan Smuts, died in 1950. Power passed into the hands of radical racialists. Macmillan's 1960 warning about the "wind of change" only made them more determined to fight to preserve their system of racial segregation or apartheid (which Smuts had opposed). Shortly afterward riots broke out in the black township of Sharpeville, and police killed more than sixty anti-apartheid protesters—the prelude to three decades of conflict in which Gandhi's name and example would be invoked more than once by resisters like Nelson Mandela and Archbishop Desmond Tutu.

1958, when Clementine was reading from *The Oxford Book of English Verse* at the dinner table.

Winston's eyes suddenly lit up. "Give it to me," he said eagerly. The book was open to a poem by Arthur Hugh Clough, "Say Not the Struggle Nought Availeth." As prime minister in 1942 he had evoked its lines in one of his most famous speeches. Now he read the lines aloud again in his old, strong voice, lines that might have been a summary of his life:

> *For while the tired waves, vainly breaking,*
> *Seem here no painful inch to gain,*
> *Far back through creaks and inlets making*
> *Come, silent, flooding in, the main,*
>
> *And not by eastern windows only,*
> *When daylight comes, comes in the light,*
> *In front the sun climbs slow, how slowly,*
> *But westward, look, the land is bright.*

"When Winston came to the last line," an observer at the table noted, "he sat up, making a vague gesture as if he were directing our eyes to the light, as he had done in the war. And then he slumped back, the effort had been too much for his tired mind."[42]

In 1960 he stopped painting. He seldom spoke anymore, did not seem to know friends, and had to be supported by nurses as he moved from room to room. Visitors might find him huddled in a chair on the yacht of his newest friend, Aristotle Onassis, or at Chartwell, where he would sit and stare into the fire for hours. Thinking, remembering, then suddenly moving a hand to stir the fire.

His ninetieth birthday on November 30, 1964, was a very different event from the public celebrations ten years earlier. It was "a half-hearted affair," his doctor of more than thirty years, Lord Moran, sadly noted. "Those near to him made suitable noises, but they knew it was all make believe, and that he did not wish to live."[43]

At eight o'clock in the morning of January 24, 1965, Winston's wish was realized. His daughter Mary was present, as was his lifelong friend Violet Bonham Carter, who watched as "his face from which all age and infirmity had dropped away," turned "young, calm, and resolute in death."

It was exactly seventy years to the day since his father had died.

By the queen's order, Churchill's body was laid in state in Westminster Abbey—the first prime minister to receive that honor since Gladstone. Around the clock for three days, in a biting winter wind, a never-ending queue of Britons filed past the coffin to pay their respects to the man whom the headline in the *Times* (the newspaper with which Churchill had fought so bitterly over India and then appeasement) called "the Greatest Englishman of His Time." At one point the line extended two miles from Westminster Bridge and the Lambeth Embankment on the east bank of the Thames, across Lambeth Bridge to Parliament Square and Westminster.

The bitterness, anger, and envy directed at Churchill all his life, from all sides, was finally gone. All that remained was the memory of the man who had saved his country in World War II; and recognition that he had come to symbolize an era in British history—and world history—that was gone forever.

Tributes poured in from every country and continent. Around the world flags flew at half-mast, stores shut, and theaters closed. Three American presidents wrote their condolences along with the pope. Canada's prime minister Lester Pearson wrote, "All Canadians are grief-stricken." Leaders from every corner of the globe and former empire offered the same sentiments. "Sir Winston Churchill's death deeply affects the Belgian people," "The whole German people share in the loss," "Nepal has lost a great friend," "It is with profound sorrow that the people of India learn of his death."[44]

Then on January 30 came the funeral. The day was gray and raw, with the same biting wind. Eight thousand police and seven thousand soldiers were in place to control the crowds, who jammed the sidewalks of the route, from Whitehall to Trafalgar Square and up the Strand and Fleet Street to Ludgate. Another estimated 300 million people— one tenth of the world's population—watched on television, from Vancouver to Bombay as the procession slowly made its way behind the Union Jack–draped coffin and gun carriage, preceded by three hundred RAF veterans of the Battle of Britain and drawn by one hundred Royal Navy seamen, to the strains of Beethoven's Funeral March. Meanwhile, the Royal Horse Artillery in St. James's Park fired a ninety-gun salute, one shot for each year of Churchill's life.

More than three thousand mourners and leaders of 110 nations attended the thirty-minute memorial service at St. Paul's. One of them was a bearded, turbaned figure, the foreign minister of India, Swaran Singh. Singh had been an intimate of Prime Minister Nehru, who had died at age seventy-five the year before. At one time Nehru had been the youthful rebel and upstart who, Churchill warned Gandhi, would exploit his popularity to gain power and whose rule over independent India would be, Churchill predicted, a "complete disaster."

But in later years Churchill and Nehru had become warily reconciled. "He has a feeling the Communists are against him," Winston joked after the Commonwealth Conference in 1955, "and that is apt to change people's opinions."[45] Churchill, however, had managed to outlive his fellow Old Harrovian. So another era had been closed, and the bitterness with it.

"When I was subaltern the Indian did not seem to me equal to the white man," Churchill recalled in 1952. It was an attitude that, he had belatedly come to realize, had hurt the Raj. Later he said that if he had been reelected in 1945, he would have tried once more to establish a constituent assembly for India. "Of course they might have got rid of us anyway," he said, referring to the Indian people, "but I'd have liked to try."

Then he had said something unlike anything he had ever said about India: "If we had made friends with them and taken them into our lives instead of restricting our intercourse to the political field, things might have been very different." That regretful musing was a final landmark on a long journey. The opening that Gandhi had wanted had finally appeared—but too late for either of them.[46]

Now the honorary pall-bearers began coming up the stairs. They included distinguished figures from Churchill's wartime years: Eden, now Lord Avon, Lord Ismay, and Lord Slim. There were also Lords Mountbatten and Attlee, the two men who, whatever their mistakes, had done what Churchill could not bring himself to do: give India its freedom. Finally the queen, queen mother, and Duke of Edinburgh arrived and led the congregation in singing Churchill's favorite hymns, including "Fight the Good Fight" and "Battle Hymn of the Republic," while the Union Jack–draped coffin stood still and silent hard by the tombs of Nelson and Wellington.

Afterward a long file of Yeomen of the Guard in red and gold coats and Grenadier Guardsmen in black bearskins and gray-blue greatcoats escorted the casket to a Port Authority barge at Festival Pier, while sixty pipers from various Highland regiments blared a lament. The great mechanical cranes of London's dockyards dipped their heads in silent tribute as Winston's body moved down London River to Waterloo Station. There it began its final trip by train to Bladon, where Winston was to be buried beside Blenheim Castle—the place where his journey had begun.

Meanwhile the hymns were over, the tributes finished, and the last trumpet notes of Last Post and Reveille were echoing away in the Whispering Gallery. The crowd in St. Paul's Cathedral dispersed. The royal family waited until Churchill's own family had left before departing. At their head was Randolph, gray-faced, prematurely aged. He would outlive his father by only three years.

Then the other dignitaries and presidents, including Charles de Gaulle, and the array of prime ministers present and past slowly filed out. One of the latter was Lord Attlee, now aging and frail. He had stumbled and nearly fallen while mounting the cathedral steps before the ceremony. Some even worried they might have to deal with two funerals for old premiers, not one. However, Attlee recovered, although he was almost too weak to last through the memorial service and needed help leaving after it was over.

Once the rest of the crowd had left, a chair was found for him as he waited for his car. Resting on his cane, he sat alone, head bowed, thinking and remembering. Then the car pulled up. Attlee stepped in and was gone.

It was seventeen years to the day since Gandhi's assassination.

CONCLUSION:
Triumph and Tragedy

TWO MEN, BORN FIVE YEARS AND four thousand miles apart, meet once when both are unknown. Then they go their separate ways and become two of the most revered figures of the twentieth century. From time to time they pass each other as they pass through history, each bent on his own course. Otherwise they find very different destinies. One saves his country and secures victory in the greatest war the world has ever known. The other cajoles a mighty nation into giving up its most prestigious possession and founds the most populous democracy on earth.

That is the usual story of Gandhi and Churchill as portrayed by historians, biographers, and even filmmakers. But it is not the whole story. Both men at the end of their lives got what they most wanted, but at the cost of what they most treasured. Gandhi and Churchill both died as heroes to their fellow countrymen and as icons to the rest of the world. But what they are celebrated for achieving is not what they had set out to do.

Winston Churchill spent his life trying to re-create the imperial grandeur that had been the touchstone of his father's generation. He discovered that grandeur as a young officer in India, and in the pages of Gibbon and Macaulay he uncovered the dream that underlay it: of a European civilization that could harmonize mankind's conflicting impulses and create a world of progress and "bright uplands." Churchill's identity as a Briton was founded on that dream, just as he cherished the empire that went with it.

When Churchill was young, the dream had been shared by others. Then it slowly evaporated, first among intellectuals, then among politicians, and finally among the British public. Among everyone, that is, except Churchill, who nurtured it and kept it alive during years of frustration and failure. He used it to inspire his nation to victory in World War II, but afterward it lost its value to others if not to him. Britons preferred to remain human beings rather than become heroes. To his sorrow Churchill was left with the fragments of his broken dream, including the dream of the Raj in India.

Gandhi too lived a dream. He had conceived that dream in London as a law student: of India as the spiritual home of mankind, of an ancient Hindu civilization that could overcome mankind's conflicting impulses and create a world of spiritual harmony and growth, of ahimsa and satyagraha or soul force.

That dream too sustained him through years of frustration and failure. He used it to inspire his nation to reach out for freedom from Britain and for independence. Then, when the goal was in sight, his vision lost its value to others if not to him. Gandhi too was left with a dream's broken fragments, while India dissolved into chaos and violence.

Gandhi's death did more to end the violence than anything he had done when he was alive. But the disaster that engulfed post-independence India did not come to a halt after 1948. The Raj was over and India was free, but it was no longer the India he—or Churchill—would recognize. It had become two countries, and then eventually three: India, Pakistan, and Bangladesh. More years of bloodshed and fighting lay ahead. Under Nehru's disastrous economic policies, India's poverty remained. Only years of retrenchment, and a trend of thinking far different from Gandhi's notion of a nation of charkhas and self-sufficient villages, would put India on the path to becoming a stable, prosperous nation.

Meanwhile military coups and the rise of anti-Western Islamic fanaticism would punctuate the sad history of Pakistan. It would fight two more savage wars with its larger rival for control of Kashmir. At one point in 1999 Pakistan and India even approached a nuclear showdown. And today, thanks to al-Qaeda, the old Northwest Frontier, or Waziristan, is as dangerous and violent a place as it was when Churchill first served there 110 years ago.

All this may have fulfilled Churchill's worst predictions of what would happen if the British left India. But he would have had no satisfaction at being proven right. His dream had been shattered, too. Despite his best efforts, Churchill could not restore Britain's pride and self-confidence in the world any more than Gandhi was able to build upon India's pre-British roots. And in striking ways, identities have been reversed. Today's democratic, modernizing, globalizing Indians seem more like Americans, Australians, and the other "English-speaking peoples" than Churchill could ever have imagined. Bangalore, the sleepy outpost where he spent a year reading and playing polo, is today a stronghold of a thriving capitalist economy, while Indian Navy aircraft carriers and warships dominate the waters of South Asia just as Churchill's Royal Navy once did.

At the same time Gandhi's New Age spirituality has found a more receptive home in the West than the Mahatma could ever have imagined. From the Beatles and the Hare Krishnas to vegetarianism and civil rights and peace studies, the impact of Gandhi's image and example has been huge. Indeed, his name may be more revered today in England and America than it is in his own home country, where, as one commentator has put it, Gandhi "continues both to divide Indians and to haunt their dreams."[1]

These cultural shifts reflect the complex realities of the modern world. It is a world that Gandhi and Churchill did so much to shape but for which their late Victorian education gave them an instinctive revulsion. They had little time to waste enjoying nuance. They both believed that the fate of civilization depended on the assertion of timeless values against the ebb and flux of the present. They believed there were higher values than getting and spending. They believed that bravery and courage were the ultimate keys to human character, whether for a man of war like Churchill or for an apostle of nonviolence like Gandhi.

But above all they believed that the personal and the political were inseparable. Gandhi spent his life insisting that Indian self-rule and rule of the self were the same thing: that people who could not do the one were incapable of the other. He may not have been far wrong. Likewise, Churchill believed that a strong nation was the necessary product of a strong people, whether as individuals like the great heroes of English history he revered (including the conquerors of India like Clive and Hastings) or as a nation or "race." To late Victorians like Gandhi and Churchill, those terms meant the same thing.

Both men lived their late Victorian creeds to the hilt. They saw the political arena as the place where their moral visions could be realized and their personal courage put to the test. Both believed that by sheer force of will and example they could redirect the course of events in India and in the world. The experience of defeat only seemed to intensify their drive and ambition. Ultimately, both men convinced themselves that their lives would have meaning only if they could secure the support of the masses for their dreams, even if the elites of their societies, Britain and India, remained suspicious and resentful, even scornful.

And to a powerful degree, they succeeded in securing that support. But both men also failed to realize that sheer will alone could not change how *others* saw the world and reacted to it. Millions would rally to both their causes; both men would earn the respect and admiration, even adulation of a generation of Britons and Indians, respectively. Each would see an essential part of their vision triumph. Both earned the permanent gratitude of their nations, as a result.

But at the end of the day those millions rallied to Gandhi and Churchill for their own reasons, as had their own closest followers. Few if any were willing to be what Churchill or Gandhi wanted them to be. Britons wanted to win the war against Hitler and Japan, but not in order to become an imperial race again. Indians wanted independence, but not in order to transcend ancient rivalries and modern national identities. In the end everyone remained true to themselves as ordinary human beings, while Gandhi's and Churchill's rivals and followers (Nehru, Jinnah, and Patel on the one side, Attlee, Mountbatten, and Eden on the other) looked ahead to their own political futures.

In short, the world refused to be reshaped in either Churchill's or Gandhi's image. It was an outcome that at first bewildered, then enraged, and finally overwhelmed them both. That was their tragedy, to set beside their triumph. The world remained obdurate in the face of their personal crusades to change it. History stayed on its steady oblivious course, despite their efforts to propel it toward horizons where it preferred not to go: in Gandhi's case, to a world without violence or exploitation, in Churchill's, to a British Empire blossoming into a robust union of English-speaking peoples.

Still, both men had left an imperishable mark on their age and a lasting legacy for coming generations. They had fought each other for the sake not only of an empire but of the future of humanity. In their forty-year rivalry, both men tasted glorious triumph and humiliating defeat. They inspired millions of devoted followers and alienated millions more. Taken together, their story is an inspiring tribute to the power of human beings to shape their own destiny, and a warning of the dangers of self-delusion and pride.

Their story is the great untold parable of the twentieth century.

SIGNIFICANT DATES

1857	The Great Mutiny or Sepoy Revolt.
1869	Birth of Mohandas Gandhi in Porbandar, Gujarat. Opening of Suez Canal.
1874	Birth of Winston Churchill in Blenheim Palace, England; Gandhi's father Karamchand moves family to Rajkot.
1885	Winton's father Lord Randolph Churchill becomes secretary of state for India; founding of Indian National Congress.
1888	Mohandas Gandhi leaves to study law in London; Winston Churchill enters Harrow, earns lowest marks in school.
1893	Gandhi leaves India for South Africa.
1894	Gandhi helps to found Natal Indian Congress.
1896–7	Churchill as lieutenant in Fourth Hussars arrives in India and sees action in Northwest Frontier province and Mamund Valley.
1899	Outbreak of Boer War.
1900	Churchill with South African Light Horse and Gandhi with Indian ambulance corps both serve at battle of Spion Kop; on return to England, Churchill elected as MP for the first time.
1901	Death of Queen Victoria.
1904	Churchill leaves Tories for Liberal Party.
1906	Gandhi and Churchill meet at the Colonial Office in London.
1907	Gandhi launches his first passive resistance campaign.
1908	Gandhi in prison for first time; Churchill becomes President of the Board of Trade and joins Liberal cabinet.

1909   Gandhi's second deputation to London; murder of William Curzon Wyllie; Gandhi writes *Hind Swaraj*.

1911   Gandhi ends his third passive resistance campaign; Churchill as Home Secretary at Sydney Street "siege."

1913   Gandhi's march to Transvaal; as First Lord of the Admiralty Churchill takes flying lessons.

1914   Outbreak of World War One. Gandhi recruits Indian ambulance drivers in London; Churchill leads Antwerp relief force.

1915   Gandhi returns to India and founds Sabarmati Ashram; Churchill launches Gallipoli offensive.

1917   Gandhi's first visit to Champaran; Churchill becomes Minister of Munitions.

1918   End of World War One.

1919   Rowlatt Acts and massacre at Amritsar.

1920   Gandhi launches his first noncooperation campaign in India.

1921   Churchill becomes Colonial Secretary; organizes Cairo Conference.

1922   Violence at Chauri Chaura; Gandhi sentenced to Yeravda jail; Churchill loses his parliamentary seat at Dundee.

1924   Gandhi released from prison; Churchill leaves Liberal Party.

1926   Lord Irwin (later Viscount Halifax) appointed viceroy of India; General Strike in England.

1927   Appointment of Simon Commission to discuss future of India.

1929   Indian National Congress meeting at Lahore approves Gandhi's plan for complete independence or Purana Swaraj; Churchill in New York City witnesses Black Thursday and Wall Street crash.

1930   Gandhi's Salt March; first Round Table Conference in London; Churchill speaks to India Empire Society opposing Dominion status for India.

1931   Gandhi-Irwin Pact; Gandhi visits London for second Round Table Conference; Churchill resigns from Conservative Party's Business Committee.

1932   British Government announces Communal Award; Gandhi's "fast unto death" and so-called Poona Pact.

1933   Adolf Hitler comes to power in Germany.

1935   Despite Churchill's opposition, Government of India Act passes Parliament; Anglo-German naval treaty.

1936   Gandhi founds new ashram at Sevagram; Hitler remilitarizes the Rhineland.

1938   Munich conference partitions Czechoslovakia; Gandhi opposes Subhas Chandra Bose's bid for re-election as president of Indian National Congress.

1939   Outbreak of Second World War. Churchill becomes First Lord of the Admiralty; Gandhi endorses Jawaharlal Nehru's manifesto demanding independence in exchange for Congress support for British war effort.

1940   Invasion of Norway; Churchill becomes prime minister; Lahore meeting of Muslim League calls for independent Pakistan; Gandhi launches his "personal" satyagraha campaign.

1941   Hitler invades Russia; Japanese attack on Pearl Harbor and invasion of Malaya.

1942   Singapore and Burma fall to Japanese invaders; British envoys led by Sir Stafford Cripps fail to break deadlock on India's future; Gandhi launches Quit India campaign, then is arrested and imprisoned in Aga Khan's palace.

1943   Gandhi launches another fast while under arrest; Great Bengal Famine begins; tide of war turns decisively in Allies' favor.

1944   Gandhi released from prison; Fourteenth Army at Imphal and Kohima holds out against Japanese invaders; Churchill opposes then agrees to Operation Overlord and invasion of France.

1945   Yalta conference; Gandhi attends Simla Conference with Viceroy Wavell; Churchill loses reelection as Prime Minister; trial of pro-Japanese Indian National Army officers at Delhi's Red Fort.

1946   Cabinet Mission's efforts to arrange Muslim–Hindu compromise fails; Muslim leaders declare Day of Action, which triggers riots in Calcutta and other cities.

1947   Lord Mountbatten named viceroy of India; meets with Gandhi and other leaders and announces Britain will leave India by August; impending partition of India sparks massacres and war over Kashmir; Gandhi struggles to end ethnic cleansing.

1948   Assassination of Mahatma Gandhi, aged seventy-nine.

1951   Tories return to power in Parliament, with Churchill as prime minister.

1955   His health failing, Churchill steps down as prime minister following general election.

1963   Death of Jawaharlal Nehru.

1965   Death of Winston Churchill, aged ninety.

GLOSSARY OF TERMS

ahimsa	nonviolence (opposite of himsa)
ashram	religious or semi-monastic community, usually centered around a guru or holy man
Bhagavad Gita	important Hindu religious text, part of the epic poem *Mahabharata*
bania	Hindu commercial caste
Bapu	"Father," a nickname for Gandhi
brahmacharya	celibacy
Brahmin	the highest Hindu caste
charkha	spinning wheel
chukka	one of the six timed periods in a polo match
dalit	outcaste or untouchable
darshan	the sighting or viewing of a holy man or site
dhoti	folded loincloth worn by Indian men
feringhi	derogative term for Europeans
guru	holy man, teacher
Harijan	"Children of God," Gandhi's term for dalits or untouchables
hartal	strike or work stoppage
jati	subcaste

khadi   homespun cotton cloth

kusan   peasant or farmer cultivator

Khilafat   movement that supported the claims of the
                   Turkish sultan as Caliph or protector of
                   Muslim holy places

Krishna or Krshna legendary Hindu hero, believed to be an
                   incarnation of the god Vishnu; the central
                   character in the Bhagavad Gita

lathi   long iron-tipped cane used by Indian
                   police

lakh   one hundred thousand

Mahasabha   ultra-orthodox Hindu brotherhood, sometimes
                   allied with Gandhi

Mahatma   "Great Soul," honorific title given to Mohandas
                   Gandhi

moksha   "release," or spiritual salvation in Hindu
                   religious philosophy

Mughals   Muslim rulers of India until 1858

nabob   wealthy man, used to describe Europeans
                   who made great fortunes in India in the
                   eighteenth century (from *nawab*)

Parsi   India's Zoroastrian minority, largely centered in
                   Bombay

purdah   custom of veiling women, common among
                   Muslims but also some Hindu castes

raj   "rule," as in "British Raj"

Ram or Rama   character in Hindu legend who appears as an
                   incarnation of the god Vishnu; hence a name
                   for God

Ramanama   recitation of the name of Rama as religious
                   rite

ramraj (ya)   "the rule of Rama," usually projected in the
                   future

Rashtriya Swayamsevak Sangh or RSS	ultra-orthodox Hindu organization
sadhu	Hindu ascetic or wandering holy man
satyagraha	literally "soul force," Gandhi's term for his program of nonviolent resistance
sepoy	Indian Army soldier, especially before and during the Great Mutiny of 1857
Shiva	one of the oldest and most important Hindu gods
sowar	Indian Army cavalry trooper
swadeshi	"belonging to one's country," used to describe goods produced in India; hence a symbol of Indian independence and self-sufficiency
swaraj	"self-rule," hence Indian Home Rule
varna	caste
varnashramadharma	Gandhi's term for an ideal Hindu society, in which caste would serve as the basis for a division of labor rather than social hierarchy
Vaishnava	Hindus who practice particular religious devotions to the god Vishnu rather than Shiva
Vishnu	important Hindu God

ACKNOWLEDGMENTS

I was in high school when I helped my father to correct proofs of his translation of the *Bhagavad Gita*. The experience fixed Arjuna and Krishna and terms like *bakhti yoga* and Mahatma, in my consciousness for the first time. Since then, my father, A.L. Herman, has been my reliable and patient mentor in all things relating to India and Indian thought. His books on Hinduism, Buddhism, and his own writings on Gandhi have been a guide and inspiration, just as his library has been a steady resource for my reading and research for more than thirty years.

Without him this book would have been inconceivable. He not only read drafts of the manuscript, and answered specific questions on fine points in Gandhi's thought and pre-Vedic and Vedic Indian history, he also laughed at all (or nearly all) my jokes. No one else makes writing a book feel more like fun than hard work.

I also owe a huge debt to the University of Virginia, and the incomparable collection of books and materials on India and Gandhi built up by the Center for South Asian Studies and its librarian at Alderman Library, Philip McEldowney. Phil also graciously agreed to read chapters of the manuscript, and gave expert advice on consulting Indian sources online. Pramit Pal Chaudhuri also read the book in manuscript form, and I owe him much for his insights into the nature and direction of contemporary India, and its legacy from the past.

Peter Rühe at the GandhiServe Foundation was patient and helpful in procuring images. Every modern Gandhi scholar owes him a debt of gratitude for his dedicated scholarship, and the wonderful Gandhi resources he has made available online.

Warm thanks also go to the Ames Library of South Asia at the University of Minnesota for allowing me to consult its wonderful collection of photographs and maps and where, as a boy, I absorbed my first lessons in the history of British India. It was at the University of Minnesota's James F. Bell Library that I did my first research on the geography of European penetration of India. The book's opening chapters also owe a great deal to the rich collection and the patient and reliable staff of the New York Public Library.

John Pocock's masterly seminar on the concept of empire held at the Folger Institute in Washington, D.C., had a decisive impact on my thinking in this book, including the place of Gibbon in Churchill's thought. Professor Will Hay of Mississippi State University provided timely and invaluable help as did conversations with Professor Iain Smith of the University of Warwick on the Boer War.

On the Churchill side, writing this book would have been impossible without Sir Martin Gilbert. His biography of Churchill and its companion volumes remain monuments of modern historical scholarship—and indispensable tools for any Churchill researcher. Sir Martin graciously agreed to read the manuscript, and although our work together on the book was necessarily limited, his cheers from the sidelines were always a morale booster when things got frustrating.

Carlo d'Este graciously and unselfishly gave me the fruits of his own research on Churchill and kindly read the manuscript, as did Richard Langworth, editor of *Finest Hour* at the Churchill Centre in Washington, D.C., who steered me clear of some early mistakes. As with other readers—my father, Philip McEldowney, Pramit Chaudhuri, Carlo d'Este, and the rest—whatever errors remain are my own.

Thanks are also due to the staff of the Churchill Archives Centre and the Chartwell Papers at Churchill College, Cambridge; Hulton Getty Images; the British Library; and the Imperial War Museum. Special thanks go to the late Russell Blackwood, Jeanne Gerbus, Greg Lindsay of the Centre for Independent Studies in Sydney, Robert Matheson, John J. Miller, Wendy Doniger, Alice Pappas, Nick Phillipson of the University of Edinburgh, Ivor Tiefenbrun of Linn Technologies in Glasgow, and Muhammed Sajjad Yussef, who all provided help in making this a better book. Apologies go to those who also helped in a myriad of ways, but whose names I've left out.

Conversations with Charles T. Matheson, Tom Veblen, and Paul Koda gave shape to the book in its early stages, and their intelligent insights, as always, appear in almost every chapter. My agents, Glen Hartley and Lynn Chu, were enthusiastic backers of the project from the beginning. My mother, Barbara Herman, read the book manuscript with her usual discerning eye and her comments had a decisive impact, starting with the opening sentence.

Thanks also go to my editor, John Flicker, for his warm and uncompromising support for the project, and his brilliant ability to bring out the book's strengths and trim its weaknesses. His team at Bantam, particularly his assistant, Noor Zaidi, and the book's designer, Glen Edelstein, showed forbearance and patience when it helped, and skill and expertise where it counted. A special debt of gratitude goes to my copy editor, Janet Biehl. Again, whatever errors that remain are my responsibility.

My wife Beth is, as she knows, the perfect wife for a writer and an historian. She sees everything with fresh eyes, asks the inconvenient but penetrating questions, and never lets me fall back on just "good enough." She fell in love with the project even before I did, and always showed interest and enthusiasm even when my own occasionally flagged. This is her book in so many ways. I hope it is a fitting tribute to her twenty years of patience, support, and love.

NOTES

PROLOGUE

1. Shepherd, *Personal Narrative* 2.
2. Ibid., 11.
3. Captain Fletcher Hayes, quoted in Collier, *Sound of Fury,* 72.
4. Quoted in Hibbert, *Great Mutiny,* 168.
5. Duberly, *Suppression of Mutiny,* 156.
6. Shepherd, *Personal Narrative,* 15–17, 32–33.
7. Hibbert, *Mutiny,* 180; Shepherd, *Personal Narrative,* 47.
8. Trevelyan, *Cawnpore,* 202.
9. Thomson, *Story of Cawnpore,* 160–61.
10. Hibbert, *Mutiny,* 192.
11. Amelia Horne, "Narrative," quoted in Ward, *Bones Are Scattered,* 329.
12. Hibbert, *Mutiny,* 203.
13. Quoted in Chunder, *Travels of a Hindu,* 2:104.
14. Quoted in Kaye, *History of Sepoy War,* 2:269.
15. Pollock, *Way to Glory,* 176.
16. Hibbert, *Mutiny,* 195.
17. Ibid., 207.
18. Trevelyan, *Cawnpore,* 312–13.
19. Hibbert, *Mutiny,* 209.
20. Ward, *Bones Are Scattered,* 438–39; Bruehl, *Crisis of the Raj,* 141–43.
21. Quoted in Kaye, *History of Sepoy War,* 2:399.
22. Quoted in Ward, *Bones Are Scattered,* 455.
23. Duberly, *Suppression of Mutiny,* 25.
24. Edwardes, *Battles of Mutiny,* 23.

25. Hibbert, *Mutiny,* 313.
26. The account of events by Lieutenant MacDowell is published in Hodson, *Twelve Years of a Soldier's Life,* 311–14.
27. Ibid., 297, 303.
28. Pyarelal, *Early Phase,* 189.
29. Ibid., 190.
30. Meer, *Apprenticeship,* 1.
31. See Arnold, *Gandhi,* 17.

CHAPTER 1. *The Churchills and the Raj*

1. Quoted in R. S. Churchill, *Winston S. Churchill,* 1:4–5.
2. Letter to Mrs. L. Jerome, November 30, 1874, in R. S. Churchill, *Companion,* 1:1:2.
3. Montgomery-Massingberd, *Blenheim Revisited,* 98, 105–7.
4. That included £3,000 from his father-in-law. Pearson, *Private Lives,* 42.
5. Ibid., 49.
6. Foster, *Lord Randolph,* 25.
7. Most men stopped work when the women and children did, since factories could not function shorthanded. See Mathias, *First Industrial Nation,* 183.
8. That cohesiveness was enhanced by the coming of steam power and the telegraph. For a readable account, see Ferguson, *Empire,* 165–71.
9. Foster, *Political Life,* 66–67. Gladstone's observations on the Churchills' lack of principle is found in *ibid.,* 127.
10. R. H. S. Churchill, *Speeches of Lord Randolph,* 30–31; James, *Lord Randolph,* 78.
11. Foster, *Lord Randolph,* 69.
12. Ibid., 172.
13. Ibid., 177.
14. Spear, *History of India,* 65–66.
15. Moon, *British Conquest,* 13–14.
16. Heathcote, *Military in British India,* 29–30.
17. Moon, *British Conquest,* 56; Moorhouse, *India Britannica,* 39.
18. The classic work is Spear, *Nabobs,* but it should be supplemented with Jasonoff, *Edge of Empire.*
19. Moon, *British Conquest,* 606.
20. Gosh, *Dalhousie in India,* esp. 41–42.
21. Farwell, *Armies of Raj,* 51.
22. Moon, *British Conquest,* 757.
23. Lloyd, *British Empire 1558–1983,* 177.
24. Moorhouse, *India Britannica,* 80; Moon, *British Conquest,* 781.
25. Hopkirk, *Great Game.*

26. Farwell, *Armies of Raj,* 51.

27. Ferguson, *Empire,* 216.

28. Moorhouse, *India Britannica,* 118–20.

29. See Cain, *Hobson and Imperialism,* 48. The actual phrase was "a gigantic system of outdoor relief for the aristocracy of Great Britain."

30. See, for example, Dalrymple, *White Mughals.*

31. Moorhouse, *India Britannica,* 136.

32. For background, see Herman, *Idea of Decline.*

33. Quoted in Hirschmann, *"White Mutiny,"* 72.

34. Chaudhuri, *Great Anarch!,* 62.

35. Quoted in Hirschmann, *"White Mutiny,"* 142.

36. Quoted in Farwell, *Armies of Raj,* 183.

37. Ibid., 180. See also Streets, *Martial Races.*

38. Farwell, *Armies of Raj,* 181.

39. Chaudhuri, *Great Anarch!,* 63.

40. Quoted in editor's introduction to Gandhi, *Hind Swaraj,* xix–xx.

41. Quoted in Moon, *British Conquest,* 773.

42. Ibid., 841.

43. Quoted in ibid., 859. The exception was the 1899–1900 famine, which struck nearly a third of India and killed somewhere between three and four million people. Its effects would have been far worse without Lytton's measures, which had culminated in 1883 in the Famine Code.

44. Moon, *British Conquest,* 772; Mathur, *Lord Ripon's Administration,* 237. The quotation is from one of Ripon's strongest supporters, the chief commissioner of Assam, but the sentiments are his.

45. Quoted in Hirschmann, *"White Mutiny,"* 54, 122.

46. Ibid., 65–66.

47. Ibid., 123.

CHAPTER 2. *Lord Randolph Takes Charge*

1. Churchill, *Lord Randolph,* 1:555–64.

2. Letter of December 13, 1884, ibid., 555.

3. Ibid., 557.

4. Letter of January 8, 1885, quoted in Foster, *Lord Randolph,* 170.

5. The classic work is Buchanan, *Development.*

6. Dilks, *Curzon in India,* 1:74.

7. Letter of January 14, 1885, in Churchill, *Lord Randolph,* 1:558.

8. Churchill, *Roving Commission,* 1–2, 4.

9. R. S. Churchill, *Companion,* 1:1:102–3.

10. Churchill, *Lord Randolph,* 1:560–61.

11. Dufferin, *Our Viceregal Life,* 1:55.

12. Churchill, *Lord Randolph,* 1:563; Foster, *Lord Randolph,* 172–73.

13. Ibid., 1:563.

14. Foster, *Lord Randolph,* 173.
15. Quoted in Beloff, *Imperial Sunset,* 1:159–60.
16. Churchill, *Lord Randolph,* 1:474.
17. Ibid., 1:476.
18. That rule changed in 1893. See Beloff, *Imperial Sunset,* 1:36.
19. Foster, *Lord Randolph,* 212.
20. Ibid., 189–90, 198.
21. Churchill, *Lord Randolph,* 1:519.
22. Foster, *Lord Randolph,* 208–9; Churchill, *Lord Randolph,* 1:525.
23. McLane, *Indian Nationalism,* 49.
24. Churchill, *Lord Randolph,* 1:473.
25. R. S. Churchill, *Winston Churchill,* I:xxix.
26. Manchester, *Visions of Glory,* 188.
27. R. S. Churchill, *Companion,* 1:1:116–19.
28. Manchester, *Visions of Glory,* 126.
29. Pearson, *Private Lives,* 66.
30. Manchester, *Visions of Glory,* 205.
31. Churchill, *Roving Commission,* 43.
32. Morgan, *Young Man in a Hurry,* 48.
33. R. S. Churchill, *Companion,* 1:1, 470–71; letter of April 22, 1894.
34. Churchill, *Roving Commission,* 62.
35. Foster, *Lord Randolph,* 383, 390.
36. R. H. S. Churchill, *Speeches,* 123.
37. Ibid., 136.
38. Quoted in Martin, *New India,* 136.

CHAPTER 3. *Illusions of Power*

1. Arnold, *Gandhi,* 16.
2. Green, *Gandhi,* 37.
3. Quoted in Payne, *Gandhi,* 16.
4. Devanesen, *Making of Mahatma,* 115.
5. Gandhi, *Autobiography,* 1.
6. Payne, *Gandhi,* 23.
7. Green, *Gandhi,* 38.
8. Payne, *Gandhi,* 20–21.
9. Gandhi, *Autobiography,* 28–29.
10. See Chaudhuri, *Great Anarch:* 44. On Brahmanism and Vaishnavism, see Lannoy, *Speaking Tree,* 206.
11. Macaulay, "Speech on Government of India," in *Prose and Poetry,* 718.
12. As noted in Roberts, *History of World,* 129, 137.
13. Gandhi, *Hind Swaraj,* 90. Buddha, in the *Dhamma-kakka-pavathana-sutta,* is quoted in Keraly, *Gem in Lotus,* 217.

14. Keraly, *Gem in Lotus,* 35.
15. See Herman, *Influences,* and Pyarelal, *Gandhi,* 192.
16. Basham, *Wonder That Was India,* 146.
17. The earliest description of the caste system dates from the third century B.C.E. and was written by the Greek traveler Megasthenes. See Ghorye, *Caste and Class in India,* 1.
18. Chaudhuri, *Continent of Circe,* 148.
19. For example, see Fuller, *Caste Today,* esp. introduction.
20. Not surprisingly, this appealed particularly to a non-Brahmin audience. Some scholars see a strong Ksatriya or warrior-class influence in the *Upanishads*; indeed another key figure in this rejection of traditional religious hierarchy, Gautama Buddha, belonged to the Ksatriya class. See Olivelle, *Upanishads,* xxxiv–xxxv.
21. Allen, *Search for Buddha.*
22. Roberts, *History of World,* 137.
23. Schulberg, *Historic India,* 82.
24. Quoted in Basham, *Wonder That Was India,* 53.
25. Ibid., 55–56.
26. Allen, *Search for Buddha,* 2, 9.
27. According to Ali, *Emergence of Pakistan,* 3.
28. See the indispensable work on popular Hinduism in pre-Mutiny India, Dubois, *Hindu Manners,* 305.
29. Moon, *British Conquest,* 236–37.
30. Quoted in Moorhouse, *India Britannica,* 49.
31. Spear, *India,* 101.
32. Mill, *History of British India.* In point of fact, British rule had actually made the caste system more rigid and insular, by codifying the laws of Dharmasastra in order to adjudicate cases in their law courts involving Hindus.
33. Macaulay, "Minute on Indian Education," in *Prose and Poetry,* 722.
34. Ibid., 723.
35. On the British rediscovery of Hinduism, the still indispensable work is Kopf, *British Orientalism.*
36. See Stokes, *Peasant Armed.*
37. Moon, *British Conquest,* 636.
38. Ferguson, *Empire,* 216.
39. Kopf, *British Orientalism,* 196.
40. Bahadur, *Causes of Indian Revolt,* 15.
41. Quoted in Foster, *Lord Randolph,* 170.
42. Brown, *Modern India,* 128.
43. Hindus (with the exception of Sikhs) were virtually cut out of a military profession that had been traditional to the image of Hindu manhood and that was now drawn almost entirely from "warlike and hardy races" like Muslim Pathans, Punjabis, and Baluchis. Farwell, *Armies of Raj,* 181.

CHAPTER 4. *Awakening*

1. Green, *Gandhi,* 57–58.

2. Gandhi, *Collected Works,* 71:132; Green, *Gandhi,* 58.

3. Payne, *Gandhi,* 40–41.

4. Gandhi, *Autobiography,* 10.

5. Ibid., 25, 26–27; Green, *Gandhi,* 75.

6. This was in July 1906. Arnold, *Gandhi,* 54.

7. Gandhi, *Autobiography,* 32.

8. Payne, *Gandhi,* 50.

9. Gandhi, *Autobiography,* 36–37.

10. Gandhi, *Collected Works,* 1: 42.

11. Hunt, *Gandhi in London,* 1.

12. In an interview with *Vegetarian* magazine in June 1891. Gandhi, *Collected Works,* 1:41.

13. Walkowitz, *City of Dreadful Delight,* 192–93.

14. Ibid., 27.

15. Gandhi, *Autobiography,* 43; Hunt, *Gandhi in London,* 16.

16. Gandhi, *Autobiography,* 40, 45–46.

17. Ibid., 40.

18. *Satapatha Brahmana,* quoted in Doniger, ed., *Laws of Manu,* xxxiii.

19. Quoted in Shulman, *King and Clown,* 29.

20. Gandhi, *Autobiography,* 42.

21. Hunt, *Gandhi in London,* 20.

22. Green, *Gandhi,* 107.

23. Hunt, *Gandhi in London,* 33–34.

24. Gandhi, *Autobiography,* 61.

25. Cranston, *HPB,* 59–60.

26. Blavatsky, *Isis Unveiled,* 2:639.

27. Cranston, *HPB,* 434.

28. Gandhi, *Autobiography,* 66.

29. Ibid., 60.

30. Hunt, *Gandhi in London,* 18.

31. Gandhi, *Collected Works,* 1:41.

32. Ibid., 1:70.

33. Green, *Gandhi,* 114–15.

34. Gandhi, *Autobiography,* 75.

35. Ibid., 88.

36. Green, *Gandhi,* 121.

37. Quoted in ibid., 120.

38. Arnold, *Gandhi,* 45.

39. Swan, *Gandhi,* 91–120, 21–22.

40. Quoted in Hunt, *Gandhi in London,* 89.

41. Gandhi, *Autobiography*, 93.
42. Ibid., 97.
43. Ibid., 99–100.
44. Ibid., 101.
45. See Fischer, *Life of Gandhi*, 49.
46. The letter ran on September 23, 1893. Gandhi, *Collected Works*, 1:60.
47. Gandhi, *Autobiography*, 121.
48. Swan, *Gandhi*, 42.
49. Ibid., 41.
50. Arnold, *Gandhi*, 51.
51. Gandhi, *Autobiography*, 151.

CHAPTER 5. *Awakening II*

1. Gandhi, *Collected Works*, 1:359–92.
2. Charmley, *End of Glory*, 275.
3. Churchill, *Roving Commission*, 89.
4. Ibid., 64.
5. Ibid., 74, 76.
6. Ibid., 102.
7. Manchester, *Visions of Glory*, 239.
8. Churchill, *Roving Commision*, 103, 104.
9. Ibid., 107–8.
10. R. S. Churchill, *Companion*, 1:2, 701.
11. Milburn, *Polo*, 15–16.
12. Churchill, *Roving Commission*, 111.
13. Gibbon, *Decline and Fall*, 1:31, 103, 83.
14. Macaulay, *Prose and Poetry*, 326.
15. Ibid., 372, 393.
16. Reade, *Martyrdom*, 497.
17. Churchill, *Roving Commission*, 115; Moran, *Churchill in War*, 208.
18. Churchill, *Savrola*, 78.
19. Ibid.
20. Lukacs, *Duel*, 39.
21. Gilbert, *Prophet of Truth*, 413.
22. R. S. Churchill, *Companion*, 1:2:751.
23. Quoted in Louis, *In the Name of God!*, 174, 172.
24. Churchill, *Roving Commission*, 121.
25. R. S. Churchill, *Companion*, 1:2.
26. Manchester, *Visions of Glory*, 250.
27. Churchill, *Roving Commission*, 122–23.
28. Ibid., 123; Manchester, *Visions of Glory*, 251.
29. Dispatch of September 21, 1897, in Churchill, *Young Winston's Wars*, 29.

30. The original articles are in Churchill, *Young Winston's Wars.* The version of
    The Malakand Field Force is from the combined volume of his war
    correspondent books, *Frontiers and Wars.*
31. Churchill, *Malakand Field Force,* 47.
32. Ibid., 55.
33. Churchill, *Roving Commission,* 131.
34. Ibid., 137.
35. Ibid., 140.
36. Ibid., 141.
37. Ibid., 142.
38. Manchester, *Visions of Glory,* 258.
39. R. S. Churchill, *Companion,* 1:2:703.
40. Manchester, *Visions of Glory,* 263.
41. R. S. Churchill, *Companion,* 1:2:924.
42. Churchill, *Roving Commission,* 163–64.
43. Morgan, *Young Man in a Hurry,* 99–100.
44. Churchill, *Roving Commission,* 194; 188.
45. Ibid.
46. R. S. Churchill, *Companion,* 1:2:978.
47. Ibid., 1:2:979.
48. As noted in Churchill, *Roving Commission,* 194.
49. Churchill, *River War,* in *Frontiers and Wars,* 66.
50. Churchill, *Roving Commission,* 133.
51. Churchill, *Malakand Field Force,* 48.
52. The phrase comes from the essay on Warren Hastings in Macaulay, *Prose
    and Poetry,* 379.
53. R. S. Churchill, *Complete Speeches,* 1:262.
54. Gilbert, *Road to Victory,* 666.
55. Ibid., 1166.

CHAPTER 6. *Men at War*

1. Gandhi, *Autobiography,* 164.
2. Ibid., 167.
3. Ibid., 165–66.
4. Ibid., 77.
5. Tendulkar, *Mahatma,* 3:11.
6. Gandhi, *Autobiography,* 171.
7. Ibid., 168–69.
8. Gandhi, "Nonviolence in Peace and War," in *Selected Writings,* 60.
9. In general, see Mosse, *Image of Man.* The quotations in the footnote
   are from Gandhi, *Autobiography,* 188; Churchill, *London to
   Ladysmith,* 394.
10. Swan, *Gandhi,* 65.

11. Interview with *Englishman,* November 13, 1896, in Gandhi, *Collected Works,* 1: 458.

12. Swan, *Gandhi,* 68.

13. Brown, *Prisoner of Hope,* 37.

14. It receives its own chapter in Gandhi, *Autobiography,* 243–45.

15. Gandhi, *Collected Works,* I; Gandhi, *Autobiography,* 151–52.

16. Quoted in Ferguson, *Empire,* 228.

17. Indeed, for the first time under Milner, Gandhi found some official support for the Natal Congress's petitions on behalf of the Transvaal. Although Milner and Colonial Secretary Joseph Chamberlain had to let the 1895 ghetto law stand, they forced the Transvaal authorities not to expel the Indians living there until 1899. Swan, *Gandhi,* 87, 88–89.

18. Gandhi, *Autobiography,* 188.

19. Ibid., 151.

20. Gandhi, *Collected Works,* 2: 316–17.

21. Quoted in Morgan, *Young Man in a Hurry,* 116.

22. Celia Sandys, *Dead or Alive,* 21.

23. On the whiskey, see Churchill, *Roving Commission,* 126–27. Scotch, as Winston pointed out, was not his father's drink. Lord Randolph had belonged to an earlier "brandy and soda" generation. But Churchill concluded, "after adequate experiment and reflection," that "whisky in a diluted form is the more serviceable of these twin genii." Later Churchill's alcohol consumption would be the subject of much speculation and gossip. He, however, always stoutly maintained that he had full control over his drinking, which usually started in midmorning with a thin whiskey and soda. In 1931 he even convinced an American physician, at the height of Prohibition, to prescribe a minimum of 250cc of alcohol per day as necessary for his health, "especially at mealtimes." See Holmes, *Footsteps of Churchill,* 16.

24. Atkins, *Incidents and Reflections,* quoted in Pearson, *Private Lives,* 102.

25. R. S. Churchill, *Companion,* I:2:1058.

26. Gandhi, *Collected Works,* 2: 332.

27. R. S. Churchill, *Companion,* 1:2:1058–99; Churchill, *Roving Commission,* 242.

28. Churchill, *Roving Commission,* 243–44.

29. Ibid., 246.

30. Ibid., 249.

31. Churchill, *London to Ladysmith,* in *Frontiers and Wars,* 395.

32. Sandys, *Dead or Alive,* 225; Churchill, *Roving Commission,* 259, 261.

33. He also dismissed Winston's promise that he would give the Boers a fair break in his published story if released, saying "he may be a chip off the old block." This was a reference to the fact that Winston's father had made a heavily publicized trip to South Africa before his death and told

the press he found the Boers dirty, lazy, and barbarous. In 1900 the remarks still stung. Morgan, *Young Man in a Hurry,* 49.

34. Ibid., 127.

35. Haldane's own account, *A Soldier's Saga,* is quoted in Morgan, *Young Man in a Hurry,* 125. The doubts about Churchill's more sanitized version of his escape grew larger in 1997, with the discovery of a 1931 letter from Haldane to his friend the fifth Viscount Knutsford saying that Churchill had "slipped off without me or the third man," meaning Sergeant Brockie. However, Sandys, in *Dead or Alive,* 113–15, points out that after the war Haldane and Churchill remained cordial friends with no sign of bitterness over the incident, and that Haldane even inscribed a copy of *A Soldier's Saga,* published in 1948, to Winston, saying, "With profound admiration from an old ally." What seems likely is that Winston acted selfishly but not thoughtlessly and convinced himself that he was not abandoning comrades but seizing his only opportunity for escape. If the roles had been reversed, Haldane and Brockie would likely have done the same thing.

36. Churchill, *Roving Commission,* 272.

37. Morgan, *Young Man in a Hurry,* 127–28.

38. Farwell, *Great Anglo-Boer War,* 138.

39. Sandys, *Dead or Alive,* 137–38.

40. R. S. Churchill, *Companion,* 1: 2:1153.

41. Dispatch of January 23, in Churchill, *Young Winston's Wars,* 215.

42. Quoted in Payne, *Gandhi,* 119.

43. Gandhi, *Autobiography,* 188.

44. Ibid., 188–89.

45. Gandhi, *Collected Works,* 3:222–23.

46. Quoted in Payne, *Gandhi,* 123.

47. Churchill, *Young Winston's Wars,* 215–16. This was in June 1945, in a conversation with then Viceroy Wavell. See Wavell, *Viceroy's Journal,* 146.

48. Gandhi, *Collected Works,* 2:354.

49. Ibid., 2:355.

50. Gandhi, *Autobiography,* 189.

51. Sandys, *Dead or Alive,* 427.

52. R. S. Churchill, *Companion,* 1:2:1149–50, 1151.

53. Ibid., 1:2:1203.

CHAPTER 7. *Converging Paths*

1. Swan, *Gandhi,* 90.

2. Gandhi, *Autobiography,* 223.

3. Ibid., 224.

4. Green, *Gandhi,* 148.

5. Ibid., 153–54.

6. Gandhi, *Collected Works,* 3:379.

7. Swan, *Gandhi,* 112.

8. Quoted in Green, *Gandhi,* 148.

9. "Gandhi and the Black People of South Africa," in Hunt, *American Looks,* 88.

10. Gandhi, *Collected Works,* 3:323.

11. Ibid., 37:261.

12. Gandhi, *Autobiography,* 265.

13. Ruskin also reinforced the anti-Darwinist message of another writer Gandhi had discovered slightly earlier, the Scots Free Church lecturer Henry Drummond. Drummond's *Natural Law in the Spiritual World,* published in 1883, argued that the governing principle of evolution was not survival of the fittest, as Darwinians claimed, but the sacrifice of the most altruistic, i.e. those who nurture and offer their help to others. Drummond's celebration of altruism was a powerful riposte to Churchill's mentor Winwood Reade and reveals once again the contrast between the Gandhi and Churchill worldviews.

14. Editorial of October 28, 1905, in *Indian Opinion*. Gandhi, *Collected Works,* 4:473.

15. Payne, *Gandhi,* 148.

16. Ibid., 149.

17. See Curzon, *Viceroy's India.*

18. Moon, *British Conquest,* 920–91.

19. Ibid., 936.

20. Ironically, the reason for his departure had little to do with the partition controversy. It was rather his clash with India's commander in chief Lord Kitchener over the future shape of the Indian Army. But in India the impact was the same: he left the most reviled public figure among Indians since James Neill. See Dilks, *Curzon in India,* vol 2.

21. Gandhi, *Autobiography,* 279.

22. Gandhi, *Collected Works,* 5:366–67.

23. Gandhi, *Autobiography,* 281.

24. Ibid.

25. Ibid., 181.

26. Ibid., 184.

27. Green, *Gandhi,* 240.

28. Gandhi, *Autobiography,* 182.

29. Quoted in Swan, *Gandhi,* 102.

30. Gandhi, *Satyagraha,* 137.

31. Back in January 1904 Gandhi had told Indian merchants who were being harassed by the government that "the person prosecuted should rise to the occasion, decline to pay any fines, and go to gaol." Quoted in Swan, *Gandhi,* 117.

32. Although Haji Habib was also chair of the BIA's Pretoria committee and president of the BIA, Abdul Gani opened the proceedings. Swan, *Gandhi,* 121.

33. Gandhi, *Satyagraha,* 146, 148.

34. Hunt, *Gandhi in London,* 64–65.

35. Gandhi, *Collected Works,* 3:426.

36. In other words, more than a million dollars in today's figures. This according to his son the biographer, in R. S. Churchill, *Winston Churchill,* 2:1.

37. Morgan, *Young Man in a Hurry,* 138.

38. Ibid., 149.

39. Bennett, *Concept of Empire,* 330.

40. Churchill, *Complete Speeches,* 262.

41. Ibid., 1:99. How free and open India's markets really were is a question for economic historians. Gandhi was about to write a stinging rebuke to the assertion that they were indeed free and open. The debate was striking, for it revealed the degree to which British politicians thought of India as *separate* from the rest of the *British* Empire.

42. Ibid., 1:263.

43. Bonham Carter, *Intimate Portrait,* 85.

44. Manchester, *Visions of Glory,* 359–61.

45. Williams and Ramsden, *Ruling Britannia,* 339. Ironically, South Africa and coolie labor were important issues in the 1906 election. However, these were Chinese, not Indian, workers, imported by High Commissioner Milner to work in South Africa's mines. Labour and Liberals branded it "Chinese slavery," and campaign posters appeared showing men wearing pigtails in chains. Churchill opposed Milner's program but hardly campaigned against it. For him, the crucial issue all along was free trade.

46. Morgan, *Young Man in a Hurry,* 187.

47. Churchill, *London to Ladysmith,* 393.

48. Quoted in Morgan, *Young Man in a Hurry,* 197.

49. Quoted ibid., 198.

50. Hunt, *Gandhi in London,* 56; Gandhi, *Collected Works,* 6:85.

51. Gandhi, *Collected Works,* 6:95.

CHAPTER 8. *Brief Encounter*

1. Hunt, *Gandhi in London,* 69.

2. Ibid., 68–69.

3. One reason was that there had been a petition drive led by Dr. William Godfrey. Godfrey, an Anglo-Indian Johannesburg doctor, had worked with Gandhi during the plague outbreaks in 1904 and had spoken at the Empire Theater meeting. However, he now denounced Gandhi as an ambulance-chasing radical lawyer who had profited personally from agitating against the government, "while Indians in South Africa

gained nothing." Copies of the petition arrived in London before Gandhi's arrival; Elgin and others had seen them. Godfrey had considerably complicated Gandhi's mission, and although he managed to allay suspicions in London, the petition shows how sharply divided the Indian community and its supporters were over Gandhi himself. Hunt, *Gandhi in London,* 58, 71–73. Characteristically, Gandhi never mentioned the issue in either *Satyagraha* or the *Autobiography*.

4. Gandhi, *Collected Works,* 6:88.
5. Payne, Gandhi, 167–68.
6. Quoted in Hunt, *Gandhi in London,* 76.
7. Gandhi, *Collected Works,* 6:188.
8. Ibid., 6:259.
9. Hunt, *Gandhi in London,* 77.
10. Gandhi, *Satyagraha,* 173.
11. Ibid., 172.
12. Colonial Office correspondence files, CO 291/103/39670, quoted in Hunt, *Gandhi in London,* 80.
13. Gandhi, *Satyagraha,* 174.
14. Quoted in Hunt, *Gandhi in London,* 66.
15. Churchill, *Complete Speeches,* 707.
16. See Herman, *Community, Nonviolence.*
17. He even says in *Satyagraha,* "I have no idea when the phrase 'passive resistance' was first used in English, and by whom" (153).
18. Hardiman, *Feeding the Baniya.*
19. Herman, *Community, Nonviolence;* Green, *Tolstoy and Gandhi;* and Green, *Origins of Nonviolence.*
20. Hunt, *Gandhi and Nonconformists;* Gandhi, *Satyagraha,* 153.
21. Hunt, *Gandhi in London,* 96.
22. Ibid., 97.
23. Gandhi, *Satyagraha,* 156.
24. The quotation is from "Yeravda Mandir," in Gandhi, *Selected Writings,* 46. Maganlal still won the prize.
25. Ibid., 156.
26. Quoted in Swan, *Gandhi,* 147.
27. Payne, *Gandhi,* 171–72; Hunt, *Gandhi in London,* 96.
28. Green, *Gandhi,* 171.
29. Gandhi, *Collected Works,* 356.
30. Payne, *Gandhi,* 174.
31. Green, *Gandhi,* 171–72.
32. Payne, *Gandhi,* 194.
33. "Further Considerations," February 29, 1908, quoted in Swan, *Gandhi,* 161–62.
34. Gandhi, *Satyagraha,* 217.
35. Gandhi, *Satyagraha;* Payne, *Gandhi,* 181–83.
36. Swan, *Gandhi,* 163.

37. Gandhi, *Satyagraha*, 249–50.
38. Morgan, *Young Man in a Hurry*, 218.
39. Bonham Carter, *Intimate Portrait*, 4.
40. Morgan, *Young Man in a Hurry*, 220.
41. Gilbert, *Companion*, 2:2, 820.
42. Brown, *Prisoner of Hope*, 343.
43. Quoted in Manchester, *Visions of Glory*, 403.
44. Bonham Carter, *Intimate Portrait*, 131.
45. Quoted in Morgan, *Young Man in a Hurry*, 255.
46. See Roberts, *Eminent Churchillians*, 213.
47. Ibid., 212.
48. Morgan, *Young Man in a Hurry*, 289. On eugenics and minimum wage law, see Freeden, "Eugenics and Progressive Thought."
49. Masterman, *C.F.G. Masterman*, 144.

CHAPTER 9. *Break Point*

1. Srivastava, *Five Stormy Years*, 147.
2. The most detailed accounts of the shooting are in ibid. and Datta, *Dhingra*.
3. Srivastava, *Five Stormy Years*, 25.
4. Letter to Hermann Kallenbach, August 7, 1909, quoted in Hunt, *Gandhi and Nonconformists*, 125.
5. Prabu and Rao, *Mind of Mahatma*, 335; Tendulkar, *Mahatma*, 2:6.
6. Srivastava, *Five Stormy Years*, 81.
7. Wolpert, *Morley and India*, 124.
8. Blunt, *My Diaries*, 2:288.
9. Letter of August 7, 1909, in Pyarelal Collection, quoted in Hunt, *Gandhi in London*, 125.
10. Payne, *Gandhi*, 186.
11. Gandhi, *Satyagraha*, 174.
12. Quoted in Payne, *Gandhi*, 190.
13. Ibid., 191.
14. Swan, *Gandhi*, 174–75.
15. Ibid., 174.
16. Ibid., 175.
17. Srivastava, *Five Stormy Years*, 150–51.
18. Ibid., 127, 64–65.
19. Hunt, *Gandhi in London*, 125, 126–27.
20. Gandhi, *Collected Works*, 10: 190.
21. Ibid., 10:159.
22. Ibid., 10:63.
23. On August 10. Ibid., 10:24.
24. Gandhi, *Satyagraha*, 313.
25. Hunt, *Gandhi and Nonconformists*, 133.

26. Letter of November 12, 1909, in Gandhi, *Collected Works,* 10: 234–35.

27. Gandhi, *Collected Works,* 10:108, 9.

28. Gandhi, *Collected Works,* 35:245–58.

29. "Letter to a Hindoo," in Tolstoy, *Complete Works,* 35:245–58.

30. Maine was an eminent legal historian and former legal member of the viceroy's council in the years following the Mutiny. His thesis would be essential to Gandhi's view of rural India for the rest of his life. See Iyer, *Moral and Political Thought.*

31. Gandhi, *Collected Works,* 10:168–69.

32. Ibid., 10:201–2.

33. Ibid., 10:315.

34. The best edition is found in Gandhi, *Hind Swaraj,* which includes the preface to the original English edition published in Johannesburg in 1910.

35. Ibid., 19.

36. The complete revised text is in ibid., 5–125.

37. Ibid., 28.

38. Ibid., 36–37, 33.

39. These were Chesterton's words, not Gandhi's, in his *Illustrated News* article.

40. Ibid., 69.

41. Ibid., 47.

42. Letter to Lord Ampthill, October 30, 1909, in Gandhi, *Collected Works,* 10:202.

43. Ibid., 10:90.

44. In the preface, Gandhi, *Hind Swaraj,* 7.

45. Srivastava, *Five Stormy Years,* 127.

46. Gandhi, *Hind Swaraj,* 5n2.

47. Blunt, *My Diaries,* 2:270. It is extremely doubtful that Churchill had any idea what Gandhi was planning. But someone may have told him about Tolstoy's *"Letter to a Hindoo,"* which proposed much the same thing.

48. Gandhi, *Collected Works,* 10:143–44.

49. Gandhi, *Hind Swaraj,* 113.

50. Green, *Gandhi,* 198–99.

51. Swan, *Gandhi,* 226.

52. Ibid., 231.

CHAPTER 10. *Parting of the Ways*

1. Churchill, *Amid These Storms,* 68.

2. Morgan, *Young Man in a Hurry,* 291.

3. Manchester, *Visions of Glory,* 420–21.

4. R. S. Churchill, *Companion,* 2:2, 1033.

5. Churchill, *Complete Speeches,* I:1028.

6. As Manchester points out in *Visions of Glory,* 416.

7. Gandhi, *Collected Works,* 10:188.

8. Quoted in Morgan, *Young Man in a Hurry,* 303.

9. Churchill, *Complete Speeches,* 2:1877.

10. Ibid., 1878.

11. Speech of May 13, 1901, in Churchill, *Complete Speeches,* 1:82.

12. Similar views are reflected in Leo Amery's conception of empire, discussed in Louis, *In the Name of God,* 68–69.

13. Quoted in Arnold, *Gandhi,* 155.

14. See Herman, *To Rule the Waves.*

15. Churchill, *World Crisis,* 1:123–24.

16. Bonham Carter, *Intimate Portrait,* 188.

17. The classic example was his fierce opposition to the increase in naval estimates demanded by the Admiralty in 1909, the resolution of which Churchill described this way: "The Admiralty demanded six [battleships]; the economists offered four; we finally compromised on eight." See also Ben-Moshe, *Strategy and History,* 11–12.

18. Jablonsky, *Great Game,* 50–51.

19. Letter of November 30, 1913, in R. S. Churchill, *Young Statesmen,* 684.

20. Morgan, *Young Man in a Hurry,* 364.

21. Payne, *Gandhi,* 264.

22. As noted by Swan, *Gandhi,* 233.

23. Gandhi, *Collected Works,* 12:147.

24. Swan, *Gandhi,* 236.

25. Arnold, *Gandhi,* 63.

26. Quoted in Brown, *Prisoner of Hope,* 90.

27. Gandhi, *Collected Works,* 11:359.

28. Ibid.

29. Swan, *Gandhi,* 236.

30. Undated letter from Sarvodaya Library, Phoenix, Natal, quoted in Swan, *Gandhi,* 242.

31. Ibid., 114.

32. Ibid., 19, 114; Arnold, *Gandhi,* 45.

33. On the tax, see Swan, *Gandhi,* 23–24, 194.

34. Payne, *Gandhi,* 258.

35. Interview with *Rand Daily Mail,* October 22, 1913, in Gandhi, *Collected Works,* 13:375.

36. Swan, *Gandhi,* 245.

37. Gandhi, *Collected Works,* 13:372.

38. Swan, *Gandhi,* 250.

39. Payne, *Gandhi,* 259.

40. See Gandhi, "Nonviolence in Peace and War," in *Selected Writings,* 61.

41. Quoted in Green, *Gandhi,* 216; Gandhi, *Collected Works,* 3:223.
42. Unfinished letter of April 22, 1914, in Gandhi, *Collected Works,* 14:154.
43. Green, *Gandhi,* 214–15.
44. Quoted in Swan, *Gandhi,* 250.
45. Ibid., 251.
46. Gandhi, *Collected Works,* 13:399.
47. Swan, *Gandhi,* 251–52.
48. Ibid., 251–54.
49. Payne, *Gandhi,* 265.
50. Ibid.
51. Quoted in Green, *Gandhi,* 140.
52. Quoted in Fischer, *Life of Gandhi,* 125.
53. Swan, *Gandhi,* 255–56.
54. Ibid., 254–55.
55. As pointed out by Swan, *Gandhi,* 256.
56. Quoted in Fischer, *Life of Gandhi,* 124.

CHAPTER 11. *A Bridgehead Too Far*

1. Churchill, *Complete Works: Early Speeches,* 7. The quotation from F. E. Smith is in Manchester, *Visions of Glory,* 20.
2. Confession of Faith, point 15; see Payne, *Gandhi,* 216.
3. Gandhi, *Autobiography,* 311.
4. Quoted in Hunt, *Gandhi in London,* 165.
5. Gandhi, *Collected Works,* 12:531; quoted in Green, *Gandhi,* 208.
6. Hunt, *Gandhi in London,* 169.
7. Quoted in Wolpert, *India,* 289.
8. Ibid., 173–74.
9. Quoted in Jablonsky, *Great Game,* 47.
10. Churchill, *World Crisis,* 1:225.
11. Which first appeared in 1911, Ben Moshe, *Strategy and History,* ibid., 16.
12. Gilbert, *Companion,* 3:2:850.
13. Jablonsky, *Great Game,* 49.
14. Quoted in Bonham Carter, *Intimate Portrait,* 275.
15. Manchester, *Visions of Glory,* 500.
16. This was Captain (later Admiral) Herbert Richmond, then assistant director of operations and a harsh critic of Churchill's policies in the Second World War as well. Quoted in d'Este, *Warlord.*
17. Gilbert, *Companion,* 3:1:180.
18. Churchill, *World Crisis,* 1:395.
19. Quoted in Addison, *Unexpected Hero,* 74.
20. Gilbert, *Companion,* 3:2:188, 191.

21. Asquith, *Letters to Venetia,* 345–46.
22. Keegan, *First World War,* 234.
23. Bonham Carter, *Intimate Portrait,* 262.
24. Farwell, *Armies of Raj,* 240.
25. Best, *Churchill and War,* 56.
26. Steel and Hart, *Gallipoli,* 6–7.
27. Gilbert, *Companion,* 3:1:436.
28. Ibid., 463.
29. As noted in Wallin, *By Ships Alone.*
30. Gilbert, *Companion,* 3:2:547–48.
31. Quoted in Fromkin, *Peace to End All,* 149.
32. Ibid., 131–33.
33. Fromkin, *Peace to End All,* 154; but also Wallin, *By Ships Alone,* and
    Churchill's own judgment in *World Crisis.*
34. Quoted in Keegan, *First World War,* 242.
35. Quoted ibid., 244–45.
36. Letter of April 29, 1915, in Gilbert, *Companion,* 3:2:835.
37. Ibid., 3:844.
38. Bonham Carter, *Intimate Portrait,* 330.
39. Gilbert, *Companion,* 3:2, quoted ibid., 341.
40. Gilbert, *Companion,* 3: 2:1250.
41. Churchill, *Amid These Storms,* 101, 103.
42. Keegan, *First World War,* 248.
43. Churchill, *World Crisis,* 168.

CHAPTER 12. *Gandhi's War*

1. Gandhi, *Collected Works,* 14:53 old style, quoted in Green,
   Gandhi, 266.
2. See letter to Gokhale, October 30, 1911, in Gandhi, *Collected Works,*
   12:84–86.
3. Payne, *Gandhi,* 288, 293; Arnold, *Gandhi,* 73.
4. Arnold, *Gandhi,* 73.
5. Brown, *Modern India,* 108.
6. Moon, *British Conquest,* 968.
7. Brown, *Modern India,* 139.
8. V. S. Srinivasa Sastri, quoted in Brown, *Rise to Power,* 42.
9. Gandhi, *Collected Works,* 14:413.
10. Srinivasa, *Five Stormy Years,* 8–9.
11. Quoted in Beloff, *Imperial Sunset,* 1:37.
12. Almost all were elected by municipalities or other official bodies. The
    other important concession for the future was giving Muslims reserved
    elected seats in the provincial councils, based on proportion of
    population. See Wasti, *Lord Minto.*

13. Spear, *History of India,* 2:179.

14. Moon, *British Conquest,* 959–60.

15. See Chapter 10 and Spear, *British Conquest,* 179–80.

16. Brown, *Rise to Power,* 30.

17. As noted in Naipaul, *Wounded Civilization,* 167.

18. Gandhi, *Autobiography,* 243.

19. Quoted in Brown, *Rise to Power,* 44–45.

20. Gandhi, *Autobiography,* 157.

21. Gandhi, *Collected Works,* 15:28.

22. Green, *Gandhi,* 184.

23. Quoted in ibid., 287.

24. Montagu, *Indian Diary,* 57.

25. The full text of the speech, with Gandhi's editing of passages that "in cold print would make the speech bad reading," is in *Collected Works,* 15:148–55.

26. Payne, *Gandhi,* 300.

27. Brown, *Rise to Power,* 27.

28. Wolpert, *Jinnah,* 28.

29. Shukla did get a chance to speak to the Congress, and at the insistence of the lawyer Prasad, it did pass a mild resolution calling for an official board of investigation of conditions in Champaran. But the issue would have been forgotten if Shukla had not decided to approach Gandhi. Payne, *Gandhi,* 305.

30. Brown, *Rise to Power,* 55.

31. Ibid., 62–63; Basu, *Rift and Reunion,* 178–79.

32. Brown, *Rise to Power,* 76.

33. Gandhi, *Autobiography,* 364.

34. Letter dated April 10, 1917, in Gandhi, *Collected Works,* 15:328–29.

35. Gandhi, *Autobiography,* 366.

36. Prasad, *Gandhi and Bihar,* 5.

37. Ibid., 15.

38. Quoted in Brown, *Rise to Power,* 65.

39. Gandhi, *Collected Works,* 15:335–36.

40. Payne, *Gandhi,* 310; Gandhi, *Autobiography,* 372.

41. Brown, *Rise to Power,* 67.

42. Quoted ibid., 68.

43. Gandhi, *Autobiography,* 370.

44. Brown, *Rise to Power,* 79.

45. Gandhi, *Autobiography,* 372.

46. Ibid., 373.

47. Quoted in Brown, *Rise to Power,* 82.

48. For example, the speech in Surat of January 31, 1922, in Gandhi, *Collected Works,* 26:56.

49. Brown, *Rise to Power,* 83–88, 101.

50. Gandhi, *Autobiography,* 388; Payne, *Gandhi,* 324–25.
51. Quoted in Brown, *Rise to Power,* 103.
52. Ibid., 27.
53. Ordinarily, Westminster paid for overseas expeditions involving Indian forces. However, New Delhi voted an extraordinary grant to pick up the entire tab. Moon, *British Conquest,* 968–69.
54. Wolpert, *India,* 294.
55. Moon, *British Conquest,* 979.
56. Quoted in Beloff, *Imperial Sunset,* 1:161.
57. Gandhi, *Collected Works,* 15:509.
58. Ibid., 15:467.
59. Editorial, *Young India,* September 17, 1925, quoted in "Nonviolence in Peace and War," in Gandhi, *Selected Writings,* 36.
60. Quoted in Brown, *Rise to Power,* 149.
61. Ibid., 146.
62. Montagu, *Indian Diary,* 58.
63. Letter of April 30, 1918, in Gandhi, *Collected Works,* 17:12.
64. Quoted in Brown, *Rise to Power,* 126.
65. Speech at Naidad, June 21, 1918, in Gandhi, *Collected Works,* 17:79.
66. Gandhi, *Collected Works,* 17:86.
67. Letter of April 29, 1918, in Gandhi, *Collected Works,* 17:8.
68. Green, *Gandhi,* 268.
69. Gandhi, *Collected Works,* 17:88.
70. Letter of July 6, 1918, in Gandhi, *Collected Works,* 17:123, 124.
71. Gandhi, *Selected Writings,* 56; Gandhi, *Collected Works,* 17:124.
72. Payne, *Gandhi,* 328.
73. Quoted in Brown, *Rise to Power,* 127.
74. Moon, *British Conquest,* 980.
75. Quoted in Brown, *Rise to Power,* 131, 129.

CHAPTER 13. *Bloodshed*

1. For example, in the United Provinces. See Hasan, *Nationalism and Communal Politics,* 181–82.
2. Churchill, *Complete Speeches,* 3:2875.
3. Moon, *British Conquest,* 987.
4. Ibid., 987.
5. Brown, *Rise to Power,* 163; Wolpert, *India,* 298.
6. Brown, *Rise to Power,* 166.
7. Ibid., 169.
8. Quoted ibid., 171.
9. Ibid., 174.
10. Collett, *Butcher of Amritsar,* 253.
11. Ibid., 430.

12. Ibid., 261; Johar, *Heritage of Amritsar,* 135.

13. According to Dyer's own testimony to the Hunter Commission. See Johar, *Heritage of Amritsar,* 35. Collett, *Butcher of Amritsar,* 261, says between ten and fifteen minutes. Dyer and his men had expended some 1,650 shells; based on this figure, many believe the actual death toll was closer to five hundred or even a thousand.

14. Payne, *Gandhi,* 341–42.

15. Brown, *Rise to Power,* 176.

16. Ibid., 232.

17. Johar, *Heritage of Amritsar,* 142; Rao, Sastri: *Political Biography,* 58.

18. Chaudhuri, *Unknown Indian,* 404.

19. Collett, *Butcher of Amritsar,* 387.

20. Brown, *Rise to Power,* 233.

21. Ibid., 232–33.

22. Quoted in Brown, *Rise to Power,* 235.

23. Ibid., 236–37.

24. "The Congress Report on the Disorders in the Punjab," is in Gandhi, *Collected Works,* 20:1–182; see also Johar, *Heritage of Amritsar,* 136, 137.

25. Gandhi, *Collected Works,* 20:178, 179.

26. Hunter Report, quoted in Brown, *Rise to Power,* 240–41.

27. Editorial, *Young India,* July 20, 1920, in Gandhi, *Collected Works,* 21:71.

28. Ibid.

29. Ibid., 20:376.

30. Charmley, *End of Glory,* 146.

31. Jablonsky, *Great Game,* 61. In 1915 Churchill envisioned creating armored vehicles on treads large enough to crush lines of barbed wire, as well as "sweep the [German] trenches with machine gun fire." Churchill was certainly indispensable in bringing the vehicle (code-named tank) into development, production, and finally deployment in the Battle of the Somme in 1916. However, Churchill himself said, "There never was a person about whom it could be said 'This man invented the tank.' "

32. Quoted in Charmley, *End of Glory,* 150.

33. Raymond, *Uncensored Celebrities,* 105, 102, 106.

34. Women over twenty-one did not get the vote until 1928. Williams and Ramsden, *Ruling Britannia,* 379.

35. Ibid., 382.

36. Curtis, *Commonwealth of Nations.*

37. Quoted in Herman, *Idea of Decline,* 272.

38. Quoted in Manchester, *Visions of Glory,* 690.

39. Quoted ibid., 605; Blunt, *My Diaries,* 276.

40. Manchester, *Visions of Glory,* 671–73.

41. Especially in the face of Germany's rearmament in the 1930s. In fact, the

Ten Year Rule was not reversed until 1935. Manchester, *Visions of Glory,* 691.

42. Wilson diary, May 21, 1920, in Gandhi, *Companion,* 4:2:1104.

43. Ibid., 4:2:1214.

44. Manchester, *Visions of Glory,* 683.

45. "My own opinion is that the offense amounted to murder, or alternatively manslaughter." Letter to Lord Crewe, July 17, 1920, quoted in Collett, *Butcher of Amritsar,* 382.

46. Churchill, *Complete Speeches,* 3:2983.

47. Collett, *Butcher of Amritsar,* 379.

48. Wilson diary, May 17, 1920, in Gilbert, *Companion,* 4:2:1098.

49. Collett, *Butcher of Amritsar,* 374.

50. Bonar-Law to Churchill, July 8, 1920, in Gilbert, *Companion,* 4:2:1140.

51. Quoted in Collett, *Butcher of Amritsar,* 379–80.

52. Ibid., 381.

53. Morgan, *Young Man in a Hurry,* 183: "He deplored anti-Semitism whenever it arose." See also Feith, "Palestine and Zionism," 210–62, esp. 261–62, and Gilbert, *Churchill and the Jews.*

54. The text is in Churchill, *Complete Speeches,* 3:3005–14.

55. Sir William Sutherland to Lloyd George, July 9, 1920, in Gilbert, *Companion,* 4:2:1141.

56. Fisher diary, ibid., 4:2:1140.

57. Collett, *Butcher of Amritsar,* 384.

58. Gilbert, *Companion,* 4:2:1136.

59. Gandhi, *Autobiography,* 116.

60. Churchill, *Complete Speeches* 3:2946.

61. Nehru, *Toward Freedom,* 50.

62. Quoted in Collett, *Butcher of Amritsar,* 401.

63. Ibid., 401.

64. Gandhi, *Collected Works,* 21:47.

65. Brown, *Rise to Power,* 252.

CHAPTER 14. *Noncooperation*

1. Hasan, *Communal Politics,* 9.

2. Minault, *Khilafat Movement,* 5.

3. Brown, *Modern India,* 127.

4. Quoted in Hasan, *Communal Politics,* 107.

5. For example, see Gandhi, *Collected Works,* 26:26. This was the result, again, of his view of Indians as united by *race*—which was actually more inclusive of Indian minorities like Muslims, than were the ideologies of either Moderates or Extremists like Tilak.

6. Brown, *Rise to Power,* 156, 202.

7. Gandhi, *Collected Works,* 20:283.

8. Quoted in Payne, *Gandhi,* 349.

9. Green, *Gandhi,* 303.

10. Hasan, *Communal Politics,* 121.

11. Brown, *Rise to Power,* 263.

12. Ibid., 264.

13. Ibid., 266; Hasan, *Communal Politics,* 134.

14. Hasan, *Communal Politics,* 135.

15. The changes are summarized in Arnold, *Gandhi,* 115–17.

16. Gandhi, *Collected Works,* 22:252.

17. Blunt, *My Diaries,* 276.

18. Churchill, *Complete Speeches,* 3:2942; Council of Ministers meeting, February 9, 1922, in Gilbert, *Companion,* 4:3:1762.

19. Ibid., 4:3:1119.

20. Clayton, *British Empire as Superpower,* 112–14.

21. Ibid., 121.

22. Catherwood, *Churchill's Folly,* 81.

23. Haldane, *Insurrection in Mesopotamia,* 215.

24. Ibid., 217–18; Catherwood, *Churchill's Folly,* 86.

25. Churchill and Trenchard, August 29, 1920, in Gilbert, *Companion,* 4:2:1190.

26. These figures are from Busch, *Britain, India, and Arabs,* 408–9.

27. Quoted in Fromkin, *Peace to End All,* 452.

28. Quoted in Catherwood, *Churchill's Folly,* 87.

29. Heathcote, *Military in British India,* 239.

30. As noted in Keegan, *First World War,* 218.

31. Catherwood, *Churchill's Folly,* 104.

32. Manchester, *Visions of Glory,* 701, 703.

33. Fromkin, *Peace to End All,* 499.

34. Churchill, *Complete Speeches,* 3:3259.

35. Churchill had no problems with the notion of a Jewish homeland, as promised by the Balfour Declaration, although an independent Jewish national state seemed an unwarranted stretch in 1922. See Feith, "Palestine and Zionism," 262.

36. As promised in the 1922 Treaty of Sèvres. Catherwood, *Churchill's Folly,* 136, 150.

37. Fromkin, *Peace to End All,* 424–26, 562.

38. Clayton, *British Empire as Superpower,* 41, 295.

39. Gilbert, *Companion,* 4:3:1644–45.

40. Quoted in Chaudhuri, *Great Anarch!,* 23, and Pearson, *Private Lives,* 228.

41. Letter of September 19, 1922, in Gilbert, *Companion,* 4:3:1986.

42. Brown, *Prisoner of Hope,* 147.

43. Krishnadas, *Seven Months,* 30.

44. Keer, *Mahatma Gandhi,* 425.
45. Brown, *Rise to Power,* 257; Rao, *Sastri,* 87; Payne, *Gandhi,* 350.
46. Brown, *Rise to Power,* 309.
47. Ibid., 312.
48. Brown, *Prisoner of Hope,* 145.
49. Brown, *Rise to Power,* 316–17.
50. Moon, *British Conqest,* 653–54.
51. Quoted in Payne, *Gandhi,* 354.
52. Krishnadas, *Seven Months.*
53. Hasan, *Communal Politics,* 165.
54. November 5, 1921, resolution, 25:59, in Gandhi, *Collected Works.*
55. Ibid., 25:127.
56. Ibid., 22:1.
57. Payne, *Gandhi,* 359–60.
58. Gandhi, *Collected Works,* 26:55.
59. Quoted in Brown, *Rise to Power,* 328.
60. Gilbert, *Companion,* 4:2:1762–63.
61. Letter of February 10, 1922, ibid., 4:2:1764–65.
62. Ibid., 4:2:1765.
63. Gandhi, *Collected Works,* 26:295.
64. Editorial, *Young India,* January 26, 1922, in ibid., 20:20.
65. Payne, *Gandhi,* 361.
66. The text of the statement is in Gandhi, *Collected Works,* 26:381–85.
67. Quoted in Brown, *Rise to Power,* 343.

CHAPTER 15. *Reversal of Fortunes*

1. Quoted in Manchester, *Visions of Glory,* 745.
2. Quoted in Gilbert, *Churchill* IV, 890.
3. Viscount Templewood, *Nine Troubled Years,* 42–43.
4. Bonham Carter, *Intimate Portrait,* 382. Churchill admitted in *Painting as a Pastime* that the colors were "delicious to squeeze out."
5. Churchill, *Painting as a Pastime,* 222, 226.
6. Pearson, *Private Lives,* 200–1.
7. Letter of February 24, 1924, in Gilbert, *Companion,* 5:1:114.
8. Charmley, *End of Glory,* 197.
9. Quoted in Gilbert, *Prophet of Truth,* 42.
10. Williams and Ramsden, *Ruling Britannia,* 384.
11. Gilbert, *Prophet of Truth,* 57–58.
12. Ibid., 59.
13. Gandhi, *Collected Works,* 27:6.
14. Ibid., 27: 7–8.
15. Brown, *Prisoner of Hope,* 182–83.
16. Letter of September 15, 1924, Gandhi, *Collected Works,* 29:155–56.

17. Quoted in Brown, *Prisoner of Hope,* 176.

18. Later he would write, "Of the English books [read at Yeravda], Gibbon takes easily the first place." Gandhi, *Collected Works,* 29:134.

19. Ibid., 27:8.

20. Ibid., 29:408.

21. Ibid., 27:9.

22. Gandhi, *Autobiography,* 442.

23. Payne, *Gandhi,* 321.

24. Quoted ibid., 376.

25. As noted in Muggeridge, *Green Stick,* 110.

26. Among the books he read was Mansar Ali's *Leaves from the Companions of the Prophet* and the Koran.

27. Interestingly, so did India's untouchables. See Ahmed, *Jinnah, Pakistan,* 101–3, 65–67.

28. Quoted in Brown, *Civil Disobedience,* 24. The figures on violence appear on 10.

29. Brown, *Prisoner of Hope,* 207.

30. The mustache was a symbol of Hindu masculinity. See Naipaul, *Wounded Civilization,* 123.

31. Quoted in Mayo, *Mother India,* 155.

32. Gandhi, *Collected Works,* 34:322.

33. Keer, *Gandhi,* 224.

34. Green, *Gandhi,* 296.

35. Desai, *Bliss It Was;* Green, *Gandhi,* 294.

36. Desai, *Bliss It Was,* 4.

37. Ibid.

38. Fischer, *Life of Gandhi,* 73–74, 75.

39. Brown, *Rise to Power,* 42.

40. Keer, *Gandhi,* 85, 509.

41. Desai, *Bliss It Was,* 4.

42. Ibid., 19.

43. Ibid., 20.

44. Quoted in Fischer, *Life of Gandhi,* 375.

45. See Green, *Gandhi,* 336.

46. Slade, *Spirit's Pilgrimage;* Green, *Gandhi,* 304. On Churchill's role in creating Anglo-Iranian, the ancestor of today's British Petroleum, see Herman, *To Rule the Waves,* 486.

47. Rolland, *Mahatma Gandhi,* 3, 5.

48. Ibid., 62, 97.

49. Ibid., 6–7, 247.

50. Ibid., 246, 33.

51. Gandhi and Rolland, *Correspondance,* Letter of March 22, 1922, 14; Green, *Gandhi,* 246.

52. Payne, *Gandhi,* 452.

53. Quoted in Gilbert, *Prophet of Truth,* 116.

54. Quoted in Charmley, *End of Glory,* 212.

55. As pointed out in Johnson, *Modern Times,* 164.

56. Quoted in Charmley, *End of Glory,* 208.

57. Gilbert, *Companion,* 5:1:305.

58. See Herman, *To Rule the Waves,* 520–21; Gilbert, *Companion,* 5:1:306.

59. See the same memorandum, ibid., 5:1:304.

60. Gilbert, *Prophet of Truth,* 159.

61. Charmley, *End of Glory,* 218.

62. Gilbert, *Prophet of Truth,* 217–19.

63. Ibid., 226.

64. Charmley, *End of Glory,* 202.

65. Ibid., 221.

66. Manchester, *Alone,* 14.

67. Ibid., 10; Gilbert, *Prophet of Truth,* 301.

68. Gilbert, *Prophet of Truth,* 302.

69. Ibid.

70. Quoted in Charmley, *Lord Lloyd,* 84.

71. Gandhi, *Collected Works,* 26:463–64. The correspondent was the American columnist Drew Pearson.

72. Ibid.

73. Ibid., 26:464, and Charmley, *Lord Lloyd,* 84.

74. Gilbert, *Prophet of Truth,* 273–78.

75. Ibid., 326.

76. Thomas Jones diary, in Gilbert, *Companion,* 5:1:1473.

77. Manchester, *Visions of Glory,* 250.

78. Gilbert, *Companion,* 5:2:86–87.

79. Gilbert, *Prophet of Truth,* 350.

80. Ibid., 595–96.

CHAPTER 16. *Eve of Battle*

1. Quoted in Chaudhuri, *Great Anarch!,* 262.

2. Ibid., 263.

3. Moon, *British Conquest,* 1027.

4. Letter of November 8, 1927, quoted in Birkenhead, *Halifax,* 241.

5. Mayo, *Mother India,* 49, 96–97.

6. Ibid., 34–35, 38.

7. Ibid., 268.

8. Ibid., 195.

9. Quoted in Gilbert, *Prophet of Truth,* 243.

10. Gandhi's review of Mayo in *Young India,* September 15, 1927, in *Collected Works,* 40:105–14.

11. Chaudhuri, *Great Anarch!,* 256.

12. Moon, *British Conquest*, 1028.
13. Quoted in Brown, *Civil Disobedience*, 26.
14. Brown, *Prisoner of Hope*, 217.
15. Gandhi, *Collected Works*, 41:447.
16. Arnold, *Gandhi*, 140.
17. Brown, *Prisoner of Hope*, 218–19.
18. Chaudhuri, *Great Anarch!*, 261.
19. Quoted in ibid., 264.
20. Chaudhuri, *Great Anarch!*, 263.
21. Brown, *Civil Disobedience*, 35.
22. One province alone, Bengal, owed nearly 140,000 rupees, while seven provinces had failed to pay their regular contributions for 1929 to the central fund. See Brown, *Prisoner of Hope*, 256.
23. Ibid., 223.
24. Gandhi to Nehru, January 17, 1929, quoted in Brown, *Civil Disobedience*, 39.
25. Brown, *Prisoner of Hope*, 224.
26. Gandhi, *Collected Works*, 46:377.
27. Quoted in Roberts, *Holy Fox*, 4–5.
28. Ibid., 20.
29. Moorhouse, *India Britannica*, 177.
30. Ferguson, *Empire*, 215.
31. Roberts, *Holy Fox*, 23.
32. Ibid., 24.
33. Templewood, *Nine Troubled Years*, 43–44.
34. Roberts, *Holy Fox*, 20.
35. Quoted in Birkenhead, *Halifax*, 224.
36. Quoted in Brown, *Prisoner of Hope*, 230.
37. Johnson, *Viscount Halifax*, 222.
38. Nirad Chaudhuri remembered: "I was utterly unconvinced the offer was sincere." *Great Anarch!*, 270.
39. Brown, *Civil Disobedience*, 64.
40. Templewood, *Nine Troubled Years*, 45; Low, *Britain and Indian Nationalism*, 22.
41. Gilbert, *Companion*, 5:2:40n2.
42. Ibid., 5:2:27.
43. Manchester, *Visions of Glory*, 845.
44. Gilbert, *Prophet of Truth*, 355.
45. Birkenhead, *Halifax*, 274.
46. The figure is in Mayo, *Mother India*, 20.
47. According to Charmley, *End of Glory*, 241.
48. This phrase actually comes from a later Churchill article, in Gilbert, *Companion*, 5:2:40n2.
49. Gilbert, *Prophet of Truth*, 356–57.

50. Louis, *In the Name of God,* passim.
51. Gilbert, *Companion,* 5:2:34–35.
52. Ibid., 5:2:115.
53. Gandhi, *Collected Works,* 47:348–49.
54. Brown, *Prisoner of Hope,* 232.
55. For example, the Punjab police official commenting on the Lahore Congress, noted in Brown, *Prisoner of Hope,* 234; Brown, *Civil Disobedience,* 79; and Chaudhuri, *Great Anarch!,* 44–45.
56. Gandhi, *Collected Works,* 47:381, 405.
57. Brown, *Prisoner of Hope,* 232, and Brown, *Civil Disobedience,* 70.
58. Sastri, *Letters of Sastri,* 183–84.
59. Gilbert, *Companion,* 5:2:110.
60. Johnson, *Viscount Halifax,* 238.
61. Birkenhead, *Halifax,* 276.
62. The account is from Nanda, *Nehrus,* 322–24.
63. Birkenhead, *Halifax,* 277, 275.
64. Quoted in Brown, *Civil Disobedience,* 79.
65. Gilbert, *Companion,* 5:2:126.
66. Ibid., 5:2:128–29.

CHAPTER 17. *Salt*

1. Keer, *Gandhi,* 518.
2. Brown, *Prisoner of Hope,* 234–35.
3. Brown, *Civil Disobedience,* 80.
4. Gandhi, *Collected Works,* 48: 206–7.
5. Gandhi, *Hind Swaraj,* 20n24.
6. Brown, *Prisoner of Hope,* 236.
7. Brown, *Civil Disobedience,* 95.
8. Gandhi, *Collected Works,* 48:390.
9. Ibid., 48:362, 365.
10. Fischer, *Life of Gandhi,* 271.
11. Payne, *Gandhi,* 389.
12. Desai, *Bliss It Was,* 11
13. Payne, *Gandhi,* 389.
14. Desai, *Bliss It Was,* 11–12.
15. Gandhi, *Collected Works,* 48:392–93.
16. Brown, *Civil Disobedience,* 101.
17. Ibid., 104.
18. Gandhi, *Collected Works,* 49:6.
19. See Irwin's Letter to the Secretary of State for India, India Office Library, Mss. Eur. C 152/6, 73, quoted in Birkenhead, *Halifax,* 282.
20. Roberts, *Holy Fox,* 34.
21. Gandhi, *Collected Works,* 49:13–17.

22. Ibid., 49:15–18.
23. Weber, *On Salt March,* 345–46.
24. Gandhi, *Collected Works,* 49:34–35.
25. Fischer, *Life of Gandhi*, 275.
26. Gandhi, *Collected Works,* 49:102.
27. Ibid., 46.
28. Chaudhuri, *Great Anarch!,* 276, 278.
29. Brown, *Civil Disobedience,* 112.
30. Remarks at a Conservative Party meeting at Thanet, August 20, in Gilbert, *Companion,* 5:2:180–81, n3.
31. Fischer, *Life of Gandhi,* 277–78.
32. Ibid., 276.
33. Brown, *Prisoner of Hope,* 238–39.
34. Brown, *Civil Disobedience,* 113.
35. Fischer, *Life of Gandhi,* 275.
36. Brown, *Civil Disobedience,* 114.
37. Chaudhuri, *Great Anarch!,* 280.
38. Gandhi, *Collected Works,* 49:34.
39. Ibid., 49:108.
40. Ibid., 49:8.
41. Desai, *Bliss It Was,* 27.
42. Brown, *Civil Disobedience,* 127.
43. Ibid., 135.
44. Quoted ibid., 138.
45. Chaudhuri, *Great Anarch!,* 280.
46. Ibid., 278.
47. Brown, *Civil Disobedience,* 124.
48. Quoted in Fischer, *Life of Gandhi,* 277.
49. Editorial, *Young India,* April 10, 1930, in Gandhi, *Collected Works,* 49:61, 62.
50. Quoted in Brown, *Prisoner of Hope,* 245.
51. Quoted in Brown, *Civil Disobedience,* 147.
52. Gilbert, *Companion,* 5:2:136.
53. Remarks at a Conservative Party meeting at Thanet, August 20, 1930, ibid., 5:2:180–81, n2.
54. Ibid., 5:2:180.
55. Moon, *British Conquest,* 1045.
56. Moore, *Crisis of Unity,* 115.
57. Moon, *British Conquest,* 1044.
58. Roberts, *Holy Fox,* 35.
59. Gilbert, *Companion,* 5:2:180–81, n3.

CHAPTER 18. *Round Tables and Naked Fakirs*

1. Charmley, *Lord Lloyd,* 173.
2. Gilbert, *Companion,* 5:2:199.
3. Letter of September 23, 1930, ibid., 5:2:185.
4. Ibid., 5:2:185–86.
5. Ibid., 5:2:186.
6. Ibid., 5:2:187, 183, 201.
7. Moore, *Crisis of Unity,* 143.
8. Ibid., 159.
9. Churchill, *Complete Speeches,* 5:4934.
10. Ibid., 5:4935.
11. Ibid., 5:4936.
12. Ibid., 5:4937.
13. Ibid., 5:4938.
14. Gilbert, *Companion,* 5:232–33 n2.
15. Quoted in Charmley, *Lord Lloyd,* 172.
16. Gilbert, *Companion,* 5:2:231.
17. Taylor, *Origins of Second World War,* 154.
18. Arnold, *Gandhi,* 151.
19. Brown, *Civil Disobedience,* 175.
20. Quoted in Payne, *Gandhi,* 404.
21. Brown, *Prisoner of Hope,* 248.
22. Payne, *Gandhi,* 404.
23. See Sarkar, "The Logic of Gandhian Nationalism: Civil Disobedience and the Gandhi-Irwin Pact (1930–31)," IHR 3:1 (July 1976), 114–46; 114.
24. Gandhi, *Collected Works,* 51:223.
25. Brown, *Civil Disobedience,* 188.
26. Gilbert, *Companion,* 5:2:243.
27. Telegram to Baldwin, January 23, 1931, in Gilbert, *Prophet of Truth,* 380.
28. Churchill, *Complete Speeches,* 5:4950, 4951, 4952.
29. Ibid., 5:4950.
30. Ibid., 5:4955, 4956.
31. Ibid., 5:4956.
32. Gilbert, *Companion,* 5:2:252.
33. Ibid., 5:2:252–53 n1.
34. Ibid., 5:2:250.
35. Ibid., 5:2:257.
36. Churchill, *Complete Speeches,* 5:4971.
37. Gilbert, *Companion,* 5:2:253–54.
38. Ibid., 5:2:258.
39. Ibid., 5:2:258–59.

40. Gilbert, *Prophet of Truth,* 388.
41. Gilbert, *Companion,* 5:2:269.
42. Gilbert, *Prophet of Truth,* 391.
43. Churchill, *Complete Speeches,* 5:4985.
44. For example, see Geoffrey Dawson to Lord Irwin, March 5, in Gilbert, *Companion,* 5:2:291, suggesting that Baldwin was on the brink of resigning.
45. Gilbert, *Prophet of Truth,* 394.
46. Ibid., 395.
47. Martin, *Battle,* 229.
48. Churchill, *Complete Speeches,* 5:4993.
49. Ibid., 5:4995.
50. Ibid., 5:4999.
51. Ibid.
52. Gilbert, *Companion,* 5:2:302.
53. Ibid., 5:2:303.
54. Martin, *Battle,* 229.
55. Churchill, *Complete Speeches,* 5:5004.
56. Gilbert, *Prophet of Truth,* 401–2.
57. Gilbert, *Companion,* 5:2:308 n1.

CHAPTER 19. *Contra Mundum*

1. Hunt, *Gandhi in London,* 182.
2. Ibid., 179–80.
3. Baldwin certainly wanted him to take the post. Irwin privately and severely protested; and Churchill wrote later that he declined the offer. But if the Tories had won by a narrow margin, he would have been hard-pressed not to accept. See Gilbert, *Prophet of Truth,* 322, 326.
4. Gandhi, *Collected Works,* 34:322.
5. Ibid., 51:221, 223.
6. Shirer, *Gandhi,* 126, 133.
7. Quoted in Fischer, *Life of Ghandi,* 287.
8. Shirer, *Gandhi,* 58–59. The other press interviews are in Gandhi, *Collected Works,* 53:337–44.
9. Gandhi, *Collected Works,* 51:223.
10. Gilbert, *Prophet of Truth,* 413.
11. Churchill, *Complete Speeches,* 5:5061.
12. Ibid.
13. Gandhi, *Collected Works,* 53: 352.
14. Roberts, *Holy Fox,* 41.
15. Hunt, *Gandhi in London,* 182.
16. Muggeridge, *Green Stick,* 110, 189–190.
17. Hunt, *Gandhi in London,* 183.

18. *Times* obituary January 31, 1948, quoted in Hunt, *Gandhi in London,* 183.
19. Templewood, *Nine Troubled Years,* 63; letter to Willingdon, November 19, 1931, quoted in Brown, *Prisoner of Hope,* 257.
20. The equally tedious details are found in Moore, *Crisis of Unity.*
21. Again, the details are ibid., 220–21.
22. Shirer, *Gandhi,* 194.
23. Chaudhury, *Gandhi and Contemporaries,* 41.
24. Quoted in Hunt, *Gandhi in London,* 185.
25. Shirer, *Gandhi,* 194.
26. Gandhi, *Collected Works,* 53:466.
27. By going off the gold standard, and without consulting the Indian government, the government also kept the rupee pegged to sterling's new lower value. Moore, *Crisis of Unity,* 215.
28. Hunt, *Gandhi in London,* 183.
29. Ibid., 186.
30. Churchill, *Complete Speeches,* 5:5114–15.
31. Ibid., 5:5061.
32. Gilbert, *Companion,* 5:2:381.
33. Churchill, *Complete Speeches,* 5:5119, 5122.
34. Gilbert, *Companion,* 5:2:380n1. They included Cain, Demosthenes, Hannibal, Cicero, Vercingetorix (the Gaul chieftain defeated by Julius Caesar), El Cid, King Harald, Mary Queen of Scots, George III, Marie Antoinette, Metternich, Napoleon, General Ludendorff, and Robert E. Lee.
35. Hunt, *Gandhi in London,* 208.
36. Gandhi, *Collected Works,* 54:87.
37. Ibid., 54:329.
38. Shirer, *Gandhi,* 150.
39. Quoted in Brown, *Prisoner of Hope,* 255.
40. Moore, *Crisis of Unity,* 246–47; Brown, *Prisoner of Hope,* 261.
41. Moore, *Crisis of Unity,* 248.
42. Gandhi, *Collected Works,* 54:343–46.
43. Payne, *Gandhi,* 434; Moore, *Crisis of Unity,* 250.
44. Gilbert, *Prophet of Truth,* 421–23.
45. Letter of January 5, in Gilbert, *Companion,* 5:2:391.
46. Ibid., 5:2:397.
47. Moore, *Crisis of Unity,* 251.
48. Lord Lloyd to Baldwin on March 3, 1931, in Gilbert, *Companion,* 5:2:292–93.
49. Shirer, *Gandhi,* 166.
50. Article for *Daily Mail,* February 5, 1931, in Gilbert, *Companion,* 5:2:258–59 n1.
51. Gilbert, *Prophet of Truth,* 413.
52. Churchill, *Complete Speeches,* 5:5028.
53. Gilbert, *Companion,* 5:3:308 n1.

54. Ibid., 5:2:436.

55. Churchill, *Complete Speeches,* 5:4971, 4973.

CHAPTER 20. *Last Ditch*

1. Payne, *Gandhi,* 434.

2. Moore, *Crisis of Unity,* 262–63.

3. Gandhi. *Collected Works,* 25:479 Old Style.

4. Quoted in Jaffrelot, *Ambedkar,* 58.

5. Moore, *Crisis of Unity,* 265.

6. Gandhi, *Collected Works,* 56.

7. Payne, *Gandhi,* 440.

8. Statement to the press, September 16, 1932, in Gandhi, *Collected Works,* 57:40.

9. Letter of September 9, 1932, ibid., 57:9.

10. Ibid., 57:30.

11. Described in letter to Mirabehn, September 15, 1932, ibid., 57:34.

12. Payne, *Gandhi,* 442.

13. Jaffrelot, *Ambedkar,* argues that Ambedkar's theory anticipates the anthropological theories of caste of Louis Dumont and others.

14. Ambedkar, *Essential Writings.*

15. Quoted in Jaffrelot, *Ambedkar,* 66.

16. Quoted in Chaudhury, *Gandhi and Contemporaries,* 43.

17. Quoted in Brown, *Prisoner of Hope,* 267.

18. Moore, *Crisis of Unity,* 265.

19. Brown, *Prisoner of Hope,* 270.

20. Payne, *Gandhi,* 457.

21. Quoted in Brown, *Prisoner of Hope,* 275.

22. Gilbert, *Prophet of Truth,* 437–38.

23. Gilbert, *Companion,* 5:2:448, 447.

24. Charmley, *Lord Lloyd,* 182.

25. See letter of July 1 to Sir John Simon, in Gilbert, *Companion,* 5:2:450.

26. Letter to Lord Sydenham, January 7, ibid., 5:2:513.

27. Quoted in Charmley, *Lord Lloyd,* 183.

28. Gilbert, *Companion,* 5:2:532; Charmley, *Lord Lloyd,* 185.

29. Gilbert, *Prophet of Truth,* 474.

30. Speech of June 27, 1932, in Gilbert, *Companion,* 5:2:449n1.

31. Gilbert, *Prophet of Truth,* 456.

32. Speech at Epping, February 23, 1933, in Churchill, *Complete Speeches,* 5:5224.

33. Gilbert, *Companion,* 5:2:621.

34. The phrase is from Charmley, *End of Glory,* 157.

35. Gilbert, *Prophet of Truth,* 472.

36. Gilbert, *Companion,* 5:2:567.

37. The remark is from a speech on January 30, 1931, in Churchill, *Complete Speeches,* 5:4968.

38. Gilbert, *Companion,* 5:2:579.

39. Slade to Churchill, September 10, 1934, ibid., 5:2:868.

40. Ibid., 5:2:918–19.

41. Gilbert, *Prophet of Truth,* 600.

42. Speech of February 20, 1935, in Churchill, *Complete Speeches,* 5:5497.

43. Quoted in Gilbert, *Prophet of Truth,* 615.

44. Ibid., 617.

45. Ross, *Emissary,* 20, 29.

46. Birla, *Shadow of Mahatma,* xv.

47. Ibid., ix.

48. Ibid., 189–90.

49. Ibid, 191.

50. Manchester, *Visions of Glory,* 883.

CHAPTER 21. *Against the Current*

1. Gilbert, *Prophet of Truth,* 619.

2. Chaudhuri, *Great Anarch!,* 437–38.

3. Ibid., 439, 445, 437.

4. Gilbert, *Prophet of Truth,* 399.

5. Tendulkar, *Mahatma,* 5:271.

6. Brown, *Modern India,* 279, 286.

7. Ibid., 287.

8. Arnold, *Gandhi,* 185.

9. Payne, *Gandhi,* 467.

10. Gandhi, *Collected Works,* 70:296.

11. Brown, *Prisoner of Hope,* 300.

12. Ibid., 301.

13. Green, *Gandhi,* 342.

14. See letter to Harilal's son Manu, June 6, 1935, in Gandhi, *Collected Works,* 67:139.

15. Kalarthi, *Ba and Bapu,* 90–91.

16. Gandhi, *Collected Works,* 69:77–78.

17. Green, *Gandhi,* 343.

18. Quoted in Payne, *Gandhi,* 473.

19. For example, Lala Lajpat Rai. See Ali, *Emergence of Pakistan,* 25.

20. Quoted in Wolpert, *Jinnah,* 71.

21. See Ahmed, *Jinnah, Pakistan,* 71–72.

22. Ali, *Emergence of Pakistan,* 25.

23. Quoted in Ahmed, *Jinnah, Pakistan,* 74.

24. Golwalkar, *We or our Nationhood Defined* (1938), quoted in ibid., 67.

25. Quoted in ibid., 74.

26. Wolpert, *Jinnah*, 152.

27. Brown, *Modern India*, 296.

28. Brown, *Prisoner of Hope*, 295; Ali, *Emergence of Pakistan*, 27–28.

29. Talbot, *Provincial Politics;* Ali, *Emergence of Pakistan*, 29.

30. Nehru, *Toward Freedom*, 365.

31. Brown, *Modern India*, 296.

32. Gandhi, *Collected Works*, 73:136; Wolpert, *Jinnah*, 160.

33. Wolpert, *Jinnah*, 163.

34. Ali, *Emergence of Pakistan*, 31.

35. Chamberlain's arrival was not the first public event broadcast by the new and primitive television—that honor belonged to the coronation of the new king George VI.

36. Roberts, *Eminent Churchillians*, 20.

37. Taylor, *Origins*, 292.

38. Gilbert, *Prophet of Truth*, 990.

39. "It was a triumph for all that was best and most enlightened in British life," writes historian Alan Taylor with an overlay of irony, "a triumph for those who had preached equal justice between peoples," including for the three million Sudeten Germans who had hitherto lived under Czech rule. Taylor, *Origins*, 184.

40. Gilbert, *Prophet of Truth*, 990, 981.

41. Churchill, *While England Slept*, 218.

42. Gilbert, *Prophet of Truth*, 1011–12.

43. Taylor, *Origins*, 76, 285.

44. Quoted in Lukacs, *Duel*, 39.

45. Gilbert, *Wilderness Years*, 141.

46. Ibid., 111.

47. For example, Charmley, *End of Glory*, and Charmley, *Churchill's Grand Alliance*, passim.

48. Quoted in Roberts, *Eminent Churchillians*, 141–42.

49. According to John Charmley, if the Government "did not actually authorize" Desmond Morton to leak its estimates of German air strength to Churchill, "ministers were not sorry he had them." *End of Glory*, 292.

50. Gilbert, *Prophet of Truth*, 918–19.

51. Hyde, *Baldwin*, 352.

52. Taylor, *Origins*, 132.

53. Roberts, *Holy Fox*, 47–48.

54. Ibid.

55. Taylor, *Origins*, 184.

56. Manchester, *Alone*, 101.

57. Gilbert, *Prophet of Truth*, 680.

58. For example, speech of March 12, 1931, Churchill, *Complete Speeches*, 5:4995.

59. Gilbert, *Companion*, 5:3:704–5.

60. Quoted in Gilbert, *Wilderness Years,* 111.
61. Gilbert, *Prophet of Truth,* 561–62.
62. Ibid., 441, 561.
63. Ibid., 977.
64. Gilbert, *Wilderness Years,* 116.
65. Ibid., 77.
66. Quoted in Gilbert, *Prophet of Truth,* 1001–2.
67. Quoted in Churchill, *His Father's Son,* 105.
68. Gilbert, *Prophet of Truth,* 610–11.
69. Pearson, *Private Lives,* 230.
70. Charmley, *End of Glory,* 300–1.
71. Churchill, *His Father's Son,* 103–4.
72. Manchester, *Alone,* 385.
73. Churchill, *His Father's Son,* 448.
74. Charmley, *End of Glory,* 300.
75. Gilbert, *Prophet of Truth,* 603.
76. Quoted in Gilbert, *Wilderness Years,* 152.
77. Gilbert, *Prophet of Truth,* 700.
78. Gilbert, *Companion,* 5:3:658.
79. Ibid., 5:3:730–31.
80. Gilbert, *Wilderness Years,* 157.
81. Dutton, *Anthony Eden,* 29.
82. Gilbert, *Prophet of Truth,* 905.

CHAPTER 22. *Edge of Darkness*

1. Taylor, *Origins,* 153.
2. Roberts, *Holy Fox,* 447.
3. Colvin, *Chamberlain Cabinet,* 146–47.
4. Gilbert, *Prophet of Truth,* 993.
5. Ibid., 999–1001.
6. Nicholson, *Diary.*
7. Gandhi, *Collected Works,* 74:79; Payne, *Gandhi,* 482.
8. Bose, *Collected Works,* 9:92.
9. Chaudhury, *Gandhi and Contemporaries,* 277.
10. Chaudhuri, *Great Anarch!,* 502–3.
11. For example, his speech, "India and Russia," February 22, 1942, in Nehru, *Independence,* 213–14.
12. Letter February 12, 1935, Bose, *Collected Works,* 8:91.
13. S. Das, *Subhas,* 307, 345.
14. Bose, *Collected Works,* 2:349, 351.
15. Chaudhury, *Gandhi and Contemporaries,* 282.
16. Bose, *Collected Works,* 8:3–30.

17. Just how bitter is reflected in Nirad Chaudhuri's memoir written fifty years after the event: Chaudhuri, *Great Anarch!,* 458–70.
18. Quoted ibid., 507.
19. Ibid., 507–8.
20. Chaudhury, *Gandhi and Contemporaries,* 283.
21. Ibid.
22. Chaudhuri, *Great Anarch!,* 510.
23. Quoted in Chaudhury, *Gandhi and Contemporaries,* 284.
24. Chaudhuri, *Great Anarch!,* 515.
25. Letter of October 24, 1940, quoted in Chaudhury, *Gandhi and Contemporaries,* 286.
26. Gandhi, *Collected Works,* 74:34.
27. Brown, *Prisoner of Hope,* 292–94.
28. Green, *Gandhi,* 345.
29. Churchill, *Gathering Storm,* 342–43.
30. Quoted in Colvin, *Chamberlain Cabinet,* 191.
31. Taylor, *Origins,* 197–98.
32. Gilbert, *Companion,* 5:3:1411–12, 1488.
33. Gilbert, *Prophet of Truth,* 1064–65.
34. Ibid., 1085.
35. Ibid., 1053.
36. The phrase is from Lord Wolmer, in a letter dated July 7, 1939, Gilbert, *Companion,* 5:3:1554.
37. Charmley, *End of Glory,* 364.
38. Quoted in Gilbert, *Prophet of Truth,* 1081.
39. Quoted ibid., 1063.
40. Ibid., 1103.
41. Manchester, *Alone,* 519.
42. Gilbert, *Prophet of Truth,* 1108.
43. Churchill, *Gathering Storm,* 406.
44. Colvin, *Chamberlain Cabinet,* 252.
45. Churchill, *Gathering Storm,* 408.
46. Quoted in Gilbert, *Prophet of Truth,* 1112.
47. Manchester, *Alone,* 543.
48. Gilbert, *Prophet of Truth,* 1113; Churchill, *Gathering Storm,* 410.

CHAPTER 23. *Collision Course*

1. Glendevon, *Viceroy at Bay,* 71–72.
2. Ibid., 73.
3. Ibid., 134. The Congress Working Committee had declared its opposition to India's participation in any future war as far back as May and did so again in August 1939. See Ahmad, *Indian Response,* 3.

4. For example, ibid., 4, and the discussion in Moon, *British Conquest,* 1086. Moon, to his credit, personally disagrees with this view.

5. According to Payne, *Gandhi,* 482. See also Parekh, *Colonialism,* for Gandhi's critique of Western civilization, esp. 82–84.

6. Gandhi, *Collected Works,* 75:241–42.

7. Quoted in Fischer, *Life of Gandhi,* 350.

8. Ibid., 350.

9. Gandhi, *Collected Works,* 76:156.

10. Ibid., 78:344.

11. Fischer, *Life of Gandhi,* 348.

12. Ibid.

13. The full quotation, recorded by an eyewitness, is: "Shoot Gandhi. And if that does not reduce them to submission, shoot a dozen leading members of the Congress; and if that does not suffice, shoot 200 or so until order is established." Roberts, *Holy Fox,* 72.

14. Churchill, *Blood, Sweat, and Tears,* 314.

15. "How to Combat Hitlerism," June 18, 1940, in Gandhi, *Collected Works,* 78: 343.

16. Chaudhuri, *Great Anarch!,* 534–35.

17. Gandhi, *Collected Works,* 76: 311–12.

18. Ibid., 76:327.

19. Nehru, *Toward Freedom,* 408.

20. Quoted in Brown, *Prisoner of Hope,* 270.

21. Quoted in Chaudhuri, *Great Anarch!,* 555–56.

22. Gandhi, *Collected Works,* 76:355.

23. Brown, *Modern India,* 299–300.

24. Ibid., 242.

25. Letter of October 11, 1937, in Gilbert, *Companion,* 5:3:789.

26. Glendevon, *Viceroy at Bay,* 144, 148.

27. Gandhi, *Collected Works,* 76:12, 58.

28. Brown, *Prisoner of Hope,* 314, 325.

29. Quoted in Ali, *Emergence of Pakistan,* 35.

30. Ibid.

31. The league did condemn Nazi aggression but warned that any Muslim cooperation depended on "justice and fair play" for Muslims, including no more constitutional concessions to the Hindus. Moon, *British Conquest,* 1087. After all, to Jinnah's mind the real enemy was not the Germans or even the British but the Indian National Congress.

32. Gandhi, *Collected Works,* 76:312.

33. Ibid., 77:241–42, 295.

34. Quoted in Chaudhury, *Gandhi and Contemporaries,* 283.

35. Quoted in Wolpert, *Jinnah,* 174–75.

36. Gandhi, *Collected Works,* 78:78–81.

37. Ibid., 78:403–4.

CHAPTER 24. *From Narvik to Bardoli*

1. Quoted in Cross, *Samuel Hoare,* 172.
2. Churchill, *Gathering Storm,* 461.
3. As noted in Lukacs, *Duel,* 29.
4. Colville, *Fringes of Power,* 113.
5. Ibid., 122, 123.
6. Quoted in Lukacs, *Duel,* 32.
7. Colville, *Fringes of Power,* 124.
8. Lukacs, *Duel,* 33.
9. Amery, *Diaries,* 3:358–60.
10. Churchill, *Blood, Sweat, and Tears,* 269.
11. Amery, *Diaries,* 3:365.
12. Ibid., 3:368–69.
13. Lukacs, *Duel,* 34.
14. Quoted in Roberts, *Eminent Churchillians,* 141.
15. Charmley, *End of Glory,* 394.
16. Colville, *Fringes of Power,* 142–43.
17. These quotations come from Halifax's notes from the meeting, quoted in Manchester, *Alone,* 669. The version of events on the ninth is taken from Colville, *Fringes of Power,* 142–43, who tells us he had the account from Churchill himself. Other versions exist, including Churchill's own in *Gathering Storm* (which misdates the meeting as May 10). Colville's seems the most accurate account, as well as the most plausible.
18. Lukacs, *Duel,* 6–7.
19. Colville, *Fringes of Power,* 142; Lukacs, *Duel,* 34.
20. Churchill, *Blood, Sweat, and Tears,* 292.
21. Speech of July 14, 1940, in W. S. Churchill, ed., *Never Give In,* 235.
22. Ibid., 346, 360.
23. Colville, *Fringes of Power,* 267.
24. The phrase is from Dangerfield, *Strange Death,* quoted in Louis, *In the Name of God,* 58n3.
25. Gilbert, *Finest Hour,* 80–81; Churchill, *Blood, Sweat, and Tears,* 348.
26. This was on April 12: Colville, *Fringes of Power,* 117.
27. Ibid., 234.
28. Louis, *In the Name of God,* 68.
29. Amery, *Diaries,* 3:76; Louis, *In the Name of God,* 172.
30. Colville, *Fringes of Power,* 236.
31. This was July 26: Gilbert, *Finest Hour,* 682; Colville, *Fringes of Power,* 236.
32. Roberts, *Eminent Churchillians,* 170.
33. Quoted in Gilbert, 480.
34. Quoted in Callahan, *Retreat From Empire,* 38.
35. Gandhi, *Collected Works,* 79:104.

36. Their discussion is summarized in Linlithgow's letter to Gandhi afterward, dated September 30, in Gandhi, *Collected Works,* 79:474–75.

37. Brown, *Prisoner of Hope,* 329.

38. Interview with *Spectator* editor Evelyn Wrench, December 1941, in Gandhi, *Collected Works,* 81:348.

39. Brown, *Prisoner of Hope,* 330.

40. Ibid., 331.

41. Ibid., 332.

42. Ibid.

43. Gandhi, *Collected Works,* 81:372.

44. Ibid., 81:356, 363.

45. Ibid., 81:374.

46. Ibid., 81:376.

CHAPTER 25. *Debacle*

1. Churchill, *Grand Alliance,* 620.

2. Ibid., 611, 620.

3. Herman, *To Rule the Waves,* 536.

4. Colville, *Fringes of Power,* 480.

5. Louis, *In the Name of God,* 145–46.

6. Louis, *Imperialism at Bay,* 125–26.

7. Ibid., 130.

8. Colville, *Fringes of Power,* 530.

9. W. S. Churchill, ed., *Never Give In,* 307–8.

10. See Chaudhuri, *Great Anarch!,* 566–69.

11. Ahmad, *Indian Response,* 28–31.

12. Gandhi, *Collected Works,* 80:197–98.

13. Bayly and Harper, *Forgotten Armies,* 192.

14. Chaudhuri, *Great Anarch!,* 590.

15. Bayly and Harper, *Forgotten Armies,* 119.

16. Ibid., 120.

17. Ibid., 122.

18. See Chapter 11.

19. Bayly and Harper, *Forgotten Armies,* 130.

20. Moran, *Churchill at War,* 17–18; Gilbert, *Road to Victory,* 30–31.

21. Gilbert, *Road to Victory,* 5, 37.

22. Ibid., 5, 37, 54.

23. Bayly and Harper, *Forgotten Armies,* 132.

24. W. S. Churchill, ed., *Never Give In,* 330.

25. Bayly and Harper, *Forgotten Armies,* 147.

26. Ibid., 146.

27. Brooke, *War Diaries,* 256.

28. Bayly and Harper, *Forgotten Armies,* 181.

29. Gandhi, *Collected Works,* 81:454.
30. Ibid., 82:6.
31. Ibid., 82:28.
32. Das, *Subhas,* 236.
33. The best eyewitness account is Hartog, *Sign of Tiger.*
34. Das, *Subhas,* 248.
35. Bayly and Harper, *Forgotten Armies,* 256.
36. Ibid., 207.
37. Moon, *British Conquest,* 1102.
38. Moore, *Cripps,* 56; Moon, *British Conquest,* 1104.
39. Gilbert, *Road to Victory,* 55, 57.
40. Moon, *British Conquest,* 1102; Moore, *Cripps,* 62.
41. Quoted in Thorne, *Allies of a Kind,* 242.
42. Quoted in Churchill, *Hinge of Fate,* 185.
43. Thorne, *Allies of a Kind,* 242–43.
44. Moran, *Churchill at War,* 36.
45. Cadogan, *Diaries,* 432–33.
46. Gilbert, *Road to Victory,* 54.
47. Harvey, *War Diaries,* 94; Gilbert, *Road to Victory,* 55.
48. Moore, *Cripps,* 74.
49. Ibid.
50. Gilbert, *Road to Victory,* 84–85.
51. Moon, *British Conquest,* 1109; Bayly and Harper, *Forgotten Armies,* 245.

CHAPTER 26. *Quit India*

1. Chaudhuri, *Great Anarch!,* 694.
2. Quoted in Brooke, *War Diaries,* 285.
3. Among them was Sapru. Brown, *Prisoner of Hope,* 335.
4. Gilbert, *Road to Victory,* 88.
5. Brown, *Prisoner of Hope,* 336.
6. Quoted in ibid.
7. Editorial in *Young India,* December 29, 1920, in Gandhi, *Collected Works,* 22:153.
8. Brown, *Prisoner of Hope,* 322.
9. May 28, 1942. Gandhi, *Collected Works,* 82:338.
10. Interview, June 14, ibid., 82:378.
11. Ibid., 81:231.
12. Quoted in Payne, *Gandhi,* 493.
13. Gandhi, *Collected Works,* 82:376.
14. Ibid., 378.
15. Ibid., 378; Payne, *Gandhi,* 494.
16. Brown, *Prisoner of Hope,* 338.

17. Gandhi, *Collected Works,* 82:197, 199.
18. Payne, *Gandhi,* 495.
19. Fischer, *Life of Gandhi,* 386.
20. Ibid., 385.
21. Gandhi, *Collected Works,* 83:205. There were actually two messages, one timed at nine a.m. and the other sometime during the day.
22. Chaudhuri, *Great Anarch!,* 703.
23. Brown, *Prisoner of Hope,* 340.
24. Bayly and Harper, *Forgotten Armies,* 248–49.
25. Amery, *Diaries,* 2:877.
26. Brown, *Prisoner of Hope,* 340.
27. Bayly and Harper, *Forgotten Armies,* 245.
28. Brown, *Modern India,* 309.
29. Bayly and Harper, *Forgotten Armies,* 191; Mollo, *Indian Army,* 162.
30. Das, *Subhas,* 572.
31. Bayly and Harper, *Forgotten Armies,* 74–75.
32. Telegram of April 7, 1941, in Gilbert, *Finest Hour,* 1047n2.
33. Churchill, *Hinge of Fate,* 178.
34. Gilbert, *Road to Victory,* 90.
35. Quoted ibid., 88.
36. Prime Minister, Record Files, Public Record Office, London, 245. 4, 48/9, quoted in Thorne, *Allies of a Kind.*
37. Gilbert, *Road to Victory,* 123.
38. Moran, *Churchill at War,* 84.
39. Gilbert, *Road to Victory,* 209–10.
40. Churchill, *Complete Speeches,* 6:6676–77.
41. Bayly and Harper, *Forgotten Armies,* 250.
42. Gilbert, *Road to Victory,* 105.
43. Bayly and Harper, *Forgotten Armies,* 272.

CHAPTER 27. *Showdown*

1. Gandhi, *Collected Works,* 83:211.
2. Ibid., 83:215.
3. Ibid., 83:275.
4. Ibid., 83:275.
5. Ibid., 83:281.
6. Fischer, *Life of Gandhi,* 390.
7. Moran, *Churchill at War,* 61.
8. Tendulkar, *Mahatma,* 3:113.
9. Chartwell Papers 20/106/74; Gilbert, *Road to Victory,* 343.
10. Chartwell Papers 20/106/91.
11. Moran, *Churchill at War,* 106.
12. Chartwell Papers 20/107/5.

13. Chartwell Papers 20/107/6.

14. Thornes, *Allies of a Kind,* 360.

15. Fischer, *Life of Gandhi,* 390.

16. Gilbert, *Road to Victory,* 348.

17. Brown, *Prisoner of Hope,* 342.

18. Chartwell Papers 20/107/21.

19. This was February 25: Chartwell Papers 20/107/26.

20. Gilbert, *Road to Victory,* 350.

21. Gandhi, *Collected Works,* 83:293–94.

22. Fischer, *Life of Gandhi,* 391.

23. Gilbert, *Road to Victory,* 350.

24. Churchill, *Hinge of Fate,* 641–42.

25. Chaudhuri, *Great Anarch!,* 706–7.

26. Bayly and Harper, *Forgotten Armies,* 282–84, 288.

27. Thorne, *Allies of a Kind,* 355.

28. Wavell, *Viceroy's Journal,* 3.

29. Louis, *In the Name of God,* 172, 173.

30. Bayly and Harper, *Forgotten Armies,* 291.

31. Wavell, *Viceroy's Journal,* 14, 23, 25.

32. Bayly and Harper, *Forgotten Armies,* 295–96.

33. Louis, *In the Name of God,* 174.

34. Moon, *British Conquest,* 1131.

35. Wavell, *Viceroy's Journal,* 33.

36. Ibid., 23.

CHAPTER 28. *Triumph and Tragedy*

1. Hartog, *Sign of Tiger,* 108–11. Bose did not travel alone. His devoted disciple Abid Hassan came along and slept in the bunk above him, while entertaining the U-boat crew with his imitations of "Nazi bigwigs" like Goebbels and Göring.

2. Ibid., 63–64. Bose welcomed the two thousandth legionary in February 1943. The final total, according to Hartog (who joined the unit as German adviser in 1944), reached four thousand. British sources bring the number down to 3100, with 300 to 400 German personnel (66).

3. German Military Intelligence Report, in Ganpuley, *Netaji in Germany,* Appendix, 183. On Hitler and *Lives of the Bengal Lancers,* see Hauner, *India in Axis Strategy,* 33.

4. Bose, *Collected Works,* 8:429.

5. Bayly and Harper, *Forgotten Armies,* 322.

6. Green, *Gandhi,* 363.

7. Quoted in Das, *Subhas,* 279–80.

8. Ibid., 249.

9. For example, Bayly and Harper, *Forgotten Armies,* 233–34, 258–59.

10. Thorne, *Allies of a Kind,* 359.

11. Brooke, *War Diaries,* 1:504.

12. Lamb, *War Leader,* 247; Louis, *Imperialism at Bay,* 283.

13. Lamb, *War Leader,* 248–49.

14. Wavell, *Viceroy's Journal,* 40.

15. Voigt, *Second World War,* 230.

16. Bayly and Harper, *Forgotten Armies,* 372.

17. Churchill, *Closing the Ring,* 486.

18. Allen, *Burma,* 237.

19. Bayly and Harper, *Forgotten Armies,* 381.

20. Churchill, *Closing the Ring,* 488.

21. Bayly and Harper, *Forgotten Armies,* 388, 390.

22. Voigt, *Second World War,* 232.

23. Bayly and Harper, *Forgotten Armies,* 393.

24. Brown, *Prisoner of Hope,* 343.

25. Wavell, *Viceroy's Journal,* 70.

26. Gilbert, *Road to Victory,* 351 n1.

27. Telegram dated May 27, in Gilbert, *Road to Victory,* 351n1.

28. Payne, *Gandhi,* 498.

29. Ibid., 502.

30. Ibid., 504.

31. Letter of March 9, 1944, in Gandhi, *Collected Works,* 84:25.

32. Brown, *Prisoner of Hope,* 343.

33. Payne, *Gandhi,* 505.

34. Wavell, *Viceroy's Journal,* 74–75.

35. Voigt, *Second World War,* 242–43, 208.

36. Brown, *Prisoner of Hope,* 345.

37. Wavell, *Viceroy's Journal,* 79.

38. Quoted in Prabhu and Rao, *Mind of Mahatma,* 68.

39. Brown, *Prisoner of Hope,* 349.

40. Ali, *Emergence of Pakistan,* 46–47.

41. Wavell, *Viceroy's Journal,* 91.

42. Lamb, *Churchill as War Leader,* 205.

43. Thorne, *Allies of a Kind,* 475.

44. Ibid., 507.

45. Moran, *Churchill at War,* 281.

46. Charmley, *End of Glory,* 587–88.

47. Moran, *Churchill at War,* 278.

48. Ibid., 278–79.

49. Letter dated February 1, 1945, in Gilbert, *Road to Victory,* 1166.

50. Louis, *In the Name of God,* 174–75.

51. Moon, *British Conquest,* 1136.

52. Louis, *In the Name of God,* 177–78.

53. Ibid., 171–72.

54. Wavell, *Viceroy's Journal,* 135.

55. Ibid., 136.

56. Ibid., 135–36.

57. Churchill, *Complete Speeches,* 7:7154–55.

58. Moran, *Churchill at War,* 305, 306.

59. Colville, *Fringes of Power,* 600.

60. Thorne, *Allies of a Kind,* 641.

61. Bayly and Harper, *Forgotten Armies,* 294.

62. Quoted in Allen, *Burma,* 633–34.

63. Brown, *Prisoner of Hope,* 355.

64. Wavell, *Viceroy's Journal,* 144–45.

65. Ibid.

66. Ibid., 147.

67. Ibid., 155.

68. Gandhi, *Collected Works,* 87:234.

69. Ibid., 87:153.

70. Ibid., 87:153–54.

CHAPTER 29. *Walk Alone*

1. Manchester, *Visions of Glory,* 27.

2. Moore, *Escape from Empire,* 25.

3. Ibid., 28–29.

4. Louis, *In the Name of God,* 165–66.

5. Colville, *Fringes of Power,* 606.

6. Chandos, *Memoirs,* 328–29.

7. Bayly and Harper, *Forgotten Armies,* 364–65.

8. Moran, *Churchill at War,* 351–52.

9. Colville, *Fringes of Power,* 611.

10. Moore, *Escape from Empire,* 3.

11. Wavell, *Viceroy's Journal,* 159.

12. Mansergh, *Transfer of Power,* 6:60.

13. Wavell, *Viceroy's Journal,* 168.

14. Moran, *Churchill at War,* 351.

15. Chaudhuri, *Great Anarch!,* 755, 794.

16. Interview with unnamed British paper, October 28, 1946, in Gandhi, *Collected Works,* 92:421–22.

17. Ibid., 92:8.

18. Ibid., 87:315.

19. Ibid., 87:359.

20. Ibid., 96:64.

21. Ibid., 87:300.

22. Mahajan, *Independence,* 73.

23. Wavell received word of Bose's death on September 21 (*Viceroy's Journal,*

174). He remained skeptical, however, and awaited further confirmation. Others are still waiting for confirmation today.

24. Gopal, *Nehru*, 1:308.

25. Bayly and Harper, *Forgotten Armies*, 448.

26. Ahmad, *Indian Response*, 119.

27. Wavell, *Viceroy's Journal*, 187, 188.

28. Mahajan, *Independence*, 88, 94–95.

29. Mansergh, *Transfer of Power*, 6:1079.

30. Hyde, *Baldwin*, 353.

31. Quoted in Gopal, *Nehru*, 1:306.

32. Quoted in Ahmed, *Jinnah*, 114.

33. Wavell, *Viceroy's Journal*, 236.

34. Ibid., 299.

35. Moon, *British Conquest*, 1147.

36. Ali, *Emergence of Pakistan*, 60.

37. Ibid., 57, 62.

38. Wavell, *Viceroy's Journal*, 298.

39. Ibid., 314–15.

40. Quoted in Ali, *Emergence of Pakistan*, 66.

41. Blame very deliberately laid in Moore, *Escape from Empire*, passim.

42. As noted in Arnold, *Gandhi*, 211–12.

43. Ali, *Emergence of Pakistan*, 69.

44. Chaudhuri, *Great Anarch!*, 811.

45. Wavell, *Viceroy's Journal*, 336.

46. Report in *Hindustani Times*, September 27, in Gandhi, *Collected Works*, 92:246.

47. Ibid., 92:329.

48. Ibid., 92:344, 355, 345.

49. Ibid., 92:358, 375.

50. Payne, *Gandhi*, 521.

51. Bose, *My Days*, 63, 85, 84.

52. Moon, *British Conquest*, 1158.

53. Gandhi, *Collected Works*, 92:382.

54. Wavell, *Viceroy's Journal*, 344–45, 401–2.

55. This was in September. See Mansergh, *Transfer of Power*, 8:454–62.

56. Wavell, *Viceroy's Journal*, 345.

57. Attlee's letter is dated January 8, 1947, in Mansergh, *Transfer of Power*, 9:490–91.

58. Quoted in Roberts, *Eminent Churchillians*, 108.

59. Churchill, *Complete Speeches*, 8:7386.

60. Ibid., 8:7444–48.

CHAPTER 30. *Death in the Garden*

1. Roberts, *Eminent Churchillians,* 80.

2. Mosley, *Last Days of Raj,* 90.

3. Mansergh, *Transfer of Power,* 10:8.

4. Payne, *Gandhi,* 526.

5. Mansergh, *Transfer of Power,* 10:47.

6. Quoted in Roberts, *Eminent Churchillians,* 82.

7. Ibid., 85.

8. Moore, *Escape from Empire,* chap. 4, *passim*; Roberts, *Eminent Churchillians,* 91.

9. Mansergh, *Transfer of Power,* 10:84; Roberts, *Eminent Churchillians,* 82.

10. Mosley, *Last Days of Raj,* 96.

11. April 1, 1947, prayer meeting, in Gandhi, *Collected Works,* 94:217.

12. Johnson, *Modern Times,* 474.

13. See, for example, Jalal, *Sole Spokesman.*

14. Quoted in Mosley, *Last Days of Raj,* 91, 110.

15. Moore, *Escape from Empire,* 206.

16. Copies of some of the letters survive in Chartwell Papers 43 A-B and 44.

17. The entire conversation is recorded in Mansergh, *Transfer of Power,* 10:513.

18. Wolpert, *Jinnah.*

19. Pyarelal, *Early Phase,* 215, 217.

20. If the plan hadn't been signed, the viceroy confessed to his press officer, "Dickie Mountbatten would have been sunk, and could have packed his bags." Mosely, *Last Days of Raj,* 127.

21. Quoted ibid., 133.

22. Roberts, *Eminent Churchillians,* 90.

23. Payne, *Gandhi,* 531.

24. Pyarelal, *Early Phase,* 215.

25. Gandhi, *Collected Works,* 96:186, 196.

26. Ibid., 96:182.

27. Payne, *Gandhi,* 533.

28. Bose, *My Days,* 225.

29. Quoted in Wolpert, *Nehru,* 408.

30. Karaka, *Betrayal in India,* 52–53.

31. Wolpert, *Nehru,* 409–10.

32. Manubehn Gandhi, *Miracle of Calcutta,* 66.

33. Chaudhuri, *Great Anarch!,* 842.

34. Quoted in Wolpert, *Nehru,* 411–12.

35. Payne, *Gandhi,* 548.

36. Masson, *Edwina,* 206–7.

37. Chaudhuri, *Great Anarch!,* 527.

38. Ali, *Emergence of Pakistan,* 259.

39. Chaudhuri, *Great Anarch!,* 834.

40. Roberts, *Eminent Churchillians,* 94.

41. Quoted ibid., 106.

42. As Andrew Roberts points out, we now know that Indian troops had moved into Kashmir well before any tribesmen crossed the border (104).

43. Churchill, *Complete Speeches,* 8:7525–26.

44. Speech of October 5, 1943, in Gandhi, *Collected Works,* 97:6.

45. Gandhi, *Collected Works,* 97:7. The phrase "unseen and more glorious empire of hearts" is Pyarelal's translation and infinitely superior to the "imperceptible rule of hearts" of *Collected Works.*

46. Ibid.

47. Quoted in Wolpert, *Nehru,* 418, 421.

48. Quoted in Green, *Gandhi,* 384.

49. Gandhi, *Collected Works,* 98:36.

50. Ibid., 98:219.

51. Payne, *Gandhi,* 555–56.

52. Gandhi, *Collected Works,* 98:227.

53. Manubehn Gandhi, *Last Glimpses,* 179.

54. Green, *Gandhi,* 381.

55. Srivastava, *Five Stormy Years,* 190.

56. Chaudhuri, *Great Anarch!,* 503.

57. Ghosh, *Murder Trial,* 67.

58. Gandhi, *Collected Works,* 98:260.

59. Pyarelal, *Early Phase,* 215.

60. Manubehn Gandhi, *Last Glimpses,* 218.

61. Pyarelal, *Early Phase,* 756.

62. Manubehn Gandhi, *Last Glimpses,* 297–98.

63. Payne, *Gandhi,* 631.

64. Pyarelal, *Early Phase,* 767.

65. Bourke-White, *Halfway to Freedom,* 232.

66. Gandhi, *Collected Works,* 98:36.

67. Chaudhuri, *Great Anarch!,* 874, 879.

68. Ibid., 876.

69. Birla, *In the Shadow of Mahatma,* 325–26.

70. Quoted in Green, *Gandhi,* 365.

71. Fischer, *Life of Gandhi,* 14.

72. Payne, *Gandhi,* 597.

73. Brown, *Modern India,* 337.

74. Payne, *Gandhi,* 599.

CHAPTER 31. *Lion in Twilight*

1. Fischer, *Life of Gandhi,* 18–19.
2. Speech of October 28, 1948, Churchill, *Complete Speeches,* 7:7722.
3. Ibid., 7:7588.
4. His speech on "the United States of Europe" was delivered in Zurich on September 19: ibid., 7:7379–82. On its relationship with the Marshall Plan, see Gilbert, *Never Despair,* 337.
5. Churchill, *Diaries,* 179.
6. Ibid., 309.
7. Churchill made this admission in September 1957. Gilbert, *Never Despair,* 1250.
8. Ibid., 333.
9. Ibid., 334.
10. Ziegler, *Mountbatten,* 461.
11. On this point, see Roberts, *Eminent Churchillians,* 127, 129–31.
12. Ibid., 131.
13. Churchill, *Complete Speeches,* 7:7671–72.
14. Ibid., 7:7721–22.
15. Churchill, *Memories and Adventures,* 59.
16. Bourke-White, *Halfway to Freedom,* 232.
17. Williams and Ramsden, *Ruling Britannia,* 419–20.
18. Churchill told his children about the strange encounter a few days later. His son Randolph urged him to write it down: Churchill was reluctant but eventually did, locking it away in a wooden box until his death. First published in the *Sunday Telegraph* a year after his funeral in 1966, it also appears in Martin Gilbert's final volume (*Never Despair,* 364–72, and in a bound version edited by Richard Langworth, under the title Randolph gave it: *The Dream* (Washington, D.C.: Churchill Centre, 2005).
19. W. S. Churchill, *Never Give In,* 446.
20. Churchill, *Memories and Adventures,* 72–73.
21. Roberts, *Eminent Churchillians,* 253; Williams and Ramsden, *Ruling Britannia,* 431.
22. Roberts, *Eminent Churchillians,* 252.
23. Quoted in Pearson, *Private Lives,* 389.
24. Churchill, *Memories and Adventures,* 60–61, 62–63.
25. This was in June 1945: Moran, *Churchill at War,* 335.
26. Moran, *Churchill at War,* 355–56.
27. W. S. Churchill, *Never Give In,* 479.
28. Clark, *Other Half,* 128.
29. Pearson, *Private Lives,* 370.
30. Moran, *Churchill at War,* 555.
31. Ibid., 653.
32. Churchill, *Complete Speeches,* 8:8607–9.

33. Moran, *Churchill at War,* 614.

34. W. S. Churchill, *Never Give In,* 498.

35. Quoted in Pearson, *Private Lives,* 373.

36. Moran, *Churchill at War,* 621.

37. On January 10, 1952. Ibid., 386.

38. Ibid., 619.

39. Morris, *Farewell the Trumpets,* 531.

40. Lloyd, *British Empire,* 344.

41. Moran, *Churchill at War,* 819; Roberts, *Eminent Churchillians,* 219.

42. Moran, *Churchill at War,* 785.

43. Ibid., 840–41.

44. Levin, *Run It Down,* 408.

45. Moran, *Churchill at War,* 670.

46. Ibid., 394, 479.

CONCLUSION: *Triumph and Tragedy*

1. Luce, *In Spite of the Gods,* 8.

REFERENCE LIST

Addison, David. *Churchill: The Unexpected Hero:* Oxford: Oxford University Press, 2005.

Ahmad, Manzoor. *Indian Response to the Second World War.* New Delhi: Intellectual Publishing House, 1987.

Ahmed, Akbar. *Jinnah, Pakistan, and Islamic Identity.* London: Routledge, 1997.

Ali, C. M. *The Emergence of Pakistan.* New York: Columbia University Press, 1967.

Allen, Charles. *The Search for the Buddha: The Man Who Discovered India's Lost Religion.* New York: Carroll & Graf, 2002.

Allen, Louis. *Burma: The Longest War, 1941–1945.* London: J. M. Dent & Sons, 1985.

Ambedkar, B. R. *The Essential Writings of B. R. Ambedkar.* New York: Oxford University Press, 2004.

Amery, Leo. *The Leo Amery Diaries,* ed. John Barnes and David Nicholson. London: Hutchinson, 1980.

Arnold, David. *Gandhi.* London: Longmans, 2001.

Asquith, H. H. *Letters to Venetia Stanley,* ed. Michael Brock. Oxford: Oxford University Press, 1982.

Atkins, J. B. *Incidents and Reflections.* London: Christophers, 1947.

Bahadur, Sir Sayyid Ahmed Khan. *The Causes of Indian Revolt.* 1858; Lahore: Book House, 1970.

Basham, A. L. *The Wonder That Was India.* New Delhi: Rupa, 1981.

Basu, Mriral Kumar. *Rift and Reunion: Contradictions in the Congress, 1908–1981.* Calcutta: K.P. Bagchi & Co., 1990.

Bayly, Christopher, and Tim Harper. *Forgotten Armies: The Fall of British Asia, 1941–1945.* Cambridge, Mass.: Belknap Press, 2005.

Beloff, Max. *Imperial Sunset,* vol. 1, *Britain's Liberal Empire, 1897–1921.* New York: Alfred A Knopf, 1970.

Ben-Moshe, Tuvia. *Churchill: Strategy and History.* Boulder, Colo.: Harvester Wheatsheaf, 1992.

Bennett, George, ed. *The Concept of Empire: Burke to Attlee, 1774–1947.* 2nd ed. 1953; London: Adam and C. Black, 1967.

Best, Geoffrey. *Churchill and War.* London: Hambledon & London Press, 2005.

Birkenhead, Earl of. *Halifax: The Life of Lord Halifax.* Boston: Houghton Mifflin, 1966.

Birla, Ganshayam Das. *In the Shadow of the Mahatma.* Bombay: Orient Longman, 1953.

Blavatsky, Helena P. *Isis Unveiled: A Master-Key to the Mysteries of Ancient and Modern Science and Theology,* vol. 2, *Theology.* New York, 1877.

Blunt, Wilfred S. *My Diaries: Being a Personal Narrative of Events,* vol. 2, *1900–1914.* New York: Alfred A. Knopf, 1922.

Bonham Carter, Violet. *Winston Churchill: An Intimate Portrait.* New York: Harcourt Brace, 1965.

Bose, Nirmal Kumar. *My Days with Gandhi.* 1953; New Delhi: Orient Longman, 1974.

Bose, Subhas Chandra. *Netaji: Collected Works.* New York: Oxford University Press, 1997.

Bourke-White, Margaret. *Halfway to Freedom.* New York: Simon & Schuster, 1949.

Brooke, Alan. *War Diaries 1939–1945: Field Marshall Lord Alanbrooke.* London: Weidenfeld & Nicolson, 2001.

Brown, Judith M. *Gandhi's Rise to Power: Indian Politics, 1915–1922.* Cambridge: Cambridge University Press, 1974.

_____. *Gandhi and Civil Disobedience: The Mahatma in Indian Politics, 1928–1934.* Cambridge: Cambridge University Press, 1977.

_____. *Modern India: The Origins of an Asian Democracy.* New York: Oxford University Press, 1985.

_____. *Gandhi: Prisoner of Hope.* New Haven, Conn.: Yale University Press, 1991.

Bruehl, Wayne. *The Crisis of the Raj.* Hanover, N.H.: University Press of New England, 1986.

Buchanan, Daniel. *The Development of Capitalist Enterprise in India.* New York: Columbia University Press, 1934.

Busch, Briton Cooper. *Britain, India, and the Arabs, 1914–1921.* Berkeley and Los Angeles: University of California Press, 1971.

Cadogan, Alexander. *The Diaries of Sir Alexander Cadogan, 1938–1945,* ed. David Dilks. New York: G. P. Putnam, 1972.

Cain, Peter J. *Hobson and Imperialism: Radicalism, New Liberalism, and Finance, 1887–1938.* Oxford: Oxford University Press, 2002.

Callahan, Raymond. *Churchill: Retreat from Empire.* New York: SR Books, 1984.

Catherwood, Christopher. *Churchill's Folly: How Winston Churchill Created Modern Iraq.* New York: Carroll & Graf, 2005.

Chandos, Viscount (Oliver Lyttelton). *The Memoirs of Lord Chandos.* London: Bodley Head, 1962.

Charmley, John. *Lord Lloyd and the Decline of the British Empire.* New York: St. Martin's Press, 1987.

_____. *Churchill: The End of Glory: A Political Biography.* New York: Harcourt Brace Jovanovich, 1993.

_____. *Churchill's Grand Alliance.* New York: Harcourt Brace, 1995.

Chartwell Papers, Churchill Archive Centre, Churchill College, Cambridge.

Chaudhuri, Nirad. *The Continent of Circe: An Essay on the Peoples of India.* Bombay: Jaico, 1970.

_____. *Autobiography of an Unknown Indian.* London: Hogarth Press, 1988.

_____. *Thy Hand, Great Anarch! India 1921–1952.* Boston: Addison-Wesley Longman, 1989.

Chaudhury, P. C. Roy. *Gandhi and His Contemporaries.* New Delhi: Sterling, 1972.

Chunder, Bholanauth. *Travels of a Hindoo to Various Parts of Bengal and Upper India.* London: Trubner, 1869.

Churchill, Randolph Henry Spencer. *Speeches of Lord Randolph Churchill, with a Sketch of His Life,* ed. Henry W. Lucy. London: George Routledge & Sons, 1885.

Churchill, Randolph S. *Winston S. Churchill,* vol. 1, *Youth: 1874–1900.* Boston: Houghton Mifflin, 1967.

_____. *Winston S. Churchill,* vol. 2, *Young Statesman, 1901–1911.* Boston: Houghton Mifflin, 1967.

_____. *Winston S. Churchill: Companion* vol. 1, pts.1 and 2. Boston: Houghton Mifflin, 1967.

_____. *Winston S. Churchill: Companion* vol. 2, pts. 1–3. Boston: Houghton Mifflin, 1969.

Churchill, Winston S. *The Story of the Malakand Field Force* (1898), in *Frontiers and Wars.* London: Eyre and Spottiswoode, 1962.

_____. *Savrola.* New York: Longmans Green, 1899.

_____. *London to Ladysmith via Pretoria* (1900). In *Frontiers and Wars.* London: Eyre and Spottiswoode, 1962.

_____. *Lord Randolph Churchill.* London: Macmillan, 1906. 2 vols.

_____. *The World Crisis.* New York: Scribner's, 1923.

_____. *My Early Life: A Roving Commission.* New York: Scribner's, 1930.

_____. *Amid These Storms.* New York: Scribner's, 1932.

_____. *Painting as a Pastime* (1942). New York: Cornerstone Library, 1965.

_____. *Great Contemporaries.* 1937; London: Fontana, 1959.

_____. *While England Slept: A Survey of World Affairs, 1932–1938.* New York: Putnam, 1938.

_____. *Blood, Sweat, and Tears.* New York: G. P. Putnam, 1941.

_____. *The Second World War,* vol. 1, *The Gathering Storm.* Boston: Houghton Mifflin, 1948.

_____. *The Second World War*, vol. 3, *The Grand Alliance.* Boston: Houghton Mifflin, 1950.

_____. *The Second World War,* vol. 4, *The Hinge of Fate.* Boston: Houghton Mifflin, 1951.

_____. *The Second World War,* vol. 5, *Closing the Ring.* Boston: Houghton Mifflin, 1951.

_____. *Frontiers and Wars.* London: Eyre and Spottiswoode, 1962.

_____. *Churchill: Taken From the Diaries of Lord Moran.* Boston: Houghton Mifflin, 1966.

_____. *Young Winston's Wars: The Original Dispatches of Winston S. Churchill,* ed. Frederick Wood. New York: Viking, 1972.

_____. *Liberalism and the Social Problem: A Collection of Early Speeches as a Member of Parliament.* Bristol: Hamlyn, 1974.

_____. *His Complete Speeches, 1897–1963,* ed. Robert Rhodes James. 8 vols. London: Chelsea House, 1974.

_____. *Memories and Adventures.* London: Weidenfeld & Nicolson, 1989.

_____. *His Father's Son: The Life of Randolph Churchill.* London: Weidenfeld & Nicolson, 1996.

_____. *Never Give In!: The Best of Winston Churchill's Speeches.* New York: Hyperion, 2003.

Clark, Kenneth. *The Other Half: A Self-Portrait.* London: John Murray, 1977.

Clayton, Anthony. *The British Empire as Superpower, 1919–1939.* London: Macmillan, 1986.

Collett, Nigel. *The Butcher of Amritsar: General Reginald Dyer.* London: Hambledon & London, 2007.

Collier, Richard. *The Sound of Fury: An Account of the Indian Mutiny.* London: Collins, 1963.

Colonial Office Records, London.

Colville, John. *The Fringes of Power: 10 Downing Street Diaries, 1939–1955.* New York: W.W. Norton & Co., 1985.

Colvin, Ian. *The Chamberlain Cabinet: How Meetings in 10 Downing Street, 1937–1939, Led to the Second World War—Told for the First Time from the Cabinet Papers.* New York: Taplinger, 1971.

Cranston, Sylvia. *HPB: The Extraordinary Life and Influence of Helena*

Blavatsky, Founder of the Modern Theosophical Movement. New York: G. P. Putnam, 1993.

Cross, J. A. *Sir Samuel Hoare: A Political Biography.* London: Jonathan Cape, 1977.

Curtis, Lionel. *The Commonwealth of Nations.* London: Macmillan, 1916.

Curzon, Lord. *A Viceroy's India: Leaves From Lord Curzon's Notebook,* ed. Peter King. London: Sedgwick & Jackson, 1984.

d'Este, Carlo. *Warlord.* New York: HarperCollins, 2008.

Dalrymple, William. *White Mughals: Love and Betrayal in Eighteenth Century India.* New York: HarperCollins, 2002.

Dangerfield, George. *The Strange Death of Liberal England, 1910–1914.* New York: Capricorn Books, 1961.

Das, Hari Hara. *Subhas Chandra Bose and the Indian National Movement.* New Delhi: Sterling, 1983.

Datta, V. N. *Madan Lal Dhingra and the Revolutionary Movement.* New Delhi: Vikas, 1978.

Desai, Narayan. *Bliss It Was to Be Young with Gandhi: Childhood Reminiscences.* Bombay: Bharatiya Vidya Bhavan, 1988.

Devanesen, Chandran D. S. *The Making of the Mahatma.* New Delhi: Orient Longman, 1969.

Dilks, David. *Curzon in India.* New York: Taplinger, 1969.

Doniger, Wendy, ed. *The Laws of Manu.* Harmondsworth: Penguin, 1991.

Duberly, Mrs. H. *Suppression of Mutiny 1857–1858.* 1859; New Delhi: Sirjana Press, 1974.

Dubois, J. A. *Hindu Manners, Customs and Ceremonies,* ed. H. Beauchamp, 3rd ed. 1906; Delhi: Oxford University Press, 1978.

Dufferin, Marchioness of. *Our Viceregal Life in India: Selections from My Journal, 1884–1888.* London: John Murray, 1890.

Dutton, David. *Anthony Eden: A Life and Reputation.* London: Arnold, 1996.

Edwardes, Michael. *Battles of the Indian Mutiny.* New York: Macmillan, 1963.

Farwell, Byron. *The Great Anglo-Boer War.* New York: W.W. Norton & Co., 1976.

_____. *Armies of the Raj: From Mutiny to Independence, 1858–1947.* New York: W.W. Norton & Co., 1989.

Feith, Douglas. "Palestine and Zionism, 1904–1922." In James W. Muller, *Churchill as Peacemaker.* Cambridge: Woodrow Wilson Center Press and Cambridge University Press, 1997.

Ferguson, Niall. *Empire: The Rise and Demise of the British World Order.* New York: Basic Books, 2002.

Fischer, Louis. *The Life of Mahatma Gandhi.* 1950; New York: Collier, 1962.

Foster, R. F. *Lord Randolph Churchill: A Political Life.* Oxford: Oxford University Press, 1981.

Freeden, Michael. "Eugenics and Progressive Thought," *Historical Journal* 22, no. 3 (1979), 645–71.

Fromkin, David. *A Peace to End All Peace: The Fall of the Ottoman Empire and the Creation of the Modern Middle East.* New York: Avon Books, 1990.

Fuller, C. J., ed. *Caste Today.* Delhi: Oxford University Press, 1996.

Gandhi, Manubehn. *Miracle of Calcutta.* Ahmedabad: Navajivan Publishing, 1959.

_____. *Last Glimpses of Bapu.* Agra: Shiva Lai Agarwala & Co., 1962.

Gandhi, Mohandas K. *Satyagraha in South Africa.* Ahmedabad: Navajivan Publishing, 1928.

_____. *An Autobiography: The Story of My Experiments with Truth.* 1948; New York: Dover, 1983.

_____. *Selected Writings of Mahatma Gandhi,* ed. Ronald Duncan. Boston: Beacon, 1951.

_____. *The Collected Works of Mahatma Gandhi.* 100 vols. New Delhi: Ministry of Information and Broadcasting, Government of India, 2000–

_____. *Hind Swaraj and Other Writings,* ed. Anthony J. Parel. Cambridge: Cambridge University Press, 1997.

Gandhi, Mohandas K., and Romain Rolland. *Correspondance, extraits du Journal et textes divers.* Paris: A. Mizhel, 1969.

Ganpuley, N. G. *Netaji in Germany: A Little Known Chapter.* Bombay: Bharatiya Vidya Bhavan, 1959.

Ghorye, G. S. *Caste and Class in India,* 5th ed. Bombay: Prakashan, 1969.

Ghosh, T. *The Gandhi Murder Trial.* New York: Asia Publishing House, 1975.

Gibbon, Edward. *The Decline and Fall of the Roman Empire.* 1779–89; Harmondsworth: Penguin, 1977.

Gilbert, Martin. *Winston S. Churchill: Companion* vol. 3, parts 1–2. Boston: Houghton Mifflin, 1973.

_____. *Winston S. Churchill: Companion* vol. 4, parts 1–3. Boston: Houghton Mifflin, 1977.

_____. *Winston S. Churchill,* vol. 5, *Prophet of Truth, 1922–1939.* London: William Heinemann, 1979.

_____. *Winston S. Churchill: Companion* vol. 5, parts 1–2. Boston: Houghton Mifflin, 1981.

_____. *Winston Churchill: The Wilderness Years.* London: Macmillan, 1981.

_____. *Winston S. Churchill,* vol. 6, *Finest Hour, 1939–1941.* London: William Heinemann, 1983.

_____. *Winston S. Churchill,* vol. 7, *Road to Victory, 1941–1945.* London: William Heinemann, 1986.

_____. *Winston S. Churchill,* vol. 8, *Never Despair, 1945–1965.* London: William Heinemann, 1988.

Glendevon, John. *Viceroy at Bay: Lord Linlithgow in India, 1936–1943.* London: Collins, 1971.

Golwalkar, Madhav Sadashiv. *We or Our Nationhood Defined.* Nagpur: Bharat Prakashan, 1938.

Gopal, Sarvepalli. *Jawaharlal Nehru: A Biography.* New York: Oxford University Press, 1989.

Gosh, Suresh Chandra. *Dalhousie in India, 1848–1856.* New Delhi: Munshiran Manoharlal, 1973.

Green, Martin. *Tolstoy and Gandhi, Men of Peace: A Biography.* New York: Basic Books, 1963.

_____. *The Origins of Nonviolence: Tolstoy and Gandhi in Their Historical Settings.* University Park: Pennsylvania State University Press, 1986.

_____. *Gandhi: Voice of a New Age Revolution.* Harrisburg, Pa.: Continuum, 1993.

Haldane, A. L. *The Insurrection in Mesopotamia, 1920.* 1922; Nashville, Tenn.: Battery Press, 2005.

Hardiman, David. *Feeding the Baniya Peasants and Usurers in Western India.* New Delhi: Oxford University Press, 1996.

Hartog, Rudolf. *The Sign of the Tiger: Subhas Chandra Bose and His Indian Legion in Germany, 1941–1945.* New Delhi: Rupa & Co. 2002.

Harvey, Oliver. *War Diaries of Oliver Harvey, 1941–1945,* ed. John Harvey. London: Collins, 1978.

Hasan, Mushirul. *Nationalism and Communal Politics in India, 1885–1930.* New Delhi: Manohar, 1991.

Hauner, Milan. *India in Axis Strategy: Germany, Japan, and Indian Nationalists in the Second World War.* Stuttgart: Klett-Cotta, 1981.

Heathcote, T. A. *The Military in British India.* Manchester: Manchester University Press, 1995.

Herman, A. L. *Community, Nonviolence and Peace.* New York: SUNY Press, 1999.

_____. *Influences: How Ancient Hinduism Dramatically Changed Early Christianity.* Stevens Point, Wis.: Cornerstone Press, 2004.

Herman, Arthur. *The Idea of Decline in Western History.* New York: Free Press, 1997.

_____. *To Rule the Waves: How the British Navy Shaped the Modern World.* New York: HarperCollins, 2004.

Hirschmann, Edwin. *"White Mutiny": The Ilbert Bill Crisis in India and the Genesis of the Indian National Congress.* New Delhi: Heritage, 1980.

Hodson, W.S.R. *Twelve Years of a Soldier's Life in India,* ed. George Hodson. 1859; Lahore: Wajidalis, 1983.

Holmes, Richard. *In the Footsteps of Churchill.* New York: Basic Books, 2005.

Hopkirk, Peter. *The Great Game: The Struggle for Empire in Central Asia.* New York: Kodansha, 1994.

Hunt, James D. *Gandhi and the Nonconformists: Encounters in South Africa.* South Asia Books, 1986.

_____. *Gandhi in London.* New Delhi: Promilla, 1993.

_____. *An American Looks at Gandhi: Essays in Satyagraha, Civil Rights, and Peace.* New Delhi: Promilla, 2005.

Hyde, H. Montgomery. *Baldwin: The Unexpected Prime Minister.* London: Hart-Davis MacGibbon, 1973.

India Office Library, British Library, London.

Iyer, Rhagavan N. *The Moral and Political Thought of Mahatma Gandhi.* Oxford: Oxford University Press, 1973.

Jablonsky, David. *Churchill, the Great Game, and Total War.* Portland, Ore.: Frank Cass, 1991.

Jaffrelot, Christopher. *Dr. Ambedkar and Untouchability: Analysing and Fighting Caste.* New Delhi: Permanent Black, 2006.

Jalal, Ayesha. *The Sole Spokesman: Jinnah, the Muslim League, and the Demand for Pakistan.* Cambridge: Cambridge University Press, 1985.

James, Robert Rhodes. *Lord Randolph Churchill.* London: Weidenfeld & Nicholson, 1959.

Jasonoff, Maya. *Edge of Empire: Lives, Cultures, and Conquest in the East, 1750–1850.* New York: Alfred A. Knopf, 2005.

Johar, S. S. *The Heritage of Amritsar.* Delhi: Sundeep Prakashan, 1978.

Johnson, A. C. *Viscount Halifax: A Biography.* New York: Ives Washburn, 1941.

Johnson, Paul. *Modern Times: The World from the Twenties to the Eighties.* New York: Harper & Row, 1985.

Kalarthi, Mukulbhai. *Ba and Bapu,* trans. Gurdial Mallik. Ahmedabad: Navajivan, 1962.

Karaka, D. F. *Betrayal in India.* London: Victor Gollancz, 1950.

Kaye, Sir John. *History of the Sepoy War in India 1857–1858.* London: W. H. Allen, 1880.

Keegan, John. *The First World War.* New York: Alfred A. Knopf, 1999.

Keer, Dhananjay. *Mahatma Gandhi: Political Saint and Unarmed Prophet.* Bombay: Popular Prakashan, 1973.

Keraly, Abraham. *Gem in the Lotus: The Seeding of Indian Civilization.* London: Weidenfield & Nicolson, 2004.

Kopf, David. *British Orientalism and the Bengal Renaissance.* Berkeley and Los Angeles: University of California Press, 1969.

Krishnadas. *Seven Months with Mahatma Gandhi.* Ahmedabad: Navajivan, 1951.

Lamb, Richard. *Churchill as War Leader.* London: Carroll & Graf, 1993.

Lannoy, Richard. *The Speaking Tree: A Study of Indian Culture and Society.* Oxford: Oxford University Press, 1971.

Levin, Bernard. *Run It Down the Flagpole: Britain in the Sixties.* New York: Atheneum, 1971.

Lloyd, Trevor O. *The British Empire 1558–1983.* Oxford: Oxford University Press, 1984.

Louis, William Roger. *Imperialism at Bay: The United States and the Decolonization of the British Empire, 1941–1945.* New York: Oxford University Press, 1978.

_____. *In the Name of God, Go!: Leo Amery and the British Empire in the Age of Churchill.* New York: W. W. Norton & Co., 1992.

Low, D. A. *Britain and Indian Nationalism.* Cambridge: Cambridge University Press, 1997.

Luce, Edward. *In Spite of the Gods: The Strange Rice of Modern India.* New York: Doubleday, 2007.

Lukacs, John. *The Duel: 10 May–31 July 1940, the Eighty-Day Struggle Between Churchill and Hitler.* Boston: Houghton Mifflin, 1941.

Macaulay, Thomas B. *Macaulay: Prose and Poetry,* ed. G. M. Young. Cambridge, Mass.: Harvard University Press, 1967.

Mahajan, Sucheta. *Independence and Partition: The Erosion of Colonial Power in India.* New Delhi: Penguin, 1989.

Manchester, William. *The Last Lion: Winston Spencer Churchill: Visions of Glory, 1874–1932.* Boston: Little, Brown, 1983.

_____. *The Last Lion: Winston Spencer Churchill: Alone, 1932–1940.* Boston: Little, Brown, 1989.

Mansergh, Nicholas. *The Transfer of Power, 1942–1947.* 12 vols. London: Her Majesty's Stationery Office, 1970–1983.

Marsh, Edward. *A Number of People: A Book of Reminiscences.* New York: Harper & Brothers, 1939.

Martin, Briton. *New India 1885: British Official Policy and the Emergence of the Indian National Congress.* Berkeley and Los Angeles: University of California Press, 1969.

Martin, Hugh. *Battle: The Life Story of Winston S. Churchill, Prime Minister.* London: Gollancz, 1940.

Masson, Madeleine. *Edwina: The Biography of the Countess Mountbatten of Burma.* London: Robert Hale, 1958.

Masterman, Lucy. *C. F. G. Masterman: A Biography.* London: Frank Cass, 1968.

Mathias, Peter. *The First Industrial Nation: An Economic History of Britain,* 2nd ed. London: Methuen, 1983.

Mathur, L. P. *Lord Ripon's Administration in India, 1880–1884.* New Delhi: S. Chand, 1972.

Mayo, Katherine. *Mother India.* London: Jonathan Cape, 1927.

McLane, J. R. *Indian Nationalism and the Early Congress.* Princeton, N.J.: Princeton University Press, 1977.

Meer, Fatima. *Apprenticeship of a Mahatma: A Biography of M. K. Gandhi.* New Delhi: Gandhi Hindustani Sahitya Sabha, 1997.

Milburn, Frank. *Polo: The Emperor of Games.* New York: Alfred A. Knopf, 1994.

Mill, James. *History of British India.* Chicago: University of Chicago Press, 1975.

Minault, Gail. *The Khilafat Movement: Religious Symbolism and Political Mobilization in India.* New York: Columbia University Press, 1982.

Mollo, Boris. *The Indian Army.* Poole: Blandford Press, 1981.

Montagu, Edwin. *An Indian Diary.* London: William Heinemann, 1930.

Montgomery-Massingberd, Hugh. *Blenheim Revisited: The Spencer-Churchills and Their Palace.* London: Bodley Head, 1985.

Moon, Sir Penderel. *The British Conquest and Dominion of India.* London: Duckworth, 1989.

Moore, R. J. *The Crisis of Indian Unity, 1917–1940.* Oxford: Clarendon Press, 1974.

_____. *Churchill, Cripps, and India, 1939–1945.* Oxford: Clarendon Press, 1979.

_____. *Escape from Empire: The Attlee Government and the India Problem.* Oxford: Clarendon Press, 1983.

Moorhouse, Geoffrey. *India Britannica.* London: Grenada, 1984.

Moran, Lord. *Churchill at War, 1940–1945.* London: Carroll & Graf, 2002.

Morgan, Ted. *Churchill: Young Man in a Hurry, 1874–1915.* New York: Simon & Schuster, 1982.

Morris, James. *Farewell the Trumpets: An Imperial Retreat.* New York: Harcourt Brace Jovanovich, 1978.

Mosley, Leonard. *The Last Days of the British Raj.* London: Weidenfeld & Nicolson, 1964.

Mosse, George. *The Image of Man: The Creation of Modern Masculinity.* Oxford: Oxford University Press, 1996.

Muggeridge, Malcolm. *Chronicles of Wasted Time,* vol. 1, *The Green Stick.* London: Collins, 1972.

Muller, James W. *Churchill as Peacemaker.* Cambridge: Woodrow Wilson Center Press and Cambridge University Press, 1997.

Naipaul, V. S. *India: A Wounded Civilization.* New York: Vintage, 1976.

Nanda, B. R. *The Nehrus: Motilal and Jawaharlal.* New York: John Day, 1963.

Nehru, Jawaharlal. *Toward Freedom: The Autobiography of Jawaharlal Nehru.* New York: John Day, 1942.

_____. *Independence and After: A Collection of Speeches, 1946–1949.* New Delhi: Karol Bagh, 1951.

Nicholson, Harold. *Diaries and Letters,* vol. 2, *The War Years, 1935–1939.* New York: Atheneum, 1967.

Olivelle, Patrick. *Upanishads.* New York: Oxford University Press, 1996.

Parekh, Bhikhu. *Colonialism, Tradition, and Reform: An Analysis of Gandhi's Political Discourse.* New Delhi: Sage Publications, 1999.

Payne, Robert. *The Life and Death of Mahatma Gandhi.* New York: E. P. Dutton, 1969.

Pearson, John. *The Privates Lives of Winston Churchill.* New York: Simon & Schuster, 1991.

Pollock, John C. *The Way to Glory: The Life of Havelock of Lucknow.* London: John Murray, 1957.

Prabhu, R. K., and U. R. Rao, eds. *The Mind of Mahatma Gandhi,* 3rd ed. Ahmedabad: Navajivan Publishing, 1968.

Prasad, Rajendra. *Mahatma Gandhi and Bihar: Some Reminiscences.* New York: Hafner, 1949.

Pyarelal, Nayar. *Mahatma Gandhi, The Early Phase,* vol. 1. Ahmedabad: Navajivan, 1965.

_____. *Mahatma Gandhi: The Last Phase,* vol. 1. Ahmedabad: Navajivan, 1956.

Rao, P. Kodanda. *The Right Honourable V. S. Srinivasa Sastri: A Political Biography.* Bombay, 1963.

Raymond, E. T. *Uncensored Celebrities.* New York: Henry Holt, 1919.

Reade, Winwood. *The Martyrdom of Man.* New York: Dutton, 1931.

Roberts, Andrew. *The Holy Fox: A Biography of Lord Halifax.* London: Weidenfield & Nicolson, 1991.

Roberts, Andrew. *Eminent Churchillians.* New York: Simon & Schuster, 1995.

Roberts, J. M. *The Pelican History of the World.* New York: Viking/Penguin, 1976.

Rolland, Romain. *Mahatma Gandhi.* New York: Century, 1924.

Ross, Alan. *The Emissary: G. D. Birla, Gandhi, and Independence.* London: Collins Havill, 1986.

Sandys, Celia. *Churchill: Wanted Dead or Alive.* New York: Carroll & Graf, 1999.

Sarkar, Sumit. "The Logic of Gandhian Nationalism: Civil Disobedience and the Gandhi-Irwin Pact (1930–31)." *Indian Historical Review* 3:1 (July 1976), 114–46.

Sastri, V.S.S. *Letters of the Right Honourable V. S. Srinivasa Sastri,* ed. T. N. Jagadisan. Bombay: Asia, 1963.

Schulberg, Lucille. *Historic India.* New York: Time-Life Books, 1968.

Shulman, David Dean. *The King and the Clown in South Asian Myth and Poetry.* Princeton, N.J.: Princeton University Press, 1983.

Shepherd, W. G. *A Personal Narrative of the Outbreak and Massacre at Cawnpore, During the Sepoy Revolt of 1857.* 1879; New Delhi: Academic Books, 1980.

Shirer, William L. *Gandhi: A Memoir.* New York: Simon & Schuster, 1979.

Slade, Madeleine. *The Spirit's Pilgrimage.* 1960; New York: Coward-McCann, 1978.

Spear, Percival. *The Nabobs: A Study of the Social Life of the English in Eighteenth-Century India.* London: Oxford University Press, 1963.

_____. *A History of India,* vol. 2. Harmondsworth: Penguin, 1973.

Srivastava, Harindra. *Five Stormy Years: Savarkar in London, June 1906 to June 1911.* New Delhi: Allied Publishers, 1983.

Steel, Nigel, and Peter Hart. *Defeat at Gallipoli.* Basingstoke: Macmillan, 1994.

Stokes, Eric. *The Peasant Armed: The Indian Revolt of 1857.* Oxford: Clarendon Press, 1986.

Streets, Heather. *Martial Races: The Military, Race, and Masculinity in British Imperial Culture.* Manchester: Manchester University Press, 2004.

Swan, Maureen. *Gandhi: The South African Experience.* Johannesburg: Ravan Press, 1982.

Talbot, Ian. *Provincial Politics and the Pakistan Movement: The Growth of the Muslim League in North-West and North-East India, 1937–1947.* New York: Oxford University Press, 1989.

Taylor, A.J.P. *The Origins of the Second World War.* Greenwich: Fawcett, 1966.

Templewood, Viscount. *Nine Troubled Years.* London: Collins, 1954.

Tendulkar, D. G. *Mahatma: Life of Mohandas Karamchand Gandhi.* Ahmedabad: Navajivan, 1960.

Thomson, Mowbray. *The Story of Cawnpore.* London: Richard Bentley, 1859.

Thorne, Christopher. *Allies of a Kind: The United States, Britain, and the War Against Japan, 1941–1945.* Oxford: Oxford University Press, 1978.

Tolstoy, Leo. *Complete Works.* New York: Thomas Crowell, 1891.

Trevelyan, G. O. *Cawnpore.* London, 1886.

Voigt, Johannes. *India in the Second World War.* New Delhi: Arnold-Heinemann, 1987.

Walkowitz, Judith R. *City of Dreadful Delight: Narratives of Sexual Danger in Late-Victorian London.* Chicago: University of Chicago Press, 1992.

Wallin, Jeffrey. *By Ships Alone: Churchill and the Dardanelles.* Durham, N.C.: Carolina Academic Press, 1981.

Ward, Andrew. *Our Bones Are Scattered: The Cawnpore Massacres and the Indian Mutiny of 1857.* New York: Henry Holt, 1996.

Wasti, Syed Razi. *Lord Minto and the Indian Nationalist Movement 1905 to 1910.* 1964; Lahore: People's Publishing, 1976.

Wavell, Archibald Percival. *Wavell: The Viceroy's Journal.* London: Oxford University Press, 1973.

Weber, Thomas. *On the Salt March.* New York: HarperCollins, 1998.

Williams, Glyn, and John Ramsden. *Ruling Britannia: Political History of Britain, 1688–1988*. London: Addison-Wesley Longman, 1990.

Wolpert, Stanley. *India*. Englewood Cliffs, N.J.: Prentice-Hall, 1965.

_____. *Morley and India 1906–1910*. Berkeley and Los Angeles: University of California Press, 1967.

_____. *Jinnah of Pakistan*. Delhi: Oxford University Press, 1984.

_____. *Nehru: A Tryst with Destiny*. New York: Oxford University Press, 1996.

Ziegler, Philip. *Mountbatten: The Official Biography*. New York: Alfred A. Knopf, 1985.

INDEX

PHOTOGRAPH CREDITS

PHOTO INSERT I

Page One
General Wheeler's battered entrenchment at Cawnpore after the Great Mutiny of 1857 (Hulton/Getty Archives)

Lord Randolph Churchill visiting India in 1885 (Churchill Archives/reproduced with permission of Curtis Brown Ltd., London, on behalf of The Broadwater Collection)

Page Two
Mohandas Gandhi with members of London's Vegetarian Society in 1890 (V. Jhaveri/ Peter Rühe)

Winston Churchill in India in 1896, as subaltern with the Fourth Hussars (Churchill Archives/ reproduced with permission of Curtis Brown Ltd., London, on behalf of The Broadwater Collection)

Page Three
Gandhi and fellow members of the Indian Ambulance Corps during the Boer War (V. Jhaveri/Peter Rühe)

The *Illustrated Police News*'s heroic version of Churchill's escape from a Boer prison (Churchill Archives/reproduced with permission of Curtis Brown Ltd., London, on behalf of The Broadwater Collection)

Page Four
Gandhi as he appeared when he met Churchill in London in October 1906 (V. Jhaveri/ Peter Rühe)

Churchill as secretary of state for the Colonies after his first and only meeting with Gandhi (Churchill Archives/reproduced with permission of Curtis Brown Ltd., London, on behalf of The Broadwater Collection)

Page Five
A rare action photograph of South African police halting Gandhi's dramatic march to the Transvaal, November 1913 (Local History Museum, Durban/Peter Rühe)

Failure of the Gallipoli campaign in 1915 (Hulton/Getty Archives)

Page Six
Gandhi meeting with Indian National Congress stalwarts in September 1921 (V. Jhaveri/ Peter Rühe)

Page Seven
Churchill as the new chancellor of the exchequer on his way to present his first budget to the House of Commons, 1925 (Churchill Archives/reproduced with permission of Curtis Brown Ltd., London, on behalf of The Broadwater Collection)

Page Eight
Gandhi using his *charkha,* or spinning wheel, at Sabarmati Ashram, 1926 (V. Jhaveri/ Peter Rühe)

PHOTO INSERT II
Page One
Mohandas and Kasturbai Gandhi after arriving in India in January 1915 (V. Jhaveri/ Peter Rühe)

Page Two
Winston Churchill and Clementine Churchill on his return to England from America, 1929 (Hulton/Getty Archives)

Page Three
The beginning of Gandhi's Salt March at Sabarmati, March 1930 (GandhiServe/Peter Rühe)

Page Four
Gandhi making salt at Bhimpur (V. Jhaveri/Peter Rühe)

Salt satyagraha in Bombay (*Daily Herald* Archive/Peter Rühe)

Page Five
Churchill speaks against Indian independence to meeting of the Indian Empire Society, December 1930 (Fox Photos/Getty Archives)

Page Six
Gandhi with Prime Minister Ramsay MacDonald and Sir Samuel Hoare at second Round Table Conference, London 1931 (V. Jhaveri/Peter Rühe)

Page Seven
A left-wing cartoonist's view of Churchill against the Government of India Bill, 1933 (Churchill Archives/reproduced with permission of Curtis Brown Ltd., London, on behalf of The Broadwater Collection)

Page Eight
Gandhi with Subhas Chandra Bose at the Indian National Congress meeting in 1938 (Hulton/Getty Archives)

PHOTO INSERT III
Page One
Winston Churchill and Viscount Halifax, 1940 (Getty Images)

Page Two
Churchill visits the bombed ruins of Coventry Cathedral, 1940 (Churchill Archives/ reproduced with permission of Curtis Brown Ltd., London, on behalf of The Broadwater Collection)

Gandhi with his longtime secretary, Mahadev Desai (V. Jhaveri/Peter Rühe)

Page Three
Churchill and President Franklin Roosevelt at Sunday services on the HMS *Prince of Wales*, August 1941 (Imperial War Museum)

The HMS *Prince of Wales* sinking after being targeted Japanese planes (Imperial War Museum)

Page Four
Quit India riot in Bombay, October 1942 (Kanu Gandhi/Peter Rühe)

Sikh soldiers in Cairo present a gift to Winston Churchill on his 69th birthday, November 1943 (Imperial War Museum)

Page Five
Churchill with jubilant crowd on V-E Day, May 8, 1945 (Imperial War Museum)

General Archibald Wavell, viceroy of India 1943–1946 (Time & Life Pictures/Getty Images)

Page Six
Aftermath of massacres in Calcutta, 1946 (photo by Margaret Bourke White; Hulton/Getty Archives)

Gandhi arriving with his grandniece Manubehn at Delhi train station, March 1947 (V. Jhaveri/Peter Rühe)

Page Seven
Gandhi's funeral, January 31, 1948 (V. Jhaveri/Peter Rühe)

Page Eight
Churchill's funeral, January 30, 1965 (Hulton/Getty Archives)

ABOUT THE AUTHOR

ARTHUR HERMAN is the bestselling author of *How the Scots Invented the Modern World,* which has sold over 350,000 copies worldwide, and *To Rule the Waves: How the British Navy Shaped the Modern World,* which was nominated for the prestigious Mountbatten Prize in 2005. He is a former professor of history at Georgetown University, Catholic University, George Mason University, and the Smithsonian's Campus on the Mall.